A HISTORY OF THE PEACE CONFERENCE OF PARIS

First printed 1924

PRINTED IN ENGLAND
AT THE OXFORD UNIVERSITY PRESS
BY FREDERICK HALL

A HISTORY OF THE PEACE CONFERENCE OF PARIS

EDITED BY

H. W. V. TEMPERLEY

VOL. VI

Published under the auspices of the British Institute of International Affairs

LONDON
HENRY FROWDE AND HODDER & STOUGHTON
THE *LANCET* BUILDING
1 & 2 BEDFORD STREET, STRAND, W.C. 2
1924

CONTRIBUTORS TO VOLUME VI[1]

BAKER, P. J., M.A., Cantab., late Whewell Scholar International Law, Cambridge. Formerly of the Secretariat of the League of Nations.

BARRETT LEARNED, H., Ph.D., sometime Professor of Modern History, Leland Stanford University, U.S.A.

BUTLER, HAROLD, C.B., Deputy Director of International Labour Office.

BUTLER, J. R. M., Fellow of Trinity College, Cambridge.

CHILDS, W. J. M.

HARRIS, H. WILSON, M.A., Cantab.

HOGARTH, D. G., C.M.G., Litt.D., Oxford.

HORNBECK, S. K., Professor, United States Tariff Commission.

KEITH, A. B., Professor in the University of Edinburgh.

LORD, R. H., Ph.D., Professor of Modern History, Harvard University.

MAURICE, Major-General SIR F., K.C.M.G., late Director of Military Operations, British War Office.

OGILVIE, A. G., M.A., Reader in Geography in the University of Manchester.

ORMSBY-GORE, the RIGHT HON. W. G. A., M.P., late Member of the Permanent Mandates Commission.

PATON, H. J., M.A., Fellow of The Queen's College, Oxford.

SIMPSON, J. Y., Professor in the University of Edinburgh.

STEERS, J. A., M.A., Scholar of St. Catharine's College, Cambridge.

TEMPERLEY, H. W. V., M.A., Reader in Modern History in the University of Cambridge.

TOYNBEE, A. J., M.A., Oxon., Professor of Byzantine History, London University.

[1] The allocation of chapters to contributors is given on pp. xxix–xxxi.

EDITORIAL FOREWORD

A FOREWORD, which closes a six-volumed survey, should be brief. The work has undergone considerable modifications as it progressed, owing partly to the advice and suggestions of critics and reviewers, partly to modifications of plan caused by the progress of events and certain unexpected modifications in the international situation. More could have been told in the first three volumes had the revelations of certain writers been available at that time. The last three volumes have been able to profit by these fortunate indiscretions. In the main, moreover, the original design has been carried out, which was to give a description of the work of the Peace Conference by writers who knew their subjects at first hand and had not infrequently influenced the events they describe.

Endeavours have been made, so far as possible, to make use of the work of American as well as of British participants in the Peace Conference, and, whenever possible, use has also been made of the works of writers of other nationalities such as Nitti and Tardieu. It is probable however, and indeed inevitable, that the work displays a certain bias in favour of British and, to a less extent, of American policies. But the reader, being warned of the tendencies of the compass, should be able to steer his course aright. In the documents given and in the quotations made from the German and other enemy documents there should be enough material wherewith to check and to criticize any tendencies of this kind.

The last and most agreeable duty of an Editor is to make acknowledgments to those who have been of service to the work for which he is responsible. Without the aid of the Committee of the British Institute of International Affairs this work could not have been produced at all. Among those who were specially active and helpful with regard to the production of Volumes IV and V, it is right to mention the names of Lord Meston the Chairman, of the two Honorary Secretaries, Mr. Lionel Curtis and Mr. G. M. Gathorne-Hardy, of Mr. J. W. Headlam-Morley, of Professor A. F. Pollard, and of Sir J. Cecil Power. It is due to the latter's generosity and public spirit that the publication of the sixth volume has been rendered possible.

It would be alike impossible and invidious to make acknowledgments to all those who have given valuable advice and help in regard to these volumes as a whole. But the editor must mention three names distinguished in history and in diplomacy, those of Sir Ernest Satow, of Sir Adolphus Ward, Master of Peterhouse, and of Sir Valentine Chirol, whose ripe judgment and profound knowledge of history and politics have always been ungrudgingly placed at his disposal. In this volume, as in all the others, the skilled aid of Miss Lilian Mattingly has been invaluable in correcting and verifying the numerous references and statements which occur in the History. Mr. J. A. Steers has acted as geographical adviser in the sixth volume.

At the same time it should be understood that, while the work of those mentioned (and of many others not mentioned) has been of the greatest assistance, they should not be held responsible for any errors which the volume may contain.

It is certain that the views expressed in these volumes will not be those of posterity. But it is hoped that a sufficient contemporary record has been given of the events and motives which prevailed at the Peace Conference.

PLAN OF THE WORK

The sixth volume deals with the various aspects of the Treaties in Northern and Eastern Europe and outside Europe. The first chapter deals with the Turkish Empire. No military or diplomatic account of its collapse has been thought necessary, for the defeat was for the moment complete, and the armistice, as related elsewhere, necessitated an unconditional surrender. The serious aspect of the question here lay in the various obligations and commitments of the Allies, first, to one another, then to King Husein and other Arab Chiefs, to Zionism, and to Greece. The nature and extent of these commitments, as will be seen, involved the encouragement of Arab nationalism in Mesopotamia, Syria, and Arabia, of Jewish nationalism in Palestine, and the penetration of Greeks into Asia Minor. These attempts in return provoked a Turkish nationalistic movement in Anatolia which was of so strenuous a nature as ultimately to transform and to revise the Treaty of Sèvres piece by piece and step by step. The great problem of the future of Constantinople was shirked and not settled in this Treaty, and the results of this inability to face the question are described to the end of 1922.

The story of the Turkish Treaty is the story of a Treaty which the Supreme Council momentarily forced on a defeated and discredited government, only to find that the provisions were unworkable because the Great Powers were not prepared to enforce them. On the other hand in Poland, with which the second chapter deals, there was a serious attempt by the Great Powers to reconstruct that great Polish nation, which had been for a century and a half partitioned between the three despotic Eastern Monarchies. As the Great Powers were prepared to enforce their views, this experiment has for the time being, at any rate, been successful. As a result of the execution of the treaties Poland has not been threatened by Germany, and has been able even to expand at her expense by the Upper Silesian decision. Contrary to all expectation she has also repelled the Bolshevik danger. The ultimate success of the experiment must depend upon time. It seemed to be necessary in the *History of the Peace Conference* to call special attention to this great constructive experiment on the part of the Allies. Contrary to the usual plan of this History a short historical introduction has been here given, for in this case, more than in any other, it was to history that the Conference appealed. Attention has also been concentrated on the ideas actually prevalent at the Conference itself and underlying the attempted solution. Developments subsequent to the Treaty of Versailles are more lightly treated, for in this, more than in any other part of the History, it becomes important to give the views of the reconstructors of the map of Europe. For just as the idea of 'Break Austria' has determined the fate of one part of Central Europe for a generation, so has that of 'Reconstitute Poland' for another. It is these ideas, not the patched or fumbling expedients by which statesmen subsequently sought to lessen their force or to delay their application, which settled the weal or woe of Central Europe. Therefore, it is the origin of these ideas and their interpretation in the Treaties which is of the greatest importance.

While chapter two deals with the still incomplete Polish experiment, chapter three deals with experiments in forming or recognizing nationalities which are still more incomplete. The shadow of the once vast Russian Empire hung over the Conference, for it was not considered impossible that it might be shortly reconstituted. Hence the Conference was slow in recognizing the Baltic nationalities and made only tentative attempts to re-establish them. As regards the Bolsheviks themselves the treatment followed has been different. For they set out by denying the authority of the Peace Conference, and hence have but a limited relation to its history. They come into it simply in so far as they conform to or approach the ordinary commercial and diplomatic relations of international society as interpreted by the Peace Conference or by individual Powers present at it. With the Bolshevik attempt to reconstruct Society in Russia and to inaugurate a world-revolution elsewhere we are only slightly concerned.

In chapter four an attempt is made to deal with the World outside Europe. The development of nationalities and of nations within the British Empire, is certainly one of the most startling of the direct, and indirect, results of the war and of the peace. Whether in Canada or Egypt, in India or in South Africa, in Malta or in Australasia the swell and pulse of new movements and new ideas can be traced. It was deeply affected by the sacrifices made and the consequent privileges claimed by the Dominions, and by the surprising solution made by admitting them to the League. For that constituted their introduction, as it were, into the family of nations. The privileges claimed by, and the duties imposed upon, a member of the League seem, in fact, hardly compatible with a dependent status, and hence admission to the League constitutes a phenomenon in the history of the Empire of the most decisive importance.

Apart from the British Empire, Japan played a most important part at the Conference. It assumed on certain occasions the status of a fifth Great Power, so that the destinies of Europe have been permanently affected by an Asiatic State. The complicated problem of Shantung, as decided at the Conference, is here fully described. The diplomatic attitude of the United States, in this as in such matters as the Russian situation or Mandates, has been outlined, while the American Treaty with Germany is published, as is believed, for the first time in this country. In the case of the United States it has been found possible in chapter five to sketch its internal disputes which have so deeply influenced diplomacy and international affairs. The omission to treat another problem, and an almost equally fascinating one, that of the influence of the war and the peace on Latin America, is regrettable. But such topics would require a volume in themselves.

The last chapter of this concluding volume is devoted to analysing the developments under that great constructive experiment, known as the League of Nations. It opens with an account of the different ideas which led to its formation and with a general description of its constitution and aims. Certain special features—Labour, Justice, Mandates, guarantees against war—are then separately considered. It is believed that the stress laid upon this feature is justified by the fact that it is now certain that some of the original provisions of the Peace Treaties are clearly obsolete and that more are obsolescent. But the League contains within itself the possibilities of a great and permanent international instrument, and provides for those necessities of growth and adaptation, for which all experience shows that no rigid treaty articles can provide. In concluding this survey it may perhaps be as well to emphasize the fact that the League could not have existed in its present form, or perhaps in any form at all, without the support and the advocacy of President Wilson.

By way of epilogue a short survey of some of the more important principles and lessons of the Peace Conference has been made. It is hoped that this will be found of some value and that some of the newer information, not previously available, has been incorporated in it. Attention has been called particularly to Mr. Lloyd George's remarkable Memorandum of the 25th March 1919, and to the manner in which the League is attempting to handle some of the problems left unsolved by the Supreme Council.

The appendices in this volume are designed to exhibit the secret Allied Agreements and certain other instruments affecting the future of the Turkish Empire ; the final award as to Upper Silesia ; the secret Allied Agreements with reference to China and Japan. In addition the text of the Treaty of the United States with Germany is added. Two other appendices give the present position of the Covenant of the League and the texts of some typical Mandates.

It has been thought necessary to add editorial notes in some cases to bring chapters up to date (i.e. to December 1922),[1] but the chapters themselves are, in general, studies of the work of the Peace Conference and not primarily of any later developments.

A separate index of names is given in this, as in every other, volume. This volume includes a general subject-index to the whole six volumes. This subject-index deals only with subjects treated in the narrative and text. The inquirer will find the complete official index of names and subjects to the German Treaty in Vol. III, pp. 380–457; and a topical index to the Austrian, Hungarian, and Bulgarian Treaties in Vol. V, pp. 477–83. It is hoped that it will be possible, by the aid of these various indices, not only to find the chief subjects of importance readily but to test the accuracy of all statements in the text by comparison with the original articles of the treaties and with other important documents.

Of passion and prejudice there has already been enough and it is hoped that the History may serve to assuage and calm rather than to inflame them. Thirty years hence men will not only view this turbulent scene with more detachment, but they will know more than we do of the darker secrets of the Peace Conference. But it is only in this generation, and by the evidence of contemporary writers, that the knowledge of certain facts and opinions can be preserved. If only a few of these are recorded or indicated in this history its purpose will have been amply achieved.

HAROLD TEMPERLEY.

[1] In the case of the Treaty of Lausanne (v. pp. 114–7) the story has been carried into 1923 for the sake of completeness, as in some other instances (v. pp. 192, 283, 616).

CONTENTS OF VOL. VI

CHAPTER I

THE NEAR AND MIDDLE EAST

PART I

A. THE SECRET AGREEMENTS AFFECTING THE NEAR AND MIDDLE EAST (1915–17)

B. BRIEF SKETCH OF TURKISH TERRITORIAL SETTLEMENTS PUBLICLY PROPOSED SINCE THE ARMISTICE

PART II

THE NON-ARAB TERRITORIES OF THE OTTOMAN EMPIRE SINCE THE ARMISTICE OF THE 30TH OCTOBER 1918

PART III

THE EMERGENCE OF ARAB NATIONALISM

A. GREAT BRITAIN AND THE ARABS UP TO THE ARMISTICE OF THE 30TH OCTOBER 1918

B. SYRIA AND PALESTINE

i. *Syria since the Armistice of Mudros, 30th October 1918*

PART IV

THE INDEPENDENCE OF EGYPT

PART V

THE LIBERATION OF PERSIA

CHAPTER II

THE RESURRECTION OF POLAND

PART I

HISTORICAL SKETCH

PART II

POLAND AT THE PEACE CONFERENCE

CHAPTER III

EVOLUTION AND REVOLUTION IN NORTHERN EUROPE

PART I

THE RECOGNITION OF THE BALTIC STATES

PART II

THE BOLSHEVIKS AND DIPLOMACY

CHAPTER IV

THE WORLD OUTSIDE EUROPE

PART I

THE BRITISH DOMINIONS

A. THE STATUS OF THE DOMINIONS BEFORE THE PEACE CONFERENCE

B. THE DOMINIONS AT THE PEACE CONFERENCE

C. THE INFLUENCE OF THE PEACE CONFERENCE AND THE LEAGUE COVENANT ON THE STATUS OF THE DOMINIONS

PART II

SHANTUNG AT THE PEACE CONFERENCE

CHAPTER V

THE ATTITUDE OF THE UNITED STATES SENATE TOWARDS THE VERSAILLES TREATY: 1918–20

CHAPTER VI

INTERNATIONAL DEVELOPMENTS UNDER THE LEAGUE OF NATIONS

PART I

THE MAKING OF THE COVENANT

PART II

THE INTERNATIONAL LABOUR SECTION OF THE TREATIES

PART III

THE PERMANENT COURT OF INTERNATIONAL JUSTICE

PART IV

THE MANDATORY SYSTEM

PART V

GUARANTEES AGAINST WAR

EPILOGUE

SOME GENERAL CONSIDERATIONS ON THE PEACE CONFERENCE AND ITS AFTERMATH

I. THE WILSONIAN PRINCIPLES AND THE NEGOTIATIONS LEADING TO PEACE

II. MR. LLOYD GEORGE'S SCHEME OF A PEACE

III. CERTAIN PRINCIPLES IN THE PEACE TREATIES

IV. PROMOTION OF INTERNATIONAL CO-OPERATION SINCE 1919

APPENDICES

MAPS

LIST OF CONTRIBUTORS TO VOLUMES I, II, IV, V AND VI

VOLUME I

Chapter	Contributor
CHAPTER I.	
Part I. The Military Defeat of Germany.	
„ II. Some Influences of Sea-Power in the War.	Admiral H. W. Richmond.
CHAPTER II.	
The German Revolution and the Conditions which prepared it.	K. W. M. Pickthorn, M.A., Fellow of Corpus Christi, Cambridge.
CHAPTER III.	
The Political Aspects of the Armistice Negotiations.	
CHAPTER IV.	
Material Effect of the War upon Neutrals and Belligerents, 1918.	H. W. Carless Davis, C.B.E., Fellow of Balliol College, Oxford.
CHAPTER V.	
The Public and Official War-Aims of the Belligerents.	H. W. V. Temperley, M.A., Reader in Modern History, University of Cambridge.
CHAPTER VI.	
Part I. The War-Aims of Labour.	C. de Lisle Burns, M.A., Cantab.
„ II. The Bolshevik Attitude at Brest-Litovsk and its Effects.	B. H. Sumner, M.A., Fellow of All Souls, Oxford.
CHAPTER VII.	
The Organization of the Conference.	C. K. Webster, M.A., Wilson Professor of History, University College of Wales, Aberystwyth.

CHAPTER VIII.

Part	Subject	Contributor
Part I.	Political and Military Working of the Armistice Commission at Spa.	
„ II.	The Work of the Supreme Economic Council.	E. F. Wise, M.A., Cantab., late of the Ministry of Food.
„ III.	Maintenance of Authority of Conference: Poland, Germany, Hungary.	

CHAPTER IX.

Subject	Contributor
The Legal Basis of International Relations Prior to the Re-establishment of Peace by Treaties.	H. D. Hazeltine, of Harvard University, U.S.A., Downing Professor of the Laws of England, Cambridge University.

VOLUME II

Subject	Contributor
Introduction.	H. W. V. Temperley.

CHAPTER I.

Part	Subject	Contributor
Part I.	The League of Nations.	Lord Eustace Percy, M.A., Oxon., M.P.
„ II.	International Labour at the Conference.	Professor J. T. Shotwell, Columbia University, U.S.A.
„ III.	Reparation and Economic Aspects.	
„ IV.	Finance and Reparation.	A. E. Siepmann.
„ V.	International Communications Policy Embodied in the Treaty.	Colonel H. O. Mance, C.B., D.S.O.

CHAPTER II.

Part	Subject	Contributor
Part I.	The Military Occupation of Germany.	
„ II.	The Military Terms.	
„ III.	The Naval Clauses—Terms.	

CHAPTER III.

The Settlement of the Western Frontiers of Germany.	C. R. Cruttwell, M.A., Fellow of Hertford College, Oxford.

CHAPTER IV.

Part I. The Schleswig Question.	H. C. O'Neill.
,, II. Meaning, Strategic and Otherwise, of the Loss to Germany of Polish Territory.	

CHAPTER V.

The Territorial Settlement in Africa.	The late G. L. Beer and Miss F. M. Graves.

CHAPTER VI.

The Legal Basis of International Relations Prior to the Re-establishment of Peace by Treaties (continued from Chap. IX, Vol. I).	Professor H. D. Hazeltine.

CHAPTER VII.

The New Germany.

VOLUME IV

CHAPTER I.

Part I. The Military Collapse of Bulgaria.	
,, II. Military Disintegration of Austro-Hungarian Monarchy.	E. M. B. Ingram, M.A., Cantab.
,, III. The Downfall of the Habsburg Monarchy.	L. B. Namier, M.A., late Lecturer Balliol College, Oxford.

CHAPTER II.

Part I. The Armistices and their Meaning.	
,, II. Brief Sketch of the Problems connected with the Austrian and Hungarian Treaties.	

CHAPTER III.

Part I.	The Treaty with Austria (Treaty of St. Germain). The Military Terms.	
„ II.	The Treaty with Hungary (Treaty of the Trianon). The Military Terms.	
„ III.	The Treaty with Bulgaria (Treaty of Neuilly). The Military Terms.	H. W. V. Temperley.

CHAPTER IV.

Part I.	The Yugo-Slavs.	R. G. D. Laffan, M.A., Fellow of Queens' College, Cambridge.
„ II.	Rumania and the Redemption of the Rumanians.	
„ III.	The Formation of the Czecho-Slovak State.	R. W. Seton-Watson, Litt.D., Oxon.

CHAPTER V.

The Treaty of London.	H. W. V. Temperley.

CHAPTER VI.

Part I.	The Czecho-Slovak Plebiscite Areas.	Robert F. Young, M.A., Oxon.
„ II.	The Klagenfurt Basin.	Roland L'E. Bryce, B.A., Oxon.
„ III.	German West Hungary.	

CHAPTER VII.

The Making of the Treaties with Austria, Bulgaria, and Hungary and the Principles underlying them.	H. W. V. Temperley.

CHAPTER VIII.

The New Bulgaria.	W. J. M. Childs.

CHAPTER IX.

Part I.	The New Austria.	A. C. Coolidge, Professor of Modern History, Harvard University, U.S.A.
„ II.	The New Hungary.	H. W. V. Temperley.

VOLUME V

CHAPTER I.

	Subject	Contributor
Part I.	Reparation and Financial Clauses in Austrian, Hungarian, and Bulgarian Treaties.	Lieut.-Colonel The Hon. Sidney Peel, D.S.O.
,, II.	Introduction to the Economic Clauses of the Treaties.	
,, III.	Commercial Policy in German, Austrian, Hungarian, and Bulgarian Treaties.	A. A. Young, Professor of Economics, Harvard University, U.S.A., President of the Tariff Sub-committee, Economic Section of the Peace Conference.
,, IV.	Enemy Property, Debts, and Contracts.	

CHAPTER II.

Subject	Contributor
The Treaties for the Protection of Minorities.	
Tables and Summaries. Statistical Tables.	B. C. Wallis, B.Sc., London, Fellow Royal Statistical Society.
Recognition of New States.	H. W. V. Temperley.

VOLUME VI

CHAPTER I.

	Subject	Contributor
Part I. A.	The Secret Agreements affecting the Near and Middle East (1915–17).	
,, B.	Brief Sketch of Turkish Territorial Settlements publicly proposed since the Armistice.	H. W. V. Temperley.
,, II.	The Non-Arab Territories of the Ottoman Empire since the Armistice of the 30th October 1918.	A. J. Toynbee, M.A., Oxon., Professor of Byzantine History, London University.

Part III. A.	Great Britain and the Arabs up to the Armistice of the 30th October 1918.	D. G. Hogarth, C.M.G., Litt.D., Oxford.
,, B i.	Syria.	
,, B ii.	Palestine and Zionism.	W. J. M. Childs.
,, C.	The Problem of Mesopotamia (Iraq and Mosul).	
,, IV.	The Independence of Egypt.	H. W. V. Temperley.
,, V.	The Liberation of Persia.	
CHAPTER II.		
Part I.	Historical Sketch of Poland.	R. H. Lord, Ph.D., Professor of Modern History, Harvard University.
,, II.	Poland at the Peace Conference.	H. J. Paton, M.A., Fellow of the Queen's College, Oxford.
CHAPTER III.		
Part I.	The Recognition of the Baltic States.	J. Y. Simpson, Professor in the University of Edinburgh.
,, II.	The Bolsheviks and Diplomacy.	H. Wilson Harris, M.A., Cantab.
CHAPTER IV.		
Part I.	The British Dominions.	A. B. Keith, Professor in the University of Edinburgh.
,, II.	Shantung at the Peace Conference.	S. K. Hornbeck, Professor, United States Tariff Commission.
CHAPTER V.		
	The Attitude of the United States towards the Versailles Treaty: 1918–20.	H. Barrett Learned, Ph.D., sometime Professor of Modern History, Leland Stanford University, U.S.A.
CHAPTER VI.		
Part I.	The Making of the Covenant.	J. R. M. Butler, Fellow of Trinity College, Cambridge.
,, II.	The International Labour Section of the Treaties.	Harold Butler, C.B., Deputy Director of International Labour Office.

Part III.	The Permanent Court of International Justice.	P. J. Baker, M.A., Cantab., late Whewell Scholar International Law, Cambridge. Formerly of the Secretariat of the League of Nations.
,, IV.	The Mandatory System.	The Right Hon. W. G. A. Ormsby-Gore, M.P., late Member of the Permanent Mandates Commission.
,, V.	Guarantees against War.	Major-General Sir F. Maurice, K.C.M.G., late Director of Military Operations, British War Office.
EPILOGUE.		
MAPS.		A. G. Ogilvie, M.A., Reader in Geography in the University of Manchester. J. A. Steers, M.A., Scholar of St. Catharine's College, Cambridge.

CHAPTER I

THE NEAR AND MIDDLE EAST

PART I

A. THE SECRET AGREEMENTS AFFECTING THE NEAR AND MIDDLE EAST (1915–17)

1. *The Four Secret Agreements.* The Secret Treaties and Agreements, four in number, forming the subject of this Chapter, are those relating to the Near and Middle East, into which the Allies entered as exigencies inseparable from the war. In chronological order they are:

(*a*) *The Constantinople Agreement, 18th March 1915.* The 'Constantinople Agreement' regarding the future of Constantinople, the Straits, and Persia, between Great Britain, France, and Russia, completed on the 18th March 1915.

(*b*) *Secret Treaty of London, 26th April 1915.* The Secret Treaty of London, under which Italy entered the war on the side of the Entente, signed on behalf of Great Britain, France, Russia, and Italy on the 26th April 1915. This treaty had a wider scope than the other agreements, for it dealt also with Italian territorial demands in Austria-Hungary.

(*c*) *Sykes-Picot Agreement, 16th May 1916.* The Agreement between Great Britain, France, and Russia (more commonly known as the 'Sykes-Picot Agreement') relating to the future of certain portions—chiefly the Arab regions—of the Ottoman Empire, completed on the 16th May 1916.

(*d*) *St. Jean de Maurienne Agreement, 17th April 1917.* The Agreement of St. Jean de Maurienne respecting Italian territorial claims in Asia Minor, made between Great Britain, France, and Italy on the 17th April 1917. This Agreement was a result of the secret pact of the 16th May 1916, from which Italy was excluded.[1]

[1] Public knowledge of these secret undertakings has been gained chiefly from Russian sources. Soon after the Bolshevik Government came into power—in October 1917—they published to the world, in an attempt to discredit the so-called capitalist Governments of Western Europe, the documents found in the archives of the Russian Foreign Office which related to these and other

In this chapter it is sought to outline, as fully as documents and other material now available render possible, the secret Agreements relating to the Near and Middle East to which various Allies subscribed during the war; and, further, to place these commitments in their proper perspective, and to exhibit them in the setting to which they inseparably belong—the gigantic struggle for national survival, which required of the nations involved in it the use of every expedient permissible in diplomacy and war. Unless considered in their true historical setting the secret Treaties and Agreements bear a distorted and entirely misleading aspect, and possess little relationship with reality.

2. *The first stage of the war, 1914–15.* The outbreak of war in 1914 between Great Britain, France, and Russia, and Germany and Austria-Hungary, left Turkey, Bulgaria, Greece, Italy, and Rumania in a position of doubtful or precarious neutrality. All expected to realize their large national ambitions at the cost of one or more of their neighbours. Each believed that participation in the war on the side of the victors would secure the attainment of these ambitions, and that upon a scale more satisfying than imagination had ever suggested during the long preceding years of peace. On the other hand, in an upheaval so wide, engaging forces so vast, and containing such ominous signs of being a struggle to the death, alliance with the losing side might well involve irreparable national disaster. Nor would a policy of indefinite neutrality be free from risk. For these neutrals undue delay in making their decision, to support one alliance or the other, might obviously land them in dangers hardly less than would unconsidering precipitancy.

(*a*) *Turkish Treaty with Germany, 4th August 1914.* The Young Turk leaders of the Ottoman Empire had, as we now know, already made their decision, and committed their country beyond recall to support of the Central Powers by a secret Treaty with Germany, signed on the 4th August 1914.

(*b*) *Bulgaria.* Bulgaria, too, under the Tsar Ferdinand, had also gone far in the same direction, though not as yet irrevocably. The part Bulgaria could play in the war was of profound

secret commitments of foreign Governments and Tsarist Russia. The revelations so made, though giving much important information, were incomplete, and in details not always quite accurate. Cp. R. S. Baker, *Wilson and World Settlement* (1922), I, 43–72; and text of discussion of the 20th March 1919, III, 1–19.

importance to each of the great hostile alliances, whichever she might decide to join. Repeated efforts, therefore, were made by the Entente Powers and by M. Venizelos, the Greek Prime Minister, to secure the adherence of Bulgaria; but she was not to be moved, even by promises of large territorial adjustments in her favour. Nothing short of decisive military successes by the Entente would have sufficed to shake the confidence of Ferdinand and his satellites in the ultimate triumph of German arms. Ferdinand adopted a policy of neutrality in outward form which moved steadily towards action with the Central Powers; and when, at last, the Entente effort to reach Constantinople had plainly failed, he caused his country to begin hostilities against Serbia on the 14th October 1915.[1]

(*c*) *Greece.* In Greece, during the earlier stages of the war, the situation was more complicated. There, indeed, King Constantine and his pro-German supporters were following a policy not unlike that of Ferdinand in Bulgaria. But Greek public opinion was divided, for M. Venizelos and his party were in favour of siding with the Entente, and the King had to go warily and with many temporizations. Thus for some time Greece was regarded as a possible ally, both by the Entente and by the Central Powers, and could be neglected by neither.

(*d*) *Italy.* At the outbreak of war Italy was the ally of Germany and Austria-Hungary, a partner of long standing in the Triple Alliance, and her position, in consequence, was one of exceeding delicacy. The sympathies of her people, however, were less with her Allies than with the Powers of the Entente. Undeniably, too, she stood to gain more by helping to defeat her age-long enemy, Austria-Hungary, than by assisting that enemy to victory and aggrandisement. Her allies, it further appeared, had decided upon their policy of war without consulting Italy, and thus had not fulfilled a precedent condition to obtaining her support under the terms of the alliance. Faced with this breach of etiquette—committed because it served the German purpose at the time—her Government held that Italy was under no valid treaty obligation to join the Central Powers, and, on the 3rd August 1914, issued a Declaration of Italian neutrality. Thenceforward, as the one Great Power of Europe remaining neutral, Italy held a commanding position in relation to both groups of belligerents.

[1] For relations of Bulgaria and Greece in 1915 *v.* Vol. IV, pp. 452–3.

(*e*) *Rumania*. Rumania was another neutral state which, by geographical position and military strength, would be able to exert a considerable influence upon the course of the war. She too had come within the orbit of the Triple Alliance, to which she had secret contingent commitments.[1] Here again the policy of the sovereign, King Charles, a Hohenzollern, was opposed by the Prime Minister, M. Bratianu, who saw that his country's interests lay with the Entente. Geographically, however, Rumania was badly placed. So long as Constantinople and the Straits were under Turco-German control she could be munitioned only precariously—or perhaps not at all—through the ports of Arctic Russia. Rumanian neutrality, therefore, was long-continued, and not until the time seemed altogether favourable did that state join the Entente under a secret treaty, signed on the 17th August 1916, with Great Britain, France, Italy, and Russia.[2] The Treaty calls for no further remark here, having already been examined in an earlier volume of the present work.

In addition to treaties and agreements designed to secure the support of neutrals for the Entente, various grave questions —which existed, or from time to time arose—between the Powers of the Entente, also had to be regulated by secret compacts. To this class belong the Agreement regarding Constantinople and the Straits; the so-called Sykes-Picot Agreement, and the Agreement of St. Jean de Maurienne. They represent, on the whole, concessions upon policy by the Allies between themselves, in order to harmonize their aims, and to maintain the unity of the Alliance in prosecution of the war. They dealt with the future at a time when the outcome of the war could not be assured. The fulfilment of each, therefore, was made contingent upon the ultimate success of the Allies being complete enough to allow of the pact being executed.

3. *The 'Constantinople Agreement' of the 18th March 1915, between Great Britain, France, and Russia, regarding Constantinople, the Straits, and Persia.* The grouping into which the belligerent Powers fell in the first week of August 1914, seemed to indicate for Russia a possibility of realizing her traditional ambitions in Constantinople and the Straits. And when, during the first week in November, hostile acts by Turkey compelled

[1] *v.* Vol. IV, pp. 213–14.
[2] Cf. Text in Vol. IV, pp. 515–17; *v.* also ibid., pp. 216–19.

the Entente Powers to declare war upon her, it was evident that a momentous approach towards the realization of Russia's dearest ambition had taken place. Between this step and complete attainment, however, much remained to be carried through. It was necessary for the Entente to obtain complete victory in the war; it was necessary for Russia to secure in advance the Agreement of Great Britain and France to her contingent annexation of Constantinople. The first lay in the lap of time, and the final decision could not be hastened, could not be prejudged. Negotiations for the second, however, might be begun—and, from the Russian point of view, the sooner the better, lest untoward developments should jeopardize success.

The matter, indeed, grew urgent when, in January and February 1915, the Russian position in Trans-Caucasia threatened to become precarious—notwithstanding the disastrous defeat inflicted on Turkish arms at Sarykamish, during the first week of January. In seeking the assistance of her allies, by suggesting an Allied expedition against Constantinople, the question of the city's future was bound to arise.

The course of the negotiations upon which Russia now entered, and the claims she and her Allies in turn put forward, may be gathered best by quoting from a secret memorandum of the Russian Foreign Office, drawn up just before Italy had entered the war on the 23rd May 1915.[1]

On the 19th February (4th March N.S.) 1915 the Minister of Foreign Affairs handed to the British and French Ambassadors a memorandum which set forth the desire to add the following territories to Russia as the result of the present war:

> 'The town of Constantinople, the western coast of the Bosporus, the Sea of Marmara, and the Dardanelles; Southern Thrace as far as the Enos-Midia line; the coast of Asia Minor between the Bosporus and the river Sakaria and a point on the Gulf of Ismid to be defined later; the islands in the Sea of Marmara, and the Islands of Imbros and Tenedos. The special rights of England and France, in the above territories are to remain inviolate.'

The claims as thus defined do not, it may be pointed out, include the Asiatic shores of the Sea of Marmara (except a small

[1] Published in the Bolshevik *Pravda* on the 20th December 1917, and in the *Manchester Guardian* on the 22nd February 1918; and see map opposite p. 6.

portion along the Ismid peninsula) nor of the Dardanelles. The memorandum continues:

'Both the British and French Governments express their readiness to agree to our wishes, provided the war is won, and provided a number of claims made by England and France, both in the Ottoman Empire, and in other places, are satisfied.

'As far as Turkey is concerned these claims are as follows:

(1) 'Constantinople to be recognized as a free port for transit of goods not proceeding from or to Russia, and a free passage is to be given through the Straits to merchant ships.

(2) 'The rights of England and France in Asiatic Turkey to be defined by Special Agreement between England, France, and Russia are recognized.

(3) 'The Sacred Mohammedan places are to be protected, and Arabia is to be under an independent Mohammedan [rule].

'The neutral zone in Persia established by the Anglo-Russian Agreement of 1907 is to be included in the English sphere of influence.

'While recognizing these demands in general as satisfactory, the Russian Government made several reservations.

'In view of the formulation of our wishes with regard to the Sacred Mohammedan places it must now be made clear whether these localities are to remain under the Sovereignty of Turkey with the Sultan keeping the title of Caliph, or whether it is proposed to create new independent states. In our opinion it would be desirable to separate the Caliphate from Turkey. In any case freedom of pilgrimage must be guaranteed.

'While agreeing to the inclusion of the neutral zone of Persia within the sphere of English influence, the Russian Government considers it right to declare that the districts round the towns of Isfahan and Yezd should be secured by Russia, and also that part of the neutral zone which cuts a wedge between the Russian and Afghan frontiers and goes as far as the Russian frontier at Zulfagar should be included in the Russian sphere of influence.

'The Russian Government considers it desirable that the question of the frontiers between Russia and Northern Afghanistan should simultaneously be solved according to the wishes expressed at the time of the negotiations in 1914.

'After the entrance of Italy into the war, our wishes were communicated to the Italian Government also, and the latter expressed its agreement, provided the war ended in the successful realization of Italian claims in general, and in the East in particular, and in the recognition by us for Italy within the territories ceded to us of the same rights as those enjoyed by England and France.'

This Russian memorandum gives a coherent summary of what had been done. Faced by an almost irresistible combination of circumstances making for Russian possession of Constantinople, Great Britain and France had safeguarded their own interests as best they could. Great Britain, in consideration for reversing her long-standing policy of opposition to Russian domination of Constantinople and the Straits, had secured an advantageous revision of the zones of influence in Persia. Of special interest, also, are clauses (2) and (3) in the section of the memorandum reciting the claims of Great Britain and France in Turkey as admitted by Russia. Clause (2) foreshadows the subsequent Sykes-Picot Agreement of the 16th May 1916. Clause (3) bears indirectly but pertinently upon the same agreement by requiring an independent Arabia under a Mohammedan sovereign. How these matters fell out will be shown later in reviewing the 'Sykes-Picot Agreement'.

The summary is supported by the contents of two official and secret telegrams revealed by the Bolshevik Government, and is further borne out by an authoritative statement in the Duma by the Russian Prime Minister of the time.

The first telegram is of the 18th March 1915, from M. Sazonoff, the Russian Minister of Foreign Affairs, to the Russian Ambassador at Paris. It recounts the favourable reception accorded, especially by Great Britain and France, to the Russian proposals contained in the memorandum of the 4th March 1915, the gist of which we have already given. The telegram in question says:

'On the 8th March the French Ambassador, on behalf of his Government, announced to me that France was prepared to take up a most favourable attitude in the matter of realization of our desires as set out in my telegram to you, No. 937, in respect of the Straits and Constantinople, for which I charged you to tender Delcassé my gratitude.

'In his conversations with you Delcassé had previously more than once given his assurance that we could rely on the sympathy of France, and only referred to the need of elucidating the question of the attitude of England, from whom he feared some objections, before he could give us a more definite assurance in the above sense. Now the British Government has given its complete consent in writing to the annexation by Russia of the Straits and Constantinople within the limits indicated by us, and only demanded security for its economic interests and a similar benevolent attitude on our part towards the political aspirations of England in other parts.

'For me, personally, filled as I am with most complete confidence in Delcassé, the assurance received from him is quite sufficient, but the Imperial Government would desire a more definite pronouncement of France's assent to the complete satisfaction of our desires, similar to that made by the British Government.'

The second telegram is one from M. Sazonoff to the Russian Ambassador in London, and is dated the 20th March 1915:

'Referring to the Memorandum of the British Embassy here of the 12th March, will you please express to Grey the profound gratitude of the Imperial Government for the complete and final assent of Great Britain to the solution of the question of the Straits and Constantinople, in accordance with Russia's desires. The Imperial Government fully appreciates the sentiments of the British Government, and feels certain that a sincere recognition of mutual interests will secure for ever the firm friendship between Russia and Great Britain.

'Having already given its promise respecting the conditions of trade in the Straits and Constantinople, the Imperial Government sees no objection to confirming its assent to the establishment (1) of free transit through Constantinople for all goods not proceeding from or proceeding to Russia and (2) free passage through the Straits for merchant vessels.

'In order to facilitate the breaking through of the Dardanelles undertaken by the Allies, the Imperial Government is prepared to co-operate in inducing those States whose help is considered useful by Great Britain and France to join in the undertaking on reasonable terms.

'The Imperial Government completely shares the view of the British Government that the Holy Moslem places must also in future remain under an independent Moslem rule. It is desirable to elucidate at once whether it is contemplated to leave those places under the rule of Turkey, the Sultan retaining the title of Caliph, or to create new independent States, since the Imperial Government would only be able to formulate its desires in accordance with one or other of these assumptions. On its part the Imperial Government would regard the separation of the Caliphate from Turkey as very desirable. Of course the freedom of pilgrimage must be completely secured.

'The Imperial Government confirms its assent to the inclusion of the neutral zone of Persia in the British sphere of influence. At the same time, however, it regards it as just to stipulate that the districts adjoining the cities of Isfahan and Yezd, forming with them one inseparable whole, should be secured for Russia in view of the Russian interests which have arisen there. The neutral zone now forms a wedge between the Russian and Afghan frontiers, and comes up to the very frontier line of Russia at Zulfagar. Hence a portion of this wedge will have to be annexed to the Russian sphere of influence. Of essential importance to the Imperial Government is the question of railway construction in the neutral zone, which will require further amicable discussion.

'The Imperial Government expects that in future its full liberty of action will be recognized in the sphere of influence allotted to it, coupled in particular with the right of preferentially developing in that sphere its financial and economic policy.

'Lastly, the Imperial Government considers it desirable simultaneously to solve also the problems in Northern Afghanistan adjoining

Russia in the sense of the wishes expressed on the subject by the Imperial Ministry in the course of the negotiations last year.'

The penultimate paragraph of this telegram throws aside all pretence that Russia's intentions in her Persian sphere of influence were anything less than annexation in the long run. 'Full liberty of action' was the compensation she took for agreeing to the extension of the British zone of influence.[1]

The allusion to Afghanistan covered a proposal put forward before the war for improving the irrigation of Russian territory in that region. Lord Islington stated in the House of Lords on the 9th January 1918, that no suggestion affecting the territorial integrity of Afghanistan had ever been made. He also stated that the Ameer had been assured that no such proposal would be made or agreed to at the Peace Conference.

4. *Later Russian developments over the Constantinople Agreement, 1916–21.*

(*a*) *The 2nd December 1916, Trepoff's Declaration.* The first official statement that the Agreement we have just outlined existed was made in the Russian Duma, on the 2nd December 1916, by M. Trepoff, the Prime Minister. The revelation was made with the express purpose of reviving if possible, the national spirit of the Russian people, and strengthening the position of the Throne and the Imperial Government. Russia was by this time far advanced in revolution, and Throne and Government alike were on the eve of downfall. The Prime Minister's statement was:

> 'An Agreement which we concluded in 1915 with Great Britain and France, and to which Italy has adhered, established in the most definite fashion the right of Russia to the Straits and Constantinople. . . . I repeat that absolute Agreement on this point is firmly established among the Allies.'

How far the Russian people had moved from their old beliefs and ideals was shown by the failure of this announcement to stir them. The fatuous self-sufficiency and blind incompetence, not only of their rulers, but of the whole ruling class in general, and the rank corruption which permeated classes yet wider, had caused the Russian State, as then organized, to become rotten. The people were turning eagerly to new ideals. They had lost faith and hope, they were, too, already war-weary; and when the moment arrived, as it were unexpectedly and

[1] *v.* also p. 209.

suddenly, in which the greatest of their national aims came within resolute grasp, that generation of Russians proved incapable of seizing it.

(*b*) *Bolshevik attitude, 1917.* After the Revolution the Bolshevik Government formally declared, in accordance with their theories, that Russia no longer had any ambitions to be satisfied by the occupation of Constantinople and the Straits. With the withdrawal of Russia from the war and from her alliances the Agreement between her and the Western Powers lapsed, and the future of Constantinople and its great water-way, a subject of endless contention and rivalry, remained for the solution of Time. It is of interest, however, to glance at subsequent Bolshevik action in Persia and Turkey relating to the Allied Agreement of the 18th March 1915.

(*c*) *Bolshevik Treaty with Persia, 27th February 1921.* By the Russo-Persian Treaty signed at Moscow on the 27th February 1921 (the text of which was published in the *Manchester Guardian* of the 31st March 1921) the 'Government of the Russian Socialist Federate Soviet Republic' formally and definitely denounced all Treaties and Agreements concluded between Imperial Russia and Persia, and all Agreements of the Imperial Government with other Powers relating to Persia.[1]

(*d*) *Bolshevik Treaty with Kemalists, 16th March 1921.* By another Treaty signed at Moscow on the 16th March 1921, between the Russian Soviet Republic and the Great National Assembly of Turkey (in other words the Turkish Angora Government), Bolshevik Russia made a similarly disinterested gesture towards Nationalist Turkey. The Treaty frees Turkey from all Agreements concluded with the Tsarist Government, and from the consequences arising from international treaties or agreements by that Government. Russia and Turkey further agree to open the Straits to the shipping of all nations, and to confide the preparation of an International Agreement on the freedom of the Straits to a Conference of Delegates from the coastal states concerned. The findings of the Conference, however, were not to be of a kind to affect the independence of Turkey, nor the security of Constantinople.

5. *The 'Secret Treaty of London', signed on the 26th April 1915, between Great Britain, France, Russia, and Italy, regarding*

[1] For further details *re* Persia *v. infra*, pp. 214–15.

the entry of Italy into the War. The Treaty of London laid down the terms on which Italy entered the War on the side of the Entente Powers.[1]

Italy had, in fact, long-standing and growing ambitions to realize. Territories peopled by the Italian race were still under the rule of the Hapsburgs; the north-eastern frontier imposed upon her by Austria after previous wars was no better than that of a defeated state. Nor was she without memories of her ancient past. She desired, from motives of security and sentiment, to make of the Adriatic an Italian Sea. With a teeming population and high birthrate she saw a great and constant emigration of her people to lands not under the Italian flag. At one time she had looked to Tunis, traditionally the nearest and wealthiest African province of old Rome, as an ideal field for Italian colonization; but there she had seen herself forestalled by France. Taught by this experience she had then, at the cost of war with Turkey, made sure of Tripolitana, another of her ancient African possessions, only to find that whatever it might have been under Rome it now presented few opportunities for Italian settlement. Italy, in truth, was under all the disadvantages of being a late arrival among the Powers anxious to acquire colonial possessions.

However, farther afield was Mediterranean Asia Minor, a rich and fertile region, sparsely peopled, its great natural resources undeveloped, its climate not very unlike that of Southern Italy, its coast not three days' voyage from Italian ports. It, too, had once been Roman territory. Towards this land Italian attention had for some time been directed, as a promising field for Italian commercial activity—perhaps even, under favourable circumstances, for Italian expansion. With wise prevision, Italy was, already, as the result of her war with Turkey in 1911, in occupation of the Dodecanese Islands, in part covering the western coast of Asia Minor. More and more, however, during recent years, it had become apparent that Germany was likely to dominate Asia Minor. The entry of Turkey, therefore, into the War on the 31st October 1914 in alliance with Germany, did not make for Italian support being eagerly thrown in the same direction.

After the Declaration of Italian neutrality on the 3rd August 1914, Italian opinion speedily hardened to the view that Italy

[1] Text is in Vol. V, pp. 384–93.

should seek the full realization of her national aims by every means in her power; and that her policy should be characterized by severe practicality—that it should, in fact, deal only with realities, and be influenced neither by prejudice nor by sentiment. Obviously Italy's claims could be more fully satisfied if she found herself on the side of the victorious Entente than on the side of the victorious Central Powers, provided that the Entente had recognized her claims in advance and undertaken to secure their fulfilment. A policy of realities, therefore, called for support of the Entente, but for support to be given under bond.

Germany, nevertheless, did not allow Italian policy to be shaped against her without making efforts to guide it in German interests. Prince Bülow was dispatched on a mission to Rome in January 1915, where he used every artifice to influence the Italian Government and Italian opinion. His efforts, however, were hampered by the fact that Italian ambitions could be satisfied only at the expense of Germany's ally Austria, and her prospective ally, Turkey.

We are not concerned here with the various articles of this long and elaborately drawn London Pact except as applying to the Near and Middle East.[1] Suffice it to say that the Treaty provided for the immediate conclusion of military and naval conventions; the first between Italy and the three other Great Powers of the Entente, the second between Italy and Great Britain and France alone; and that Italy undertook to prosecute the War with all her resources, and to conduct her operations jointly with her allies against *all* enemy powers. Other articles define with careful exactitude the huge territorial additions Italy was to receive from Austria and her position in Albania:

ARTICLE 8. 'Italy shall receive entire sovereignty over the Dodecanese Islands which she is at present occupying.

ARTICLE 9. (This article is of great importance but is fully quoted below under § 10 *a*.)

ARTICLE 10. 'All rights and privileges in Libya at present belonging to the Sultan by virtue of the Treaty of Lausanne are transferred to Italy.'

ARTICLE 12. 'Italy declares that she associates herself in the declaration made by France, Great Britain, and Russia to the effect

[1] For other treatment *v.* Vol. IV, pp. 288–91, and for Albania, ibid., p. 340.

that Arabia and the Moslem Holy Places in Arabia shall be left under the authority of an independent Moslem Power.

ARTICLE 16. 'The present arrangement shall be held secret.'

In addition to this Italy acceded on the 26th April 1915 to the Anglo-French-Russian Declaration of the 5th September 1914 by which the three Governments agreed not to conclude a separate peace, and that, 'whenever there may be occasion to discuss the terms of peace, none of the Allied Powers shall lay down any conditions of peace, without previous agreement with each of the other Allies'. It was further agreed that after the declaration of war by Italy, a new declaration of the Four Powers on the above lines should be signed and published.

With her desired expansion in Europe clearly defined and covenanted for, her interest in maintaining the balance of power in the Mediterranean recognized, and the assurance of receiving a proportionate equality of treatment with her great Allies in any partition or disposal of Ottoman territory in Asia that might result from the struggle, Italy declared war on Austria-Hungary on the 23rd May, and on Turkey on the 20th August 1915.

How far the provisions of the Treaty of London were realized in regard to Turkey-in-Asia, and the influence they exercised, will best be seen when we consider the Sykes-Picot Agreement and the Agreement of St. Jean de Maurienne.

6. *The Sykes-Picot Agreement and the Sherif of Mecca.* To make the origins and purposes of the Sykes-Picot Agreement clear it becomes necessary now to glance at a still earlier secret understanding.

Faced with the realities just described, and in prosecution of the War in the East on behalf of herself and her Allies, Great Britain, during the year 1915, obtained the support of the Sherif of Mecca against the Turks. The Sherif was already covertly hostile to the Young Turk Government of Turkey, and had refused his backing to the *Jihad* decreed by the Turkish Sultan as Caliph of Islam. He already had large ambitions for himself, his family, and the independence of the Arab race. He aimed at nothing less than the creation of an Arab State, or a Confederation of Arab States, which should embrace the Arab peoples of Syria, Mesopotamia, and the greater part of Arabia, with himself as Sovereign or Suzerain.

The understanding with the Sherif was arrived at in a series of letters between him and Sir H. McMahon, who at that time was British High Commissioner in Egypt. The correspondence remains unpublished, but has been officially described, both in the House of Lords and the House of Commons during 1921 and 1922, as being of a somewhat 'inconclusive' nature. That it pledged Great Britain to large measures of policy has never been disputed, though questions have arisen regarding certain details. These, however, do not concern us here.[1]

While undertaking to support the scheme of Arab independence Great Britain excluded from its operation the Turkish vilayet of Adana, containing the towns of Alexandretta, Adana, and Mersina, and the Syrian districts lying west of the line Aleppo–Homs–Hama–Damascus. The reasons given for excluding these territories were that they contained a non-Arab population and that there France had special claims.

Subject to these reservations, and to the Sherif of Mecca making an effective rising against the Turks, Great Britain pledged herself to freeing the Arab population from Turkish rule, and to establishing, not necessarily over the whole area, an independent Arab State. In this guarantee France subsequently joined. Important results were expected from an Arab rising led by the Sherif of Mecca—Warden of the Holy Places—not only in a military sense, but still more for its effect upon the World of Islam and the prestige of the Sultan-Caliph at Constantinople. Nor can it be said that expectation was not justified by results, for the rising proved to be of incalculable advantage to the Allied Cause.

(*a*) *French attitude.*[2] Although France concurred, and gave her support to the projected rising, she viewed with distrust and anxiety the prospect of far-reaching military successes being achieved by the Arabs themselves. When the rising seemed likely to come about she pressed her demands upon Great Britain for an Agreement regarding Asiatic Turkey. She desired execution of the provision in the Constantinople Agreement—of the 18th March 1915—which required the definition of Anglo-French rights in these regions by agreement between Great Britain, France, and Russia. She desired, in fact, to obtain of Great Britain a binding and definite recognition of French ambitions in Syria and Cilicia. Not-

[1] *v.* Part III of this Chapter, *passim*.

[2] *v.* also Chap. I, Part III, A, § 4, pp. 127–28.

withstanding the presence of German armies on French soil, French public opinion and the French Government supported these claims with remarkable energy and persistence.

In a way there was abundant reason for this urgency on the part of France. The Arab leaders already held her in deep suspicion, and made no secret of their hostility to her pretensions in Syria. They knew that Great Britain had nothing except goodwill for the Arab aims, and for the unification of the Arab race; they knew that for these aims France had nothing but irremovable hostility. In short they recognized that Arab and French aspirations in Syria were entirely incompatible.

(*b*) *Franco-British compromise.* The general situation, therefore, was somewhat as follows:

Honour demanded that previous British undertakings to the Sherif of Mecca and the Arabs should be amply fulfilled. It was at the same time urgently necessary to maintain concord and unity of effort between the chief European Allies, and—more difficult still—between European Allies and Arab Allies. It was necessary to harmonize the territorial ambitions of France and Russia with the vital and traditional interests of Great Britain, not only in the Ottoman hinterland of the Persian Gulf, but also in the international water-way formed by the Suez Canal and the Red Sea. And it was necessary to provide for the future of Palestine—or at least of Jerusalem—without placing this region, held in world-wide sanctity, under unqualified Arab rule. At this time, too, the clash of interests between France and the Arabs, and, therefore, between France and Great Britain, threatened to become acute.

In these circumstances of difficulty the British and French Government respectively appointed, towards the end of 1915, the late Sir Mark Sykes and M. Georges Picot, to prepare the terms of settlement as far as might be possible. The outcome of their labours was a draft of the so-called Sykes-Picot Agreement.

The draft represented no more than the compromises capable of attainment at the time, compromises between interests that were in almost direct and unvarying opposition. In this form the Agreement was then submitted to the Tsarist Government of Russia, who recognized, subject to certain restrictions, the arrangement come to between Great Britain and France. The conclusion of the Agreement by the several Powers concerned was effected during the end of April and the month of May 1916. It well may be that maintenance of the interests for which Great Britain stood, Arab interests, as well as British, had not been rendered less difficult during the early months of 1916 by the contemporaneous desperate struggle for life in which France was engaged before Verdun.

7. *Terms of the Sykes-Picot Agreement, 16th May 1916.* Secrecy was regarded as essential to the usefulness of the Agreement. Knowledge of its terms, even of its existence was kept, at the time, both from the Italian Government and the Sherif of Mecca. But of this Secret Agreement, as of others into which the Tsarist Government of Russia had entered, the Bolsheviks published details [1] as soon as they came into power. The Secret Memorandum of the Russian Foreign Office, dated 6th March 1917 and giving these particulars, runs as under:

'As a result of negotiations which took place in London and Petrograd in the spring of 1916 the Allied British, French, and Russian Governments came to an Agreement as regards the future delimitation of their respective zones of influence and territorial acquisitions in Asiatic Turkey, as well as the formation in Arabia of an independent Arab State, or a federation of Arab States. The general principles of the Agreement are as follows:

'(1) Russia obtains the provinces of Erzerum, Trebizond, Van, and Bitlis, as well as territory in the southern part of Kurdistan, along the line Mush–Sairt–Ibn Omar–Amadjie–Persian frontier. The limit of Russian acquisitions on the Black Sea coast will be fixed later at a point lying west of Trebizond.

'(2) France obtains the coastal strip of Syria, the vilayet of Adana, and the territory bounded on the south by a line Aintab–Mardin to the future Russian frontier, and on the north by a line Ala Dagh, Kaisariya, Ak-dagh, Jildiz-dagh, Zara, and Egin–Kharput.

'(3) Great Britain obtains the southern part of Mesopotamia with Baghdad, and stipulates for herself in Syria the ports of Haifa and Akka.

'(4) By Agreement between France and England, the zone between the French and British territories forms a confederation of Arab States, or one independent Arab State, the zones of influence in which are determined at the same time.

'(5) Alexandretta is proclaimed a free port.

'With a view to securing the religious interests of the Entente Powers, Palestine, with the Holy Places, is separated from Turkish territory and subjected to a special régime to be determined by agreement between Russia, France, and England.

'As a general rule the contracting Powers undertake mutually to

[1] In the *Izvestia* on the 24th November 1917, reproduced in translation in the *Manchester Guardian* on the 19th January 1918.

recognize the concessions and privileges existing in the territories now acquired by them which have existed before the War.

'They agree to assume such portions of the Ottoman debt as correspond to their respective acquisitions.'

8. *Relation to Treaty of Sèvres and Tripartite Agreement.* The Sykes-Picot Agreement exercised a patent influence upon the course of subsequent events in the regions to which it applied, notwithstanding that the Russian Revolutionary Government repudiated the provision concerning Russia. The disclosure of its existence and terms led speedily to the collateral Agreement of St. Jean de Maurienne between Italy, France, and Great Britain. The disclosure also strained the loyalty of the Sherif of Mecca and his sons towards their Western Allies, and, in particular, fanned Arab hostility against the French. But for the larger and more serious problems to be solved it served its purpose well enough for the time—it provided a working arrangement between Great Britain and France which abated causes of dangerous friction, and, in some degree, determined the course of future developments.

With certain variations the Agreement became the basis of territorial change and control imposed by the Treaty of Sèvres and the related Tripartite Agreement, upon the Ottoman Empire in Asia.

The more important of these variations were:

(*a*) That Ottoman territory assigned to Russia remained Turkish; and that the greater part of the vilayet of Adana assigned to France likewise remained under Turkish sovereignty.

(*b*) That in place of annexation the system of mandates was adopted by the Peace Conference for the Arab areas in occupation by France and Great Britain; and that these two Powers were invited to become the mandatories.

(*c*) That Palestine, instead of being placed under international control, was made a separate mandated area, under Great Britain as mandatory, with special provision for the creation of a National Home for the Jews.

(*d*) And that, by arrangement between Great Britain and France, the Mosul district was transferred from the

French area of the Sykes-Picot Agreement to the British area.

A later development was that by the Agreement of Angora[1] France retroceded to Turkey some 10,000 square miles of the territory intended to be placed under mandate, including nearly the whole part of the Baghdad Railway which the Treaty of Sèvres had withdrawn from Turkish sovereignty.

The shortcomings of the Agreement in providing for the complete fulfilment of Arab territorial and political aims do not require more than passing mention in this chapter. They are fully treated elsewhere. As has been shown, these shortcomings were inevitable in the presence of imperative French claims to Syria. But the Anglo-French pledge to redeem the Arab peoples from Turkish rule has been carried to completion beyond doubt or question, as also the undertaking to set up a Sovereign Arab State or States. In this matter Great Britain, at least, has honoured her promises to the full extent of the obligations she undertook. The Sherif of Mecca, as King Husein, rules over the Sovereign Arab State of the Hejaz. His son Feisal has been crowned King of Iraq with Baghdad as capital, and the British mandated territory of Mesopotamia, extending from the Persian Gulf to Syria, as his realm. And in Trans-Jordan, an Arab country included in the mandate for Palestine, another son, Abdullah, has been established as ruler. That the various Arab States of Central and South-Western Arabia should not be anxious to come under the rule or suzerainty of King Husein is a matter for Arab settlement alone, and is entirely outside the operation of British undertakings.

But the outstanding grievance of Arab Nationalists against the Sykes-Picot Agreement remains unabated, and without prospect of remedy, that the admission of France to Syria, even in the position of mandatory, places the Arab peoples under the control of two separate foreign powers, with the obviously consequent loss of Arab unity and of the hope of ever attaining it. In order to show his opinion of the Allied treatment of the Arab question King Husein of the Hejaz forbade his representatives at Paris to sign the Treaty of Sèvres, and has not joined the League of Nations.

9. *The Agreement of St. Jean de Maurienne, 17th April 1917,*

[1] 20th October 1921 ; for text *v. infra*, pp. 33–4.

between France, Great Britain, and Italy, regarding Italian claims in Turkey-in-Asia. The Agreement of St. Jean de Maurienne defined the gains, territorial and economic, to be received by Italy in Asiatic Turkey in fulfilment of the undertaking contained in Article 9 of the Agreement of London, completed on the 26th April 1915. Already, Great Britain, France, and Russia had settled between themselves, by the Sykes-Picot Agreement, what were to be their own gains in Asiatic Turkey; the Agreement of St. Jean de Maurienne was intended to be the corollary instrument between the same Powers and Italy in respect of Italian rights. How it failed of its intended purpose forms an episode of war-time diplomatic history not as yet disclosed, though report makes no secret of the cause of failure. Nor have the terms of the Agreement ever been published. But there is no difficulty in piecing together from a variety of sources a broad outline of its origin, purposes, and chief provisions.

As has been said, the Sykes-Picot Agreement was negotiated and completed without the knowledge of the Italian Government, who seem to have remained ignorant of its very existence for several months. It is evident, however, that at the beginning of the year 1917 that Government were already in possession of the Agreement, and were negotiating with the other chief Allies for a precise and binding recognition of Italian claims in South-Western Asia Minor, admitted in principle in Article 9 of the Treaty of London. It is evident, moreover, that the Italian Government were pressing their demand for this definition and recognition with no little insistence. They were seeking, in fact, to secure that Italian interests in Asiatic Turkey should be placed on the same definite and explicit footing, between the several Allies, as had been secured for the interests of France, Russia, and Great Britain by the Sykes-Picot Agreement.

(*a*) *Treaty of London, 26th April 1915.* The governing passages of Article 9 runs as follows:

'Generally speaking, France, Great Britain, and Russia recognize that Italy is interested in the maintenance of the balance of power in the Mediterranean, and that in the event of a total or partial partition of Turkey-in-Asia, she (Italy) ought to obtain a just share of the Mediterranean region adjacent to the province of Adalia, where Italy has already acquired rights and interests which formed the subject of an Italo-British Convention. The zone which shall eventually be allotted to Italy shall be delimited, at the proper time, due account being taken of the existing interests of France and Great Britain.

'The interests of Italy shall also be taken into consideration in the event of the territorial integrity of the Turkish Empire being maintained and of alterations being made in the zones of interest of the Powers.

'If France, Great Britain, and Russia occupy any territories in Turkey-in-Asia during the course of the War, the Mediterranean region bordering on the province of Adalia within the limits indicated above shall be reserved to Italy, who shall be entitled to occupy it.'

It will be well now to see just what Ottoman territory falls within the operation of these vague terms. 'The Province of Adalia' is clear enough—it could only mean the independent sanjak of Adalia. But 'the Mediterranean region adjacent to the province of Adalia', and 'the Mediterranean region bordering on the province of Adalia', contain sweeping possibilities. These definitions might certainly be held to include the independent sanjak of Itchili and the vilayet of Adana to the east, and the independent sanjak of Menteshe and the great and wealthy vilayet of Smyrna (or Aidin), in the north-west. It might even be possible to make these definitions cover the whole or part of the inland vilayet of Konia and the independent sanjak of Karahissar, both of which border the narrow, coastal 'province of Adalia' on the north, and come within the Mediterranean region. Further uncertainty was introduced—though not, perhaps, to the complete advantage of Italy—by use of the words 'just share'. On what basis, for instance, was Italy's 'just share' to be computed? The principle of Italian rights admitted in the Treaty of London had, in fact, been given an application so elastic and uncertain, that when exact definition of such rights was attempted the widest discrepancies of interpretation appeared.

10. *Italy and the St. Jean de Maurienne Agreement*, 17th April 1917. Discussions with Italy on these various points came to a head in April 1917. On the 17th of that month the Prime Ministers of France, Great Britain, and Italy met at St. Jean de Maurienne and there endeavoured to hammer out terms of agreement upon the questions at issue. The conflict of national interests and aims which had arisen and required solution before agreement could be reached is partially revealed in the comments of the Italian press at the time. Thus the Rome *Tribuna* of the 25th April indicated how large were the Italian

claims with which the meeting of Prime Ministers had to deal. This journal spoke of :

'. . . the zone from Smyrna inclusive through the vilayet Konia up to the limit Adana', as the 'zone adapted for the satisfaction of those Italian interests of which the first stone was laid by the concession of Adalia and the possession of the Dodecanese.'

And on the 27th April the *Corriere della Sera* of Milan wrote :

'. . . while English interests mainly centre on Mesopotamia, French on Syria, and Italian on the vilayets of Smyrna, Konia, and Adana there was a lively difference and discussion . . . on certain points, and, more especially, on Smyrna, Adana, and Alexandretta . . . French opinion claimed all Syria up to the Anti-Taurus, while English opinion pointed to Alexandretta as the natural Mesopotamia outlet to the Mediterranean. To settle these differences, reciprocal and conciliatory arrangements were necessary, giving compensations and indemnities, where occasion arose, on the general principle of keeping to prevailing agreements with a minimum of renunciations.'

Reading between the lines of these comments it appears that Italian claims included the sanjaks of Adalia, Menteshe, and Itchili, and the vilayets of Smyrna and Adana—all on the Mediterranean seaboard—and part at least of the huge inland vilayet of Konia. These areas, apparently, were proposed as a zone for Italian occupation or annexation. But it appears, further, that Italian claims included an additional zone, a sphere for exclusively Italian interests though remaining under Turkish sovereignty. This second zone must have comprised portions of the vilayets of Brusa and Konia, and of the independent sanjaks of Kutahia, Karahissar, Nigde, and Kaisari. The two zones together covered the southern half of the whole Anatolian peninsula ; the zone proposed for annexation formed by much the greater part of this immense territory, and included the whole southern and south-western coast-line (*v. infra* p. 25).

11. *Adjustment of conflicting claims.* Other matters apart, Italian claims were in serious conflict with the Sykes-Picot Agreement, for the vilayet of Adana and a portion of the sanjak of Kaisari had already been ear-marked for France by that instrument. It was such directly opposing interests that had to be harmonized at St. Jean de Maurienne. And neither the British nor the French Prime Minister was in a strong position to deny to Italian demands advantages similar to those already secured to Great Britain and France.

The Agreement of St. Jean de Maurienne, so far as we know its terms, rejected the Italian claim to the vilayet of Adana and part of the sanjak of Kaisari, but conceded wellnigh everything else. It assigned with these exceptions, to Italy, the annexable zone she sought, including the vilayet and city of Smyrna—these alone a gain of inestimable importance—the sanjaks of Menteshe, Adalia, and Itchili, and the greater portion of the inland vilayet of Konia. It conceded, too, the wide zone of special Italian interest.

But, as has been said, these enormous Italian gains were never brought to realization. Just why, and in what circumstances, has not been officially disclosed, even by the Italian Government whose hopes had been disappointed. Report, however, is not silent on the matter, and credits the Russian Government with the cause. The story is, in brief, that Russian consent to the Agreement of St. Jean de Maurienne was necessary; that this consent was not given; and that, therefore, the instrument which might have placed some 70,000 square miles of Asia Minor under Italian sovereignty failed to attain validity.

The influence of this dead Allied compact survives only in the Tripartite Agreement annexed to the Treaty of Sèvres—of which both have since been profoundly modified (*v.* pp. 114–17). Under this Agreement Italy was accorded, not an annexable zone, but 'an area in which the special interests of Italy are recognized'.[1] This area covers nearly the same territory which, under the Agreement of St. Jean de Maurienne, was assigned to Italy in the two zones of annexation and of interest.

[1] For Text *v.* App. I, Part II. For Mosul Secret Agreement *v.* this chapter Part III, C, § 4.

CHAPTER I

THE NEAR AND MIDDLE EAST

PART I

B. BRIEF SKETCH OF TURKISH TERRITORIAL SETTLEMENTS PUBLICLY PROPOSED SINCE THE ARMISTICE[1]

1. *Speeches of Mr. Lloyd George, 5th January, and of President Wilson, 8th January 1918.* An account has been given of the actual secret obligations and commitments of the Allied Powers with regard to the ultimate territorial settlement of the Turkish Empire. A short summary will here be made of the attempts to translate these agreements into practice and to announce them in public. The first Allied public announcement, indicating their commitments was in the Balfour Note to President Wilson of the 18th December 1916, which referred to one of the Allied 'war-aims' as the 'setting free of the populations subject to the bloody tyranny of the Turks; and the turning out of Europe of the Ottoman Empire as decidedly foreign to Western civilization'. Whatever this meant or did not mean, it certainly meant depriving the Turks of Constantinople and Eastern Thrace. On the 5th January 1918, Mr. Lloyd George, in a speech defining British 'war-aims', said 'nor are we fighting to deprive Turkey of its capital, or of the rich and renowned lands of Asia Minor and Thrace, which are predominantly Turkish in race . . . while we do not challenge the maintenance of the Turkish Empire in the homelands of the Turkish race, with its capital at Constantinople—the passage between the Mediterranean and the Black Sea being internationalized and neutralized—Arabia, Armenia, Mesopotamia, Syria, and Palestine are, in our judgment, entitled to a recognition of their separate national conditions. What the exact form of that recognition in each particular case should be need not here be discussed, beyond stating that it would be impossible to restore to their former sovereignty the territories to which I have already referred'.

[1] Complete to December 1922.

Whatever else this meant it meant that the Turks were not going to be turned out of Constantinople and Eastern Thrace. Mr. Lloyd George added that conditions had been ‘ changed ’ by ‘ new circumstances, like the Russian collapse and the separate Russian negotiations ’.[1] He claimed, both then and since, that the chief representatives of other parties, including Labour, agreed with him.

Mr. Lloyd George's proposed assignment of Eastern Thrace and Constantinople to the Turks, committed Great Britain alone. But on the 8th January 1918 President Wilson made the famous speech of ‘ the Fourteen Points ’, which stated that ‘ the Turkish portions of the present Ottoman Empire should be assured a secure sovereignty, but the other nationalities which are now under Turkish rule should be assured an . . . unmolested opportunity of autonomous development, and the Dardanelles should be permanently opened . . . to the ships and commerce of all nations under international guarantees ’.

This was a definite pledge, and formed part of the pre-Armistice Agreement which both Germany and the Principal Allied and Associated Powers agreed to be morally binding for the Peace Settlement. It is not very clear what it means, for Wilson apparently retained the Turkish formal suzerainty even over Arabia, Mesopotamia, etc., and gave only a ‘ secure sovereignty ’ to ‘ the Turkish portions of the Ottoman Empire ’. But ‘ the Turkish portions of the Ottoman Empire ’ are hard to define. Are Thrace and Constantinople, for instance, such ‘ Turkish portions ’ ? We know what Mr. Lloyd George thought on the 5th January 1918. For on the 22nd March 1920 he declared to an Indian deputation that both the Greek and Turkish censuses ‘ put the Mussulman population of Thrace in a considerable minority ’, and, on the 27th February 1920, he declared that the majority of the population of Constantinople was Turkish, in each case referring to his speech of the 5th January 1918. Thus he thought most of East Thrace Greek, and perhaps Western Thrace as well.

2. *Arrangements between the Armistice and the Peace Conference, 1919–20.* The Armistice with the Turks of the 30th

[1] On the 10th November 1914, Mr. Lloyd George spoke of the Turks as ‘ a human cancer, a creeping agony in the flesh of the lands which they misgovern, rotting every fibre of life. . . . I am glad that the Turk is to be called to a final account for his long record of infamy against humanity ’.

October 1918 was a purely military arrangement, stipulating for the surrender of all Turkish forces and permitting the Allies to occupy all necessary strategic points, notably such as were necessary to the command of the Bosporus, and Dardanelles. It will perhaps make the situation clearer if we divide the actual territorial arrangements under the following headings: (*a*) Arabia, Mesopotamia, Palestine, Syria; (*b*) Smyrna; (*c*) Constantinople and the Straits; (*d*) Thrace; (*e*) Armenia.

(*a*) *Arabia, Mesopotamia, Palestine, Syria.* The Allied Powers were already in effective occupation of these areas at the Armistice, and the Turkish forces had been hopelessly defeated by Generals Allenby and Marshall. The severance of these areas from Turkish sovereignty was practically accepted by all parties. But President Wilson's views to a certain extent prevailed, for the Peace Conference agreed to have Mandates for Syria, Palestine, and Mesopotamia.[1] As regards other Arab territories these had been practically promised independence on the basis of self-determination by the joint Franco-British declaration of the 7th November 1918 which referred vaguely to their national aspirations.

(*b*) *The decision to allow the Greeks to occupy Smyrna, 6th May 1919.* This area might have been held to be assigned to Italy under the St. Jean de Maurienne Agreement. But the consent of Russia was necessary to the validity of this instrument and, as it had never been given, the agreement lapsed. On the 3rd and 4th February M. Venizelos appearing before the 'Ten' definitely claimed the Smyrna area. In the Greek Territorial Commission the French and British supported the Greek claim to Smyrna, while the Americans denied the Greeks any claim to the sovereignty of any part of Asia Minor. The Italians were hostile, and practically withdrew from the Commission.[2] Shortly afterwards the Italian Delegation left Paris in consequence of President Wilson's attitude over Fiume (24th April).[3] This was the opportunity of M. Venizelos and he used it with the greatest ability. Unknown apparently to the American expert advisers, unknown naturally to the Italians, the 'Big Three', as they now were, in deep secrecy not only authorized but invited

[1] Wilson refused to accept the Secret Agreements and wished arrangements to go by consent of the peoples, *v.* R. S. Baker, *loc. cit.* I, 73–5, 79.

[2] Bowman—in House and Seymour, *What Really Happened at Paris*, New York, 1921, p. 194.

[3] *v.* Vol. IV, pp. 300–1.

Venizelos to occupy Smyrna with Greek troops.[1] This decision appears to have been taken between the 5th and the 11th May, and it was carried into effect on the 15th May with the support of British, French, and American warships. It resulted at once in horrible atrocities and massacres of the Turks by the Greeks, but, serious as these were, they were not the worst result. Venizelos appeared before the Council of Five on the 16th July to explain these circumstances, and, as is well known, appeased them by suggesting that insults to French troops marching into Strasburg might have provoked similar measures of retaliation. But these terrible incidents were not the most serious part of the business. It is, of course, technically true that under the Armistice the Allies had the right to occupy any area in the Turkish dominions, which they might consider necessary for the enforcement of order. Technically, too, it was an Allied and not a Greek, occupation. But every one knew, as is more fully explained below (p. 44), the real meaning of this move. It was an admission of the Greek claim to Smyrna and to the surrounding hinterland. Whether that claim was to take the form of annexation or mandate or merely occupation, was immaterial. It was a definite assertion of Greek claims on some territory in Asia Minor and, as such, necessarily provoked the vigorous resistance of Turkish nationalists, as well as the vigorous protests of Italy.[2] It was significant that Mussulmans of India, with the Maharajah of Bikanir in the foreground, at once brought protests before the Peace Conference. The 'Smyrna affair' is also important as showing that the American attitude, as laid down in the 'Fourteen Points', was beginning to be modified by events.

(c) *The American Mandate for Constantinople and the Straits.* As regards the 'Freedom of the Straits', as laid down both by Wilson and Lloyd George, there seems to have been no dispute. France seems to have been equally firm.[3] A special point was made of securing this in the Armistice, though that might of course refer to purely temporary measures. But the principle seems to have been generally accepted as both desirable and necessary. It was, however, largely dependent

[1] House and Seymour, op. cit., pp. 194–5, R. S. Baker, *op. cit.* II, 192–5. The American figures for Smyrna sanjak were 375,000 Greeks, 325,000 Mohammedans, and 8,000 others. *v.* Statistics at end of this Part for figures dealing with Smyrna zone as defined in Sèvres Treaty.

[2] On 12th May Italy was permitted to send a land force to Adalia.

[3] Poincaré, *Revue des Deux Mondes*, 12th February 1920, says that a French memo to this effect was presented to the Conference.

on one condition, and that was that a large force should be maintained in European Turkey under the control of a single Power. That could only be done by the United States. The idea was mooted as early as February 1919, and seems to have been regarded with some favour by President Wilson, though he always made it clear that such a matter could be determined only by the people of the United States themselves. Later, on the 16th April, Colonel House is reported as saying, ‘ they have all come to think that the only true solution is to have the United States take it, for while they all oppose each other, none of them opposes the United States. But I don’t know that our people in America want any mandates at all in Europe or Asia ’.[1] The Peace Conference bore this in mind. The Viceroy of India in May 1919 informed the British Government, ‘ Moslem feeling is already deeply stirred. Educated opinion is probably prepared for extensive territorial losses, but not for the loss of Constantinople, especially in view of the recent announcements made by the Prime Minister and Lord Robert Cecil ’.[2] The meaning of these utterances was, however, obscured by the fact that the Allies in their reply of the 16th June to the Germans went out of their way to proclaim their adherence not only to the ‘ setting free of the populations subject to the bloody tyranny of the Turks ’ but also to ‘ the turning out of Europe of the Ottoman Empire as decidedly foreign to Western civilization ’. These phrases of the former letter of the 10th January 1917 to Wilson, once intended to cover a Russian annexation of Constantinople, were now apparently invoked to provide an opportunity for an American Mandate. It must, however, have been very confusing to the Turks, especially as their delegates had about the same time received a severe public letter, signed Clemenceau, which represented their aims and aspirations in no very amiable light. In private, however, the French Government advocated the retention of the Sultan in Constantinople at this time.[3] According to Lord Robert Cecil ‘ no one ever suggested turning the Caliph out of Constantinople ’,[4] and he was in a position to know the truth in 1919. But these utterances must certainly have suggested this

[1] 16th April 1919, Col. House *v.* C. T. Thomson, *The Peace Conference Day by Day*, pp. 310–11 ; Lloyd George in Commons, 27th February 1920.
[2] Quoted by Mr. Lloyd George in House of Commons, *The Times*, 27th February 1920.
[3] Pichon in *Revue des Deux Mondes* of the 12th February 1920.
[4] House of Commons, *The Times*, 27th February 1920.

possibility. In fact the design seems to have been to 'Vaticanize' the Sultan, and to govern the Straits and Constantinople through the Agency of a Mandatory Power.

(i) *America refuses the Mandate.* On the 27th June President Wilson stated to some press representatives that he personally favoured the United States Mandate for Constantinople, but that this was, primarily, a matter for the American people to decide. But the very hostile reception of the President's peace proposals in America soon made it doubtful even in early autumn as to whether they would accept any mandates at all or even exercise any serious influence over the Turks.

(ii) *Franco-British decision as to Constantinople, December 1919–February 1920.* That the uncertainty of the American attitude delayed the signing of the Turkish Treaty is evident from the speech of Mr. Lloyd George at Sheffield (17th September 1919) 'We cannot settle Turkey till we know what the United States is going to do'. By the end of September, however, Wilson's serious illness practically ended any hope of securing American influence. This caused great fluctuations in Allied policy. According to Poincaré, Clemenceau actually discussed a suggestion of Lloyd George for turning the Turks out of Constantinople during his visit to London at the end of December 1919.[1] On his return to France, however, Clemenceau reverted to his former view, and Mr. Lloyd George speedily adopted it. On the 18th February 1920, Admiral de Robeck, British High Commissioner at Constantinople, officially announced that he had been instructed to make public 'the fact that the Allies had decided not to deprive Turkey of Constantinople'. Mr. Lloyd George in a speech in the House of Commons on the 27th February 1920, endorsed this pledge and, according to M. Poincaré, 'advanced the most brilliant arguments in support of those previously made to him by M. Clemenceau, but which the French Prime Minister had subsequently been induced courteously to abandon'. Meanwhile the Allies (March) sent strong forces to Constantinople and expelled the Kemalists.

The decision as to Constantinople was now final,[2] but the results of the vacillation were not. To quote M. Poincaré once more 'these changes of view gave renewed vigour to our worst

[1] *Revue des Deux Mondes*, 12th February 1920.

[2] The Allied ultimatum to Turkey of the 19th July 1920 suggested the question would be reconsidered if the Turks refused to sign the Treaty of Sèvres.

enemies, supplied elements which irritated them, and favoured their resistance to the Peace Conference'. But in fact the provisions of the Treaty of Sèvres were decided at San Remo on the 24th April 1920.

(*d*) *Thrace.* On the 5th January 1918, Mr. Lloyd George had said 'nor are we fighting to deprive Turkey of the rich and renowned lands of ... Thrace, which are predominantly Turkish in race'. The Western Thrace question was settled by the Bulgarian Treaty which ceded it to the Allied and Associated Powers, Art. 48, 27th November 1919: that of Eastern Thrace was bound up with Constantinople. It is well known that the British members of the Greek Territorial Commission backed the claims of Greece to Eastern Thrace, to which Western Thrace was necessarily an adjunct.[1] It is also known that the American Delegation, always tender to Bulgaria with whom the United States were not at war, did not support these claims, and even advocated advancing the Bulgarian frontier to the Enos–Midia line.[1] The Italians appear steadily to have opposed all concessions to Greece in this area. On the 22nd March 1920, Mr. Lloyd George stated to an Indian Caliphate Delegation that, according to both Greek and Turkish censuses, the Mussulman population was in a considerable minority. 'If that is true, and the principle of self-determination is to be applied, the whole of Thrace would certainly be taken away from Turkish rule.' In point of fact Greek forces had just occupied Eastern Thrace with the consent of the Allies. This principle was maintained in the Allied ultimatum to Turkey on the 19th July 1920. 'The Allies can make no modification in the clauses of the Treaty which detach Thrace and Smyrna from Turkish rule, for in both areas the Turks are in a minority.'[2]

3. *The Territorial Terms of the Treaty of Sèvres and related Agreements, 10th August 1920.* The Treaty of Sèvres was finally signed on the 10th August 1920. Representatives of the United States and the Kingdom of Hejaz were not present, and the Serb-Croat-Slovene representatives refused to sign.

[1] Bowman in Seymour and House, *What Really Happened at Paris*, p. 192. According to Tardieu, *L'Illustration*, 11th December 1920, pp. 452–3, the French in 1919 did not agree to the British 'tracé de la frontière gréco-turque en Thrace'. They seem, however, to have favoured some Greek extension to part of Eastern Thrace.

[2] *v.* Statistical Tables end of this section, p. 39.

The Territorial terms were as follows:

(*a*) Arabia, Palestine, Mesopotamia, and Syria.[1]

(i) *Arabia.* The King of Hejaz was recognized as independent and the Holy Places placed under his care. The boundaries of Turkey were drawn so as to exclude her from control of any other Arabian States or of Syria, Palestine, and Mesopotamia, and Turkey also renounced in favour of the Principal Allied Powers any rights over territory outside Europe that lay beyond her new frontiers (Art. 132).

(ii) *Palestine and Mesopotamia.* Palestine was to be entrusted to a Mandatory Power selected by the Principal Allies who were also to define her boundaries. Syria and Mesopotamia were 'provisionally recognized as independent states' and to be 'advised and assisted' by a Mandatory Power in each case. The frontiers and selection of Mandatories was to be arranged for by the Principal Allies. It had already been practically arranged in 1919 that France should be the Mandatory of Syria, and Great Britain of Palestine and Mesopotamia. The boundaries of the latter had also been extended to include Mosul, though originally assigned to the French sphere under the Sykes-Picot Agreement.[2] The Powers had anticipated matters at San Remo on the 5th May 1920 when France was definitely selected as the Mandatory for Syria and Great Britain for Palestine and Mesopotamia. These arrangements were, therefore, in a sense confirmed at Sèvres. Simultaneously on the 10th August 1920 another arrangement was made for extending the sphere of economic (and to some extent) political interests of certain powers in parts of the new Turkey. This Tripartite Agreement between France, Italy, and Great Britain arranged for certain spheres of 'special interest' for Italy in what was, roughly, the south-west part of Asia Minor lying outside the Smyrna area, and a similar sphere of 'special interest' for France in Cilicia (i.e. north of the Syrian boundary). The new Franco-Turkish frontier now gave up to France the whole Gulf of Alexandretta (Iskanderun) and the important section of the Baghdad railway from Karakein as far as Nisibin.

(*b*) *Smyrna and the Greek Isles.* The town of Smyrna and

[1] Turkey also renounced all rights over Egypt, Sudan, Cyprus, Libya (Tripoli), Morocco, Tunis.

[2] Tardieu, *L'Illustration*, pp. 452–53. These boundaries together with the Franco-British boundary of Palestine were adjusted by a Franco-British Convention of the 23rd December 1920 (Cmd. 1195, Misc. No. 4, 1921), Parl. Paper.

the Ionian hinterland were to be under Greek administration for five years, at the end of which a plebiscite was to decide their fate. Various arrangements were also made as to certain Greek islands.[1]

(*c*) *Constantinople and the Straits.* Full provision was made for the internationalization of the Straits and for the demilitarization of contiguous areas. The Turkish boundary was drawn in the west near the Chatalja lines, Constantinople remaining under Turkish sovereignty.

(*d*) *Thrace.* Western Thrace had already been ceded to the Allies as a whole, and was now ceded by the Allies to Greece by a separate Treaty of the date the 10th August 1920. Eastern Thrace was ceded to Greece up to the Chatalja lines.

(*e*) *Armenia and Kurdistan.* Turkey agreed to recognize Armenia as 'a free and independent State', and to accept a frontier for Armenia to be decided by the President of the United States in the area of the vilayets of Erzerum, Trebizond, Van, and Bitlis.

Kurdistan was to receive an autonomous government, with a possible modification of its frontier in favour of Persia.

4. *Results of the Sèvres Treaty.* This general arrangement was characterized by Mr. Lloyd George in the House of Commons on the 24th June 1920 as 'a policy of releasing all non-Turkish populations from Turkish sway. . . . If we allowed Mustapha Kemal or any man of his type to break down that policy Europe would have failed dismally in its duty'. It was easy enough to coerce the Government at Constantinople, but Kemal had revolted and stirred up the army. He could defy anybody in Anatolia and declined either to accept the Treaty or to be coerced. It seems clear that he began threatening both the British positions on the Ismid peninsula and the Greek ones to the east of Smyrna in June 1920. With Allied support and a British loan the Greeks then proceeded to attack Kemal and not only defeated him but captured Brusa the old Turkish capital. These brilliant operations ended with the parliamentary

[1] Turkey ceded Imbros and Tenedos to Greece and recognized Greek sovereignty in Lemnos, Samothrace, Mytilene, Chios, Samos, and Nikaria. The Dodecanese were ceded to Italy in the Sèvres Treaty. But an agreement between Italy and Greece had been signed the 14th May 1920 by which all of them except Rhodes were ceded by Italy to Greece, and this was itself an adaptation of a previous agreement signed the 29th July 1919 between Venizelos and Tittoni. Rhodes was to return to Greece when Great Britain returned Cyprus. *v. infra*, pp. 37–40.

defeat and fall of Venizelos (November 1920). The return of ex-king Constantine to Greece in face of Allied opposition for a time compromised the situation. Mr. Lloyd George, however, continued to lend moral support to Greece, declaring with reference to Asia Minor, 'The friendship of the Greek people was vital to us in that part of the world, a part of the world which was vital to Great Britain, more vital than to any other countries of the world' (22nd December 1920).[1] The signs of strong Turkish resentment of this attitude became apparent in January 1921. The Kemalists now defied their own Constantinople Government and adopted 'the National Pact', a document originally drawn up by some Turkish deputies at Constantinople in January 1920. It was adopted as a national programme by the Angora National or Kemalist Assembly early in 1921.[2] They demanded 'the security of Constantinople' and the union under Turkish sovereignty of all parts of the Ottoman Empire 'inhabited by an Ottoman Moslem majority'. This certainly meant, in Kemalist eyes, that both Smyrna and Eastern Thrace should be returned to Turkey, while they claimed that a free plebiscite should be held in Western Thrace to determine 'its juridical status'. The situation at the beginning of 1921 was that the Greeks had won brilliant but precarious successes in Asia Minor, and that the Kemalist tide was slowly gathering in intensity. Kemal at Angora was defying Constantinople, the Greeks, and the Allies at once.

5. *The London Conference, February–March 1921.* (i) With the view of obtaining some settlement a Conference of the Great Powers was held in London in February 1921, to which both Greek, Turkish Constantinopolitan, and Kemalist or Angoran, representatives were summoned. The terms offered by the Great Powers to the parties were, in reality, a revision of the Treaty of Sèvres in favour of the Turks. The military clauses were whittled down.

(ii) As regards Smyrna it was proposed to retain a Greek force in the town itself, but to place the Ionian area under a gendarmerie controlled by the Allies, and to have a Christian Governor of the whole area under the League of Nations. The

[1] As at this period a Greek division in the Ismid peninsula was actually under the command of General Harington, the British Commander at Constantinople, there was some Greek-British co-operation. This arrangement ended in March 1921, *v.* Lord Crawford, House of Lords, 21st April 1921.

[2] Text in App. II, Part II.

arrangement was to be subject to review by the League of Nations on the demand of either party at the end of five years.

(iii) The demilitarized area round the Straits reduced in extent, and an early evacuation of Constantinople (though not of Gallipoli and Chanak) was offered.

(iv) As regards Eastern Thrace it was proposed to hold a statistical inquiry into the character of its population. But internationalization was definitely refused.

(v) As regards Armenia certain threats were made as to not evacuating Constantinople if Armenian massacres continued.

It is known, however, that at this time negotiations took place between the Kemalists and France and Italy respectively, which suggested separate agreements. These are the true origin of the later Agreement of Angora.

Both Greeks and Turks rejected these terms, and at the end of March hostilities were resumed. The Allied Governments declared their intention of observing a perfect neutrality between the contending parties. It was made clear, however, that Constantinople was excluded from the field of operations and that the Allies would not sanction its capture by the Greeks.[1] Ultimately the Greeks penetrated far into the interior of Asia Minor and even got within measurable distance of Angora. But their offensive wave had become exhausted and by the autumn the attempt had failed, and the Greek situation had become extremely serious.

6. *France and the Angora Agreement, 20th October 1921.* The situation had rapidly worsened from the point of view of the Allies. The Italians had been negotiating as early as April 1921 for the withdrawal of their troops from Asia Minor, and this evacuation had already advanced far by June. In that same month a Conference of the Allies at Paris offered once more to mediate between Greece and Turkey but without effect. Then France sent out M. Franklin-Bouillon to the Kemalist Government at Angora. According to Lord Curzon assurances were given by M. Briand that he 'had been forbidden to discuss with the Angora Government the larger question of peace',[2] and was only negotiating for the French evacuation of Cilicia

[1] Mr. Lloyd George in reply to Col. Aubrey Herbert, Commons, 18th April 1921.

[2] These and subsequent quotations in Parl. Paper Cmd. 1570. Correspondence respecting the Angora Agreement. The text of the Angora Agreement will be found in App. II, Part II, b.

together with such matters as exchange of prisoners, protection of minorities, etc. To the amazement of the world it was announced shortly afterwards that, on the 20th October 1921, France had concluded a separate Agreement with the Angora Government. This Agreement had, however, been already foreshadowed by the Franco-Kemalist negotiations of March 1921.

(*a*) *Lord Curzon's protest, 5th November 1921.* Lord Curzon addressed a note on the 5th November to the French Government protesting against this Agreement. He pointed out that Article 1 provided that ' the state of war will cease between the high contracting parties '. This meant more than a local armistice for that ' is still technically a state of war '. The Agreement also implied ' formal recognition of the Grand National Assembly at Angora as the sovereign authority in Turkey, in which case a peace concluded with Angora would be contrary to the Franco-British Treaty of the 4th September 1914, and to the London Pact, of November 1915 '. He recorded his opinion also that Articles 3 and 6 ran counter to the provisions of the Treaty of Sèvres for the protection of minorities and ignored the responsibilities assumed by the French Government for the protection of minorities in the zone of their special interests under the Tripartite Agreement. He next referred to the revision of the North Syrian frontier by which the area of the Gulf of Alexandretta and the Baghdad railway from Adana to Nisibis and Jeziret Ibn 'Umar had been handed back to Turkey by France. Great Britain had not been consulted though the area in question had been conquered by British forces. The arrangement might involve ' serious strategic consequences to her (Great Britain's) position in Mesopotamia '. In conclusion Lord Curzon suggested that the arrangement ' has the appearance of being a separate Agreement concluded by one of the Allies with an enemy Government without consultation with the remainder '.

(*b*) *French explanation, 17th November 1921.* In reply on the 17th November the French Government denied that it had ever agreed to remain in Cilicia under the Tripartite Agreement and that evacuation was a ' necessity '. They denied also that this local agreement constituted either a *de facto* or *de jure* recognition of the Angora Government. As regards the Baghdad railway the French Government pointed out that a section of it actually was in French Mandated territory (the Maidan Ekbez to Chobun Bey section) and that this section would be closed to the Turks in case of hostilities between them and Great Britain. They denied further that there were any secret clauses in the Agreement. Lord Curzon, in reply to this not very convincing apologia, maintained his objections to the transfer of the Baghdad railway. He declined, however, explicitly to reserve the attitude of the British Government, as 'The French Government admits that when peace is finally concluded the different agreements which have been negotiated up to date, including the Angora Agreement, will require to be adjusted with a view to taking their place in a general settlement'. The division between the Allies was thus made evident, and gave great encouragement to the Turks. It probably does a good deal to explain the failure of the renewed attempt at mediation between the belligerents made in February and March of 1922. A further pressure was provided by the premature disclosure of the views of the Indian Government which demanded the Allied evacuation of Constantinople, the placing of the Holy Places under the Sultan, and the surrender of Eastern Thrace by the Greeks.

7. *The Paris Conference, February–March 1922.* As has recently been revealed, the situation of the Greeks was known by the negotiators to be desperate in February 1922.[1] Consequently the terms finally offered to both belligerent parties by the Principal Allies exhibited a still further modification of the Treaty of Sèvres in favour of the Turks. They included (i) a proposal for an armistice which the Greeks had already accepted, together with permission to the Turks to have a total peace-army of 85,000 men, as compared with 50,000 only under the Treaty; (ii) the whole Smyrna area was to revert to Turkey; (iii) the Straits question was altered by the proposed restitution of Turkish sovereignty over the Asiatic side of the Straits. But the demilitarized zone was to extend sixty miles east of Chanak. The European shores of the Straits were to be constituted a zone of Allied military occupation as far as Rodosto, on the Sea of Marmara. An early evacuation by Allied troops of Constantinople was promised; (iv) a compromise was offered over Eastern Thrace. It was to be partitioned between Greeks and

[1] *v.* The Gounaris Correspondence. Debates in Commons and Lords, 7th, 11th–12th December 1922.

Turks, the Turkish frontier being advanced westward from the Chatalja lines to Rodosto ; (v) in the case of the Armenians certain vague formulae were used about 'the satisfaction of their traditional aspirations for a national home' invoking, of course, the aid of the League of Nations. These concessions were accepted by the Greeks and the Turkish Government, but the Kemalists demanded that Greek evacuation of Anatolia should begin at once and be completed within four months. Failing that the Kemalists refused to grant an armistice. On the 15th April the Allies replied that they could not agree to immediate evacuation. After this the negotiations languished.

8. *The Italian separate Agreement, April 1922, and the Kemalist capture of Smyrna, September 1922.* Matters were not improved by the announcement, made to the British Government on the 24th April, by the Italians, that they had concluded an agreement with the Constantinople Government 'by which the latter undertook to examine favourably Italian applications for railways, mines, and public works in Asia Minor'. They gave, however, 'formal assurances that the Agreement contained no counter concessions or undertakings on their part'.[1] This was, however, a further indication of the growing Kemalist power and the difference of Britain's policy from that of her two great Allies.

In May the Kemalists were reported to have committed appalling atrocities 'as part of a systematic policy for the extermination of Christian minorities in Asia Minor'. But the British Government once more endeavoured to intervene by sending a Commission of inquiry to Trebizond and threatening a reconsideration of the Paris proposals in case these measures had no effect.[2] These negotiations remained practically without result. Hostilities were resumed. The Kemalists began to move down in force against the Greeks, the latter retaliated by threatening Constantinople. On the 4th August Mr. Lloyd George stated that, while the Allies would not allow the Greeks to attack Constantinople, protection of the Christian minorities in Asia Minor would be insisted on. The general tone of the speech was unfavourable to the Kemalists and highly eulogistic of the Greek Army. Within little more than a month from this date the Kemalists had swept the Greeks

[1] Mr. Chamberlain, House of Commons, 3rd May 1922.
[2] Mr. Chamberlain, House of Commons, 15th May 1922.

out of Asia Minor and captured Smyrna. The Turkish sword had cut the diplomatic knots, and the dream of Greek expansion in Asia was over.

9. *Results of non-ratification of Sèvres Treaty.*

(*a*) *Mesopotamia, Syria, and Palestine.* The results of the non-ratification of the Sèvres Treaty had now become very serious. The formal cession of territory, such as that of Mesopotamia, Syria, and Palestine, did not really take effect until the coming into force of the Treaty. None the less in the latter part of July 1922 the Council of the League assigned the Mandates for Syria to France and for Palestine to Great Britain as from the 1st August. The view was apparently now advanced that, despite the non-ratification of the Treaty, these areas had ceased to be under Turkish sovereignty.[1]

(*b*) *The Dodecanese.* The Italian Government took a different view as regards the Dodecanese. They announced on the 8th October 1922 that they considered their agreement with Greece (14th May 1920) to cede to her these islands had lapsed owing to the non-ratification of the Sèvres Treaty. On the 14th October it was stated that Great Britain had sent a note to Italy, protesting against this denunciation having

[1] The assignment of the Mesopotamian Mandate was delayed for technical reasons, but it appears to have been held that its independence of Turkey was established. The change of view necessitated by the non-ratification of the Sèvres Treaty is illustrated below in the change in the preamble of the Palestine Mandate. A similar change was made in the preamble of the French Mandate for Syria.

Draft of the Mandate for Palestine as submitted by Mr. Balfour on the 7th December 1920, to the Secretariat-General of the League of Nations for the approval of the Council of the League of Nations.	Mandate for Palestine as confirmed by the Council of the League, 12th August 1922.
'Whereas by Article 132 of the Treaty of Peace signed at Sèvres on the 10th day of August 1920, Turkey renounced in favour of the Principal Allied Powers all rights and title over Palestine; and Whereas by Article 95 of the said Treaty the High Contracting parties agreed to entrust by application of the provisions of Article 22, the Administration of Palestine, within such boundaries as might be determined by the Principal Allied Powers, to a Mandatory to be selected by the said Powers; and'	'Whereas the Principal Allied Powers have agreed, for the purpose of giving effect to the provisions of Article 22 of the Covenant of the League of Nations, to entrust to a Mandatory selected by the said Powers the administration of the territory of Palestine, which formerly belonged to the Turkish Empire, within such boundaries as may be fixed by them; and'

been made without previous consultation with the other Principal Allies.

(*c*) *Armenia.* The boundaries of Armenia as defined by President Wilson at the end of 1920, gave a large extension of territory to her. But it was impossible to execute the award in face of the anarchy in the country and the Kemalist and Bolshevist resistance.

10. *The Agreement of Mudania, 11th October 1922.* Events marched as rapidly as the Kemalist troops, who entered the neutral zone and came within fighting distance of the British troops at Chanak. The French troops withdrew, and on the 17th September Italy announced in a semi-official *communiqué*, that, while ' defending the principle of the liberty of the Straits . . . she could not contribute with her own military contingent in case of the spread of the hostilities '. The British Government, however, stood firm, reinforced her troops and her fleet, and on the 16th September issued an invitation to the British Dominions and to the Balkan States ' to take part in the defence of the zones '. They also announced that the Turkish troops would not be allowed to cross into Europe. On the 21st the French and Italian troops withdrew from Chanak. On the 25th Mr. Lloyd George informed the press that the freedom of the Straits would be defended, but that ' we are not putting up any fight about the sovereignty in Eastern Thrace '. This indicated a concession to the Turks which they could not have obtained by force of arms.[1]

On the 11th October an Agreement was signed at Mudania between the three Allied Generals at Constantinople, the Kemalist General Ismet Pasha, and the Greek General Mazarakis. The preamble announced that the Allied Governments had ' decided to hand over Eastern Thrace and Adrianople to the Grand National Assembly of Turkey '. An armistice was to be enforced as from midnight on the 14th–15th October. On that date the Turks were to retire to stated distances from Chanak and the Ismid peninsula in Asia. In Eastern Thrace the Greek evacuation was to begin at once, and the Turks were to occupy up to the right bank of the Maritza. The Allies were temporarily to hold that bank and the Karagach suburb of Adrianople, pending settlement at a Conference. The Turks

[1] It had in fact already been made in a Note of the Allied Powers to the Kemalists of the 23rd September inviting them to a Conference.

had been prepared to fight for Eastern Thrace, the British for the 'Freedom of the Straits'. The British had surrendered Eastern Thrace, and the Turks in effect promised to guarantee the 'Freedom of the Straits'.

11. *The Lausanne Conference, November–December 1922.* The Conference, held at Lausanne in November–December, did not register any serious departure from these territorial concessions. The Allies proposed the following:

(i) The exclusion of the Turks from Syria, Mesopotamia, Palestine, and Arabia was maintained.
(ii) Smyrna was handed back unconditionally to the Turks.
(iii) Constantinople was evacuated but provisions made for small demilitarized zones on the Gallipoli peninsula.
(iv) Eastern Thrace was handed back unconditionally to the Turks.
(v) Vague stipulations for providing 'a national home' for Armenians and protecting Christian Minorities in Asia were made.

On the last day of December 1922 (the concluding date of this volume) the Turks had not assented to these terms.

The net result is that the problem is likely to work itself out in terms of force, the only influence to which the Turks submit or which they fully understand. (*v. infra* pp. 114–17).

STATISTICAL TABLES

RELATING TO SMYRNA, WESTERN AND EASTERN THRACE

(*Note.* It was accepted by the Peace Conference as a principle that Turkish figures subsequent to 1912, in view of massacres, emigration, &c., could not be relied on.)

SMYRNA.

Greek zone as defined in Sèvres Treaty.

	Greeks.	*Turks.*	*Others.*	*Total.*
Greek figures (1912) . .	553,500	310,000	91,000	954,500
		Moslems.		
Turkish figures (1914) . .	300,000	540,000	44,000	894,000
American Dr. Magie (1914) .	509,000	470,000	78,000	1,057,000

THRACE.

Western.*

	Greeks.	*Turks.*	*Bulgars.*	*Others.*	*Total.*
(Bulgarian Thrace) .	44,000	124,000	29,500	3,000	200,500

* *N.B.* Above are Greek figures of 1912, of which the accuracy is not seriously disputed.

	Greeks,	*Turks.*	*Bulgars.*	*Others.*	*Total.*
Eastern. (West of Chatalja.) (Turkish Thrace.)					
Greek figures of 1912 .	395,515	344,011	67,843		805,369
Turkish official of 1894 [1]	304,537	265,359	72,758		642,654
Grand Total Greek figures 1912 (Eastern and Western Thrace)	439,515	468,011	97,343		1,002,869

[1] Except for sanjak of Chatalja where the Turkish figures are dated 1897.

Note on certain Aegaean islands. The islands of Imbros and Tenedos were ceded to Greece under the Treaty of Sèvres. Certain other islands, including Lemnos, Samothrace, Mytilene, Chios, Samos, and Nikaria, were left by Article 5 of the Treaty of London (30th May 1913) to the decision of certain Powers, who assigned them to Greece in a note of 13th February 1914. Turkey, however, refused to recognize this decision, but was obliged to cede them to Greece in the Treaty of Sèvres (Article 84). These cessions did not include the Dodecanese and islands within three miles of the coast of Asia.

CHAPTER I

THE NEAR AND MIDDLE EAST

PART II

THE NON-ARAB TERRITORIES OF THE OTTOMAN EMPIRE SINCE THE ARMISTICE OF THE 30TH OCTOBER 1918 [1]

1. *The Nature of the Settlement in the Near and Middle East.* The making of peace in the non-Arab territories of the former Ottoman Empire was like the weaving of Penelope's web. The material was unravelled as fast as it was put together. Two additional features in the story have, however, to be considered, if the metaphor is to be worked out. In the first place, the threads successively unpicked from the original design were straightway taken and woven into another, and a more durable, pattern ; and, in the second place, there was a transposition of the mythical tasks of night and day. Penelope used to weave by day and unweave during the secret watches. But the Supreme Council after the Armistice, like the Allied Governments during the War, generally wove their Oriental policies in darkness and mystery, while the contrary process of disintegration and recomposition, which remorselessly overtook their handiwork, went forward in comparative publicity.

The unravelling began at the very moment when the preliminary sketch of the official design was being completed. In April 1917, the Secret Agreement contracted [2] at St. Jean de Maurienne by the British, French, and Italian Prime Ministers, determined the prospective share of Italy in the direct and indirect partition of the Ottoman dominions. In the same month, two successive Liberal Russian ministries, holding office before the second or Bolshevik Revolution and indisputably entitled to speak in the name of the Russian people, solemnly and publicly renounced all annexations and indemnities. Thus

[1] *This part deals only with the situation up to June* 1922.

[2] In pursuance of Art. 9 of the Agreement of London, dated the 26th April 1915. *v.* Part I, § 9, pp. 19–20.

Russia abandoned her Eastern claims under the Secret Treaties [1] at the moment when Italy was staking hers out; and from that time onward the political destinies of the East shaped themselves simultaneously on two distinct planes, which came to bear less and less relation to one another. The Secret Agreements made before the Armistice governed the negotiations at Paris and thereafter, and the substance of them was embodied in the Treaty of Peace with Turkey, signed at Sèvres on the 10th August 1920, and still more faithfully in the Tripartite Agreement of the same date, between the British Empire, France, and Italy, respecting Anatolia. On the other hand, the self-denying ordinance of Russia, to which successive Russian Governments adhered throughout the subsequent internal convulsions of the Russian state and people, set in motion a train of very different forces.

(*a*) *Results of Russia's collapse.* The disappearance of the Russian military power, while relieving the peace-makers at Paris of some obvious embarrassments, involved them at the same time in others. If Russia had not collapsed, her geographical and strategical position would have enabled her to enforce with ease whatever settlement the victorious Powers might have agreed upon for the northern provinces of Turkey. But her fall had left an immense gap in the iron ring of hostile armies by which Turkey had previously been encircled. The Western members of the Alliance, though able to break the Turkish resistance on the two southern fronts, to impose a severe armistice, to occupy the Arab provinces effectively, and to control the remainder of the Empire as far as this could be done from the sea, had not a sufficiently long arm to hold the Turkish population down by force in the Anatolian interior. Here they could only establish a military and administrative supervision—a supervision which was, as it happened, quite effective during the six months that elapsed between the Armistice of the 30th October 1918 and the disembarkation of Greek troops at Smyrna on the 15th May 1919, but which depended, in the last resort, not upon adequate military force but upon the prestige of the victors and the willingness of the

[1] Claim to Constantinople and certain territories commanding the Bosporus and Dardanelles, recognized by the British and French Governments in 1915 (*v. supra* pp. 5–8); and claim to the north-eastern territories of Asiatic Turkey, recognized in the Secret Sykes-Picot Agreement of 16th May 1916. *v. supra* pp. 16–17),

vanquished to accept a just verdict at their hands. In this situation, the Allied statesmen ought to have made peace with Turkey quickly, and to have offered her terms which were scrupulously moderate and equitable, seeing that, in this region at any rate, the consent of the conquered was indispensable for any genuine settlement. In fact, however, they procrastinated and failed to agree. First, the settlement of accounts with Germany (a far more urgent matter from a Western point of view) absorbed the thoughts and energies of the few individuals in whose hands political power was unduly concentrated as a result of the War. Then, the ghosts of old rivalries, dating back not only to the generation immediately before the Anglo-French Entente but to the Napoleonic Wars and even to the diplomatic encounters of Francis I and Henry VIII, rose up disconcertingly between them, found voice in a war-stricken and hysterical Press, and repeatedly frightened the negotiators away from this haunted Oriental ground. In consequence, the settlement with Turkey was perpetually postponed ; but events did not wait upon the leisure or the moral courage of the Allied and Associated plenipotentiaries. Every month of diplomatic inactivity rendered the British, French, and Italian troops which had been retained, since the Armistice, in Mesopotamia, Syria and Cilicia, Trans-Caucasia and Constantinople, more and more impatient to be demobilized. The cordon drawn round the unoccupied continental core of the Turkish Empire began to wear thin. Some sections of it were breaking. Would the control-officers scattered over Anatolia still be able to keep command of the situation ?

This was the practical problem with which the Supreme Council at Paris were confronted as a result of their procrastination, and their policy regarding it was the critical issue in the Eastern Question as it shaped itself after the Armistice. Two sharply opposed alternatives were open to them. Either they could make peace immediately upon terms which, while putting an end to Turkish dominion in the Arab and Balkan countries, would leave the Turkish ' homelands ' substantially intact, and would not drive the Turkish nation to despair. Or, on the other hand, they could postpone the settlement until such time as they felt more capable of grappling with it, and could retain their eventual power of enforcing their will by commissioning one or more of their lesser Eastern Allies to undertake military commitments which their own soldiers and tax-payers were becoming increasingly unwilling to shoulder. This second alternative had the supreme attraction of putting off a comparatively uninteresting and at the same time delicate and even dangerous task. But political, like monetary, bills have to be sold at a discount, and Greece, the small Power from whom a military sacrifice in ready money was solicited, would naturally not be prepared to perform services without receiving a commission. Hence, on the 6th May 1919, the Supreme Council (in agreement with M. Venizelos), decided that the military commitments in Northern Turkey which the Russian Empire (had it survived) would have undertaken in return for the acquisition of Turkish Armenia and Constantinople, and which the Western Powers, in the absence of Russia, could not undertake themselves, should be taken over by Greece on consideration of her acquiring Smyrna and an adjacent zone on the mainland of Anatolia.

(*b*) *The bargain with Greece.* The territory contemplated as the reward for the services of Greece, and eventually assigned to her (provisionally) under the Treaty of Sèvres, was not large compared with the areas respectively ear-marked by Russia, France, Italy, and Great Britain in the previous Secret Treaties. Moreover, Greece had a claim on grounds of nationality which was not possessed by these other Powers. At Smyrna, and in other parts of the Sèvres zone, there was a substantial Greek element in the population. The percentage of Greek inhabitants was unknown, for no census had ever been taken, and, two years after sending the Greek troops to Smyrna, the Allied Governments confessed their ignorance on this point by proposing themselves to appoint a commission to inquire into statistics of population both in the Smyrna zone and in Eastern Thrace.[1] Still, the Greek element was admittedly important, and the collation of existing estimates (nearly all of them *ex parte*) enabled the Supreme Council to maintain, at the time when they were drafting the Treaty, that in the Smyrna zone the Greeks were actually in a majority. This belief will hardly be shared by any one who has travelled over the district. In 1921, the Turks still had the appearance of being in a strong majority in the countryside, and of constituting approximately half the population of Smyrna city. At the same time, even

[1] Conference of London, February–March 1921, *v. supra* p. 33.

when the question of this Greek population is regarded (as it should be) as an item in the problem of minorities, it is an important and difficult example of this problem, and the Greek kingdom had a legitimate interest in the satisfactory solution of it.

Here, however, the fatal error in the policy of the Supreme Council came in, for, when full weight had been given to the claims of the Greek minorities in Anatolia and to the right of Greece to do her best for them, it remained a fact that the disembarkation of Greek troops at Smyrna was the worst conceivable means of attempting to meet the situation. In the first place, Smyrna, though it has not the same hold upon the imagination and sentiment of the Turks as Constantinople, is of greater importance than the capital to the economic life of Anatolia (the 'homeland' of the Osmanli nation). It is of infinitely greater importance than the north-eastern provinces claimed simultaneously by the Russian Empire and by the Armenians. In the second place, Turkish fear and resentment were bound to be aroused by the encroachment of Greece upon Anatolia far more keenly than by that of any other Power. Of course, if Russia had actually acquired the Armenian vilayets and Constantinople (as her Allies had recognized her right to do in 1915 and 1916), the remnant of a nominally independent Turkey would have fallen almost as completely under her control as Khiva and Bokhara. But for a century and a half before the European War, the Turks had become more and more conscious of the strength of the old Russia. Since the Russo-Turkish War of 1768–74, a prophecy had been current that the sceptre of Osman would pass to a fair-haired dynasty; the Russian protectorate, so nearly established over Northern Turkey during the 'thirties' of last century, had been regarded ever since as inevitable by the Turkish population of Anatolia. They might fear and loathe the prospect; but, had Russia emerged victorious from the European War, they would neither have been surprised at the doom imposed on them, nor have attempted to resist it. Nor, again, did they attempt—before the Greek landing in May 1919—to resist the imposition of British, French, and Italian military and political control, for though (as has been explained above), that control rested on rather slender foundations, it did not inflict any deadly wound on Turkey's pride or menace the vital interests of the Turkish people. The Turks admitted to themselves that the Western Powers were in every way their superiors; their control (even if exercised largely in their own interest) would be a lighter yoke than the rule of Abdu'l-Hamid or that of the Committee of Union and Progress; and, above all, the Western nations were not likely to send swarms of colonists to Anatolia and to expropriate the Turks from their homeland and last citadel.[1] For these reasons, the Turks showed as little inclination to resist Western control as, under other circumstances, they would have shown to resist Russian annexation.

(*c*) *Effects of the Greek landing at Smyrna, 15th May 1919.* The Greek landing produced an utterly different reaction. The Turks did not regard the Greeks as their superiors or even as their equals; they were mortally afraid of the consequences if the Greek State were to gain a foothold on the Anatolian mainland; and, on the other hand, they were not afraid of meeting Greece in single combat. The fear that a Turkish population would be supplanted, in the literal physical sense, by a Greek, was the strongest element in their emotions. For a century, Greece had steadily been acquiring Ottoman provinces in Rumelia, and in these provinces the Turkish element had subsequently dwindled away. From the Turkish point of view this was bad enough, even when it was only affecting Turkish minorities overseas. It became a question of life and death when the process began in Anatolia. If once Greece pushed her frontier on to the Anatolian mainland, the Turks foresaw that she would continue to advance, engulfing territories in which the Turkish element was still in the majority, and beyond which the Turkish nation had no city of refuge into which it could retire. For these reasons, the news of the Greek landing at Smyrna on the 15th May 1919 (and of the regrettable excesses which accompanied it) produced an electric effect upon the Turkish population through the length and breadth of Anatolia (an effect which the Supreme Council and M. Venizelos had failed to foresee). The 'will-to-war' was again aroused; a national consciousness (in the full Western sense of the term) was awakened; and eventually a Government of National Defence was established at Angora, which was not (as its opponents declared) a hoax staged by a few adventurers,

[1] Except possibly the Italians, and they were the least capable of the three Powers of imposing their will by force.

but the organized and formidable effort of a nation fighting for its existence.

The outcome of this was a new war, for the Greeks, on their side, were not prepared to give in. They hated and looked down upon the Turks as much as the Turks hated and looked down upon them. They felt it an obligation of honour to protect the Anatolian Greeks (who had been compromised by their landing); they had the elation of having been on the victorious side in the War and at the Peace Conference, and the expectation (produced by the experience of a century) that Greece must increase and Turkey must decrease. Finally, they had a romantic tradition that everything that had belonged to the Mediaeval East Roman Empire, or even to the Ancient Greek World of city-states in its widest extension, was theirs by right of inheritance. Thus, the Turkish efforts to resist the Greek invasion aroused corresponding efforts on the part of Greece to break the resistance of the Nationalists. Both parties mobilized their resources until, at the beginning of the campaign of July 1921, each had 200,000 soldiers under arms. The military conflict was indecisive (for inevitable reasons which are irrelevant here) and resulted in stale-mate. But, long before this, the Anatolian War had swept away almost every vestige of Allied control. As early as March 1920 the control officers disappeared from the scene, on both sides of the front; by February 1921 the Powers (with no means of action left except diplomacy) were unsuccessfully attempting to mediate between the belligerents. In May 1921, two months before the beginning of the chief military operations in Anatolia, they officially declared their neutrality in a joint proclamation issued by their High Commissioners at Constantinople.

This confession of impotence was utterly incompatible with the assumption of omnipotence that pervades the text of the Treaty of Sèvres. The two planes of development had diverged so far that they could never again merge into one another, and it was evident that the statesmen could not much longer straddle between the two, but would have definitely to abandon one in favour of the other. At the date when this chapter was written (mid-June 1922), the drama had not yet been played out, but the *dénouement* could already be foreseen with reasonable certainty. The plane of the Secret Treaties was doomed, for, although a number of imposing and voluminous state papers had been produced upon its surface, they had not seriously affected the lives and sentiments of nations or individuals. On the other hand, the plane of action upon which the Russians had entered when they repudiated annexations in April 1917, upon which the Supreme Council had entered when they sent Greek troops to Smyrna in May 1919, and upon which the Turks had entered when they resisted this step by force of arms and organized their National Movement, had proved itself to be the plane of reality, to which the ideals in the minds of diplomatists would have to conform. Even in the realm of state papers, this plane of action had asserted its superiority. State papers must be judged, not as potential archives, but as instruments of the will of human beings; and, from this point of view, the two Russian manifestos of April 1917, the Angora National Pact of January 1920, the Russo-Turkish Treaty of March 1921, and the Franco-Turkish Angora Agreement of the 20th October, (*v.* pp. 33–4) were of greater importance than the stately edifice of the Treaty of Sèvres and its pendants. The Supreme Council's original design was destined to be supplanted by the new web woven on a plane not of their choosing, and in a pattern not to their taste.

The broad lines of this pattern were becoming visible. It was not going to be a product which could exactly be described as a 'peace-settlement' or be brought into a precise and exclusive relation to the foregoing European War. In the Near and Middle East, at any rate, that War (overwhelming catastrophe though it had proved itself to be there also) was indivisible from a long series of events preceding it. Hence the re-establishment of equilibrium after these events, rather than after the specific upheaval of the War, was the essence of a settlement, if there was to be one. As a matter of fact, if one examines more closely the confused, painful, and long drawn-out drama, which held the Oriental stage after the brief interval between the 30th October 1918 and the 15th May 1919, one can discern that, amid the waste and suffering and destruction, a settlement (in the wider sense of the word) was emerging. Its nature can be made clearer by a recital of its principal concrete features.

2. *Liquidation of the Ottoman Empire.*

(*a*) *Western nationalistic influences.* The liquidation of the old Ottoman Empire (which began as early as 1699) was entering upon its final phase. This Empire, with its internal 'cultural autonomies' and its external economic, juridical, and even political servitudes to foreign states, had been completely non-Western in its structure. It was now giving place to a mosaic of sovereign, independent, 'self-coloured' national states consciously constructed on the Western model. Hitherto, the process had gone no farther than the secession and reorganization of the non-Turkish populations in the border provinces, leaving the trunk of the Empire maimed and bandaged, but not itself inwardly transformed. But the appearance of a Turkish National consciousness in Anatolia, and the formation of a Turkish National State by the same procrustean methods as had been employed in the creation of Serbia, Greece, Rumania, and Bulgaria, changed the character of the conflict and foreshadowed its termination, by assimilating the conflicting forces to one another. The truceless struggle between the Western and the Middle Eastern tradition, between the new and the old, was now replaced by the less hopeless strife of molecules approximating to one another in structure, which, in the process of nature, might eventually arrive at an organic harmony.

This definite triumph of Western Nationalism (which was affecting not only the Turks but the Arab populations south of them, the Persians and Afghans to the east, and even the 'Turanian' kinsmen of the Osmanli in Transcaucasia and Central Asia) was, in the truest sense, the settlement of an issue which had long been doubtful and had always been important. The political development of these peoples had not been bound to take this peculiar turn. Down to the last quarter of the seventeenth century, it seemed that the original institutions of the Ottoman Empire—under which the nationalities, while distinguished by religion and economic employment, were not segregated geographically nor divided by unbridgeable linguistic gulfs—might arrive at an equilibrium by working out a satisfactory system of cultural autonomy. Then, from 1699 to 1814, it seemed as though the Ottoman Empire would be wholly dismembered, and the gobbets swallowed and digested by other multi-national empires (the Hapsburg, Romanoff, and Bourbon Powers) of the dynastic and bureaucratic type then prevalent in Western Europe. Indeed, when, after 1814, the 'nationality solution' entered into competition with the other two, and produced the embryos of modern Yugo-Slavia and Greece, the new tendency seemed to be hopelessly overmatched by the forces already in the field. For a century, however, it gained ground upon them, and the rise of the Turkish National Movement, coinciding in date with the break-up of the Hapsburg and Romanoff monarchies, decided the issue.

(*b*) *Need of stabilizing frontiers.* One important aspect of this triumph of a particular political principle was that the abnormal instability of frontiers in the East, which had characterized the conflict of incompatible principles during two full centuries, might now die down.

(*c*) *The minorities problem.* The most valuable consequence of such a stabilization of frontiers would be that the problem of minorities might become soluble for the first time since 1699. The progressive changes of frontier, brought about by the operation of the Western concept of political nationality in Near and Middle Eastern minds during the preceding two centuries, had been causally related (in several ways) to the progressive worsening of the position of minorities, during the same period, both in the pollarded trunk of the Ottoman Empire and in the new national states fashioned out of its former branches. In the first place, the ideal of a nationally homogeneous population exclusively occupying a sharply defined national territory—an ideal which arose naturally out of West European conditions—acts as a subversive and even a homicidal force among populations in which nationalities happen to be geographically intermingled and economically interdependent. The mere introduction of the idea into such an environment almost inevitably entails violence and bloodshed, and when once the geographical segregation of national groups, by these methods, has begun, the process generates a chronic condition of fear, which in turn generates violence and bloodshed by a vicious circle of states of mind. The evil becomes more acute as the process approaches completion, for when the various local majorities have respectively succeeded in organizing themselves into national states, their chief remaining opportunity of expanding at one another's expense is to lay hands on territories adjoining their frontiers, in which the presence of minorities of their own nationality gives them a certain pretext and a certain leverage. As the struggle for existence goes on and the tension increases, the presence of alien minorities in border provinces, or even in the interior, becomes a constant source of anxiety to the ruling majority in every national state, especially in the case of states which have been losing rather than gaining ground. In such cases, fear creates a temptation first to oppress the minorities, then to evict them, and in the last resort to exterminate them by systematic massacre. This horrible tendency, which has been increasing during the past two centuries, not only among the Turks but among all the non-Western populations of the area affected by the Western nationality idea, can only be combated by removing its cause. If frontiers became stable, the fear prevalent on either side of them would diminish with time, and effective machinery for the protection of minorities would become easier to put into operation.

(*d*) *New religious outlook.* A fourth element in a permanent settlement, which had to be taken into consideration at the time when this chapter was written, was a possible change of Western sentiment towards the Turks and the Greeks, or, on a wider range, towards the Islamic and the Oriental Christian worlds. For centuries the development of the 'Eastern Question' had been profoundly influenced by the traditional sympathy of the Western public for 'Christians' and 'Europeans' and by their antipathy towards 'Moslems' and 'Asiatics'. But, between 1914 and 1922, many factors had been unsettling this ancient habit of mind. The European War had made an almost unprecedented schism in Western society. The Entente nations on the one side, and the Germans, Austrians, and Magyars on the other, had persuaded themselves, in the heat of the struggle, that their Western adversaries of the moment were more barbarous and 'unspeakable' than their non-Western allies. Their mutual disillusionment had shattered their ancient common faith in the unity and superiority of Western civilization, and after the Armistice they had each begun to realize that they were not altogether innocent themselves of the crimes of which they believed their opponents to be guilty. In this chaos of moral valuations, 'Philhellenism' and 'Turcophobia' were also losing their sharpness of outline. Englishmen found themselves disinclined to believe that Greeks were nobler than Irishmen or Turks baser than Germans. Moreover, the victorious Western nations, which had not only retained but enlarged their Oriental dependencies, had concrete motives for levelling the old moral barriers. There was not merely the motive of expediency (a motive which was not necessarily unscrupulous, since the maintenance of internal peace in these dependencies during the critical post-war period was of great importance to the world). There was also a genuine sentiment of gratitude towards those Indian and North African Moslem soldiers who had helped the French and British to defeat the Germans. This comradeship in arms with Moslem fellow-citizens made it difficult thenceforth for the Western peoples to feel that the Turk, merely because he was a Moslem, was therefore beyond the pale. Thus, at the time of writing, the old prejudices and predilections were in process of transformation, and it was difficult to foretell how they would reshape themselves. They might either kindle still more destructive passions, or else give place to more liberal and rational relationships than had previously subsisted between the great divisions of mankind.

3. *Boundaries and character of the area with which this section is concerned.* These considerations no doubt appear vague and general, yet they are important in themselves, and in June 1922 it was difficult yet to discern the form of the coming settlement in the East with greater precision or in fuller detail. The section is concerned not only with a limited period—that subsequent to the 30th October 1918—but with a limited area. Egypt and the Arab countries in Asia—areas which did, after the European War, experience something more like a peace settlement in the usual sense of the word—have been dealt with elsewhere.[1] There remains, however, to be considered the whole northern half of the former Ottoman Empire, an area with an extreme length of little less than a thousand miles, and an extreme breadth of nearly four hundred. Its boundaries on the west were the European hinterland of the Black Sea Straits (known as 'Eastern Thrace') and the Aegean Sea; on the north-east the Trans-Caucasian territories retained or recovered *de facto* by Russia; on the east Persia, a country which between 1907 and 1917 had seemed doomed to partition, and which had been unable to prevent the belligerents from fighting all over its territory during the War, but which had been miraculously reprieved by the break-down of Russia; and on the south by the Mediterranean and (further east) by the Arab provinces of

[1] Part III, *passim*, Arabs; Part IV, Egypt; and Part V, Persia.

the old Ottoman Empire, the independence of which had been recognized, on the one hand, by the Turkish Nationalists in the first article of their National Pact (28th January 1920), and on the other hand by the victorious Western Powers in the Treaty of Sèvres (10th August 1920), in the Covenant of the League of Nations, and, to a partial extent, even in the Secret Treaties.

(*a*) *Geographical unity of Anatolia ; Angora Agreement,*[1] *20th October 1921.* This area had certain important features of unity. The first of these was geographical, and was discovered, at points widely distant from one another, by the French and the Greek General Staffs, when, after the Armistice, they attempted, in Cilicia and the Smyrna zone respectively, to occupy militarily certain limited lowland districts along the littoral. They found that the lowlands were not divided by any pronounced physical barrier from the central plateau. This plateau, with its pendant strips of coast, forms a peninsula washed on three sides by the sea ; and, before this section was written, the Turkish Nationalist Government at Angora had extended their frontiers, and established their effective authority, up to the edge of the plateau at almost every point where it abutted on to the main mass of the Asiatic continent. On the north-eastern rim of the Anatolian table-land, they had forced the Armenian Republic of Erivan, in December 1920, to cede to them the two districts of Kars and Ardahan, which the Russian Empire had conquered from the Ottoman Empire in 1878. This cession had been confirmed in the Russo-Turkish Treaty signed in March 1921 at Moscow, and re-confirmed in a Treaty signed in the following October at Kars, on the one side by the Angora Government, and on the other by the three Soviet Republics in Transcaucasia, which were nominally the allies of, but actually the dependents of, the Soviet Government at Moscow. On the southern flank of the plateau, the whole situation was changed by the Agreement signed on the 20th October 1921, at Angora, by M. Franklin-Bouillon for the French Republic and by Yusuf Kemal Bey for the Government of the Great National Assembly.[1] Not only did it procure the French evacuation of the Cilician plain (a district which the Treaty of Sèvres had left under Turkish sovereignty), but it also brought about the retrocession by France to Turkey of a long strip of territory

[1] *v.* Text, App. II, Part 2, *b*.

running, west to east, from the Gulf of Alexandretta to the left bank of the Tigris opposite Jeziret-ibn-ʿUmar. The Turkish frontier was thus not only pushed southward again to within a few miles of the port of Alexandretta and the city of Aleppo, but the Amanus tunnel, and the entire track of the Baghdad railway, from the bridge over the River Jaihan in Eastern Cilicia to the temporary terminus at Rasu'l-ʿAin in Northern Mesopotamia, were brought once more under Turkish sovereignty, except for the loop running down to Aleppo.

The geographical unity of the region was thus emphasized by the fact that on the land side, where the physical boundaries of the plateau-peninsula are of course least sharply drawn, the political and military frontiers of the Turkish National Government had been carried up to, but nowhere very far beyond, the foot of the escarpment. A second feature of unity was that, throughout this area, adherents of Islam were in a decided majority; a third, that these Moslem majorities were also almost entirely Turkish [1] in their vernacular language and in their national sentiment, except in the extreme north-east, between Trebizond and Batum, where the Moslem majority consisted of Lazes (a nationality speaking a Georgian dialect), and in the south-east (the vilayets of Kharput, Diarbekr, Bitlis, and Van), where it consisted of Kurds.

A fourth feature of unity was the fact that the whole of this region was claimed for Turkey in Art. I of the National Pact. In this article, the members of the Ottoman Parliament, subscribing to the Pact, first renounced the claims of Turkey to ex-Ottoman provinces inhabited by Arab majorities and situated south of the Armistice-line laid down on the 30th October 1918. On the other hand, they claimed that the non-Arab Ottoman Moslem population north of this line constituted an indivisible political unit, *de facto* and *de iure*, and, since the element thus defined was in a majority throughout the rest of the Empire, they demanded the whole of that area for the new Turkey on the principle of self-determination. In other articles they called for a plebiscite in Western Thrace, where there was a Moslem (partly Turkish and partly Pomak Bulgarian) majority, and assented to the taking of a second plebiscite in the Transcaucasian districts of Kars, Ardahan, and Batum—

[1] The chief exceptions being Greek-speaking refugees from Crete and Circassians from the Caucasus.

districts in which the Moslem (Turkish and Georgian) population may possibly have been more numerous than the Georgian and Armenian Christians, though no light had been thrown upon this by the first plebiscite, taken under almost farcical conditions,[1] during the Turkish military occupation in 1918.

(*b*) *Armenia and the Harbord Report, 16th October 1919.* A fifth feature of unity, which is of permanent historical interest and might have been of the utmost practical importance, was the view presented in the report (dated the 16th October 1919) of a military mission, under the command of Major-General James G. Harbord, which the United States Government had dispatched to Armenia.

'The Covenant of the League of Nations contemplates that "certain communities *formerly* belonging to the Turkish Empire" shall be subject to a mandatory power for an unstated period, thus appearing to recognize in advance the dismemberment to some degree of that Empire. [The italic is ours] . . .

'A power which should undertake a mandatory for Armenia and Trans-Caucasia without control of the contiguous territory of Asia Minor —Anatolia—and of Constantinople, with its hinterland of Rumelia, would undertake it under most unfavourable and trying conditions, so difficult as to make the cost almost prohibitive, the maintenance of law and order and the security of life and property uncertain, and ultimate success extremely doubtful. With the Turkish Empire still freely controlling Constantinople, such a power would be practically emasculated as far as real power is concerned . . .

'Conceded that there shall be a mandate for Armenia and Trans-Caucasia and one for Constantinople and Anatolia, there are many considerations that indicate the desirability of having such mandates exercised by the same power. If separate powers exercised such mandate, the inevitable jealousies, hatreds, exaggerated separatist tendencies, and economic difficulties would compel failure. With all its faults, the Turkish Empire is an existing institution, and it has some rusty blood-stained political machinery which, under control of a strong mandatory, can be made to function. The peoples in question live in adjacent territory and, whether they wish it or not, are neighbours. A single mandatory for the Turkish Empire and the Trans-Caucasus would be the most economical solution. No intelligent scheme for development of railroads for Trans-Caucasia and Armenia can be worked out without extension into Anatolia . . .

'It has been very evident to this Mission that Turkey would not object to a single disinterested power taking a mandate for her territory as outlined in the Armistice with the Allies, and that it could be accomplished with a minimum of foreign soldiery, where an attempt to carve

[1] Practically the whole Christian population having previously fled the country.

out territory for any particular region would mean a strong foreign force in constant occupation for many years . . .

'Syria and Mesopotamia, however, not being considered essential to the settlement of the Armenian question or as being the field for possible American responsibilities and interests in the Near East as contemplated in the instructions to the Mission . . ., have been considered by us as excluded from our considerations, as is for a similar reason Arabia.'[1]

The above passages have not been quoted in order to prejudge the very controversial political questions with which they deal. At the time when this section was written, both official and unofficial opinion in the West was inclined to feel that, on the balance, the arguments in favour of establishing a territorially segregated 'National Home' for the Armenians were stronger than those against this method of handling the Armenian problem. The purpose of the quotation is, first, to show why this area was treated as a unit in the History of the Peace Conference after the European War; and, secondly, to enable the reader to see in advance why the attempts which were actually made, after the Armistice, to deal with the region piecemeal, turned out in many ways so disastrously, notwithstanding the strong countervailing reasons for embarking upon these experiments. Even for the historian, the dissection of this unit into subdivisions is not altogether satisfactory, and the classification adopted in the following survey is given with the warning that each topic is only artificially abstracted and has an intimate bearing upon every other. At the same time, the subject can probably be treated with least inconvenience under the following headings: The Straits and Constantinople, with their European hinterland in Eastern Thrace; the Greek minority in the area and the disposal of Smyrna; the Armenian minority in the area and the establishment of an Armenian 'National Home'. The constitution of the future Turkish National State. And lastly, the problem of protecting the considerable minorities, of almost every nationality and denomination in the Near and Middle East. These are bound to be left on the wrong side of the line after any partition of the region, or of some particular part of it, into sovereign independent territorial national states,

[1] General Harbord's Report, 16th October 1919, is printed in full in No. 151, June 1920, pp. 275–302, *American Association for International Conciliation.*

however disinterestedly and equitably the frontiers may be drawn.

4. *The Boundaries in detail.*

(*a*) *The Straits, Constantinople, and Eastern Thrace* (*Treaty of Sèvres,* Arts. 36–61, 84, 178–80). The problem of the Black Sea Straits, to which those of Constantinople and Eastern Thrace are incidental, is a point of very much greater international importance than the others with which this section is concerned. Warfare between Greeks and Turks in Anatolia may arouse dangerous passions in the Western World on the one side and in the Islamic World on the other; the fate of the Armenians may touch the conscience of all mankind; but the control of the Straits is a matter of life and death for half Europe, and of grave concern for half the nations and states of the world. There are great countries inside the Straits which have no other available channel for exchanging their products with those of the rest of the world; and these products are so important (especially during the post-war reconstruction period) that the rest of the world cannot do without them. The control of the Straits has been a vital question since the dawn of history. The Trojan War was probably fought on account of it; the issue of the Peloponnesian War was decided by it; the ancient Greek colony of Byzantium was founded, and afterwards transformed into the imperial capital of Constantinople, in order to secure it; the commercial prosperity of mediaeval Venice and Genoa largely depended upon it. The question has grown more acute in modern times, as the improvement in artillery has made it more and more difficult to force a passage against the will of a Power occupying the shores. The invention of floating mines has made the position of any party in possession practically impregnable—at any rate, against attacks from the outer or Aegean side, that is, in a direction contrary to the current maintained by the discharge of the Black Sea water.

The changes produced by the European War in the map of Central and South-Eastern Europe and of Russia complicated the question still further, by depriving large land-locked areas (like the basins of the Danube, Dnieper, and Volga) of easy alternative outlets to the Adriatic and the Baltic. Austria and Hungary were now cut off politically from Trieste and Fiume, Russia from Libau, Riga, and Reval, and Bulgaria from the Aegean. When the new frontiers were drawn, it was evident that, however successfully these political barriers might eventually be overcome by economic co-operation, a certain diversion of trade was inevitable, and the stream thus diverted was bound to seek an exit into the Black Sea, and out through the Straits into the Mediterranean.

Geologically, the Bosporus and the Dardanelles are both ex-river valleys, ultimately turned into salt-water straits by the subsidence below sea-level of the area in which they were situated. Geographically, it is illuminating to regard them as a river still, with the Sea of Marmara and the Black Sea as lakes strung along their course, and with the Danube and the rivers of Southern Russia as their tributaries. When the Straits are envisaged in this way, the immensity of their 'basin' becomes apparent, and the watershed of this 'basin' is far from being the boundary of the commercial hinterland dependent on the lowest reaches of the water-way, that is, on the section between the northern entrance to the Bosporus and the southern exit from the Dardanelles.

The economic problem, and the political problems which it carries in its train, were dormant, however, during the sixteenth and seventeenth centuries, when the Ottoman Empire included Budapest, Bukarest, and the Crimea, as well as Varna and the still undeveloped sites of modern Constanza, Odessa, Nikolayev, Kherson, and Novorossisk. The 'basin' of the Straits, vast though it was, was largely under the direct or indirect sovereignty of the state which commanded the Straits by maintaining its capital at Constantinople. Those Russian portions of the 'basin' which lay outside the Ottoman sphere of influence were still economically undeveloped, and traded little (at least in bulky commodities) with the outer world. The difficulties began after 1699, when Austria had started to push down the Danube and Russia to obtain a footing on the Sea of Azov. They became acute towards the close of the eighteenth century, when Rumania and the Crimea were partly or wholly detached from Turkey, while at the same time the steppes were opened up to agriculture, to supply food for the new industrial urban populations of Western Europe. It was as if, when the Middle West of North America was opened up by settlers coming from the Atlantic sea-board across the Alleghanies, New Orleans had still remained under the French flag, so that the new farming population of the prairie states could never be sure whether, in any given year, it would be able to export its grain, and import its agricultural machinery and other manufactured goods, by the water-way of the Mississippi. That situation would have led to bloodshed, as the parallel situation in the 'basin' of the Straits has led to it repeatedly during the last two hundred years. In America, however, where society was recently planted and was still capable of transplantation and grafting, it was comparatively easy to erase frontiers and to make the territories of states coincide with the units of economic geography. The whole Mississippi basin was incorporated into the United States, the prairie hinterland of the St. Lawrence into the Dominion of Canada. An attempt to attain similar 'natural frontiers' was the economic and social force behind the old imperialism of Tsarist Russia. But in this part of the world human life was old, and, with the progress of time, political frontiers have furrowed the map more and more deeply and thickly, like the wrinkles of age. During the eighteenth century, it looked as though the dominion over the 'basin' of the Straits would pass from the Osmanli to either the Romanoff or the Hapsburg. But the control of a strategic position is difficult to divide; the rivalry between the two expanding empires checked the progress of both; and under the shadow of the 'Balance of Power' the new-fangled Western doctrine of nationality seeded itself in the minds of the native populations and produced the phenomenon of 'Balkanization'. Russia grasped, once more, at Constantinople in 1915, but in reality her prospects of acquiring it had vanished with the establishment across her path of the sovereign independent national state of Rumania (1861–78), just as the *Drang nach Osten* of the Hapsburg Monarchy had its way stopped by the rise of the national state of Serbia. The break-up of the Hapsburg and the Romanoff Empires in 1917–18 removed, once and for all, the possibility of solving the question of the Straits by any kind of political reunification of their hinterland. In this part of the world, as has been explained above, nationalism definitely triumphed, as a consequence of the European War. But that only made a solution of the Straits Question much more difficult as well as much more necessary. Without some international control of the Straits, in which the principal maritime Powers should participate as well as all the riverains of the 'basin', the political map resulting from the War could not fail to reduce the economic situation *ad absurdum*. Under the Treaty of Sèvres, Constantinople was to remain the capital of Turkey, and, in June 1922, it was probable that Turkey would obtain more rather than less of the European littoral of the Straits assigned to her under the Treaty. But even if all the territorial claims set out in the Turkish National Pact were realized, Turkey, while retaining her sovereignty over all the shores of the vital water-way, would still only possess an insignificant portion of the economic hinterland. It would include that part of Anatolia, possibly a third of the whole peninsula, which finds its commercial outlet at ports along the coasts of the Marmara, the Bosporus, and the Black Sea. The remainder of the hinterland—Trans-Caucasia, Southern Russia, the Danube Basin, and Bulgaria—would be under other sovereignties, and nothing but some effective international control of the Straits would make the situation tolerable either for them or for the shipping interests of Great Britain, France, Italy, and the United States.

The difficulty was concrete. It had arisen before the War and would recur after it, if and whenever Turkey again became a belligerent. The capital of a belligerent state is one of the principal objectives of its enemies; and, under modern conditions of warfare, an attack on Constantinople, whether by sea or by land, would almost inevitably entail the closure of the Straits to commercial traffic. Thus a local war between Turkey and Greece or Turkey and Bulgaria might paralyse the economic and financial organization of Russia and Rumania, ruin great shipping interests in distant countries, and adversely affect the prosperity of the world. The 'Freedom of the Straits', if it meant anything, meant that commerce should be able to count on a free passage through them, whether the riverain Power or Powers were at peace or at war.

(i) *The 'Freedom of the Straits'*. The 'Freedom of the Straits', in this sense, was provided for in the Treaty of Sèvres. The relevant provisions fall under three heads. In the first place, the sovereignty over the Gallipoli Peninsula and all Eastern Thrace up to the Chatalja lines was transferred from Turkey to Greece, in order to ensure that, whether or not it should prove possible to inaugurate a successful scheme of international control, no single state, at any rate, should thereafter exercise sovereignty over the entire littoral. Greece and Turkey were unlikely to find themselves on the same side in any war, and if either Power attempted at any time to use its command of part of the shore-line in order to hold up the traffic, it would be comparatively easy to bring it to reason by military operations based on the territory of the other state, whereas a state commanding the entire littoral had been proved, during the European War, to possess the power of closing the Straits with impunity. This redistribution of territory was certainly open to grave objections on other grounds. It was of doubtful justice from the point of view of nationality, and if Constantinople was to remain the Turkish capital, it was hardly wise to bring the frontier of a hostile state up to within a few miles of its suburbs. At the same time, it did afford a practical, if crude, guarantee for the maintenance of the freedom of the Straits, and, in so far as it did this, it promoted an international interest of first rate importance. In June 1922, it was becoming evident that the dispositions of the Treaty of Sèvres in regard to Thrace [1] would have to be altered, but it remained none the less clear that, in considering the nature and extent of these alterations, the maintenance of the freedom of the Straits could not be left out of account.

The second head comprises those articles in the Treaty (178–80) which placed a military sanction in the hands of Great Britain, France, and Italy. A zone of territory was laid down, including the whole of the Asiatic and the European shores of the Dardanelles, Marmara, and Bosporus, and the adjoining territorial waters,[2] within which the three principal Allied Powers alone were to have the right of maintaining armed forces, while Turkey and Greece, the territorial sovereigns, were prohibited from doing the same (with two insignificant exceptions). All fortifications in this zone were to be dismantled permanently.

A third group of articles (37–61) defined the freedom of the Straits and set up a 'Commission of the Straits' to regulate it. The definition (which agrees with that given above, in the present section) ran as follows (Art. 37):

'The navigation of the Straits, including the Dardanelles, the Sea of Marmara, and the Bosporus, shall in future be open, both in peace

[1] These dispositions were given practical effect a month before the Treaty was signed, by a military occupation of the territory on the part of Greece with the sanction of the Allied Governments.

[2] Art. 178. Also the islands of Lemnos, Imbros, Samothrace, Tenedos, and Mitylene, and all those in the Sea of Marmara. (*v.* p. 40).

and war, to every vessel of commerce or of war and to military and commercial aircraft, without distinction of flag.

'These waters shall not be subject to blockade, nor shall any belligerent right be exercised nor any act of hostility be committed within them, unless in pursuance of a decision of the Council of the League of Nations.'

The 'Commission of the Straits' was to be composed (Art. 40) of representatives appointed respectively by the United States of America (if and when that Government was willing to participate), the British Empire, France, Italy, Japan, Russia (if and when Russia became a member of the League of Nations), Greece, Rumania, and Bulgaria and Turkey (if and when the two latter states became members of the League of Nations). Each Power was to appoint one representative. The representatives of the United States of America, the British Empire, France, Italy, Japan, and Russia were each to have two votes. The representatives of Greece, Rumania, and Bulgaria and Turkey were each to have one vote.

The Commission, so constituted, was to have two distinct though logically connected functions. On the one hand, it was to organize and administer the freedom of the Straits; on the other hand, it was to report upon any interference with it.

The first and normal function of the Commission was conceived in very wide terms. On the analogy of the older Danube Commission, everything relating to 'conservancy' was brought within its jurisdiction. It was charged (Art. 43) with the execution of harbour works and with lighting and buoying, and with the control of pilotage and towage, anchorages, wrecks and salvage, and lighterage, as well as with the application in the ports of Constantinople and Haidar Pasha of the régime prescribed in Arts. 335–45 of the Treaty for 'ports of international concern'. It might raise loans, buy out existing rights and concessions, and take up concessions on its own account. It was to levy dues from merchant shipping passing through the waters under its control, and to exercise jurisdiction over their crews (Arts. 50–3), though alterations in existing dues were only to be made with the prior assent of the Council of the League of Nations and for the execution of duties specifically assigned to the Commission by the Treaty. The Commission was further empowered to raise a special police force under foreign officers (Art. 48); to enjoy diplomatic privileges and immunities (Art. 41); to exercise its powers in complete independence of the local authority; and to have its own flag, its own budget, and its separate organization (Art. 42).

Thus, in its administrative functions, the Commission was endowed by the Treaty with something approaching to sovereignty, but, on the other hand, it did not acquire the sanction, possessed by most sovereign bodies, of imposing its own will by force. In this sphere, its function was passive and advisory. By Art. 44, the Commission, in the event of its finding that the liberty of passage was being interfered with, was to inform the representatives at Constantinople of the Allied Powers furnishing the occupying forces provided for in Art. 178. These representatives were thereupon to concert with the naval and military commanders of the said forces such measures as might be deemed necessary to preserve the freedom of the Straits. Similar action was to be taken by the said representatives in the event of any external action threatening the liberty of passage of the Straits.

These articles relating to the Straits, Constantinople, and Eastern Thrace were the least unsatisfactory part of the Treaty of Sèvres (as far as it related to the non-Arab part of the former Ottoman Empire, which is the subject of this section). In view of the unwillingness of the American nation to undertake responsibilities in this part of the world, these provisions represented an honest and not incompetent attempt to grapple with a difficult problem, and the instrument embodying them was duly signed by the Governments of Athens and Constantinople, as well as by those of the principal and minor Entente Powers (with the exception of the Serb-Croat-Slovene Kingdom and the Hejaz). But the Treaty was not ratified, and the problem itself was not necessarily capable of solution in the settlement after the European War. There were at least four obstacles. The most immediate was the traditional rivalry between France and Great Britain; behind that there were the fears and ambitions of Turkey and Greece; and farthest in the background, though ultimately the most formidable of all, lay the interests of Russia, resting on permanent geographical factors which could not be affected by the substitution of Lenin for Nicholas or of the works of Karl Marx for the Orthodox Liturgy.

(ii) *Anglo-French rivalry.* The Anglo-French rivalry was the first obstacle to assert itself. The trouble began immediately after the Armistice, with the sudden elimination of the overwhelming common fear of Germany, and the joint occupation of Syria and Constantinople. The question of which nation was to exercise the military command over the various Allied contingents at Constantinople became the subject of interminable and ill-humoured diplomatic negotiations, but this did less harm than the accomplished fact of the naval ascendancy of Great Britain. Sea-power was bound to be the principal sanction for maintaining in the Straits that régime which the Treaty envisaged, chiefly for technical reasons of strategy, but partly also because the three guarantor Powers could keep warships on the spot with relatively little increase in their normal expenditure on their Mediterranean squadrons, while the maintenance of military garrisons would involve totally new expenditure which none of the Governments concerned could permanently persuade their tax-payers to provide. It was evident, therefore, that if the provisions of the Treaty were to be maintained by material sanctions, those sanctions would practically be co-extensive with the respective naval forces of Great Britain, France, and Italy, operating in the ratio of their relative strength. Such a sanction, however, could be expressed as 'British naval predominance in the Straits' from an Anglophobe point of view, and this view gradually gained strength in France. This current of French feeling was partly fed by traditional beliefs (probably erroneous, but none the less disquieting to those who held them) regarding the circumstances in which an Anglo-French condominium in Egypt had once given place to a solely British occupation. Resentment at the alteration of the Secret Treaties in favour of Great Britain, on the questions of Mosul and Palestine, also played its part. But the most important factor was the actual diplomatic and administrative ascendancy of Great Britain at Constantinople and in the Straits after the Armistice, an ascendancy which was not only unmistakable but impressive, whether or not British naval predominance was the cause of it. Before the Treaty was signed by the French Government, a section of French public opinion had made up its mind that, in the interests of France, even a restoration of unfettered Turkish sovereignty over the Straits was preferable to the confirmation of this British ascendancy, which appeared to be the only alternative. This party in France did not, after the signature of the Treaty, either cease to preach its doctrine or fail to gain fresh adherents.

(iii) *Greek attitude.* The mental reservations of the Greeks regarding the Treaty offered a certain justification for such an attitude on the part of France. It is true that M. Venizelos, in laying the claims of his country before the Peace Conference, had pointedly refrained from asking for Constantinople and the other strategic positions commanding the Straits, on the express assumption that some kind of international control would be established there. That, however, did not mean that either Greece or her Prime Minister had abandoned their ultimate aspirations in that quarter. They calculated that if Eastern Thrace were annexed to Greece and the frontier carried up to Chatalja, while at the same time Turkish sovereignty at Constantinople were subordinated, in effect even more than in theory, to foreign military and administrative control, the Greek element was bound very soon to become predominant, in every respect, in the population of the city. If the situation created by the Treaty continued long enough, Constantinople might, therefore, pass to Greece by a bloodless and perhaps hardly perceptible revolution. But many Greek observers thought that they discerned a short cut to their goal. In their sanguine imagination, that British naval ascendancy in the Straits, which the French feared but which the Greeks welcomed, was bound to become, if it had not already become, a conscious object of British policy. In that event they were confident that Great Britain could not dispense with the local support of Greece. Mr. Lloyd George, they thought, would assign to Greece the place in the British scheme of world-policy which Disraeli had assigned to Turkey. The seeds of this relationship, they believed, were sown in the provisions of the Treaty, and if only they were given a chance to germinate, the Treaty would involve ultimate advantages for Greece far greater than those allotted to her explicitly in the text of it. Thus the Greeks did not desire the permanent working of the régime laid down in the Treaty, though they looked forward to a process of evolution, and not to a violent reversal.

(iv) *Conferences of London, February–March 1921, and of Paris, March 1922; Turkish attitude.* The Turks, on the other hand, naturally desired a reversal, because they took the same view of the facts as the Greeks and the French, and had an interest identical with that of France, and contrary to that of Greece, on the assumption that the facts had been correctly interpreted by these three parties. It is true that, as a result of the Conferences held respectively at London in February and March 1921, and at Paris in March 1922, a number of modifications of the Treaty were proposed by the Allied Powers, in order to make the terms more palatable from the Turkish point of view. The contingent expulsion of Turkey from Constantinople (Art. 36) in the event of her failing to execute certain provisions of the Treaty, was to be waived. The zone reserved exclusively for military occupation by the three principal Allied Powers was to be confined to the positions commanding the Dardanelles, and Turkey was to be allowed to maintain an effective garrison in Constantinople. As regards the Commission of the Straits, while no diminution of its functions or of the area in which they were to be exercised was suggested, Turkey was to be given not only two votes, like the principal Powers represented, but the permanent presidency. Finally, the frontier between Turkey and Greece in Eastern Thrace was to be carried substantially further westward, so as to give Turkey a militarily defensible line, out of range of Constantinople, running from Ganos on the Sea of Marmara in a north-north-easterly direction to a point on the Bulgarian frontier.

These concessions, in the aggregate, were very considerable, but they could hardly satisfy the Turks because they would not fundamentally alter the general situation. The British aspiration to naval ascendancy (if correctly diagnosed) and the Greek aspiration to eventual sovereignty over Constantinople would not be inhibited, and the Turks were encouraged to be intransigent by the (possibly correct) belief that these modifications were likewise inadequate from the French point of view. The rival Turkish Governments, of Constantinople and of Angora, agreed in holding out for the retrocession of: (i) Adrianople; and (ii) the Gallipoli Peninsula. If the Allies satisfied the latter claim they would, of course, not only exclude Greece from the possession of any territory militarily commanding the Straits, but they would replace all such territories under the sovereignty of Turkey. If these territorial claims were conceded, both Constantinople and Angora expressed themselves ready to agree to the freedom of the Straits; but, at any rate in the

National Pact, this concession was accompanied by a significant reservation.[1]

'The security of Constantinople, the capital of the Empire and the seat of the Caliphate and of the Ottoman Government, must be beyond the reach of any infringement. When once this principle has been formulated and admitted, the undersigned are ready to subscribe to any decision which may be taken, in common accord, by the Imperial Government on the one hand and by the interested Powers on the other, in order to assure the opening of the Straits to world commerce and to international communications' (Art. 4).

This claim involved, and consciously involved, the restoration of full Turkish naval and military control over the water-way and its littoral, and such control, as has been explained already, is incompatible with the freedom of the Straits in the only genuine meaning of the phrase. In peace-time, perhaps, there might be little danger that Turkey would use such military and naval control in order to interfere with the Commission of the Straits in the exercise of its rights and duties as laid down by the Treaty. In peace-time, even under the old régime, when the functions assigned to the Commission were still attributes of Turkish sovereignty, the Turkish Government did not unduly interfere with the shipping which availed itself of the waterway. The fundamental, and insuperable, difficulty of the Turkish claim lay in the proneness of Turkey to be involved in any war which arises anywhere east of the Atlantic and west of the Straits of Malacca. It would be quite unsafe to assume that Turkey will be more immune from war in the future than she has been in the past; and, under the conditions specified by her, the freedom of the Straits would invariably be interrupted whenever she was at war. If the zone of the Straits were to return within the military (as distinct from the political) frontiers of Turkey, it would become the legitimate, and indeed the essential, military objective of her adversaries. The only means of permanently neutralizing this zone is to prohibit the military utilization of it by Turkey herself as well as by her potential enemies, and to place it, instead, under the naval and military control of other parties representing the general interests of the world. The logic of these facts can hardly be questioned, and the Turkish attitude regarding the provisions

[1] Text of National Pact of Angora in App. II, Part 2a.

of the Treaty relating to this question was, therefore, a serious obstacle to a settlement.

(v) *The Russian attitude.* The particular settlement envisaged by the Treaty might possibly find its most serious opponent in Russia. Between May 1919 and June 1922, the relations of Russia to Turkey had approximated to those which prevailed during the interval between the Russo-Turkish Treaty of Unkiar-Skelessi (8th July 1833) and the Anglo-Austro-Prusso-Russian Agreement concerning the Pacification of the Levant (15th July 1840). There was, in fact, an extraordinary similarity between the two situations in which these peculiar relations arose. In the earlier period, the Turks had lost their Arab provinces to Mehmed Ali, and were threatened in their 'homelands' by the advance of the Pasha of Egypt's forces to Kiutahia, the strategic centre of Western Anatolia. After the Armistice of 1918, the Arab provinces were again lost, and the Turkish 'homelands' again threatened by a foreign military invasion, though on this occasion Kiutahia was occupied, not by the same military Power as had driven the Turkish forces out of Syria, but by a separate enemy, the Greeks, conducting an independent campaign from a base on the Aegean coast. In the two cases, a broadly parallel situation produced a parallel *rapprochement* on Turkey's part towards Russia. The loss of the Arab provinces made Turkey too weak to stand alone, and the hegemony of the great Northern Power, however alarming, was at least preferable to the conquest and subjection of the remnant of Turkey by a neighbouring people formerly subject to her. In both cases, again, Turkey was driven into Russia's arms by the fact that her local enemy enjoyed the formidable support of another Great Power—France having stood behind Mehmed Ali, as Great Britain afterwards stood behind Greece. In the earlier instance, the growing ascendancy of Russia over Turkey, to which the *rapprochement* between two parties of such unequal strength inevitably led, was interrupted by the successful conclusion of a general understanding between all the Great Powers, which resulted in a relaxation of the local pressure upon Turkey and in a general resettlement of Near and Middle Eastern affairs. In June 1922, it was impossible to say whether the current situation would eventually resolve itself in a similar *dénouement*, or whether, on this second favourable occasion, Russia would establish her suzerainty permanently over the area dealt with in this section, including the Straits and Constantinople. In consequence of the Revolution, Russia enjoyed two advantages which she had never possessed before. By abandoning centralization in favour of local national autonomies in the vast block of territory and population under her sovereignty, she had given way at last to the spirit of the times, and so improved her chances of making that block still larger—in the form of a multi-national federation. In the second place, a number of the minor nationalities in Russian territory which had thus acquired territorial autonomy, spoke Turkish vernaculars and were adherents of Islam. Indeed, the Moslem Turkish population of Russia was more than twice as numerous as that of Turkey herself, and now that these Turkish Moslems had obtained opportunities for self-expression inside the Russian State, it was conceivable that the lesser mass of Turks would be attracted by the greater. The ancient question of the Straits might yet be solved by a federation of riverain national states, including Turkey, under Russia's presidency. One thing only was certain. The solution would not take the exact form contemplated in the Treaty of Sèvres.

(*b*) *The Greek Minority and the Disposal of Smyrna* (Arts. 65–83).

(i) *The Greek Minority.* The two points comprised in this heading were linked together in the policy of the Supreme Council and in the dispositions of the Treaty of Sèvres; but they were not essentially connected, and, in June 1922, it seemed probable that they would be settled, if at all, independently of one another. Certainly the zone on the Anatolian mainland delimited round Smyrna in the Treaty (Art. 66) and provisionally assigned to Greece (Art. 69), contained some of the districts of Anatolia in which the Greek element was at its highest percentage of the total local population, and even spots (such as the towns of Aivali and Moskhonisia, parts of the Cheshmé peninsula, and certain quarters of Smyrna city) in which it was in an overwhelming majority. But it also contained important districts, like those of Bayndyr, Tiré, and Ōdemish in the upper basin of the Cayster river, in which the Greeks were in an insignificant minority; while, on the other hand, important Greek minorities were to be found far beyond its boundaries. In the absence of census-returns, any figures are conjectural, but it is at any rate probable that, of all the Greeks resident in

Anatolia at the time of the Peace Conference at Paris, when the frontiers of the 'Smyrna zone' were plotted out, 66 per cent., at the lowest estimate, were resident in districts outside those frontiers. Moreover, the separation of the Smyrna zone from Turkey and the attachment of it to Greece could not be defended on the ground that it was to be a 'reservation' for all the Greeks of Asiatic Turkey, on the analogy of the 'Indian Reservations' of the United States. The North American Indians were a nomadic and also a dwindling race. The Anatolian Greeks were sedentary, they were increasing in number, and they were scattered among a non-Greek majority for a definite economic reason. It is true that there were Greek peasant communities along the littoral of the Trebizond and Samsun provinces, and a very few similar communities in the neighbourhood of Kaisari and Konia, which might have been transplanted to vacant agricultural lands elsewhere—with great economic loss and personal suffering, no doubt, but still without altogether depriving them of their means of livelihood. But even if the transplantation of these populations were really contemplated by the Supreme Council and by M. Venizelos at the time of the Peace Conference, there was no special reason for settling them in the neighbourhood of Smyrna. In soil, in climate, in distance from their homes (measured by what is the only practicable route in the East for successful mass-migrations on a large scale, that is, the passage by sea), Smyrna was as alien to them as Macedonia or Thrace, and they might just as well have been settled in the great vacant spaces existing in those fertile but under-populated European provinces. These peasant communities, however, were not the main problem. The bulk of the Greek element in Anatolia, inside the Smyrna zone as well as outside it, in Smyrna city as much as at Amasia or Trebizond, consisted of people engaged in commerce (great and small) and in the professions. They were differentiated from the surrounding majority not only by their nationality but also by their economic occupation, and while their national consciousness (a state of mind borrowed at a recent date from Western Europe and adjusted to totally different conditions) might incline them to segregate themselves from the Turks and to live exclusively among their own kind, the necessity of gaining a livelihood made it imperative for them to stay in the environment to which economic motives had originally attracted them. To concentrate all the Greeks of Anatolia in the Smyrna enclave would be rather like collecting the representatives of half a dozen professions in the United Kingdom into a single county and removing from that county all other previous residents, in order to make room for the new-comers. Such a *tour de force* would be still more fantastic if the county selected for this experiment were London or Lancashire, and if this ‘reservation’ were then divided from the rest of the country by a political frontier. Yet this is not an unfair hypothetical parallel to the actual provisions of the Treaty in regard to Smyrna.

Smyrna was, in fact, the most inappropriate site which could be selected for the centre of such an enclave. If the statesmen were bent on making the experiment, they could have discovered districts in Anatolia where it might at least have had more chance of success from the geographical and economic point of view. On the Aegean coast, for example, not very far north of Smyrna, there was the purely Greek town of Aivali [1]—a community subsisting on the produce of its olive groves, and in the commercial sense almost isolated from the hinterland. Or there was the district of Trebizond, isolated from the rest of Anatolia by a wall of mountains parallel to the coast of the Black Sea, where, during the Middle Ages, a Greek State had maintained a separate existence for more than two and a half centuries. It is true that, at the time of the Peace Conference, the Greek element in this district probably did not amount to more than 10 per cent. of the local population, but at any rate the geographical and economic difficulties here might possibly not have proved insuperable. The selection of Smyrna, however, as the centre of the Greek enclave in Anatolia meant the ruin of the chief port in the country and a corresponding dislocation of the economic life of the interior. In May 1919 Smyrna was a commercial city with a mixed population (Turkish, Greek, and Western), in which no single element possessed an unmistakable absolute majority, though such a majority was claimed by both the Turks and the Greeks. Smyrna had risen to this eminence not as a local administrative capital, but as the *entrepôt* of trade between the Anatolian peninsula on the one hand, and Western Europe and America on the other. This trade had attracted Greeks and had largely

[1] Just within the northern boundary of the Smyrna zone as actually demarcated.

increased the Greek element in the population of the city during the preceding 150 years. But the commercial connexions between Anatolia and the West through the port of Smyrna had been built up, since the latter part of the sixteenth century, by colonies of French, Dutch, British, and other Western merchants who had settled there; and the producers and consumers who indirectly came into contact with one another at this mart, were not Greeks for the most part. They were the Western World on the one side and the predominantly Turkish population of the interior of Anatolia on the other. The commercial hinterland of Smyrna in the interior had been steadily extended by Western enterprise, the chief instruments of this extension being the two railways, built respectively with French and British capital, which had been started after the Crimean War and successively prolonged and ramified until the outbreak of the European War. In all this economic development, the Greeks took little more than a middleman's part, and even in this they were overshadowed in importance (though not, of course, in numbers) by the local Western colony.

Thus the occupation of Smyrna by Greek troops in May 1919 was immediately felt over more than half Anatolia. The Turks, realizing that it portended the separation of Smyrna from Turkey in the forthcoming Treaty, resisted the Greek invasion by force of arms, as has already been mentioned. The consequence was a new war, which spread all over Western Anatolia and which paralysed the commerce of Smyrna by setting up a military front between the port and the hinterland.[1]

The prejudicial effect of these events upon the position of the Christian minorities on the Turkish side of the front was analysed in General Harbord's report:

> 'The events of Smyrna have undoubtedly cheapened every Christian life in Turkey, the landing of the Greeks there being looked upon by the Turks as deliberate violation by the Allies of the terms of their armistice and the probable forerunner of further unwarranted aggression. The moral responsibility for present unrest throughout Turkey is very heavy on foreign Powers.'

By June 1922, the forebodings of the American Mission of Inquiry had not only been fulfilled, but the Turkish populations in the Smyrna area had also been ill-treated by the Greeks.

[1] Organized atrocities started in April 1921 on the Greek side, in June 1921 on the Turkish.

The consequences for the minorities would, indeed, have been bad enough even if the decisions of the Supreme Council could have been carried into effect instead of being frustrated by resulting in war. If this fresh war had not broken out, the Smyrna zone would almost certainly have become a Greek 'reservation', whether that was the Allied intention or no. By gentle or by violent pressure the Turkish population in the zone would have been squeezed out, while, on the other hand, the Greek village-shopkeepers and urban merchants, professional men and artisans from all the rest of Anatolia would have been herded into it, with the result of bringing economic ruin to both these sets of enforced emigrants, and of undermining the prosperity of the entire country. In the light of what actually happened, however, such a *dénouement* would have been relatively a happy one. By June 1922 it had become probable that, wherever the frontiers might eventually be drawn, some such inter-migration of minorities would have to be arranged. The inconclusive military operations had degenerated into a war of extermination, and feeling on both sides had been so much embittered that it was hardly credible that Greek and Turkish elements could continue to live together in the same towns and villages, as they had done in the past.

The picture is one of almost unrelieved gloom; and yet the Smyrna question, if rightly handled, ought neither to have been so important nor so difficult to solve as the problem of the Straits. Great and growing though the commerce of Smyrna was, it did not concern half the world, like the traffic passing through the Bosporus and Dardanelles. Turkey and Greece were the only parties politically involved, and the issue was comparatively simple. The Smyrna question acquired the paramount importance that it did through the accident that the Supreme Council committed a greater blunder in dealing with it than in their handling of any other part of the Eastern settlement—a blunder so hopeless that it produced a fresh war, and a protracted one. This Graeco-Turkish War in Anatolia, and its adverse influence upon the relations between the Western and the Islamic Worlds, were the features which invested the Smyrna question with the historical importance to which it undoubtedly attained.

(ii) *Projected constitution of the Smyrna zone.* It remains to glance at the details of the constitution sketched out in the

Treaty (Arts. 65–83) for the Smyrna zone, but the reader must bear in mind that these articles have no more than an academic interest. They had not been put into effect, though two years had passed since the Treaty had been signed. On the one hand, the Treaty had never been ratified; and, on the other, the territory of the zone had become a theatre of war, in consequence of the Greek landing, long before the relevant part of the Treaty was cast into its final form. As early as February 1921, all parties saw that at any rate this portion of the Treaty could not stand. In the meantime, the districts actually under Greek military occupation, which extended far beyond the Sèvres frontiers, were governed partly by a Greek Civil High Commissioner with dictatorial powers and partly by the Greek military authorities.

The Smyrna zone, as defined geographically in Art. 66 of the Treaty, lay wholly within the two areas in which the right of Italy to establish her direct and indirect authority respectively had been recognized by the French and British Governments in the Secret Agreement of St. Jean de Maurienne (April 1917). This instrument, however, contained a legal flaw, as has been mentioned in a preceding section, and the claims of Italy were still further weakened in May 1919 by the *de facto* occupation of Smyrna on the part of Greece, which was accomplished with the approval and assistance of the three other principal Allied and Associated Powers. The occupation occurred at a time when the relations between Italy and her Allies were strained almost to breaking point over the question of the Adriatic, and it was precipitated by a belief that she was intending to create a *fait accompli* at Smyrna in her own favour. Eventually, Italy acquiesced in the assignment of the zone to Greece, and the signatures of her plenipotentiaries were not withheld from the Treaty of Sèvres, in which the title of Greece was given recognition. Various reasons for this remarkable self-effacement on Italy's part may be conjectured. Her own title was weak; M. Venizelos had made concessions to her in other directions; but the determining factor may well have been the danger—very real during 1920—of revolution at home, and the unmistakable repugnance of the Italian working-class towards any further adventures in overseas imperialism involving fresh sacrifices of soldiers' lives. In June 1920, only two months before the signature of the Treaty of Sèvres, Italian troops at

Trieste and elsewhere, when ordered to Albania as reinforcements, refused to embark; and the Italian Government had virtually to capitulate to the Albanian national leaders.[1] In these circumstances, the claims to territory in Anatolia which had been staked out by Italy at St. Jean de Maurienne, had little intrinsic value; and, besides this, the experience of the Greeks, since their landing, had already demonstrated that the prize of Smyrna could only be secured, if at all, at a formidable cost in blood and treasure. Italian statesmen found it better policy to let the Greeks be, to take advantage of them as a foil, and to play for future benefits by assuming towards the Angora Government the rôle of a friend in need. Whether this policy would have borne fruit, as far as the competition between Italy and Greece was concerned, will never be known, for it failed through an omission to reckon with France. At the critical moment, after the labours of nearly three years, Italy was eclipsed in the favour of the Turks by the brilliant diplomatic triumph of M. Franklin-Bouillon.[2]

Meanwhile, the Treaty of Sèvres awarded to Greece, not indeed the immediate and absolute sovereignty over the whole vilayet of Aidin except the sanjak of Denizli (the area which M. Venizelos had claimed when he laid his case before the Council of Ten), but the provisional administration of a smaller territory. The boundaries of this territory (laid down in Art. 66) included, approximately, the two sanjaks of Smyrna and Manisa, less the port and district of Scala Nuova on the south, but with the addition, on the north, of Aivali and Moskhonisia. The frontiers were artificial. They cut river-valleys and railways at right-angles, and bore little or no relation to the distribution of nationalities. Towards the south, alone, they followed a physical line of division. On this side, they coincided with the water-shed of the Cayster valley, but in order to conform here to what was the natural line from the physical point of view, they had to include in their sweep a particularly large district containing an almost purely Turkish population.

In the zone thus carved out of Anatolia, Turkish sovereignty was technically not abolished but suspended. Turkey was made to transfer to the Greek Government the exercise of her rights

[1] *v.* Vol. IV, pp. 343–5.

[2] Franco-Turkish Agreement at Angora of the 20th October 1921. Text in App. II, Part 2b. *v. supra* pp. 33–5.

of sovereignty over the city of Smyrna and the said territory (Art. 69). The Greek Government was to be responsible for the administration (Art. 70), to appoint the officials who were to conduct it (Art. 70), to maintain military forces in the zone (Art. 71), to establish (if it chose) a customs boundary along the frontier line and to incorporate the zone in the Greek customs system (Art. 76). As for the inhabitants, such of them as were of Turkish nationality and could not claim any other nationality under the terms of the Treaty were to be treated on exactly the same footing as Greek nationals, and Greece was to provide for their diplomatic and consular protection abroad (Art. 79). These provisions make it evident that, had the Treaty been ratified and thereby been brought into operation, the provisional nature of the Greek administration would have been somewhat fictitious, and that Greece would have had treaty sanction for assimilating the administration of the zone, to all intents and purposes, to that of her own dominions.

There were, however, certain qualifying provisions of genuine importance. A local parliament was to be set up with an electoral system calculated to ensure proportional representation of all sections of the population, including racial, linguistic, and religious minorities. Within six months of ratification, the Greek Government was to submit an electoral scheme to the Council of the League of Nations, whose approval was obligatory (Art. 72); but since Greece was already occupying the zone *de facto*, any difference of opinion between the Council of the League and the Greek Government would merely have the effect of leaving the zone for a longer period under arbitrary Greek administration, without any constitution at all. The value of the electoral law was also diminished by the provision that the relations between the Greek administration and the local parliament were to be determined by the said administration in accordance with the principles of the Greek Constitution (Art. 73). What if that Constitution were to prove incompatible with local franchises!

A more valuable safeguard was contained in Arts. 75 and 86, which, taken together, extended to the Smyrna zone the benefits of the ‘ Minorities Treaty ’ which was signed by Greece on the one part and by the principal Allied Powers on the other on the same date and at the same place as the Treaty of Peace with Turkey.

Finally, when a period of five years [1] should have elapsed after the coming into force of the Treaty, the local parliament might, by a majority of votes, ask the Council of the League of Nations for the definitive incorporation in the Kingdom of Greece of the city of Smyrna and the zone. The Council might, as a preliminary, require a plebiscite under conditions which it would lay down. In the event of incorporation in these circumstances, Turkish sovereignty was to cease (Art. 83). Apparently, a request for the reincorporation of the zone in Turkey was not placed within the competence of the local parliament, and the choice was to be confined to one between complete incorporation in Greece or the continuance (for an unspecified period) of the interim régime. Since, however, even this latter contingency was not expressly provided for, it was apparently presumed that, after the five years, the complete incorporation of the zone in Greece was a certainty. This article deserves more severe stricture than almost any other in the Treaty, for, in order to save the faces of the Supreme Council, it exposed the non-Greek population of the zone to possible dangers of the gravest character. The logical dilemma is absolute. Either the makers of the Treaty expected that the population of the zone would not appreciably change in composition during the five years' interval, or that a substantial change would occur.[2] In the former alternative, why did they not ascertain the wishes of the population at the earliest possible date,[3] as they arranged to do in Masuria, Upper Silesia, the Klagenfurt district, and other plebiscite areas ? In the latter alternative, by what means was a change, so substantial as possibly to produce a different verdict on the question of ' self-determination ', expected to be brought about ? In nearly all instances in which the Supreme Council decided that the local population was to be consulted, it generally arranged, that the consultation should take place at the earliest possible moment, and also that, during the necessary interval, the district in question should be brought under effective inter-

[1] During this interim period, citizens of the zone were not to be subjected to compulsory military service (Art. 74), but, as the Treaty was not ratified, this safeguard did not come into force, and, by June 1922, Ottoman Greeks had been conscripted in considerable numbers for the Greek Army.

[2] The repatriation of Greeks deported by the Turkish Government before the Armistice has not to be taken into account, as Art. 72 provides that the local parliament itself shall not be constituted until this has been carried out.

[3] i.e. immediately after the completion of repatriation.

Allied supervision, and even in some cases under military control. It was obvious that the prospect of a plebiscite would be an incitement to the outbreak of violence between the rival nationalities, if they were left to themselves. But these statesmanlike precedents, established by the Supreme Council itself, were ignored in the case of the Smyrna zone. The final decision was deferred till a date five years later than the ratification of the Treaty, and in the meantime the local nationalities were not merely left uncontrolled, but a sovereign state akin to one of them was deliberately placed in full command of the territory during the critical period of waiting. Under such conditions, few states could have resisted the temptation to misuse their power. It is not, of course, suggested that the Supreme Council exposed Greece to this temptation with the intention that she should succumb to it. The charge against them is rather that they carelessly introduced into the Treaty a piece of shocking diplomatic workmanship through a loss of nerve. Conscious of the unsoundness of their policy, and of the improper considerations (suggested at the beginning of this section) on which it was largely based, they shrank, at the last moment, from awarding the zone to Greece outright. From their point of view, Art. 83 was no more than a tactful circumlocution, and they did not trouble to think out its possible consequences for parties that were far more vitally concerned than they were.

(iii) *International Clauses.* The most creditable provisions of the Treaty with regard to Smyrna were those which attempted to preserve the intercourse between the port and its former economic hinterland, irrespective of the much narrower political frontiers which the Treaty had set up. In Arts. 335–45, a liberal régime was prescribed for the administration of a number of ports (including both Smyrna and Constantinople) which were scheduled as being ‘ ports of international concern ’. Not only was the free use of these ports, on a footing of equality, secured to all states members of the League of Nations, but provision was made (Arts. 341–4) for the establishment of a ‘ Free Zone ’ in each of them. Goods imported into this zone were to be exempt from the customs of the state locally sovereign, and to pay nothing but a ‘ statistical duty ’ not exceeding 1 per mille *ad valorem* (Art. 342). Persons, goods, postal services, ships, vessels, carriages, wagons and other means of transport coming from or going to the ‘ Free Zone ’ and crossing the territory of the state under whose sovereignty or authority the port was placed, were to be deemed to be in transit[1] across that state if they were going to or coming from the territory of any other state whatsoever.

In addition to this, freedom of transit (extending to postal, telegraphic, and telephonic services) was accorded to Turkey over the territories and in the ports detached from her, in order to ensure to her free access to the Mediterranean and Aegean Seas (Art. 349). Moreover, in the case of Smyrna, it was laid down specifically, in a special article (Art. 350), that Turkey should be accorded a lease in perpetuity, subject to determination by the League of Nations, of an area which should be placed under the general régime of free zones laid down in Arts. 341–4, and should be used for the direct transit of goods coming from or going to that state (Art. 350).

These arrangements were excellent in themselves. Indeed, economic agreements on this model are essential in all those regions of the Near and Middle East in which multi-national empires have been superseded by a mosaic of comparatively small national states as a result of the triumph of the Western nationality idea. At the same time, the benefit of such attempts to make political frontiers innocuous from the economic point of view can only be secured in cases in which the political settlement itself has been more or less peaceably accepted by the several parties concerned. In the present instance, if the Turks had resigned themselves to the provisional establishment of Greek administration in the Smyrna zone, and to the prospective annulment of Turkish sovereignty over this territory after the lapse of five years, the economic arrangements of the Treaty might have operated to reduce the dislocation which the political dispositions of the Treaty would inevitably have caused. On the other hand, from the moment that the attempt to enforce these political dispositions had precipitated a new war, the economic safeguards were bound to become a dead letter. In June 1922, they were inoperative both *de iure* and *de facto*—*de iure* because the Treaty had never been ratified, *de facto* because the economic hinterland of Smyrna was devastated by military operations and cut in two by a military ‘ front ’.

[1] By Art. 328, goods in transit were exempted from customs duties and from discriminating freight-charges.

(*c*) *The Armenian Minority and the Armenian 'National Home'* (Arts. 88–93).

(i) *Armenia up to the Treaty of Sèvres.* The position of the Armenians in Anatolia was in most respects parallel to that of the Greeks. They were a widely distributed minority, consisting partly of peasant communities [1] and partly of urban colonies, exercising the same professions and performing the same economic functions as the Greek urban communities in other districts. In general, the Armenians and the Greeks filled the same rôle in the eastern and western portions, respectively, of the area with which this section is concerned, though the distribution of the two communities overlapped in Pontus, Central Anatolia, Smyrna, and Constantinople.

The Armenians had attained their greatest prosperity in the period between 1821 and 1878. After the outbreak of the Greek War of Independence, which compromised the vast Greek interests in the Ottoman dominions outside the frontiers of the new Greek national state, the Armenians to a large extent inherited the position which the Ottoman Greeks had formerly enjoyed in the public and private service of their Turkish masters. At the same time, that part of the Armenian nation which lived in Trans-Caucasia, beyond the Ottoman frontiers, greatly benefited by the establishment of Russian rule south of the Caucasus Mountains (1783–1864). Their position changed for the worse, however, after the Russo-Turkish War of 1877–8. During the negotiation of the San Stephano and Berlin Treaties, the Armenians became a pawn in the game of Anglo-Russian rivalry in Asia. At San Stephano the Russians stipulated for reforms, in favour of the Armenians, in the north-eastern provinces of Asiatic Turkey which they had occupied during the war, and for the continuance of the Russian military occupation of these provinces until the reforms had been carried out. The British negotiators at Berlin insisted that the Russian evacuation of the provinces in question should be immediate and unconditional, but they could not dismiss the project of ameliorating the condition of the local Christian minority, when once the Russians had put it forward. They therefore introduced provisions for reforms into the Treaty of Berlin,

[1] Which were at their highest percentage in the vilayet of Van and in parts of Bitlis and Erzerum, as the Greek peasants were in Pontus and in the neighbourhood of Smyrna. *v.* Harbord Report above cited.

though in vaguer terms than those employed in the Treaty of San Stephano, and without adequate guarantees. The Russian military occupation, the attraction of the Armenian Question into the orbit of Western international politics, and the momentary concentration of public attention in the West upon the 'Eastern Question', had somewhat the same effect upon the Armenians as the Anglo-French struggle in the Levant, and the military occupation of the Ionian Islands, had had upon the Greeks during the Napoleonic Wars (1798–1814). It produced a mental ferment and a sudden influx of Western ideas. Western political nationalism infected the Armenians, just as it had previously infected the Greeks, Serbs, Rumanians, and Bulgars, and was afterwards to infect the Turks and the Arabs. The Ottoman Government began to look upon Armenian aspirations with fear and hostility, and at the same time Armenian Nationalism made itself obnoxious to the Russian Tsardom, a Power still organized on the eighteenth-century dynastic and not yet on the nineteenth-century nationalistic Western model. Indeed, the Russian Government, being more energetic and efficient than the Turkish, usually repressed the Armenians with a heavier hand; and in 1895–7, when the Armenians in Turkey were massacred, they received no succour from the two Great Powers morally responsible for looking after them. Russia ostentatiously held aloof, and the naval power of Great Britain was impotent to produce any effect in the interior of the Anatolian plateau. The massacres recurred again in Cilicia, during 1909, and then, on an unprecedented scale, during the European War, when Russia and Great Britain were united against Turkey, when the Armenians had been alienated by past atrocities and the fortunes of the Ottoman Empire in greater jeopardy than they had ever been. The war of extermination was not initiated or even approved by the mass of the Turkish population, and some officials ventured to oppose it, but it was deliberately organized and put into execution by the 'Union and Progress' Government at Constantinople.

Thus, though the process by which multi-national empires in the East were replaced by national states, did not seriously affect the Armenians until it had entered upon its last phase, they suffered from it more severely than any other local population during the forty years between the Treaty of Berlin and the

Armistice of 1918. The reason for this was that the geographical distribution and economic functions of the Armenians were particularly unsuitable for the constitution of an Armenian national state. When the Greek national movement began, there were at any rate some districts, like the Islands and the Morea, in which there was a homogeneous, or very nearly homogeneous, Greek population, and such districts could be made, and in fact were made, the nucleus for a Greek national state on the French pattern. The Armenians, however, had no such local base of operations. It is true that they were in a plurality in the Ottoman vilayet of Van [1] and in the Russian Government of Erivan, as well as in parts of the adjoining districts; but even in this region the Turkish, Kurdish, Georgian, and Azerbaijani elements were so strong that there was nothing approaching a homogeneous Armenian population. Moreover, while in the Greek, Serbian, Rumanian, and Bulgarian cases, the doctrine of the Balance of Power had decreed that territories detached from Turkey should be formed into independent states, and should not be added to the dominions of any Western Empire, the Trans-Caucasian borderland between the Russian and Ottoman Empires was so remote from the West-European centre of gravity that Russia was able, even in 1878, to take for herself what Turkey lost in this quarter, without encountering insurmountable opposition from Great Britain or the Hapsburg Monarchy. Thus the Ottoman Armenians, in their almost impracticable aspirations for territorial independence, had behind them, not a sympathetic independent state of their own nationality, as the Anatolian Greeks had in the Greek Kingdom, but an alien Russia—willing to use the Armenians to further her own ambitions, but thoroughly hostile to Armenian national aims. Indeed, while the nucleus of an independent Greek national state has existed since 1821, the independent Armenian national Republic of Erivan only came into existence at the close of 1917, as a consequence of the Bolshevik Revolution and the dissolution of the old Russian Empire.[2]

A representative of the Armenian Republic signed the

[1] The Moslem population being split between the Turkish and the Kurdish nationalities.

[2] The gain to the Armenians, however, was largely cancelled by the blow to Armenian interests in Tiflis, Baku, Batum, and other commercial centres in Trans-Caucasia outside the boundaries of Erivan, which the simultaneous creation of the national states of Georgia and Azerbaijan involved.

Treaty of Sèvres, and provision for an independent Armenia was made in that instrument (Arts. 88–93). It must be noted in passing that, if the Secret Treaties had stood, the Armenian Question could never have been raised at the Peace Conference. The utmost extent of territory that was ever claimed by the Armenians themselves, had been swallowed up in the two conterminous zones, carved respectively out of north-eastern and south-eastern Anatolia, which had been placed at the disposal of Russia and France in the Sykes-Picot Agreement of May 1916. It must not be assumed, however, that this abortive arrangement would have been entirely to the Armenians' disadvantage. It was no doubt discreditable to the Entente Powers, which, at that very time, were exploiting Armenian atrocities in their propaganda and were encouraging Armenians to enlist in their armies by affecting to favour their national aspirations. If the Sykes-Picot Agreement had come into force, an Armenian national state would never have come into existence. On the other hand, the principal area of distribution of the Armenian nationality would have been brought under the comparatively effective and impartial rule of nations foreign to the area, and the Armenians would thus have been shielded from the worst eventualities.[1] As things actually turned out, these eventualities overtook them. This area, like the remainder of the area dealt with in this section, escaped from external control (except for the anarchic influence of the Western idea of nationality working in Eastern minds), and there was a renewal of the merciless struggle for existence between the local nationalities, in which the Armenians, being the weakest numerically[2] and the most widely scattered, inevitably went to the wall.

(ii) *President Wilson's arbitration.* The Treaty of Sèvres did much for Armenia on paper. Turkey, in accordance with the action already taken by the Allied Powers, had to recognize Armenia as a free and independent state (Art. 88); and Turkey and Armenia agreed to submit to the arbitration of the President

[1] Though this cannot be asserted with confidence of the Russian zone, since, during the Russian military occupation of 1916–17, General Yudenich assigned lands, left vacant by the deportation of the Armenians at the hands of the Ottoman Government to Cossack colonies, for which Trans-Caucasians (i. e. practically all Russian Armenians) were ineligible.

[2] Since the atrocities of 1915 in Turkey and the consequences in Trans-Caucasia of the Bolshevik Revolution and the Turkish invasion.

of the United States of America the question of the frontier to be fixed between their respective territories in the Ottoman vilayets of Erzerum, Trebizond, Van, and Bitlis and to accept his decision thereupon, as well as any stipulations he might prescribe as to access for Armenia to the sea (Art. 89). The frontiers between Armenia and Azerbaijan and Georgia respectively were to be determined by direct agreement between the states concerned. If in either case the states concerned had failed to determine the frontier by agreement at the date fixed by the decision of the President of the United States, the frontier line in question was to be determined by the Principal Allied Powers (Art. 92).

President Wilson accepted the task of arbitration which the Principal Allied Powers (aware of their inability to employ effective sanctions) had shrunk from undertaking themselves. In due course, he announced a line which awarded to Armenia the major part of the four provinces specified in the Treaty. It started from the Black Sea coast, well to the west of Trebizond (which was thus awarded to Armenia), and described the arc of a circle, running in a south-easterly direction, so as to include in Armenia Erzerum, Mush, and Van, before it finally impinged upon the Turco-Persian frontier.[1] This award would have provided a territory capable, from the economic and administrative point of view, of constituting an independent state, though, for years to come, the Armenians could not have risen to be a majority of the population. But neither the President's award, nor the articles of the Treaty in virtue of which it was made, bore any relation to the events which were actually taking place in the districts in question.

(iii) *The Bolsheviks and Armenia.* The permanent geographical features of Anatolia and Trans-Caucasia could not be affected by the victory of the Western Powers in Palestine, in France, and on the sea, or by the drafting of the Treaty of Sèvres, which ultimately followed. As before, the political destinies of this region remained in the hands of Turkey and Russia, and other Powers could only have a voice in the local settlement indirectly, through possessing either Turkey or

[1] The cynical reader will be amused to learn that the territory thus assigned, by a disinterested arbitrator, to an independent Armenia, almost precisely coincided with the zone placed by France and Great Britain at the absolute disposal of Russia in the Secret Agreement of May 1916.

Russia as their ally. Had the Tsardom survived, or had General Denikin's campaign succeeded, Great Britain and France and Italy would have had a *de facto* Government of Russia as their partner (though it is evident that, in either case, they would have had little actual influence over Russian policy as far as the Armenian Question was concerned). As it turned out, they not only lost their Russian partner, but manœuvred the revolutionary Governments at Moscow and Angora into forming a counter-entente for resistance to the eastern aims of the victorious Entente of the West. On the wide plane of international politics, this strange regrouping of forces resulted in an inconclusive trial of strength, and in June 1922 it seemed that the Western Entente on the one hand, and the Russo-Turkish Entente on the other, were bound sooner or later to come to an understanding. But, long before this, Armenia had fallen a victim to this conflict of greater Powers. The Government of the new Republic of Erivan had been of a 'Tashnakist' (or in Russian terminology 'Menshevik') complexion. Like Georgia and Azerbaijan, it had broken with the Bolsheviks; but, unlike them, it took care to keep on good terms with Denikin, because from the Armenian point of view a 'White' Russian restoration was a less unpleasant alternative than conquest by the Turks, while the chief menace to Georgia and Azerbaijan was from the side of Russia. The Erivan Government were also devoted adherents of the Western Powers, to whom they continued, with pathetic persistence, to look for salvation. These affiliations, however, were equally obnoxious to Moscow and to Angora, to whom a 'pro-Denikin' and 'pro-Entente' state, intervening between their territories, was a common danger. At that time the Bolsheviks, having disposed of Denikin, had got possession of the Black Sea port of Novorossisk and of the overland railway route to Trans-Caucasia via Baku. From Novorossisk they immediately began to send the Turkish Nationalists munitions, money, and other sinews of war. But the sea-route to Trebizond was precarious. The Entente navies still commanded the Black Sea, and the Greek fleet might at any moment blockade the north-eastern ports of Anatolia. It was essential, on military grounds, to open up an alternative route by land, and these considerations sealed the doom of Armenia. In the autumn and early winter of 1920, the Red Army and the Turkish Nationalist Army simultaneously took the offensive. Kiazym Kara Bekir Pasha captured Kars, and imposed on the Erivan Republic a treaty [1] ceding the western and south-western half of its exiguous territory to Turkey.[2] On the other flank, the Soviet troops, which had already conquered Azerbaijan and were about to conquer Georgia, invaded Erivan from the north-east, bringing with them a Soviet Armenian Government. The Tashnakists fell, the Armenian Bolsheviks reigned in their stead, and it was they who signed the treaty with Kara Bekir.

(iv) *The situation in 1921–2.* These deplorable events were taken into account by the Western Powers at the London Conference of February–March 1921. Among the concessions which they offered to Turkey on this occasion was the abandonment of the 'Wilson Line', on condition that the Turks would agree to the establishment of an Armenian 'National Home'. The phrase was borrowed from the famous 'Balfour Declaration' promising a 'National Home' to the Jews in Palestine. Its meaning was impenetrably obscure, and while no doubt that was an advantage in a war-time promise, it was already proving very awkward in Palestine now that the occasion had arrived for honouring the bond. The importation of this ambiguity into the Armenian Question might therefore be considered a doubtful blessing. On the other hand, the 'Wilson Award' was still-born, for the Allied statesmen would not have referred the question to the President if they had felt capable of solving it themselves, and the American people had already displayed in the most decisive fashion their determination to incur no further commitments west of the Atlantic. The new proposal was therefore at any rate not more impracticable than its predecessor, and, in the case of the Armenians, there was a crying need which fixed and defined the meaning of the Balfourian phrase.

As has been suggested above, it would have been better

[1] Signed at Alexandropol, and afterwards confirmed in the Russo-Turkish Treaty signed at Moscow in March 1921, and in the Treaty signed at Kars in the following October between Angora on the one part and the three Soviet Republics of Trans-Caucasia on the other.

[2] The Turkish Nationalists aimed at recovering the three districts of Kars, Ardahan, and Batum, which Russia had taken from Turkey in 1878. The cession of these three districts was one of the provisions of the Treaty of Brest-Litovsk, which, as between the Nationalists and the Bolsheviks, had never become invalid. Under the new treaties of 1920–1, Turkey acquired Kars and Ardahan, while Batum was placed under a Russo-Turkish condominium.

for the Armenians if Nationalism had never gained an entrance into the Eastern consciousness. But, for good or evil (and, in the case of the Armenians, hitherto wholly for evil), that momentous event had occurred. The Armenian minorities in Anatolia and Trans-Caucasia had already suffered all possible evil from the progress of Nationalism among the Turks, Georgians, and Azerbaijanis. They had been ruined, evicted, and massacred. The survivors of the atrocities of 1915 in Turkey, who had escaped at the time to the Russian lines, were still crowded, in June 1922, on to the remnant of the Erivan territory. There were over 300,000 of these refugees; the territory was quite unable to support such an addition to its population; and the mortality from starvation and disease was terrible. The numbers were swelled by refugees from Azerbaijan and Georgia. Moreover, the evacuation of the Cilician plain by the French in the early winter of 1921, in accordance with the Franklin-Bouillon Agreement, was accompanied by the departure from that province of almost all the Armenians who had been repatriated there since the Armistice. Some of these refugees found a temporary shelter in Northern Syria, and a few in Greece, but they had no prospects of permanent settlement. The scattered Armenian nationality had been uprooted everywhere. The only chance of preserving the lives of the survivors was to concentrate them in some territorial 'reservation', however small, which they might call their own. If the East was to be reorganized in a mosaic of national blocks, an Armenian block must be inserted somewhere in the pattern, or the nation would perish altogether.

At the Conference held at Paris in March 1922 the Foreign Ministers of the three Western Powers referred the question of the Armenian 'National Home' to the League of Nations, and, by June 1922, no further action had been taken. The Armenian colonies in Western Europe favoured a site in Cilicia, on the ground that a 'Home' established there could be protected by the sea-power of the Entente, while a 'Home' in the region of Erivan would be at the mercy of Turkey and Russia. The first part of this argument was disproved by the precedents. Sea-power had done nothing for the Cilician Armenians in 1909, 1915, or 1922.[1] The second proposition was true, but not

[1] The diplomatic difficulties were also insuperable, for Great Britain had surrendered her title to intervene in Cilicia to France in the Tripartite Agreement

necessarily fatal to the establishment of the 'Home' in that quarter. In the first place, the greater part of the surviving Armenians was already concentrated there. It would be far easier to transport 50,000 Cilician refugees to Erivan than three-quarters of a million Armenians [1] from Erivan to the south. Concentration was their only hope of survival, and the argument in favour of settling Greek emigrants from Pontus or Karaman in Macedonia rather than in an enclave round Smyrna told equally in favour of gathering the Armenians together in the neighbourhood of Erivan rather than starting an alternative national centre round Adana. The principal argument, however, concerned Russia. It is true that a national home round Erivan would be in the power of Turkey and Russia, but would these two states always exercise their power for the same ends in the future, and if their policy diverged, would not the power of Russia inevitably be exercised in favour of Armenia? If an Armenian National Home were established in this quarter, it was evident that Russia would have a vital interest in its preservation. Russia (whatever her constitution and her foreign relations) could hardly live without controlling the oil-field of Baku. If Azerbaijan (in which Baku is situated) were to join forces with Turkey, that control would be in jeopardy. The establishment of an Armenian 'National Home' between Turkey and Azerbaijan would, therefore, be a valuable safeguard from the Russian point of view. There was much to be said in favour of establishing the 'Home' in proximity to a Great Power which would have not only the means of protecting it, but an interest in doing so. But in June 1922 the settlement of this question still lay beyond the horizon.

5. *The Future Turkish State.* The subjects hitherto discussed in this section did not occupy the major part of the Treaty of Sèvres. The majority of the articles were concerned with what was to be left of Turkey—with the territorial extent, sovereign rights, and political, economic, and juridical obligations of the future Turkish State. But in June 1922 these portions of the Treaty were even more difficult to discuss than the others, because the uncertainty regarding them was still greater. On the one hand, the Treaty imposed so comprehensive a system of servitudes as to extinguish the sovereign independence of

of the 10th August 1920, and France had surrendered hers to Turkey in the Angora Secret Agreement of 20th October 1921.

[1] Including the original Armenian inhabitants and the refugees.

Turkey in fact if not in name. On the other hand, the Turks themselves, captivated by the Western doctrine of Nationalism and stimulated by the comparative freedom of action which they had enjoyed during the War,[1] were demanding the abolition even of pre-war shackles and restraints, and were altogether refusing to contemplate the imposition of additional restrictions. The Turkish attitude (which was not a new phenomenon, but had been taking shape during the past two generations), was summed up in the sixth and last article of the National Angora Pact:

'In order to ensure our national and economic development, and with the object of endowing the country with a systematic up-to-date administration, the signatories of the present Pact consider the enjoyment of an entire independence and a complete liberty of action as a *sine quâ non* of national existence.'

This proposition was quite irreconcilable with the principles underlying the Treaty of Sèvres, and it was difficult to see how any compromise could be effected. In June 1922 the issue was still being fought out by force. In the Turkish territories occupied by the Greeks and by the three Western Powers, Turkish sovereignty was effaced even more completely than the Treaty had intended—these territories being still (June 1922) under a foreign military occupation. On the other hand, the complete sovereign independence claimed in the Angora Pact had been established *de facto* in the vastly larger territories controlled by the Nationalist Government at Angora. Neither party recognized the legality of the other's position, and the position of neither was ultimately tenable if that of the other remained unchanged. It was impossible to forecast how long this situation would continue, but if a conjecture were permissible in regard to the ultimate result, it might be prophesied that, however far short the Turks might fall of attaining the ideal put forward in the Angora Pact, they would at least recover more substantial mastery in their own house than they had enjoyed at any time since the signature of the Treaty of Kuchuk Kainarjy in 1774. As early as the London Conference of February–March 1921 the Allied Powers offered Turkey concessions in regard to the restrictions upon her sovereignty

[1] The Ottoman Government denounced the Capitulations before they intervened in the War, in respect not only of the Entente Powers but of Germany and Austria-Hungary. Germany subsequently negotiated with Turkey a fresh series of treaties, to replace the Capitulations, on a basis of eciprocity.

which the unratified and unexecuted Treaty had sought to impose, and though these suggestions led to no agreement at the moment, they pointed to the direction which an adjustment would inevitably take if it were made. In this state of uncertainty, it is useless to do more here than briefly to summarize the provisions of the Treaty under this head, in order to present the reader with a starting-point for studying the revision which was bound to follow. The relevant provisions may conveniently be analysed under the following sub-headings: (1) Territorial extent of Turkey; (2) Local diminutions of her sovereignty; (3) Allied Control over her Army and Navy (Treaty, Part V, Arts. 152–207); (4) Allied Control over her Finance (Treaty, Part VIII, Arts. 231–60, +2 Annexes); (5) The Capitulations (espy. Arts. 128, 136, 149, 261, 264, 316, 426), Minorities (Art. 140–51).

(*a*) *Territorial Extent*. This has been described by implication, in the other sections of this chapter dealing with Syria and Mesopotamia, and in the previous portions of this section dealing with Eastern Thrace and the Straits, the Smyrna Zone, and Armenia. According to the Treaty, the territory of Turkey was to be coextensive with the area with which this section is concerned, except for the Smyrna Zone and the ex-Ottoman districts assigned by the 'Wilson Award' to Armenia. It was, however, doubtful in reality whether either of these regions would ultimately be detached from Turkey, while under the Franklin-Bouillon Agreement of the 20th October 1921 Turkey had already recovered a strip of territory along the Syrian border.

(*b*) *Local Diminutions of Turkish sovereignty*. These were imposed, without extinguishing Turkish sovereignty altogether, in the Zone of the Straits, in Kurdistan, and in the 'areas of special influence' assigned to Italy and France in the Tripartite Anglo-Franco-Italian Agreement which was signed simultaneously with the Treaty of Peace.[1] The Zone of the Straits has been dealt with (*v*. pp. 60–5).

In the case of Kurdistan, an inter-Allied Commission was, within six months from the coming into force of the Treaty, to draft a scheme of local autonomy for the predominantly Kurdish areas lying east of the Euphrates, south of the southern

[1] The Smyrna Zone does not fall within this category, as the permanent extinction of Turkish sovereignty was contemplated there at the end of five years.

boundary of Armenia, as determined by the 'Wilson Award', and north of the frontier of Turkey with Syria and Mesopotamia—that is, in effect, for all territories east of the Euphrates over which Turkish sovereignty was otherwise to continue (Art. 62). If within one year from the coming into force of the Treaty the Kurdish peoples within the areas thus defined were to address themselves to the Council of the League of Nations in such a manner as to show that a majority of the population of these areas desired independence from Turkey, and if the Council then considered that these peoples were capable of such independence and recommended that it should be granted to them, Turkey was to renounce all rights and title over these areas. In that event, no objection would be raised by the Principal Allied Powers to the voluntary adhesion to such an independent Kurdish State of the Kurds inhabiting that part of Kurdistan which had hitherto been included in the Mosul vilayet (Art. 64). The last clause in this article was interesting, since it involved a possible diminution of the area included in the British mandate for Mesopotamia—though the principal Kurdish (and oil-bearing) districts under that mandate would not be affected, since they fell within the boundaries of the ex-Ottoman vilayet of Baghdad. These clauses must not, however, be taken too seriously, since in March 1921 the Allied Governments declared themselves ready, in regard to Kurdistan, 'to consider a modification of the Treaty in a sense in conformity with the existing facts of the situation.'

The territorial provisions of the Tripartite Agreement were, diplomatically, on a weaker basis than those embodied in the Treaty of Peace, for Turkey herself was not a party to this instrument, and was therefore under no obligation to facilitate its execution to her own detriment. On the other hand, territories of more vital importance than Kurdistan, both to her and to the Allies, were at stake. In Art. 5 of this Agreement, and in the map officially attached to it, two zones in Anatolia were demarcated which corresponded respectively to the zone at the absolute disposal of France in the Sykes-Picot Agreement of May 1916, and to the two zones placed severally at the absolute and the restricted disposal of Italy in the Secret Agreement of April 1917. In the case of the French zone, the coincidence of area was exact. The Italian zone was diminished by the excision of the districts round Smyrna (see pp. 74–5 above), but extended, as if in compensation, towards the north-west. In every aspect, however, except the cartographical one, there was a great gulf fixed between the provisions of the public Tripartite Agreement and those of its secret predecessors. Under the new instrument, the Contracting Powers undertook, in the event of the Turkish Government, or the Government of Kurdistan, being desirous of obtaining external assistance in the local administration or police of the areas in which the special interests of France and Italy were respectively recognized, not to dispute the preferential claim of the Power whose special interests in such areas were recognized to supply such assistance. This assistance was to be specially directed towards enhancing the protection afforded to racial, religious, or linguistic minorities in the said areas (Art. 2). These arrangements represented a half-hearted attempt, on the part of France and Italy, to secure the benefits promised to them in the Secret Agreements, crossed with an effort, on the part of Great Britain, to secure additional protection for minorities as a *quid pro quo*. Whether, under certain circumstances, the provisions of the Tripartite Agreement might have led to the establishment, *de facto*, of the very different situation avowedly contemplated in the Secret Agreements, seems doubtful. In the present instance, however, the issue was speedily determined by the fact that the Turkish nation still had the 'will-to-war' for territorial stakes in Anatolia, while no such will existed among the populations of Italy and France. The title acquired by France in the Tripartite Treaty was tacitly abandoned in the Franklin-Bouillon Agreement with Angora, a diplomatic *coup* which incidentally cut away the ground from under the feet of Italy. By June 1922, it already seemed safe to regard the Tripartite Agreement as a dead letter in so far as Turkey was concerned, though it might still give any one of the signatories an advantage over the others in questions affecting its special zone.

(*c*) *Allied Control over the Turkish Army and Navy.* The provisions under this head did not differ in principle from those imposed on other defeated ex-enemy states. The numbers of the Turkish Army were to be limited, voluntary enlistment only was to be allowed (Art. 165), and an Allied control was to be established to see that the details of these stipulations were carried out.

Apart from the Sultan's bodyguard, the armed forces at the disposal of Turkey were to consist of two elements: troops of gendarmerie intended to maintain order and security in the interior and to ensure the protection of minorities and special elements intended for the reinforcement of the troops of gendarmerie in case of serious trouble and eventually to ensure the control of the frontiers. The former were to be limited to 35,000 and the latter to 15,000 men, including all ranks and services (Arts. 152–7). Officers supplied by the various Allied or Neutral Powers were to collaborate, under the direction of the Turkish Government, in the command, the organization and the training of the gendarmerie (Art. 159). Enlistment was to be open to all subjects of the Turkish state equally, without distinction of race and religion, the Moslem and non-Moslem elements of the population of each region being, so far as possible, represented on the strength of the corresponding legion of gendarmerie (Art. 165). Stocks of munitions, and the output of fresh stocks by local manufacture, were also to be limited in amount (Arts. 173–4). The naval (Arts. 181–90) and air (Arts. 191–5) clauses corresponded to the military. All these clauses were to be executed by Turkey and at her own expense under the control of inter-Allied 'Commissions of Control and Organization' (Art. 196), and the rights, duties, and emoluments of these commissions were elaborately provided for (Arts. 197–205).

Though the Treaty was never ratified, the Allied Powers established their control effectively over the naval and air forces of the Ottoman Empire, and, during the first six months after the Armistice, they succeeded in bringing the old Ottoman Regular Army down to 19,000 men. But this process was interrupted and reversed after the Greek landing at Smyrna, and by July 1921 there were 200,000 Turkish and 200,000 Greek troops on a war-footing on the mainland of Anatolia. In these circumstances, any prediction regarding the eventual size, organization, and control of the Turkish Army was impossible.

(*d*) *Allied Control over Turkish Finance.* While the military, naval, and air clauses of the Treaty of Sèvres were in general conformity with those contained in the Treaties of Versailles, St. Germain, Trianon, and Neuilly, the financial clauses were very much more drastic—not in respect of the amount of reparation which it was proposed to extract from Turkey, but in view of the fact that there was a virtually complete suppression of her financial independence. Even when the pre-war financial servitudes of the Ottoman Empire were taken into consideration, the Treaty contained a startling innovation of principle. It is true that Turkey had been partly in the hands of her foreign creditors since 1881, but these creditors had been private individuals; the Ottoman Government had compounded with them by transferring to the service of the Debt the proceeds of certain specific revenues; and though those revenues were thenceforth administered by the Council of the Ottoman Public Debt, a body representing the creditors, the Council was in law a private corporation, whose privileges and activities did not conflict with Turkish sovereignty. The test of this arrangement was its practical working, and it is generally admitted that, during the thirty-three years previous to the European War, the relations between the Council of the Debt and the Government had been harmonious, and the system mutually advantageous to the creditors and to Turkey. The Treaty, however, thrust the Council of the Debt into the background, and even contemplated its eventual dissolution (Art. 246), in favour of a Financial Commission representing the British, French, and Italian Governments and armed with extraordinary powers.

By the Treaty of Versailles (Part VIII, Annex 1), Germany had been made responsible for the reparations due from her former Allies, and the Entente Powers, therefore, waived[1] their claims for reparation from Turkey in the Treaty of Sèvres (Art. 231). At the same time, 'desiring to afford some measure of relief and assistance to Turkey,' they 'agreed with' the Turkish Government that the Financial Commission abovementioned should be appointed, and proceeded to define its powers, of which the principal were the following. The budget to be presented annually by the Minister of Finance to the Turkish Parliament was to be submitted, in the first instance, to the Financial Commission, and was to be presented to Parliament in the form approved by that Commission. The Commission was to supervise the execution of the budget and the financial laws and regulations of Turkey. This supervision was to be exercised through the medium of the Turkish Inspectorate of Finance, which was to be placed under the

[1] With certain reservations.

direct orders of the Financial Commission, and whose members were only to be appointed with the approval of the Commission (Art. 232). The Commission was also to have the last word in the regulation of the Turkish currency (Art. 233), and the Turkish Government was not to contract any internal or external loan (Art. 234), or to grant any new concession either to a Turkish subject or otherwise (Art. 239), without its consent. The Turkish Government was to transfer to the Financial Commission all its rights under the provisions of the Decree of Mouharrem [1] and subsequent Decrees. The Council of the Debt, after being purged of the representatives of bond-holders belonging to states which were 'ex-enemy' from the point of view of the Allied Powers, was to continue to operate as in the past. Indeed, the services of the Council were to be used by the Commission as widely as possible for the collection of Ottoman revenues, beyond the limits of the revenues assigned to the service of the Debt.[2] The administration of the Customs was to be under a Director-General appointed by and revocable by the Financial Commission and answerable to it. No change in the schedule of the Customs charges was to be made except with the approval of the Commission. In order to increase the Commission's powers, its creators even contemplated setting aside the rights of private property. The three Governments were to decide, by a majority and after 'consulting' the bond-holders, whether the Council should be maintained or replaced by the Financial Commission on the expiry of the current term of the Council (Art. 246). The Commission was given authority to propose, at a later date, the substitution for the pledges at present granted to bond-holders, in accordance with their contracts or existing decrees, of other adequate pledges, or of a charge on the general revenues of Turkey (Art. 247).[3] Further,

[1] Of December 1881, establishing the Council of the Debt, and transferring certain Ottoman revenues to its administration.

[2] There were good precedents for this, and it was a fruitful suggestion.

[3] After the ratification of the Treaties of Versailles, St. Germain, and Trianon, the former holdings of German, Austrian, and Hungarian nationals in the Ottoman Debt passed to the Reparations Commission, and the bulk of the remainder was held by private corporations or individuals of Allied nationality. In regard to these holdings, the powers assumed by the Allied Governments in Arts. 246–7 of the Sèvres Treaty were no doubt justified, for private Allied creditors would never have got anything out of Turkey at all but for the power and willingness of their respective Governments to coerce her. But as regards neutral (e.g. Dutch) creditors, these Articles could hardly be legally binding.

the Commission was to be entitled to assume, in agreement with the Turkish Government and independently of any default of the latter in fulfilling its obligations, the control, management, and collection of all indirect taxes (Annex II, Art. 3).

No member of the Commission was to be responsible, except to the Government appointing him, for any action or omission in the performance of his duties (Annex II, Art. 4). On the other hand, a certain safeguard was provided by the stipulation that the Commission should publish annually detailed reports on its work, its methods, and its proposals for the financial reorganization of Turkey, as well as regarding its accounts for the period (Annex II, Art. 5). Its existence was to come to an end as soon as the claims of the Allied Powers against the Turkish Government, as laid down in Part VIII of the Treaty, had been satisfied and the Ottoman pre-war Public Debt had been liquidated (Treaty, Art. 257). The date thus prescribed would have been so distant as hardly to be worth taking into account, and the Financial Commission would have become, to all intents and purposes, a permanent institution, had not circumstances prevented it from ever taking up in fact the powers so lavishly conferred upon it on paper.

(*e*) *The Capitulations.* This technical term covers a body of relationships between Turkey and certain foreign Powers which, by long tradition, have come to be regarded as a coherent whole, though it would be almost impossible to codify them in a precise and logical form. The Capitulations consist partly of written treaties, partly of customary rights; they concern not only the diplomatic relations of states, but the personal status of individuals; and they extend from the political into the juridical, financial, and economic spheres of social intercourse. Their main common characteristic is that they are a peculiar relationship only to be found existing between parties belonging respectively to two different classes: Western or Westernized States and their nationals, on the one hand, and non-Western States like Turkey, on the other. The relationship which they establish is essentially unequal and lacking in reciprocity. They impose servitudes on the inferior party without securing to it any corresponding rights as against the other. This inequality, however, has grown imperceptibly, and was not inherent in the relationship from the beginning. It has developed in consequence of a differentiation in the power, efficiency, and degree of civilization of the respective parties, and being thus based on a broad and genuine diversity, it is more difficult to remove than if it were nothing but an arbitrary injustice. The problem of the Capitulations presents itself, in fact, as a dilemma. It is generally admitted that some, at any rate, of the privileges thereby secured, in Turkish territory, to the Governments, nationals, and 'protected persons' of foreign Powers are indefensible; and that, in general, the existence of the Capitulations is a formidable barrier to Turkish administrative and judicial reform. On the other hand, until reform in these spheres is effected, foreign interests in the country (which have established themselves there in reliance upon the Capitulations, and which in some cases perform valuable if not indispensable services to Turkey) can hardly be expected to surrender the privileges which alone safeguard them against the dangers of still unremedied misgovernment. The Turks have long felt that they cannot breathe until the strangle-hold of the Capitulations is broken, and they accordingly denounced them, unilaterally, as soon as the Great Powers of Europe had begun to fight one another. On the other hand, the Allies, after the Armistice, refused to recognize a denunciation which could not be justified in international law. The Turks, however, persist in regarding the abolition of the Capitulations as only second in importance, from their point of view, to their territorial claims in the first five articles of the National Pact of Angora.[1] It is evident that no satisfactory solution can be found except through negotiation and compromise, but the provisions concerning the Capitulations which were inserted in the Treaty of Sèvres erred in the same direction as the Turkish denunciation of 1914. They took a high line on a matter in which neither party was sufficiently master of the situation to be able to practise high-handedness with any permanent success.

According to the Treaty, the capitulatory régime resulting from treaties, conventions, or usage was to be re-established in favour of the Allied Powers which directly or indirectly enjoyed the benefit thereof before the 1st August 1914, and was to be extended to the Allied Powers which did not enjoy the benefit thereof on that date (Art. 261). The Allied Powers did, at the same time, provide in the Treaty for the replacement of the Capitulations, on their judicial side, by a new system; but they proposed to carry this change through on their own motion,

[1] For text v. pp. 605–6.

without giving Turkey herself so much as a vote in deciding what was perhaps the most important outstanding problem of her domestic politics. An Anglo-Franco-Italo-Japanese Commission was to be set up within three months of the coming into force of the Treaty, to prepare, with the assistance of technical experts representing the other Capitulatory Powers, Allied or Neutral, a scheme of judicial reform to replace the existing capitulatory system in judicial matters in Turkey. This Commission might recommend, after consultation (i.e. not necessarily agreement) with the Turkish Government, the adoption of either a mixed or a unified judicial system. As soon as the Principal Allied Powers had approved the scheme, they would inform the Turkish Government, which was to accept the new system in advance. The Principal Allied Powers reserved the right to agree among themselves, and if necessary with the other Allied and Neutral Powers concerned, as to the date on which the new system was to come into force (Art. 136). Thus Turkey might have imposed upon her a substitute more objectionable to her than the Capitulations themselves, with no means of opposing the change other than by communicating her views to the all-powerful inter-Allied Commission.

On the other hand, Turkey was offered the prospect of certain compensations. The traditional prerogatives and immunities granted by past Sultans to the non-Moslem races of Turkey, while reconfirmed in a general manner by the Treaty, were to be overridden (if the case arose) by any modification of the Turkish judicial system which the Treaty might introduce (Art. 149). Even more important was the provision that (subject to certain reservations and conditions) the Financial Commission should be entitled to authorize the application by Turkey to the persons or property of the nationals of the Allied Powers of any taxes or duties which should similarly be imposed on Turkish subjects in the interests of the economic stability and good government of Turkey (Art. 264).

All judicial decisions given in Turkey by a judge or court of an Allied Power between the 30th October 1918 and the coming into force of the new judicial system referred to in Art. 136 were to be recognized by the Turkish Government, and the latter was, if necessary, to secure the execution of such decisions (Art. 426). This provision was intensely humiliating to Turkish pride, but might otherwise have had no serious permanent consequences. Far more serious was the provision that any company incorporated in accordance with Turkish law and operating in Turkey which was at the time, or should thereafter be, controlled by Allied nationals, should have the right, within five years from the coming into force of the Treaty, to transfer its property, rights, and interests to another company incorporated in accordance with the law of one of the Allied Powers whose nationals controlled it, all this being without prejudice to the full transmission to the new company of the original company's rights and privileges (Art. 316). More momentous still was the stipulation that—notwithstanding any provisions of Turkish law to the contrary—Turkey must recognize any new nationality which had been or might be acquired by her nationals under the laws of the Allied Powers or new states, and must regard such persons as having, in consequence, in all respects severed their allegiance to their country of origin (Art. 128). If advantage were taken of this clause on any large scale by foreign Governments (e.g. by Greece or Italy) on the one hand, and by Turkish nationals (e.g. by those of Greek or Armenian race), on the other, it was evident that the effective exercise of Turkish sovereignty in Turkish territory might become impossible. Certainly this clause had the effect upon the Turks of exasperating them against all the provisions of the Treaty regarding the Capitulations, thus making an agreed settlement of this problem still more difficult to achieve than it would in any case have been.

(*f*) *The Protection of Minorities* (Arts. 140–51). Provisions falling under this head have already come under consideration in previous parts of this section. The dangerous facilities for change of nationality, discussed just above, were of course introduced into the Treaty on this account (though the ultimate effect, when the all-important factor of the psychology of the Turkish majority is taken into account, might well be the opposite of that intended). Additional local sanctions for the protection of minorities were incorporated, as has been mentioned, in the Tripartite Agreement (Arts. 1, 8, and 9). A special stipulation in favour of the Assyro-Chaldeans and other racial or religious minorities scattered among the Kurds was included in the provisions relating to Kurdistan (Art. 62); and the Allied Governments were careful to repeat this when they offered concessions to Turkey regarding other aspects of the

Kurdish question in March 1921. The protection of minorities was, indeed, one of the most difficult and at the same time urgent problems raised by the political remoulding of the Near and Middle East on the lines of nationality, because, as has been emphasized already, the nationalities in this area were intimately intermingled, and could never be completely sorted out into homogeneous and territorially segregated blocks of population. Subject minorities of every nationality were therefore bound to find themselves, at the end of the process, left outside the boundaries of their national state; and, conversely, every national state was bound to find alien minorities still embedded in it. The welfare of these several minorities, and loyalty on their part towards the respective majorities and the majority Governments, were therefore desirable in the interest of all parties concerned, and these objects could only be secured by general provisions applied to, and accepted by, each minority and each state in the area, without distinction of nationality or denomination. Common interest, however, did not actually produce an atmosphere of reasonableness and moderation, and this owing to several causes.

In the first place, these Eastern peoples, with the fanaticism of converts, were carrying the Western creed of nationalism to extremes from which the Western World, with its greater experience and common sense, had generally recoiled. In their uncontrollable thirst for absolute sovereign independence within the frontiers of their own national state, they were ready to sacrifice the kindred minorities abroad rather than to allow rights secured to these to become precedents for the establishment of similar rights for the aliens domiciled in their own territories. During the post-armistice period, the Turks, Greeks, and Armenians displayed a remarkable and profoundly discouraging unanimity of feeling on this point. It was almost the only doctrine upon which they agreed, and they could hardly have chosen a more disastrous one for the purpose. Everywhere the minorities succumbed, and their tragedy seldom became known to the world until it was too late to avert it. Genuine horror at their fate, and sincere attempts to devise and bring into operation some general scheme for saving the remnants of them from extinction, emanated, for the most part, not from their more fortunately situated kindred who found themselves in a local majority and were absorbed in the ruthless exploitation of their advantage, but from the public and the statesmen of Western Europe and North America.

In the second place, there were two rival and hardly compatible concepts of the status of minorities in the field. On the one hand, there was the traditional Middle Eastern system of cultural autonomy, evolved under the ancient Persian and Arab Empires and reproduced in the 'millets' set up by the Osmanlis. A 'millet' (which may be translated 'nation' or 'denomination' with equal inexactness) was a minority corporation recognized by the public law of the land and enjoying far more extensive ecclesiastical, scholastic, and even judicial autonomy than modern Western Governments, with their zeal for uniformity, have ever tolerated. On the other hand, the 'millet' organization, while securing to its members great liberty of action in their mutual relations, generally left them on a footing of gross inequality with the ruling denomination or nation in the state, and offered them almost no protection at all against illegal oppression or against occasional outbreaks of homicidal violence. In contrast to this Middle Eastern tradition, the improvement in the position of minorities in the West (which set in very tardily and did not become a strong current in Western politics until after the French Revolution) proceeded on quite different lines. The modern Western state, always jealous of rival forms of corporate life, did not show much enthusiasm for giving the minorities the opportunity of self-protection and self-expression in their corporate capacity. It preferred to give the individual equality with all other individuals in the eye of the law. In other words, it reconciled the enfranchisement of minorities with the preservation of its own full sovereignty by tacitly excluding from the purview of the state those sides of social life in which the differences dividing minority from majority happened to express themselves.

This principle was at the bottom of the minority clauses incorporated, after the European War, in the main treaties of peace, or else embodied separately in subsidiary instruments. Inasmuch, however, as these safeguards were to apply, for the most part, to Oriental or semi-Oriental countries and populations, provisions were freely borrowed from the Oriental system; and the result was a syncretism which betrayed its origin in a sudden, overwhelming need, and lacked the surety of touch which can only be derived from experience and tradition.

This characteristic was apparent in Part IV of the Sèvres Treaty, which was put together out of the three following elements: (1) Special and most essential provisions for righting, to the small degree possible, the wrongs committed against Ottoman Greeks and Armenians since the outbreak of the European War (Arts. 142–4); (2) Provisions more or less closely corresponding [1] to those of the standard 'Minority Treaty' evolved by the Peace Conference, as exemplified in the Treaty signed at Sèvres, on the same date as the Treaty of Peace with Turkey, by the Principal Allied Powers on the one part and by Greece on the other (e.g. Arts. 140, 141, 145, 147, 148, 150); (3) A stipulation that the Turkish Government should confirm and uphold in their entirety the prerogatives and immunities of an ecclesiastical, scholastic, or judicial nature granted by the Sultans to non-Moslem races in virtue of special orders or imperial decrees, as well as by ministerial orders or orders of the Grand Vizier (Art. 149).

This combination of incongruous elements was a weakness; and, indeed, it might have been perceived *a priori* that the 'millet' system had become an anachronism. It was part and parcel of the old Oriental conception of society which the invasion of Western nationalism had overthrown. That system, with its defects and its good qualities, had grown up as a unity, and it was impracticable to preserve one fragment of it while accepting the ruin of the remainder.

The Turkish Nationalists, very significantly, took their stand without hesitation on the new ground, and made their attitude public in Art. 5 of the National Pact of Angora:

> 'The rights of minorities will be confirmed by us on the same basis as those established to the profit of minorities in other countries by the *ad hoc* conventions concluded between the Entente Powers, their adversaries, and certain of their associates. On the other hand, we cherish the firm conviction that Moslem minorities in neighbouring countries will enjoy the same guarantees where their rights are concerned.' (*v.* p. 606).

Thus the Turks repudiated the 'millet' system in the same instrument in which they abandoned their prescriptive title

[1] The correspondence was not complete. For example, freedom of religious practice was only secured to all inhabitants of Greece so long as the practices of the particular religion were 'not inconsistent with public order or public morals' (Minority Treaty, Art. 2). In the case of Turkey, the same freedom was introduced, but without the qualification (Peace Treaty, Art. 141).

to be an imperial people ruling over alien majorities. The two steps were consistent, for both were logical corollaries of the Western nationality idea. It was evident that Part IV of the Treaty would have to undergo corresponding modifications, and that safeguards for minorities in Turkey could in practice only be secured as parts of a charter of universal application. Even on this basis, however, it must be confessed that, already by June 1922, the outlook was not promising. Rigid reciprocity of conditions might overcome the obstacle of pride, and might induce Oriental nations to accept restrictions on their sovereignty, for the benefit of minorities, which they would obstinately reject so long as there was any suspicion of differential treatment. But it was to be feared that, even if a common charter were drafted amicably, and in conference, by the several states concerned, they would concur in restricting its provisions to the utmost degree possible, in their common infatuation for the sovereignty of the national state. This, too, is on the supposition that the Eastern settlement took the most favourable course. In reality, however, any round table conference between the states concerned did not appear, in June 1922, to be a very likely contingency. It seemed more probable that the Near and Middle East would remain, for an indefinite period, in a state of war, and that the mixed nationalities would become more and more exasperated against one another. In these circumstances, the protection of minorities *in situ* might prove impossible, and statesmanship might have to resort to intermigration—a desperate remedy in the East, where it involves an appalling amount of mortality and of economic destruction. In regard to territories undergoing a change of sovereignty, the Treaty of Sèvres contained the customary clauses regarding the right to opt, within a given period of time, for whichever nationality the individual inhabitants of the transferred territory might prefer, with the proviso that persons opting for a state other than that which was in future to be sovereign over their homes, must transfer their residence to the country of their choice (Arts. 123–7). This represented the ordinary practice of Western Europe, with the additional feature that Turkey was bound over to carry out any measures which might be prescribed with this object by the Council of the League of Nations (Art. 127). At the same time, the principle was wisely extended in the Treaty of Sèvres so as to cover, not merely territories undergoing a change of sovereignty, but the whole area with which this section is concerned. Turkey was to recognize such provisions as the Allied Powers might consider opportune with respect to the reciprocal and voluntary emigration of persons belonging to racial minorities. Within six months of the coming into force of the Treaty, Greece and Turkey were to enter into a special arrangement relating to the reciprocal and voluntary emigration of the populations of Turkish and Greek race in the territories transferred to Greece and remaining Turkish respectively. In case agreement could not be reached as to such arrangement, Greece and Turkey were to be entitled to apply to the Council of the League of Nations, which was to fix the terms of such arrangement (Art. 143). At the Conference held in Paris in March 1922, the Allied Powers referred the question of minorities to the League once again. It was fraught with difficulty, yet the League was in a better diplomatic position than any other party concerned for discovering a solution.

EPILOGUE, AUGUST 1923

6. (*a*) *Defeat of Greeks and Armistice at Mudania, 11th October 1922.*

By mid-June 1923, just a year after the preceding sections of this Part were written, Penelope's web had been unravelled almost to the last threads, and the rougher fabric woven out of the torn and tangled materials progressively discarded from the first design was on the verge of completion. Long before the Treaty of Lausanne was signed, however, the Treaty of Sèvres had become an historical curiosity, and the space devoted to it in the present work might therefore at first sight seem disproportionate. Yet the preservation of historical curiosities is one of the functions of history, and the Treaty of Sèvres, while its positive provisions fall under that category, was at the same time, in its negative aspect, a phenomenon of permanent historical importance. A treaty thus conceived was doomed from the outset to failure, but the impossible experiment need never have been attempted, and in that case the relations between the victorious Western Powers and the Near and Middle Eastern peoples after the Armistice of 1918 would undoubtedly have taken a very different course from that which they actually followed. From this point of view, the attempt and the error embodied in the abortive diplomatic instrument exercised an enduring influence upon international affairs, and students of its after-effects might, for many years to come, turn back with interest to a 'scrap of paper' which had stimulated such practical and effective opposition.

Between June 1922 and June 1923 the attempt to impose peace terms upon Turkey by force through the agency of the Greek Army, upon which the Principal Allied Powers had embarked in 1919, had ended in a sensational disaster. On the 26th August 1922 the military stale-mate, which had characterized the preceding eleven months of the Graeco-Turkish War in Anatolia (since the failure of the Greek offensive against Angora), was terminated by a complete collapse of the Greek Army's *moral*. An attack launched by the Turkish Nationalist forces encountered no serious resistance; a fortnight's marching carried the victors from Afiun Kara Hissar to Smyrna; within a few days more, every Greek soldier on the Anatolian mainland had been either taken prisoner or shipped away; and the screen which the military effort of Greece had interposed, since the summer of 1920, between the Turkish Army and the meagre Allied garrisons at the Straits and Constantinople, was suddenly torn down. During the three weeks following the Turkish reoccupation of Smyrna, the Principal Allied Powers, who were not yet formally at peace with the impotent Government of the Sultan-Caliph at Constantinople, found themselves in imminent danger of war with the Government of the Great National Assembly at Angora, with whom they had as yet established no definite relations either of amity or of belligerency. The tension was not really relaxed till the 11th October 1922, when a new Armistice Convention was signed at Mudania by General Harington on behalf of the Allied Powers and Ismet Pasha on behalf of Angora—a Convention to which Greece acceded three days later.[1] The object of the Mudania Armistice was to prepare the way for a fresh peace conference, in which a settlement was genuinely to be negotiated with the Turks by the Allies instead of being nominally imposed upon them. In the meantime, the diplomatic situation was simplified by the

[1] *v.* also §§ 10–11 of Part I B. pp. 38–9.

formal abolition of the Sultanate and of the Sublime Porte at the hands of the Great National Assembly. The Assembly vested the sovereignty of Turkey in its own corporate personality on the 1st November, and the ex-Sultan-Caliph Vahyd-ed-Din Khan was evacuated from Constantinople on board a British warship on the 17th of the same month. The revisionary peace conference between the Allied signatories to the Treaty of Sèvres and the now sole and undisputed Nationalist Government of Turkey was opened on the 20th November 1922 at Lausanne, and its second session was still dragging on, owing to a temporary deadlock over a single remaining point at issue, at the time when the present postscript was written, seven months later.

(b) 20th November 1922, Opening of Lausanne Conference.

At that date the situation was still technically indeterminate, since no general treaty in substitution for that of Sèvres had been signed or ratified; but in reality a peace settlement was this time in sight and a formula for agreement had been found on the most important questions. A new draft was in fact put into shape at Lausanne by the Allied Delegations before the close of the first session; and although this session eventually broke down on certain issues, many sections of the Allied draft, particularly those dealing with territorial questions and with the future régime at the Straits, proved acceptable to the Turkish representatives. A settlement of the frontier between Turkey and Iraq in Kurdistan—the single major territorial issue on which there had been no agreement—was provided for by an informal arrangement (described below) between the British and the Turkish Governments; and separate instruments concerning the exchange of Greek and Turkish populations, the release of able-bodied men, and the reciprocal restitution of interned civilians and the exchange of prisoners of war and interned civilians, were signed by the two Governments concerned. By June 1923 it was thus possible to give, in brief, a substantially correct account of what the settlement was to be. In attempting this, it seemed simplest to take the arrangement of the previous sections as a guide, and to note in order the principal changes produced by the intervening twelve months in the situation as there described.

(c) *Territorial arrangements.*

(i) *General.*

The events of these months had primarily been disastrous to Greece, and the renunciation on her part of virtually all the territorial gains assigned to her by the Sèvres Treaty at Turkey's expense was no longer an open question at the Lausanne Peace Conference, since it had been one of the essential preliminary conditions of the Mudania Armistice. Since, however, Greece had originally embarked upon her unfortunate enterprise in Anatolia on the initiative and for the benefit of the Allied Powers, her defeat carried with it the frustration of the Allies' war aims against Turkey as well as her own; and although the Allies had by successive steps abandoned and disavowed their agent before the final disaster overtook her, they were themselves overtaken by poetic justice before the new conference had run its tedious and laborious course. Having exacted the sacrifice of the Greek claims to the Smyrna zone and Eastern Thrace as the price of the Mudania Armistice, the Turks compelled the Allied Powers at Lausanne to surrender in succession their contemplated control over the Straits, their traditional privileges under the Capitulations, and even to some extent the contractual rights of their nationals who happened to be the Turkish Government's concessionnaires or creditors, before they could be brought to sign a peace treaty. If Turkey's success was to be measured in terms of her Angora Pact, her triumph was absolute, but it also had its tragic side; for the parties most intimately affected by the deplorable events of the past four years had not been the Greek, Turkish, and Principal Allied Powers and Governments but the populations of the Graeco-Turkish war zone. These unhappy people, who had not had the least voice in the drafting of the Treaty of Sèvres, were ruined, uprooted, and destroyed by its consequences with no discrimination whatever of nationality or religion. Turkey, with her depopulated territory and devastated villages, towns, and railways, emerged from the ordeal in hardly less miserable a condition (judged by any practical or human criterion) than Greece with her multitudes of destitute, bereaved, and disease-stricken refugees; and a fraction even of the Allied nations was involved in a comparable disaster through the ruin of the western colonies at Smyrna and the prospective ruin of those at Constantinople.

(ii) *Minorities.*

In general outline the liquidation of the old Ottoman Empire, as sketched in a previous section, had proceeded during these twelve months according to expectation. Almost the last vestiges of the earlier system had been obliterated by the rising tide of Western Nationalism; on a basis of national majorities, frontiers had made a distinct approach towards stabilization; the few surviving minorities (e. g. the Turks in Western Thrace and the Greeks and Armenians in Constantinople) seemed likely on the whole to benefit (though precariously) by the relaxation of tension; and the attitude towards one another of the Western, Near Eastern, and Middle Eastern peoples had changed or was changing beyond recognition.

(iii) *Territorial Unity.*

The territorial unity of the area with which this section is concerned, which has been discussed previously from several points of view, was asserted politically at Lausanne by the complete realization of Article I of the Turkish National Pact.[1]

(iv) (1) *Constantinople and Thrace, Smyrna, Armenia.*

In detail the Pact was realized on the North-West by the re-establishment of unrestricted Turkish sovereignty over Constantinople and Eastern Thrace up to the Bulgarian frontier and the Talweg of the Maritsa, and by the practical restoration of Turkish naval and military control over the coasts and waters of the Bosporus, the Sea of Marmara, and the Dardanelles. Along the new European frontiers of Turkey, her sovereignty was only to be limited by the creation of a neutral zone to a depth of about 30 kilometres (a zone of equal depth being created simultaneously on the Greek and Bulgarian side). The demand (Pact, Art. III)[1] for a plebiscite in Western Thrace was waived, but Turkey succeeded in recovering a fragment of this territory also. During the first

[1] *v.* p. 605.

session she was assigned, on the western bank of the Maritsa opposite Adrianople, the terminus of the tramway running to the nearest station on the broad-gauge main line of the Oriental Railway at Karagach. During the second session Greece further retroceded to Turkey, by direct agreement, the suburb and railway-station of Karagach itself, together with several miles of the railway on either side, in settlement of the Turkish claim to reparations for devastation which Greece acknowledged herself to have committed in the Anatolian campaign. As regards the 'Freedom of the Straits', the territorial guarantee consisting of the division of the sovereignty over the European and Asiatic shores of the Dardanelles and the Marmara between two different states was of course extinguished by the retrocession of Eastern Thrace to Turkey. The military sanction previously placed in the hands of Great Britain, France, and Italy likewise disappeared. Four zones (one on each side of the Bosporus and the Dardanelles) were taken over from the Sèvres scheme, though with important reductions in their area, but they were no longer to be open to the Allied and closed to the Turkish forces, but were to be demilitarized for all parties (as well as the Aegean islands commanding the southern entrance to the waterway); and demilitarization was interpreted in terms far less favourable to the Allies than to Turkey. Any right of the Allies to the potential occupation or precautionary inspection of these zones was forfeited *ab silentio*; while on the other hand it was expressly stipulated that Turkey might maintain a garrison in Constantinople, as well as in its insular and Asiatic suburbs, up to a maximum strength of 12,000 men; that she might utilize the demilitarized zones for lines of communication between her forces in Asia and Europe; and that she might anchor her fleet in the demilitarized waters. The Commission of the Straits was likewise maintained, though with diminished functions and powers, and was placed under Turkish presidency and under the auspices of the League of Nations. The three Principal European Allied Powers and Japan further pledged themselves to resist any violation of the security of the demilitarized zones or of the freedom of navigation (elaborately provided for, in the case of warships as well as merchant-ships, according to the possible permutations and combinations of belligerency or neutrality on the part of the various parties concerned).

Whether this Convention saved the faces of the Principal Allied Powers is a question that must be left to the reader; but it is obvious that it did not settle the concrete problem of the Black Sea Straits as sketched at the beginning of the previous Section 4 (i).

(iv) (2) *Smyrna; The Migratory Clauses.*

The disposal of Smyrna no longer presented the Allied diplomatists with the insoluble difficulties that had baffled them at Sèvres, having been accomplished by the worst possible method (that is, by war) in the only possible sense, that is, by the reunion of the artificial enclave of the Smyrna Zone with the remainder of the Anatolian Peninsula under the full sovereignty of the Turkish State. Unhappily, however, the violent solution of this wantonly created problem had already proved fatal to the Greek minority in Anatolia, the wholesale flight or expulsion of which to Greek territories overseas had accompanied the evacuation of the Anatolian mainland by the Greek Army. During the first session at Lausanne the Greek and Turkish Governments signed a separate convention for the compulsory interchange of Turkish nationals of the Greek Orthodox religion and of Greek nationals of the Moslem religion established on their respective territories as delimited by the new frontiers. The only parties exempted were the Greek inhabitants of Constantinople and the Turkish inhabitants of Western Thrace. The deportees were to be free to take with them their movable property without restriction or charge. Unportable as well as juridically 'immovable' property was to be registered and valued in both countries by a mixed commission, which was to include three neutral members chosen by the Council of the League of Nations and was always to operate under neutral chairmanship; the proceeds of liquidation were to be paid over to the Government in whose territory the property was situated and credited to the Government into whose territory the former private owner had migrated; and the two accounts were to be balanced, any difference between the total amounts debited and credited respectively to the two Governments having to be paid over in cash by the Government to which the balance proved adverse. At the same time the individual emigrants were to be informed by the Commission of the valuation at which their former property had been liquidated, and were to be entitled to receive from the Government of their new country property equal to and of the same nature as that which they had left behind. This compulsory intermigration was much criticized, both inside and outside the Conference, at the time when the Convention was being negotiated. The flight or expulsion of nearly all the Greek minorities from Turkey was, however, an accomplished fact, and the establishment of the Mixed Commission was the only means of possibly mitigating the economic hardships of their lot, while the introduction of reciprocity, though it might bear hardly upon the individual Moslem inhabitants of Greek territory, at the same time enabled the Greek Government, in the last resort, to make more room for the multitudes of Greek refugees from Anatolia and Eastern Thrace who were flocking across the new frontiers.

(iv) (3) *The Armenian Minority.*

The Armenian Minority suffered a fresh blow through the collision between Armenian irregulars and Turkish troops which occurred in the Armenian quarter at Smyrna a few days after the Turkish occupation and which appears to have been the immediate cause of the great fire. The armed resistance to the incoming Turkish Army was reported to have been organized by Armenians from elsewhere, but the Smyrna community inevitably paid the penalty for the activities of their compatriots. At the time of writing, the Armenian community in Constantinople and a few other smaller isolated groups (such as the Catholic Armenians in the town of Angora) were all that remained within the Turkish frontiers of the former Armenian population of the Ottoman Empire. During the first session at Lausanne, suggestions on the part of the Allied Governments for an Armenian 'National Home' in Turkish territory met with a categorical refusal from the Turkish plenipotentiaries, and were not pressed because the Allies had no power to insist on them. The territorial arrangements (mentioned in a previous section) which had already been made independently by the Turkish Government at Angora and the Soviet Government at Moscow in regard to Trans-Caucasia were wisely passed over in silence and thereby implicitly recognized at Lausanne. By June 1923 it was still more evident than it had been in June 1922 that if the Armenian nation had any political future, it lay on the Russian and not on the Turkish side of the Russo-Turkish frontier.

(v) The twelve months' interval had also decided the irreconcilable conflict between the standpoint of the Treaty of Sèvres and that of the Angora Movement in regard to the future of the Turkish State by a 'knock-out blow' in favour of Angora. The territorial claims asserted in Article I of the Angora Pact were not only endorsed at Lausanne with the single exception of Southern Kurdistan, but within the frontiers thus attained the Turkish Government succeeded in establishing its complete sovereignty.

(v) (1) *Southern Kurdistan.*

Southern Kurdistan, which had been included by the Treaty of Sèvres in the area mandated to the British Empire under the name of Mesopotamia, also fell within the scope of Article I of the Angora Pact as being inhabited by a non-Arab Ottoman Moslem (though a Kurdish and not a Turkish) majority. After each party had marshalled its historical, ethnological, geographical, strategic, and economic arguments on this issue during the first session at Lausanne, without any approach towards agreement, the British plenipotentiary announced his intention of referring the case to the League of Nations. Eventually the Turkish Government accepted the arbitration of the League in return for an undertaking on the part of the British Government to postpone the appeal to the League until twelve months after the ratification of the prospective Treaty of Lausanne, with a view to arriving, if possible, at a direct settlement with Turkey during the interval. Pending this, both parties were to maintain the *status quo.*

(v) (2) *No local diminutions of Turkish sovereignty.*

There was no further question of the local diminutions of Turkish sovereignty involved in the provisions of the Treaty of Sèvres regarding Northern Kurdistan and in the Tripartite Treaty (of the same date as the Peace Treaty of Sèvres) between the British Empire, France, and Italy.

(v) (3) *No restrictions on Turkish military and naval forces.*

There was no further question of Allied control over the Turkish Army and Navy.

(v) (4) *Turkish finance.*

There was no further question of Allied Control over Turkish finance. More than this, Turkey was released from any claim on the part of the Allied Powers to reparations on account of the European War. At the time of writing, the outstanding financial issue was that between the Turkish Government and the pre-war private creditors of the Ottoman Empire. The creditors were asserting a contractual right to receive their dividends in sterling; the Turkish Government was declaring itself unable to discharge its obligations in that currency at the prevailing rate of exchange, and was offering to pay in French francs at their contemporary value. Many compromises had been suggested, but none had been accepted so far by both the parties concerned.

(v) (5) *The Capitulations and the Guarantees.*

At Lausanne the Allied Powers did not challenge the abolition of the Capitulations but concentrated their efforts on securing the maximum amount of juridical guarantees in substitution for them. The practical wisdom of these efforts was questionable, for the efficacy of the Capitulations had lain less in the written word than in the naval and military ability of the Capitulatory Powers to enforce their own interpretation of these traditional privileges. Even if comprehensive paper substitutes for the Capitulations had been successfully imposed upon the Turkish Delegation at Lausanne, it was evident that under post-war conditions there would have been little or no material force forthcoming in order to impose them in Turkey; and this effect might well have been to exasperate Turkish feeling against foreign residents without securing to the latter any compensatory protection. As it turned out, however, Allied nationals in Turkey were preserved from this possible peril by the ill-success of their Governments at Lausanne. During the second session (in which this question was one of the principal items on the agenda) it was agreed that, for a transitional period of five years, the Turkish Government should select four legal councillors, who were to be nationals of States that had been neutral during the European War, from a panel drawn up by the International Court at the Hague. These councillors were to reside respectively at Constantinople, Smyrna, Samsun, and Adana. They were to have no judicial functions, but were simply to observe the working of the Turkish courts, facilitate appeals, and bring complaints to the notice of the competent Turkish authorities. The Allied negotiators, in their last stand, attempted to insist that the Turkish authorities should be required to inform the local councillor before they proceeded to arrest a foreign national; but the Turks victoriously carried even this final position, and it was decided that, when an arrest had been effected, the councillor should be informed of the accomplished fact as expeditiously as possible.

(v) (6) *The Protection of Minorities.*

The problem of protecting minorities was simplified by the almost complete extrusion of the Greek minority from Turkey, which was sanctioned after the event by the Graeco-Turkish Convention for compulsory interchange which has been described above. As far as the issue remained a practical one (as it still did in several important areas of Greece and Turkey, such as Western Thrace and Constantinople), it was settled at Lausanne on the lines of the minority clauses or treaties imposed, after the European War, upon defeated or aggrandized States in Europe, and not on the lines of the traditional Middle Eastern 'Millet' System which had previously prevailed in the Ottoman Empire. Superficially, the loss of the cultural autonomy of the 'Millets' was as heavy a blow to the minorities as that of the extra-territoriality of the Capitulations was to the foreign colonies. In the one case, however, as in the other, the theoretical status was of doubtful value in itself, while the actual situation had already been transformed by a process of historical evolution, of which the juridical revolution was a consequence and not a cause.

(*d*) *Signature of Peace.*

The Treaty of Lausanne was actually signed on the 24th July 1923 (almost three years after the signature of the Treaty of Sèvres), and was ratified by the Great National Assembly of Turkey at Angora on the 23rd August of the same year. Many of the arrangements discussed above were provided for, not in the principal instrument, but in a number of conventions and protocols signed by some or all of the parties, partly during the first and partly during the second session of the Lausanne conference. Certain questions were disposed of in unilateral communications, the most important of which was the Declaration regarding the administration of justice in Turkey made by the Turkish delegates on the same date as the signature of the Treaty. On further points, the interpretations or intentions of one party were elucidated in letters addressed to the other parties. Finally, in regard to several economic and financial matters (among them the question of the currency in which the foreign bondholders of the Ottoman Debt were to be paid) the heads of the Allied Delegations formally reserved their right to reopen the issue should their Governments fail to be satisfied by the Turkish Government's action. These, however, were small matters compared with those on which formal and precise agreement had been reached; and the Treaty of Lausanne, with its Annexes, seemed destined, in all human probability, to inaugurate a more lasting settlement, not only than the Treaty of Sèvres, but than the Treaties of Versailles, St. Germain, Trianon, and Neuilly. At first sight this judgment might appear paradoxical in the case of an instrument which had been so tardily and laboriously constructed, and which bore in its text such conspicuous marks of its painful gestation. But closer consideration might suggest that the very difficulties which had attended its birth were the best guarantees of its vitality. The preceding treaties were easily and rapidly drafted in comparatively logical form because they were the work of one party only and were imposed by the victors upon the vanquished without negotiation. In other words, they lacked the essence of diplomatic instruments, which is that they should embody adjustments between two or more programmes and points of view. The merit of the Lausanne Treaty (with all its obvious imperfections) was that it represented an agreement between the principal parties concerned, in which each had to make sacrifices and bear disappointments but none was subjected to impossible commitments or intolerable humiliations.

The Turks substantially secured their national independence and sovereignty within their ethnographic frontiers. On the other hand, the liberation of the ex-Ottoman Arab provinces in Asia completed the liquidation of the former Ottoman Empire by exempting the last non-Turkish majorities from Turkish rule (with the exception of certain Kurdish populations which remained, and others which might be reincluded, within the Turkish frontiers). Of all the parties concerned, the minorities lost, or stood to lose, the most; but the violent catastrophes (massacres, exoduses, deportations, epidemics, and beggary) which had overtaken them were the consequences, not of the Lausanne settlement (which was subsequent to these calamities), but of the disastrous policy of the Principal Allied Powers during the four years following the Armistice. In point of status, the minorities were in any case bound to be affected by the redistribution of the Near and Middle East into national states—an inevitable process for which particular governments or statesmen were not responsible. The 'Millet System' and the 'Capitulations' were anachronisms which could not last, and in the Treaty of Lausanne, with its Annexes, their disappearance was recorded. It should be noted, however, that both the native non-Moslem communities and the foreign commercial colonies retained their juridical autonomy in matters of 'personal statute'; that the rights secured to the native minorities were now placed, with Turkey's consent, under the auspices of the League of Nations; and that foreign residents were guaranteed exemption from military service, forced loans, and capital levies.

The best augury for the success of the Treaty was the spirit in which it was received on both sides. Inasmuch as it registered a melodramatic discomfiture of the Principal Allied Powers within less than five years after their apparently overwhelming triumph in the European War, the late victors might have taken it with a bad grace as a bitter humiliation, while the victors of the moment, with their sympathizers in other parts of the non-Western world, might have exulted over it as a first success in a counter-offensive against the existing ascendancy of the West. Happily, however, the long-drawn-out negotiations, wearisome and at times exasperating though they were, had the effect of damping down the war-spirit and of calling out much-needed reserves of rationality and moderation.

In the allied countries it was frankly recognized that the Turks had scored a success and that it would be undignified, as well as impolitic, to grudge them the fruits of it. At the same time the Turks admitted, to themselves no less than to the world, that the harvesting of these fruits in the social and economic field would be a more difficult task than their political and military achievements, and that the latter would be barren unless they were followed up with unremitting determination. The better feelings which at this time prevailed on either side were felicitously expressed in a statesmanlike message from the Agha Khan (who had been present at Lausanne during the last phase) to the Moslems of the British Empire and the world. At this momentous stage in their relations, both West and East thus showed a disposition to profit by their recent tragic experiences in common, and to shrink from further provoking the Envy of the Gods.

TREATY OF LAUSANNE (24 JULY 1923) RATIFIED BY TURKEY, 23 AUGUST

Territorial Adjustments mainly in Europe. *Certain Aegean Islands.* The decisions taken with respect to cession to Greece in 1913–14 (*v.* p. 40 n.) are confirmed with some exceptions.

Greece obtains Mytilene, Chios and Nikaria, Lemnos and Samothrace. (Articles 12–13.)

Turkey receives Imbros and Rabbit Isles. (Article 14.)

Italy (*v.* p. 31 n.) obtains the Dodecanese (Article 15), including Rhodes, Astropalia[1], Calki, Scarpanto, Casos, Pscopis[2], Misiros, Calymnos, Leros, Patmos, Lipsos, Sini (Symi) and Cos and adjacent islets, and Castellorizzo.

Bulgaria's frontier is readjusted as compared with the Treaty of Neuilly.

Greece's frontier stops at the Maritza.

Demilitarization Areas. Straits Convention. (24 July 1923, annexed to treaty).

Thrace. A demilitarized zone stretches from the Aegean between Makri and Ibrile Burun to the Black Sea between Ambaler and Serbes Burun.

The Straits Area. Following are demilitarized.

(*a*) The Constantinople area on both European and Asiatic shores of the Bosporus.
(*b*) All the islands of the Sea of Marmara except Emir Ali Adas.
(*c*) The European and Asiatic shores of the Dardanelles (area reduced from Treaty of Sèvres).
(*d*) Samothrace, Lemnos (both Greek); and Imbros, Tenedos, and Rabbit Isles (all Turkish).

[1] Also known as Stampalia. [2] Also known as Tilos.

CHAPTER I

THE NEAR AND MIDDLE EAST

PART III

THE EMERGENCE OF ARAB NATIONALISM

A. GREAT BRITAIN AND THE ARABS UP TO THE ARMISTICE OF THE 30TH OCTOBER 1918

1. *Beginnings of Arab Nationalism.* The relations of Great Britain with Arab peoples have been for a century more frequent and intimate than those of any Power except the Ottoman. In the Arabian Peninsula during that period hers were the only territories held by a Christian state, the only foreign Protectorates, and the only effective foreign treaties with native rulers. The three adjacent seas were acknowledged peculiarly her sphere, and habitually were patrolled by her warships alone. With Arab-speaking peoples outside the Peninsula her relations were, of course, less exclusive. France has long ruled or occupied large Arab or Arabised provinces in Northern Africa and one smaller district on the western Red Sea coast, while at the same time she has observed a protective attitude towards certain Syrian communities, and others less important in Northern Mesopotamia. Italy imposed herself a generation ago on Arab elements in Eritrea, whence her influence passed over the Red Sea to the Yemen coast; and subsequently she annexed a North African province. While Germany hardly affected Arabs except through a Turkish medium, and Spanish relations with them were confined to Moorish territory, Holland and the United States must be reckoned Powers with Arabian interests, though both were concerned with Arabs chiefly as immigrant aliens. Since Great Britain, however, could set off against all these interests those created by her occupation of Egypt, by her East African Protectorates, and by a diplomatic position hardly less important in Syria than that of France, and much more important in Mesopotamia, the balance on the whole account remained greatly in her favour.

On this account primarily (secondary reasons co-operating) the first fomenters of Arab Nationalism were disposed to seek support from Great Britain before applying to other Powers. Arab Nationalism is of recent growth. Though the individualistic instinct of the race and its intolerance of any but a minimum of administrative control have manifested themselves in word and deed ever since the establishment of the Ottoman Empire south of the Taurus, they did not find expression in terms of nationalism before the present century; nor, when they had begun in an unavailing regret for lost spiritual primacy with an ideal, rather religious than political, did they foster cohesion or beget a programme of action until 1908. The general call by the young Turks to constitutional liberty was misinterpreted in Syria as licence for racial and local groups to decentralize themselves and take in hand their own local government. Of what followed—of the formation of Arab committees with headquarters at Constantinople or Damascus or Beirut and branches in the Arab provinces; of their formal suppression one by one at the hands of the Turks during the years 1909 and 1910 till, after the Balkan War, little more survived of the movement than a secret understanding among Arab officers in the Ottoman Army and a freemasonry of discontent among Arab intellectuals, landed notables, tribal and family chiefs, and ambitious men of substance—of all this it is needless to speak further here, since through lack of single aim, of effective organization, and of strong leading, nothing practical came of it before the outbreak of war in 1914. Moreover, thanks to energetic measures which the Turks proceeded to take during the following year in Syria, no revolutionary organization that existed there before 1914 was able to exert any influence worth mentioning on the course of the War or to further appreciably the ultimate victory of the Arab cause.

2. *First steps in the War, 1914.* Nevertheless, these abortive Syrian activities, like those also of a stillborn nationalist movement in Lower Iraq, initiated contemporaneously by Seyyid Talib en-Nakib of Basra, had important indirect results. Advertising the existence of widespread Arab discontent, they caused representatives of Great Britain and France in the East to take cognizance of an Arab factor in the Eastern Question. In particular Lord Kitchener and his staff in Egypt—the land which offered the readiest asylum to Syrian malcontents—had

their attention so directed. During the spring of 1914 Abdullah, second son and Foreign Secretary of Husein, Emir of Mecca, while on a visit to the Khedive, made the British Residency aware of his father's desire for administrative autonomy in his Sherifate, where, a year before, Talaat and the Committee of Union and Progress had begun to take measures to increase central control. Lord Kitchener, therefore, who had long been concerned about German penetration of the Ottoman Empire, was already contemplating the possibility of an autonomous Arabia between Teutonized Turkey, on the one hand, and Egypt and India on the other, before war was so much as dreamed of. Nor should it be forgotten that the Syrian committees, by provoking Jemal Pasha to the drastic purgation, which, in 1915, filled Emir Husein's antechamber with refugees and his heart with mingled pity and fear, started the chain of cause which was to eventuate, in 1916, in the outbreak of the Hejaz revolt.

(*a*) *First negotiations with Emir Husein, 1914.* In August 1914, a prospect of Turkey actively joining the Central Powers was not overlooked; and as the weeks brought ever fresh news from Ottoman provinces of mobilization and popular hostility towards nationals of the Allies, Lord Kitchener foresaw a day approach when the Moslem world would be summoned by the Caliph to wage Holy War upon British, French, and Russians. Should this call evoke a general response, grave trouble would arise both in Africa and in the Indies. Bethinking himself, therefore, of Nationalist or Separatist feeling in the Arab block, which divides Turkish Moslems from those controlled by ourselves and France, and desiring to procure a religious counterpoise to the Caliph's call, sufficient to prevent local religious sentiment from overriding political ties, he decided to invite the Holy Arab Cities to abstain from such *jihad*. In the first days of autumn, Abdullah received a message of inquiry about the intentions of Husein, should *jihad* be proclaimed, and a hint of mutual advantage that, in the event of the Ottoman Empire becoming involved in the War, might result from co-operation of Hejaz with the Allies. The reply, received on the eve of Turkey's declaration, committed Husein to no positive action, but indicated that he would take, of his goodwill, no measure in the Turkish interest. On the next day, when Turkey had come into the War, an assurance was sent to

Husein of our support of his dynastic independence, and our readiness to assist in the liberation of the Arabs, subject, in his case and theirs, to active participation on our behalf. A month later an unequivocal promise from Husein, that he would abstain from helping our enemy, dispelled all present fear of the Holy Cities endorsing the Holy War.

There the matter was to rest awhile. Until many months later no communication passed between ourselves and the Emir. We, for our part, found no good occasion to press him to develop his benevolent neutrality into active co-operation. He, for his part, had to test, by letters and embassies, the temper and intentions of other Arab leaders, and also was minded, before burning his boats, to watch the progress of our war with Turkey, for which purpose he had sent his third son, Feisal, to Syria and to Constantinople. For the moment he filed our pledges, the one given to himself, and the other, as he interpreted it, to all of Arab race in Asia, and not merely Arabs of the Peninsula. Though later communications from London made it evident that, in fact, those responsible for framing the second part of our pledge had not in view the Arabs of Asia outside the peninsula any more than those of Africa, the wording justified Husein's interpretation, and sowed seeds of misunderstanding not only with him and with our Allies, but also with the Government of India.

(*b*) *Government of India negotiates with Sheikh of Koweit and Ibn Saud, 1915.* The Government of India hastened to take similar measures to detach powerful Arabs of the Peninsula from the Holy War. The Sheikh of Koweit was encouraged to repudiate his nominal, and always unwilling, allegiance to the Turkish Sultan; and our Agent at his court, Captain Shakespear, went up to Riadh, to use persuasion with Abdul Aziz ibn Saud. Before his hapless end on the 24th January 1915, Shakespear learned that Mecca was consulting Riadh about the propriety of passive resistance to the *jihad* summons. Like Husein, Ibn Saud had been initiated some time before this date into the councils of the Syrian Arab Movement; and by expelling the Turks from Hasa and Katif, in 1913, he had manifested willingness to take action in its cause. Latterly also he had been solicited by Seyyid Talib to support Nationalist action in Iraq which might forestall a foreign occupation. He was, therefore, not likely to take the Turkish side in any event. In the first week of November 1914, the Government of India proclaimed to the Indian Moslems that the Arab and Mesopotamian Holy Cities (with express inclusion of Jiddah) would remain outside our operations of war. Such an unconditional pledge, going farther than the policy already formulated by the Imperial Government, was modified ten days later by an instruction from London that no operations were to be attempted in Arabian territories by our sea or land forces, except at the request of, or in co-operation with, local Arabs. A proclamation followed, which was circulated in Egypt and the Sudan. It recited our ancient friendship towards Arabs, and pledged its continuance provided they should take no hostile action. The distribution of this declaration, by sea-planes in Hejaz and by aeroplanes in Palestine and Syria, was discontinued some months later on representations from Husein to the effect that the papers fell among illiterate men, who, carrying them for interpretation to enemy quarters, found themselves punished for unlawful possession.

(*c*) *Plans in the West. Syria and Alexandretta, 1915.* A strategic plan for detaching the Arab-speaking from the Turkish-speaking lands was ready when Turkey entered the field against us, and preparations for military offensives on both their western and their eastern flanks were in hand. No Arab leader, however, not even the Emir of Mecca, was made party to this plan. On the west, it was not proposed that Syrians or other Arabs be armed or encouraged to rise, until the main Turkish forces should have been penned back by an Allied landing in the district of Alexandretta: otherwise local populations, committed to rebellion, might rush into premature action. Our consideration in this matter was to avail them little in the event: for, when the landing at Alexandretta had been abandoned in deference to French objections, and the Turkish High Command had learned what might have been, such drastic treatment was dealt out to all Syrians suspect of Nationalism that any possibility of a serious rising was eliminated.

(*d*) *Indian Government and Mesopotamia.* On the eastern flank, however, the plan was realized. Here the native population, for geographical reasons, could not be screened by a zone of British military occupation and left to work out its own salvation; and the direction of policy and of operations fell naturally into the hands of the Government of India, which used troops not expected to accord well with Arabs, and was unwilling to renounce in advance the territorial rights of military conquest. Therefore, native co-operation was not invited, except in the maintenance of peaceful order behind our war-front; an offer by the Muntafik chief, Ajeimi, to take and hold Basra for us was ignored; and Seyyid Talib, waiting at Koweit, was advised that India would be a safer residence than Iraq. Thereupon Ajeimi and numerous Bedouin elements took part, though half-heartedly, in Turkish operations for the recovery of Basra. Subsequently the risk of arming the tribes with weapons of precision was considered greater than the value of their military co-operation; and it was not till after our capture of Baghdad, and then only in the western desert fringe, and with a view not to our Mesopotamian operations but to the ultimate reduction of Medina by famine, that Bedouin elements were encouraged to fight. The missions of Colonel Leachman, and others, had a consistently sedative and contra-propagandist purpose, which was fulfilled if the tribes behind our front remained passive, while those ahead were still hostile. No suggestion of ultimate sovereign independence was ever conveyed to the Mesopotamian Arabs by anyone who conducted our operations or administered territory in our occupation; nor, in our proclamation issued upon the fall of Baghdad, was anything foreshadowed beyond self-government under tutelage. This Indian policy, however, though it could be, and was, consistently carried out in war-time, was inconsistent with the recognition of Arab solidarity to which the Imperial Government had assented already, and continued more and more to commit itself, as will be seen.

3. *British Commitments, 1915.* In the spring of 1915 Great Britain was still free from any obligation to assist Arabs in warfare against Turks: but she was no longer free from obligations to recognize Arab independence, whenever and wherever it should be self-established, and, further, to accept the substitution of an Arab Caliphate for the Turkish, if the Moslem world were to pronounce for it and bring it to pass. In the Arabian Peninsula, in particular, she had committed herself to the establishment and support of an Arab sovereign state, controlling the Holy Cities. All these commitments, announced already to the Arab world in November 1914, were confirmed by the distribution of a second proclamation in the following June. From this position to active alliance, was but a short

and inevitable step; and in more Arab quarters than one we had betrayed already our desire and intention to take it. This aim was manifested not only in the conditional clause of the Imperial Government's undertaking with Husein of Mecca, but also in the Indian Government's conversations with Ibn Saud; and this latter government advanced a step farther by the negotiations which it authorized the Aden Administration to initiate first with a prominent sheikh on the Yemen border, Mohammed Nasir Mukbil of Mawia, and next, with Mohammed el-Idris (commonly called Idrisi), prince of Sabbia in the Asir Tihamah. Apprehensive (with good reason) of a Turkish invasion of the Aden district, and even of attack on the weak garrison of the port, the Government of India had desired to enlist on our side the Yemenite Imam, but deferred negotiations to a more favourable opportunity in view of his known Shiite fanaticism against all Christians, and his recent accord with the Ottoman occupiers of his land. Idrisi, less potent, but more ambitious, not only had been lately at war with the Porte and its loyal Asiri tribes, but subsequently had rejected Turkish overtures, among them one from Enver Pasha himself, conveyed in a special letter written in December 1914. When, in early April 1915, the Government of India, without previously consulting those concerned in negotiations with western Arabs, ratified a treaty with this Arab, under which he agreed to attack the Turks in the Yemen Tihama and we to protect his coasts the while, it went the whole of the way; and as no more than a natural consequence Aden proceeded to supply Idrisi with munitions of war.

(*a*) *Arrangement with Ibn Saud.* With Ibn Saud the relations of the Government of India developed only a little less quickly to the same end. The conversations interrupted by Shakespear's death were resumed, and in November 1915, were crowned by a treaty of alliance signed at the port of Ajer. In consideration of a guarantee of his territories against all external aggression, Ibn Saud undertook to have the same friends and the same enemies as Great Britain, and in foreign relations to await her sanction. In all its explicit provisions this treaty followed the model of pre-war Gulf pacts: but the circumstances under which it was made implicitly committed both parties to active co-operation against the common enemy in being.

(*b*) *Husein's letter, August 1915.* Three months before it was signed, other steps had been taken towards what was to prove our final and comprehensive commitment to military alliance with Arabs. In the early days of August 1915, a letter written in July by Emir Husein came to hand at Cairo. The attitude assumed by the writer and the proposition that he made were equally unexpected. Husein, claiming to speak for an Arab Nation-to-be, asked Great Britain to acknowledge the potential sovereign independence of all the Arabs of Asia from the Indian Ocean to the 37th parallel N. latitude, and from the Red Sea and Mediterranean shores to the borders of Persia, Aden territory alone excepted. This overture had been inspired, and the nature of its terms had been determined (as we learned in due course), by Syrian exiles at the Sherifian court, who prevailed over doubts excited by Feisal's report of our ill-success in Gallipoli, by appealing to the natural sympathies of Husein for Syrian distress, and to his fears lest Ahmed Jemal Pasha's reign of terror might reach Hejaz. If there was to be any Arab Nation to be made, or a prince of the Abadilah House to make it, little time was to be lost.

This letter, with its proposed extension of the War into a remote and peculiarly inaccessible theatre of operations, and its claim that Arab sovereignty be recognized outside the Peninsula in areas which, in the event of even complete victory over the Turks, were unlikely to be at the free discretion of the British Government, caused much searching of hearts. On the one hand, stood the obligation created by our own earlier overture to Husein himself, as well as our fear of an extension of the *jihad*, recently revived by certain effects of the ill-success of our arms in the Eastern theatres, and also a new doubt for the safety of the Red Sea route. On the other hand had to be weighed the undefined but lately reasserted French interests in Syria, and also the declarations and intentions of the Government of India in regard to Mesopotamia. A temporizing reply served only to draw from Husein an emphatic reiteration of the Arab territorial claim, which, as he held, we were unsympathetically ignoring. But, by the time this second letter came to hand, arguments in favour of encouraging him to revolt had been reinforced by information that, if we did not grip the Arab Nationalists, and especially the Arab party among Ottoman officers, the German advisers of Turkey would do so.

(*c*) *The British Reply, November 1915.* Since, however,

conversations with the French Foreign Office about the prospective status of Syria, in the event of an Allied victory, were already contemplated, any encouragement of Husein had to be tempered with reservations. Our reply reached Mecca early in November. It conveyed the most definite commitment into which, up to that date, Great Britain had entered with Arabs. While it explicitly ruled out of the negotiations all the Turkish-speaking districts which Husein had claimed as Arab, and all Arab societies with whose Chiefs we already had treaties—while, further, it reserved to French discretion any assurance about the independence of the Syrian littoral, or the freedom from tutelage of the interior, i. e. the districts of the four towns, Damascus, Homs, Hamah, and Aleppo—while, by reserving other Arab regions in which France might prefer peculiar interests, it left the Mosul district and even, perhaps, Palestine, in doubt—while, finally, it stated expressly that no guarantee for the unconditional delivery of either Lower or Upper Iraq to the Arabs could be given by us ;—in spite of all these reservations and exceptions it recognized an Arab title to almost all the vast territories which Husein had claimed, including Mesopotamia, and therein promised our support to Arab independence, subject only to limiting but not annulling conditions. This our recognition and support was to depend, of course, on abstention by the Arabs from helping the enemy's side and on their positive co-operation with ours. An offer, which the Emir had made, of exclusive commercial advantages to Great Britain, was ignored in favour of a stipulation that the future European advisers of the Arab independent states should be only British. This last condition also was allowed eventually to lapse *sub silentio*.

Husein lost no time in nailing to the counter our acknowledgment of a prospective Arab title to Iraq. On behalf of the Arab Nation he agreed to an indeterminate British occupation of so much as was in our hands at that moment—i. e. part of Lower Iraq only—but against a compensatory payment, whose amount and term should be settled later. He agreed to nothing about Upper Iraq, and to none of our reservations about Syria or Palestine ; and during the interval which had still to elapse before the Revolt, he would never budge from his original position, but on the contrary took every occasion to insist on the integrity of the Arab national claim to those lands, conceding only Cilicia to our insistence that it was Turkish. Beirut in particular, he protested, the Arabs would never dismiss from their case. We, for our part, neither modified our reserves, nor gave them greater precision. At the end of the year Husein, convinced at last that territorial questions were insoluble at that stage of the war, wrote to put them aside against the hour of an Allied victory, asking only for a pledge that Arab belligerents should not be deserted by the Allies in the conclusion of peace, and for financial and other help towards his preparations for action. These requests were agreed to ; and, with a last warning that in peace Great Britain would regard her obligations to France with the same eyes as in war, Husein was left to pick his day for revolt.

4. *Effect of Husein's move on French policy ; Russian attitude, 1916–17.* The importance of this negotiation was not limited by its definite commitment of Great Britain to co operate in an Arab rising. Questions of Arab title, however imperfectly they might have been determined, were bound, by the mere fact of being raised, to affect others than the Arabs and the Turks. In fact they did affect two governments, which had taken no direct part in the negotiation, the Government of India and the Government of France. That the policy of the first in its Mesopotamian sphere was compromised irretrievably by the Imperial Government's admission of Lower and Upper Iraq into negotiations with a professed spokesman of an Arab Nation, was sufficiently obvious. It did not fail to evoke a protest from Simla. As for the French Government, a new Arab factor was introduced into the conversations with Great Britain about Syria, which had already been long contemplated and actually began in November 1915. Though the possibility of a successful Arab rising under Husein was minimized in those conversations, and the probability of any rising in Hejaz taking effect upon Syria was ignored, an Arab claim to some measure of independence in Syria could not but be envisaged. In the event, while the conversations began and ended with an assumption that the French had an indefeasible right to exclusive paramountcy in all Syria north of Palestine, and resulted in recognition of a similar paramountcy for British influence south of the French limit, an Arab right to independence under varying degrees of tutelage, whether by one Power or by all the Powers, within those zones, as without

them, was conceded explicitly or implicitly by both parties. In the Agreement, in which the conversations issued after their conduct had been delegated to Sir Mark Sykes and M. Georges Picot on the 16th May 1916, the Russian Government having become a party, the three governments engaged mutually to support and recognize an Arab National State in the interior of Syria with probable centre at Damascus, whenever established by the Arabs themselves.[1] This Agreement was signed in May 1916, when the actual outbreak of an Arab rising was still uncertain and seemed remote.[1] In the following year Russia ceased to be party to it and published its terms. Husein and the Arabs generally would hear of it for the first time in December 1917, and then not unnaturally protest that, since they had not been privy before belligerence to an Agreement determining the political status of a section of their nationals, they could not be expected to subscribe to it after bearing a part in their own liberation.

5. *Husein's Revolt, May 1916.* The situation as between the Allies and the Arabs remained static far into 1916. On the one side great difficulties were encountered in our effort to supply Husein with the means of warfare ; when spring was far advanced, nothing like adequate munitions had been introduced into Hejaz. On the other side, Husein continued to presume (though without warrant of any kind) that, previous to action on his part, the Allies proposed to land in Syria. He declined to forecast any precise date for his own rising, and, as we had reason to know, had received from his son, Feisal, discouraging reports (well enough founded) of our progress in the Eastern theatres of the War. The only steps taken by him during this period, which signified a will to action, consisted in some preparation of the Bedouin tribes owing allegiance to his Emirate, and of the minds of the Meccan townsfolk ; and in tentative, and ultimately abortive, overtures to Idrisi and to the Imam Yahya of Yemen. In March he asked unexpectedly that our blockade of the Hejaz coast be more rigidly enforced, in order that his people might be persuaded more quickly of the price they were paying for sufferance of the Turk. But by May 1916 it had become very doubtful whether he would be

[1] For fuller treatment *v.* above, Chap. I, Part I, §§ 6–8, cp. R. S. Baker, I, 75, who says the French did not know the terms of the Husein Agreement till March 1919.

able or willing to take the field within any interval during which his active co-operation would serve the purposes of our warfare.

With surprise, therefore, Cairo received, late in May, from a patrol-ship in the Red Sea, a telegraphic message to say that Husein's hour was at hand, and his son, Abdullah, must meet British representatives at once. These, hastening in a cruiser to a desert shore south of Jiddah, found not Abdullah but his youngest brother, Zeid, and learned that not only had the elder son already gone to collect the tribes, but the two other brothers, Ali and Feisal, were closing on Medina. The raising of South Hejaz was timed for the third day. The die was cast and the British officers were to be consulted only about the future, about immediate reinforcement of Husein with funds, supplies, and munitions of war—to procure which, inclusive of batteries with Moslem crews, he was assured that no pains should be spared—and about Allied co-operation in Syria, of which no immediate prospect could be held out. The motive of Husein's sudden resolve was said to be news of large reinforcements in Medina. Later, more was learned about these. The Ottoman Command, advised by its Allies to turn to better account the strong position gained a year previously by Ali Said Pasha over against Aden, had enrolled a picked expeditionary force, which was to march south through Hejaz to Yemen. With it started a party of Germans, expert in wireless telegraphy and propagandist work, who might extend operations to East Africa. Jemal Pasha, however, by forbidding these Christians to approach the Holy Cities, obliged them to detrain at el-Ala and go down to the coast. There, unable to proceed by sea, they tried to pass south by land, but got no farther than Yambo. Now, as detachments of the expeditionary force appeared one after another in Medina, Ali and Feisal warned their father that the garrisons in South Hejaz might shortly be so strengthened as to preclude all successful revolt; and on this advice Husein took his action.

(*a*) *First stage, May to September 1916.* The course of the Hejaz Revolt is not our concern here. It is hardly necessary to insist that, although Husein, in seeking a personal as well as a national interest, chose his own time, used at the first only his own personnel, and repudiated our control, he was instigated and encouraged by us to rebel in our interest. And he maintained his rebellion even when disappointed of the Allied co-operation, which he had looked for in the northern Arab lands. It is less notorious, but not less true, that he and his sons were constantly exhorted by us to promote the expansion of their local revolt into a pan-Arab rising. As time went on, their forces were more and more equipped, directed, and guided by us towards a goal outside Hejaz, till in the end Feisal came to command what was a flying right wing of Allenby's invading army in Palestine and Syria. To the first phase of the Revolt, which ended with the fall of Taif, and the Pilgrimage of September 1916, it is true that we rendered little direct assistance, beyond supplying funds, stores, and munitions: but, nevertheless, it should not be forgotten that our naval guns and planes co-operated with the Sherifian forces at Jiddah, two Egyptian batteries from the Sudan helped to reduce both Mecca and Taif, and our ships not only enabled Husein to occupy Lith and Yambo, but also assured his main base at Rabegh, where British and French officers acted on shore as agents for supplies. Moreover, through the British representative at Jiddah, projects for operations on the confines of Syria and for inciting Arabs outside Hejaz to join the Movement were propounded without any intimation being given to Husein that he should confine his own aims and activities to his Emirate.

(*b*) *Second stage, September 1916 to January 1917.* In the second phase of the Revolt, which ended with the occupation of Wejh in January 1917, less was said to Husein about Syrians or other Arabs outside Hejaz for a threefold reason. First, because temporary danger of local collapse had discouraged in both parties thoughts or plans of wider movements: second, because Husein's own conception of his future relation to the Arab lands grew embarrassingly imperial (on this account the Allies refused to recognize in November 1916, his self-conferred title of King of the Arabs, and restricted him to the Kingship of Hejaz): third, because as our own advance towards Palestine progressed that autumn after the battle of Romani, we ceased to contemplate a Syrian rising as essential to our success. On the other hand, our direct control of and participation in the Sherifian operations, and our direction of them northwards became more patent during this phase. Aeroplanes with British pilots, for which Husein asked at the beginning of August 1916, were flying inland from Rabegh in December. In response to requests from Feisal early in September, and subsequently from his father, a British brigade was all but embarked for Rabegh: a project for a British occupation of Akaba was long and seriously contemplated: and direct liaison with Feisal through Colonel T. E. Lawrence resulted in the northern Arab army being supplied for a northward advance which originally had been suggested by ourselves. We ensured its success by naval operations at Wejh: and, once Feisal was established there, we steadily increased our contribution of British, French, and Egyptian personnel, and watched complacently his negotiations for eventual extension of the Revolt to the Syrian borders.

(*c*) *1917.* In the two following phases, which saw the Sherifian head-quarters moved ever northwards from Wejh to Akaba (August 1917) and from Akaba to the neighbourhood of Maan, where they remained till the summer of 1918, the control of the Revolt fell more and more into our hands. British and French officers were advising all the Sherifian leaders; they accompanied and directed the raids upon the railway; they fought in cars and aeroplanes; and it was on British advice that Akaba was seized as a base from which touch with our Palestine army might be established. There a large camp was formed practically under British control; thence went inland detachments of British, British-Indian, and French-Algerian troops to fill gaps in Feisal's effectives, officers to serve on his staff, and British camel-corps to render the railway south of Maan once for all useless to the Turks. There too, with our full knowledge, active measures were taken, from October onwards, to bring Syrian tribes into the field. The area of Sherifian operations was extended into Trans-Jordan; the help of Sherifian tribes was requested for Allenby's movements across the river; and plans were concerted between his staff and Feisal's for co-operation in a decisive thrust towards Damascus. That these plans were acted upon in the fifth and final phase of the Revolt is known to every one from the dispatches of our own Commander-in-Chief. Feisal's force was deputed to deal with one enemy army, while Allenby dealt with the rest, the Arab operations up to the Arab occupation of Damascus on the last day of September being carried out step for step in accord with a general plan, formed and rendered feasible by ourselves.

(*d*) *1918.* It was not, however, only the commanders of Allied military and naval forces who committed us to an identification of the Sherifian cause with Arab Nationalism in general. Although the Allied Governments maintained silence till 1918 about the Tripartite Agreement of 1916, and habitually ignored in their communications with Husein his pretension to a determining interest in the future status of more than Hejaz, their diplomatic representatives admitted the subject of Syria into more than one conversation with him, and gave to him as spokesman of his Nation certain provisional undertakings about its future and that also of Mesopotamia. Moreover, before Feisal's forces had penetrated beyond the Bekaa, we communicated to certain representative Syrians in Cairo an assurance that, subject to unspecified interests of France, Great Britain would recognize Arab sovereignty in all places liberated by Arab (i.e. Sherifian) arms during the War. These last words were interpreted by the Arabs to convey a prospective as well as a retrospective pledge; and in virtue of them Feisal would claim in the event both Damascus and Beirut, and take hardly the refusal which we could and did base on the clause conditioning our promise as a whole.

6. *British commitments to Husein and Feisal.* In general terms, the import of this condition was known by this time to both Feisal and his father: for the Turks had taken care to pass on what they had learned in the previous autumn from the Russian revelation of the Agreement of 1916. The Arab leaders were aware also of the other limitation of ultimate freedom of action in Syria, to which Great Britain and her Allies had committed themselves by the Balfour Declaration of the 2nd November 1917, although it cannot be said that Husein understood its precise import.[1] The subject of Palestine was not raised specifically with or by him until he was already aware of both the Secret Agreement and the Balfour Declaration—that is, not before the end of 1917. Palestine had been claimed implicitly for the Arab Nation by his original manifestos in the autumn of 1915; and when in our final reply we had reserved districts west of Damascus in particular and also others in general, in which the French might prefer special interests, he may, or may not, have thought that Palestine was in our mind—if indeed it was so. Certainly he never withdrew his claim. But equally certainly he had foreseen throughout that his Christian Allies would stipulate for some exceptional treatment of that part of the Arab area; and when the Balfour Declaration was communicated to him officially, in January 1918, he took it philosophically, contenting himself with an expression of goodwill towards a kindred Semitic race, which he understood (as his phrase made clear) was to lodge in a house owned by Arabs.

[1] That Palestine should be 'a national home for the Jews'; *v. infra* pp. 137–38.

7. *Position at the Armistice, 30th October 1918.* When the Allied warfare ceased everywhere in the Arab area—not till three months after the general Armistice so far as Hejaz and Yemen were concerned—the position was this. The Turks had been evacuated from all districts (except Yemen, where some soldiers and civilians had transferred their allegiance, temporarily or permanently, to the Arab ruler). Of the princes who had ever admitted any sort of vassalage to the Porte, all were enjoying independence *de facto* and assured sovereignty. Three of the four, who had co-operated really or nominally in our war, namely Idrisi, the Sheikh of Koweit, and Ibn Saud, were severally in treaty relations with us, though all were not in accord with all. The last named, whose original pact with Great Britain had been expanded into an offensive and defensive alliance, was augmented in status by our recognition of a new title, Sultan, which we supported, under certain conditions, with a subsidy. Idrisi, who had yielded all north of Hali Point, with a bad grace, to King Husein, was compensating himself with expansion into the Yemen Tihamah. The fourth prince, Husein himself, was bound to us by no express Treaty; but he had entered into possession of the independent Emirate, which we had undertaken to recognize and to guarantee, up to boundaries beyond any within which his predecessors for many generations had exercised effective control. If, by the strict letter of International Law, all these sovereignties had to await confirmation by the Treaty of Peace, their validity in the future, as in the present, was not doubtful. Not so assured, however, was the status of the Asiatic Arabs outside the Peninsula. Their territories (except the perennially independent deserts) were being held in suspense under alien, if benevolent, military occupation. No Arab sovereignty was recognized yet in any part of the extra-peninsular Arab area; but provisionally, native civil administration was being suffered in inland Syria and Trans-Jordania. That this status of a part was no more than an instalment of what had been provided for all the Arab lands by the Secret Agreement of 1916 seemed to Arabs to lessen its worth as a recognition of their own share in the work of liberation. If so much was to have been done in the dry tree, what should be done in the green? To ask in effect this question Feisal went to Paris.[1]

[1] *v. infra* pp. 136–37 *sqq.*; and R. S. Baker, *op. cit.* I, 75–6.

CHAPTER I

THE NEAR AND MIDDLE EAST

PART III

EMERGENCE OF ARAB NATIONALISM

B. SYRIA AND PALESTINE

1. *Syria since the Armistice of Mudros, 30th October 1918*

1. *Boundaries of Syria.* Syria, like Macedonia or Albania, was before the War a term of loose application. It usually included Palestine and some territory east of Jordan. But since the War, more particularly since the Paris Peace Conference, the name Syria has acquired a more exact political meaning. Palestine, with Trans-Jordan or the territory east of Jordan, has become a mandated dependency of the British Empire, with a definite northern frontier. The western frontier of Iraq—another mandated British dependency—is also definite. So, too, is the southern frontier of Turkey. Syria at the present time, therefore, is the portion of Asiatic Turkey which has been placed under mandate to France, and is bordered by the Mediterranean, by Palestine, by Trans-Jordan, by Iraq, and by the new Turkey.

Such are the boundaries of modern political Syria. But in the present Chapter we shall, when necessary, refer to events and movements in the wider geographical and historical Syria covered by the name before the War.

2. *Agreements affecting Syria.* The history of Syria since the Armistice of Mudros (30th October 1918) is mainly a story of disappointed aspirations—of nationalist and racial ambitions circumscribed and repressed, though not entirely thwarted, by a secret agreement concluded between three of the Entente Powers as an unavoidable exigency of the War.

The provisions of this undertaking (the so-called Sykes-Picot Agreement of the 16th May 1916) [1] were adopted by the

[1] *v.* Chap. I, Part I, A, § 6, 7; pp. 13–19; for negotiations with the Sherif, *v.* Part III, A, § 3, pp. 123–27, 132.

Paris Peace Conference as forming a predetermined basis for the settlement of the regions to which the undertaking applied.

But Syrian history of the period has also been influenced by two other undertakings, or pacts. The first is that comprised in the somewhat loose series of promises given by Great Britain to the Sherif of Mecca in 1915. By itself it would have been entirely favourable to the realization of Syrian and Arab aspirations; but in combination with the subsequent Sykes-Picot Agreement the Arab prospects created by British promises were, to say the least, greatly confused and diminished. The other undertaking is the much better known Balfour Declaration of the 2nd November 1917, whereby the British Government declared their policy of creating in Palestine a National Home for the Jews. In spirit, if not in form, this Declaration recorded an understanding between the Entente Powers and world Jewry, and was an acknowledgment of support given or to be given by Jewry to the Allied cause. These various agreements and understandings broadly represent the degree in which Syria and the remainder of the Arab regions were inextricably involved in vital Allied interests—interests, let it be said, whose origins and existence date from a time far earlier than the outbreak of the War. Each agreement was a war-measure, called into being not merely, nor even chiefly, for the protection of the interests of individual Allies, but still more for the general purpose of securing Allied victory. Each has been dealt with elsewhere.[1] Suffice to say that but for them, but, indeed, for the Sykes-Picot Agreement alone, the whole course of recent Syrian history would have been entirely different.

3. *French and British policy in Syria.* The history of Syria during the period assigned to this Chapter begins with the Armistice of Mudros, when the whole country was in effective occupation of a British Army which had swept it free of Turco-German forces in one great campaign. Even the success of this campaign, a success of momentous advantage to the Allied cause, contributed to Allied difficulties in the ultimate settlement of Syrian questions. The same French sentiments, susceptibilities, and ambitions, which the Sykes-Picot Agreement had been designed to soothe or to satisfy, were grievously wounded by the fact that the conquest of

[1] *v.* pp. 13–18.

Syria was made by British arms. A French detachment, flattered by the courtesy title of a division, and a yet smaller Italian detachment, had displayed their respective flags under Lord Allenby's command. But nothing, certainly not the pretentious telegrams which appeared at the time in the French press, that the French 'Division' had taken Beirut, could dilute the plain truth that in the brilliant conquest of Syria France had taken an insignificant part. From the inhabitants of Syria, least of all, could this fact, so injurious to French prestige, be hidden.

French public opinion deluded itself with the fond notion that the majority of the inhabitants of Syria regarded France with love, and longed for French protection. The truth was that, apart from a number of wealthy Syrian families whose cultural home was Paris, the greater proportion of the mixed population of Syria distrusted and disliked both France and the French. They might be divided, as indeed they were, in the form of their political aspirations. For some favoured complete Syrian independence, some independence as part of an Arab Confederation, and many others pinned their hopes on a period of benevolent protection by Great Britain. And even among those who rejected foreign control, the majority, at least, turned towards Great Britain for sympathetic support and protection rather than towards France, for reasons that it is needless to analyse, or to emphasize. Suffice to attribute this preference to the personal knowledge of the Syrian people that a great and victorious British army had just passed through their country as deliverers, and to the successful Arab movement in the Hejaz for independence which had been fostered by British promises to the Sherif of Mecca (now King Husein of the Hejaz), and made possible by generous British support in gold, arms, munitions, and food extended to their Arab Allies.

4. *Relations with the Sherif of Mecca.* The manner in which this Arab movement was brought into close relationship with the movement for Syrian independence calls for a few words at this point.

In moving their troops northward to the head of the Gulf of Akaba, in July 1917, and thence towards Syria, King Husein of the Hejaz and his son, the Emir Feisal, were actuated by a clear and definite policy. Their ultimate aim was the creation of an Arab Empire extending from the Red Sea to Persia and from the Yemen to the Mediterranean. But this grandiose scheme, as they knew well, could not be realized, if at all, for many years. It must, at best, be preceded by an intermediate stage, which, they believed, might be within their power to attain at the conclusion of the War. Their immediate aim, therefore, was to secure the establishment of independent Arab States covering the Arab regions which had been, or still were, under Turkish rule, and to unite these states in a Confederacy under King Husein as Suzerain, or perhaps as Sultan.

The Hejaz was already an independent sovereign state. Great Britain was pledged by her undertakings to the Sherif of Mecca to 'recognize and support' Arab independence within certain areas which included the greater part of Syria. British operations against Palestine and Syria, therefore, indicated plainly what the next step in the Arab scheme should be. From Akaba, onwards, the Arab army under the Emir Feisal was to cover the right flank of the British advance towards Syria. The Arab leaders sought at this stage to found in Syria another independent state, to be ruled by the Emir Feisal, a state that should include Damascus as capital and be, by population, wealth, and influence, the key State of the future Arab Confederation. With Feisal and his troops actually in Syria the Sherifian leaders hoped to realize this vital part of their ambitions. They knew of French designs on Syria, of French hostility towards this aspect of Arab nationalism, and they may have suspected the existence of the Sykes-Picot Agreement. But they hoped, at the conclusion of the War, to present France with the accomplished fact of a Syrian Arab State sufficiently consolidated and strong to render the execution of French designs difficult and unprofitable, if not altogether impracticable.

The terms of the Sykes-Picot Agreement were revealed to the King of the Hejaz by the Turkish enemy as the result of Bolshevik disclosures at the end of 1917. The Arab leaders were startled by the revelation; but their belief in the good faith of Great Britain wast strong, and the discovery did not affect their loyal co-operation with their British Ally. They became the more anxious, however, to obtain an actual footing in Syria, where they still hoped to defeat French aims and prevent execution of the terms of the Agreement. They hoped, too, that Great Britain and France would fall out, and that, at worst, the Agreement would be revised.[1]

5. *Opinion in Syria.* But in Syria itself the execution of the Arab scheme was faced by difficulties. Various committees for securing Syrian independence existed and the aims of these did not altogether coincide with the aims of the Sherifians. Many Syrian leaders, in fact, were opposed to the idea of Arab domination. Educated Syrians regarded Arabs of the Hejaz as uncivilized tribesmen compared with themselves, and Sherifian rule as a danger to be resisted, even though the Emir Feisal himself was well known in Syria, where, before the War, he had many friends.

Among the Syrian population of Christians and Moslems the Christian element was almost negligible in political influence. The Moslems comprised two broad classes—the *intelligentsia*, and the remainder. The *intelligentsia* were lax in the profession and practise of their Faith, cosmopolitan in their interests, and filled with western political theories. As they controlled the press and were the writers in it, their views, as far as caution permitted, found general expression. From this class chiefly were drawn those who, by means of various committees, agitated for Syrian independence. But though active in political agitation and intrigue they displayed little readiness to incur danger or sacrifice in support of their views. They were most active in the safety of Cairo, Paris, Rome, and New York. They were industrious and vehement in prompting; but they looked to others to free them from the Turk—to England, to France, and, upon Syrian terms, to the Sherifian Arabs.

The remainder of the Syrian population were Arabic-speaking Moslems, ignorant, no doubt, but a people to whom their Faith meant something. They had decided leanings towards Pan-Arabism, some, even, towards Pan-Islamism. It was upon obtaining the support of this class, the largest element in the population, that the Sherifian leaders mainly depended for success.

6. *Feisal in Damascus, October 1918.* In this situation the Emir Feisal played his cards well. Before the British and Arab advance reached Damascus he had obtained the secret support of various Syrian committees. And his official entry into

[1] *v.* also Part III, A, §§ 5–6, pp. 28–32; and also pp. 131–33.

the ancient Syrian capital, on the 3rd October 1918, was exceedingly well calculated to impress the population and rally it to his side. After severe fighting, which had ceased outside Damascus only two days earlier, he entered at a gallop, at the head of 1,500 Arab cavalry shouting and firing as they went—he entered, in fact, as previous Arab Emirs of history had done, only that he came as a deliverer, at the head of Arab troops. After this dramatic introduction, and having first obtained Lord Allenby's sanction, he had the Arab flag hoisted over the city: his next important step was to nominate one of his Syrian Arab supporters, Ali Pasha Riza el Rikabi, as Military Governor. These two highly significant acts were thus officially explained in the House of Commons on the 31st October. Lord Robert Cecil:

> 'General Allenby was authorized on 1st October to allow the Arab flag to be hoisted at Damascus, and this has presumably been done. In accordance with the laws and usages of war the occupied enemy territory is under military administration. The Military Governor of Damascus, Ali Pasha Riza el Rikabi, is responsible to Lord Allenby.'

On the 7th October the Emir Feisal issued a proclamation to the Syrian people in which he announced, in the name of his father, King Husein, that an independent government, for the whole of Syria, had been formed at Damascus. The proclamation also stated that Ali Pasha Riza el Rikabi had been appointed Arab Commander-in-Chief; that the Syrian people must prove by their acts that they were worthy of independence; and that the new Government had its foundation equally in all Arabic-speaking peoples, whatever their race or faith.

Installed thus at Damascus under the Arab flag, and with a provisional Government professing to represent an independent Syria, the Emir Feisal ingratiated himself with the people, Christian as well as Moslem, and diminished opposition to his rule by adopting Syrians as his advisers and appointing them to places in the administration he was forming. He even obtained suitable Syrians from outside the boundaries of Syria. Educated Syrians found him, too, a figure and personality that disarmed their general prejudice against an Arab Prince from the less civilized interior becoming their ruler. His aim was to revive the ancient Emirate of Damascus; and in pursuit of this purpose, satisfactory to Syrian Moslems and harmonizing well enough with King Husein's project of a Confederation of Arab States, the Syrian and Sherifian movements for independence virtually joined forces. So far the Sherifian scheme for Syria had gone well.

With the Emir established thus the British and French Governments concluded a convention on the 20th October, regulating the administration of the country during the British military occupation. Broadly, it provided for French administration being set up in certain areas, but under the control of Lord Allenby.

At this stage active hostilities between the Allies and Turks were ended by the Armistice of Mudros (30th October 1918). It found British troops in occupation of Syria and Palestine; and the Emir Feisal endeavouring to strengthen and consolidate his position, but anxious to avoid giving unnecessary cause of offence to the French; for with initial success had come a more accurate perception of the difficulties before him. He and his father still hoped, however, to prevent the French obtaining a definite footing in Syria.

7. *The Franco-British Declaration, 7th November 1918.* Syrian history now becomes for a time the story of a triangular struggle of conflicting interests. The story of the Emir Feisal's efforts to realize his ambitions; of French hostility to the Sherifian movement in Syria, and, later, to the Emir himself; and of British endeavours to honour the undertakings given to the Arabs and the French. The struggle was carried on not only in Syria, but at the Peace Conference as well, when that assembly began to take up Eastern problems. Bearing upon the struggle may be noted a dawning British recognition of the fact that, under the Sykes-Picot Agreement, the conquest of Palestine and Syria had been little more than a vicarious sacrifice by Great Britain. Complete execution of the Agreement was impracticable owing to the course of events, and some other arrangement was required. And the more so that the French showed every sign of exacting to the letter the rights conferred upon them by the agreement.

On the 7th November 1918, an important Joint Declaration by Great Britain and France, regarding British and French war aims in the East was issued to the press. Its vital passages are:

'The object aimed at by France and Great Britain in prosecuting in the East the war let loose by German ambition is the complete and definite emancipation of the peoples so long oppressed by the Turks, and the establishment of National Governments and administrations deriving their authority from the initiative and free choice of the indigenous populations.

'In order to carry out these intentions France and Great Britain are at one in encouraging and assisting the establishment of indigenous Governments and administrations in Syria and Mesopotamia, now liberated by the Allies, and in territories the liberation of which they are engaged in securing, and in recognizing these as soon as they are actually established. Far from wishing to impose on the populations of these regions any particular institutions, they are only concerned to ensure by their support and by adequate assistance the regular working of Governments and administrations freely chosen by the populations themselves. . . . Such is the policy which the two Allied Governments uphold in the liberated territories.'

This Declaration had a great influence upon Eastern opinion, not only in Syria, but in Arabia, Egypt, Mesopotamia, and Palestine. Among Syrians and Arabs it was regarded, rightly or wrongly, as superseding or at least qualifying, the provisions of the Sykes-Picot Agreement. It is evident that nothing in the verbal form of the Declaration was inconsistent with a strict adherence by the Allies to the terms of that Agreement. But the spirit, apparently, was quite different. The promise that the native populations should exercise the right of self-determination regarding the form of National Government under which they should live was thought conclusive. Indeed, it convinced the people that they were to have a free choice in wider questions than, perhaps, the Declaration ever intended, and fanned the spirit of nationalism in the Arab countries. After the armistice on the Western front Syrian expectation turned towards the approaching Peace Conference. In the meantime the British Government were taking steps to obtain a revision of the Sykes-Picot Agreement.

During December 1918, M. Clemenceau came to London and endeavoured to persuade Mr. Lloyd George to recognize the Agreement anew. Mr. Lloyd George is credited with having replied that as to Cilicia and Syria he saw no difficulty, but that he desired the Agreement amended with regard to the Mosul Vilayet and Palestine. He asked that Mosul should be included in the British sphere of influence. He also asked for Palestine—the Balfour Declaration, it may be noted, was issued by the British Government on the 2nd November 1917.

After his return to Paris M. Clemenceau consented to the surrender of the Mosul Vilayet. He admitted, too, that the French Government wished to escape the expense of administering Palestine, though they would have preferred to see that area under international control.[1]

On the 30th January 1919, the question of still further revising the Sykes-Picot Agreement seems to have been discussed at an interview in Paris between Mr. Lloyd George and Sir M. Hankey, and M. Clemenceau and M. Pichon. At this meeting, and subsequently—so the French allege—Mr. Lloyd George put forward proposals for further great reductions of the area to be assigned to France. The French Government, however, regarded these proposals as absolutely inacceptable, and quite incapable of being defended in the French Chamber.

8. *Feisal in Europe.* British advice to the Emir Feisal to come to terms with the French had not been wanting so far. But in furtherance of their desire to bring about a settlement acceptable alike to the Arabs and French, the British Government now invited the Emir to visit London as their guest, for further consultation before the Peace Conference should assemble. He came, in fact, as the representative of his father, the King of the Hejaz. A British cruiser brought him to Marseilles, where he landed on the 26th November, and he then proceeded to Paris as the guest of France. He called on President Poincaré on the 6th December, and subsequently was shown over the French front, and treated with the honour due to the representative of an ally of France.

Emir Feisal arrived in England on the 10th December 1918, and two days later was received and decorated by the King with the Chain of the Royal Victorian Order. His stay in England was marked by a display of great cordiality and goodwill which left him in no doubt of the sincere desire of the Government, as well as of the whole country, to do what was possible in furtherance of legitimate Arab and Syrian aspirations. At the same time it was made clear to him that Great Britain had no intention of falling out with France on Syrian questions, and he was advised to accept French control in Syria. This advice appears to have convinced him of its sincerity, though not of its soundness; at least it corrected his views as to the realities of the Syrian situation. He was,

[1] *v.* also Part III, C, § 4. pp. 181–82.

however, tied by the instructions of King Husein and by the large and growing expectations of Syrian opinion, which became more and more opposed to any division of the country. It remained for him now to lay the Arab claims before the Peace Conference and await its decision.

Meanwhile the Emir's visit to Paris and London had inevitably given fresh impulse in France to discussion on the future of Syria, and to reiterated assertion of the inalienable rights of France in that country. At this time the Central Syrian Committee of Independence, a body hostile to the Sherifian movement, and formed to subserve French aims, addressed a letter to M. Clemenceau drawing his attention to the necessity of maintaining Syrian unity. In his reply, written while the Emir Feisal was still in Paris, the French President of the Council did not commit himself to more than reassuring generalities, behind which appeared, however, the resolve of the French Government to maintain the rights acquired under the Sykes-Picot Agreement. He stated that the French Government were determined to ensure that Syria should work out her own evolution to a peaceful civilization; and that, at the approaching Peace Conference, they would defend the interests of the Syrian nation to the utmost in discussion with the Allies.

9. *French policy declared, 29th December 1918.* Speaking in the French Chamber on the 29th December, M. Pichon put the views of the Government more plainly. French rights in Syria, the Lebanon and Cilicia, he said, were based upon historic tradition, upon agreements and contracts, and upon the aspirations of the inhabitants. Referring to the Franco-British agreements affecting these regions he declared that France admitted the complete freedom of the Peace Conference, and its right to give the agreements their proper conclusion; but that these agreements were binding both upon England and France, and that, as between Great Britain and France, the rights recognized in them had already been acquired.

In shaping their Syrian policy at this time the French Government could not ignore the strong hold which the Emir Feisal and the Sherifian movement had already secured among the Syrian population. In a sense the Emir was in possession in Syria, and was supported in his claims by a majority of the people. It became, therefore, the aim of French policy to use the Emir, if possible, as the means of securing peaceful Syrian acquiescence in the control of the country by France.

10. *Feisal and the Arab Delegation at Paris, 1919.* The Emir returned to Paris from England on the 7th January 1919, in order to attend the Peace Conference which was to assemble on the 18th January. On the 4th February a French army order announced that he had received the Croix de Guerre with Palms, and summarized his exploits as Commander of the Hejaz Army.

As already remarked, the Emir had learned much during his visit to London and Paris. He had at last recognized that, in the relationship existing between Great Britain and France, there was no prospect of Great Britain seeking or accepting the Mandate for Syria. But Arab opposition to France, and to the control of Arab territory by more than one foreign Power, was in no way diminished by this discovery. As an alternative to Great Britain the Sherifian leaders now appear to have turned towards America. Before the Conference met the Emir had, in fact, said privately that he proposed to submit to it a project for a Confederation of Arab States, free of Turkish domination, and placed under the guidance and protection of the United States.

On the 6th February, the Emir, accompanied by Colonel T. E. Lawrence, stated the Arab case to the Conference—to the President of the United States, and the Prime Ministers and other representatives of the Allied and Associated Powers and Japan.

The views of the Arab Delegation were well enough known in advance. They were that the Arab-speaking regions, including Syria, Mesopotamia, Jezireh, Nejd, and the Yemen—the Hejaz was already independent—should be given their individual independence under an Arab suzerain, and the whole placed under a single mandatory. In the course of time it was hoped that the Confederation so established would be able to stand alone. With these as their hopes the Arab Delegation were opposed to the division of Arab territory into spheres of influence assigned to different foreign Powers.

But in placing the Arab case before the Conference the Emir and his advisers do not seem to have thought it politic to be quite so explicit. The Emir, who asked for no extension of his father's territories, confined himself to pleading for the independence of all the Arab countries, and urging that together they formed a racial and economic unit. He does not appear to have referred to the question of what Power or Powers should be given control. It is said that he asked for an international Commission of Inquiry on the subject.

11. *The Franco-British dispute over Syria, February—March 1919.* The Conference took up Syrian and Arab questions again on the 13th February by hearing the views of the Central Syrian Committee, and of Dr. Howard Bliss—himself born in Syria—well known as President of the American College at Beirut. The Syrian Committee represented the French interest, and the views they expressed were strongly hostile to the aims of the Emir Feisal and the Sherifians as far as these aims affected Syria. Dr. Bliss, on the other hand, supported the proposal for investigation by an International Commission.

Meanwhile a struggle was going on within the Conference itself upon Syrian and Arab matters, a struggle between Great Britain and France represented by Mr. Lloyd George and M. Clemenceau. Mr. Lloyd George held that subsequent developments had rendered the Sykes–Picot Agreement of 1916 impracticable and largely inoperative, and that radical revision was necessary. As we have seen, he had already secured M. Clemenceau's consent to important modifications as to the Mosul region and Palestine. But these changes had left Syrian questions untouched, and it was in Syria that the present difficulties had arisen regarding Arab independence and the claims of France. In Mr. Lloyd George's view still further modification of the Agreement was needed—a need, he claimed, recognized by the Allies, in the latest expression of their Eastern policy embodied in the Anglo-French Declaration of the 7th November 1918, which had, in effect, already abandoned the instrument of 1916. M. Clemenceau, however, stood out stiffly for the complete and unchanged validity of the Agreement as between Great Britain and France.

In following the decisions of the Conference it has now become possible to refer to the secret minutes [1] of a meeting of the Supreme Council, held in Paris on the 20th March 1919.

M. Pichon began by outlining the Sykes–Picot Agreement,

[1] Given in *Woodrow Wilson and World Settlement*, Vol. III, pp. 1–19, by R. S. Baker. Heinemann, 1922.

the French view of the situation created by it, and the subsequent negotiations between the Governments of Great Britain and France for amendment of the Agreement. He stated that what France asked for now was (1) that the whole Syrian region should be treated as a unit, and (2) that, as the mandatory system had been adopted since the Agreement was signed, France should become the mandatory of the League of Nations in this region.

In reply Mr. Lloyd George stated that if the Conference asked Great Britain to take the mandate for Syria, Great Britain would refuse. The British Government had definitely so decided because otherwise it would be said in France that they had created disturbances in Syria in order to keep the French out. The question of the extent to which Great Britain and France were concerned in these regions had been cleared up during the interview at which he had asked M. Clemenceau for Mosul and the adjacent territory and Palestine.[1] There was no question between Great Britain and France regarding Syria.

Mr. Lloyd George then recalled that the whole burden of the Syrian campaign had fallen upon Great Britain. The British Empire, including India, had maintained in the Near East 900,000 to 1,000,000 men. Their casualties had exceeded 125,000. The cost of the campaign to the British people had run to many hundred millions of pounds. The French troops taking part in the war in Syria had been so few as to make no difference. Sometimes they had been useful, but not on all occasions. During 1917 and onwards the heaviest casualties in France were those incurred by the British. He referred to this fact in order to show that the reason Great Britain had made such efforts in Palestine was not because she had not borne her part in France.

Passing to the territorial aspect of present French claims in Syria Mr. Lloyd George pointed out that M. Pichon had omitted one important fact in the statement just made. He had not explained that the coastal zone of Syria, assigned to France by the Sykes–Picot Agreement as an area in which France might establish direct or indirect administration as she thought fit, did not include the cities of Damascus, Homs, Hama, and Aleppo. Those cities lay within the zone of French influence

[1] See pp. 141–2, 181–2.

in which area France, under the Agreement, was 'prepared to recognize and uphold an independent Arab State or Confederation of Arab States . . . under the Suzerainty of an Arab Chief'. Was France, Mr. Lloyd George asked, prepared to accept that ?

This, however, was not a question between Great Britain and France, Mr. Lloyd George continued, but a question between France and an agreement which Great Britain had signed with King Husein of the Hejaz.

M. Pichon here remarked that all he asked was that, if the League of Nations gave a mandate over these territories, France should have that part set aside for her.

Mr. Lloyd George said that could not be done. The League of Nations could not be used for setting aside the British bargain with King Husein. He asked whether M. Pichon intended to occupy Damascus with French troops. If he did it would clearly be a violation of the treaty with the Arabs.

M. Pichon replied that France had no convention with King Husein.

Mr. Lloyd George then quoted extracts from the letter of the 24th October 1914, sent by Sir H. McMahon (at the time British High Commissioner in Egypt) to the Sherif of Mecca. These extracts (reproduced in the minutes of the meeting) showed that the only strictly Syrian area excluded from the territory over which Great Britain undertook to recognize and support Arab independence was the narrow portion of Syria lying west of the districts of Damascus, Homs, Hama, and Aleppo.

Continuing, Mr. Lloyd George said that it was on the basis of this letter that the Sherif of Mecca had put all his resources into the field and helped most materially to win the victory. France had for practical purposes accepted the British undertaking to the Sherif of Mecca in signing the 1916 Agreement. This had not been done by M. Pichon, but by his predecessors. He was bound to say that, if the British Government now agreed that Damascus, Homs, Hama, and Aleppo should be included in the sphere of direct French influence, they would be breaking faith with the Arabs, and that contingency they could not face.

At a later point M. Pichon asked how France could be bound by an agreement the very existence of which was unknown to her when the 1916 Agreement was signed.[1] She had undertaken to uphold ' an independent Arab State, or Confederation of Arab States ', but not the King of the Hejaz.

At this stage President Wilson pointed out that Russia had been one of the parties to the 1916 Agreement, but had now disappeared, and the partnership of interest had therefore been dissolved. However, the only question from the American point of view was as to whether France would be agreeable to the Syrians. It might not be his business; but, if the question was made his business by being brought before the Conference, the only way to deal with it would be to discover the desires of the population of these regions.

12. *Wilson's Commission of Inquiry.* President Wilson, in effect, proposed that a Commission of Inquiry, composed of an equal number of French, British, Italian, and American representatives, should be sent to Syria, Palestine, Mesopotamia, and Armenia. This Commission was to have complete freedom to tell facts as they found them. Finally, the meeting accepted the Commission, and President Wilson, at Mr. Lloyd George's request, undertook to draft its Terms of Reference.

For unity of narrative the history of the Commission had better be completed now. Investigation on the spot by an international body was violently opposed in France and by the Syrian Committee. The French Government, indeed, conscious that the result of such an inquiry would be against their Syrian claims, used every effort to prevent the investigation. By the third week in May the Commission had not yet been constituted. British and American representatives had been nominated, but M. Clemenceau still hesitated. The French Government finally abandoned the project and the British Government felt it impossible, in the circumstances, for them to do otherwise than withdraw also.

President Wilson, however, was resolved to have an inquiry, and at the end of May dispatched an American Commission, of which Mr. H. C. King and Mr. C. R. Crane were the leading members. At the end of July the Commissioners had completed their investigations in Syria and Palestine. Their report—subsequently famous as the King-Crane Report—was sup-

[1] It was subsequently admitted that the French Government of the time had been aware of the terms of the British undertaking to the Sherif of Mecca. *v.* also § 18, p. 62.

pressed, perhaps as being too plain spoken and likely to embarrass both the American Government and the Peace Conference if published. However, the general purport of their findings soon became known, official secrecy notwithstanding. Their survey, the report stated, had established that a large majority of the Syrian population desired absolute and unqualified independence ; that failing such independence America would be preferred as the Mandatory Power, and, failing America, Great Britain ; but that strong opposition to control by France had been revealed. The report showed, further, that general agreement existed in favour of Palestine and Syria being placed under the same mandatory. It may be remarked here, without attempting explanation, that on the points just mentioned the report was probably in close accordance with truth. This American inquiry produced no practical results, for before the return of the Commission to Paris the more important treaties had been signed, and President Wilson had left for home.

13. *Further disputes.* With Syrian matters before the Conference standing in abeyance, the Emir Feisal left France in the middle of April 1919, visited the Pope at Rome, and embarked at Taranto for the East on a French battleship the day following.

Towards the close of the Emir's stay in Paris Mr. Lloyd George had strongly urged him to come to agreement with M. Clemenceau. An interview resulted, at which, it is said, the Emir gave the French President of the Council a verbal promise to the effect that co-operation between the Arabs and French would be possible on the basis of Arab independence being established. Indeed, French and Syrian reports credited him with having actually completed an agreement with M. Clemenceau ; and immediately after his return to Syria his public utterances were regarded in France as being admirably correct.

But his apparent complacency towards France was not long-lived. Differences between Arab and French aims were too wide and deep to be removed by a desire for peaceful settlement on the part of the leaders. When the Emir arrived in Syria from Paris, in April, he found guerilla warfare of a kind already in progress between the Arabs and French in those coastal districts of Syria to which the British had admitted

French troops and French administration under Lord Allenby's control. The Emir could not prevent these disturbances—he would have been equally powerless had his own position been much more secure than it was. About the middle of May he addressed an informal meeting of Syrian Notables, assembled at Damascus, and explained what he had endeavoured to do in Paris, what he had asked of the Peace Conference. He had asked for the complete independence of the whole Arab nation, from Egypt to Persia; but, recognizing geographical facts and the difficulties imposed by lack of ready means of intercommunication, he had also asked that each geographical subdivision of the Arab region should have a separate and independent government. He desired the Notables to say whether or not they approved and would support him. Almost unanimously those present, including chiefs and leaders of the Lebanon, the Hauran, and Trans-Jordan, as well as of the more narrow Syria, expressed their approval and pledged their assistance. The Emir then undertook to convoke a Syrian Assembly.

Feisal recognized now that for him there was a choice of alternatives—either whole-hearted support of the Arab cause against French pretensions, or loss of his position as Arab leader and prospective sovereign of a Syrian Arab State. From this point onwards he seems to have thrown in his lot definitely with the anti-French party, and to have felt that the chief hope of preserving Syria from French control lay in the strength of the armed resistance the Arabs could offer. Out of deference to French susceptibilities the British authorities subsequently refused to allow the meeting of the promised Assembly. The Emir, however, endeavoured to enlist, arm and equip a Syrian army, and at least succeeded in obtaining many volunteers for the force.

Doubtless the outlook of the Arab leaders was affected by knowledge of the growing tension which, at this time, existed between the Governments of Great Britain and France regarding Syria. With no ill will on the British part, indeed, notwithstanding many proofs of British disinterestedness, French anxiety as to recognition of the claims of France, as to the ultimate realization of French ambitions in Syria, had greatly increased since the Peace Conference assembled. French public opinion, turned always with passionate regard towards

Syria, saw in the continued British occupation only a sinister agency—an agency which alone prevented the immediate transformation of a romantic national dream into actuality most happy and desirable. British promises to the Arabs, Arab assistance to the Allies, the wishes of the Arab population, even the British conquest of Syria, all were conveniently put aside whenever France approached Syrian questions. The British Government, as has been seen, had declared unequivocally that Great Britain would not accept the Mandate for Syria, even if offered her. Their great interest in Syria at this time lay in securing that British undertakings to the Sherif of Mecca and the Arabs should be substantially honoured; their great difficulty that the Syrian policy of France conflicted with the execution of these undertakings. But British anxiety on this score was regarded by the French as mere subterfuge to eliminate France from Syria. British officers and officials in the Near East were openly charged with influencing the native population against France; with throwing obstacles in the way of French officials; with revealing the calculated purpose of making a French occupation of Syria impossible. The prolonged delay in concluding peace with Turkey also added greatly to Allied difficulties, for Turkish and Syrian questions were closely interwoven. It is scarcely remarkable that, amid such Allied differences and confusion, the Arab leaders pursued an anti-French policy, or that they regarded possession of an effective army as the one argument which would secure the final settlement of Syrian questions in accordance with Arab desires.

14. *Provisional Franco-British Agreement, September 1919.* At the end of May or beginning of June the Emir Feisal seems to have received information from the Arab representative who had remained at the Peace Conference that the withdrawal of the British garrison in Syria was contemplated. At about the same time he learned that the proposed inter-Allied Commission of Inquiry regarding the Syrian Mandate had fallen through. Hitherto the Arab leaders had hoped that, in spite of British statements to the contrary, Great Britain might, after all, accept the Mandate for Syria. The news regarding the proposed withdrawal of British troops, and the abandonment of the Commission of Inquiry, appears to have convinced the Emir and his supporters that the British Government,

as far as they were concerned, had definitely resigned Syria to France. Arab hopes now turned more than ever towards the United States, especially as the American Commission had come out and begun its investigations.

Matters drifted on thus until the middle of September 1919. Early in the month Mr. Lloyd George and M. Clemenceau reached a provisional agreement upon Syrian questions, and the arrangement was approved by the Supreme Council. In outline it provided that, until the Treaty of Peace with Turkey was concluded, French troops should replace British garrisons in Syria, and that, thenceforward, Great Britain would have no responsibilities there. But it also provided that the area reserved by the Sykes-Picot Agreement for an independent Arab State, in other words, the area east of, and including the cities of Damascus, Hama, Homs, and Aleppo, should be occupied not by French troops but by Arab; in fact Baalbek was fixed as the nearest point of French occupied territory to Damascus. However, the Arab State so foreshadowed was to look to France alone for support and advice.

It should be noted at this point that the area reserved from French occupation under the agreement between Mr. Lloyd George and M. Clemenceau, was approximately the region known as 'Occupied Enemy Territory (East)' during the British military occupation. We have seen how Damascus was placed under Arab administration from the first by Lord Allenby. The area so committed to Arab rule was subsequently extended until it included the area bounded on the west by the Lebanon, the river Jordan, and the Dead Sea, on the north by a line which passed roughly east and west a little north of Aleppo, and on the east by the desert. The cities of Damascus, Hama, Homs, and Aleppo all were included within this military district of 'Occupied Enemy Territory (East)'. It was under Lord Allenby's supreme control, and British troops were in the four cities just named, but the administration was Arab, and Arab troops formed the greater part of the occupying force. This Syrian region had been set apart and placed under the Emir Feisal by the deliberate purpose of the British Government in preparation for the future Arab State, and in specific fulfilment of British pledges to the Arabs. Hence the British reservation withholding the whole of this region from French occupation after British troops should have withdrawn from

Syria, and British responsibilities there have ceased. But under the provisional arrangement the southern part of 'Occupied Enemy Territory (East)', in other words, the portion now known as Trans-Jordan, was to remain under British control, though with an Arab administration.

For Great Britain the provisional arrangement between Mr. Lloyd George and M. Clemenceau fulfilled alike British undertakings to France, contained in the Sykes-Picot Agreement, and British pledges to the Sherif of Mecca. The weakness of the arrangement lay in a cause outside these earlier commitments. It lay in the obvious intention of France to adopt her own interpretation of promises, actual or implied, which the Allies had given to the Arabs. One of these promises—the Declaration of the 7th November 1918—we have already mentioned; the other was contained in the Covenant of the League of Nations, and runs as under:

> 'Certain communities formerly belonging to the Turkish Empire have reached a stage of development where their existence as independent nations can be provisionally recognized subject to the rendering of administrative advice and assistance by a mandatory until such time as they are able to stand alone. The wishes of these communities must be a principal consideration in the selection of the Mandatory.'

Between the Declaration of the 7th November and the Covenant of the League, it is clear that the Arabs were justified in expecting that the exercise of self-determination promised them should at least extend to the choice of the Mandatory Power under whose control they were to be placed. They were opposed to the division of Syria between two mandatories: they were fiercely opposed to France as mandatory either for the whole or part of Syria. Yet Great Britain—an acceptable mandatory—was precluded by her earlier commitments to France from accepting the position: and America—the other acceptable mandatory—was by this time showing a resolve to avoid all mandatory responsibilities in the Old World. If the decision of the British Government to withdraw from Syria were final and irrevocable, and if the United States definitely resolved to refuse the Mandate, there remained for the Arabs only the acceptance of French control or the securing of complete Syrian independence. In this situation the Arab leaders still hoped that the Peace Conference might reach a solution in accordance with the spirit of the November Declaration and the Covenant of the League.

15. *General Gouraud, French High Commissioner in Syria, October 1919.* At the middle of September 1919 the Emir Feisal again came to London at the invitation of the British Government. They desired to discuss with him the situation in Syria created by the pending British evacuation; and that he should reopen negotiations with the French Government. He is understood to have protested against the withdrawal of British troops from Syria and the replacing of them by French troops, even in those parts of the country not reserved for Arab administration by the provisional arrangement. The British Government made it clear, however, that the British occupation could be continued no longer, and urged him to go to Paris and come to terms with France.

On the 9th October, General Gouraud was appointed French High Commissioner for Syria and Cilicia, and Commander-in-Chief of the Army of the Levant. Meanwhile the British evacuation went on. It was clear that the terms of the provisional arrangement between Mr. Lloyd George and M. Clemenceau would be executed.

The Emir accordingly went to Paris, and was received by M. Clemenceau on the 21st October. Negotiations between them, however, do not appear to have made much progress. The fundamental requirements of each were too opposed to be reconciled; the ultimate aims of each lay in opposite directions. But Feisal succeeded in persuading M. Clemenceau to defer the French occupation of Baalbek—the nearest point proposed for French approach to Damascus—as a matter on which Arab opinion was already dangerously inflamed. On the questions of the Syrian Mandate and Syrian independence Feisal now appealed to the Supreme Council.

The attitude of the British Government at this time is shown by the answers given to two questions in the House of Commons. On the 30th October Mr. Bonar Law said:

'No final statement as to the future government and administration of Syria can now be made. The settlement of the future of these territories rests with the Peace Conference, which has not, so far, been able to consider the question of Peace with Turkey because the United States of America have not as yet defined their attitude in regard to the responsibilities they may be able to undertake. So far as Syria is concerned the British Government announced to the Peace Conference last March that in no circumstances would Great Britain be prepared to undertake a mandate for Syria. Owing to the delay in the conclusion of the Treaty of Peace already mentioned we are making arrangements with the French Government and the Emir Feisal for the immediate withdrawal of British troops from Syria, and for the assumption of the duties of occupation by the French and Arabs pending the conclusion of the Treaty of Peace. . . .'

On the 19th December Mr. Lloyd George added this statement:

'The situation in Syria is a part of the larger question of the future of Turkey, arrangements for the examination and settlement of which were discussed at the recent meetings in London. Conversations between the French Government and the Emir Feisal are proceeding in Paris, and have not yet reached a termination. I am happy to say that in consequence of these conversations and of the military arrangements between the British and French Governments the tension in Syria has sensibly relaxed.'

This may have been true enough regarding Great Britain and France; but it was unduly optimistic regarding France and the Arabs. Indeed, the Arab aspect of the situation was daily becoming more threatening and dangerous. By the beginning of December 1919, British troops had been withdrawn from Cilicia and Syria in accordance with the terms of the provisional agreement, and French troops had taken their place. Great Britain, therefore, would stand more or less removed from later developments.

But the possibility of serious conflict between France and the Arabs had not escaped the attention of those directing the growing Nationalist movement in Turkey. Such a conflict might be made to provide valuable assistance in the attainment of Nationalist ends; it was an opportunity for embarassing the Allies, or one of the Allies, not to be neglected. With Cilicia occupied by French troops Turkish Nationalists, further, had their own intimate cause of quarrel with France, and were already preparing to begin hostilities there. They had no love for the Sherifian movement or for Sherifian leaders: but in a common cause old quarrels might be forgotten—or at least conveniently put aside for settlement at a future opportunity. Turkish Nationalist agents, therefore, using the convenient theories of Pan-Islamism, and expounding the community of interest existing between Turkish Moslems and Syrian Moslems as members of the universal world of Islam, became active in inflaming Arab opinion against the French. Many Syrian Moslems, in fact, adopted the view that union with Nationalist Turkey would be preferable to their country passing under the control of France.

A word should be spared here to the attitude of the Arab Nationalists regarding Palestine. Up to the time of the British evacuation of Syria the relationship between Palestine and Syria had been a question of little practical importance. Under the agreement between Great Britain and the Sherif of Mecca, Palestine—as lying west of the Damascus–Aleppo line—was excluded from the area destined for an independent Arab State. Besides, the Emir Feisal had declared his agreement with the proposals of the Zionist leaders as laid before the Peace Conference. But as Arab Nationalism grew, and especially after the British evacuation, when the prospect of Syria and Palestine coming under the same Mandatory Power disappeared, an agitation arose for Palestine being included in an independent Syria, as containing an inseparable part of the Arab nation. The prospect of organized Jewish settlement, presented in alarmist and exaggerated form, contributed much to the agitation. Nor is it a subject for surprise that, this stage having been reached, the Emir Feisal and other Arab leaders should urge the unity of Palestine and Syria as a matter of policy. But, although the growing insistence upon this claim by the Emir and Syrian Arabs may be recorded, the matter, as far as it affected the period of Syrian history now under review, remained more or less theoretical, and calls for no further mention here. Whatever should be said upon it belongs rather to the subject of Palestine.

16. *The San Remo Decision, 24th April 1920.* As has been seen, Feisal appealed to the Peace Conference again, at the beginning of November, in another effort to secure a settlement of the Mandate question in accordance with Arab desires or, failing that, to obtain complete independence for Syria. The distribution of Mandates for the Near East was, in fact, soon to be settled. Unqualified Syrian independence was a proposal which stood no chance of acceptance by the Conference, if only for the reason that the granting of such independence would mean the definite end of French dreams in the Levant. The Emir had to await the decisions of the Conference

regarding Mandates; and he left France for the East on the 13th December.

By the end of January 1920 France, now in complete military occupation of Cilicia and the parts of Syria not reserved for the Arab State, had her hands fully occupied. The Turkish Nationalists had begun hostilities, and guerilla warfare was general in north-western Syria. Within a month the Nationalist Turks had compelled the French to retire from the Sanjak of Marash with severe losses, and were threatening Adana and the Cilician plain.

On the 10th March a Congress of Syrian Notables, sitting at Damascus, offered the crown of Syria and Palestine to the Emir Feisal, who thereupon accepted it with the position of King. How far the Congress was representative of the Arab people need not be discussed here. That it met and took the steps it did were political moves, prearranged in the hope of influencing the decisions of the Peace Conference. Incidentally it may be mentioned that the same Congress, at the same time, nominated the Emir Abdullah, second son of the King of the Hejaz, for the Kingship of Iraq or Mesopotamia.

Confronted by this situation the Governments of Great Britain and France, on the 15th March, repudiated the action of the Arab Congress, again informed the Emir that the future of the Arab regions could be decided only by the Peace Conference, and requested him to attend the next meeting of that body. The Emir replied that he would send a representative.

Meanwhile the Conference met at San Remo, where, on the 24th April, it decided that both Syria and Iraq should become independent States, subject to a Mandatory Power until they were able to stand alone. The Conference further decided that the Mandates for Iraq and Palestine should be assigned to Great Britain, and for Syria to France. In communicating these decisions to the Emir Feisal the British Government once more urged him to come to Paris for the next meeting of the Peace Conference as a course favourable to recognition of his kingship by the Conference.

The decisions of the Conference gave rise to many protests throughout Syria, and the strongest indications of hostility to France as mandatory. In deference to the feelings of the people the Emir Feisal announced that as King of Syria he could not acquiesce in any part of Syrian territory being placed under foreign domination. It appears, too, that at this stage he felt that another visit to Paris would be misunderstood in Syria, and be prejudicial to his position; he therefore temporized with the request of the British Government that he should attend the Peace Conference.

While events in Syria were shaping thus France was conducting a difficult war in Cilicia against the Turkish Nationalists, and action against Feisal and the Syrian State had to be postponed. However, by the beginning of July the situation in Cilicia had become safe, and a French Army of some 90,000 men was concentrated in Syria. On the 14th July General Gouraud dispatched an ultimatum to the Emir. The ultimatum required unconditional recognition of the French Mandate; immediate reduction of the Syrian Army, and the abolition of conscription; the unimpeded circulation of Franco-Syrian currency; French military occupation of the Rayak–Aleppo railway, including Aleppo; and the punishment of those Arabs who had been guilty of attacking French forces.

17. *General Gouraud expels Feisal from Syria, July–August 1920.* We need give only the barest outline of what followed. In view of the overwhelming strength at the disposal of General Gouraud the Emir accepted the terms of the ultimatum. Great disorders, however, arose at Damascus, where it was found necessary in the interests of peace for Sherifian troops to suppress by force violent popular demonstrations in favour of war. Nevertheless, the Arab desire for hostilities against France was not to be restrained. On the 22nd July an attack was made on a French outpost by Arab horsemen; and on the 23rd July the French replied with a general offensive against the positions held by Syrian troops. The battle resulted in the rout of the Syrian Army, with great loss in men and material, and the occupation of Damascus on the 25th July. Aleppo had fallen a day earlier to a French force from the north hitherto engaged in opposing the Turks.

On finding themselves in possession of Damascus the French declared the Emir Feisal deposed, and ordered him to leave Syria—which he did by retiring into Palestine. They then set up a new Syrian Government on conditions, including the payment of an indemnity, dictated by themselves as conquerors. The plea of military necessity, arising in operations for the restoration of order in the mandated territory of Syria, was invoked to cover French action and the occupation of Damascus and Aleppo; and the same necessity was supposed to explain the occupation of Hama and Homs—both these towns being on the line of railway between Damascus and Aleppo.

So fell the Emir Feisal's independent Syrian State—a State created and fostered by Great Britain in fulfilment, or partial fulfilment, of her pledges to the Arabs. It fell because its existence was in direct conflict with French ambitions, in circumstances which prevented British influence being made effective for its preservation—it fell, in short, because its own armed strength was insufficient to ensure its survival.

18. *British attitude to Syria, 1920.* It is difficult to define with exactness the situation thus created for the British Government by French action in Syria. On the one hand were British pledges which had brought the Arabs into the War as Allies; and later British policy in Syria which, in fulfilment of those pledges, had laid the foundations of an independent Arab State in Occupied Enemy Territory (East), and, on the evacuation of Syria by British troops, had sought to perpetuate that State by specifically excluding, under the provisional agreement of September 1919 with the French Government, this area from occupation by French troops. In addition were the promises contained in Article 22 of the Covenant of the League of Nations and the Joint Allied Declaration of the 7th November 1918. On the other hand were the Sykes-Picot Agreement, and the large fact that the Supreme Council had conferred the Mandate for Syria and the Lebanon on France with, of course, a very definite responsibility for the exercise of control within the territories so mandated.

Between these commitments and promises—both particular and general—French responsibilities under the Mandate, and actual French action, any clear-cut solution for the difficulties of the British Government was exceedingly hard to find. In fact, if reasons of high expediency be recognized, it may be admitted at once that a clear-cut solution of British originating was an impossibility.

The best exposition of the situation, as well as of the views upon it held by the British Government, is to be found in the record of questions and answers on the subject in the House of Commons on the 19th July 1920, and of the long debate which followed the same day.

It is impracticable to give here more than the barest outline of these important Parliamentary discussions. They should be read in full in the unrestricted pages of 'Hansard' if the various implications of the Syrian situation of the time are to be understood by the layman of Middle Eastern affairs.

In the greater number of questions asked was evident the unavowed purpose of challenging French action in Syria, of invoking British support for the Emir Feisal. Behind the barriers of custom and rule which impeded plain speaking in the House of Commons regarding an Allied Power, it was sought to show that French action was in conflict with British pledges to the Arabs. That it was in conflict, too, with Article 22 of the Treaty of Versailles (Covenant of the League of Nations); with the Joint Allied Declaration of November 1918; and with the Agreement of September 1919 between the British and French Governments. And that the Mandate for Syria not having been as yet assigned to France by the League of Nations, but so far only by the Supreme Council, French action was wanting in international legality. It was asked whether in these circumstances France had submitted the terms of her ultimatum to the Arabs to the Supreme Council, and whether the terms of the Mandate itself for Syria had yet been submitted to the Allied Powers. It was suggested that Great Britain was under pledge to support the Arabs; that at least His Majesty's Government should make immediate representations to France.

To the particular question addressed to the Prime Minister, Mr. Bonar Law, Leader of the House, replied:

'I understand that the French Government, owing to the attacks made on their forces by Arab troops, and, as they believe, the generally hostile attitude of the Syrian Government, issued an ultimatum on the 14th July demanding, by the 18th July, the control of the Rayak–Aleppo Railway, unconditional acceptance of the French mandate, the introduction of French-Syrian currency, and the surrender for punishment of the Arabs who fought against them. The ultimatum was not submitted to the Supreme Council. The terms of the mandate for Syria have not yet been submitted to the Allied Powers.

'As regards the last part of the question, His Majesty's Government, who had for some time, but unsuccessfully, been urging the Emir Feisal to come to Europe to discuss the outstanding questions with the Supreme Council, do not consider that they can usefully act upon the information at present at their disposal, but they are in communication with the French Government on the matter.'

In answer to other questions, Mr. Bonar Law replied:

'I have said that we are in communication with the French Government. I do not accept the statement of my Noble Friend [Lord R. Cecil] that what has happened is against the Treaty of Versailles. As regards the question of my Noble Friend it [French action] is not inconsistent with the French mandate and the assumption that it [the French mandate] is given confirmation [by the League of Nations]. I do not think I can say anything more. It is very difficult, I think, to judge action which is taken on the responsibility alone of the French Government.'

After a further exchange of questions and answers the adjournment of the House was moved 'for the purpose of discussing a definite matter of urgent public importance, namely, "the immediate danger to British interests in the Middle East arising from the threatened new hostilities in Syria."' The motion was supported by more than forty members, and the debate followed later in the evening.

The debate contained not only a close examination of the Syrian situation and British responsibilities arising therein, but also Mr. Bonar Law's explanation of how the British Government regarded the matter. The debate cannot be summarized here; it is too long and does not lend itself to clear abridgement—it should, if possible, be read in full in 'Hansard'. But this much can be said in indication of the line followed by Mr. Bonar Law. He represented that the granting of the Mandate to France by the Supreme Council was not incompatible with British pledges to the Arabs, and that, under the Mandate, France had wide discretionary powers, the exercise of which could not well be challenged by any individual State. He said, also, that the French Government had given assurances that French military occupation of the territory excluded from such occupation by the Agreement of September 1919 between Great Britain and France would be merely temporary. For the rest of Mr. Bonar Law's able handling of a difficult and dangerous matter it may be remarked that, in the course of the debate, he accepted, as applicable with truth to the Syrian situation, an aphorism uttered by the late Lord Randolph Churchill—'We have this eternal conflict between what has happened and what should have happened.'

One other point remains to be mentioned in confirmation of a statement made in an earlier part of the present chapter. In reply to a question during the debate Mr. Bonar Law explicitly declared that the correspondence between His Majesty's Government and the Sherif of Mecca containing the British pledges to the Arabs, had been fully disclosed to the French Government at the time.[1]

The overthrow of the Emir Feisal greatly incensed the King of the Hejaz and caused dangerous excitement in the Arab regions east of Jordan. For a time it seemed that the French might have to meet serious Arab attacks from the Hauran and Trans-Jordan (both of which districts had been in the area ruled by the Emir Feisal) supported by King Husein and the Sherifian family. But the danger of organized hostilities passed away, largely owing to the influence exerted by the British Government in discountenancing Arab action.

19. *The problem of Trans-Jordan.* Violent expression of Arab resentment against France and the French occupation of Syria could not, however, always be restrained. On the 20th August 1920, Arabs attacked a train near the border of Syria and Trans-Jordan and killed two members of the new pro-French Syrian Cabinet as well as French officers and soldiers who were on board. The attack was made on the Syrian side of the border but it reflected Arab feeling in Trans-Jordan.

This territory, though included in the Palestine Mandate, and under the Government of Palestine, was not occupied by British troops, and had no organized British administration. It was loosely supervised through local chiefs guided by resident British Political Officers. How to control the tribes of Trans-Jordan without military occupation, without appearing to derogate British undertakings to the Arabs, and yet to ensure that the region should not become an Alsatia, a scene of turbulent unrest, and a danger to French Syria, was a problem to which the British Government gave serious consideration. The solution eventually adopted was to form an autonomous Arab State of the territory, with the Emir Abdullah, second son of King Husein, as its ruler, assisted by British advisers. In this way a central Arab authority was set up; an authority with sufficient prestige, responsible for the maintenance of order, and yet acceptable to the in-

[1] *v.* § 11, p. 147.

habitants. At the same time it was obvious that the pledges of the British Government to the Sherif of Mecca and to the Arabs were being fulfilled in this part of the Arab countries.

20. *The problem of Iraq.* A similar policy was followed later in the British mandated area of Iraq. The policy followed there has an important bearing upon the period of Syrian history now under review, and therefore calls for mention here.[1]

When the British Government decided in 1921 to establish Iraq as an independent Arab State they allowed the Emir Feisal to become a candidate for the throne, subject to election by the people. That this opportunity should have been given him was both just and wise. He had shown himself a valuable and loyal ally during the most doubtful and difficult period of the War. British policy had laid the foundations of his Syrian State from which he was ejected by the French in circumstances precluding any British intervention. He had supported this disaster with dignity, and without seeking to make trouble, recognizing that it was not, at the time, in the power of his British ally to assist him. It was natural, therefore, that the British Government should regard him with sympathy and goodwill, and be ready, and, it may be, even glad to accept him as King of Iraq if chosen by the people. The more so, too, that as a possible ruler for this Arab State he had much in his favour—his personal appearance and manner, the prestige of his family, his reputation among men of his race for his part in the War and for his efforts to establish Arab independence in Syria. Moreover, he possessed a knowledge of the West, of the tangled skein of European politics, of the British position in the Middle East and in the world; he had already had experience in statecraft and in the thankless task of ruling Arabs. He was accepted by the people of Iraq, and crowned king in the course of August 1921, and has since filled this difficult position with general approval and greater success than is generally admitted.

Of course the French found unofficial, if not official, cause for offence in the elevation to the throne of Iraq of a Prince they had chosen to regard as an enemy. That sentimental disadvantage, however, was, perhaps, a small matter when balanced against the weighty advantages of the Emir being

[1] *v.* Part III, *passim.*

accepted by the Arabs of Iraq as their king, with Baghdad as his capital and the whole of Iraq as his kingdom, and the aspirations of the Arab race for independence being thus in large part attained. And not the least of these advantages was that, with the creation of an autonomous Arab State east of Jordan, it demonstrated the fulfilment of those British pledges to the Sherif of Mecca and the Arabs, on the strength of which they had come into the War.

21. *Franco-British Boundary Settlements, 23rd December 1920–7th March 1923.* We now must leave the overthrow of the Emir Feisal and the independent Syrian State by France, and the subsequent measures adopted by the British Government in fulfilment of their pledges to the Arabs, and pass to an outline of what has happened since in the Syrian area placed by Mandate under French control.

With Great Britain as mandatory in Palestine and Iraq, and France in Syria and Lebanon, it was necessary that the frontiers of these mandated areas should be definitely laid down. During the latter part of 1920 a convention was negotiated between Great Britain and France having such delimitation as its chief purpose.

The Syrian–Iraq boundary presented no difficulties. The line agreed upon left to Great Britain the Mosul region which had already been the subject of negotiation and agreement in principle between Mr. Lloyd George and M. Clemenceau at the Peace Conference.

The frontier between Syria and British mandated territory in the south involved various contentious questions, and was not so easily settled. The successful economic development of Palestine in the future depended on water-supply, both for power and irrigation. Water adequate for these purposes and at sufficient elevation existed only in streams flowing through the border districts between Syria and Palestine—in the Litani River, the Upper Jordan, the Yarmuk River, itself the chief tributary of the Jordan from the East. But these streams, either in whole or in part, lay within the Syrian area provisionally assigned to France by the Sykes-Picot Agreement—Palestine then not having been envisaged as a possible area of industrial development and closely settled population.

At the Peace Conference, indeed, Mr. Lloyd George had asked for a Palestine restored to its ancient confines of ' Dan unto Beersheba', and M. Clemenceau is understood to have conceded the claim in principle. But just what, geographically, did the name Dan imply? Doubtless Dan of old included the basin of the Upper Jordan, very likely of the Litani, too. With the future of the Jewish National Home before them the Zionist Organization rightly pleaded that Palestine should include not only the basins of the Upper Jordan and the Litani, as part of Dan, but the northern half of the basin of the Yarmuk—all of which areas fell within the territory claimed by France under the Sykes-Picot Agreement. The attainment of such advantageous frontiers for Palestine was, however, out of the question at this time. On all Syrian questions the French had ever been difficult and uncompromising, as on matters closely affecting vital French interests. They now declined to make any concession of Syrian territory except a small extension which brought the northern extremity of Palestine up to (but not including) the town of Beisan—which of old was Dan. They also insisted on retaining the eastern shores of the Sea of Galilee. But they granted Palestine the privilege of using, within French territory, the surplus waters of the Upper Jordan and the Yarmuk (though not of the Litani) for irrigation and the production of electric power, when the requirements of French mandated territory should have been satisfied. After protracted negotiations the French Government would yield so much but no more, and the frontier between Syria and British mandated territory was provisionally settled accordingly.

A significant article affecting Cyprus[1] which appears in the Convention must be mentioned here. It provides that, owing to the strategical position of Cyprus in regard to Syria, the British Government shall not open negotiations for the cession or alienation of the island without the previous consent of the French Government.

The Convention[2] defining the boundaries of Syria with Iraq and Palestine and matters connected therewith, was signed on the 23rd December 1920. It provided for the demarcation of the frontiers by an Anglo-French Boundary Commission, and the conclusion of an agreement between

[1] *v.* also pp. 195. 205 and n.

[2] Known as the 'Franco-British Convention of December 23, 1920, on certain points connected with the Mandates for Syria and the Lebanon, Palestine, and Mesopotamia' (Cmd. 1195).

the two governments upon the frontier line thus finally determined.

This Agreement [1] was signed on the 3rd February 1922. It was ratified by the British Government on the 7th March 1923, and came into effect three days later.

The line as eventually determined by the Boundary Commission differs slightly at some points from that defined in principle in the Convention of 1920. The chief change is that the whole of the Sea of Galilee remains in Palestine.

22. *French policy in Syria ; Angora Agreement, 20th October 1921.* It was in quite a different manner that the French Government dealt with the northern frontiers of the region assigned to France by the Supreme Council. In Cilicia the French were faced by the Nationalist Turks, who showed no signs of acquiescing in loss of territory there, however resigned they might be to surrendering the more strictly Arab countries. Besides, the French Government were already cherishing Eastern ambitions in which France should succeed to the position of political influence and economic advantage in Turkey held by Germany in 1914; and Turkish hostility to France was incompatible with the success of their plans. Moreover, the French people had become critical and restive under the growing cost in money and blood required to maintain the French position in Cilicia and Syria.

On the 20th of October 1921, the French Government, therefore, concluded a remarkable agreement with the Turkish Government at Angora, which, making a bold bid for Turkish friendship, changed the outlook and in a large degree affected Syria.[2] Under this pact, negotiated by M. Franklin-Bouillon, France not only restored Cilicia to Turkish sovereignty and evacuated the province, but surrendered a part of the area placed in her keeping as mandated territory by the Supreme Council. France, in fact, abandoned the line laid down by the Treaty of Sèvres as the frontier between Turkey and territory mandated to France, and substituted a new line. It began at Pyas, a few miles north of Alexandretta, passed eastwards thence to a point on the Baghdad Railway some thirty miles north of Aleppo, and thereafter followed the course

[1] This Agreement was published as a White Paper (Cmd. 1910) on the 1st August 1923.

[2] For text *v.* App. II, Part II, B, and for British protest Part I, B, § 6, pp. 33–5.

of that railway to Nisibin in such a way as to place the actual railway line in Turkish territory. From Nisibin the new frontier turned north-east to the Tigris at Jeziret Ibn Umar. The territory included within the frontier of the Treaty of Sèvres and the new frontier and thus surrendered, comprises about 9,000 square miles.

Criticism of the French Government for their action cannot, apparently, be supported by the argument of illegality. The Treaty of Sèvres, on which these matters hung, had not been ratified, and was therefore non-existent as a binding instrument; nor had the Mandate for Syria been issued by the League of Nations. Neither were Allied pledges as to freeing the Arabs from Turkish rule unduly strained by the surrender, for the territory shows no preponderating Arab element in the population.

The Pact of Angora gave France at least a temporary security against the Nationalist Turks, and by removing French public alarm on the score of staggering credits, heavy casualties, and an uncertain future in the Levant, may be said to have strengthened the French hold on Syria.

The territorial organization of Syria and Lebanon adopted by the French after they had consolidated their position merits a little attention now as indicating how they regard these mandated areas.

Under the Sykes-Picot Agreement, France was to enjoy complete liberty of action in the portion of Syria bordering on the Mediterranean—the area including the Lebanon—in other words, these districts were destined for French annexation. But the mandatory system subsequently adopted by the Peace Conference at Paris rejected the whole principle of annexation, and replaced it with the principle of trusteeship.[1]

23. *French policy in Lebanon.* Nevertheless, the policy of France as mandatory has been to treat the Lebanon upon a different footing from Syria. One of the earliest acts of General Gouraud after the expulsion of the Emir Feisal, was to visit the chief town of the Maronites, in the Lebanon, and announce the creation of a Greater Lebanon State. This was done by attaching the plains of Bekaa, not occupied by a Lebanese population, to the Lebanon district. As long ago

[1] The text of the Syrian and Lebanon Mandates are given in App. V, Part III.

as 1862, General Gouraud said, it had been the purpose of France to reincorporate the Bekaa with the Lebanon, and now, after all these years, France had realized her ideals. He further announced the decision of the French Government that henceforward no inhabitant of Lebanon would be allowed to emigrate. The motive behind this mediaeval ordinance lay, perhaps, in the fact that the Lebanese in general were by tradition sympathetic towards French ambitions in Syria, and thus formed an invaluable asset which could not be allowed to diminish itself.

The internal policy subsequently followed by the French in these mandated areas always sought to foster the idea that the Lebanon State was a political entity apart from the rest of Syria. That, while it had economic interests in common with its Syrian hinterland, its political interests and aspirations were, or should be, quite divorced. The French Administration, in fact, already regarded the Lebanon as being an integral portion of France, in much the same way as Algeria, and their policy was based upon this unavowed but governing assumption.

The remainder of Syria was eventually divided into the three States of Aleppo, Damascus, and of the Alouites, the latter being the country of the Ansariya—the Mediterranean littoral extending from a point north of Tripoli to the Orontes River.

There was at first no attempt at providing representative government, either in Lebanon or the Syrian States. Even when the election of representatives to the State Councils was adopted and the Syrian States were officially called 'autonomous', the form of government remained a façade behind which French officials exerted complete power. Perhaps it is as yet too soon to expect that greater progress should have been made with native self-government.

24. *Conclusion.* In June 1922, a decree was issued providing for the provisional federation of the autonomous States of Syria, but excluding the Lebanon. The Federal Council consists of five members from each of the States of Aleppo, Damascus, and of the Alouites, with the President of the Council as the President of the Federation. The Council sits alternately at Damascus and Aleppo, one year in each city.

This short survey of recent Syrian history would be needlessly incomplete if closed without some reference to the delay which has supervened in promulgating the Syrian Mandate.

The Mandate for Syria and Lebanon was conferred on France by the Supreme Council on the 4th April 1920, confirmed 5th May. The terms were to be prepared by the mandatory, and then submitted to the Council of the League of Nations for approval and promulgation. The Mandate for Palestine was conferred on Great Britain at the same time. In preparing these instruments the British and French Governments discussed the terms in consultation with each other, and the draft Mandates for Palestine and for Syria and Lebanon when deposited with the Council of the League in December 1920, had then been examined and agreed upon by both of the mandatory governments. The draft Mandates so submitted were approved by the League on the 24th July 1922; they were then ready for promulgation.

But at this stage the Italian Government opposed the promulgation of the Syrian Mandate before various matters regarding Syria, in dispute between France and Italy, should have been cleared up. Executive decisions by the League have to be unanimous, and unanimity as to promulgating the Mandate could not be obtained; on this point, therefore, a deadlock arose.

The difficulty was partially surmounted by the League deciding to approve the Mandate, and defer promulgation until the dispute was ended; and that whenever settlement was reached promulgation should follow automatically. Meanwhile, the League requested France to administer Syria and Lebanon in accordance with the Mandate as approved.

It may be mentioned here that the deadlock produced by the dispute has also prevented the Mandate for Palestine becoming operative, for the French Government have insisted upon the simultaneous promulgation of both Mandates.

So far [1] the dispute remains unsettled.

[1] September 1923.

B. PALESTINE AND ZIONISM

II. *Palestine since the 30th October 1918.*

The history of Palestine since the Armistice of Mudros has been shaped chiefly by the influence of three agreements or undertakings already described or referred to in other chapters of the present volume. These agreements are: the British commitments to the Sherif of Mecca in 1914–15, the Sykes-Picot Agreement of 1916, and the Balfour Declaration of 2nd November 1917.[1] For Syria, Arabia, and Iraq—for the more strictly Arab regions—the two first named have been of dominating influence. For Palestine, on the other hand, the Balfour Declaration has had by far the chief importance. In a political sense, indeed, Palestine of the present day is the direct outcome of that British—or Allied— policy expressed in the vague but pregnant sentence of sixty-eight words which constitutes the Declaration.

Any attempt, however brief, to outline the recent history of Palestine must concern itself largely with the Declaration and its results, how the remarkable policy represented by the Declaration came to be adopted, how the Declaration itself harmonized with other Allied Agreements and declarations affecting Palestine and its inhabitants, and how the broad principles expressed or implied in the Declaration were given administrative form, and thus in application influenced the whole current of Palestinian life and history.

1. *The Balfour Declaration* (House of Commons), 2nd November 1917.

'His Majesty's Government views with favour the establish-
'ment in Palestine of a National Home for the Jewish People,
'and will use its best endeavours to facilitate the achievement
'of this object, it being clearly understood that nothing shall
'be done which may prejudice the civil and religious rights of
'existing non-Jewish communities in Palestine or the rights
'and political status enjoyed by Jews in any other country.'

This apparently simple pronouncement, so brief, so casual in manner, yet so careful in phrasing, was, in truth, the resultant of various conflicting and involved interests of world-wide influence

[1] For commitments to Husein *v.* pp. 123–7, 132–3; for terms of Sykes-Picot Agreement *v.* pp. 16–17, 128; *v.* also maps opp. p. 6 and p. 32.

and importance. A brief reference to these interests and their interplay is essential to the purpose of the present chapter.

Much is heard of the Declaration as an instrument conferring upon the Jewish race unwarrantable privileges in a land from which that race had been effectively dispersed. There has been remarkably little said as to the reasons of high policy which impelled the Allies to adopt the purpose of the Declaration as one of their war aims.

To some extent altruistic motives influenced certain Gentile protagonists of the Zionism expressed in the Declaration. At a time when justice for oppressed races and small peoples had become an Allied slogan it was at least consistent to include the Jews among those whose wrongs might be righted as an outcome of the War. But we well may doubt how far such considerations, standing alone, would have carried the Allied Governments towards accepting the restoration of the Jewish people to Palestine as a war aim. The truth is, of course, that for Great Britain and her Allies the policy indicated in the Declaration was most definitely a war measure, well calculated to yield results of immense importance to the Allied cause. And, further, that for Great Britain special reasons existed why she should adopt and support the policy of the Declaration.

These may be found in the obvious advantages of covering the Suez Canal by an outpost territory, in which important elements of the population would not only be bound to her by every interest, but would command the support of world Jewry. That was the long view of British Imperial interests, taken in 1916 and 1917 ; it counted for much then, but for even more after the war.

But apart from exclusive British interests, the Declaration may be described as essentially a war measure adopted by the Powers of the Entente in the furtherance of their own vital interests. Defined in greater detail, it was a bold, imaginative, and statesmanlike effort to prevent the incalculable and universal influence of Jewry being exerted on the side of the Central Powers—as, indeed, it was, to a serious extent, then being exerted—and to transfer this highly important influence to the cause of the Entente. Nor was it a project of sudden origin, or hastily embraced. The advantages to be gained if the policy of the Declaration were adopted had long been urged ; opposition to that policy had long been active. Before the British Government gave the Declaration to the world it had been closely examined in all its bearings and implications, weighed word by word, and subjected to repeated change and amendment. Unless full weight be given to these antecedent facts, no correct judgment upon the Declaration and its policy in operation can be formed.

2. *The Zionists and the Declaration.* Zionism had been a living and ambitious force in the Jewish world long before 1914. While awaiting its real opportunity it had, in 1905, rejected the tempting offer of territory for the creation of a Zionist State in Uganda, under the British flag. It had steadily looked to Palestine as the one land which could provide the historical connexion essential to Zionist aims. The entry of Turkey into the war brought the hitherto impracticable dreams of Zionism within the bounds of possible attainment. If the goodwill of the Allies, particularly of Great Britain, could be secured, and provided that ultimate success should attend the Allied arms, much might be done to realize the dearest ambitions of Zionism. It lay with Zionist leaders to bring their ideal before the British Government as a scheme likely to be of advantage to the Entente.

Suffice to say that at this crisis of its fortunes Zionism was fortunate, that in Dr. C. Weizmann and Mr. N. Sokolov it found two leaders equal to the great occasion, that British Statesmen, including Mr. (now Lord) Balfour, Lord Milner, Mr. Lloyd George, Lord Robert Cecil, immediately recognized the political importance and value of the Zionist suggestions, and that in the subsequent long negotiations and discussions by which the aims of Zionism were harmonized with the political realities of the situation, the British negotiators were Mr. Balfour and the late Sir Mark Sykes, both of them convinced and ardent supporters of Zionist aspirations. These British representatives and the Zionist leaders just named must be credited with the chief part in framing the policy of the Declaration.

Support of Zionist ambitions, indeed, promised much for the cause of the Entente. Quite naturally Jewish sympathies were to a great extent anti-Russian, and therefore in favour of the Central Powers. No ally of Russia, in fact, could escape sharing that immediate and inevitable penalty for long and savage Russian persecution of the Jewish race. But the German General Staff desired to attach Jewish support yet more closely to the German side. With their wide outlook on possibilities they seem to have urged, early in 1916, the advantages of promising Jewish restoration to Palestine under an arrangement to be made between Zionists and Turkey, backed by a German guarantee. The practical difficulties were considerable; the subject perhaps dangerous to German relations with Turkey; and the German Government acted cautiously. But the scheme was by no means rejected or even shelved, and at any moment the Allies might have been forestalled in offering this supreme bid. In fact in September 1917 the German Government were making the most serious efforts to capture the Zionist movement.

Another most cogent reason why the policy of the Declaration should be adopted by the Allies lay in the state of Russia herself. Russian Jews had been secretly active on behalf of the Central Powers from the first; they had become the chief agents of German pacifist propaganda; by 1917 they had done much in preparation for that general disintegration of Russian national life, later recognized as the revolution. It was believed that if Great Britain declared for the fulfilment of Zionist aspirations in Palestine under her own pledge, one effect would be to bring Russian Jewry to the cause of the Entente.

It was believed, also, that such a declaration would have a potent influence upon world Jewry in the same way, and secure for the Entente the aid of Jewish financial interests. It was believed, further, that it would greatly influence American opinion in favour of the Allies. Such were the chief considerations which, during the later part of 1916 and the next ten months of 1917, impelled the British Government towards making a contract with Jewry.

But when the matter came before the Cabinet for decision delays occurred. Amongst influential English Jews Zionism had few supporters, at all events for a Zion in Palestine. It had still fewer in France. Jewish influence both within and without the Cabinet is understood to have exerted itself strenuously and pertinaciously against the policy of the proposed Declaration.

Under the pressure of Allied needs the objections of the anti-Zionists were either over-ruled or the causes of objection removed, and the Balfour Declaration, as we have seen, was published to the world on 2nd November 1917. That it is in purpose a definite contract with Jewry is beyond question. Subsequently the Declaration was accepted and endorsed by the Governments of France, Italy, and Japan.

That it is in purpose a definite contract between the British

Government and Jewry represented by the Zionists is beyond question. In spirit it is a pledge that in return for services to be rendered by Jewry the British Government would ' use their best endeavours ' to secure the execution of a certain definite policy in Palestine. No time limit is set for performance; completion alone appears to have been intended as the conclusion of the contract. It would thus seem to be an agreement incapable of being greatly varied except by consent.

How far the implied services of Jewry have been or may yet be rendered cannot be estimated, and must always remain a matter of opinion. The Declaration certainly rallied world Jewry, as a whole, to the side of the Entente. The war was won by the Entente; and to the Declaration as a measure to that end may be attributed a share in achieving the great result. And it is possible to understand from many sources that directly, and indirectly, the services expected of Jewry were not expected in vain, and were, from the point of view of British interests alone, well worth the price which had to be paid. Nor is it to be supposed that the services already rendered are the last—it well may be that in time to come Jewish support will much exceed in importance any thought possible in the past. That, however, is a possibility for Palestine of the future to demonstrate.

3. *The Declaration in relationship to other Allied Agreements.* The Declaration was the latest of the three chief agreements bearing on Palestine. Each had been made independently of the other; two were secret agreements; all had been made under the compulsion and stress of war; and between the negotiations for each, entirely unforeseen changes of policy had been forced upon the Allied Powers. Complete harmony between the provisions of these various agreements might not therefore always have been preserved.

No difficulties worth mentioning arose between the Declaration and the Sykes-Picot Agreement. But between the Declaration and the undertakings to the Sherif of Mecca an unfortunate discrepancy of territorial definition is alleged. It turns upon the question whether Palestine was or was not excluded from the territory in which the British Government pledged itself to support Arab independence. The complete correspondence embodying the negotiations and pledges has not been published; for the purpose of this chapter the matter is purely theoretical and requires no discussion; it is enough to say, therefore, that the British Government maintained their reading of the letters that Palestine was so excluded. But it may be remarked that had the Sherif's son, the Emir Feisal, not been ejected from Syria by the French, much less might have been heard of his father's claim to Palestine.[1]

4. *Palestine after the War.* With Palestine thus secured territorially as a National Home for the Jews, we come at this point to a brief outline of subsequent events.

Zionism pleaded its cause before the Supreme Council at the Paris Peace Conference on 27th February 1919.[2] The proposals made by the Zionist representatives were: That the Powers should recognize the historic title of the Jews to Palestine, and their right to re-establish there their National Home. That the sovereign possession of Palestine should be vested in the League of Nations, and the Government entrusted to Great Britain as Mandatory of the League. They also asked that certain specific provisions should be included in the Mandate. The chief of these were: For the establishment of such conditions as would in the end permit the creation of an autonomous commonwealth. To promote Jewish immigration and close settlement on the land. That the Mandatory should accept the co-operation in economic matters of a Council representing the Jews of Palestine and the world, and leave matters of Jewish education to the same Council. And that the Mandatory should confer the widest possible measures of self-government upon localities.

Long delay followed before the Supreme Council could arrive at its decisions. During this period Anglo-French rivalries in regard to Syria and Palestine became acute; the Emir Feisal and the Arab movement for an independent Syria played their part; the Arab Nationalist movement also developed in Palestine; and anti-Zionist Jewish influence exerted itself against the scheme of the proposed Jewish National Home in Palestine.

But on the 25th April 1920 the Supreme Council, sitting at San Remo, allocated the Mandate for Palestine to Great Britain.[3] The Council also adopted the division of Ottoman territory in Syria as provisionally arranged between Great Britain and France in the Sykes-Picot Agreement. In the Treaty of Sèvres, signed on 10th August, 1920, Zionist claims regarding Palestine were recognized and the promises of the Balfour

[1] *v.* further, pp. 25, 30, 126–7, 140–1, 180–2. [2] Cf. Vol. I, p. 246.
[3] *v.* pp. 505–6, 519, 521–3 and App. V. 645.

Declaration incorporated in the text of the Treaty. On 20th July 1920 civil government was established in Palestine, and the first British High Commissioner, Sir Herbert Samuel, entered upon his duties.

(a) *Frontiers of Palestine.*

The frontier separating Palestine from French Syria gave rise to much negotiation between the British and French Governments. This subject has, however, already been dealt with elsewhere in the present volume,[1] and requires no special mention here except to remark that as ultimately fixed it was not to the advantage of Palestine.

(b) *The Palestine Mandate.*

The preparation of the Draft Mandate for Palestine and Trans-Jordan was the next important step by the British Government as Mandatory. It was effected in consultation, not only with Zionist representatives, but with the French Government, in order to secure such general agreement of terms between the Palestine Mandate and the French Mandate for Syria as might be advisable. The Draft was submitted to the League of Nations on 7th December 1920, and approved in July 1922. Promulgation was delayed, as explained in the Syrian chapter of this work.[2]

As interpreting and expanding into practical administrative form the compressed enunciation of policy contained in the Declaration the text of the Mandate[3] well repays careful study. In effect the Mandate grants to Zionism nearly all that Zionist representatives asked for at the Paris Conference in 1919. On the other hand, its provisions guard with scrupulous care the civil and religious rights and interests, and even the susceptibilities, of the diverse races inhabiting Palestine. While establishing the conditions necessary for the creation of the National Home for the Jewish People, it accords no rights to individual Jews as citizens that it does not equally accord to individuals of any other race or faith. The policy of the Declaration may be justifiable or unjustifiable, the adoption of that policy wise or unwise. But conceding that the policy must now be executed, the terms of the Mandate are difficult to criticize except in a spirit of factiousness.

[1] *v.* pp. 37 n., 164–6, and maps opp. pp. 32 and 116.
[2] See p. 169.
[3] Cmd. 1785, 1922.

(*c.*) *Arab opposition to execution of the policy of the Declaration.*

With the earliest measures for establishing a civil government Arab opposition to the prospect of a Zionist Palestine redoubled. Adopting the wild and extravagant utterances of extreme Zionists as representing the truth, the Arab population created for themselves a future of offensive Jewish domination speedily ending in complete dispossession. Under the pressure of such apprehensions Moslem and Christian Arabs made common cause. The old-time friendly tolerance of Jews gave place to a hatred in which the compelling influences of race, faith and fear all found violent expression. Serious riots occurred at Jerusalem in April 1920, and in Jaffa in May 1921. The Report[1] of the Commission of Inquiry which investigated these outbreaks provides an exhaustive and admirable survey of the situation in Palestine at the time, and exhibits the difficulties attending execution of the policy of the Balfour Declaration.

Meanwhile a Palestinian Arab Congress had registered a formal protest against the Declaration, demanded the repeal of past legislation, and the creation of a National form of Government representative only of the Arabic-speaking population.[2] In order to make Arab opposition to Zionism effective, the Congress established a permanent organization to unify and direct Arab efforts, collect funds, and ensure continuity for the movement. This Moslem-Christian movement, in fact, soon became powerful and secured influential external support. In February 1922 the Congress dispatched a Delegation to London to press the opposition of the Moslem-Christian population to the whole policy of the Balfour Declaration. The negotiations and correspondence which followed[3] with the Colonial Office were protracted and marked by plain speaking, and laid bare the fundamental fact of the situation—that what the Arab Congress demanded would, if conceded, render impossible the fulfilment of British pledges to the Jewish people. On 22nd July 1922 the British Government therefore reaffirmed the Balfour Declaration, and there, both in principle and practice, the matter remains.

[1] Cmd. 1540, 1921.

[2] The census of 1922 shows, in round figures, a population including 589,000 Moslems, 83,000 Jews, 73,000 Christians, 8,500 others.

[3] Published as Cmd. 1700, 1922.

CHAPTER I

PART III

EMERGENCE OF ARAB NATIONALISM

C. THE PROBLEM OF MESOPOTAMIA (IRAQ AND MOSUL)

1. *Introduction.* The entry of Turkey into the war forced us to attack the Turkish Empire through its Arab subjects. The plan was adopted of an advance from the various extremities of the Turkish Empire. In each of these campaigns, and in the Mesopotamian campaign most of all, military success was bound to lead first to the destruction of the existing government, and next to some attempt to construct a substitute. Assuming the actual soundness, from the political point of view of the war, of a campaign in Mesopotamia, there was no reason to stop, in fact there was every reason not to stop, between the landing at Fao and the setting up of an administration for the whole of the occupied territory.[1] If oil protection was the object, it would doubtless have cost us less to protect Abadan and the pipe-line than it actually did cost us to extend our arms and at the same time our civil obligations over the three vilayets of Baghdad, Basra, and Mosul, though in the two latter there was also valuable oil. But the advance to these was apparently due to a political desire to avenge the surrender of Kut and to uphold our prestige. If the campaigns in any one theatre cost relatively more than elsewhere, it does not follow that their contribution to the general result is to be dismissed as not worth while.

2. *Situation at the Armistice, 30th October 1918.* The conquered territory was administered on the only possible lines, the higher officials and political officers in nearly every case being lent by the army, the subordinate clerical staff drawn from India. In posts between these two grades Iraquis

[1] Sir W. Robertson, *Daily Express*, 22nd February 1923, is reported as saying 'Troops were sent to Mesopotamia in 1914 to guard our oil interests; but policy was allowed to override strategy, and troops pushed on and on, till they got to Mosul.'

were employed, whenever suitable or willing. But these two necessary provisoes limited the field of choice. We were at war with the Turkish Empire, and most of its officials, the only people in the country with administrative experience, retired with the Turkish armies.

The Armistice brought under our control an area equal to about half the United Kingdom. The communications of this area consisted, in addition to the rivers, of about 650 miles of railway and 10 miles of macadamized roads. The administration of an area so large and so badly served by communications put a great strain on the army and on the civil government. It was a remarkable achievement, out of the resources at hand, to provide a coherent and efficient form of government for the whole.

Whatever the official view of the future of Iraq, this view ought to have governed the measures taken for the settlement of the country. The transfer, after the fall of Kut, of the control of Mesopotamia from India to the Home Government made no apparent difference to the official policy. The British had a chance if not a duty to improve the social, economic, and political conditions of a backward people. They saw the life of the Arab 'solitary, poor, nasty, brutish, and short' without perhaps realizing that the Arab preferred it so. But even if the Arab did prefer it so, it does not follow that the Arab was right, or that we were wrong in trying to improve him. It may be that we went too fast, and that, instead of aiming at the best, we should have been content with the second best. Our proclamation soon after the landing, and General Maude's after the fall of Baghdad, at least implied an obligation to give the Arabs our best. And anything short of that would have exposed us to the more formidable charge of depriving them of one government without giving them anything better in its place.

It must be remembered too that after the fall of Baghdad in March 1917 the battle line was separated from the base at Basra by a distance of 350 miles as the crow flies and 470 miles measured along the shortest possible route by rail, road, or river. An efficient administration of the country, that is an administration by British officials, was essential even with the security of the military occupation.

3. *Question of the Mandate.* This administration, surviving the

Armistice, was found to be too enterprising and too expensive. It is easy to say that this result ought to have been foreseen. It is not easy to discover either how early it actually was foreseen, or what different system could have been adopted. But in any case with the beginning of the negotiations for the Peace Treaty, the problem of Iraq ceased to be a local administrative problem and became part of a world-wide political problem.

This might seem, indeed, already to have been indicated in the Anglo-French Declaration of the 7th November 1918, which stated that the object of British and French in the East was 'the establishment of national governments and administrations deriving their authority from the initiative and free choice of the indigenous populations' and to recognize these governments as soon as they shall have been effectively established. This was aimed primarily at Syria and the Hejaz, but was applied of course by Iraquis to Mesopotamia. Almost simultaneously the theory of the Mandate made its appearance.

In the sketch given by General Smuts of the working of the Mandatory System there was nothing to show that the work of the Mandatory was to be other than slow or expensive. The discussions on the form of Mandate to be applied to Iraq had little effect on, and were equally little affected by, the course of events in Iraq. As a matter of fact, scarcely any progress was made in the assignment or drawing up of Mandates until May 1919, and after that the whole question of Mandates over countries formerly in the Turkish Empire was postponed until the announcement of a decision by the United States. The Mandate for Iraq was not formally accepted by Britain until May 1920. The delay in its publication and still more the delay in the signing of the Peace Treaty with Turkey, however unavoidable, had disastrous results in Iraq.

Between the Armistice and the actual publication of the terms of the Mandate it might have been possible, at the expense of efficiency, to introduce into the government a greater number of native officials. But any form of government in this period was bound to be subject to many embarrassments. The first of these was the progress of the Arab movement in Hejaz and Syria. This had been indispensable to our military success in Palestine, but it very soon committed us to an explicit general recognition of Arab independence so far as we could promote it, in return for an implicit obligation on the part of the Arabs to help us in the war. The fact that we had discouraged Arab co-operation in Mesopotamia was not likely to help us, after the establishment of an Arab kingdom in Hejaz and Syria, still less after President Wilson's pronouncement on self-determination, followed by an opinion said to emanate from the same source, that Mesopotamia might be regarded as one of the countries ready for self-determination; all of which seemed to be confirmed by the Anglo-French proclamation of the 7th November 1918.

4. *Negotiations as to oil and Mosul at the Peace Conference, 1918–19.* It has already been pointed out that the French and British interests in the Middle East had seriously conflicted with one another. They differed about Arab policy, about spheres of influence, and also about control of oil. It was the latter which came to the front in connexion with Mesopotamia.

(*a*) *Discussions of Clemenceau and Lloyd George, December 1918.* Prior to the War British commerce had interests in Mesopotamian oil, indirectly through the Anglo-Persian Oil Company, which drew its chief supplies from Persian territory, and directly through the Turkish Petroleum Company. The capital of the latter was 75 per cent. British and 25 per cent. German. On the 28th June 1914 it obtained from the Turkish Government the exclusive right to all oil in the vilayets of Mosul and Baghdad.[1] This transaction was completed before the War, and the 25 per cent. German capital was liquidated during the War. By the beginning of 1916 it had become necessary for the British and French Governments to delimit their spheres of influence in the Middle East, and in this act of partition Mosul was, under the Sykes-Picot Agreement, assigned to France.[2] But at the time of the Armistice the French were at a disadvantage in having only a few battalions in Syria, while the British had not only conquered Syria with Arab help, but were also firmly fixed in the occupation of

[1] Tardieu, *L'Illustration*, 19th June 1920, *v.* also a debate on the subject of oil in the House of Commons, 10th March 1922.

[2] *v.* above, Chap. I, Part I, A, §7*b*, pp. 15–17; Part III, B, § 7, pp. pp. 141–2. According to Tardieu, *loc. cit.*, Sir E. Grey obtained from M. Cambon, 15th May 1916, a declaration that France was ' ready to sanction, in the regions which should be attributed to it or should be liberated by its action, the different British concessions of a date preceding the War'. This covered the Turkish Petroleum Company, and the declaration was ratified by both Governments 17th May 1916. Cp. R. S. Baker, III, pp. 1–19.

Mosul. Further, the Turkish Petroleum Company had been recognized by the French Government as having the exclusive monopoly of oil in the vilayets of Mosul and Baghdad.

The story is not fully known, but the following is the statement of M. Tardieu.[1] He states that M. Clemenceau arrived in London in December 1918 fully primed with the facts. Mr. Lloyd George demanded a British, instead of an international, administration in Palestine and a transfer of Mosul from the Franco-Arab to the British-Arab sphere. M. Clemenceau indicated approval of these demands on three conditions: (1) France to obtain some share in the oil of Mosul by modification of the agreement (15th–17th May 1916); (2) full support to France against American objections; (3) if the Mandate system prevailed—Damascus and Aleppo, Alexandretta and Beirut were to be under one Mandate (the French).

(*b*) *Berenger-Long Oil Agreement, 18th April 1919.* Negotiations were resumed at the Peace Conference and an oil agreement negotiated between M. Berenger and Mr. Walter (Lord) Long (8th April):

(i) France to receive 50 per cent. of all the oil rights which the two countries could obtain in Russia, Rumania, and Galicia.

(ii) France to receive 34 per cent. of disposable oil in British Colonies.[2]

(iii) Great Britain to receive 34 per cent. of disposable oil in French Colonies.

(iv) France to receive the German share (25 per cent.) of the capital of the Turkish Petroleum Company in Mosul and Baghdad.

(v) Great Britain to have the right of carrying a pipe-line from Mosul across French Mandated territory to the Mediterranean.

(vi) *Negotiations fail over Mosul, May–December 1918.* This question of oil concession was, however, complicated by that of territorial control. On the 21st–22nd May M. Tardieu declares that two discussions (*très vives de ton*) took place between M. Clemenceau and Mr. Lloyd George. They ended by M. Clemenceau saying: 'If you had told me in December (1918)

[1] *L'Illustration, loc. cit.*, cp. R. S. Baker, *Wilson and World Settlement*, Vol. I, pp. 70, 74, 76.

[2] Crown Colonies must be meant.

that the cession of Mosul would entail, in addition, the cession of an immense territory I should, from that moment, have declined to assign you Mosul.'[1] The Berenger-Long Agreement had been ratified by the French Foreign Office on the 16th May, but M. Clemenceau declined to assent to it as being contingent on a satisfactory territorial adjustment. An attempt to renew the accord failed again in December, and the question, according to M. Tardieu, was still unsettled when M. Clemenceau resigned on the 20th January 1920. It is usually unsafe to question the facts of M. Tardieu, but M. Briand did so in the French Chamber on the 25th June 1920. He declared that, in one of those informal conversations, of which no record exists, during the Peace Conference, 'The French agreed to abandon Mosul and Palestine' at a moment which was full of difficulties for them. M. Tardieu contradicted him in a speech, giving the version of the facts above cited, which seem to be confirmed by Mr. Baker.

5. *The Mesopotamian Mandate assigned.* Whatever be the correct explanation, the oil and territorial questions had been settled by May 1920.

(*a*) *San Remo Oil Agreement, 24th April 1920.* The San Remo Oil Agreement signed on the 24th–25th April 1920 was a modification of the Berenger-Long Agreement.[2]

(i) France was to receive 50 per cent. of oil rights acquired by the two countries in Rumania, but, as regards 'the territories of the late Russian Empire' no proportion was mentioned, and also nothing was said about Galicia.

(ii) and (iii) Great Britain to receive not less than 33 per cent. (instead of 34 per cent.) of disposable oil in British Crown Colonies, same proportion for British in French Colonies in North Africa, but not in Tomini or New Caledonia where oil is reported.

(iv) and (v) France to receive the 25 per cent. (i.e. German share) of the Turkish Petroleum Company and to facilitate transport of oil by pipe-line or rail from both Mesopotamia and Persia across French Mandated areas to an East Mediterranean port.

[1] Tardieu, *loc. cit.*; according to R. S. Baker, Vol. I, pp. 78–9, Mr. Lloyd George and M. Clemenceau both stated that they knew nothing of the oil agreement till the 22nd May 1919.

[2] *v.* Text of San Remo Agreement in App. II, Part I.

(*b*) *Assignment of the Mandate, 3rd May 1920, and Sèvres Treaty, 10th August 1920.* It is not clear why M. Briand had consented to an arrangement which M. Clemenceau is said to have refused. But at this time the Emir Feisal, the son of King Husein, and the leader of the Arab revolt, was posing as king at Damascus and asserting his claims over Syria. The French press asserted that British support was promised against Feisal, provided Mosul was handed over to her Mandatory area. At any rate, it was announced on the 5th May that France had been assigned the Mandate over Syria, and that Great Britain had received that of Mesopotamia including Mosul. In July 1920 General Gouraud deposed Feisal, chased him out of Syria, and entered Damascus in triumph on the 7th August. On the 10th August the Treaty of Sèvres was signed in which Turkey 'provisionally recognized Syria and Mesopotamia as independent states subject to the rendering of administrative advice and assistance by a Mandatory until such time as they are able to stand alone'. In each case the Mandatory was already chosen.

6. *The Rebellion in Mesopotamia, August 1920.* Whatever be the true history of these complicated negotiations, it is quite clear that uncertainty and misunderstanding prevailed up to the last moment. The uncertainty as to the policy of the Home Government was naturally reflected in the attitude of the officials on the spot in Mesopotamia and had the worst possible effects. New American wine was fermenting in old Arabian bottles. A wild unreasoning hope as to complete national independence on the Wilsonian model had been actually suggested to the Iraquis by some official actions. Thus the Civil Commissioner in the winter of 1918–19 was instructed to ask the local population three questions: (1) Whether they were in favour of an Arab State including the vilayets of Mosul, Baghdad, and Basra under British tutelage; (2) if so, whether the new state should be under an Arab Emir; (3) and in that case, whom would they suggest? The disturbing novelty of consulting the natives seems to have excited them greatly without resulting in the production of many helpful answers.

Later on disturbances began to break out. At the end of 1919 a really serious movement broke out in favour of Feisal and of a federated Syria and Mesopotamia under his rule. British outposts were attacked on the Euphrates and forces dislodged from certain outlying points. This was a great blow to British prestige. The pro-Feisal movement, as above related, spread to Syria and fanned the flames in Mesopotamia. On the 5th May the assignment of the Mandate to Great Britain was announced. On the 3rd June two British officers and their staff were murdered by Arabs at Tel Afar, west of Mosul. All the elements of a revolt were now present, discontent of wild tribesmen, pan-Arab feelings among tamer townsmen, wild religious enthusiasm. It was in vain that the British Government announced on the 20th June that Mesopotamia was to be constituted 'an independent State under guarantee of the League of Nations' and that 'due regard' would be paid 'to the rights, wishes, and interests of all the communities of the country'. The proclamation also said that Iraq was 'subject to the Mandate of Great Britain'. The rebellion broke out, and the crisis was a dangerous one. During one anxious and critical month (August 1920) the safety of the communicating line between Baghdad and the outer world depended upon the loyalty of one or two sheikhs. Then the tide turned, and the rebellion gradually subsided. With it fell the previous system of government, and Sir Arnold Wilson made way for Sir Percy Cox, who was instructed to conciliate the native population (October 1920). At the same time (December 1920) a Middle East Department was created and placed under the Colonial Office which Mr. Winston Churchill now controlled.

7. *The Cox System, 1921.* The new system of government was a provisional one, pending the decision by a national Assembly of the future constitution of the State. Like the old one it was expensive but it was at least more effective. An Arab Ministry was formed, presided over by the Nagib of Baghdad, the former British secretaries or directors became their advisers. Similarly Arab notables appeared as Mutasarrifs, with British political officers in the background. The 'stopgap' system can never be ideal, but this one seems to have tided over an awkward period.[1] The real question was, what was to be the future constitution, and in the winter of 1920–1 the shadow of a republic dissolved into the more definite outlines of a constitutional monarchy. But who was to be the monarch, and how was he to be elected? After much hesitation a choice was made.

[1] A series of sensational articles on Mesopotamian politics appeared in *The Times* of the 27th December 1921 and following days.

The Arab stone which the French had rejected in Syria became the head of the corner in Mesopotamia. The British Government finally decided to back Feisal. Early in June 1921 it was announced that Feisal was on his way to Iraq. Mr. Winston Churchill announced (14th June 1921) 'that no obstacle would be placed in the way of his candidature . . . and that, if he was chosen king, he would receive the support of the British Government'. But so much emphasis was laid on Feisal's coming simply as the guest of the people of Iraq, that British officials had every excuse for not knowing how they were to act towards him. This is why Feisal complained that their attitude was other than he had been led to expect. At any rate he came, and was received with demonstrations as spontaneous as his agents could make them.

8. *Feisal, King of Iraq, 23rd August 1921.* It does not seem certain that there was any wave of national enthusiasm for him. Basra wanted direct rule by the British, as most likely to secure commercial stability. The north wanted either a Turkish or a British or an Arab government or none at all, but not Feisal. The great Sheikhs of the middle Euphrates regarded him, compared with themselves, as a foreigner and an upstart. His success at first was due largely to British support and less largely to his own reputation. Afterwards his own personality was his greatest asset.

On the 11th July the Council of State unanimously declared Feisal king, with the proviso that his government was to be constitutional, representative, and democratic. This resolution was supplemented by a referendum, which proved nothing except that the people were still amenable to the declared wishes of the British Government. On the 23rd August Feisal was installed as king, having been chosen by 'a great majority'.

The stage-management of his reception into Iraq had been so peculiar that the situation was full of anomalies. In theory he was a constitutional ruler, but without a constitution, and a king by popular consent, though he still had to find his way into the hearts of his subjects. He was surrounded by pitfalls, into some of which he fell heavily. Anti-British feeling showed itself in many incidents. All the time a treaty was being negotiated between him and the British Government which met with all sorts of hitches and embarrassments. At last on the 12th October 1922 the Treaty of Iraq was signed between Feisal and the British Government, and Iraq [1] emerged as an apparently independent but protected state.

9. *The Draft Mandate, 7th December 1920, and American criticism, 1921–2.* To understand the situation created by the Iraq Treaty it is necessary to refer to the international situation. Much mystery was preserved as to the Draft Mesopotamia Mandate.[2] It came before the Assembly on the 9th December 1920 but its terms were not disclosed. Finally the Draft saw the light in February 1921, owing to the enterprise of an American reporter. It met at once with criticism. Lord Sydenham declared that it should be amended, and Lord Robert Cecil expressed the fear that Mesopotamia was to be a recruiting ground for the British army and that Mesopotamian troops were to be used for that purpose.

(*a*) *Military Defence.* The Draft Mandate empowered the Mandatory Power to maintain troops for the defence of the territory. Local forces could be raised in the Mandated area by the Mandatory until the entry into force of the Organic Law.

(*b*) *Internal.* The Turkish capitulations were abolished in this area (Art. 5), but the Mandatory was to secure under the judicial system : (i) the interests of foreigners (Art. 6) ; (ii) the law and jurisdiction now existing regarding the religious beliefs of certain communities (Art. 6). The Mandatory was also to ensure complete religious toleration and freedom of conscience (Art. 8).

(*c*) *External.* The Mandatory was empowered to control the foreign relations of Mesopotamia, to issue exequaturs to foreign consuls, and to have the consular and diplomatic protection of Iraquis outside their own territory (Art. 3).

(*d*) *Commercial.* No discrimination against the nationals of any state a member of the League as compared with the nationals of the mandatory or any foreign state, in transport, commerce, navigation, industry, i.e. generally in trade or oil (Art. 11).

The questions raised by this last provision provoked vigorous remonstrance from the United States in a controversial correspondence, given more fully elsewhere (Chap. VI, Part IV, § 7). The American point, as regards Mesopotamia, was that equality of treatment in trade, and in fact to the commerce of all nations,

[1] *v.* App. II, Part III, B. [2] *v.* Text, App. II, Part III, A.

whether members of the League or not, was a part of the general principles of the Peace Treaties, and that this was infringed by the San Remo Agreement (Art.7) that the Turkish Petroleum Company 'should be under permanent British control'. The British reply was that, while 'equitable treatment' would be given to American traders, the Turkish Petroleum Company had secured pre-war rights from Turkey which must be respected. 'The (San Remo) Agreement aims at no monopoly, it does not exclude other interests, and gives no exclusive right to the Mandatory Power, while the Mesopotamia State is free to develop the oil-fields in any way it may judge advisable, consistent with the interests of the country' (Lord Curzon to J. W. Davis, 9th August 1920). This position was fortified by quotations and facts suggesting that the United States was by no means a practiser of the doctrines of 'equality of trade' and the 'open door' on the American Continent in reference to states like Costa Rica and Hayti.

The Americans returned to the charge, obtained from the League the drafts of the Mandates before they were decided on by the Council, and put forward the further claim that no Mandates shall be revised without the consent of America. They caused great embarrassment to the League, and to their attitude is probably due the fact that the Mesopotamian Mandate is not yet confirmed by the Council. It does not, however, appear that the League is prepared in fact to exclude them from such equality of commercial treatment as is accorded to all members of the League in Mesopotamia, but the British Government has not surrendered its claim, as of right, to exclude any non-member of the League from such benefits.

10. *The Iraq Treaty, 12th October 1922.* Though the Draft Mandate is not yet approved by the Council of the League, it has had much influence upon the Iraq Treaty. In fact the obligations of Great Britain to the League, as defined in the Draft Mandate, necessarily preceded the Treaty, which defines the obligations of Great Britain to Feisal and Iraq. The articles of the Treaty represent what is in fact a scheme for governing Iraq, by British advice and assistance, somewhat in the same way as it was proposed (though fruitlessly) to govern Persia.[1]

(*a*) *Military.* Same as in the Draft Mandate, but Great

[1] *v.* This Chap., Part V, §§ 6–10, pp. 211–17, *passim.*

Britain agrees to provide certain support and armed assistance to the King of Iraq (Art. 7).

(*b*) *Internal.* A British High Commissioner and Consul-General, together with other British advisers, will reside in Iraq, and no officials other than British or Iraquis can be appointed without British consent. In 'all important matters affecting the international and financial obligations and interests of His Britannic Majesty for the whole period of the Treaty', i.e. twenty years, the King of Iraq 'agrees to be guided by the advice of His Britannic Majesty' (Art. 4). He is also to 'fully consult the High Commissioner on what is conducive to a sound financial and fiscal policy'. He undertakes further to 'accept and give effect to such reasonable provisions' as may be devised by the Mandatory for the judicial and other protection of foreigners.[1] These are to form the subject of a special agreement to be presented to the League (Art. 9). Religious freedom and toleration are to be provided for in the Organic Law (Art. 3) as in the equivalent provisions in the Mandate.

(*c*) *External.* The King of Iraq has somewhat more independence than Mesopotamia would have under the Mandate.[2] He can appoint his own diplomatic representatives but, where he is not represented, the protection of Iraqui nationals will be entrusted to Great Britain. He issues exequaturs himself to foreign representatives 'after His Britannic Majesty has agreed to their appointments' (Art. 5).

(*d*) *Commercial.* This is the same as in the Mandate except that Great Britain is permitted to admit to equality of trade, not only members of the League, but 'any state to which His Britannic Majesty has agreed by treaty that the same rights should be ensured as it would enjoy if it were a member of the said League (including companies incorporated under the laws of such state)' (Art. 11). This provision enables the United States (and the Standard Oil Company) to be admitted through 'the open door', if Great Britain so wishes.[3]

(*e*) *Relations to the League.* Arrangements are made for the various agreements to be submitted to the League, but

[1] Iraq is to consent to 'reasonable' provisions re immunity of foreigners. In Articles 5 and 6 of the Syrian Mandate foreigners are more fully protected.

[2] i.e. if drawn on the Syrian model (*v.* Art. 3) which gives the Mandatory sole control of the external relations of the Mandated State.

[3] There is no passage on 'concessions' like that in par. 4 of Art. 11 of the Syrian Mandate.

almost no allusion is made to the Mandate as such. Further differences between the two parties as to interpretation of the Treaty are to go to the Court of International Justice under Art. 14 of the Covenant. Great Britain is to use her good offices 'to secure the admission of Iraq to membership of the League as soon as possible' (Art. 6). The Treaty, however, is to last for twenty years (Art. 18), unless before that date Iraq is admitted to the League 'in which case notice of termination shall be communicated to the Council of the League of Nations'. The main differences between these arrangements and those proposed with reference to Persia are that the League supervises and can protect the interests of Iraq, in a way which it could not have done with respect to Persia. Until the various separate agreements are negotiated it is unsafe to say exactly what the Treaty actually implies in the way of British influence and control, or even as regards its relation to the League. But it would appear that the Council of the League can exercise considerable influence in various ways, and that the Permanent Court of Justice can deal with the Treaty as regards 'interpretation' though nothing is said as to application, and the disputes referred to are apparently those between the two contracting parties. The League's consent would seem necessary to the termination of the Mandate in one form or another.

It is clear that the present Treaty is, to a certain extent, provisional and anomalous, for it comes into force *before* and not *after* the Mandate. It comes into force on ratification by both parties, and is therefore not subject to the preliminary approval of the Council of the League. As regards amendment, the Draft Mandate (Art. 18) provides for the consent of the League to modification of the terms, but by Art. 18 of the Treaty this can be done by consent of Great Britain and Iraq. There is no provision for an annual report to the Council of the League. Most of the difficulties will be removed or cleared up if the League refuses to register the Treaty. Mr. Fisher on the 17th November 1922 stated the general position to the Council as follows:

'His Majesty's Government have obligations, however, not only towards Iraq, but also *vis-à-vis* the League of Nations, for apart from the necessity to submit the draft mandate to the League, Art. 96 of the Treaty of Sèvres, Art. 22 of the Covenant of the League of Nations lays down that the degree of authority, control or administration to be exercised by the mandatory shall, if not previously agreed upon by the

Members of the League, be explicitly defined in each case by the Council . . .

'It will be understood that the proposed Treaty will serve merely to regulate the relations between His Majesty's Government, as mandatory Power, and the Arab Government of Iraq. It is not intended as a substitute for the mandate, which will remain the operative document defining the obligations undertaken by His Majesty's Government on behalf of the League of Nations.'

11. *General Conclusion.* For the present situation in Iraq circumstances are doubtless responsible, and good reasons can certainly be adduced for every step taken by Great Britain at the time. Yet there were certain principles of Eastern policy laid down long ago by the Duke of Wellington which apply to this situation. He once opposed the transfer of the capital of India from Calcutta to Delhi, on the ground that this would be to remove the capital from the operation of British sea-power. If for Calcutta we read Basra, and for Delhi Baghdad, the warning is appropriate. Again, he once told Czar Nicholas that an advance in Asia might be advisable, but, if made, was irrevocable. A punitive or military expedition might be one thing, but an attempt to set up civil administration was quite another. If that was done you could never draw back because of the resultant loss of prestige and of the military dangers attendant upon it. Here again his warning is timely. As a military measure the capture of Baghdad or even of Mosul may have been sound, but the establishment of civil administration and the hesitations of the Home Government confronted us with problems of quite another order, for which the soldiers were not responsible.[1] Hence the danger of the present position.

Whether withdrawal is possible or not is for those with the requisite knowledge to decide. The administration has been enormously costly ; in 1921 we still had 100,000 troops and had spent about a hundred millions of money in Mesopotamia. Under the Turks a garrison of 16,000 troops only had been maintained at vastly less expense. The strategic situation has altered much for the worse. For Mesopotamia was intended to be held in conjunction with Persia, and both were to be under British influence. Now Persia, Afghanistan, on the east, the Bolshevists and the Turks in the north, are all either hostile or

[1] *v.* Opinion of Sir Henry Wilson in *Daily Mail*, 30th May 1922 would seem to prove that he was not responsible for remaining at Mosul. Sir W. Robertson (Speech, *Daily Express*, 22nd February 1923) lays the responsibility on the politicians for going to Mosul.

disinclined to assist our schemes of defence or protection. Mesopotamia is an outwork, with a bastion at Mosul, thrust deep into enemy country. She depends for her life, like a diver, upon a long slender communicating tube which is open to the danger of puncture or severance. No country, which lies so far from the sea and from British sea-power, is really safe from attack.[1]

The commercial arguments for remaining are not easy to understand. It does not seem ever to have been proved that trade follows the flag, still less that the flag must be steeped in oil. The anarchic disorders of Mexico and of Persia have not prevented enterprising British companies from maintaining their hold upon, and deriving large profits from, oil wells.

The humane arguments of remaining to improve the lot of the inhabitants and the condition of the country would be more convincing if it was certain that they really prefer British to Turkish rule, that the Iraquis are capable of forming a nation, that Feisal is really their choice, or that Mosul was desirous of remaining with them. Ultimately the decision will rest with the Turk. For, if the Iraquis continue to regret their old masters, it is difficult to see how we can ultimately prevent them from returning to Turkish sway. The Turks till December 1922 steadily demanded the restoration of Mosul.[2] For the British Empire, as for the Turkish, no graver problem exists than that of Iraq and Mosul.

The final conclusion would appear to be that the Iraq Treaty has been allowed to precede the Mandate, because the British Government wishes to conciliate Iraq by regarding her in some sense as a sovereign state, which she is not, and cannot be, under the Mandate. This step has resulted in Iraq obtaining some concessions which she would not have received under an ordinary mandate. But her position, while improved against the League, is to some extent weakened as against Great Britain. In the end, however, a *modus vivendi* will probably be found, and, like other backward states, Iraq will ultimately find her best friend in the League.

[1] Sir Henry Wilson, *loc. cit.*

[2] Mosul contains Turkish elements, but does not appear at present to be predominantly Turkish in sentiment. The British *pros* and Turkish *cons* on the subject are given adequately in *The Times* of the 24th January 1923. [By Article 3 Treaty of Lausanne (24 July 1923, ratified by Turkey 23 Aug.) the frontier between Turkey and Iraq is to be arranged in nine months between Turkey and Great Britain. Failing an arrangement the dispute will be settled by the League.]

CHAPTER I

THE NEAR AND MIDDLE EAST

PART IV

THE INDEPENDENCE OF EGYPT

THE special status of Egypt as a part—if a rather shadowy one—of the Turkish Empire necessitates its consideration in connexion with the Turkish and other Treaties of Peace.

1. *Pre-war Status of Egypt.* The British control of modern Egypt began with the revolt of Arabi Pasha against the Khedive which caused Great Britain to intervene in 1882 to restore order. In this intervention other interested Powers, though invited, declined to take part, and Great Britain found herself confronted with the Egyptian problem alone. The previous position of Egypt in the Turkish Empire is not easy to describe or to define. Its substantial emancipation from Ottoman rule dated from the days of Mehemet Ali, who obtained hereditary rights for his successors, and of his son Ibrahim, who had carried his victorious arms so far into Asia Minor as to threaten the break-up of the Ottoman Empire. From the fifties onward Egypt began to amass debts and to attract foreign capitalists. The Suez canal, created by French enterprise, led to international agreements in which Great Britain, as a large purchaser of shares and as requiring to safeguard her route to India, was specially interested. The régime just previous to 1882 was a peculiar one. Concessions made by Turkey to Egypt had always been of a unilateral character, i.e. had been theoretically conferred by the Sultan on the Khedive, though in practice they were often yielded at the sword's point. From 1840 right up to 1882 a long series of firmans had defined the position, the most important being that of 1879,[1] which confirmed the Khedive's rights with regard to the conduct of foreign relations. It is important to remember that, before Great Britain appeared on the scene, ' Egypt was an autonomous nationality under the

[1] It however withdrew from Egypt the right of contracting loans, renewed the annual tribute at £750,000 (Turkish), and limited the Egyptian army to 18,000 men.

suzerainty of the Sultan of Turkey.'[1] Egyptian Nationalists, therefore, had a fair case for contending that, before British intervention took place, Egypt really enjoyed a measure of independence. This is the key to the whole subsequent history. Egypt, at any rate in her own eyes and probably both in theory and fact, never has been in the position of a British Colony demanding 'self-government', 'Dominion status', or 'nationhood'. Hence according to the Egyptian view it was not a question of Great Britain conferring privileges or liberties on Egypt. It was simply a question of allowing her to revert to that condition of relative independence which she had possessed before the English arrived.

2. *The British Status in Egypt.* On her entry into Egypt Great Britain declared that she was merely occupying the country temporarily to secure order and to protect the property of foreign residents and would depart as soon as these objects were attained. This theory was upheld by both British parties, and in 1887 Sir Henry Drummond Wolf was dispatched to Constantinople to sign a Convention which should arrange for an evacuation in three years. The Sultan at the last moment withheld his signature and the overture broke down. None the less, the 'national status' of Egypt was, in theory at least, unimpaired. The British position was in no way legalized. The Khedive in law governed Egypt with an Egyptian Cabinet, an Egyptian Legislative Council, and an Egyptian Assembly. The British 'Agent and Consul-General', like similar representatives of other Powers, merely conveyed the views of his Government to the Khedive. In practice, however, the 'special position' of Great Britain was recognized.

The British officials, though in theory advisory, technical, or consultative, had a predominant influence in the administration, but from 1892 onwards their numbers were very restricted. The British Army of occupation ensured order and facilitated a British reorganization, and the command and control of the Egyptian Army Force were British.

To the susceptible Oriental mind this practical control did not outweigh the theoretical advantage of Egypt's position, which served as an implied pledge that the occupying Power did not mean to alter the status of Egypt. Sir Eldon Gorst, the successor of Lord Cromer, even went so far as to say that the

[1] Milner Report, Egypt, No. 1, 1921, Cmd. 1131, p. 7.

'fundamental idea' of British policy was to fit Egypt for self-government 'while helping them in the meantime to enjoy the benefit of good government'. Lord Kitchener, who succeeded him. was less communicative, and one action of his brought into sharp contrast the unreality of theory and fact. When the Italians were fighting the Turks in Tripoli in 1911 Lord Kitchener prevented Egyptian officers or men from going to aid the Turks in Tripoli and refused to permit the Turkish armed forces in Palestine to cross Egypt into Tripoli. It was a form of suzerainty familiar in the East, by which the suzerain (i.e. the Sultan of Turkey) was prevented from marching troops through the district of which he was suzerain. This, however, affected the rights of the Sultan rather than those of Egypt, and excited no special emotion in Egyptians.

3. *The War: a British Protectorate declared.* On the outbreak of war, Abbas II, the notoriously Anti-British Khedive, was in Constantinople. The course taken by Great Britain was intended to avoid hurting the Egyptian susceptibilities, as is shown by the fact that Great Britain annexed Cyprus [1] the day she declared war on Turkey, 5th November 1914. She did not annex, she merely declared a protectorate over Egypt. The proclamation, issued on the 18th December 1914, ran as follows:

'His Britannic Majesty's Secretary of State for Foreign Affairs gives notice that in view of the state of war arising out of the action of Turkey, Egypt is placed under the protection of His Majesty, and will henceforth constitute a British Protectorate.'

'The suzerainty of Turkey over Egypt is thus terminated, and His Majesty's Government will adopt all measures necessary for the defence of Egypt and protect its inhabitants and interests.'

This Proclamation does not suggest that the Protectorate was a war-measure, or that 'the defence of Egypt' by Great Britain was limited merely to defence in the War. Both assertions have since been made by Egyptian Nationalists.[2] It seems fair to point out, however, that other official utterances containing vague assurances about 'accelerating progress towards self-government', etc., were certainly made. One

[1] *v.* also pp. 165, 205 and n.

[2] See Sultan Husein's views given to Sir V. Chirol, *Egyptian Problems*, 1920, p. 132.

result of the Protectorate, which subsequently caused great annoyance,[1] was that the British Government dispensed with an Egyptian Minister for Foreign Affairs and placed the Egyptian Foreign Office under the British High Commissioner who had replaced the 'Agent and Consul-General' as supreme British representative. A graver step than the proclamation of the Protectorate was taken on the 19th December, when a further Proclamation declared Abbas II deposed and stated that the succession had been offered to and accepted by Prince Husein Kamel, with the title of Sultan of Egypt. The title was no doubt meant to indicate Egypt's independence of Turkey, but the deposition of the Khedive by Proclamation after, and not before, the British Protectorate had been proclaimed, suggested that Great Britain was the real ruler and the new Sultan wholly dependent upon her.

4. *Egyptian Dissatisfaction during the War.* The course of the War was not calculated to dispel these illusions. There seems to be no doubt that the recruiting for the Egyptian Labour and Camel Transport Corps, the requisitioning of animals and goods from the natives, and even the collection of subscriptions for Red Cross funds were carried out by Egyptian native officials in a manner which gave rise to all sorts of intimidation and corruption.[2] As these measures were intended to aid Great Britain in the War, she was naturally blamed for them. All this lent stimulus to the Egyptian Nationalist agitation against British rule in Egypt. This was based partly on the inevitably growing discontent of a native population with a foreign ruler, partly on the dislike of Moslems for Christians. It received a notable accession from the theory of self-determination proclaimed by President Wilson. It derived much also from the Anglo-French Declaration of the 7th November 1918, which stated that the objects of France and Great Britain in the East were the 'establishment of national governments deriving their authority from the initiative and free choice of the indigenous populations', and declared their intention to be 'to recognize these governments as soon as they have been effectively established'.[3] The example of the King of the Hejaz, the exploits of Lawrence and of Feisal, brought home to the Egyptians the conviction that the long-expected

[1] It was not till 1919 that this was stated as a grievance.
[2] Cf. Milner Report, pp. 10–11. [3] For Text, pp. 140–1.

hour of independence was at hand. If Arabs could be free, why not also Egyptians ?

5. *Egyptian Demands in 1918, Zaghlul and Rushdi Pasha.* Towards the close of 1918 Sir Reginald Wingate, the British High Commissioner, had warned the Home Government that the ferment of these ideas would soon have its effect in Egypt. Public opinion there was shortly inflamed by various incidents. Zaghlul Pasha and other Nationalists demanded on the 13th November to be allowed to proceed to London with demands for a programme of 'complete autonomy'. The Prime Minister —Rushdi Pasha—simultaneously proposed an official mission to London on lines which had the approval of the new Sultan. His contention, more guarded than that of Zaghlul, was that the Peace Conference would consecrate the British Protectorate and that, before it did this, he was entitled to know what the Protectorate meant and what rights it gave to Egypt. Under the Sultan of Turkey the Egyptians had certain defined rights; what rights had they as against Great Britain under the Protectorate ? The British Foreign Office declined to receive Zaghlul, and suggested that Rushdi's visit was 'inopportune' and should be deferred.

6. *The Deportation of Zaghlul, March 1919.* This dilatory attitude on the part of Great Britain produced serious consequences. Rushdi resigned, and early in March, Zaghlul declared his intention of leading a delegation to lay the legitimate aspirations of Egypt 'before other countries', and sent a heated petition to the Sultan. In punishment for this, after approval by the British Government, the Acting High Commissioner deported Zaghlul and three of his adherents to Malta early in March. This action led to violent outbreaks in the second and third weeks involving looting, arson, severing of railways and telegraphs, murder of British officers, and finally open revolt in four provinces. Lord Allenby, the Commander-in-Chief in Egypt and Syria, was at Paris on the 12th March where he was advising on Syrian and Arabian affairs. He returned to Egypt as 'Special High Commissioner' on the 25th, and by that time the military situation was under control. Lord Allenby took various conciliatory steps, and in the meantime released Zaghlul and his three associates from their deportation at Malta. They made use of their freedom to proceed forthwith to Paris, where they formed one of the numerous unrecognized

deputations of nationalities clamouring for recognition, justice, existence, or self-government. By the time they arrived in Paris, however, the question of Egypt, for good or for evil, had been settled by the various Powers at the Peace Conference.

7. *Attitude of Powers other than England towards Egypt from the outbreak of War to the Peace Conference.*

(*a*) *France.* Previous to the War certain other Powers were almost as much interested in Egypt as Great Britain herself. France had been led by history, by tradition and inclination to exercise influence in Egypt, and had more than once caused great embarrassment to Great Britain. But the Anglo-French Agreement of 1904 altered all this. It was accompanied by a declaration signed in London in which Great Britain declared that she had 'no intention of altering the political status of Egypt'. In return 'the Government of the French Republic, for their part declare that they will not obstruct the action of Great Britain in that country, by asking that a limit of time be fixed for the British occupation or in any other manner'. During the War the British Government did alter the status of Egypt, but the French Government showed every desire to assist and support their Ally, and was one of the first to recognize the British Protectorate.

(*b*) *Powers other than France.* The interests of other Powers were not, like the French, largely political, but chiefly commercial and economic, yet in Egypt the two were inextricably intertwined. By the system of Capitulations, which applied to Egypt as being part of the Ottoman Empire, fifteen states [1] had secured extra-territorial rights of a very extensive character. These included not only certain commercial concessions, but exemption from courts of local jurisdiction, inviolability of domicile and protection from arrest, and most important of all —immunity from personal taxation without assent of their Government. In practice foreigners were (and in 1922 still are) liable only to the house and land tax, and no purely Egyptian legislation applicable to foreigners can be enforced without the consent of the Capitulatory Powers. These privileges really created fifteen centres of extra-territorial jurisdiction upon the soil of Egypt within the Egyptian state. They were not easily

[1] Austria-Hungary, Belgium, Denmark, France, Germany, Great Britain, Greece, Holland, Italy, Norway, Portugal, Russia, Spain, Sweden, United States.

to be justified or maintained in the face of the great improvement in Egyptian administrative and judicial methods, though much of this was due to British influence. The British Consul-General had been tacitly allowed to take the lead before the War, but under a British Protectorate the British High Commissioner might exercise different powers, for it was the avowed British purpose to substitute one authority for fifteen in dealing with Capitulatory matters, and her scarcely less evident purpose to curtail, in some measure, the privileges of all Capitulatory Powers (as, e.g., in regard to taxation) where they injured Egypt's economic development. Hence it was exceedingly difficult to obtain the recognition of a British Protectorate from other Powers, whose merchants were naturally desirous of maintaining their special position. Between the 18th December 1914 and the Armistice of the 11th November 1918, Belgium, France, Greece, Portugal, Russia, and Serbia had given this recognition. After the Peace Conference began to sit it became highly important that other Powers should follow suit. Italy—whose interests were important—delayed very long, and did not finally give recognition. The United States finally recognized the British Protectorate on the 23rd April 1919.[1] Five neutral powers[2] remained, together with two Enemy Powers—Germany and Austria-Hungary. With the last two it was easier to deal.

8. *Enemy Powers deprived of Capitulatory Rights.* In the Draft Treaty to Germany, presented on the 7th May 1919, according to Art. 147 (unaltered in the revised Treaty of the 28th June) 'Germany declares that she recognizes the Protectorate proclaimed over Egypt by Great Britain on December 18, 1914, and that she renounces the régime of the Capitulations in Egypt. This renunciation shall take effect as from August 4, 1914.'[3] A series of other articles (148–53) effectively deprived Germany of economic, financial, or commercial interests in Egypt. Art. 154 contained a significant provision—'Egyptian goods entering Germany shall enjoy the treatment accorded to British goods'.

Austria and Hungary were compelled by similar articles in their treaties to recognize the British Protectorate and also to

[1] Mr. Lansing, no believer in 'self-determination', says he urged this recognition on President Wilson in September 1918.

[2] Denmark, Holland, Norway, Spain, Sweden.

[3] *v.* Text in Vol. III, pp. 184–6.

renounce all Treaty and contract rights acquired by the former Austro-Hungarian Monarchy.[1]

Germany did not, however, surrender without a struggle. She declared that she was 'obliged, without consulting the Egyptian people, to recognize the protectorate over Egypt by Great Britain and . . . to violate Egypt's right of self-determination'.[2] Her protests were disregarded at the Peace Conference, but they were noted by Zaghlul, and the appeal to 'self-determination' added fuel to the flame of Egypt's nationalistic aspirations.

9. *The Treaty of Sèvres, 10th August 1920.* The international aspects of the Egyptian question were practically terminated by these separate recognitions, and by the various Treaties, and finally by that of Sèvres of the 10th August 1920 whereby Turkey renounced all her rights in, or title, over Egypt as from the 5th November 1914, and recognized the British Protectorate (proclaimed on the 18th December 1914).[3] This Treaty has not, indeed, been ratified, but the Turkish aspect of the question is not of a serious character, except from the strict standpoint of international law. Her rule had long been nominal, and regret or desire for the Turk formed no part of the Egyptian agitation. It was not Pan-Islam, but self-determination and 'Egypt for the Egyptians' which were the burning watchwords of that movement.

10. *The Milner Mission and the Milner-Zaghlul Conference, 18th August 1920.* As a result of the agitations of 1919 it was announced in May of that year that Lord Milner would head a special Mission to Egypt to inquire into disorders, to report on the existing situation and to suggest a form of Constitution. Unfortunately, in view of the increasing agitation, its departure was delayed till the end of November, and it was received with great demonstrations of hostility by unofficial persons and with

[1] Austrian Treaty, Art. 102–9, Hungarian Art. 86–93 ; *v.* Text, Vol. V, p. 204.

Bulgaria was also compelled to recognize the Protectorate but, as she had no capitulatory rights, was merely compelled to renounce all claim to them, *v.* Bulgarian Treaty, Art. 63, Text, Vol. V, p. 318.

[2] *v.* Vol. II, pp. 299, 363.

[3] Art. 101–12. Art. 101 runs thus : 'Turkey declares that in conformity with the action taken by the Allied Powers she recognizes the Protectorate proclaimed over Egypt by Great Britain on December 18, 1914.' Not all Allied Powers had recognized the British Protectorate. The French (and decisive) version runs 'La Turquie qu'en conformité avec l'action prise par les Puissances alliées'.

great reserve by Egyptian officials.[1] The mission returned to England in March 1920, and through the moderating influence of Adli Pasha, Zaghlul Pasha was persuaded to come to London with some of his adherents to discuss with Lord Milner the possibility of arriving at a solution of the Egyptian question. A memorandum was eventually drawn up and signed by Lord Milner on the 18th August 1920, the adoption of which Lord Milner was prepared to recommend to the British Government in return for Zaghlul pledging himself to urge its adoption on his countrymen in Egypt. The Memorandum first suggested that a Treaty should be signed between Egypt and Great Britain, in which the latter recognized the independence of Egypt as a constitutional monarchy with representative institutions, Egypt in turn agreeing to confer on Great Britain 'such rights as are necessary to safeguard her special interests', and to give the guarantees to foreign Powers necessary to secure their relinquishment of Capitulatory rights. In the second place it provided for a Treaty of Alliance between the two countries in which Great Britain should support Egypt in defending her territorial integrity, while Egypt offered, in case of war, to give Great Britain all the assistance and facilities in her power, 'within her own borders'. Egypt was to have the right of diplomatic representation in foreign countries, but would undertake not to adopt in foreign countries an attitude inconsistent with the alliance, or create difficulties for Great Britain or enter into agreements with foreign Powers prejudicial to British interests.

Egypt was to give Great Britain the right of maintaining a military force on Egyptian soil to protect her imperial communications, but this force was not to constitute a military occupation of the country nor to prejudice the rights of the Egyptian Government. Internally, a Financial Adviser and an official in the Ministry of Justice were to be appointed by Egypt in concurrence with His Majesty's Government. Finally, Great Britain was to negotiate the whole question of Capitulations. Lord Milner made clear in a separate letter to Adli Pasha of the same date that the Sudan had been deliberately excluded from the discussion. Zaghlul was unwilling to commit himself to the

[1] The Milner Mission consisted of Viscount Milner, Sir Rennell Rodd, General Sir J. G. Maxwell, General Sir Owen Thomas, M.P., Sir C. J. B. Hurst, J. A. Spender with Mr. A. T. Loyd and Captain E. M. B. Ingram as Secretaries.

policy of the Memorandum without first testing the feeling of his countrymen towards it. Some of his colleagues proceeded to Egypt and found a disposition to accept with some detailed modifications. On their return, October 1920, to London, negotiations were resumed, but failed to result in the agreement anticipated. The Milner Mission then proceeded with their Report and finally signed it on the 9th December 1920.

11. *Lord Allenby's Proposals, November 1921–January 1922.* During the next ten months much futile negotiation over a draft treaty took place, but the attitude of both parties caused difficulties. Egypt declined a draft treaty and refused absolutely to go further until the Protectorate was finally abolished. Next, on the 17th November 1921, Lord Allenby reported to Lord Curzon [1] that his British Advisers were unanimously of the view 'that a decision which does not admit the principle of Egyptian independence, and which maintains a protectorate must entail serious risk of revolution throughout the country' . . . 'Unless His Majesty's Government are prepared to give substantial satisfaction to expectations which Egyptians have legitimately formed on the basis of apparent policy of His Majesty's Government during the past two years, it will be impossible to form any Ministry.' 'Strong military force' could, of course, be used, but 'liberal concessions' were necessary. Lord Curzon suggested that this argument was 'to a large extent unsound'. Lord Allenby replied (6th December) that he wanted to be able to promise the Sultan 'a higher degree of independence' than the British Government 'are clearly disposed to grant'. He added, on the 11th December, that 'no Egyptian . . . can sign any instrument which in his view is incompatible with complete independence. Consequently it is necessary definitely to abandon the idea that the Egyptian question can be settled by means of a Treaty'.

On the 21st December, Lord Allenby, in consequence of the renewed violence of Zaghlul's attitude, prohibited him from further political activities, arresting him on the 23rd and subsequently deporting him to the Seychelles. Violent agitations ensued and a new Ministry under Sarwat came into office. On the 12th January 1922, Allenby asked for the approval of the

[1] Egypt, No. 1, 1922, Cmd. 1592, p. 5. One point in dispute was that Great Britain claimed the right of military occupation unlimited in time and space, never before in fact exercised. On the 3rd December 1921 the British Government's note indicated a return to the policy of force, which was subsequently abandoned.

Government, for the following statement to the Sultan of Egypt. Great Britain was prepared to recommend to Parliament, without waiting for the conclusion of a treaty, the abolition of the protectorate and the recognition of Egypt as an independent sovereign State, and the re-establishment forthwith of the Egyptian Ministry for Foreign Affairs, and consequent diplomatic representation of Egypt abroad. The régime of martial law was to be abolished as soon as an Egyptian Indemnity Act had been passed, and could be suspended 'in respect of all matters affecting the free exercise of political rights of Egyptians'. After this new state of affairs was established, the two Governments would conclude an agreement on the following four points: (*a*) security of communications of British Empire; (*b*) defence of Egypt against all foreign aggression or interference direct or indirect; (*c*) protection of foreign interests in Egypt and protection of minorities; (*d*) the Sudan. Lord Allenby made it clear that, in his opinion, the country could not be governed any longer without concessions on these lines.

12. *The British Declaration to the Sultan, 28th February 1922.* Lord Allenby was summoned to England to explain his views. As a result they were accepted *in toto*, except that the *status quo* as to the four points (*a*), (*b*), (*c*), and (*d*) was to be maintained pending the 'free discussion and friendly accommodation on both sides to conclude agreements in regard thereto between His Majesty's Government and the Government of Egypt'. Till such time the discretion of the British Government, as regards (*a*), (*b*), (*c*), and (*d*), was 'absolutely reserved'.

These sentiments were communicated to the Sultan on the 28th February in the form of a unilateral declaration, thus showing that Great Britain claimed definitely to have certain concessions and to reserve certain matters. The Protectorate was abolished and Egypt recognized as 'a sovereign independent state'. As regards other foreign states, however, the situation is made sufficiently clear in Mr. Lloyd George's explanatory telegram to British Dominion Governments of the 27th February. 'In communicating the substance of this declaration to foreign Powers, we propose to announce that the termination of the British Protectorate over Egypt involves no change in the *status quo* as regards the position of other Powers in Egypt. We propose to declare that the welfare and integrity of Egypt are necessary to the peace and safety of the British Empire, which will, therefore, always maintain as an essential British interest the special relations between itself and Egypt long (*sic*) recognized by other Governments, and in calling attention to these special relations as defined in the declaration recognizing Egypt's independence, we propose to declare that we will not admit them to be questioned by any other Power, that we will regard as an unfriendly act any attempt at interference in the affairs of Egypt by another Power; and that we will consider any aggression against the territory of Egypt as an act to be repelled by all means at our command.'

13. *General Principles.* The settlement thus outlined has two aspects, internal and international. The 'sovereignty and independence', which Egypt has received, seem of a limited character. Zaghlul, the man who had done most to win Egypt's independence, was actually deported just before Egypt received 'the right to manage her own internal affairs'.[1] Further, both the Capitulatory régime or its substitute, and certain arrangements enabling Great Britain to interfere in certain matters of finance and justice, seem hardly reconcilable with 'independence' or 'sovereignty' as normally understood. This seems to be even more the case as regards external affairs. Egypt is to have her own Foreign Office and diplomatic representatives but it is clear that, in most things, Great Britain will act as intermediary between her and Foreign Powers, who are very seriously warned against interference. The arrangement is 'equivalent', in Lord Allenby's words, 'to the declaration of a British Monroe doctrine over Egypt,' though even the most strenuous disciples of Monroe have never said 'hands off' to foreigners in a more determined manner.

14. *The Sudan and Cyprus.*

(*a*) *The Sudan.* The status of the Sudan is important both to Egypt, to Great Britain, and to Foreign Powers, and that is one of the reasons why foreign states are recommended not to question these matters in which the rights of the British Empire are so vitally involved. The status of the Sudan is defined by the Anglo-Egyptian Convention of the 19th January 1899, which lays it down that Great Britain was 'by right of conquest' entitled 'to share in the settlement and future working and development' of the Sudan. By this claim and in virtue of this Convention, the authority of the Turkish Sultan was definitely excluded, as also was the Capitulatory régime of

[1] On 4th April 1923 he was released from Gibraltar by British authorities on the ground of ill-health.

Egypt, and 'no foreign consuls should reside in the country without the consent of the British Government'. The Governor-General, who has supreme military and civil power, was to be appointed by the Khedive of Egypt on the recommendation of the British Government. The arrangement seems clear. The Sudan is an Anglo-Egyptian Protectorate virtually controlled by Great Britain. Thus the flags of the Egyptian Sultan and the British King float side by side over the Sudan, but all the administration is British. Mr. Lloyd George in Parliament on the 1st March 1922 stated that we 'will never allow the progress that has already been made and the greater promise of future years to be jeopardized'. He further added that Great Britain could not 'agree to any change in the status of that country (the Sudan) which would in the slightest degree diminish the security for the many millions of British capital which are already invested in its development'. All this evidently relates to a period preceding that at which the Mandate theory came into force. The legal situation seems to be that the status of the Sudan was settled by a pre-war arrangement in which Egypt herself took part but which she is now apparently claiming to discuss if not to revise. Foreign Powers are frankly told that they will not be permitted to interfere. In point of fact it would appear that they have already renounced such rights by the Treaty of Sèvres but this was not ratified, and is now superseded by the new Treaty of Lausanne.[1]

(*b*) *Cyprus*. By the Treaty of Sèvres (Art. 115–17) the High Contracting Parties (i.e. the Allies as well as Turkey) recognized the annexation of Cyprus proclaimed by the British Government on the 5th November 1914. Turkey renounced all rights or title over Cyprus including tribute. Turkish nationals born or habitually resident in Cyprus will acquire British, and lose Turkish, nationality. This arrangement is, however, unratified.

[1] Treaty of Sèvres, Art. 113. 'The High Contracting Parties declare and place on record that they have taken note of the Convention between the British Government and the Egyptian Government defining the status and regulating the administration of the Soudan, signed on January 19, 1899, as amended by the supplementary Convention relating to the town of Suakin signed on July 10, 1899.'

Art 114. 'Soudanese shall be entitled when in foreign countries to British diplomatic and consular protection.'

By Art. 16–17 of Lausanne Treaty (24th July 1923, ratified by Turkey 23rd Aug.) Turkey renounced all titles over Egypt and the Sudan as from 5th November 1914, and (Art. 20) recognized the British annexation of Cyprus from the same date. *v. supra*, pp. 165, 195.

CHAPTER I

THE NEAR AND MIDDLE EAST

PART V

THE LIBERATION OF PERSIA

1. *Introductory*. Persia is a country enormous in extent but, on the whole, barren and unproductive except in the Caspian provinces and the oil area in the south. The chief interest she possessed for other Powers before the War was to form a 'buffer-state' between Great Britain and Russia. The latter Power was steadily expanding southwards and had, ever since 1879, been attempting to penetrate into North Persia. The chief volume of Persian trade was with the Caucasus and the north and Russia's interest was, therefore, evident. The inability of the Persian Government to protect traders, the badness and scarcity of her communications, naturally led Russia to constant interference. British interests were less evident and less aggressive. Great Britain obviously desired to maintain maritime control of the Persian Gulf, and had had a long trading connexion with this area and its hinterlands. Hence British interests in Persia were connected also with Mesopotamia. However, in the first decade of the twentieth century, British interests became directly involved with the security of the oil fields of Persia from which the British fleet was to draw increasing supplies of fuel. This interest was naval and, therefore, vital. The energetic Anglo-Persian Oil Company obtained concessions in South-west Persia in the Karun valley and in the Baktiari area, and had built pipe-lines to the coast, and established oil refineries near the mouth of the Shat-el-Arab at the Isle of Abadan. Here again, and in a more important manner, British interests were concerned alike with Persia and with Mesopotamia. In peace time these concessions involved no infringement of Persian sovereignty, and, in fact, supplied a revenue to Persia and gave Great Britain an interest in preventing her from falling under the control of another foreign Power. None the less British interests began to be bound

up with those of Russia when Germany pressed on with the Baghdad railway. In the Agadir period, and subsequently, Great Britain often had to co-operate with Russia in demands on Persia, not because she approved of them, but because her interests outside Persia compelled her to support Russian claims. None the less the British desire was, if possible, to maintain Persia's independence.

2. *The Anglo-Russian Agreement, 31st August 1907.* From 1881 to 1914 the history of Persia has been a history of penetration by Russia and of attempts by Great Britain to nullify or resist the effects of that penetration and to hold on to the coast and control the Persian Gulf. By means of a Russian bank and of Russian loans and Russian commerce the Tsarist Government arrived at economic control, and by a force called the Persian Cossack Brigade (ultimately Division), officered by Russians, they endeavoured to secure material control at need. British diplomacy, without force and without adequate funds, was thought to have secured a notable triumph in 1906 when British support enabled Persian Nationalists to secure a constitution, and forced the Shah to abandon his despotic control of the Government. But the young Mejliss or Parliament had great difficulties to overcome, which were increased by Russian intrigue, by the death of the old Shah, and the accession of an anti-constitutional tyrant.[1] For reasons above mentioned, Great Britain entered into an agreement with Russia on the 31st August 1907, which was very disadvantageous to the former. Both Powers engaged to respect the 'strict independence and integrity of Persia'. Each Power bound itself to seek no concessions whatever in regions conterminous to the frontier of the other. The spheres were then defined, the Russian including Ispahan and Yezd and Teheran, and the British the province of Kirmán, the south-eastern corner of Persia conterminous with Baluchistan and Afghanistan. Persia was not informed of this agreement, which so gravely affected her, until after its conclusion,[2] and Afghanistan expressed her disapproval.

This arrangement was, in several ways, to the disadvantage

[1] Muhammed Ali; *v.* Professor E. G. Browne's *Persian Revolution of 1910*, Cambridge (1908). He holds strongly to the view, upheld also by other great authorities, that the constitutional movement might well have succeeded.

[2] The text and explanatory letter are in Shuster, *Strangling of Persia*, pp. 25–30.

of Great Britain. The Karun valley, including the important oil centre near the coast and mouth of the Tigris, was not in the British sphere, and, but for the War, the Baghdad railway would certainly have given Germany a strong footing there. The British sphere was largely a sandy waste with only one important town (Kirmán), and was intended simply to provide a barrier against Russian advance. The districts adjoining the British-Indian frontier were to remain a desert. The Persian objection to this agreement was natural and correct. Their traditional policy was to play England off against Russia. When the two Powers were agreed, this was no longer possible. Further, the policy of Tsarist Russia was not honest, for she 'undoubtedly aimed at the annexation of Northern Persia, and we (i.e. Great Britain) in self-defence, would ultimately have been obliged to take over the southern provinces'.[1] If this is the case, Persia and her friends had some reason for denouncing the Agreement. It is, however, pretty certain that the Agreement did hamper Russia, and that, without it, the Russian annexation would have proceeded more rapidly. In a secret telegram of the 20th March 1915, from the Russian Government to Count Benckendorff in London, M. Sazonoff confirmed Russia's 'assent to the inclusion of the neutral zone of Persia in the British sphere of influence'. He added ominously 'the Imperial Government expects that in future its full liberty of action will be recognized in the sphere of influence allotted to it, coupled in particular with the right of preferentially developing in that sphere its financial and economic policy'.[2] 'Full liberty of action' here must mean Russian annexation, and the fact that it is demanded suggests that England had previously hampered such annexation.

3. *Mr. Shuster, 1911–14.* The Russians soon showed their hand, inspiring intrigues everywhere, harbouring troublesome refugees, creating incidents, and finally sending Russian troops into Persian territory. The Shah Muhammed Ali began fighting the Constitutionalists but on the 16th July 1909 he

[1] Sir Percy Sykes, *Persia*, p. 148. On 4th December 1911 Benckendorff wrote that the terms 'Integrity and Independence of Persia' possessed 'little real importance', and Sazonoff indicated on his visit to England (September 1912) that the neutral zones might have to be annulled. Siebert, *Collection of Entente Documents* (American translation), pp. 91, 132.

[2] Secret document published by Bolsheviks in *Manchester Guardian*; reproduced in F. Seymour Cocks, *Secret Treaties*, pp. 22–4; *v.* also *supra*, Chap. I, Part I, A, § 3 *sub fin.*, pp. 8–9. *Morning Post*, 25th Aug. 1923.

was deposed by the Mejliss who chose as Shah Ahmad Shah—a boy of twelve. The old Shah took refuge with the Russians and was then supported by them in his attempt to regain the throne. Great Britain, however, did nothing to aid him, and his attempt finally ended in 1911.

The Persian Government had already invited an American, Mr. Morgan Shuster, to reform their finances. He arrived early in 1911 and showed great energy in his task, but Russia interfered and finally insisted on his withdrawal. 'His failure was most regrettable, and the only consolation is, that, had he been tactful and suitable in every way, Russia would sooner or later have found means by which to oust him.' [1] Other authorities go further than this and hold that he was suitable in every way. Anyhow it is certain that he was loved by the Persians, who ascribed his fall to the fact that he had sought to establish the independence of Persia and to regenerate the nation.[2] And the fall of Shuster finally confirmed Persia in the view that one great Power had vowed her destruction, and that Great Britain, if not an accomplice of Russia, was at least unable to be an effective restraint upon her. Matters went from bad to worse, and in 1914 the anti-British feeling in Persia was only less acute than the anti-Russian.

4. *Persia in the War, 1914–18.* Persia declared her neutrality at the outbreak of war, but the Government was unable to keep order and, in so far as they had a policy, were hostile to Russia and consequently to the Entente which supported her. The German Minister saw his opportunity and practically reigned supreme at Teheran. Russian forces speedily occupied the north and north-western area, and, despite some remonstrances from the British Minister, showed every intention of annexing territory. In the south the British occupied the Turkish port of Basra to protect the oil refineries on the Isle of Abadan and sent a military force to occupy Bushire in Persian territory.[3] An effective control of Persia had been established in 1917, when, as a result of the Russian Revolution, the Russian troops gradually melted away. Great Britain was

[1] Sir Percy Sykes, *op. cit.*, p. 152.

[2] Shuster, *op. cit.*, p. 96, says: 'The British Minister let it be known he favoured the financial plans . . . which we were endeavouring to put into effect.'

[3] During the War the British Government also acquired some five million one-pound shares of the Anglo-Persian Oil Company for the nation.

then forced to act alone. Generals Douglas and Sykes held firmly on to the coast and built a good road between Bushire and Shiraz. In 1918 General Dunsterville with a small force marched through Persia, and, after many romantic adventures, finally occupied Enzeli on the Caspian. Another British force occupied East Persia from Transcaspia to the frontier of Baluchistan. The manifest aim of these movements was to draw cordons across Persia to prevent German, Turkish, or Bolshevist agencies from reaching Afghanistan or the Indian frontier and sowing dissension there. The Armistice removed the German danger, but the others remained. The Bolshevist propaganda, equally well adapted to Persia, India, or Afghanistan, was formidable enough, and, in the near future, the country might be invaded by Bolshevist or Turkish troops, or by a combination of both.

To secure a strong, stable and friendly state on the flanks of India and Mesopotamia Great Britain aimed at controlling the armed forces of Persia after the Armistice. This was not easy. Many of the gendarmerie organized by Swedish officers were pro-Turkish in sympathy, and the South Persian Rifles, into which some of them entered, were disaffected and had already mutinied. The South Persian Rifles, however, became an efficient force in 1919. The Persian Cossacks, still under Russian officers, were equally or even more untrustworthy. British forces were separated from one another by immense distances, and the Persian people were hostile or unfriendly. Subsidies issued on a lavish scale to these and other forces served temporarily to quiet them but seem ultimately only to have encouraged them in disloyalty to their paymasters.[1] Probably the wiser course would have been to retire altogether from North Persia (the old Russian sphere) and concentrate on the coast so as to protect the oil fields. But it has been argued that this course was not really possible after the Armistice, and that complete evacuation or control of the whole country were the only two courses open.

At the beginning of 1919 the well-known Arab expert, Sir Percy Cox, was appointed temporary Minister at Teheran, and made a great effort to negotiate a working arrangement with the Persian Government.

[1] It has been reckoned that these sums in 1919 and 1920 came to about £225,000 monthly or nearly three millions a year, without reckoning personal or local subsidies.

5. *Persia at the Peace Conference.* A Persian Delegation arrived at the Peace Conference. Their demands were of considerable interest as they mark the attempt of Persians to state their national claims in public. These demands were three:

(*a*) *Political.* Abrogation of the Anglo-Russian Agreement of 1907. They further demanded the abolition of consular courts and withdrawal of consular escorts.

(*b*) *Economic Independence.* Persia demanded reparation for the devastation of areas and destruction of property by the various armies which had entered Persia during the War. She also claimed freedom from concessions and a control of her own economic destinies.

(*c*) *Territorial.* This last demand was reminiscent of the old days of Persia's glory. Oblivious of the present she demanded the Oxus for her boundary, thereby claiming Transcaspia, Merv, and Khiva. In the western and north-westerly directions she actually claimed Asia Minor to the Euphrates, i.e. Kurdistan, Diarbekir, and Mosul.

All these demands were made at a time when the Government were entirely unable to organize, administer, or control the Kingdom of Persia within the pre-war boundaries.

So far as the Peace Conference was concerned, Persia secured an invitation to become a member of the League, as was seen in the Draft Treaty with Germany presented on the 7th May. Otherwise she was not allowed to state her case. Her Foreign Minister, Mushavim-el-Mamaulik, was with the Delegation but was not permitted to visit England, because he was anti-British in his sentiments. This did not prevent Great Britain from coming to terms with the Teheran Government by a secret agreement in London, negotiated by Prince Firuz Mirza—another Persian Minister.[1]

6. *The Anglo-Persian Agreement, 9th August 1919.* This important agreement was completed and published on the 9th August. Before stating its terms it may be well to state that two letters were simultaneously addressed to the Persian

[1] *v.* Text, § 6, pp. 212–13.

Government which contained the British answer to their Peace Conference demands. (p. 211). As regards :

(*a*) *Anglo-Russian Agreement of 1907*. Great Britain consented to co-operate in the revision of Treaties, i.e. to abrogate all Anglo-Russian Agreements, but said nothing as to abolishing consular escorts and courts.

(*b*) *Economic Independence*. To support Persia's claim for damage suffered at the hands of *other belligerents*. The Persian claim for abolition of consular courts and escorts was not accepted.[1]

(*c*) *Territorial*. To agree to a rectification of the frontier at certain points.[2]

The Agreement was as follows :

'PREAMBLE : In virtue of the close ties of friendship which have existed between the two Governments in the past, and in the conviction that it is in the essential and mutual interests of both in future that these ties should be cemented, and that the progress and prosperity of Persia should be promoted to the utmost, it is hereby agreed between the Persian Government on the one hand, and His Britannic Majesty's Minister, acting on behalf of his Government, on the other, as follows :

'1. The British Government reiterate, in the most categorical manner, the undertakings which they have repeatedly given in the past to respect absolutely the independence and integrity of Persia.

'2. The British Government will supply, at the cost of the Persian Government, the services of whatever expert advisers may, after consultation between the two Governments, be considered necessary for the several departments of the Persian Administration. These advisers shall be engaged on contracts and endowed with adequate powers, the nature of which shall be the matter of agreement between the Persian Government and the advisers.

'3. The British Government will supply, at the cost of the Persian Government, such officers and such munitions and equipment of modern type as may be adjudged necessary by a joint commission of military

[1] There would seem to be no doubt that Persia alone could not protect aliens within her borders. In 1917 the Governor of Ispahan was proved to have received blackmail from robbers, and there is plenty of evidence to show that this was a common practice among provincial governors.

[2] The only attempt to carry this out appears to be a vague suggestion in Art. 62 of the Treaty of Sèvres (10th August 1920) providing for the local autonomy of Kurdistan. A Commission composed of British, French, Italian, Persian, and Kurdish representatives was to 'visit the spot to examine and decide what rectifications, if any, should be made in the Turkish frontier where, under the provisions of the present Treaty, that frontier coincides with that of Persia.' In old days the Persian frontiers had stretched, at one time or another, far west of the Euphrates, had reached the Caucasus on the north, and the Indus on the east.

experts, British and Persian, which shall assemble forthwith for the purpose of estimating the needs of Persia in respect of the formation of a uniform force which the Persian Government proposes to create for the establishment and preservation of order in the country and on its frontiers.

'4. For the purpose of financing the reforms indicated in clauses 2 and 3 of this agreement, the British Government offer to provide or arrange a substantial loan for the Persian Government, for which adequate security shall be sought by the two Governments in consultation in the revenues of the customs or other sources of income at the disposal of the Persian Government. Pending the completion of negotiations for such a loan the British Government will supply on account of it such funds as may be necessary for initiating the said reforms. [By a separate agreement Persia contracted for a British loan of £2,000,000 at 7 per cent.]

'5. The British Government fully recognizing the urgent need which exists for the improvement of communications in Persia, with a view both to the extension of trade and the prevention of famine, are prepared to co-operate with the Persian Government for the encouragement of Anglo-Persian enterprise in this direction, both by means of railway construction and other forms of transport; subject always to the examination of the problems by experts and to agreements between the two Governments as to the particular projects which may be most necessary, practicable, and profitable.

'6. The two Governments agree to the appointment forthwith of a committee of experts for the examination and revision of the existing customs tariff with a view to its reconstruction on a basis calculated to accord with the legitimate interests of the country and to promote its prosperity.' (*v. infra*, p. 214). Signed at Teheran, 9th August 1920.

7. *Persian hostility to the Agreement.* The Agreement was no sooner published than it met on all sides with hostile criticism. It was asserted in Paris that this arrangement had been concluded behind the backs not only of the Persian delegates present at Paris, but also of the Peace Conference as a whole. The French papers were bitter, and Viscount Grey criticized severely the secrecy of the negotiations as inconsistent with the Covenant of the League. The United States is declared, on good authority, to have protested strongly against the whole arrangement, and the American Legation in Teheran formally denied that they had given any approval to it. Persian feeling, so far as national or popular opinion could be discerned, was very hostile. The secrecy of the negotiation caused deep suspicion in Persia. All sorts of allegations, mostly uncomplimentary, were made. A deeper feeling was stirred by the proposal for employing British advisers throughout. Persian policy had been either to employ neutral foreigners, such as Belgian customs officers,

Swedish gendarmes, or American financiers, or to play off the advisers of interested powers—German, Russian, or British—one against the other. With experts all of one nation this game would be impossible. Moreover, Persians knew well that it is one thing to get experts into a country and quite another thing to get them out, and the chaotic state of the country promised a long stay for the visitors. Persians had another objection to an All-British personnel. The bureaucracy from ministers to local tax-gatherers, from provincial governors to gendarmes, would be kept strictly within their legal salaries, and everything would be governed in a uniform and systematic way. This was not agreeable to those who loved irregularity. All sorts of arguments, large and small, noble and base, political and national, tended to inflame public opinion against the new bargain with the alien.

Some efforts were made to counter this propaganda. On the 17th August 1919, Mr. Cecil Harmsworth, Under-Secretary for Foreign Affairs, denied that 'the (British) Government proposed or that the Persian Government would have consented to create anything in the nature of a protectorate' and Lord Curzon spoke even more emphatically in the same sense. A few days later the Shah was induced to visit England. But the Shah, even had he been friendly, could not ratify the Treaty. For one important fact had been forgotten, Persia was still governed by the Constitution of 1906, and by Art. 24 every treaty, covenant, or concession had to be approved by the Mejliss, except secret treaties. The Anglo-Persian Agreement had been published, and therefore had to be ratified by the Mejliss.[1] This circumstance was probably overlooked, for the Mejliss had not sat since 1915. It had never been a body easy to control, but, if it had been immediately summoned, some authorities have thought that it would have approved the Agreement.

8. *The Bolshevik Intervention, 1920, and Perso-Russian Treaty, 27th February 1921.* During 1919 and the spring of 1920 some progress was made, and the Customs Tariff was actually revised, though without giving Great Britain any preference. A reorganization of the army was planned but, before it could

[1] The accusation that there were secret articles in the Agreement appears to be groundless. In any case, if it were correct, such articles would not be binding for, by the Supplementary Fundamental Laws of 1907, Art. 53, 'The secret clauses of a Treaty cannot in any case annul the public clauses of the same'. *v.* Shuster, *Strangling of Persia*, pp. 294, 305.

materialize, a tremendous blow was struck at British prestige. The Bolsheviks intervened in force. A Bolshevik fleet in the Caspian appeared off Enzeli, slowly pushed back the slender British forces, seized the ships abandoned there by Denikin, and landed troops in large numbers. After much hesitation and delay the Persian Cossacks, still led by ex-Tsarist officers, advanced against the Bolsheviks. After some spectacular successes they had to fall back in a state of demoralization and to find shelter in the British lines. General Ironside, the newly appointed British commander, showed a resolute front to the Bolsheviks and insisted on the dismissal of the Russian officers in the Cossack division. But it had already been determined to withdraw British forces from the north. In the month of February the Bolsheviks achieved a great diplomatic coup, and the Persian Cossacks a great military one. First the Bolsheviks signed a treaty with Persia, cancelling Persia's debt to Russia, offering to withdraw their troops, and handing over all Russian concessions and public works, as roads, railways, harbours, etc., to Persia.[1] This was spectacular enough, for it exhibited Russia as disinterested and Great Britain as the exploiter of Persia. What followed was still more spectacular. A Persian, Reza Khan (Sirdar Sipah), managed to corrupt the Persian Cossacks, and induced them to advance on the capital. On the 21st February Teheran fell and Reza Khan, posing as a liberator, made Seyd Zia, a Persian journalist, Prime Minister. Both Russian and Persian influences had proved alike anti-British.

9. *Denunciation of the Anglo-Persian Agreement, June 1921.* Seyd Zia, the new Prime Minister, was, however, not wholly a puppet. He denounced the Anglo-Persian Agreement, 'in order', as he said, 'to do away with misunderstandings between the Persian and English peoples.' Apart from that he was enlightened enough to desire British friendship, and made some efforts to secure it. But by the end of April the British forces had practically evacuated North-west Persia, so that he was left with only Cossacks to make head against Bolsheviks. In March, Rothstein, a Bolshevik minister, had arrived at Teheran. Before the end of May Zia was driven from office, and the influences that succeeded were wholly anti-British. Reza Khan had caused his fall, and, since then, he has been the 'uncrowned king' of Persia.

[1] Except only the valuable fisheries in the Caspian.

In June 1921 the Mejliss met, and the Shah, in his opening speech, alluded to the 'happy demise' of the Anglo-Persian Agreement. Arrangements were made for disbanding the South Persian Rifles, and finally for getting rid of all British advisers civil or military. The Government completed its work of expelling British influences by granting oil-concessions in the five northern provinces to the American Standard Oil Company. By the D'Arcy concession the Anglo-Persian Oil Company hold a monopoly of oil production in all Persia except these five provinces, and had actually purchased the Russian rights in the northern provinces, which were now handed over to the Standard Oil Company.[1] American financial advisers were once again sought by the Mejliss. The negotiators of the Anglo-Persian Agreement were denounced as traitors, and friendly relations established with Afghanistan, Azerbaijan, and Kemal Pasha, i.e. with the covert or open foes of Great Britain.

The British view of these transactions was stated with some vigour by Lord Curzon in the House of Lords on the 27th July 1921. He described the instability of Persian ministries, the atmosphere of perpetual and invincible intrigue, the hatred, suspicion, and hostility which had made all British efforts vain. Persia had definitely rejected British aid and British influences. She preferred the Bolshevik Government to us, or at least feared them too much to adhere to us. Hence all British officials and British forces were being withdrawn. He himself had been a friend of Persia for thirty years.[2] Persia had of her own will made her own choice as she was free to do. But, if the choice was hers, so also would be the consequences.

10. *Persia and the League. Conclusion.* Persia has made some attempts to benefit by her admission to the League. Immediately after the Bolshevik aggression in May 1920 she appealed to the League, and the matter was discussed before the Council on the 15th and 16th June. The 'Economic Weapon' was useless against the Bolsheviks and the League could do nothing. So the Council commended Persia, approved her undertaking direct negotiations with the Bolsheviks, deferred their decision, and asked to be informed of the march of events. The result of these direct negotiations must certainly

[1] Some working arrangement between the two companies seems subsequently to have been arrived at.

[2] One authority says that this 'statement was not well received, and, to put it mildly, was not concurred in by the Persians'.

have exceeded expectation, and Persia may have ascribed some of the result to the League. The Shah in opening the Mejliss stated somewhat naïvely in June 1921 that foreign troops were being withdrawn from the country and that it was hoped to obtain reparation for the damage they had done through the League of Nations. In connexion with the Agreement Great Britain had offered to support such a claim against foreign belligerents *other than herself*, but by the denunciation of that Agreement this obligation ceased. It is not easy to see how reparation can be obtained from the other belligerents, viz. the Turks, the Germans, the Bolshevik and the anti-Bolshevik Russians, since they are not members of the League. But Persia has continued her faith in the League and her chief delegate in 1921 made a most eulogistic speech on the League's labours at the Assembly. It is also of importance that she is still (December 1922) the only independent Mohammedan State in the League.

The situation of Persia has not been unlike that of Albania. Each was hampered, both before and since the War, by obligations and agreements between foreign States which she was physically helpless to resist and yet spiritually unable to accept. Each desired to remain neutral in the War and each failed to do so. In the case of each nation, a combination of circumstances has led to the withdrawal of occupying troops and to freedom from external interference. The method of emancipation has, however, been different. Albania owes her frontiers, her existence, her recognition to the League ; Persia owes more to the Bolsheviks than to anyone else. In that lies her danger for the future. But, whatever her defects, she has shown in the past an inexhaustible capacity for refusing to accept foreign domination, and her future is at present in her own hands.

CHAPTER II

THE RESURRECTION OF POLAND

PART I

HISTORICAL SKETCH

PRINCE LICHNOWSKY, writing not long before the Armistice, declared that the 'Polish question is perhaps the most difficult of all questions', and that 'it now forms for Germany the gravest problem of the war and of the peace'.[1] Later experience, particularly that of the Peace Conference, has justified this opinion, at least with regard to the exceptional difficulties of the problem.

At bottom it is a question of a people who have never enjoyed the advantage of clearly-marked natural frontiers or of an adequate and assured access to the sea, and whose political frontiers have fluctuated in astonishing fashion down to the time when their state was wiped out of existence; with the result that to-day this nation is scattered in larger or smaller numbers over a vast area—an area half as large again as Germany; the domain in which it has a numerical preponderance is very much smaller than the domain over which it once ruled or in which its culture is still predominant; and it is a very difficult problem to assign to it frontiers that will satisfy its just claims and its vital needs without at the same time infringing upon the rights of neighbouring peoples. For a clearer comprehension of the problem, it is indispensable to glance at the geography of the country and to consider certain aspects of its history.

1. *The Geography of Poland.* Poland lies almost exactly in the centre of Europe. It forms part of the great plain which begins in France, extends across northern Germany and Russia, and terminates at the Urals. It lies at the point where this plain, which is comparatively narrow in the west, widens out like a fan, owing to the southward bend of the Carpathians, to spread henceforth from the Baltic to the Black Sea. This position at what may be called the neck of the funnel, or the gateway from the broad plain of the east to the narrower one

[1] Article in the *Berliner Tageblatt*, 2nd September 1918.

of the west, has placed Poland athwart what has always been the great commercial and military highroad between east and west, and also upon several important routes between north and south (the route from the Black Sea to the Baltic via the Vistula, and that from the Baltic to the Mediterranean via Cracow and the 'Moravian Gate'). This position has brought great advantages and perhaps even greater dangers. It has given the country an exceptional importance as a distributing centre and a highway for transit trade; but, on the other hand, situated at the meeting-place of the Germanic, the Scandinavian, the Slavic, and—for centuries—the Asiatic worlds, Poland has been terribly exposed to attacks from all sides, and has been for centuries the great battle-field of Eastern Europe, much as Belgium has been in the West. To-day the Poles in Europe number between 25 and 30 millions,[1] and are wedged in between the two giant nations of the Continent, the Germans and Russians, who outnumber them respectively in the ratio of 2 and 3 : 1.[2]

The dangers of this exposed central location are increased by the fact that Poland has no good natural frontiers. The only boundaries that nature has provided in this region are the Carpathians on the south and the Baltic on the north, but neither of these barriers has fully served its purpose either as an ethnographic or a political limit. On the south the Polish population overlaps the mountain crest for a considerable distance; so did the frontiers of the old Polish state, and so in part do the frontiers of the newly created Poland. On the north, old Poland was never able to hold a sufficient frontage on the Baltic, and the Polish population has allowed itself to be crowded away from the sea-coast except for a narrow strip along the shore just west of Danzig. On the east and west hardly any serious barrier is to be discovered. The great European plain is broken only by the numerous rivers, which serve, not so much to separate the peoples, as to unite and to mingle them. The valleys of the Oder, the Warta, and the Netze have brought the Germans into Poland; and the Niemen, the Pripet, and the Dniester have carried the Poles far into Lithuania and the Ukraine. The one real obstacle to ethnic and political expansion

[1] An exact figure cannot be given in the present state of our statistics.

[2] This is on the basis of deducting the Ukrainians and White Russians from the Great Russians.

that the plain presents, is the great area of marshes and forests in the Pripet valley. That gloomy and ill-favoured region never attracted Polish colonists, who advanced in great waves into the fertile lands on both sides of it: north-east into the Grodno and Vilna regions, and south-east, towards Lemberg, Volhynia, and Podolia. Hence the strangely bifurcated appearance presented to-day by the eastern limits of the Polish ethnographic area (or at least of the area with a large percentage of Polish population) and hence the difficulty of drawing a good eastern frontier for Poland. The Polish advanced positions at Vilna and Lemberg form two exposed salients, cut off from each other by the wedge-like Pripet region with its enigmatic population, which may be White Russian or Ukrainian, but is certainly not Polish.

The river valleys at any rate afford Poland whatever natural unity she possesses, particularly the great central stream, the Vistula. The latter river has always been the great artery of the country's economic life, and scarcely any other European nation has its settlements concentrated in one river valley in like degree. Poland might, indeed, be described as the basin of the Vistula, plus the valleys of certain adjacent rivers which offer easy access to the Vistula, are in part connected with it by canals, and virtually form one network of water-ways with it. This complex of closely connected rivers has vastly facilitated Polish expansion in the past, and offers magnificent commercial possibilities for the future—the chance to open good and easy connexions with the Danube, the Niemen, the Dnieper, i.e. with half of Eastern Europe. But the proper exploitation by Poland of her splendid water-routes has always depended, and in the future will probably depend, on her control of the great port at the mouth of the Vistula—an inadequate control in the past, and not too secure a one at present.

2. *The Territorial Development of the old Polish State*. Poland was originally a rather small state. The early Polish kingdom, as it grew up between the tenth and twelfth centuries under its first dynasty, the House of Piast, included what has been called in recent times 'Congress Poland'[1], Western Galicia, Silesia, Posnania, West Prussia, and (at times) Pomerania. In short it embraced the region between the Oder and the

[1] The small kingdom set up by the Congress of Vienna in 1815 and incorporated in Russia a few years later.

Vistula, and not much more. At any rate, it extended farther to the west and possessed a broader frontage upon the Baltic than was to be the case in later times.

In the twelfth and thirteenth centuries the realm went through a period of division, weakness, and confusion, owing to frequent partitions and civil wars among its princes. Unfortunately for Poland, this period coincided with one of the greatest ages of German expansion and colonization, the most successful period in the thousand years' history of the Teutonic *Drang nach Osten*. It was at this time that Brandenburg, Mecklenburg, Pomerania, and Silesia [1] passed under German control and were flooded with German colonists. Even more serious was the fact that in the thirteenth century the Teutonic Knights established themselves in East Prussia, assimilating or exterminating the original Prussians,[2] and founding there a German colony which has always remained a thorn in the side of Poland. In 1309 the Knights succeeded in seizing West Prussia as well, thus bridging the gap between their older possessions and Germany, completely cutting off Poland from the Baltic, and inaugurating that struggle for the mouth of the Vistula which has gone on intermittently ever since.

When Poland in the fourteenth century pulled herself together again as a united kingdom, it was too late to think of recovering most of the lands lost during the preceding period. To one of these losses, namely, that of West Prussia, the Poles could not be permanently reconciled, for it imperilled their most vital interests. The recovery of that province was the

[1] Silesia began to detach itself from Poland from 1163 on, after it had come to have a separate line of dukes of its own (a branch of the House of Piast). In the thirteenth century these dukes were more and more drawn into the political and cultural orbit of Germany and estranged from Poland. They filled up their lands with German colonists, who came to predominate in all parts of the duchy except the south-eastern corner, 'Upper Silesia', where the Polish element has maintained its numerical superiority down to the present day. About the beginning of the fourteenth century, the dukes of Silesia transferred their allegiance from Poland to the Kingdom of Bohemia, which was then one of the leading states in Germany. The Piast dukes lingered on as vassals of the Bohemian Crown until their line died out in 1675. Silesia passed along with the Bohemian lands to the Hapsburgs in 1526. As a result of the War of the Austrian Succession, about nine-tenths of it fell to Prussia in 1745, but the southern fragments—the old duchies of Troppau and Teschen—continued to form 'Austrian Silesia' down to 1918. (*v.* Vol. IV. pp. 348–50).

[2] A people who, as is well known, were neither Germans nor Slavs, but closely related to the Letts and Lithuanians.

aim of the ensuing Hundred Years' War between Poland and the Teutonic Knights, a struggle that has the very greatest importance in Polish history and is marked by the historic victory over the Germans at Tannenberg (Grünwald) 1410.

Looking for allies and additional resources for this struggle, Poland turned to the East and began her *Drang nach Osten*, a momentous expansion which presents many analogies to, and was the direct result of, the Germanic movement called by that name. The initial success in that direction was the conquest of Eastern Galicia (1340–77), the first encroachment by Poland upon the domain of the Ukrainian nationality, and the beginning of a problem that has been very much before the world in the past two years. An even more brilliant success was the personal union between Poland and Lithuania in 1386, a capital date in the history of Eastern Europe. For Lithuania was at that time a huge state, stretching from the Baltic to the Black Sea, including nearly the whole of the White Russian and the Ukrainian peoples, a realm built up within a couple of generations by able rulers and the valour of the little Lithuanian nation, which formed scarcely one-tenth of the population of its vast empire. The union between Poland and Lithuania created a realm which was for a long time the strongest power in Eastern Europe, and which remained down to the Partitions the second or third largest state on the Continent.

Reinforced by this immense accretion, Poland was able to carry through to a successful conclusion the struggle with the Teutonic Knights. By the Peace of Thorn, which crowned her victory (1466), West Prussia, including Danzig and the mouth of the Vistula, was reunited to Poland, although with extensive rights of local self-government, while East Prussia was left to be held by the Knights as a fief of the Polish Crown.[1]

An even more important result of the union of 1386 was the gradual fusion of Lithuania with Poland. In this partnership, which has scarcely a parallel in European history, Poland, the smaller but more culturally advanced state, constantly predominated and—without a struggle or even serious friction—

[1] In 1525 the King of Poland allowed the Teutonic Grand Master, Albert of Hohenzollern, who had become a Protestant, to secularize East Prussia and turn it into a duchy hereditary in his family. In 1618 this duchy passed to the Brandenburg branch of the Hohenzollerns. The Great Elector succeeded in freeing East Prussia from Polish suzerainty by the treaties of Wehlau (1657) and Oliva (1660).

to a large degree absorbed and assimilated her associate. The connexion between the two states, which originally consisted solely in their possession of a common ruler, was gradually tightened until in 1569 it was turned into a permanent organic union. By about the same period the nobility of Lithuania and to a large extent the Christian population of the towns had voluntarily accepted the Polish language, customs, and nationality; and Polish colonists had settled thickly in many parts of the Grand Duchy.[1] Polish culture reigned in Vilna, Minsk, Lutsk, and Kameniets, almost as much as in Cracow or Warsaw.

This process of Polonization did not, however, extend to the lower classes of the population. It is true that one great obstacle was largely removed by the foundation of the Uniate Church in communion with Rome,[2] to which the bulk of the Orthodox populations in Galicia had by the eighteenth century adhered. But the masses of the Lithuanian, White Russian, and Ukrainian peasantry still clung to their respective languages and national customs, and opposed an insuperable barrier to the solid establishment of Polish nationality throughout most of the eastern territories.

It is scarcely necessary to speak here of the many fluctuations of the Polish frontiers during the sixteenth and seventeenth centuries, or of the reasons for the stagnation and decadence into which Poland, like many other countries, had fallen during the eighteenth century. But it may not be out of place to survey briefly the situation of the Republic just prior to its dismemberment, for the Poles to-day are continually driven to make the comparison between the new Poland that is being created, and the old 'historic' Poland that existed before the Partitions.

3. *Poland in 1772.* On the eve of the First Partition Poland ranked as the third largest state on the Continent, with an area of 282,000 square miles, while in population it stood fourth, with over 11 million people. Its frontiers extended from the Baltic and the Carpathians to the Dnieper and the Dvina. It included nearly the whole of that broad isthmus between the Baltic and the Black Sea which leads from Eastern continental Europe to the peninsular Europe of the West.

[1] i.e. Lithuania.

[2] A body founded in 1596, which accepted the supremacy of the Pope but was allowed to preserve the Slavic liturgy and many special rites and practices of the Orthodox Church.

Within these boundaries Poland perhaps formed more of a natural geographic unit than does the new Poland of to-day. At least, Polish geographers have generally held that the area defined above has a high degree of physical unity with respect to its structure, climate, products, river systems, and other features, and that from this standpoint 'historic Poland', stretching from sea to sea, was the ideal political arrangement for this region, the only arrangement that would make the picture fit the frame.

Whatever be the merits of such views, the old Polish state suffered from the fact that its population was far from homogeneous. The Poles can scarcely have formed more than 50 per cent. of the population, at the most; more than one-third of it was made up of Ukrainians and White Russians, and the remainder consisted of Germans, Jews, Lithuanians, Letts, Armenians, and Tartars. It may be surmised that if this state had lasted on into the nineteenth century, it would have had to face very serious troubles from nationalist movements, which have disrupted most other states containing a similar medley of peoples.

Old Poland was also weakened by the fact that while it was a Republic both in name and in fact,[1] political rights and privileges were restricted almost entirely to the nobility; a prosperous Polish middle-class was sadly lacking; and the peasants were held in serfdom. This gave the state a perilously narrow basis. It tended to make the masses of the population rather indifferent to the fate of the Republic; it tended to make Polish patriotism a monopoly of the nobility and of the clergy.

Economically, the country was then miserably poor and backward, from causes into which it is impossible to enter here. The cities, apart from Warsaw and Danzig, were small and unimportant; commerce and industry were almost non-existent; agriculture was the one mainstay of economic life.

Politically, the Republic had by the middle of the eighteenth century fallen into a sad state of impotence and lethargy. The defects, abuses, and eccentricities of the Polish constitutional system of that time are sufficiently well known. But since this gloomy chapter of Polish history has, in the minds of so many people in the West, obscured all the earlier, brighter period, it

[1] Although it had had an elected king as its nominal head.

deserves to be pointed out that the old Polish state in its best days—in the sixteenth and seventeenth centuries—had been a rather creditable and attractive experiment. It was the largest and most ambitious experiment with the republican form of government that the world had seen since the days of the Romans. It was the first experiment on a large scale with a federal republic down to the appearance of the United States. In the sixteenth and seventeenth centuries this Republic was the freest state in Europe, the state in which the greatest measure of constitutional, civic, intellectual, and religious liberty existed. In an age of religious persecution and chronic religious wars, Poland knew few such troubles; it offered almost complete toleration and an asylum to those fleeing from persecution in all Western lands. And if in the eighteenth century the Republic had fallen into evil days, the errors and shortcomings of that period can be paralleled in many other European countries, and they are certainly not to be taken as proving that the Polish nation is permanently incapable of independent statehood. One is no more entitled to predict that a free Poland will hasten to repeat the mistakes of the eighteenth century, than one would be to hold up against the present-day Italians the similar faults of their ancestors of the same period. The childish unfitness of Italians for self-government was once a commonplace of politics, just as was the conception of the Germans as only a 'nation of thinkers and dreamers'.

4. *The Partitions of Poland* (*1772*, *1793*, *1795*, *1815*). At the moment when Poland had reached the lowest stage in her decline, the three great aggressive monarchies that surrounded her, Russia, Austria, and Prussia, united to despoil her of certain territories which they coveted. By this First Partition (1772) Catherine II appropriated a part of White Russia (the later 'governments' of Vitebsk and Mogilev); Frederic II took West Prussia (though without Danzig); and Austria acquired most of what is now Galicia.

This drastic lesson served to arouse the Poles from their lethargy and to start a very promising movement for political, economic, and social reforms. But the neighbouring Powers were not disposed to tolerate this revival. Once more they fell upon the Republic, and whereas they had partitioned it the first time because it was weak and 'anarchical', on the next occasion they dismembered it because it was growing inconveniently strong. By the Second Partition (1793) Prussia annexed Danzig and Posnania, while Russia seized all the country as far as a line which, curiously enough, corresponds rather closely to the Polish-Russian frontier marked out a few months ago by the Treaty of Riga.

This intolerable humiliation provoked the uprising led by the national hero, Kosciuszko, a last desperate effort on the part of the Poles to free themselves. By way of punishment for this brave attempt, the three great Powers then combined to destroy Poland entirely (Third Partition, 1795).

Of the moral side of these transactions it is hardly necessary to speak here. The world has long since passed judgment, and the almost unanimous opinion of all disinterested critics has been that the dismemberment and annihilation of this peaceful and inoffensive state was one of the worst international crimes that modern Europe has witnessed.

After Napoleon's half-hearted attempt to restore Poland, the Congress of Vienna in 1815 made a new distribution of the Polish territories, which then lasted with slight changes down to the outbreak of the World War. By this Fourth Partition Russia was left in possession of about 82 per cent. of the area of 'historic Poland'; 10 per cent. falling to Austria; and 8 per cent. to Prussia. But since 'historic Poland' and 'ethnographic Poland' (i.e. the area within which the Poles form the majority of the population) do not by any means coincide, it may be pointed out that under the arrangements of 1815 about three-fifths of the ethnically Polish race were left under Russian rule, one-fifth under Austria, and one-fifth under Prussia.[1]

5. *Poland since the Partitions.* The history of Poland from the time of the Partitions down to the outbreak of the World War may be divided into two periods. During the first of them (down to 1863) the nation, refusing to believe that the unparalleled wrong done to it could endure for more than a short time, made no less than nine efforts to regain its freedom by arms. This was the period of perpetual conspiracies, ever-recurring insurrections, and of heroic but fruitless sacrifices; the period when most of the élite of the nation lived in exile,

[1] While our statistics are pretty unreliable, especially the Russian ones, it may be said that in 1910 there were in Prussia about 4 million Poles; 4·3 million in Austria; and at least 13 million in Russia. *v.* Statistical Tables, Vol. II, p. 214.

forming the Polish Legions in the armies of Revolutionary France and of Napoleon, making themselves, later on, the knights-errant of liberty in every foreign land, ready to shed their blood generously whenever a chance presented itself to fight for the freedom of other peoples (1830, 1848–9); the period, too, when the splendid efflorescence of Polish literature attested the vitality and power of the national genius, and a galaxy of romanticist poets sang the hopes and sufferings of 'the martyr nation' with poignant beauty and pathos.

After the failure of the insurrection of 1863, however, the Poles could not but recognize that the methods hitherto pursued were hopeless. As long as the three great military monarchies of Eastern Europe remained erect and united in their common purpose of keeping their victim enchained, the restoration of a free and united Poland was an impossibility. Hence after 1863 the Poles in the main renounced conspiracies, rebellions, and indeed any hope of fulfilling their national aspirations save in the very distant future. Many of them turned away in despair from politics and threw themselves into 'work on the foundations', i.e. the economic upbuilding of the nation. Others devoted themselves to such modest opportunities for political work as the existing conditions afforded. The one aim was to survive as a nation: to keep patriotism alive, and to quicken and invigorate it among the masses of the people; to prepare the nation materially and morally for the future day when, through a fundamental change of circumstances, Poland might emerge from the tomb.

(*a*) *Russian, and* (*b*) *Prussian, Poland.* There can be little need of again describing here the régime of oppression, persecution, and attempted denationalization to which the Poles were subjected during most of the nineteenth century. That régime was particularly accentuated in Russian Poland from 1863 onwards; in the Austrian share during the period down to 1866; and in Prussian Poland after the advent to power of Bismarck. The effort to drive the Polish language from the schools, the courts of justice, and all administrative intercourse; to suppress Polish institutions and organizations of every sort; to uproot the sense of Polish nationality, or at least to render impossible every external manifestation of it—such methods were characteristic of what Poland has experienced at the hands of all three masters. The Tsarist government distinguished itself by its intermittent outbreaks of exceptional brutality, such as the exploits of Muraviev, ‘ the Hangman ’, the dragonnades in the Cholm territory, or the prohibition of the speaking of Polish in any public place (in Lithuania). The Prussian government pursued a less lurid, but more continuous and methodical, system of oppression. Not content with merely holding down the Poles, it undertook the more positive policy of ‘ swamping ’ them with Germans. Every one knows at what cost and with what perfect absence of moral scruples this government laboured since 1886, through its Colonization Commission and other agencies, to tear away from its Polish subjects the land that had been theirs for a thousand years and to re-people it with Germans. The culmination of this policy was the unparalleled Act of 1908, which authorized the government to expropriate any Polish landowner at its discretion.

(*c*) *Austrian Poland.* At all events, the pressure to which the Poles have been subjected was never uniform in all three parts of their country. There has always been some one part in which conditions were more tolerable, and patriotic work could still be carried on. If Russian Poland served in such a rôle from 1815 to 1830, during the brief existence of the constitutional kingdom founded by Alexander I, and Prussian Poland formed a haven of refuge during the mid-nineteenth century under the mild rule of Frederick William IV, Austrian Poland in the last fifty years became ‘ the Polish Piedmont ’. Forced by her expulsion from Germany in 1866 and by her dualistic reorganization in 1867 to seek a new equilibrium of forces and to bid for the loyalty of her Polish subjects, Austria accorded to the Poles of Galicia a wide measure of local autonomy and, indeed, she virtually turned over the government of that province to them. Hence, Galicia could become the great centre of every sort of Polish intellectual, economic, and political activity, the headquarters of every national movement, a school whose output of parliamentarians, of trained administrators, and of soldiers is of no slight importance for the new Polish state that has just been created. Doubtless it was a far from perfect school, for Galicia has not escaped all traces of the contaminating political atmosphere of Austria ; but, at any rate, it afforded the chief, and in many respects the only, training for national self-government that the Poland of to-day has received.

(*d*) *Modern tendencies.* The variety of political and economic régimes under which the Poles have lived for more than a hundred years has not failed to produce a considerable differentiation and even a certain estrangement between the three long-sundered parts of the nation. Every visitor to the country to-day is struck by the differences in ideas, habits, and character between the hard-headed, practical, rather unsentimental Posnanian Poles, among whom illiteracy is almost unknown and who have taken on much of the Prussian love of order, regularity, and efficiency; the Galician Poles, with their passion for politics and their tendency to slow, easy-going Austrian ways; and the Russian Poles of the 'Congress Kingdom', with their 50 per cent. of illiteracy, their much more backward economic and social conditions, their political inexperience and doctrinairism—all legacies of the Russian period—and their greater devotion to art, to literature, and to the things of the spirit. While the unity of the nation has not been fundamentally broken down, it will assuredly be a task of much difficulty to establish uniform laws and institutions where such a diversity has hitherto existed, and to overcome the manifold and subtle effects of more than a century of disunion.

Among the other changes that the last hundred years have produced, one must mention the decided weakening of Polish influence and of the Polish element in many regions that belonged to the old Republic. The partitioning Powers have not laboured altogether in vain. At the beginning of the nineteenth century Polish culture and the Polish language still reigned throughout almost the whole of historic Poland, at least in this sense that the educated and socially predominant classes adhered to them. Since that time 'Polonism' has met with grave losses. The country gentry, who were its chief representatives in the more easterly territories, have lost a great part of their estates or of their influence, through the policy or the reprisals of the Russian Government. By means more efficacious than edifying Nicholas I and his successors brought back to the bosom of the Orthodox Church millions of Uniate peasants in White Russia and the Ukraine, millions who, as long as they remained obedient to Rome, had been oriented towards Poland rather than Russia. Furthermore, two at least of the peoples once united with the old Polish state have now developed pronounced nationalist movements of their own—the Lithuanians and the Ukrainians. Almost inevitably both movements have assumed a marked anti-Polish tendency, since both had to fight against the Polish culture that had long predominated among their peoples and had quite seduced their upper classes away from them. However incomplete these revivals of long-dormant nations may be, they have, at all events, made it clear that the restoration to Poland of her frontiers of 1772 is out of the question to-day.

Nevertheless, these losses and setbacks to the Polish cause have been compensated, in part at least, by gains elsewhere. If the Polish element has lost ground in territories where it was widely but thinly disseminated and represented chiefly by the *intelligentsia*, it has continued to make progress, even in the time of Poland's servitude, in regions where it was more concentrated and where, in particular, there was a Polish peasantry on which to build. There has been a steady and impressive increase of Polish population in Eastern Galicia.[1] And in the heart of 'historic Lithuania', in the region around Vilna especially, it would seem that the Polish language has been making wide conquests in the most recent decades. Some evidence of this appears even in the statistics prepared by the Tsarist Government, although in the case of the regions affected by the Polish question those statistics were in general so 'tendencious' and so much 'made to order' that, in the opinion of the present writer, they afford no safe basis for determining the exact ethnographic situation. If one can accept the concurrent testimony of the census taken by the Germans in 1915–16 and the one taken by the Poles in the winter of 1919–20, there is now a continuous belt of predominantly Polish territory extending from the Congress Kingdom through the Grodno and Vilna districts as far as the Dvina. For certainty as to the details we may have to wait until a census is taken that is less exposed to controversy than the ones just mentioned. Yet it seems probable that the Polish element in the central zone of 'historic Lithuania' has gained a degree of strength or even numerical preponderance of which the old Russian statistics and the current ethnographic maps give no adequate conception.

[1] 1857—20 per cent. of Poles; 1890—31·2 per cent.; 1910—39·6 per cent. While it is true that this gain is partly due to the fact that the Jews, forming 12 per cent. of the total population, have within the period in question transferred themselves from the German to the Polish column, there can be no doubt that the Poles alone have increased more rapidly than the Ukrainians.

In the west the Poles have also made gains, although of a rather different sort. Here it has been a case of awakening a national movement among Polish-speaking populations which had long been separated from Poland and were apparently quite destitute of any Polish national consciousness. Such has been the work accomplished in the past half century in Upper Silesia and in Teschen, regions that had been politically detached from Poland since the fourteenth century. Such was the task undertaken by a few patriots, among the Protestant Poles (' Masurians ') of East Prussia, who had never been directly under Polish rule at all; but here the national revival was only in its first faint beginnings at the time when the World War broke out.

Of even greater importance than these gains around the periphery has been the internal transformation that Poland has undergone since the middle of the nineteenth century. The emancipation of the serfs and the agrarian reforms that grew out of that measure have produced a class of laborious, thrifty, and on the whole prosperous peasant landowners, a class which, as a result both of the propaganda carried on by the intellectuals and of its own hard experience under foreign domination, soon came to rally to the national movement. In Prussian Poland, during the bitter struggle of the last thirty years for the land, in face of the colonizing enterprises of the Government, the peasants have been the mainstay and the salvation of the Polish cause. Meanwhile, Russian Poland, since the ' sixties ' of the last century, has been going through an astonishingly rapid industrial development, which made that region one of the chief manufacturing centres of the Russian Empire. This helped to produce a numerous, active, and enterprising middle class, an element hitherto sadly lacking in the social structure of the nation, and a large class of industrial working-men, who have also displayed a patriotism no whit inferior to that of the old ruling classes.

In short, in the last half-century a new Poland has arisen, far stronger, richer, more harmoniously developed, more fitted for self-government than the old Poland of the *szlachta*[1] and the clergy. If the generation that had witnessed the fiasco of 1863 had renounced politics and had almost despaired of Poland, the generation that appeared at the close of the century

[1] The gentry, great and small.

and which is now upon the stage, grew up with a more hopeful and self-confident spirit, proud of the material progress that was being made, full of faith in the new democratic society that was being created, ready to believe that the day of deliverance was not so far off after all. And from the time when the revolution of 1905 gave the first premonition of the internal dissolution threatening Russia, and still more after the Bosnian crisis of 1908 had shown the probability of a great war in which the partitioning Powers would be matched against each other, the Poles began to look forward to and prepare for that Armageddon which alone could set them free.

CHAPTER II

THE RECONSTITUTION OF POLAND

PART II

POLAND AT THE PEACE CONFERENCE

1. *General Introduction.* Poland lies in the very centre of Europe in a situation which, while geographically advantageous in many respects, is rendered difficult by the proximity of two of the greatest Powers of Europe, Russia in the east and Germany in the west. If we take into account all people who are Poles by race and language within the area claimed as Polish, they amount to some 20 millions—a number relatively large in comparison with the general average of European nations, but dangerously small in comparison with the totals of her two powerful neighbours.[1] The Carpathians offer a certain protection in the south, but at the same time in their character as a barrier they direct all movements, whether military or economic, into a channel running east and west, and neither to the east nor to the west is Poland provided with strong natural defensive frontiers. Her position is made worse by the German enclave of East Prussia, which leaves her only the most inadequate connexion with the sea. The situation is further complicated by the existence on her eastern borders of races who in the past formed part of the kingdom of Poland, and are a source of strife between Poland and Russia. These races are, going from north to south, the Lithuanians (a non-Slavonic race), the White Russians, and the Little Russians (known also as Ukrainians and Ruthenians). The Poles claim that the White Russians and Little Russians are distinct from the Great Russians or Muscovites, and they always refer to them (contrary to the ordinary English usage) as White Ruthenians and Ruthenians.

Now it is clear that the most elementary justice demanded the setting up of a Polish state with some reasonable chance of life, nor was any alternative possible to the Peace Conference,

[1] *v. supra*, Part I, § 4, pp. 225–6.

even if it had been desired. Russia was in anarchy, Austria had broken up, Germany was crushed. No malevolence could prevail against the resurrected state, and the judgment of history had been passed (or so it seemed to the Poles) upon the three criminal Powers who had so often sinned against the Polish nation.

The basis of the present settlement and the ground for future hopes lay, however, not in the weakness of Poland's enemies, but in the existence of the Polish nation and the strength of Polish patriotism. In face of the widespread impression (resting partly upon certain historical facts, but more largely upon German propaganda) that the Poles are a nation of selfish individualists dominated by a reactionary and unscrupulous aristocracy, it is well to stress the fact that the chief strength, and perhaps in some ways also the chief weakness, of Poland lies in her extreme and sometimes exaggerated idealism. The passionate patriotism which was always present in the Polish upper class of *szlachta* (a class which includes not only the great nobles but many people who so far as wealth is concerned are little superior to the peasants) spread during the dark days of the nineteenth century to all classes of society. The expression of this patriotism by the poets has often taken on the colours of mysticism. The Poles regarded themselves as the Chosen People, chosen not for victory but for suffering. Poland was the Messiah among the nations, by whose broken body and shed blood salvation was to be wrought for all the nations of the world. As the Partitions of Poland had been the greatest crime of the old régime, so her resurrection was to usher in a new era of peace. The dangers of this doctrine—its tendency to produce sudden recklessness on the one hand and helpless acquiescence on the other—roused just protests in Poland itself and led to a more practical doctrine of hard work, hard thinking, and economic effort. None the less Polish patriotism has never ceased to retain something of the intensity and the idealism of this earlier view. All Poles believe in the historic mission of Poland as an apostle of liberty and as an outpost of Western civilization against what they regard as the barbarism of the East. It was this which enabled the Polish people to stand fast when it seemed as if a wave of Bolshevism might sweep over Europe. It was this also which made them sensitive to what some of them regarded as an unwarranted interference and mistrust on the part of the Entente Powers.

Again, it is this idealistic patriotism rather than mere arbitrary ambition or economic interest which has been and is the primary cause of the Polish attitude towards the border countries of the East. Poland claims, and claims on the whole with a certain degree of justice, that these countries belonged to her in the past not by conquest but by free union. The Polonization of the upper classes in these countries was not the result of organized oppression but rather of the superior Polish culture. The hostility of these people to the Poles is explained as temporary and artificial the work of a few intellectuals in German or Austrian or Russian pay. Poland without these areas in which she has been the chief source of civilization will be still a mutilated body; force will be still victorious over right. National ambitions are seldom the product of cold reason or even of selfish interest—they would be easier to deal with if they were—and it is useless to attempt to understand the Polish question without some consciousness of this romantic attachment to the border countries and of the way in which these countries are inextricably bound together with Poland in the Polish mind. To the Pole the sharp categories applied by the foreigner appear divorced from reality. He remembers rather how Mickiewicz, a Lithuanian noble with a White-Russian name, writing as a Polish patriot in the Polish tongue, begins *Pan Tadeusz*, the greatest classic of Polish literature, with the impassioned outburst, 'Lithuania, my country, thou art like health'.

2. *Polish Claims*. Hence, whatever may be thought in regard to its wisdom, nothing could be more natural and more inevitable than that the ultimate desire of the Poles should be for frontiers approximating to the historic frontiers of 1772. It is unnecessary to examine here the Polish demands in detail, and, indeed, these varied considerably from time to time, but it is possible to state their claims in general outline.

As against the Germans they demanded that the ethnographic frontier should be the determining factor, and that, where it was necessary to modify the ethnographic frontier because of economic or other considerations, that modification should be to the advantage of Poland. They interpreted the ethnographic frontier strictly as including all regions in which

Poles by race and language were in a majority, and they were inclined to assume that Polish race and language implied in all cases a wish to be united to the new Polish state. In addition they went considerably further than the Entente Powers in their desire to modify the ethnographic frontier to their own advantage for economic and other reasons. Perhaps in certain cases they asked for more than they really expected to receive and sometimes damaged their position by asking too much. On the other hand, they had a real claim to be treated generously in Posnania and West Prussia, where the strength of the Germans had been founded upon an international crime and built up by methods of organized oppression.

As against the Czechs the Poles insisted on their full ethnographic claims and refused to consider demands for modification in favour of Czecho-Slovakia on economic grounds.

In the east their demands were varying and obscure. They gave up the strictly ethnographic principle, and demanded not only Eastern Galicia but at least some portion of White Russia and the Ukraine, on grounds of defence or economics or history or culture. Their attitude was, however, modified to a certain extent by hopes of securing a 'free union', notably with Lithuania, but they were in some cases rather disinclined to envisage the possibility that freedom should involve freedom to refuse as well as to accept union. Perhaps it would be fair to sum up the Polish attitude here by saying that they demanded a certain portion of these regions in any case, but hoped that a more or less free choice might induce still wider regions to throw in their lot with Poland. The idealists laid more stress upon the latter considerations, while conservative politicians concentrated more upon what they regarded as the minimum claim necessary to Polish safety, and, therefore, over-riding all other considerations in a region where nationality was relatively undeveloped.

3. *Smaller Nationalities.* As regards the attitude of these small nationalities towards the Polish claims, it is sufficient to say here that in all cases there was some larger or smaller national movement, recent perhaps, but apparently growing, and certainly vociferous, reinforced by or even confused with the hatred of the peasant for his Polish landlord. These national movements differed in strength and in character, and it was possible to argue about their intensity and per-

manence, but in all cases they were directed definitely against the Poles.

4. *Claims of Larger Nationalities.*

(*a*) *The Czechs.* Apart from these small nationalities the other peoples directly interested in the solution of the Polish question were the Czechs, the Russians, and the Germans. Of these the Czechs put forward claims in the district of Teschen primarily upon the grounds of certain economic needs alleged to be vital to the new state of Czecho-Slovakia. Otherwise their differences with the Poles were on matters of relatively slight importance.[1]

(*b*) *The Russians.* The Russians, whose interests were affected at many more points, suffered from having no representatives who could speak for the country as a whole. With the Bolsheviks the Conference had no official dealings, while the other Russian representatives had behind them only portions of the former Russian Empire, and, being unrecognized, were unable to put forward authoritative claims. As a consequence the case of the Russians was inadequately expressed and imperfectly appreciated. Their general position was that they accepted the independence of Poland within her ethnographic limits, but disputed all claims to territory farther east.

(*c*) *The Germans.* The Germans, on the other hand, could speak with the authority of their government behind them, and although they were without power to affect the decision, their protests were followed by a certain number of concessions. They disputed the justice of the settlement in all respects, but accepted the cession of at any rate parts of Posnania, while protesting hotly against the proposals in regard to Danzig, West Prussia, and Upper Silesia.

5. *Attitude of Principal Allied and Associated Powers.*

Such, then, were the various claimants. The decision lay with the Conference as a whole, but primarily with the Principal Allied and Associated Powers, the United States, France, Great Britain, Italy, and Japan. The decisions taken by the Five Powers were in all cases unanimous, and there is no need to dwell much upon the differences which preceded the final decision. It will generally be sufficient to set forth, irrespective of their origin, the main considerations which were urged and weighed before the final decisions were ultimately reached.

[1] A full treatment is given in Vol. IV, pp. 348–67.

As, however, a certain amount of information leaked out during the progress of the negotiations, it may be well at this stage to give some quite rough indication of the general attitude adopted by each of the Great Powers primarily concerned.

On the central point all the Powers were agreed—that it was necessary to establish a Polish state and to establish it with a real chance of existence, that is to say with the greatest possible stability and strength. Opinions differed only as to the manner in which Poland could be made most strong and most stable—a question very intimately bound up with considerations as to what was just as between her neighbours and herself.

(*a*) *France.* France, conscious of her historic friendship with Poland, proud of her part in building up and training the Polish army, and above all ever mindful of a common menace from Germany which threatened both countries alike, may be said to have constituted herself the principal advocate of Polish expansion. She was not, however, unconscious of the difficulties involved, nor did she wish to go as far as the Poles themselves. In one case, that of Teschen, she supported the claims of the Czechs against the contentions of the Poles.

(*b*) *United States.* America had displayed very early an interest in the question of Polish independence and, like France, had memories of historic ties with Poland. As regards the frontier with Germany, the Americans were, like the British, conscious of the danger of including too many Germans in the new Polish state. In the earlier stages of the negotiations the American and British points of view approximated very closely, but in the later stages, notably in regard to Danzig and Upper Silesia,[1] the Americans displayed considerable reluctance before accepting the further modifications introduced on the initiative of the British. In other regions the Americans upheld the Polish claims with great energy, particularly in regard to Teschen and Eastern Galicia.

(*c*) *Italian and Japanese views.* The Italians had no special

[1] It should be mentioned that the *thirteenth point* (*v.* Vol. I, pp. 434–5) is really ambiguous as regards plebiscites: 'An independent Polish State should be erected which should include the territories inhabited by indisputably Polish populations, which should be assured a free and secure access to the sea, and whose political and economic independence and territorial integrity should be guaranteed by international covenant.' Is Upper Silesia inhabited by an indisputably Polish population or not?

interest or strong views in regard to the frontiers with Germany. They supported the Poles in Teschen against the Czechs and in Eastern Galicia against the Ruthenians. As regards territory formerly Russian they felt strongly the obligations incurred by the alliance with Russia, and held that while it was desirable to give to Poland the ethnographic frontier which had been recognized by Kerensky's government, it was undesirable to go farther in deciding the fate of regions in which the Russians were concerned. The decision on these matters had in the end to be postponed.

The Japanese were not directly interested in the Polish question so far as it was settled by the Conference. The boundary with Russia, with which they were more immediately concerned, never came up for final decision.

(*d*) *British views.* The British delegation were most conscious of the disadvantages involved in including large numbers of Germans within the Polish frontiers and were the prime movers in the direction of diminishing their numbers and also in securing a special position for Danzig and in providing plebiscites for regions whose allegiance might be regarded as doubtful. They also supported the claim of the Czechs in Teschen. As regards the east they felt strongly both the dangers which the Poles would incur by expansion and the necessity of securing the self-determination of the border peoples. They felt this not only as regards former Russian territory but also as regards the much-debated question of Eastern Galicia.

It is clear, therefore, that Great Britain was the only Power which found itself in the unhappy position of opposing or seeking to limit the Polish claims in all the main questions where there were substantial differences of opinion.[1] The wisdom or unwisdom of the British attitude can be judged only by history, but it is necessary to insist that this attitude arose from no unfriendliness towards Poland. It arose rather from a deeply rooted belief that if Poland was to be strong both

[1] *v.* Lloyd George's Memo., 25th March 1919 (Cmd. 1614, 1922): 'I am, therefore, strongly averse to transferring more Germans from German rule to the rule of some other state than can possibly be helped. . . . The proposal of the Polish Commission that we should place 2,100,000 Germans under the control of a people which is of a different religion and which has never proved its capacity for stable self-government throughout its history, must, in my judgment, lead sooner or later to a new war in the east of Europe.'

internally and externally it was necessary that self-determination should be the guiding principle of the settlement. Internally Poland must in any case possess very large minorities of Jews on the one hand and Germans on the other—neither of them likely to make the wheels of political life run more smoothly. If besides this inevitable alien minority Poland were to receive in the west more than the necessary minimum of Germans and in the east quantities of unwilling Lithuanians, White Russians, and Ruthenians her political effectiveness would decrease with the increase of her size, and she would become like the former Austrian Empire, a conglomerate of nationalities incapable of securing even-handed justice and of working a democratic form of government. Externally she would be surrounded by a ring of enemies, smarting under a sense of injustice, preaching a gospel of irredentism, fostering faction within her borders, and waiting an opportunity—which would not be difficult to find—for military aggression. And these enemies would be two of the greatest Powers of Europe—Russia and Germany. Germany, indeed, would always have causes for dispute with Poland. It was, however, possible and desirable to reduce these causes to the minimum demanded by justice. In such circumstances the Poles would be wise to avoid all possible cause of quarrel with Russia, even if it meant in some cases recognizing Russian claims whose justice they disputed. Above all, it was dangerous to take advantage of Russia's temporary weakness and annex border peoples without securing a free expression of their wishes. Such action, as it separated Russia and Germany in space, would bring them together in spirit and might easily result in a new and this time perhaps a final Partition of Poland from which no human power could save her. Considerations of this kind were alien to the ardent and idealistic Polish temperament, for that very reason it is necessary to stress their importance.

Such were the main lines of divergence where divergence existed, and it must be strongly emphasized that only after the fullest discussion of the principles involved in each case did the Conference arrive at its final decisions. Nevertheless, it cannot be doubted that, contrary to the opinion usually expressed in England at the time, the negotiations suffered not as a result of dilatoriness—though every day that passed made solution more difficult—but as a result of haste. However much time was devoted to each particular problem as it arose there was little or no opportunity for a comprehensive survey of the problem as a whole. Yet it is possible by solving separate problems in isolation with a reasonable amount of justice to produce a total result which is inconsistent and even unjust. The lack of a comprehensive survey was felt to some extent even on the West taken as a whole by itself. It was felt still more—at least from the British point of view—in regard to the different methods of settlement proposed for the West and for the East.

6. *Tendencies at the Conference.* The Conference manifested —at any rate, as far as the frontier with Germany was concerned—two main tendencies in discussion. The first tendency, which may be called the tendency of the old diplomacy, was based upon the view that friends should be strengthened at the expense of enemies, or that the innocent should be strengthened at the expense of the guilty. It showed itself, not in crude demands for the manifestly unjust, but by insisting that in all doubtful cases the benefit of the doubt should be given to Poland. The second tendency, which we may still believe, or, at any rate, hope to be the tendency of the new diplomacy, rested on the principle of doing justice to enemies as well as friends. It involved the belief that a solution on this principle alone could be permanent since it might in the end receive the support of those who suffered from the application of the principle in any particular case, inasmuch as they would gain by its establishment in international affairs as a whole.

In spite of a widespread impression in England to the contrary it was, on the whole, the second tendency which prevailed. As far, at least, as the frontier with Germany is concerned, strategic considerations were for the most part completely ignored—notably in regard to Danzig and the Polish corridor. This was done deliberately in the belief that in this way alone could justice be secured, and that subsequent disputes would be settled not by force of arms but by the League of Nations. It is, as we shall see later, mere nonsense to suppose that the Conference was following in these matters a policy of simple revenge. It may be added that in regard to regions which had been taken away from Poland by a gross international crime and Germanized by unashamed political injustice, it was neither unreasonable nor unjust to give

Poland the benefit of the doubt in cases where doubt really existed.

Considerations involving a distinction between friends and enemies did not properly speaking arise in regard to the eastern and southern frontiers of Poland, but the relations of the Great Powers with the Bolsheviks not only deprived the Russians of adequate opportunities for stating their case, but also secured for the Poles a degree of consideration which they would not have received if Russia had still been regarded as an ally. The French at least appear to have felt that the duty of the Conference was to create a large Poland as a barrier against the Bolsheviks and as an ally of France in any future war against Germany.

In the attempt to secure justice as between nation and nation it was universally agreed that nationality must be the chief basis of the settlement. It was equally agreed that in certain cases it was necessary to modify or even over-ride considerations of nationality by reference to other factors and especially by reference to economic factors. Modifications on strategic grounds received much less support, but the economic factors when they were intimately bound up with geography sometimes involved strategic considerations as well. History was not and could not be altogether ignored. Religion was taken into account mainly negatively, that is so far as it threw doubt upon the national sympathies of people who clearly belonged to a particular nation by race and language, but were of a different religion. Differences of opinion were concerned solely with the extent to which these other factors might justly be allowed to over-ride considerations of nationality pure and simple, and it was no unusual thing to find the positions taken up by the representatives of the Great Powers exactly reversed in dealing with different problems.

The necessity of taking into account factors other than nationality, at least in matters of detail, becomes obvious as soon as any attempt is made to deal with concrete problems. It is often supposed that a solution in terms of nationality is the simplest thing in the world, whereas in reality it is one of the most difficult.[1] It is clearly impossible to have islands of one country situated on the territory of another, and there are geographical facts which preclude the construction of an inter-

[1] *v.* on this, Vol. IV, pp. 429–34.

national frontier after the fashion of a jig-saw puzzle. In all such cases it is necessary to decide contrary to the wishes of one or other of two bodies of people, and to do so on grounds of general justice, taking into account questions of history and religion and the economic interests both of the territories immediately concerned and of the nations which lay claim to these territories.

In no region is this more true than in the area claimed by Poland. Apart from the awkwardly placed enclave of East Prussia (in the north of which the German conquest of the native Borussi—a people akin to the Lithuanians—was ruthless and complete) there has been an overflow of Germans into Poland and of Poles into the border countries in the east. There are of course differences in the two cases. The German overflow was, on the whole, originally in the nature of peaceful penetration, but after the Partitions it had been reinforced by the deliberate action of the Prussian Government, especially since 1870. The Polish overflow was due mainly to the Union of Lithuania and Poland, to diplomacy rather than to war, to the superiority of Polish culture, and to natural economic causes. So far as history was concerned the two cases differed, but in their results they were practically the same. Hence, over considerable areas in both west and east, there are large and diffused minorities of alien race and language, possessed of disproportionate influence, belonging to or believing themselves to belong to a higher civilization and culture, controlling most of the means of production, and constituting in general the middle or upper classes. In the towns this alien element tends to become actually a majority, and even in the country districts there may be considerable islands where the native element is in a definite minority. In such cases are we to prefer the will of the ill-educated majority to that of the well-educated minority? Are we to determine the fate of the more compact and wealthy islands by the will of the larger but more sparsely inhabited country districts which surround them? Are we, in short, to prefer quantity to quality or vice versa? One method would be to make a clean cut by majorities on both sides, and to ask the minority in each case to lend their aid to the states in which they would find themselves. This method was the method definitely adopted in the west to the detriment of the Germans. In the east the weight of opinion outside the British

Delegation was in favour of adopting another method to the advantage of the Poles. The people immediately concerned are naturally unable to take a dispassionate view of the situation. Their passions are aroused, their pride is affected, and they refuse to consider the possibility of putting large bodies of their countrymen under the government of 'barbarians'. This in the case of the Germans could be set aside and the principle of the will of the majority could be made to prevail. The Poles in the east were in a position of greater strength, and they pleaded that the only alternative to the satisfaction of their demands was to hand over the border peoples to what they regarded as an equally alien race of Muscovites and Bolshevists. Their plea was at least partially accepted in regard to Eastern Galicia in spite of the various alternative solutions put before the Conference. The problem of the other border countries remained unsettled.

The difficulty of applying the principle of nationality is increased by the fact that national divisions are in this region somewhat uncertain in themselves. There are considerable areas where the national aspirations of the inhabitants have been called in question.[1] It is alleged that the national movements are recent, that they are the work of a few intellectuals without backing among the people, even that the people in some cases are so little developed that they are indifferent to nationality and ready to take on any stamp which may be imposed upon them. The Poles urged this strongly in regard to their border nationalities, the Germans did the same in regard to all Poles who had been severed from Poland before the Partitions and to some who had belonged to Poland as late as 1772. The German plea was met by instituting plebiscites

[1] It should be observed that these questions often give rise to linguistic controversies which are singularly unprofitable. The Germans contend that many Poles within former German territory speak a dialect quite distinct from educated Polish. The Czechs maintain the same view as regards certain of the Polish-speaking people in Teschen, Zips, etc., *v.* IV. 350, 364. Similarly the Poles lay great stress on the differences between the White Russian and Little Russian dialects on the one hand and Great Russian on the other. In regard to such contentions it is well to remember (*a*) that a dialect always differs and may differ very greatly from the educated language to which it is most nearly related, and (*b*) that while nationality cannot be determined on linguistic grounds alone it is generally desirable that people speaking different dialects of the same language should be included in the same state. What really matters, however, is the will of the people and their natural affinities, not the linguistic subtleties of pedantic grammarians.

for the areas whose historical connexion with Poland was remote.

7. *The method of decision by Plebiscite.* Despite many serious difficulties the plebiscite remains the best and, indeed, the only way of determining nationality in areas where the real wishes of the inhabitants are subject to doubt. For this purpose it was used in all parts of Germany where Poles by race had long been cut off from their native country. It was also used, however, in certain instances to meet a momentary political situation rather than to obtain information which was lacking. Here also a comprehensive survey of the problem would have been of considerable value, and might have led to the abolition of certain plebiscites and the institution of others.

This secondary use of the plebiscite is, however, in itself an indication of another difficulty with which the Conference had to contend. It was quite impossible to ignore the actual situation of the moment and to base decisions entirely upon the permanent factors involved. During the period of the Conference great events were happening and these could not fail to influence the decisions. There were grave troubles in connexion with the armistice between Poles and Germans in Posnania, and also in regard to the transport of Haller's army through Germany; there were difficulties in regard to German troops in Lithuania and the Baltic Provinces; there were complaints about the conduct of the German Government in Upper Silesia and West Prussia. Between Poland and Czecho-Slovakia there was continual friction in regard to Teschen. Within Poland itself there were a series of anti-Jewish excesses. All these things—not to mention the countless difficulties which affected Poland less directly—delayed and hampered decisions in the Conference and inflamed the passions of the peopleto be affected by the decisions.

8. *The fait accompli in East Galicia.* Again the actual power and character of the governments involved could not be entirely ignored, and it is useless to disguise the fact that the Poles, by presenting the Conference with a *fait accompli* in Eastern Galicia, materially affected the settlement.[1] The Poles were strong enough to assert their will in the disputed area itself, and pressure exercised by the Conference might easily have led to such an outburst of passion as would have swept away the Polish Government and left nothing but anarchy in

[1] *v.* Vol. I, pp. 335–8; Vol. IV, pp. 84–5, 95, 103–5, 135.

its place. The Poles in this way gained both by their strength and by their weakness.

9. *Bolshevism.* Above all, the shadow of Bolshevism hung over everything and rendered obscure things which ought to have been clear. The alleged danger that the Bolsheviks were about to advance through Eastern Galicia to join the Bolsheviks of Hungary undoubtedly affected the views of the representatives of the Great Powers.[1] The Poles could with every reason occupy portions of the border countries in order to free them from anarchy and to defend Poland itself against attack. Yet while these countries were being fought over, it was impossible to secure self-determination, and hazardous, if not foolish, to legislate for a quite uncertain future. There were, indeed, hopes that first Kolchak and then Denikin could succeed in establishing a Russian Government with which it would be possible for the Poles and the Allied Powers to treat in regard to the ultimate fate of the disputed territories. It was partly such hopes which prevented the Conference from dealing with these regions, but these hopes were gradually destroyed. The difficulties caused by this situation were enormous. Threatened by Bolshevik armies and assailed by Bolshevik propaganda, weakened by war and famine and disease, the border peoples were, to say the least, not in the best condition to establish a stable form of government. The Poles, on the other hand, even apart from national ambitions, could hardly be expected to hand over willingly to a Bolshevik régime large areas where members of their race constituted the bourgeois element and possessed the bulk of the land. It is no easy matter in such circumstances to secure ideal solutions of problems which are in themselves sufficiently difficult, and it is well for critics of the Conference to remember that there are some tasks which are almost too great for mortal men.

10. *The Settlement.* The complicated details of the Polish settlement can be grasped most easily if they are considered in four main divisions as they affect: (*a*) German territory, (*b*) the boundary between Poland and Czecho-Slovakia, (*c*) Eastern Galicia, and (*d*) territories formerly Russian. The boundary between Poland and Russia is still undetermined, and thus all that can be done under the fourth heading is to indicate briefly the nature of the problems involved.

[1] *v.* Vol. I, pp. 353–5; Vol. IV, pp. 159–61.

(*a*) *Poland and Germany.* The Polish Commission was appointed on the 12th February 1919, and was instructed on the 26th February to report on the boundary between Poland and Germany. Its report was completed on the 12th March and formed the basis of the subsequent settlement. Certain modifications, as is well known, were introduced by the Supreme Council in regard to Danzig and the neighbouring regions. Later, after the German Observations on the Draft Treaty had been received, still further modifications were introduced in regard to Upper Silesia, and the frontier between Germany and Poland was also altered in some points of detail.[1]

The original proposals of the Commission were roughly as follows:

(i) That the Memel district should be ceded to the Principal Allied and Associated Powers.

(ii) That a plebiscite should be held in the region of Allenstein.

(iii) That in Posnania and West Prussia the westernmost limit of Polish ethnographical majorities should, with certain modifications, be made the frontier between Poland and Germany.

(iv) That Danzig and the whole length of the Danzig–Mlawa–Warsaw railway should be included in Poland.

(v) That in Upper Silesia all regions which had a Polish ethnographical majority should be assigned to Poland, while a small area in the extreme south should be given to Czecho-Slovakia.

The last three proposals require a specially detailed discussion, both because they were subsequently modified and because they have been subjects of controversy.

(*b*) *The Memel district.*[2] The Memel district (which concerns Lithuania and not Poland though it was dealt with by the Polish Commission) is a small area in the extreme north-east of East Prussia lying between the river Niemen or Memel and the former frontier of East Prussia and Russia. It contains some 2,500 square kilometres and about 150,000 inhabitants. Practically

[1] *v.* extracts from German Observations and Allied Reply, Vol. II, pp. 283–5. For a brief general treatment with statistics of populations involved, *v.* Vol. II, pp. 207–15.

[2] For German Observations and Allied Reply, *v.* Vol. II, pp. 290–1, 364, 366–7, 382, 391.

all the country districts are inhabited by a majority of Lithuanians who in this region are Protestants, whereas their countrymen in Russia are Roman Catholics. The town of Memel itself is largely German, and, if the town and the country districts are taken together, the population is about half German and half Lithuanian.

It must be remembered that East Prussia was originally inhabited by people of Lithuanian stock called the Borussi who are usually said to have been exterminated by the Teutonic Knights. It is only in the eastern districts that the Lithuanian speech, whatever be the case with the Lithuanian race, still prevails. The Lithuanians indeed claimed extensive regions west and south of the Niemen on the ground that these were still inhabited by people of Lithuanian race who had given up using the Lithuanian speech in quite recent times. It was, however, felt by the Conference that the process of Germanization had gone too far to be reversed and that it was unreasonable to take into account the islands of Lithuanian-speaking people who still lingered on in the midst of Germanism. East of the Niemen the case was different. There the country districts were definitely Lithuanian and there was a strong Lithuanian movement in spite of all German efforts at repression—efforts which, it may be mentioned, continued even during the Conference itself. If wider interests were taken into account it was impossible to argue that this small area was essential to Germany. On the other hand, it formed the only possible outlet to the sea for some two million Lithuanians and for the White Russians who inhabit the upper reaches of the Niemen. In such circumstances it was felt that the national aspirations of the small town of Memel could hardly stand in the way of the vital economic needs of several millions of people, and that the economic interests of the town itself would be furthered by allowing it to go with its hinterland.

The reason why this area was ceded to the Allied and Associated Powers was that no Lithuanian Government was at that time recognized by the Conference. It is still (July 1921) under inter-Allied control with a French officer in supreme command.[1]

(c) *The Allenstein Plebiscite.*[1] The Allenstein (Olsztyn) district as defined by the Peace Conference consists (with some

[1] Cp. Vol. II, pp. 201–11, Allenstein, 213, but see note at end of chapter.

modifications) of the former Regierungsbezirk of Allenstein—the most southern region of East Prussia. It contains over 12,000 square kilometres and over 550,000 inhabitants. Of these latter slightly more than half are Polish in race and language, though the Germans call them Masurians and lay stress on the divergences of the local dialect from educated Polish speech. On the other hand, this area has for centuries been under the domination of East Prussian Germans, and as a result the Poles as well as the Germans are Protestants. The only exception is a district, situated, curiously enough, in the extreme north, which belonged to the bishopric of Ermeland or Warmia and was thus a part of Poland till 1772. Within this bishopric (the southern part of which alone is included in Allenstein while the northern part extends to the Baltic east of Danzig) both Poles and Germans are Catholic. The Poles in the Allenstein region are for the most part peasants. The national movement among them is comparatively recent and apparently limited in extent. The country is sparsely inhabited and of little agricultural value—a labyrinth of hills and lakes and bogs. As such it offers an admirable zone of defence to the country which includes it within its frontiers.

This was agreed to be a region which could not be assigned to Poland without a clear expression of the will of the people. History and religion connected the inhabitants with Germany, race and language with Poland. The German-speaking minority was unusually large and was widely distributed. It was recognized that, since the people were politically undeveloped and the Polish national movement was of recent origin, large numbers of Poles might vote for Germany out of ignorance and timidity rather than out of real conviction. The Conference was conscious that this area would probably be assigned to Germany as a result of the plebiscite and yet that the ties of race and language might in the end prove more powerful and lead to a strong Polish movement when it was too late to be effective. It was, however, necessary to take the facts as they were and to leave the future to look after itself. A plebiscite met the actual situation fairly and it was impossible to do more.[1]

The plebiscite was held on the 11th July 1920. 363,209 votes were cast for union with East Prussia, 7,980 for union

[1] For Selections from German Observations and Allied Reply *v.* Vol. II, pp. 289–90.

with Poland. The whole area with insignificant modifications was assigned to Germany.

(*d*) *West Prussia and Posnania.* The important question of Danzig and the Mlawa railway being reserved for special consideration later, we are here concerned only with the western frontier of Poland in West Prussia and Posnania. The frontier as originally proposed by the Polish Commission and presented to the Germans in the first draft of the Peace Treaty was modified in six places after the German reply had been received.[1] The original proposal, which had been subscribed to by representatives of all the Great Powers, was the result of an honest attempt to do justice as between Poland and Germany. It, however, took into account factors other than ethnography to an extent which was afterwards thought, particularly by the British representatives, to be excessive, and while much could be said in defence of its solutions in regard to any particular problem, the result as a whole, owing to the general tendency to give the benefit of the doubt to Poland, was unduly unfavourable to the German claims.

There were three areas in particular where Germany had been treated with extreme severity. All three areas were inhabited by a large majority of Germans, but they had been assigned to Poland on various grounds. In the north a small part of Pomerania was assigned to Poland in order to fit in better with the existing railway lines and in a lesser degree to widen a little the exceedingly narrow Polish corridor. At Schneidemühl an area beginning round the town and extending north-eastwards along the Schneidemühl–Konitz railway received similar treatment in order to prevent the Germans from having a base for the concentration of troops against the exposed Posnanian salient. Further, in order to secure an adequate defence for the Posnanian salient to the south, it was proposed to make the river Bartsch the boundary between Poland and Germany, thus assigning to Poland some 800 square kilometres of Middle Silesia inhabited by perhaps 40,000 people, of whom a quite insignificant fraction are Poles. The first and third of these proposals were specially open to criticism, as the two areas in question had never in the whole course of history formed part of a Polish state and their annexation could not but be regarded by Germans as a violation of every right of nationality.

[1] For Selections from German Observations and Allied Reply *v.* Vol. II, pp. 285–7.

All three areas were assigned to Germany in the final version of the Treaty of Peace.

When it was proposed to modify the original proposals in respect to these three areas, it was pointed out in the Commission specially appointed by the Supreme Council to deal with this question and that of the plebiscite in Upper Silesia that, if the Polish Commission had assigned on economic and strategic grounds certain ethnographically German districts to Poland, they had also on similar grounds and in accordance with a principle of compensation assigned certain ethnographically Polish districts to Germany. It was urged that it was for this reason desirable to reconsider the cases where ethnography had been departed from to the detriment of Poland and not only the cases where it had been departed from to the detriment of Germany. As a result of this reconsideration three areas which had previously been assigned to Germany were finally assigned to Poland. The three areas thus assigned to Poland were the north-west corner of the Kreis of Schlochau, a small district to the south of Filehne, and a strip of territory in the extreme west of Middle Silesia. All three areas are inhabited by a majority of Poles.

These changes, therefore, improved the frontier line from the ethnographic point of view. There may be objections to some of them on economic and administrative grounds, while strategic considerations have simply been swept aside. As regards the two Governments especially affected it was argued that any concessions to the German case would be productive of arrogance and bad faith in Germany and would weaken the German consciousness of defeat. On the other hand, concessions indicated a willingness on the part of the conqueror to be fair to a defeated enemy, and made it easier for the German Government to sign the Peace without losing its authority and so perhaps plunging Germany into anarchy. As to the Poles, they were much more concerned with rescuing a few more Poles from German tyranny than with the strategic and economic disadvantages resulting to Poland from the change in the original proposals. On the whole, they appear to have regarded the proposed modifications with approval.

These changes are, however, matters of relatively little importance. They affected quite small areas and relatively small bodies of men. Of the resulting line as a whole it may be said, indeed, that the balance is still in favour of Poland from the exclusively ethnographic point of view. Practically every Polish peninsula—if we may employ that term to indicate a Polish arm extending into territory otherwise inhabited principally by Germans—has been included in Poland. Apart from a few villages in Pomerania the only noteworthy exception appears to be the country districts round Bomst, and there, if the town is counted along with the country districts, the Germans appear to have a slight majority. No such effort was made to include all German peninsulas in Germany, and, indeed, it would have been impossible to do so without temporarily paralysing the means of communication in Posnania, as these small German peninsulas are almost always centres of railway communication.

If, however, it is possible, as it well may be, to criticize the new frontier in certain of its details there should be no reasonable doubt that the principle upon which the whole line is based is fundamentally just. That principle is to make the Polish frontier follow the westernmost limit of the area inhabited by a majority of Polish-speaking people and to allow Germany no territorial compensation for the widespread German minority and the considerable number of German islands scattered over Polish territory. Two considerations which support this method of treating a minority apply in West Prussia and Posnania as as they apply nowhere else. The first is that the German overflow is due largely to the fact of the Partitions, and the second is that it has been artificially fostered by the German Government at the expense of its Polish subjects. But even apart from these two special considerations the principle itself is surely sound. In a civilized community it is the majority as a whole which must decide. We have no right to prefer the wishes of the economically and socially superior minority to those of the mass of the people. Indeed, it is easier in some ways for the well-to-do and the educated to adjust themselves to a new government than it is for the poor and the oppressed. It is easier also for the townsman to migrate if he wishes to retain his nationality than it is for the peasant. As to the principle of compensation, it is wrong, or at most right within narrow limits. The fact that over a large area there is scattered a minority whose wishes have to be over-ridden is no reason for selecting arbitrarily a portion of that area and disposing of it contrary to the wishes of the majority of its inhabitants. To do so is merely to commit an arbitrary injustice on one body of people because it has been necessary to commit an injustice on another, or rather it is to commit an arbitrary injustice on one body of people to balance a just and necessary hardship under which another body of people is suffering. It is to ignore altogether the principle of self-determination which, if it means anything, must mean self-determination by majorities.

It is, of course, infinitely regrettable that there should be so large a number of Germans in the territory assigned to Poland. It is a misfortune for the Germans concerned and not less of a misfortune also for Poland. But it is idle to speak as if these Germans were arbitrarily and unnecessarily included in Poland, or as if a few modifications of the frontier or the retention by Germany of a few square miles around Danzig would easily get rid of them. No other result is possible unless the Germans are deliberately transplanted to their original home. The history of the last hundred and fifty years has been a deliberately organized German invasion of Polish territory so that over almost the whole area there is one German to every two Poles. If, therefore, some two million Poles are to be returned to Poland in West Prussia and Posnania, it is absolutely inevitable that with them must go at least a million Germans. However regrettable this may be, there is no gainsaying the fact. It may, however, be possible to derive some consolation from the reflection that the German census exaggerated slightly the number of Germans thus affected and that a large number of the Germans settled in this area are colonists and officials deliberately planted there by the German Government for the Germanizing of its Polish subjects. When it is remembered that German officials are immensely more numerous than English in relation to the work to be done, that in Germany not merely administrative officers and police, but also teachers and even workers on the railway are Government officials, and further, that from all these offices, even the smallest, the Polish subjects of the German Government were excluded, the actual inclusion of a considerable number of Germans in the new Poland may seem in some respects a working out of historic justice. The Poles displayed moderation and practical sense in allowing large numbers of these officials—some of whom had been bitter enemies of Poland—to retain their positions, but it is in the interests of all parties that the German Government should find some work for them to do in their own country.

It should also be added that, according to German official figures, the Polish rate of increase on German territory is almost exactly double the rate of increase of the Germans themselves. The Polish rate of increase is in fact almost incredible in these regions and the thorough German methods of sanitation ensure that it is not balanced here, as it is to some extent elsewhere, by a correspondingly large infantile mortality. It is precisely this fact which led the German Government to import Germans from elsewhere at the public expense and to attempt to Germanize the Poles by force. This fact too must surely be taken into account in determining the frontiers. The removal of the artificial factors which have kept up the German proportions, will allow natural forces to work, and these will tend in a few years to make many of the precarious German islands disappear altogether from the ethnographical map.

If the fundamental principle is sound, what is to be said of its application ? Setting aside minor details which may be questioned, the area in which the decision of the Conference may most easily be criticized is the area which is loosely referred to as the Bromberg area. This is more than a German island, it is a chain of islands or almost a narrow promontory stretching up the Netze valley and extending past Bromberg to the valley of the lower Vistula. This German promontory was deliberately created by the German Government, which since the time of Frederick the Great has aimed at cutting off the Poles from the sea by stretching a belt of Germans along this line of communications. The promontory is thus largely artificial and in the area of Bromberg itself the majority is to some extent made up of German railway and other officials and their dependents in the widest sense of the word. Even if it were not, adherence to purely ethnographical considerations would produce a wholly impossible frontier, and could hardly be advocated as a reasonable solution. As the case stands it is necessary and just that this area should be assigned to Poland.

The only practical alternative would be to assign to Germany all the territory extending north of the Bromberg area to the Baltic, i.e. in other words, to abolish the Polish corridor to the sea. It is often assumed that this Polish corridor to the sea, which involves the cutting off of East Prussia from the rest of

Germany, is bound up with the question of Danzig and is based on purely economic grounds. Nothing could be farther from the truth. The question of Danzig is a question of whether the corridor is to be economically effective, but the Polish corridor exists quite independently of Danzig. A glance at any ethnographic map based, as it must be, on German figures shows at once that a definite belt of territory containing a majority of Poles extends from the main body of Polish territory to the sea west of Danzig and cuts off the Germans of East Prussia from the Germans in the west. It is not only history and economics which justify this Polish corridor, it is the ethnographic facts themselves. The Germans suggest, of course, that the Poles in this area are not Poles but Kashubians, and can point to differences between their dialect and educated Polish almost as remarkable as the differences which exist between High and Low German. No one suggests, however, that these people are really German in sympathy, and they are Catholics like most of the other Poles. Only by a flagrant piece of injustice to these people could this area be assigned to Germany. East Prussia was historically and still is a German colony detached by Polish territory from the rest of Germany.

If we pass beyond the region immediately concerned to the two countries affected it is infinitely more important to a nation of over twenty million inhabitants to have access to the sea and direct contact with Western Europe than it is for some two million Germans in East Prussia to have a land connexion with the rest of Germany. East Prussia retains her connexion with Germany by sea, and it is by sea that most of the trade between East Prussia and Germany has in fact been carried on. If it be said that the needs of Poland might be adequately met by rights of transit over German territory to the Baltic, it is still more true that the smaller needs of East Prussia can be adequately met by rights of transit across Polish territory to Germany, and such rights are in fact given by the Treaty. No doubt there is a blow to German pride in this solution, but it is a blow to that German, or rather Prussian, pride which has received its strength and its evil character precisely from the subjection of others by force in this very region. The opposite solution would involve a blow not only to Polish national pride but also to the sentiment of justice which is here manifestly on the side of the Poles.

It may indeed be argued that just or not this is a decision to which Germany will never submit, and that it would be well to avoid future trouble by allowing her to have her way at once. The naked right of the stronger is, however, a curious basis upon which to found a Peace, which was intended to inaugurate an era of justice for all nations and to protect the rights of small nationalities. Every principle supposed to underlie the Peace demands that in this area justice should be done, and for the future, in this as in other cases, it can only be hoped in spite of indications to the contrary that the decision may secure in the end the support of all nations including Germany herself on the simple ground that it is just.

(*e*) *Danzig and the Mlawa Railway* (*Marienwerder*). By the original proposals of the Polish Commission Danzig and the whole length of the Danzig–Mlawa–Warsaw railway was to be made Polish territory. The first criticisms of these proposals raised in the Supreme Council affected only the question of the Mlawa railway and assumed the justice of the proposals in regard to Danzig. Later the question of Danzig itself was raised and the original proposals of the Polish Commission considerably modified. But the solutions of both questions were in their final form before the first draft of the Treaty was presented to the Germans: (1)

(i) *Mlawa railway* (*Marienwerder*);[1] *plebiscite result.* Of these two questions that of the Mlawa railway is important, though very much less so than that of Danzig. Unless this railway is given to Poland the shortest route between Danzig and Warsaw must lie in German hands. The serious disadvantage of this to Poland is obvious, and its seriousness is not diminished by the fact that the circuitous route which remains open can with difficulty be made adequate to the economic requirements of the country. It need hardly be said that the strategic disadvantages are even more serious. The Polish Commission believed, and, indeed, reiterated its belief in the teeth of the Supreme Council, that in the circumstances it was necessary to override the wishes of the local inhabitants because of the vital importance to Poland of this line of communications. The Supreme Council took, however, the opposite view in the end. It was pointed out that with the exception of a relatively small area (the area of Stuhm which was histori-

[1] Cp. Vol. II, pp. 210–11, 213.

cally Polish and has by no means lost its Polish character) all this territory had belonged to East or Ducal Prussia for centuries and was inhabited by Germans whose national sympathies were undoubted. The strategic argument was set aside, the economic was met by giving Poland rights of transit, and a plebiscite was decided upon for the whole predominantly German area (generally called the Marienwerder area) between the railway and the Vistula.[1] In this case the plebiscite is clearly not necessary to ascertain the wishes of the inhabitants about which there is no reasonable uncertainty except in the area of Stuhm, but it probably helped to calm Polish opinion which had been excited by the unauthorized publication of the proposals of the Polish Commission and greatly resented any changes which it regarded as detrimental to Poland. The plebiscite was held on the 11th July 1920; 96,923 votes were recorded for union with East Prussia, 8,018 for union with Poland. With certain modifications the whole area was assigned to Germany.

(ii) *Danzig.*[2] The crucial question is, however, the question of Danzig. The inhabitants of Danzig are for the most part German in race and language, and many people in England—even among those who disapprove of the Italian attitude towards the parallel problem of Fiume—speak as if it were self-evident that Danzig ought to remain in Germany in accordance with the principle of nationality. Yet surely the principle which ought to be applied is clear. As a general rule it is desirable to follow the wishes of the majority of the inhabitants in regard to nationality, but there are certain exceptions. One is where an island of one national character is surrounded by territory of another national character. The other—and this is the case of Danzig—is where the national aspirations of a small body of men clash with the vital necessities of a much larger body of men. In both cases the interests of the smaller body must give way to those of the larger. The relative size of the two communities of course affects the force of this principle, and another determining factor is the extent to which the needs of the larger body can really be called vital.

Now it is hardly possible to find a clearer case than the case of Danzig. The construction of another harbour on the Polish

[1] *v.* Extracts, German Observations and Allied Reply, Vol. II, pp. 289–90.
[2] Ibid., Vol. II, pp. 291–3, and *v.* also p. 214.

coast was seriously investigated by experts at the Conference and found to be impracticable. We have, therefore, to consider the needs of a nation of over twenty million inhabitants occupying the whole basin of the Vistula with certain ramifications and extensions particularly to the west. Every law of geography insists that the natural outlet for this country, possessed of all sorts of economic possibilities and now in process of being industrialized, is by the mouth of the river around which and upon which the whole fabric of Polish society has been built. It is futile to expect that the main bulk of Polish products should pass down the Dniester through foreign territory to the Black Sea or even follow the difficult route, also through foreign territory, to the Adriatic by way of the Moravian gates. By far the greater part of Polish trade must pass by way of the Vistula and the port of Danzig. Surely, if any nation has a claim to direct contact with the outer world it is the nation which is certainly the largest and perhaps the most highly developed of all the new nations established or re-established by the Peace. Nor is this merely an economic question. If a powerful nation like Germany, whose history has not shown her to be over-scrupulous, is to control the main outlet of Polish trade, she will in the end make Poland a mere vassal. It is bad enough that the corridor given to Poland should be so inadequate in comparison with her economic needs, and it is a regrettable necessity that both sides of that corridor should be held by a hereditary enemy. Poland may, however, be able to live with German fingers on either side of her windpipe. She cannot live with a German finger in her throat. For the Polish nation the possession of Danzig, in some form or other, is a matter not of mere economic convenience but rather of life and death.

On the other side, it is impossible to claim that the retention of Danzig is essential to the existence of the German state. So far is this from being the case that it has been a deliberate German policy to restrict the development of Danzig with the result that a city, which has a situation not incomparable to that of Hamburg, remains considerably smaller than the East Prussian garrison and university town of Königsberg—a result which is obviously not due entirely to the Russian system of tariffs. Further, as has already been pointed out, the question of Danzig is not bound up with the question of cutting off East Prussia from the rest of Germany. That would have to be done in any case on purely ethnographical grounds, even if Danzig were to remain in German hands. The German interest is, therefore, primarily one of national sentiment, and there is no doubt that, as a result of the historic connexion of Poland with the town, her sentiment for Danzig is as strong as that of Germany.

The town of Danzig was, like other Polish towns in the Middle Ages, composed of German traders who settled in Polish territory for purposes of commerce. Owing to its proximity to Germany it retained its German character and its special privileges long after the other towns had ceased to do so. Its loyalty to Poland during the whole period was undoubted. It was annexed to Germany against the wishes of its inhabitants, who persisted in their preference for Poland even till so late as 1815. No doubt a century of German rule has brought about a change of attitude, but it is impossible to prefer the interests of some 170,000 Germans in Danzig (or even of some 360,000 if the surrounding territory be included) to the vital necessities and the historic claims of the Polish state. Further, the union between Danzig and Poland, if it is contrary to the national sentiment of the inhabitants, is entirely favourable to their economic interests. There were clear indications even at the time of the Conference that this was realized by some of the Danzig merchants, and there are still clearer indications of it to-day. Danzig, if the Polish state prospers, will become in no long time a first-class port, and it may well be that its German inhabitants may find it difficult not to prefer their economic interest to their national pride. It may be added that, if the artificial barriers maintained by the German and Russian Governments are removed, the working of natural economic laws is likely to bring an influx of Polish traders to the town as it increases in size.[1] It is only by artificial means that Danzig can be prevented from becoming what nature intended it to be—a Polish port.

It was on such considerations that the Polish Commission recommended the inclusion of Danzig in the Polish state. The report had to be completed within a very brief period and contained one grave omission in that no recommendations were made as to the status which Danzig was to have within the

[1] For extracts from German Observations and Allied Reply see Vol. II, pp. 291–3; for statistics *re* Danzig, *v.* II, 215.

Polish state. It was in fact doubtful at the time whether such recommendations were within the terms of reference of the Commission. The question was finally raised in the Supreme Council on the initiative of the British. It was felt strongly that the national aspirations of the inhabitants could not simply be overlooked. The solution finally adopted may be criticized as unnecessarily vague (although this vagueness was no doubt deliberate) and it may be urged that it would have been better to have restored to Danzig its historic status of autonomy within the Polish state, and to have recognized explicitly the sovereignty, or at any rate the suzerainty, of Poland. The proposals adopted did not go so far in recognition of the Polish claim, and the real situation will not be clear until the Treaty [1] to be made between Poland and Danzig has been tested in practice. The Peace Treaty lays down only the general principles upon which the Special Treaty is to be based (Art. 104). The city, together with the German area around it, becomes a Free City under the League of Nations. A High Commissioner appointed by the League of Nations is to act as a sort of arbitrator between Danzig and Poland. Polish suzerainty is not expressly recognized, but Poland is to control the foreign relations of the Free City and is to exercise a sort of economic control (now defined in a subsequent Treaty) over the means of communication. Danzig is to be within the Polish Customs Union. As neither of the two parties involved can do without the other, it should be possible with the exercise of a little common sense on both sides to produce a quite workable arrangement, and

[1] [The treaty between Poland and the Free City of Danzig was signed the 27th October 1920 and accepted by the city the 9th November 1920, from which date it came into force. The Constitution was approved by the High Commissioner on the 11th May 1922. The essential feature of both systems is that the High Commissioner (in 1922 the British Lieut.-General Sir R. C. Haking) decides all disputed questions as between Germans and Poles. A right of appeal to the Council of the League exists and has been frequently exercised. As is remarked in the text it is impossible at present to tell how the system will work out. Certainly much will depend on the individual High Commissioner. It seems clear, however, that a single individual as arbitrator between two nationalities is far superior to an international Board (as, e.g., in the Saar valley). A French President of an international Board in the Saar is evidently a different thing from a British High Commissioner mediating between Germans and Poles in Danzig. A study of the appeals, etc., referred to the League from Danzig suggests that both Germans and Poles recognize that it is to their interest to adopt working solutions of disputed and delicate questions. The success of the experiment will be proved by the gradual lessening of appeals to the League.—*Editor's note.*]

it may be hoped that a union of interests may lead later to a union of hearts, as it did in the past.

It can hardly be doubted that this solution is as just as could be obtained in the circumstances—if anything it takes too much account of local feeling and too little of Polish needs. The Poles, however, after their first protests, have acquiesced in these arrangements, and will, it is to be hoped, settle down to work them out in a spirit of practical compromise.

Only one thing remains to be added. If the Polish problem could have been dealt with as a whole, Poland would have been willing to acquiesce in almost any sacrifice elsewhere in order to secure Danzig. It was, however, not the Polish question but the German question which of necessity formed the centre of gravity of the Conference. Poland had to be dealt with piecemeal, and having secured certain rights over Danzig the Poles naturally accepted these as a matter of course and began to stress the importance of other things.

(*f*) *Upper Silesia.*[1] The final solution of the Danzig question was determined before the first draft of the Treaty had been presented to the Germans. In the case of Upper Silesia the original proposals of the Polish Commission were accepted without modification by the Supreme Council and were embodied in the Draft Treaty. As a result of the German criticisms the original proposals were seriously modified, and this modification was one of the most important concessions which the German Delegation secured. The details were determined by a specially appointed Commission which dealt also with the minor changes made in the western frontier of West Prussia and Posnania.

The proposals in the Draft Treaty were simple. The western boundary of the ethnographically Polish area was made the frontier between Germany and Poland. The only noteworthy exception was the undoubtedly German peninsula of Leobschütz, a peninsula with an extraordinarily narrow isthmus which intruded between the Poles to the north and the Austrian or Czecho-Slovak frontier to the south in a fashion so awkward that its retention by Germany made a practicable frontier impossible unless a considerable part of ethnographically Polish territory were to remain within the German state. It

[1] *v.* Vol. II, pp. 211, 213 on economic and strategic importance, and pp. 287–8, 391, for extracts from German Observations and Allied Reply.

is to be noted further that of the territory cut off from Germany by the original proposals a small strip of country west of the Oder in the extreme south was inhabited by a Czech population. It was intended to assign this territory, together with a part of Leobschütz, to the Czecho-Slovak state, and proposals for determining this part of the frontier between Czecho-Slovakia and Poland were drawn up by the Polish and Czecho-Slovak Commissions in joint sittings. Owing, however, to the subsequent changes in regard to the treatment of Upper Silesia as a whole only the small area inhabited by Czechs was assigned to the Czecho-Slovak state.[1]

The area which it was thus intended to cut off from Germany contained some 11,000 square kilometres with a population of nearly two millions. Of these two million inhabitants almost exactly two-thirds are Poles and one-third are Germans. The number of Czechs is quite insignificant. The proportion of Poles to Germans is the same as that which prevails generally in what was formerly German Poland, and it should be noted that, in spite of its small size, this area contains almost as many Poles as there are in the Polish regions of Posnania, which cover an area considerably more than double the size. Here, as elsewhere, the strength of the Germans lies in the towns, in some of which they have a clear majority. The area to the east of the Oder is of very great industrial importance owing to the presence of coal, and in a lesser degree of iron-ore.

The Polish Commission in its original proposals, therefore, merely followed the same principles which were universally accepted as applying to Posnania and West Prussia. There were, however, certain differences between the two cases. Posnania had been Polish during the whole course of Polish history down to the Partitions, and West Prussia had been Polish during the greater part of that history. Upper Silesia had, however, separated from the rest of Poland very early as a result of dynastic quarrels, and its connexions had been with Bohemia, and finally through Bohemia with the Habsburgs, until Frederic the Great succeeded in securing it by force of arms in 1742. Its economic development had been due to Prussian enterprise and Prussian capital, although—it may be well to remember—the labour was mostly contributed from the side of the Poles, who are of course the original inhabitants of the country.

[1] *v.* Vol. IV, pp. 366–7.

The Germans in their reply to the demands of the Peace Treaty in regard to Poland singled out the case of Upper Silesia for special criticism. Their reply laid stress upon two main lines of argument: (1) that Upper Silesia was economically necessary to Germany and unnecessary to Poland, and (2) that the will of the inhabitants was in favour of remaining in Germany.

(1) The first argument has a certain amount of truth in it, although it was somewhat exaggerated. The loss of Upper Silesia in addition to that of Alsace-Lorraine will seriously diminish the wealth of Germany, will involve a certain readjustment of the German economic system, and naturally will make it harder for Germany to perform her Treaty obligations in regard to Reparation. Nevertheless she will still retain in the Westphalian coal-fields the largest coal-area in Western Europe. It is also true that the present needs of Polish industry (which is still relatively limited as a result of Russian mismanagement and oppression) could be adequately met from the coal-mines in Russian and Austrian Poland. But it is to be hoped and expected that Polish industries will expand enormously if freed from the artificial restrictions against which they have had to struggle in the past. It is very important to Poland that she should have an adequate opportunity of continuing her industrial development, nor is there any reason to believe that she will be unwilling to sell her superfluous coal to Germany, who was further given certain rights of purchase in the final version of the Treaty.[1] There is clearly no conclusive argument on the purely economic side taken by itself. It is only in the most exceptional circumstances that need for a commodity justifies the annexation of the country which contains it, and in spite of the hardship that a region developed by German capital should pass to the Polish state it is hardly possible to prefer the national aspirations of the capitalist to those of the labouring classes who constitute the majority of the population.

[1] *v.* Vol. III, p. 162, Art. 90 of Versailles Treaty: 'Poland undertakes to permit for a period of fifteen years the exportation to Germany of the products of the mines in any part of Upper Silesia transferred to Poland in accordance with the present Treaty. Such products shall be free from all export duties or other charges or restrictions on exportation. Poland agrees to take such steps as may be necessary to secure that any such products shall be available for sale to purchasers in Germany on terms as favourable as are applicable to like products sold under similar conditions to purchasers in Poland or in any other country.' But see also App. III to this volume.

(2) The more serious contention of the German Delegation was, however, that the real wishes of the bulk of the population were in favour of Germany. This German contention was perfectly familiar to all those who had studied the Polish question. Just as in East Prussia it was a favourite German device to call certain Poles Masurians, and in West Prussia to call other Poles Kashubians, so in Upper Silesia the Poles were described as speaking Wasser-polnisch, and their Polish character was said to be as diluted as their language. In the 'German Observations' these customary assertions were supported by figures in regard to voting of a somewhat misleading character. The figures, when analysed, appeared to indicate a Polish majority in the disputed area, and it was only a small body of Protestant Poles in the north (outside of the industrial districts) whose national sentiment as a whole was considered open to reasonable doubt. There was, indeed, a somewhat artificial movement for the independence of Upper Silesia which was fostered by the Germans and apparently ignored by the Poles, but the independence of Upper Silesia would mean in the end its dependence upon Germany, and it was agreed not to take this possibility into consideration in the Treaty. Speaking generally, the Polish movement in Upper Silesia had the majority of the population behind it in the Polish districts before the War, and it appeared probable that this movement had been strengthened by the resurrection of the Polish state. If, however, there was any doubt about the question it was only reasonable that it should be settled by a plebiscite, and this is the solution which was adopted in the final version of the Treaty of Versailles.

It must not, however, be disguised that the opposition to the plebiscite was very strong. This opposition rested not only on the theory that it was an error to make any concessions to the Germans, but also on considerations affecting this particular case. It insisted on the difficulty of providing the troops necessary to maintain order, and it laid special stress upon the illegitimate pressure exercised upon the Polish lower classes by priests and pastors, officials and teachers, capitalists and managers. To meet this contention the period before the taking of the plebiscite was in this instance unusually prolonged. There was a real danger that the Polish movement, which was certainly gaining strength, had not yet attained sufficient force

MAP V
ILLUSTRATING UPPER SILESIAN AWARD 1921

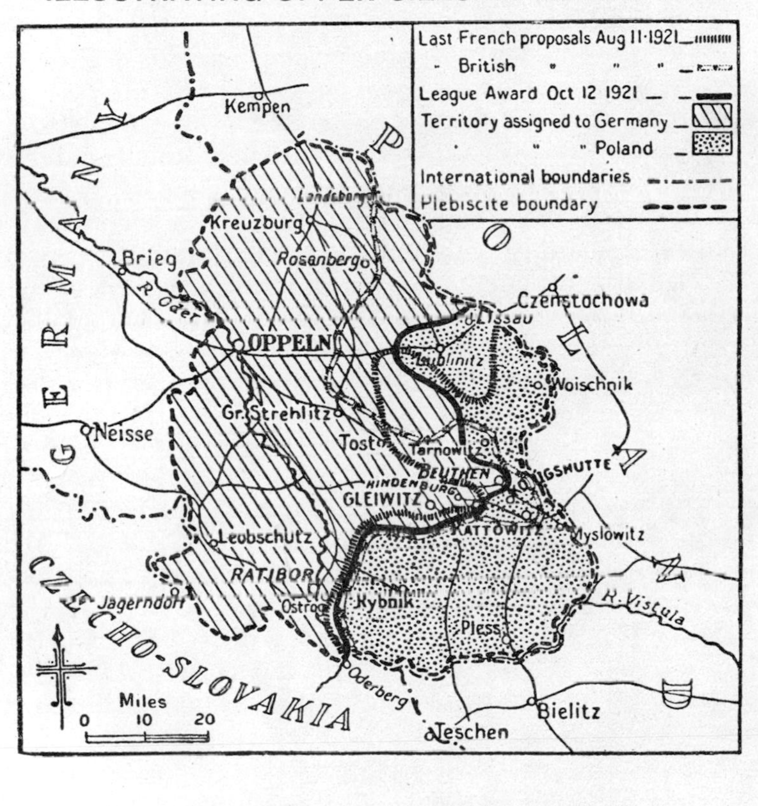

to enable the Polish labourer to judge clearly the issues which were at stake. The uneducated Polish voter is liable to be affected by German statements that he will lose his industrial insurance, and perhaps even his livelihood, if he votes for union with Poland. The result might be a vote which did not express the real wishes of the people, and might be bitterly regretted in later years by the majority of the population. Such a state of affairs would be certain to cause trouble both locally and in Poland. There is no need to disguise the reality of this danger, but its seriousness was estimated differently by different observers.

On the other hand, it was thought to be an enormous gain to Poland if the district should join Poland by an explicit affirmation of its wish to do so. The Germans, no doubt, would probably maintain, even in such a case, that illegitimate pressure was exercised upon the voters and that the decision was not the expression of the real will of the people, but was due to a desire to escape the heavy taxation in Germany and to other accidental causes. Yet even if such contentions should be urged, a free vote was bound to affect the attitude of the more reasonable among the Germans to this question. It was bound to affect to an even greater extent the general attitude of the civilized world.

It may be noted in conclusion that the general trend of the Conference in regard to this, and, indeed, to all other parts of the Polish problem in German territory, was to lay more and more stress on the principles of nationality and self-determination and to attach less and less importance to economic and strategic considerations.[1]

For the actual results of the plebiscite and the Silesian Award by the League see Map, Appendix III, Part II.

(g) *Poland and Czecho-Slovakia.* The question of the frontiers between Poland and Czecho-Slovakia, though they caused the Conference almost as much trouble as those between Poland and Germany, can be dealt with much more briefly. There are really only three problems involved—the problem of

[1] *v.* e.g. Annex to Art. 88 of Versailles Treaty (Vol. III, p. 161). After the plebiscite in Upper Silesia the Commission were to recommend a boundary between Germany and Poland. 'In this recommendation regard will be paid to the wishes of the inhabitants as shown by the vote, and to the geographical and economic conditions of the locality.' This has been generally interpreted as putting national claims in the foreground. *v.* App. III.

Upper Silesia; the problem of Teschen; and the problem of Zips and Orava. All these are treated in Vol. IV, pp. 348–66.

11. *Eastern Galicia.* Of all the questions affecting Poland that of Eastern Galicia was perhaps the most complicated and the most difficult of solution. All the general difficulties in regard to the determination of Poland's eastern frontier are found here in their most aggravated form; and there are in addition several special difficulties peculiar to this area. The Polish minority is more numerous and more widely distributed, the national antagonisms are more bitter, and the economic stakes are of greater value. Eastern Galicia is to the Poles very much what Upper Silesia is to the Germans, although it is perhaps fair to say that in regard to Eastern Galicia considerations of national sentiment are stronger, and those of economic interest perhaps weaker, than is the case in regard to Upper Silesia.

Galicia as a whole (apart from certain minor modifications which need not detain us) has been Austrian since 1772, and the Austrian connexion has produced a type of civilization different from that both in German and in Russian Poland. In particular during the last half-century the Poles in alliance with the Austrian Government have possessed great privileges and have enjoyed political preponderance—not always, it is alleged, by legitimate methods. The division between Western and Eastern Galicia is merely a judicial one—Cracow being the judicial centre of the one and Lemberg (Lwów) the judicial centre of the other. Western Galicia is solidly Polish, with a small minority of Jews. Eastern Galicia is inhabited by Ruthenians, Poles, and Jews.

As regards the international status of this country, Austria ceded the whole of Galicia to the Principal Allied and Associated Powers by the Treaty of St. Germain in September 1919.[1] The Principal Allied and Associated Powers assigned Western Galicia to Poland by the 'Certain Frontiers' Treaty which they signed at Sèvres on the 10th August 1920 (Vol. IV, pp. 135–6; vol. V, p. 169), but the Poles refused to sign this Treaty apparently on the ground that they could not accept any

[1] Treaty of St. Germain, Art. 91: 'Austria renounces so far as she is concerned in favour of the Principal Allied and Associated Powers all rights and titles over the territories which previously belonged to the former Austro-Hungarian monarchy, and which, being situated outside the new frontiers of Austria as described in Art. 27, Part II (Frontiers of Austria), have not at present been assigned to any State.' *v.* Vol. IV, pp. 134–5; Vol. V, p. 169.

separate treatment for Eastern Galicia. The whole of Galicia, and certainly Eastern Galicia, is still in international law the property of the Principal Allied and Associated Powers.[1]

It may be said at once that there was never any intention on the part of any of the Great Powers to exclude the whole of Eastern Galicia from Poland. The solid Polish bloc crosses the division between Western and Eastern Galicia and extends to the line of the River San. The line, which the British Delegation proposed as the Eastern frontier of Poland proper in this area, ran to the east of that river and included in Poland the whole solidly Polish area besides a strip of mountainous country in the south inhabited by the Lemkians, a body of mountaineers whose national affinities and sympathies were all with Russia but whose geographical situation rendered it apparently inevitable that they should remain within the Polish frontiers.

The Eastern Galicia, whose fate was so hotly debated at the Peace Conference, was, therefore, not identical with the former judicial division of the Austrian Empire, and it is misleading to quote figures applying to the latter in support of contentions in regard to the former. Eastern Galicia will be used here throughout as meaning that part of Eastern Galicia lying to the east of the frontier proposed by the British Delegation.

In the sense here adopted Eastern Galicia is an area of slightly under 50,000 square kilometres. Its inhabitants number slightly over four and a half million—a number sufficiently large to render its ultimate fate of very serious importance. Of these—to judge by the census of religions—just under 3,000,000 or 63 per cent. are Ruthenians, just over 1,000,000 or 23 per cent. are Poles, and a little over 500,000 or 12 per cent. are Jews. The linguistic census includes most of the Jews among the Poles, as the Austrian system took into account not the mother-tongue—which in the case of the Jews is Yiddish—but the language of ordinary intercourse, and did not acknowledge Yiddish as a language. In view of the doubtful attitude of the Jews towards the Polish State, it is generally regarded as fairer to consider them as distinct from the Poles proper.

The Ruthenians maintain that the number of Poles is grossly exaggerated and that the Poles are in reality only some 500,000 or 600,000. It is, however, safer to accept the census in

[1] Written before the assignment of East Galicia to Poland in March 1923, *v.* note, p. 283.

spite of its Polish bias and to regard the Poles as constituting something under a quarter of the whole population, nearly two-thirds of which is composed of Ruthenians.

The Ruthenians, who are simply a branch of the Little Russian race, are for the most part peasants with a small class of *intelligentsia* who are their leaders; in religion they are Uniates accepting the Roman faith but following the Orthodox ritual. The Jews are petty traders in the towns and villages, and supply a certain proportion of the professional classes. The Poles constitute the upper and professional classes with their dependents, but there is a considerable number of peasant settlements in the country districts, and the towns (which apart from Lemberg never rise above 50,000 inhabitants) are on the whole divided between Poles and Jews.

The distribution of the two chief races is very mixed. There is a considerable Polish minority almost everywhere and in places even in the country districts the Poles are actually in a majority. There is, for example, a chain of Polish islands running east towards Lemberg somewhat similar in character to the German island of Bromberg in Posnania. Lemberg itself and the country round it are in majority Polish, and there are certain areas, curiously enough in the extreme east, where the Poles are in a definite majority. Eastern Galicia is in short a Ruthenian sea with a large number of Polish islands rising above the surface in a curiously irregular manner.

The attitude of the Poles towards this area is simple. They claim the whole of it as an essential and integral part of Poland. Its historical connexion with Poland has been longer and closer than that of the territories lying farther to the east. The Polish minority is larger and more influential than elsewhere and especially since the national passions have been inflamed by tales of atrocities. Polish sentiment cannot tolerate the idea that a million fellow countrymen should be placed under the rule of 'barbarians'. They feel especially strongly in regard to Lemberg, a Polish town of some 200,000 inhabitants with a large Jewish minority and a small number of Ruthenians. They cannot forget the recent and heroic defence of the town by its inhabitants against its Ruthenian assailants when even boys and girls took part in the fighting. They claim also the oil-wells of Drohobycz as having been developed by Polish enterprise and as being vital to Polish needs. In short, they regard the whole of Eastern Galicia as their just right, but claim with special passion the western parts with the two important centres of Lemberg and Drohobycz. Further, they attach enormous importance to a common frontier with Rumania and the establishment of a continuous Polono-Rumanian front against Bolshevik Russia.

The attitude of the Ruthenians is alleged to be less clear and more equivocal. They are a people less developed than the Poles and, apart from a small body of *intelligentsia* who are fanatically anti-Polish, they have no upper class to supply them with leadership and traditions. It is even contended that as a whole they have no political and national self-consciousness. Although, however, there may be differences of opinion as to the extent and the profundity of Ruthenian national feeling, to the dispassionate observer two things are perfectly clear. One is that national consciousness is much stronger in this region than it is among the people of the same stock in the Russian Ukraine. The other is that during the last fifty years there has been a steady increase in national feeling and in bitterness against the Poles, a bitterness enormously increased by the local war during the Peace Conference and undoubtedly manifesting itself in a number of atrocities committed upon Polish landlords. The Ruthenians have been compelled to submit to the superior force of the Poles, but it is not credible that they welcome their own subjection.

The position of the Ruthenians was, however, enormously weakened in Paris by their own internal discord, which, as is seen in the past history of the Poles themselves, appears to be the special temptation of a defeated people. So far as can be judged the majority of the Ruthenian people pride themselves on their separate nationality and express a hostility to Great Russia second only to their hostility to the Poles. There is, however, a considerable minority lying chiefly along the slopes of the Carpathians and in certain other regions who are definitely pro-Russian and regard themselves as simply a branch of the one Russian race. Hence the representatives of Eastern Galicia came to Paris speaking with two voices, and this made it easier for their opponents to maintain that they were a people politically undeveloped and nationally ill-defined. Such uncertainty served in some quarters to confirm the Polish claim.

Each party also laid itself open unnecessarily to a special argument—thus weakening its own case and distracting attention from the real situation. The Russophil party wished to bring Russia to the very summits of the Carpathians. Who, it was asked, could support the responsibility of causing such a menace to the stability of Europe, especially at a time when Russia was in the hands of Bolsheviks? The Ruthenian or Ukrainian party, on the other hand, proclaimed their intention of acting as the 'Piedmont' of Ukrainia, and of becoming a centre of propaganda in Russia on behalf of an independent Ukraine. Who would venture to set up such a storm-centre in the heart of Europe, a source of sedition and disruption for the Russian Empire? In this way by focussing attention not only on their own disunion, but also upon academic questions of no possible practical importance at the moment, the two parties allowed the fundamental contention upon which they were really united to become obscure, that it was contrary to every principle of self-determination to hand over three million people to the Polish State without securing for them the right to make some free and public expression of their will.

As to the Jews, they do not appear to have given much expression to their opinions one way or the other. As a small and not very popular minority it was no doubt dangerous for them to do so, especially when fighting was going on and the issue hung in the balance. They appear wisely to have waited upon events.

Such then was what may be called the internal situation—on the one hand, a strong Polish minority accustomed to command, determined to maintain its position, and backed by a vehement national sentiment throughout the length and breadth of Poland; on the other, a Ruthenian majority doubtfully equipped for government, bitterly hostile to its Polish masters, and divided against itself. During the greater part of the Peace Conference the two nations were more or less continuously at war, the lines running in such a way that Lemberg was held by the Poles and the oil-wells of Drohobycz by the Ukrainians. The local difficulties were in themselves already sufficiently serious.

When one turns, however, to the possible solutions which the Peace Conference had to consider, the difficulties appear only to increase. To declare the whole country independent would have satisfied the Ruthenians, but the Poles would certainly not have submitted, and even if they had there was no guarantee that the Ruthenians could have set up a stable government or that the Polish minority would be adequately protected. To hand the whole country over to the Poles could be done only by force of arms and would be manifestly unjust. It was necessary to seek some sort of solution which would at least attempt to do justice between the contending parties.

It may be said with confidence that there was no possible solution which did not receive serious consideration by the Polish Commission in Paris. Even the most improbable contingencies were envisaged, including such remote possibilities as a temporary occupation of the whole territory by Czecho-Slovakia or Rumania. All the Delegations in Paris, except the British, were, however, strongly in favour of assigning the whole territory as a natural unit to Poland in some form or other and with such safeguards and limitations as might be thought necessary. There were, indeed, proposals to split up the country by a frontier running east of Lemberg and Drohobycz. Such a frontier would have assigned to Poland a large area in which the majority was definitely Ruthenian; it would not have satisfied the Poles; it would have meant bitter hostility on the part of the Ruthenians; and it would have left the portion of Eastern Galicia excluded from Poland a mere mutilated fragment resting on nothing and incapable of existing by itself. These proposals were, however, put forward as desirable only in case the British view should be accepted, that sooner or later the Ruthenians should be given a real opportunity for self-determination. If the future fate of the country was to be left in any reasonable doubt, then such doubt, it was maintained, should not be allowed to affect Lemberg and Drohobycz, both of which should be secured for Poland. The possibility of self-determination—if this should be thought desirable—ought to be given only to the east of the Lemberg–Drohobycz line.

There were two serious possibilities before the Conference; one was to attempt to secure a free expression of the people's will under proper international safeguards, the other was to give Poland some sort of authority and control at least for a time.

Of these the first was very difficult—its opponents said impossible. An immediate plebiscite could not be held unless the country was occupied by a neutral force, it would have taken place at a time when men were inflamed by passion and little inclined to vote from a reasonable consideration of the true interests of the country. Further, what alternatives could be put before them at a time when Russia was in chaos, and independence would lead to internal troubles and perhaps, it was urged, to co-operation of some sort with the Bolsheviks? Clearly it was desirable that the plebiscite should be postponed till passions were cooler and Europe had taken definite shape again after passing through the furnace of war and revolution. But to secure this it would be necessary to have some sort of supervision by the League of Nations. If a representative of the League of Nations arrived without forces in a country seething with civil war what chance was there that his wishes would be obeyed? On the other hand, it was impossible to send a large international force to this remote inland area with hostile forces all around and the Bolsheviks hammering at the gates. Similarly, what Great Power would accept from the League of Nations a temporary mandate over this country at a time when troops were urgently needed elsewhere, when demobilization was being demanded, and when all the nations were on the point of exhaustion? Even if a Great Power did accept such a mandate the result would be economic dislocation and political instability, and the country would continue to be a hotbed of agitation and strife until some permanent settlement was secured. Poland, it was urged, was the only Power in the vicinity, Poland alone could bring about a permanent and immediate settlement, and Poland was both willing and anxious to undertake the responsibility.

In spite of strong protests from the British Delegation these considerations appeared to be conclusive to the majority of the Powers at the Peace Conference. The matter was, however, to some extent taken out of their hands. As related elsewhere, in May 1919 the Poles attacked successfully and the Polish advance stopped after protests from Paris only when the greater part of Eastern Galicia had been occupied by Polish troops.[1] Subsequently (on the 19th June) the Poles were authorized to continue their advance to the borders of Eastern Galicia on the ground, which later events hardly confirmed, that what remained of the Galician-Ukrainian army was no

[1] Vol. I, pp. 335–7.

longer in a position to resist the Bolshevik army which at that time appeared to be engaged in an attempt to join up with the Hungarians. The British proposal that at the same time a High Commissioner should be appointed by the Allies to safeguard the interests of the Ruthenians was rejected. The Poles thus received authorization from Paris for a military occupation of Eastern Galicia modified only by some vague references to ultimate self-determination; and although this was not intended to prejudice the final political decision, it committed the Conference to a Polish solution of the question, until such time as the final decision should be taken.

The Ruthenians naturally considered that they had been betrayed by Paris, and their bitterness at the betrayal was increased by two special considerations. In the first place they maintained that in reliance upon the promises of the Allies and the proposals for an Armistice they had removed troops from the Polish front and sent them against the Bolsheviks. This is to some extent borne out by the subsequent adventures of a body of Galician troops who fought on various sides in South Russia. In the second place, they believed that the Polish success was possible only because of the arrival in Poland of Haller's army—an army which had been equipped and trained by the Allies. Even apart from these special considerations they regarded Paris as having yielded to *force majeure* on the part of the Poles and as having turned a deaf ear to the just demands of the weak and the oppressed.

It was in this hopeless situation that the Paris Conference set itself to work out for Eastern Galicia some sort of local autonomy within the Polish State. A great deal of labour was devoted to the preparation of a statute defining the extent of East Galician autonomy. The difficulties in the way of any kind of Ruthenian autonomy were, however, by this time almost insurmountable. National bitterness and hatred were too strong. If the local authorities in Eastern Galicia were given real power the result could only be a deadlock between them and the Polish Government. If they were not, the whole thing was little better than a farce. Home Rule can be worked only where there is goodwill between the local and the external authorities, and the possibility of such goodwill in this area had by now altogether disappeared. The Conference, however, persisted in its intentions in the face of these difficulties, and after a great deal of somewhat confused discussion, in which the representatives of Great Britain were usually in a minority of one, a decision was reached on the 20th November 1919. The Poles were to have a mandate over Eastern Galicia for twenty-five years. At the end of that time the League of Nations was to consider the whole question afresh.

The Poles objected very strongly to any such solution, since they regarded Eastern Galicia as a part of Poland proper and resented interference from outside. The Great Powers appear to have had little enthusiasm for the scheme, and finally on the 22nd December 1919 these proposals, on the initiative of the French, were quietly shelved. The result is that this problem has received no solution from the Peace Conference. Eastern Galicia is still in International Law the property of the Principal Allied and Associated Powers, but it is occupied and administered by the Poles without obligations or conditions of any kind.[1]

This state of affairs can hardly be regarded as satisfactory from any but the Polish point of view. The Ruthenians have no guarantees for the protection of their liberties, and they complain bitterly of Polish injustice and of Polish attempts to colonize them on the German model. Above all, they have no assurance that in the course of time they will be allowed an opportunity for the free expression of their will as to their ultimate fate as a nation. No doubt the difficulties in the way of intervention by the League of Nations were enormous from a practical point of view, and they have grown more serious with the lapse of time, but it is hard not to feel that these difficulties might have been surmounted and ought to have been surmounted—perhaps that they could even yet be surmounted. As things stand, four and a half million people have by a tragic collocation of circumstances been deprived of their rights of self-determination, and a new Ireland has been set up in the heart of Europe—with what consequences no man may know.

12. *Poland and Russia.* The question of the Eastern Territories is still unsettled.[2] The local difficulties are enormously increased by the present conditions in the former Russian Empire which in this area add to the conflict between national ambitions, a conflict between different systems of government

[1] Certain Frontiers' Treaty, Vol. IV, pp. 135–6.
[2] *v.* note and map p. 283.

and economic organization, or, as the Poles would prefer to express it, a conflict between European democracy and civilization on the one hand, and the tyranny of a band of fanatical idealists and professional criminals on the other.

It is of course universally recognized that ethnographically Polish territory must be in Poland, and this covers almost the whole of Congress Poland. The Polish Commission spent some time in drawing up a frontier including in Poland all that was certainly Polish without prejudice to the ultimate allotment of territory farther east. This frontier excluded from Poland on the north-east a part of the Government of Suwalki which, though it formed part of the Congress Kingdom, is inhabited by Lithuanians. It included in Poland, on the other hand, a considerable portion of the Government of Grodno which had lain outside the Congress Kingdom. South of Brest-Litovsk it coincided with the former frontier of the Congress Kingdom including within Poland the whole of the Government of Kholm, which is inhabited by a majority of Ruthenians similar in language and religion to the Ruthenians of Eastern Galicia but nationally less self-conscious. The British Delegation, indeed, wished to exclude the two southern powiats of this Government from Poland on the ground that here there was a specially compact Ruthenian majority which ought to be given the same rights of self-determination as their kinsmen in Eastern Galicia. The line was accepted by the Supreme Council in December 1919 and became known later, together with its continuation in Eastern Galicia, as the Curzon line. The Polish occupation, however, extended beyond it towards the frontiers previous to 1772.

Subsequent events leading up to the Treaty of Riga are sketched in Chapter III, Part II. It should be observed here, however, that the Curzon line at the time it was drawn up was only a provisional minimum frontier, and that both the French and the Americans believed that the final frontier line should be farther to the east. It should be noted also that by the Treaty of Versailles (Art. 87) Poland undertook to accept the decision of the Principal Allied and Associated Powers as regards her future frontiers, so that in law the question is an open one until such a decision is finally made.

All that can be done in the present chapter is to indicate very briefly the reasons which lay behind the claims of the Poles to expand in the east and the difficulties of the problem as it presented itself to the Peace Conference.

Although the Poles claimed much of what was before the War Russian territory and is certainly not ethnographically Polish, it is a mistake to regard their claims as merely a striking example of national chauvinism and imperialistic folly. The Russian Bolsheviks are dangerous neighbours, and, apart from the historical connexion of these territories with Poland, the Poles believed that it was their task to rescue the border peoples from a race at least as alien to them as their own, and that by so doing they might save a large part of Europe from the false doctrines and foul practices of the Bolshevik Government. Once more, as in the old days, Poland must bring to these peoples the blessings of liberty and order. Once more she must enter upon the historic mission of defending European civilization from the barbarism and tyranny of the East. This conviction was, of course, much strengthened by the startling Polish victory over the Bolsheviks before Warsaw in the middle of 1920.[1]

Even if the question be regarded from a somewhat less exalted standpoint it is easy to see reasons behind the Polish claim. There were three main courses possible. The first was that Poland should abandon these territories to the Bolsheviks. But if these territories did not wish to be Bolshevik why should they be forced to become so, and was it not too much to ask that the Poles should peacefully make over to the Bolsheviks territories in which their compatriots constitute the greater part of the bourgeoisie and still possess a very great portion of the land? The second was that these intermediate peoples should become independent. But without Polish help their independence would immediately fall before a Bolshevik invasion, and even apart from that it is more than doubtful whether any of them (with the exception of the Lithuanians who are in contact with the sea and can secure foreign help) is capable or even desirous of organizing or maintaining any kind of stable national government. The third course was that the Poles should take these people under their protection, should become responsible for their defence, and should introduce such order and institutions as were suitable for their needs. It is small wonder that the Poles preferred the last course, and it is

[1] *v.* Chap. III, Part II, § 9 *d*, p. 321.

a misconception to maintain that in so doing they were necessarily actuated only by blind folly and criminal ambition.

On the other hand, there are certain considerations which quite naturally do not appeal to the Poles, but which ought not to be overlooked. A Polish occupation, even if it could be maintained against the Bolshevik armies, almost inevitably meant that the fate of millions of people would be decided without any opportunity for self-determination. It may be that self-determination, owing to the undeveloped condition of the people, is difficult or inexpedient, but the fact remains that those members of the border peoples who have become vocal are bitterly opposed to the Polish claims. That their influence would be likely to make the task of Poland difficult can hardly be disputed, for the Polish landlords cannot avoid arousing the dislike which is usually aroused by their class, and the peasants cannot but be influenced in their ideas by the fact that the rest of Russia has forcibly expropriated the landlords. When the economic equilibrium has been disturbed and when in addition the economic antagonism involves the Pole on one side, and the White or Little Russian peasant on the other, it is easy for even a few fanatical idealists to awaken the dormant consciousness of nationality and to turn an economic conflict into a national one. It is far too common an assumption that because a national movement like any other must begin in a small and rather unrepresentative body of men it is unlikely to become a permanent and powerful force. Nationality is probably a much more serious factor in the situation than the Poles are wont to admit.

The feeling of nationality may be specially dangerous in this case because in spite of artificial attempts to regard it as distinct from and opposed to the Russian, as well as the Polish, nationality, it may at any moment in the case of the White and Little Russians become merged in a general Pan-Russian movement. The Russians themselves regard these people as simply branches of the one Russian people, and, apart from the Poles and the Ruthenian leaders in Galicia, it is difficult to find any large body of people who take a different view. The Poles might possibly have been able to develop a non-Polish, non-Russian national feeling in these areas, but the chances were heavily against their being successful, and there is little doubt that at the present time such a feeling is relatively insignificant.

One thing, however, is clear. A Polish occupation of these regions means the hostility of every Russian, Bolshevik or Monarchist, Liberal or Reactionary. In the end this must involve, as we suggested in our introduction, an alliance of Russia and Germany against Poland. It is almost impossible that Poland could hold her own against such an alliance. A solidly united and homogeneous country might perhaps in favourable circumstances be able to do so, but the very facts which are the source of Russian hostility are likely to be also a source of Polish weakness. The permanent occupation of these regions means that millions of men of a different race and language and of an admittedly inferior civilization would constitute part of the fabric of the Polish State. They would tend to make democratic government difficult because political education is necessary to the smooth working of democratic institutions. They might easily make it altogether impossible if they came into conflict with their political superiors. If, on the other hand, the Poles gave up the democratic ideal and attempted to rule these people with a strong hand, they might indeed succeed in securing a numerical increase to their army, but it would be at the expense of admitting the enemy within their gates.

It was such considerations and not any lack of sympathy or failure to grasp the difficulties of the situation which led the British Delegation in particular to feel very great hesitation as to the ultimate wisdom of the Polish policy of expansion in the East.

It may be well to indicate briefly in conclusion the special character of the three separate problems, Lithuania, White Russia, and the Ukraine, so far as they affect Poland.

13. *The Lithuanians*. The Lithuanians are a non-Slavonic people numbering some 2,000,000. In religion they are Roman Catholics. Their ethnographic frontier is defined with reasonable clearness. Their leaders are bitterly hostile to the Poles and they have at present an organized government which has now been recognized by the Allies and by the Poles. They are quite distinct in race and language from both Poles and Russians and the national movement if not very profound is certainly far too strong to be ignored. They are thus in a position entirely different from that of the White and Little Russians. They have before them some real possibility of

independence, though the Poles hope that they will enter into some sort of union with the Polish State comparable to that which existed in the past. Considering the smallness both of their numbers and of their territory it is difficult to see how they can maintain complete independence with Germany on the one side and Russia on the other.

It should be noted further that their ethnographic frontier circles round the town of Vilna on the north and west. Vilna itself is a Polish town with a very large Jewish element and is situated just inside White Russian territory. As it was the former capital of Lithuania the Lithuanians attach great importance to its possession.[1]

14. *The White Russians.* The White Russians are a people numbering about 6,000,000 lying between the Lithuanians to the north and the Pripet marshes to the south, and extending from the frontiers of ethnographic Poland to east of the Polish frontiers of 1772. They are the most backward and undeveloped of all Slavonic peoples. They are Roman Catholics in the west and Orthodox in the east. It is these western Catholics especially that the Poles wish to bring within the frontiers of Poland on the ground of similarity of religion and even, it is maintained, of language.

It should be mentioned here that the Poles assert the existence of a narrow band of Polish-speaking territory running from the Polish ethnographic frontier as far as Vilna. This is flatly contradicted by the Russian census of 1897, but it is to some extent supported by a partial census taken during the German period of occupation. The matter could be settled only by an independent commission of linguistic experts or by a plebiscite carried out under an impartial authority. Even if such an area does exist it is doubtful whether its geographical position is such as to justify its inclusion within the Polish frontiers.

15. *The Little Russians or Ukrainians.* The Little Russians or Ukrainians cannot fall far short of 30,000,000 if we include the Ruthenians of Galicia and other parts of Austria-Hungary. They lie to the south of the White Russians but extend far beyond them to the east. Their national movement is strong chiefly in Galicia (where they are Uniates) though it has spread into Russia (where they are Orthodox) to a very limited extent.

[1] The Poles have recently shown a desire to annex Lithuania, *v.* Chap. III, Part I, § 4, p. 309, and note on p. 283.

They were the first branch of the Russian race to make their presence felt in history, and the Russian Empire began originally in the Little Russian capital of Kiev.

It is clearly impossible for the Poles to take in hand the protection of a race so much more numerous than their own. The Polish attitude towards them is a little difficult to understand. In Eastern Galicia, where the national movement is strong, it is in conflict with the Poles. In Russia, where it is weak, it appears to have Polish support. The Poles can clearly have little influence upon it to the east of the Dnieper, but they appear to have been anxious to establish some sort of Little Russian autonomy to the west of the Dnieper in Volhynia, Podolia, and Kiev. Their hope was no doubt that they might be able in this way to see Russia split into two and so avoid the presence of one powerful neighbour to the east, but it may be doubted whether this policy was not too complicated and whether it ever had before it any chance of success.

16. *Future prospects.* It is altogether idle to attempt anything in the nature of prophecy in regard to the future prospects of the Polish State. The utmost that can be done is to indicate briefly some of the more important factors in the situation, many of which have already been suggested by the previous examination into more detailed questions.

It is clear in the first place that Poland is a large country with great possibilities in front of her. In the present uncertainty with regard to frontiers it is impossible to estimate the extent of Polish territory, but it may be pointed out that the territory inhabited by definitely Polish majorities amounts to something like 90,000 square miles, while if the territory claimed for Poland on historic and other grounds be taken into account the total would amount to something like 300,000 square miles. The Poles themselves number over 20,000,000, excluding the three or four million Poles who live outside the former kingdom, of whom about $1\frac{1}{3}$ millions are in the United States of America. As we have seen, Poland must in any case contain also some millions of Germans and some millions of Jews. If even the most moderate demands of the Poles were satisfied there would in addition be large numbers of Little Russians (Ruthenians), White Russians, and possibly Lithuanians, so that the total number of inhabitants would hardly be less than 30,000,000, and might be very much more.

The economic possibilities of the country are also enormous. The results obtained by the introduction of German methods of agriculture into Prussian Poland, one of the least naturally fertile parts of Poland, give some indication of the future which might lie before Polish agriculture if modern methods were adopted in the Polish plain, or the still more fertile plateau regions to the south. The richest part of Upper Silesia, with its coal, iron, zinc, and lead, and part of Teschen, have now been added to Poland, and East Galicia with its oil is under Polish control. Thus the mineral wealth of the country will be enormous, and even without these there is coal in the Congress Kingdom and in Western Galicia, while the hills round Kielce are rich in iron-ore, copper, and lead. In industry also the development of textiles in such towns as Kalisz, Lodz, Warsaw, and Bialystok had been phenomenal before the War, especially in view of the very unfair Russian methods of competition. The War and the German occupation have given all this industry a terrible set-back, and Poland, like other Central European countries, finds it difficult to get the raw materials to restart her industries. Yet in view of the very great ability in industrial and engineering enterprises which the Poles were manifesting before the War it is not unreasonable to hope that, if once successfully restarted, Polish industry might develop in a very remarkable and rapid way.

The temporary difficulties which Poland has to face are, of course, exceedingly formidable. The country has been invaded by a typhus epidemic. The lack of raw materials and machinery affects every branch of the national life. Even apart from the Russian war and all the consequences arising from it, in particular the very low rate of the Polish exchange, there are most serious economic problems to be solved both in the way of securing a reasonable subsistence for the workmen and of satisfying the demands of the peasants for land. The economic problems of the west of Europe are serious enough, but in the east all these problems are aggravated, and conflicts are conducted with much greater bitterness on both sides.

The solution of all these problems is made more difficult by the special circumstances of the Polish State. We have already alluded to the weaknesses arising from the presence of too many nationalities within the Polish frontiers, and it may be added that the presence of so many Jews with their own language, religion, customs, and aspirations gives rise to many difficulties which are not always treated in the most reasonable way by either side. But it must be remembered further that the Poles themselves since the Partitions have become accustomed to different types of civilization, law, and administration in different parts of the country, and that there are thus enormous obstacles in the way of their working smoothly and harmoniously together. It is to be hoped that the different types of character thus produced may in the end all contribute to the special excellences of the Polish State, and that the Poles may be able to adapt for themselves the better features of all the countries under which they have suffered. To begin with, however, these differences do little but add to the enormous difficulties of organizing a new system of government.

If the Poles had enjoyed a great deal of political experience during the last hundred years these difficulties might not indeed be so serious. The exact reverse, however, is the case. In Austria they have certainly possessed a considerable amount of political power, but Austria can hardly be considered the best school for statesmen. In Germany they have profited by German science and German education, and they have displayed the most remarkable qualities in organizing their co-operative system in the teeth of German opposition, but it appears to be doubtful how far this experience has fitted them for the wider functions of government. The aim of the Russian Government seems to have been the weakening of the moral fibre of the nation, and if that aim has been only partially successful, it is undoubtedly the case that the educational level of the Polish peasant in Russian territory is deplorably low. The critics of Poland very often make too little allowance for the enormous difficulties she has had to face.

In the perilous adventure of reconstituting a new state the Poles are supported by the intense and fervent patriotism of a whole people and by a deep-rooted and passionate love of liberty. No doubt both of these may have their bad side as well as their good. Patriotism may so easily become imperialism, and liberty may so easily become licence, yet without these it is impossible to lay the foundations of any state. No one has ever doubted that the Poles possess the heroic virtues of courage and fidelity, nor again that they are capable of the highest achievements in literature and art and of what may be called the flowers and graces of civilization. All these great qualities may well make men hopeful of a great future for their country. Yet the very ardour of their temperament exposes them to special temptations, and there is a real danger that in aiming too high they may once again be brought low. The great question of the future is whether they will be able in addition to the qualities they have to develop others, less attractive perhaps but no less necessary, the common-place qualities of steadiness, thoroughness, perseverance, the capacity for organization and co-operation, and in general the humbler virtues of the business man. The history of the Poles in Prussia suggests very strongly that they may, and this is borne out by the way in which the smaller nobility or squirearchy has begun to take to commerce and industry as well as to the professions. The great need of the future for Poland is work and peace. The development of industry and commerce, as well as of agriculture, can alone give them that solidity which it is doubtful if they at present possess.

This brief review cannot but suggest that the prospects in front of Poland are full of danger, although there is much in the situation which gives occasion for hope. Germany almost certainly and in all probability Russia also are likely to be her enemies. In the course of time both of these countries are bound to recover most if not all of their former strength. Poland will have to walk very warily between these two great nations, and it is essential that she should be free from domestic discord and internal weakness. The next fifty years will be fraught with fate for her and for the other countries of Central Europe. It is to be hoped that the whole energies of the country may be concentrated on the one task of laying her foundations safe and sure.[1]

[1] *Editor's Note.*—On 15th March 1923 The Principal Allied Powers, under Article 87 of the Treaty of Versailles (Vol. III, pp. 157–8), assigned the following boundaries to Poland, East Galicia, and the Vilna area from Grodno to south of Dvinsk. They also recognized the boundary line of the Treaty of Riga concluded between Poland and Russia at Riga (*v.* map and Chap. III, Part II, § 9 e. See Mr. Bonar Law's explanation (20 March 1923, Hans. Ded., cols. 2320–1). Memel was in January 1923 assigned under Article 99 of Versailles Treaty (Vol. III, p. 168) to Lithuania.

CHAPTER III

EVOLUTION AND REVOLUTION IN NORTHERN EUROPE

PART I

THE RECOGNITION OF THE BALTIC STATES

1. *General.* Russia was really never so much a National State as a State composed of several nationalities, and consequently it was noticeable that with the progress of the War a process of crystallization of the various constituent national elements, which had set in previous to 1914, was now going on apace. Of the Border peoples from Finland in the north-west to the Tartars in Trans-Caucasia—all of them non-Slavonic with the exception of the Poles—most had, at the commencement of the War, affirmed their loyalty to the Russian Government, through their representatives in the Duma.[1] Their national self-consciousness was at very different stages of development, yet they felt, in varying degrees, none more acutely than those of the Baltic Provinces with their German social stratum, that Russia could not ultimately threaten their national aspirations to the same extent as the more relentless Prussian will to dominate. The course of the War, marked as it was in each of these States by local circumstances that only intensified the national and separatist feeling of these Border peoples, and reaching its climax, so far as Slav Russia was concerned, in the establishment of the Soviet Government and the Treaty of Brest-Litovsk, led, therefore, naturally to the disintegration of the Empire of the Tsars, a process which was rendered the more easy as the result of the Allied victory. In following this movement in the Baltic States, characterized as it was by features common to them all, it will be found convenient to attempt to trace its main outlines in the case of Finland, Esthonia and Latvia, and Lithuania respectively.

[1] Finland had no representatives in the Duma, and paid an annual sum to Russia in lieu of military service.

2. FINLAND

The case of Finland demands separate notice if for no other reason than that it had always held a peculiar and privileged position within the Russian Empire. It was a country with a Constitution of its own, the maintenance of which had been definitely guaranteed to the Finnish people when their country was annexed by its conqueror, Alexander I, in 1809. It was a country with national aspirations and traditions of statehood to which its highly educated people jealously clung, and of which the Russian Government in its most arbitrary, and therefore least intelligent, acts was never able to deprive them. Yet these very people as a whole, in spite of the dark periods in the past, were to the last strangely reluctant, to snap entirely the bond that had held them to Russia; even with the Provisional Government of 1917 they were prepared to enter into new relations which would leave matters of foreign policy and military defence in the hands of Russia, if only the Diet were allowed supreme control in all domestic affairs. Events, however, developed in such a way that on the 6th December 1917, the Diet proclaimed the independence of Finland as a sovereign state.

(*a*) *Results of the War.* The Great War, opening during a period at which an intensified Russification of Finland was being attempted, had naturally found that country less wholehearted in its support of the Russian Government than other regions of the Empire. Nevertheless if Finns to the number of 2,000 crossed over to Germany, and were eventually incorporated as the 27th Jäger Battalion which saw service on the Riga front, no less a number served in various capacities with the Russian forces. At first upset and damaged, the economic life of the country later received a tremendous stimulus through the imperial demands upon its manufacturing centres; these developed at the expense of the agricultural interests and needs of the country, so that by 1917 food conditions began to be difficult. Although one of the earliest acts of the Russian Provisional Government, after the Revolution of March 1917, was to restore the constitutional autonomy of Finland which had been taken away under the Bill for Imperial Legislation (1910) and other similar later Acts, still the Provisional Government did not take kindly to the fundamental assumption of the Finns that with the abdication of the Tsar the personal bond that held their country to Russia was dissolved and that it was in consequence a free country. Under the Finnish Constitution, even as amended in 1906, all executive power lay with the Senate, a body nominated by the Tsar, and only capable of submitting proposals to be considered by him as Grand Duke of Finland. But it was in particular the growing unrest in Russia—for the sense of nationality had long ere this reached mature development—that drove Finland to the extreme step of cutting loose entirely from that unhappy country. The impulse to separation was strongest among the bourgeois who had prospered during the War; the Social Democrats, who were in sympathy at any rate with the earlier stages of the Russian Revolution, were not so set upon complete independence, and toyed with ideas of a status in relation to Russia comparable to that of a British Dominion. Still in a slight majority in the Diet, the latter party, while putting through democratic legislation such as the eight hours' day, began to look towards the now restless Russian garrisons, in addition to their use of the strike, as a means of impressing the bourgeois parties with the necessity of yielding to their demands. With the refusal of the Russian Provisional Government to go any further in the matter of Finnish independence, the situation became still more serious; and on the 18th July 1917 the Diet, as the one authority directly representing the people, assumed the supreme power in Finland without reference to the Senate, Governor-General, or Russian Government. The latter replied by dissolving the Diet, and fixing the new elections for October, when the Social Democrats were returned in the minority. Meanwhile the internal unrest grew, fostered by a food shortage, obtrusive capitalism, and an alien army of occupation daily getting more out of hand. The Soviet Government was now in power, and while the Finnish bourgeois parties were only thereby strengthened in their determination to cut loose from Russia, the Social Democrats found themselves drifting into sympathy with the Bolsheviks, as the result of the treatment meted out to the Diet by the Provisional Government. They attempted to try and secure by force what their numerical inferiority prevented them, at any rate for the time being, securing by constitutional methods. After the Russian Revolution the Social Democrats, who were then in the majority in the

Diet, had replaced the police, many of whom were Russians, by a local 'militia' whose composition became so progressively 'Red' that the bourgeois parties organized a corresponding White Guard. The Social Democrats had also organized a Red Guard all over the country to safeguard the fruits of the Russian Revolution. These Red bodies continued to make common cause with the Russian soldiery, whose removal the Diet had been unable to obtain from the Russian Government; and the general sense of insecurity and unrest was increased by the growing undiscipline and terroristic acts of the Reds, due to the fact that their pay had ceased. It was under these circumstances, in the belief that 'the only means to save Finland from famine and anarchy is to declare her a Sovereign Power', that the Declaration of absolute Independence was made by the Diet, being carried by the bourgeois White majority against the Socialist proposal that it should be realized by means of a mutual friendly understanding with Russia. The Soviet Government had meanwhile replaced some of the Russian troops in Finland by others that were definitely Russian Red Guard troops who were deliberately sent with the purpose of fomenting disturbance in Finland. This having been done it was possible for the Soviet Government to grant formal recognition of Finnish Independence on the 4th January 1918, in which course they were followed by Sweden, Germany, and France.

(*b*) *The 'White' Reaction*, 1918–19. All the elements, economic, social, and political, were now in existence for a far-reaching conflagration, and with a cue given by the forcible closing of the Russian Constituent Assembly by the Bolsheviks on the 19th January, it was not difficult for the extremer elements amongst the Social Democrats, aided by arms and munitions as well as Red troops from Russia, to carry out a *coup d'état* which put them in possession of Helsingfors on the 29th January 1918. The civil war which followed was really of the nature of a class war—an endeavour to establish 'a dictatorship of the proletariate' in one of the most democratic countries in the world, which was resisted with equal determination. Success lay initially with the Reds. But their programme had never made much impression in the north-western part of Finland. The bourgeois Government made Vasa its headquarters, and the White Army, the bulk of which was drawn from the White Guards, was rapidly organized under General

Mannerheim, with considerable assistance from the survivors of the German-trained Jäger Battalion. Appeals by members of the Government to Sweden for assistance in men and arms received tardy consideration owing to the political situation, and apart from volunteers nothing was eventually done. A more immediate response was given by Germany, who saw the prospect, not merely of reasserting her position in the Baltic and possibly of re-establishing a reactionary government in Russia, but also of striking at the Allied forces at Archangel and Murmansk.[1] The Germans landed in the Aland Islands on the 3rd March and on the mainland under Von der Goltz nine days later. In the interval, a very one-sided Commercial Treaty between Germany and Finland was drawn up and signed. By forced marches Von der Goltz moved on Helsingfors, while the White Army meanwhile took the industrial centre of Tammerfors. On the 12th April Von der Goltz entered Helsingfors, and by the 26th May General Mannerheim was also able to make a solemn entry into the capital in token of the cessation of hostilities. The Russian elements had been pushed across the border, and about 74,000 Finnish Social Democrats were prisoners of war. Any hopes that the former had cherished of using a Bolshevized Finland as a base for a further campaign in Scandinavia were at an end.

Not unnaturally, though quite unconstitutionally, the bourgeois or Conservative parties now sought to exclude the Social Democrats from participation in the work of the re-assembled Diet; as it was, the actual representation of that party was only a single member, the others having fled or being prisoners of war. The Swedish and Old Finn parties in particular, showed as a whole very marked pro-German leanings, and succeeded, in spite of the opposition of the Young Finns and Agrarians in getting a decision on the 19th October by 64 to 41—a total vote of little more than half the membership of the Diet—to offer the 'Finnish Crown' to a German princeling. This step was taken with a view to securing the maintenance of social order and close political co-operation with Germany. The German troops were invited to remain in the country,

[1] The whole subject is treated with a certain frankness in Von der Goltz's *Meine Sendung in Finnland und im Baltikum* (1920). He omits, however, to mention that the German General Staff had a secret understanding with the Finnish pro-Germans about the establishment of a German monarchical régime in Finland. In short, the whole expedition was as much a German as a Finnish idea.

German officers reorganized the Finnish army, out of the successful White Guards ; and the idea of a Greater Finland, which should include the nearly allied population of Eastern Karelia, seemed practicable to many members of the Conservative parties. The defeat of Germany, however, put an end to the pro-German schemes of what was after all a minority. The Conservative Government of Mr. Paasikivi had to resign, and was succeeded on the 26th November by a new Coalition Ministry under Mr. Ingman. The Commercial Treaty with Germany was annulled, and the German troops left the country. The acting Regent, Mr. Svinhufvud, who had held this position since the 18th May, also resigned, and on the 12th December the Diet elected General Mannerheim to succeed him. Under amnesties enacted by these two Regents more than half of the Red prisoners of war were liberated. The new Government also dissolved the Diet and fixed the new elections for March 1919.

(*c*) *Position after the Armistice ; British recognition, 6th May 1919.* The economic condition of Finland at this time was perilous in the extreme, and it is only right to mention the part played by the Allies in solving the food problem in particular. As soon as the Commercial Treaty between Finland and Germany was annulled, and guarantees for the withdrawal of the German troops were secured under the Armistice Convention, the Allied Governments took steps to sell large quantities of food to the Finnish Government. An agreement to this effect was arranged on the 10th December 1918 in London between Mr. Hoover and Dr. Holsti, the Finnish representative in London. Further, in the matter of the recognition of Finnish independence by the Allies, while France gave early recognition, which was withdrawn after the Diet vote of the 9th October 1918, Great Britain proposed to recognize it in April 1918, while the German troops were in the country, provided that Finland would maintain her neutrality during the war. The Germans, in their endeavour to secure Finnish co-operation on their side, gave definite undertakings to arrange for the recognition of Finnish independence by all states at the Peace Conference which should follow the end of the war. The question of the recognition of Finnish independence was discussed anew by the Allied Powers on the 3rd May 1919, and the British recognition followed three days later.

As the result of the new elections, the Socialist representation numbered 80 out of 200, while 50 votes were representative of the Conservative or Extreme Right parties, and 70 of the Centre parties. The Diet having been convoked immediately, a new Government came into power in April. The Premier was Mr. Castren, and his Cabinet consisted of representatives of all the bourgeois parties. A Bill was introduced with the object of giving the country a democratic Republican constitution. In spite of the Conservative opposition this Bill was passed and became Fundamental Law on the 17th July. On the basis of it the Diet elected Dr. K. J. Stahlberg, who had been leader of the Progressist (Young Finn) party, to the highest office of the state. In the beginning of August the Government resigned, having accomplished its main purpose of carrying through the constitutional reform, and a new Government was formed by Professor Vennola, consisting of Centre party politicians only.

(*d*) *Relations with Russia, advance on Petrograd, 1919.* We must now return to the question of Finnish relations with Russia. Soon after the close of the Finnish civil war, the German Government had invited the Finnish and the Russian Governments to send delegates to Berlin, with a view to the conclusion of a definite peace between these countries. Negotiations were commenced in August, but ended in complete failure, chiefly owing to the refusal of the Russian delegation to accept any of the principal Finnish proposals. As the Russians were not aggressively inclined at the time, it was found possible to reduce the war strength of the Finnish army gradually, although local hostilities had not definitely ceased. In the autumn of 1919, however, the adventure of General Yudenitch induced the Conservative parties in Finland, who numbered 50 votes in the Diet, to advocate active intervention openly. The same minds that conceived the idea of a Greater Finland were convinced that a rapid march of the newly organized Finnish army on Petrograd under the victorious Mannerheim, in co-operation with Yudenitch, would mean the capture of that city and the ultimate fall of Bolshevism, and that Russia, receiving her capital again from Finnish hands, would out of gratitude respect for all time the independence of that people. The 80 Socialists in the Diet were bitterly opposed to the idea of granting assistance to, or co-operating with,

Yudenitch, and urged the Government to make peace with Russia. The two Centre parties, comprising 70 members, likewise considered new hostilities inopportune, but on the other hand, found no sufficient reason for fresh efforts to initiate peace proposals. In the meantime the Finnish Government had been in close touch with the Esthonian, Latvian, and Polish Governments, and had learned that only the Esthonians, who had just concluded a successful war of defence, were inclined to conclude an immediate peace with Russia. The situation was sufficiently perplexing, for it was clear that what Finland needed above all was a period of peace in which to strengthen and develop her new independence, reorganize her economic life, and heal the bitter feuds engendered by the civil war with all the difficulties it entailed. For the Government to join in any unprovoked attack on Russia would simply have been to challenge afresh the extremer Socialist elements, while on the other hand, the call for aid and incorporation in the Finnish state from some of the East Karelians was difficult to resist. In the solution of her problems, Finland was supremely fortunate to possess from the time of the Castren Ministry onwards so sagacious and far-seeing a Foreign Minister as Dr. Rudolf Holsti.

In the spring of 1920 events took a turn unfavourable to the hopes of the Finnish war party; for with the evacuation of the Archangel regions and Murmansk by the Allied forces of the north, the whole military situation was changed. As long as White Russian forces remained in occupation of Eastern Karelia, Finland had practically no cause for anxiety. Now she suddenly saw her eastern frontier exposed to the possibility of Bolshevik concentrations, with the situation in Eastern Karelia more problematic than ever. With a view to averting any chance of fresh hostilities on a large scale, the Finnish Government entered into preliminary *pourparlers* with the Russian Government in the hope of arranging an armistice until peace negotiations could be renewed. Plenipotentiaries met at the frontier on the Karelian Isthmus, but failed to agree as to the terms of an armistice. In April the Finnish Government resigned, and was succeeded by a bourgeois Coalition under Professor Erich. This Cabinet decided to accept a Russian invitation to open peace negotiations, and as the new Prime Minister and some other members of the Cabinet belonged to the Conservative parties, the Government policy encountered no opposition in the Diet.

(*e*) *Peace Negotiations with the Bolsheviks, 1920.* Peace negotiations commenced at Dorpat in Esthonia on the 12th June, but were adjourned on the 14th July, owing to the unwillingness of the Russian Government to accept the Finnish terms; in particular the question of the destiny of Eastern Karelia proved a very difficult one on which to reach agreement. Simultaneously with these negotiations the Russian Government reopened hostilities against Poland, and carried their initial success to the precincts of Warsaw. Public opinion in Finland solidified under the pressure of events towards acceptance of the Russian promise of local autonomy in Eastern Karelia. The negotiations were resumed on the 28th July. The Finnish delegates strove further to secure the right of national self-determination for the Karelians, but without any positive result. The Social Democrats and the Swedish Party, representing together a small majority in the Diet, declared themselves opposed to further efforts in this direction. The Peace Treaty was subsequently signed on the 14th October. The Diet empowered the Government to ratify the Treaty, which came into force on the 1st January 1921.

The Governments of Professors Vennola and Erich alike did very much for the country by the laws which they carried for organizing the state finances and for social reforms. Efforts were also continually directed towards mitigating and overcoming the bitterness prevailing between the bourgeoisie and labour and other aftermath of the civil war. By a Bill introduced on the 28th May 1920, the Government were authorized to request the admittance of Finland into the League of Nations. A formal request was addressed to the Secretary General on the 30th June, and on the 16th December 1920, Finland was unanimously accepted into the membership of the League.

3. ESTHONIA AND LATVIA

(*a*) *General.* In the case of these two countries, inhabited by peoples of very different race but with a history that had had much in common, the struggle for freedom and for national independence was an even more remarkable process than in the case of Finland. The severest phases came after all the exhaustion of the Great War, when both states were fighting with both Germany and Russia, and backed by no previous experience of what constructive statesmanship meant. We are still too close to the events to get a true perspective, but it may be confidently asserted that when the full story comes to be told, the epic of the Esthonian and Latvian struggle for independence will rank high amongst the world's records of such performances. 'A people without an *épopeé*,' said Goethe, 'can never become of much worth,' but in the recent elaboration of their *épopeé* these peoples proved their worth.

It would be a mistake to suppose that the political situation in these two Baltic Provinces about the time of the Allied Armistice with Germany was the direct result either of the war, or of the fact that a Communist Government had established itself in Russia, or of the declaration of the Allies that they were fighting for the small nationalities, or even of the glamour surrounding the mystic word 'self-determination'. Rather did these circumstances provide the conditions under which a movement, or national self-consciousness, which came distinctly into being in these Provinces during the sixties of the previous century, rapidly developed into maturity and expressed itself in significant action. This deepening desire for freedom of economic and cultural development had already manifested itself in the rising of 1905, and, in the defence of Latvian territory during the war against the Germans, and later against the pro-German Bermondtists and the Bolsheviks alike, showed itself to be a very real thing. It must not be forgotten that from the spring of 1915 right up to the spring of 1920, Latvia had been,[1] almost without a break, an arena of military action. In their retreat the Russians used every effort to leave this once flourishing country a desert. Owing to the removal of machinery, raw materials, and the workers into the interior, and the deliberate destruction of what could not be removed, the large industries characteristic of Latvia, and particularly of Riga, were entirely destroyed, so that in this respect Latvia had suffered more than any other region of the former Russian Empire. Attempts had been

[1] Lack of space alone prevents a corresponding measure of detail in the case of Esthonia, where events concerned with the main issues were broadly parallel, although, owing to her more northerly position, she suffered much less in the Great War.

made to remove rolling-stock and all means of transport by sea or river, and whatever was left behind of this nature or in the way of grain or cattle or supplies had been seized by the German occupational authorities and either used by them or transferred to Germany, along with many loads of timber. But, more particularly, although troops that were native to these regions fought magnificently in defence of what was their homeland, no real defence of Courland or Livonia had been attempted by the Russians. The fight made by two battalions of Lettish reservists before Mitau inspired the idea of purely Lettish detachments in the regular army. Permission was obtained from the Russian commander-in-chief, and in July 1915 the Lettish Duma delegates issued a recruiting appeal which resulted in the formation of eight regiments from the refugees and by transfer of nationals from other regiments. Their daring gallantry on various occasions during the years 1915–17, and especially before Riga, led to their being described by the Kaiser in a field speech as the 'eight stars on the Riga front' which would have to be extinguished before that city fell into his hands. Yet the Russians continued to retreat, and circumstances in connexion with the evacuation of Riga on the 3rd September 1917, produced a very profound impression, and deepened the conviction that there had been a systematic betrayal of these regions by the Supreme Command. Two-thirds of the inhabitants of Courland were now refugees all over Russia, and it is not surprising that out of these refugees and regiments alike the Bolsheviks eventually recruited a certain number of adherents. On the other hand, many returned to fight for Latvia, while the Lettish organization charged with the care of these refugees, and operating from Petrograd so long as this was possible, not merely kept alive their national feeling, but proved a good training ground for men who were later called upon to create and mould the future state.

Already after the Russian Revolution in March 1917, and especially after the later Bolshevik *coup d'état*, it became clear to the Lettish patriots that they had nothing to hope for from Russia, and that they must take the destinies of their country into their own hands. This was the more evident since the commander of the German forces of occupation, after the fall of Riga, called into existence various Landtags and Landesrats, arbitrarily composed of representatives of the German baronial class, who began to plan for some form of annexation to, or incorporation in, the German Empire. Accordingly the Lettish National Council, composed of representatives of the different Lettish democratic political parties, outstanding Lettish organizations and individuals, constituted itself at Walk on the 16th November 1917, and proceeded to take steps for proclaiming and establishing the independence of Latvia. At the All-Russian Constituent Assembly which met in Moscow on the 5th January 1918, the Lettish Deputy Goldman announced that Latvia now regarded herself as an autonomous unit whose position, international relations, and internal organization were matters for the decision of her own Constituent Assembly. The Lettish National Council held a second session in Petrograd on the 17th and 18th January 1918, at which Latvia, that is Courland, South Livonia, and Latgalia, was declared an independent democratic republic. Protests were also made on behalf of the Lettish people against any attempt to divide up the country, as also against any attempt at a conclusion of peace that implied any limitation of the rights of peoples to self-determination. Similarly, representatives of the Esthonian people had met at Reval in November 1917, and in the name of the right of self-determination had proclaimed Esthonia a sovereign state, and carried the resolution into effect by the establishment of a Government in Reval on the 24th February 1918.

(*b*) *German Occupation, 1918.* Meanwhile, during the interruption of the Peace negotiations at Brest-Litovsk, the Germans occupied Estland and Livonia, so that, with the exception of a part of Latgalia, the whole of Latvia and Esthonia was in German hands. In conformity with the terms of the Treaty of Brest-Litovsk, Courland together with the district and city of Riga was placed under a German protectorate; the remainder of the country (as also Estland) was to remain under German occupation until peace and order were restored, while the destiny of Latgalia was to be settled later. The agitation for union with Germany was vigorously carried on by the various Rumps of the Landesraten, e.g., that of Courland, praying the Kaiser on the 8th March 1918 to accept the Grand-ducal crown of Courland, and expressing the hope that Courland, Livonia, Esthonia, and the island of Oesel might be formed into a state and united to Germany. To these and similar representations made at Berlin and supported in person, the Kaiser replied that he would 'mit Rat und Tat zur Herbeiführung dieses Zustandes helfen'. Between requisitions, wholesale arrests, suppression of the press, and restriction of personal liberty, the occupation everywhere took on the character of a 'terror'. These details are mentioned partly because they illustrate and confirm the conviction, expressed at the time by a few observers, that it was in her East European, rather than West European, frontier that Germany was really interested, that Courland was the last of the territories occupied by her that she would wish to surrender, and that at the time of the Armistice negotiations no less attention ought to have been given to the situation on her eastern frontier than was given to the situation in the west. More particularly, they serve to indicate the intensity of the difficulties under which the Esthonian and Lettish patriots alike had to carry on their struggle for independence.

(*c*) *British and Allied Attitude towards recognition, 1918.* During the spring and summer of 1918 it was apparent, particularly from the situation in Poland and Czecho-Slovakia, that the countries where Bolshevism made least appeal were those of nascent nationality. They wanted to be themselves; hence disorder and class warfare had no interest for them. It looked as if the best card to play against Bolshevism at that particular stage was the support of incipient nationality, wherever discerned. Examination of the Baltic border states showed the existence of a will to resist Germanism and Bolshevism alike, to which there was nothing comparable in any party of Slav Russia proper. So there developed in certain quarters the idea of helping the non-Slavonic Russian Border States, both on the Baltic and in Trans-Caucasia, in their struggle for independence, primarily in the interests of their self-determination, but also with a view to stabilizing conditions in a zone around Russia, from which, with the help of the co-operative societies, food and industrial necessities might be introduced into that unfortunate country. It is to the lasting credit of Great Britain, to which country more than any other these border states looked for guidance and assistance, that this policy of interest in them as a whole commended itself to her first amongst the Great Powers, the only drawback being that it was not more extensively, opportunely, and energetically carried out. There was, however, always the difficulty that France and the United States of America were consistently opposed to it, for reasons of their own which have since proved to be unjustified.[1] As it was, the Esthonian National Council was recognized *de facto* by the British Government on the 3rd May 1918, and similar recognition was given to the Lettish Council on the 11th November 1918.

(*d*) *The Armistice and its execution.* At the time of the cessation of hostilities between Germany and the Allies, the former country had overrun the Baltic Provinces, and from the terms of the Armistice Convention of the 11th November 1918 it became clear that the attention directed to the conditions on the eastern border had been based on inadequate information, although sound information was at hand. The French and Italian political representatives on the Council of the Allies were unfortunately of the opinion [2] that to believe in a Bolshevik danger to the Baltic States and elsewhere was 'to let ourselves be deceived by German propaganda'. Unfortunately also, Mr. Balfour withdrew his more energetic and practicable proposals in view of Marshal Foch's opinion that they were not realizable. The French, however, were naturally engrossed with their own frontier, and were less interested in the East German frontier. The result was that, while the principle of the evacuation of territory by Germany in east and west was agreed upon, an Allied Commission was appointed to superintend that

[1] President Wilson defined his attitude as follows in a note on Russian affairs delivered to the Italian Embassy at Washington, published in the press the 12th August 1920. 'By this feeling of friendship and honourable obligation to the great nations whose brave and heroic self-sacrifice contributed so much to the termination of the war, the Government of the United States was guided in its reply to the Lithuanian National Council on the 15th October 1919 and in its persistent refusal to recognize the Baltic States as separate nations independent of Russia. The same spirit was manifested in the Note of this Government of the 23rd March 1920, in which it was stated with reference to certain proposed settlements in the Near East, that no final decision should or can be made without the consent of Russia. In line with these important declarations of policy the United States withheld its approval from the decision at the Supreme Council at Paris, recognizing the independence of the so-called Republics of Georgia and Azerbaijan.' He further stated that, though recognizing the independence of Armenia, the United States 'has taken the position that the final determination of its boundaries must not be made without Russia's consent and agreement'.

[2] Partial accounts of these proceedings are gradually being made public (cf. Mermeix, *Les Négociations secrètes et les Quatre Armistices, avec Pièces justificatives*; R. S. Baker, *Woodrow Wilson and the World Settlement*). The sooner the whole account is published the better; it will afford an admirable world lesson in comparative statesmanship. For a general account of the evacuation *v.* Vol. I, pp. 341–6.

evacuation in the west, but no corresponding Commission was appointed for the east. And not merely so, but clauses XII and XIII in the Armistice Convention under which that evacuation was regulated were so clumsily drawn up that their ambiguity was easily exploited by the Germans in their endeavour to hold the fruits of their conquests in the east. Indeed, not till more than a year after the Armistice were conditions on the eastern frontier in the way of being settled according to the intention of the Allies, and in one instance, at least, such settlement is still outstanding

Under Art. XII of the Armistice Convention the Germans were to withdraw from territory which formed part of the Russian Empire at August 1914, 'as soon as the Allies shall consider this desirable, having regard to the interior conditions of these territories', while under Article XIII the evacuation was to commence 'at once'. A 'Progressive Bloc' of Lettish patriots, representative of many parties, who had been secretly organizing the life of their country under the leadership of Mr. Ulmanis, and alike protesting against incorporation with Germany, were now joined by the members of the National Council, who had left Petrograd, fleeing before the Bolsheviks; and a conjoint National Assembly was held at Riga on the 18th November 1918, under Mr. Tschakste, which proclaimed the sovereign independence of Latvia, and elected a Provisional Government to take charge of affairs during the coming critical days, until a Constituent Assembly could be elected on a normal basis. Meanwhile, the Bolsheviks had crossed the Narova on the northern Esthonian border on the 28th November, and at various points on the Latvian frontier a few days later. The Germans, who wished to avoid all conflict with the Bolsheviks, at the same time did everything in their power to hinder the Esthonian and Lettish Provisional Governments in their endeavours to organize local forces of resistance. The German maintenance of control of telegraphs and railroads, together with their removal of arms and ammunitions, was all part of a policy directed in the hope that Esthonians and Letts alike would request their assistance in the imminent struggle with the Bolsheviks, and thus provide the legal excuse which they required for remaining on in these countries, in which they had established themselves specifically to protect them and to introduce peace and order there. Under the nerveless action of the Allies as a whole, it looked more than once as if the local German nobility with the aid of the occupational forces might succeed in their design of crushing the young Nationalist Governments or rendering them helpless against the Bolshevik invaders, with whom the Balts [1] might have come to terms later with the help of the German Government. Great Britain was, however, giving assistance with arms, ammunition, and food-stuffs, while the presence of units of a Baltic squadron at different times in Reval and Libau gave both active and moral support. Further, Finland rendered valuable assistance to Esthonia in the forms of a volunteer force and of a loan, while Danish and Swedish volunteers also fought side by side with the Esthonians against the invaders. In Latvia the conditions were for a time even harder, that country being as yet entirely under German control, while a movement of slow retreat from Esthonia had begun. Further, the Provisional Government had no funds and only a few companies of soldiers badly armed.

(*e*) *Von der Goltz in the Baltic.* By January 1919 the Government was compelled to evacuate Riga, and retire to Libau, the Germans having retreated to the line Libau–Shrunden Goldingen. In and around Libau the Lettish Government strove to build up an army of defence from the patriotic students and peasants who were concentrating on that town. Common action on the part of the Latvian army with the Balts and Germans against the Bolsheviks was hindered by the fact that at every point Von der Goltz, the German commander, made it apparent that he wished to be master of the country. Sent to the Baltic Provinces, according to his statement,[2] originally for the defence of East Prussia against the Bolsheviks, he arrived at Libau on the 1st February, and quickly 'I conceived my task in the larger sense of the future of Germany'. His idea was to try still to carry out the eastern policy of his country which had been upset by the recent course of events, by coming to an understanding with the White Russians under the common standard of a campaign against the Bolsheviks, and so to build up a close understanding with the Russia that was to be. Russia would have need of German merchants and

[1] A term applied to the element in the population of German extraction. They formed 6 per cent. of the population and held 60 per cent. of the land.
[2] *Op. cit.*, p. 127.

technical men, for her *intelligentsia* had been destroyed. Germany needed land for many of her ex-soldiers; why not settle them in the devastated border provinces which their industry would soon restore to their former prosperity? By promises of land out of that third part of their estates which the Baltic barons agreed to devote to this purpose, Von der Goltz was able to maintain an effective force of German volunteer soldiers alongside of the Balts, prepared to see the business through on these conditions, even when the growing pressure of the Allies began to insist on the evacuation of these provinces by the German forces. The only obstacles to success were the young National Governments. A first plot failed, but on the 16th April Von der Goltz with the aid of the Balts overthrew the Lettish Provisional Government, which took refuge on a ship at Libau under British protection. Thereafter he proceeded to attack the Bolshevik forces, and with the assistance of the Balts and also of some Lettish national units which saw as their primary duty the necessity of ridding their country of the Bolshevik, recaptured Riga on the 22nd May 1919. In the north of Latvia a mixed force of Lettish and Esthonian nationals had also been successfully operating against the Bolsheviks. They, however, stood in the way of the German commander's project of a reconquered Latvia, which was to be supplemented by a revolution provoked against the Provisional Government in Esthonia. The result was a realignment of Esthonian and Lettish national forces against the Germans and Balts, which resulted in the defeat of the latter in June.

(*f*) *Expulsion of the Germans from the Baltic Provinces.* An Allied Commission had now been appointed to supervise matters in the Baltic States, and under its authority the Lettish Provisional Government was reinstated at this stage, and concluded an Armistice with the Germans on the 3rd July, under which the Germans agreed to withdraw from Riga and evacuate Courland. Five days later the Provisional Government returned to Riga and recommenced the work of consolidating the Latvian army; an endeavour was also made to conciliate the Balt element by offering them representation in the Government, and so secure their co-operation in the common struggle against the Bolsheviks. The purely German forces did not carry out the terms of the Armistice and remained within the limits of Courland, where they were reorganized and joined by units composed of liberated Russian prisoners of war. Von der Goltz's recall having been insisted on by the Allies, he was succeeded by the adventurer Avaloff-Bermondt, who continued for some time to inspire this 'Russian Army of the North-West', which was as much a danger to the young Border States as in its original purely German composition under Von der Goltz. Very quickly it showed itself in its true light as an anti-Lettish, rather than anti-Bolshevik, force, and by the 8th October was marching once more on Riga. Supported by Allied men-of-war the Latvian army under General Balod successfully held the passage to the Dwina, although the city was under the fire of Bermondt's forces for a month. Supplies began to fail, and the Bermondtist rabble was compelled to retreat, perpetrating acts of vandalism and wanton destruction surpassing anything that Latvian property had suffered previously at Russian, German, or Bolshevik hands. On this occasion the evacuation of Courland was complete. Inspired by its success, the Latvian army after a month of preparation commenced a fresh campaign in January 1920, with a view to driving the Bolsheviks out of Latgalia, the only part of Latvia still remaining in their hands. Here again the operations were completely successful by the end of the following month, and carried no farther than strictly ethnographical, rather than strategical, reasons demanded. Elections were held for the Constituent Assembly in the middle of April, and at its first meeting on the 1st May 1920, Mr. Tschakste, the president of the National Council, was elected President of the Assembly.

(g) *Peace Negotiations, Recognition of Latvia and Esthonia by Supreme Council, 26th January 1921.* The new Government under Mr. Ulmanis concluded an armistice with Germany on the 15th July 1920 and a Treaty of Peace with Russia on the 11th August. On the 26th January 1921, Latvia and Esthonia were recognized *de jure* by the Supreme Council of the Allies and on the 22nd September admitted as members of the League of Nations. As in the case of Latvia so also with Esthonia, only after a Peace Treaty had been signed with Russia on the 2nd February 1920, following a heroic defence against vastly superior numbers, did the Esthonian people have a chance for the first time of organizing the economic life of their country, and setting their internal affairs in order. A Constitution corresponding closely to that of Switzerland and of the German

Republic was passed by the Constituent Assembly on the 15th June 1920. Under it citizens of both sexes from the age of twenty have the right to vote, or stand for election to the Diet. The membership of the latter is 100, elected for a term of three years. The initiative for legislation does not lie solely with the Diet; thus 25,000 electors may claim a plebiscite, or propose a new law.

4. LITHUANIA

(*a*) *German intervention, 1915–17.* In the case of Lithuania, the progress in self-determination has not been so outwardly marked, partly because the peculiar geographical situation of that country, lying directly between Russia and Germany, has made an interest in its position and native richness and fertility something not easily surrendered by either of these countries, and partly because, owing to a long past period of close relationship with Poland, it has seemed naturally desirable in many Polish minds that history should be made in some sort to repeat itself. Yet this does not mean that there has been any less determination on the part of the Lithuanian people to become a sovereign independent state, or that their recent past has not had its episodes of attempted Russification and denationalizing treatment during the early stages of the war as in the cases of Latvia and Esthonia, which only deepened the resolve to be free from domination whether from the east, west, or south. In the earlier revolution of 1905, Lithuanians alone of all the constituent peoples of Russia held a convention (4th and 5th December) of about 2,000 delegates in their historic capital of Vilna, demanding autonomy for their country (represented by the four Governments of Vilna, Kovno, Grodno, and Suwalki) and a Diet of their own at Vilna. Again, in the same city, on the 18th–22nd September 1917, another representative gathering of over 200 delegates was held during the German occupation, after a long period of discussion with the military authorities and subsequent preparation and organization, at which the Taryba or National Council was elected, consisting of twenty Lithuanian members and six representing national minorities,[1] and expression was given to the demand that for the free development of Lithuania, it was absolutely necessary that

[1] Of these the Jews and White Russians did not co-operate before the last months of 1918; the Poles never co-operated.

she become ' an independent State, organized on democratic principles within her ethnographical frontiers '. German policy with regard to Lithuania, while ultimately favourable to cultural autonomy, was tending rather at this time in the direction of annexation, and it therefore seemed desirable to create some sort of Lithuanian Council which might be persuaded or forced to co-operate with the military authorities as an auxiliary organ with limited powers. The Lithuanian difficulty was how to concede that measure of agreed co-operation with the Germans which was set down as a condition of their being allowed to hold the Conference at all, without endangering the primary object of national independence. As no elections could be held, an organizing Committee was compelled to select the delegates from each of the districts of the country, having due regard to class and comparative strength of political parties.

(*b*) *The Taryba, 1917–18.* The Taryba at once set to work on its two principal tasks of creating and organizing the Lithuanian State, and of attempting to restore, or at least ameliorate, the economic and social condition of the country. This meant that it had to protest vigorously against the unnecessarily heavy requisitioning and consequent insufficient feeding of the population, the banditism of escaped Russian prisoners of war, exploitation of the forests, forced labour, and against the attempt to introduce the compulsory teaching of German in primary schools, with the prospect always of being forcibly dissolved by the local German authorities. It also endeavoured to get into touch with Lithuanian refugees in other parts of Europe, and the emigrant population in the United States of America, as also, on the one hand, to put its case for the self-determination of the country before the representatives of the Allies, and, on the other, seek by establishing relations with certain groups in the Reichstag and with the Central Government at Berlin to secure some investigation of the actions of the military authorities in Lithuania, and recognition of the independence of the country. On the 29th November 1917, Count Hertling, the newly appointed Chancellor, recognized, in a speech in the Reichstag, the right of Lithuania, Courland, and Poland to dispose of their own destinies. It was, however, very speedily made clear in Berlin to representatives of the Taryba that such recognition of independence and support of Lithuanian claims at the Peace Conference would have to be purchased by a perpetual alliance with Germany which should find expression in military, transport, customs, and currency conventions. The success against Russia, however, stiffened the German attitude; Brest-Litovsk had the result that the direction of Lithuanian affairs fell back once more almost completely into military hands. A new formula was proposed by Germany in the verbiage of which the independence of Lithuania seemed less recognizable than before. By declaration, on the 11th December 1917, the Taryba in view of all the circumstances adopted and signed the earlier agreed formula, in which amongst other points, Vilna was recognized as the capital of the Lithuanian State. But this action in no way modified the German attitude on the spot, even although Lithuania had now formally asked for 'the aid and protection' of the German Empire. Nor would the Germans allow Lithuanian delegates to appear at Brest-Litovsk and explain the circumstances under which they had declared the independence of the Lithuanian State. In consequence the Taryba asked the German Government for a definite answer on these three points. Does Germany recognize Lithuania as an independent State? Does she agree to hand over the administration of the entire country to the Taryba? Does she agree to withdraw her troops from Lithuania? To the first question only was a definite answer given by letter on the 27th January 1918, stating that while the German Government recognized Lithuania as an independent State, in terms of the resolutions of the 11th December 1917, it reserved the right of deciding at what moment this recognition should be made: further, the aforesaid conventions had still to be drawn up. The Taryba decided that if Germany did not grant recognition, it would annul the rest of the understanding expressed in the aforementioned resolutions. On the 16th February 1918 it reaffirmed the re-establishment of an independent Lithuanian State 'founded on a democratic basis with Vilna as capital, and the dissolution of all political connexions that had existed with other peoples. The Taryba declares at the same time that the basis of this State and its relations with other States will be definitely fixed by a Constituent Assembly', which ought to be convoked as soon as possible and elected by all the inhabitants on a democratic basis. Count Hertling very truly replied that this declaration overturned the basis on which the German Government was prepared to recognize the independence of Lithuania, and that it could not do so under these modified conditions.

These details are mentioned in order to show that, even under a German occupation of all Lithuania that had lasted since September 1915, and in opposition to a Government that was peculiarly anxious to annex their industrious, orderly, and law-abiding population and their rich territory, the Lithuanian representatives struggled persistently to effect the recognition, in theory and practice, of the independence of their country. At the same time the hard facts of the situation had also to be taken into account, and particularly when the threat of a Bolshevik invasion began, later, to assume the form of a reality. Since a German withdrawal was a possibility under the terms of the Armistice, it was only natural that the new State, without resources in funds, munitions, or trained troops, and from its peculiarly inland position unable to receive consignments of arms from the Allies, should take assistance from Germany. For the moment the situation was that Germany had complete control of the country, and having been successful in her negotiations at Brest-Litovsk, was no longer prepared to give even the most shadowy recognition of Lithuanian independence except on her own terms. Recognition was finally granted by the Kaiser on the 23rd March 1918, on the original basis, with the additional condition that Lithuania should bear a part of the German war costs, as having been liberated by that country.

(*c*) *Situation in 1918*. In Lithuania the actual situation in no way improved as the result of these negotiations. The local German authorities endeavoured to thwart or embarrass the Taryba on every occasion in its now recognized task of trying to build up the State. They even tried to start an agitation in favour of a personal union between Lithuania and Saxony or Prussia. By harsh requisitions and propaganda of various kinds they produced growing restlessness and unsettlement, and under various pretexts hindered free movement about the country and isolated Vilna. None the less the Taryba held to their task, and by attempting to institute a bureau for dealing with complaints against the occupational authorities, as also by trying to take up such matters as the repatriation of Lithuanian refugees from Russia, the still harsh requisitions, attempts at Germanization in the schools, the reorganization of Vilna University and the professional schools, strove to discharge their responsibility to the Lithuanian people. At every turn resistance was encountered from the local military authorities on the ground that Lithuanian administration could not begin till after the end of the war: in no sense would they allow that the Taryba either possessed sovereign rights or was an organ of government. Foiled partly in their endeavours, isolated from Allied support, disquieted by suggestions of forced union of Lithuania with Saxony or Prussia, and by 'tendencious' articles in the local German press to the effect that Lithuania had not a sufficiency of citizens capable of administering the country, and realizing also that the agreed close relations could not be maintained between a monarchical Germany and a country with any other kind of constitution, the Taryba rather abruptly decided on the 11th July 1918 to call Duke William of Urach, a German Catholic princeling, to 'the throne of Lithuania'. It was believed that he could trace descent in some degree from an old Lithuanian king called Mindangas, but a majority of the Taryba was more influenced by the practical argument that, in the circumstances, the formation and consolidation of a Lithuanian state would proceed more rapidly under a constitutional monarch.[1] The project had an unfortunate issue. On the one hand, a minority of the Taryba rightly maintained that this question of the form of a Constitution was one on which a Constituent Assembly alone had a right to decide. On the other hand, the German Government resented this independent action on the part of the Taryba, and maintained that in the matters of a Constitution and candidates to the throne alike, it must be consulted: the Taryba was also reminded that the question of a personal union between Saxony and Lithuania had not yet been decided. More than ever, if possible, Germany was treating Lithuania as occupied enemy territory, and doing nothing by way of practical recognition or securing an international status for her. Meanwhile, however, events were moving in a direction which tended to weaken the German grip on Lithuania. Following the speech of the new Chancellor, Prince Max of Baden, in the Reichstag on the 5th October 1918, in which he stated, in replying to Mr. Wilson, that the German

[1] It was also believed that Duke William might influence the Centrum in the Reichstag to prevent annexation to Prussia.

Empire saw no objection to nations organizing their State and government in their own way, by virtue of their right to self-determination, the President of the Taryba was informed on the 20th October of the decision of the German Government to delegate legislative and administrative power to a Lithuanian Government which it was now the business of the Taryba to organize. Although anxious to withdraw its troops at the earliest possible moment, the Government was still disposed, he was assured, to satisfy the often expressed desire of the population and leave troops and the necessary means of transport in the country yet awhile. The Taryba immediately took up the question of the still harsh requisitioning and of the organization of a militia for national defence. This meant a request to the German Government for arms, and also for a loan of three million marks in connexion with the reconstruction of the State, the formation of a Government, and the organization of the militia. Towards the last proposal the Germans showed no cordiality, hoping in this way to compel the people to request their continued presence in the capacity of protectors. Delay also characterized their attitude in relation to the other requests. Meanwhile, the Taryba worked out the basis of a Provisional Constitution and empowered its President to nominate a President of the ministers who should constitute the Provisional Lithuanian Government. In this way, on the 5th November, Professor Voldemaris was designated President of a Cabinet which he formed six days later. On the 2nd November, the Taryba formally departed from its resolution of the 11th July in which 'the throne of Lithuania' was offered to Duke William of Urach, and referred the final solution of the question of the régime to the Constituent Assembly.

(*d*) *Germans evacuate Lithuania, 1918–19 ; de facto Recognition by Great Britain, 24th September 1919.* After the Armistice Convention Germany showed almost as little desire to evacuate Lithuania as she did in the case of Courland. Lithuania, still unrecognized and unaided by any of the Entente Powers, found her position daily more precarious. Threatened by the Bolsheviks, the Lithuanians were disturbed by German propaganda to the effect that the failure of the Allied Powers to recognize Lithuania as an independent State was due to their intention to unite Lithuania either to Poland or to

Russia, and that accordingly she would be better off with a German orientation. A new Taryba had been elected in January, and in April Mr. Smetona, President of the Taryba, was made President of State. Renewed attempts were made to secure the moral support of the recognition of Lithuanian independence by the Entente, for with it went the assurance to the young Lithuanian army that their fight would then really be one for the maintenance of their independence. Not, however, before the 24th September 1919 did Great Britain grant *de facto* recognition to the Lithuanian Government, being followed generally by the other Powers—exactly seventeen months after the *de facto* recognition had been accorded to Esthonia (3 May 1918) and ten months after the *de facto* recognition of Latvia (11th November 1918).

(*e*) *The Bolshevik Intervention, 1919–20*. The Germans, putting their own interpretation on Art. XII of the Armistice, had evacuated Vilna without notice. This involved the removal of the Lithuanian Government to Kovno, and the Bolsheviks entered the city on the 5th January 1919. The progressive evacuation of the country by the Germans was accompanied by a wholesale plundering of public and private property, while the Bolsheviks followed them at a distance of 15 to 20 kilometres. The Lithuanian Government had begun recruiting for its army in the beginning of January, and speedily about 20,000 men were enrolled in regiments. These were initially supplied with arms and ammunition in part by Germany who still occupied the western part of Lithuania in March 1919, and was beginning to be apprehensive about the danger of Bolshevism to herself. Assistance was later furnished by Great Britain. As soon as it was possible, the Lithuanian army took the offensive, but owing to insufficient munitions was unable to push its victorious onset to the limit of attempting to expel the Bolsheviks from Vilna, and halted on the line Ponievicz–Wilkmerge–Landwarowo–Troki. The Poles, advancing against the Bolsheviks from the direction of Lida, entered Vilna on the 20th April 1920. Thereafter, the history of the Lithuanian State becomes entangled against its will with that of the romantic yet aggressive Polish State. On the 12th July 1920, Lithuania having expelled the Bolsheviks from her territory, concluded with Soviet Russia at Moscow a Peace Treaty under which Vilna and its territory were conceded to her. Russia was now apparently anxious to establish connexions with the outside world through the Border States, but her success in stemming the Polish onslaught towards Kiev brought with it a stiffening of the terms of the Treaty. Both during the subsequent Russian offensive and Polish counter-offensive, the Lithuanian Government observed a neutral attitude.

(*f*) *The Polish intervention, 1920–2.* With the retreat of the Bolsheviks, the territorial disputes between Lithuania and Poland, especially in respect of Vilna and its district became acute, and on the initiative of Poland reference was made to the Council of the League of Nations on the 5th September 1920. A provisional line of demarcation between the two armies, the so-called Curzon line was mutually agreed upon on the 20th September at the instance of the Council, but the Poles failed to observe the agreement. On the 7th October a Control Commission appointed by the League arranged a further agreement at Suwalki with the object of avoiding further occasion of hostilities by closing the road to Vilna where the Lithuanian Government were in possession, to the Poles. Two days later Vilna was occupied by the Poles under Zeligowski, in contravention of the Suwalki agreement, the Lithuanians having been attacked by superior forces, and deciding to retire. The Polish Government disarmed Zeligowski but did nothing to expel him.

The nerveless and helpless attitude of the League of Nations in face of this initial *coup de force*, produced a sense of impunity in one of the parties to the quarrel. It seemed a repetition of the manœuvres of Korfanty in Silesia. Thus arose a feeling of exasperation and consequent intransigence on the part of Lithuania that all the subsequent able handling of the situation by the Council of the League could hardly overcome. It was also unfortunate in the interests of the appearance of impartiality that the chief of the League's Control Commission should have been selected from a nation already tied by military and commercial conventions to one of the parties to the dispute.[1] The United States granted Lithuania recognition (30th July 1922). Lithuania was received into the membership of the League of Nations on the 22nd September 1921, and *de jure* recognition was also afforded by the leading Allied Powers on the 20th December 1922.

[1] *v.* Map and note at end of Chap. II, p. 283, In January 1923 the Principal Allied Powers assigned Memel to Lithuania, and on 15th March the Vilna area to Poland.

5. *Mutual Relations of the Baltic States ; General Conclusions.* Mutual relations between the various Baltic States have been growing closer and more cordial. The natural relations between Finland and Esthonia, which were temporarily cooled during the 1918 rapprochement of Germany and Finland, were subsequently restored by Finnish aid in the form of volunteers and a loan during the Esthonian struggle against the Bolsheviks. Latvia and Esthonia are fortunate in having all their frontiers delimited, contrasting in this and other respects with Lithuania. Defensive military, political, and economic agreements are in various stages of development. In particular the idea of a defensive League has engaged the attention of the leaders of the various States. In January 1920 the Finnish Government convoked the first Baltic Conference at Helsingfors which was attended by representatives of Poland, Lithuania, Latvia, Esthonia, and Finland. The idea of a Baltic Alliance was accepted in principle, and close economic co-operation was organized. A second Conference was held at Riga in August 1920, for which the Latvian Government had elaborated an extensive programme. Owing to the Bolshevik invasion of Poland, and the Polish and Lithuanian dispute, the net result was not great. On the 17th March 1922, a political agreement was signed at Warsaw between Poland, Latvia, Esthonia, and Finland. But the Finnish Diet, under the lead of the Socialists, who were adverse to any agreement with the Baltic States even for the purpose of defence against Russia (while the Right parties did not consider that it went far enough as a defensive alliance), brought about a change of Cabinet, and consequent delay. None of the Baltic States but perceives that their future in great part depends upon their ability to make Russia feel that she is not cut off from the Baltic ports, and their policy in face of this situation has been broad-minded. They are doing everything that they can to facilitate Russian transit ; Reval harbour, for example, is being enlarged with this in view. Russia on her part shows herself desirous of carrying out her side of the economic conditions laid down in the Dorpat Peace Treaty of the 2nd February 1920, in spite of her disordered transport and other difficult internal conditions. On the wall of the building now used as Foreign Office in the capital of one of these States is a Latin inscription, 'In Concordia Res Parvae Crescunt.' Its lesson is rapidly being assimilated by them all.

CHAPTER III

EVOLUTION AND REVOLUTION IN NORTHERN EUROPE

PART II

THE BOLSHEVIKS AND DIPLOMACY [1]

1. *General.* The opening of the Peace Conference in January 1919 found Russia dominated by a Soviet Government enjoying what was then generally believed to be the last brief phase of its precarious tenure of power. Two years before, in March 1917, the first revolution, which drove the Tsar from Petrograd, had taken place. In November of that year Kerensky and his moderates had fallen in their turn before the subversive forces kindled by the fierce appeals of a Lenin and a Trotsky. In March 1918 the Peace of Brest-Litovsk had been signed with Germany, Russia thereby surrendering Poland, Lithuania, the Baltic Provinces, and the Ukraine.

January 1919, therefore, found Russia at peace with Germany but engaged on almost every frontier in a desperate struggle with adversaries supported for the most part by her former allies. At Omsk, in Siberia, the anti-Soviet Admiral Kolchak was established, endeavouring, with American and Japanese assistance, to push westward across the Urals to join hands with an anti-Soviet Archangel Government resting on British, American, and Italian bayonets. At Murmansk another Allied expedition was based on Northern Russia's only warm-water port. General Yudenitch did not begin his march on Petrograd till later in the year; but in the Baltic region Germans were supporting the local troops, Esthonians and Letts, against the Bolsheviks. Poland was doing her best to

[1] No attempt is made in this chapter to deal with the internal, or even with many of the external, aspects of Bolshevism. Lenin denied the authority both of the Peace Treaties and of the League of Nations, and Russia's History, therefore, lies outside the History of the Peace Conference. The attempt is here made to show how political events and economic necessities gradually brought Soviet Russia within the orbit, first of the commerce, and then of the politics, of Western Europe.

drive her eastern frontier deeper into Russia. In the Ukraine Petliura, who had lately obtained the chief power, was threatening Russia's western governments. And in the Crimea, General Denikin, with Allied fleets to supply him and guard his rear, was driving towards the basin of the Don.

At Paris all these rival sections had their champions and most of them their accredited representatives. M. Sazonoff, the former Foreign Minister, represented Omsk, M. Tchaikovsky Archangel, while Professor Miliukoff, the Social Revolutionary leader, Prince Lvoff, M. Savinkoff, and General Gutchkoff, the Octobrist, were all prepared to support any plan that would effect the downfall of the Soviet Administration. And round them had gathered a number of émigrés of distinction, attracted to Paris by the hope that external action by the Western Powers would achieve that internal upheaval in Russia which would enable them to regain their old authority and what was left of their material possessions.

2. *The Prinkipo proposal, 22nd January 1919.* In point of fact the Russian situation was practically the first problem to which the heads of the Allied delegations in Paris applied themselves. The first meeting of the Peace Conference proper took place on the 18th January, and on the morning of the 21st President Wilson read to the Council of Ten a report drawn up by Mr. W. H. Buckler, then attached to the American Embassy in London, on his recent conference with the Soviet representative M. Litvinoff at Helsingfors.

There had, however, already been conversations between the heads of the Allied States, notably one which took place at the Quai d'Orsay on the 16th January, at which the alternative policies regarding Russia were exhaustively examined. It was on that occasion that Mr. Lloyd George, who observed incidentally that General Denikin was merely occupying a little backyard near the Black Sea and that Admiral Kolchak would appear to be at heart a monarchist, presented the three policies between which in his view it was necessary to choose. The first was military intervention, the second the establishment of a 'cordon sanitaire' between Russia and the rest of Europe, and the third the British plan of calling the leaders of all the Russian factions to Paris in the hope of bringing them to some agreement in concert with the Allies.

The latter proposal was immediately and vigorously contested by M. Clemenceau, who imposed an absolute veto on any invitation of Soviet representatives to the French capital. Another rendezvous had therefore to be found, and President Wilson accordingly proposed that ' the various organized groups in Russia should be asked to send representatives to some spot like Salonika, there to meet representatives of the Allies to see if a basis of agreement could be discovered.' In actual fact the meeting-place fixed in the proclamation issued over President Wilson's name on the 22nd January was the island of Prinkipo in the Sea of Marmara, the date proposed for the meeting being the 15th February.

The meeting never was held, either at Prinkipo or anywhere else. The Paris representatives of the four so-called Governments of Omsk (Kolchak), Ekaterinodar (Denikin), Archangel, and the Crimea refused definitely to meet the Bolsheviks, and the former Cadet leader, Professor Miliukoff, publicly deplored the issue of the invitation. The Soviet Government itself, when it received President Wilson's proclamation after an unexplained delay, transmitted a qualified acceptance, declaring that, if the Powers would undertake to refrain from interference in Russian internal affairs, ' the Russian Soviet Government is disposed to enter into immediate conference on Prince's Island or at some other place, be it with all the Entente Powers or with some of them separately, or even with some Russian political groups at the request of the Entente Powers '.

President Wilson's proclamation had contained the stipulation that the conference should be preceded by a truce among the parties invited, and that aggressive action against Finland or any part of pre-war Russia should cease. There could be no truce if the anti-Bolshevik forces preferred to go on fighting, and Mr. Lloyd George was severely economical of fact when he told the House of Commons in the following April that the Soviet Government ' would not accede to the request that they should cease fighting '. In any case, the proposal was quietly permitted to lapse, though the three Baltic Republics of Esthonia, Latvia, and Lithuania had accepted the proposal.

3. *The Bullitt Mission, 18th February 1919.* Between February and April the Council of Four, as it had then become, was almost wholly engrossed with the German peace, and Mr. Lloyd George in the memorandum he circulated privately on the 25th March contented himself with observing that ' it

is idle to think that the Peace Conference can separate, however sound a peace it may have arranged with Germany, if it leaves Russia as it is to-day'. By that time, however, a step had been taken round which controversy long continued to centre. On the 18th February Mr. William C. Bullitt, a member of the American Commission to negotiate Peace, received instructions from Mr. Lansing, then Secretary of State, 'to proceed to Russia for the purpose of studying conditions, political and economic, therein for the benefit of the American Commissioners plenipotentiary to negotiate peace.'

A full statement was made by Mr. Bullitt as to the nature and outcome of his mission before the Foreign Relations Committee of the American Senate in September 1919. He was instructed, according to this testimony, to go to Russia 'to attempt to obtain from the Soviet Government an exact statement of the terms on which they were ready to stop fighting', and he was empowered by Colonel House, a member of the American Commission, to indicate the willingness of the United States Government to support proposals for an armistice on all fronts, the re-establishment of economic relations (for Russia was still under Allied blockade), and the conditional withdrawal of all Allied troops from Russian soil. Mr. Bullitt gave it in evidence that he had discussed his mission with Mr. Philip Kerr, Mr. Lloyd George's private secretary, and had prepared in collaboration with him an outline of possible conditions of peace. Mr. Kerr, added Mr. Bullitt, stated that he had discussed the whole matter with Mr. Lloyd George and Mr. Balfour.[1]

4. *The Bolshevik Offer, 14th March.* The immediate outcome of the Bullitt Mission was a document drawn up on the 14th March by M. Tchitcherin and M. Litvinoff containing terms which the Soviet Government undertook to accept provided they were tendered not later than the 10th April. Those terms may be thus briefly summarized.

(1) Short armistice pending a peace conference.
(2) All *de facto* Governments in Russia to retain the territory they hold.

[1] [Mr. Wilson does not appear to have denied Bullitt's statements when brought to his notice, though he did not affirm them. Mr. Lansing, so far as he was concerned, 'found it impossible to make an absolute denial,' *The Peace Negotiations*, 1921, p. 242. Mr. Lloyd George called the whole statement 'a tissue of lies'. Ed. note.]

(3) Economic blockade to be raised and trade relations restored.
(4) Soviet Russia to have unhindered transit to ports on former Russian territory.
(5) General amnesty and resumption of diplomatic relations.
(6) Allied troops to be withdrawn and Allied assistance to anti-Soviet Governments to cease.
(7) The Soviet Government and other Governments on former Russian territory to 'recognize their responsibility for the financial obligations of the former Russian Empire to foreign States parties to this agreement and to the nationals of such States'.

These proposals were immediately telegraphed from Helsingfors to the American Delegation and Mr. Bullitt himself returned forthwith to Paris. Thirty-six hours after reaching there he breakfasted with Mr. Lloyd George (who had been furnished with copies of the Helsingfors telegrams), General Smuts being also present. The British Prime Minister, according to Mr. Bullitt's evidence, attached great importance to the report the American emissary had brought back, and urged him to make it public. He spoke, however, of British public opinion as a fatal obstacle to the action he personally would desire to take.

5. *Mr. Lloyd George on the Bullitt Mission, 16th April 1919.* The report was never published, President Wilson vetoing that course. The appointed day, the 10th April, passed with no action taken, and on the 16th April, just over a fortnight after his conversation with Mr. Bullitt, Mr. Lloyd George rose in the House of Commons and made the following statement in answer to a direct question by Mr. Clynes:

> 'We have had no approaches at all. Of course there are constantly men of all nationalities coming from and going to Russia, always coming back with their own tales from Russia. But we have had nothing authentic. We have no approaches of any sort or kind. I have only heard of reports that others have got proposals, which they assume to have come from authentic quarters, but these have never been put before the Conference by any member of the Conference at all. There was some suggestion that there was some young American who had come back. All I can say about that is that it is not for me to judge the value of these communications. But if the President of the United States had attached any value to them he would have brought them before the Conference, and he certainly did not.'

That declaration—the ethics of which may, perhaps (in

words employed by Mr. Lloyd George later in another connexion), be left to the unprejudiced judgment of posterity[1]—ended any possibility that might have attached to the Bullitt Mission, and advocates of peace with Russia were left to discover some new method of approach. It was found, or appeared to be found, through the agency of Dr. Fridtjof Nansen, inspired, there is reason to believe, by Mr. Hoover, who held strongly that contacts with Russia established on a humanitarian basis might have valuable political results.

6. *The Nansen Proposal, 3rd April 1919*. What Dr. Nansen, writing as a neutral, proposed to the individual Members of the Council of Four on the 3rd April was the organization of a commission for the relief of Russia, the enterprise to be strictly non-political and carried out under neutral management. After a fortnight's consideration the Council of Four addressed to Dr. Nansen a letter accepting his proposal on conditions embodied in the following paragraph:

> 'That such a course (local distribution on purely humanitarian basis) would involve cessation of all hostilities within definite lines in the territory of Russia is obvious. And the cessation of hostilities would necessarily involve a complete suspension of the transfer of troops and military material of all sorts to and within Russian territory.'

On that basis Dr. Nansen transmitted, or endeavoured to transmit, his proposal to the Soviet Government. There were, however, difficulties, not all unavoidable, in the matter of wireless communication, and it was over a fortnight before his communication reached Moscow. It met with an immediate response in the shape of a characteristically prolix and argumentative Note from M. Tchitcherin, the purport of which was that the letter of the Council of Four, in its insistence on the cessation of hostilities and the suppression of the movements of troops and material, had interwoven military and political proposals with a humanitarian plan; that the Soviet Government would be ready to enter into the former questions with its adversaries, i.e. the Entente Governments, direct; and that meanwhile it would be glad to send delegates to meet Dr. Nansen somewhere outside Russia and discuss the possibilities.

7. *The Question of recognizing Admiral Kolchak*. This suggestion, like those handed to Mr. Bullitt some six weeks

[1] *v.* note on p. 314.

earlier, was not judged worthy of consideration and the Nansen proposal went the way of the Prinkipo proposal and the Bullitt Mission. The next steps taken, indeed, constituted an adventure in quite another direction. Admiral Kolchak, the anti-Bolshevik commander at Omsk, having about this time made a substantial advance westward, the Allies, while temporizing over the proposal to accord him official recognition, announced their intention to support him with money and supplies conditionally on his undertaking to call a Constituent Assembly in the event of his victory over the Bolsheviks.

At the same time the Siberian leader was to undertake to recognize the independence of Finland and Poland, and in the case of the Baltic States and the Caucasian territories to recognize their autonomy pending a final settlement in co-operation with the League of Nations. Admiral Kolchak declined to give a definite assurance with regard to the independence of any portion of former Russian territory, holding this to be a matter for the Constituent Assembly when it came into being; but on other points, including the recognition of the debts of the Tsarist Government, his reply was sufficiently satisfactory to the Allies to lead them to promise him support within the limits already indicated.

Unfortunately for any hopes based on this rapprochement, Admiral Kolchak forthwith began a series of forced retirements and his star from that moment continued steadily to decline. It was indeed not in him, but in General Denikin in Southern Russia, that the Allies placed reliance in the later months of 1919, but Denikin, after reaching Kiev in September, and Oral in October, found himself like the Siberian commander swept back by the tide of Bolshevik resistance. General Yudenitch, operating in the north against Petrograd, suffered a like fate, and in November Kolchak's stronghold of Omsk fell before the Red Army. Thus 1919 closed with the Allies' hopes for the White invaders shattered into ruins.

8. *The Bolsheviks and the Baltic States, February–August 1920.* Not unfittingly the new year ushered in new policies. Henceforward two processes were in constant and simultaneous operation, neither of them making rapid or prosperous headway, but neither ever brought completely to a standstill. One was the attempt at the opening up of commercial relations between Russia and the West, the other the gradual cessation of

hostilities between Russia and her neighbours. Among these the three Baltic Republics of Esthonia, Lithuania, and Latvia concluded peace in February, July, and August respectively, in each case on terms that must be regarded as broadly reasonable.

9. *The Bolsheviks and Poland.* Between Russia and Poland the struggle was longer and more bitter. That was due not merely to the fact that Poland, with the 20 odd millions of inhabitants which the Peace Treaties then gave her, was capable in herself of developing considerable military strength. The protraction of her contest with the Bolsheviks was due much more to the action of the Allies, and in particular of France, whose policy was based on the theory of a powerful Poland as counterpoise to Germany on the one hand, and as a barrier against Bolshevism on the other. In consonance with that theory, General Haller's Polish legion, raised in France, where it had served down to the Armistice, was transported in April 1919 to Poland via Danzig.[1]

When 1920 opened Poland was in a position of no little danger. Kolchak was beaten, Denikin was beaten, the Baltic Republics were near the end of their resistance. The Poles, still executing a policy conceived in Paris, were left to face what, but for the diversion in the south caused by the attacks of General Wrangel (whom the French recognized later in the year as the head of a *de facto* Government), would have been the whole strength of the Soviet Army. The military aspect of the struggle has, however, no special relevance here except in so far as it throws light on the attitude of the Entente Powers, with Poland as their agent, towards the Soviet Government, and of the Soviet Government towards them.

The history of the relations between Russia and Poland in the year 1920, down to the Peace of Riga in October, is a history of strange alternations of victory and defeat, with peace conversations, among which the negotiations initiated at the Spa Conference in July are conspicuous, proceeding simultaneously with little intermission.

(*a*) *The Supreme Council's advice, February 1920; Poles capture Kiev, 8th May.* Poland, as has been said, down to the end of 1919 was acting in large measure as agent for the Allies, and endeavouring broadly to hold the line from which the

[1] *v.* I. 340-1.

Germans fell back after the Armistice, but on the 24th February 1920 the Supreme Council, meeting in London, declared that with regard to the communities bordering on Russia the Allied Governments

'cannot accept the responsibility of advising them to continue a war which may be injurious to their own interest. Still less would they advise them to adopt a policy of aggression towards Russia. If, however, Soviet Russia attacks them inside their legitimate frontiers, the Allies will give them every possible support.'

Poland did not seriously regard that formal warning. The frontier laid down for her provisionally by the Allies in Paris—the Curzon line as it was called—had not at this time been disclosed, but it was revealed later as running roughly from Grodno through Bialystock down to the Bug at Brest-Litovsk and thence along that river to near Sokol, and finally south past Przemysl to the Carpathians.

With that line few Poles, the historic frontier of 1772 occupying all their thoughts, would have been satisfied in January 1920. While the Bolshevik armies were still pre-occupied with Kolchak and Denikin, Polish forces captured Dvinsk and moved south-east towards Kiev. February and March were occupied in resultless peace negotiations and towards the end of April the great Polish offensive, undertaken in conjunction with a Ukrainian army under Petliura, was launched. The result was a considerable success, culminating in the fall of Kiev on the 8th May. That was the high-water mark, the Bolshevik armies massing, regaining the Ukrainian capital, and pressing the Poles steadily back.

(b) *The Supreme Council and the British advice to Poland, July 1920.* By the time the Supreme Council met at Spa in July the Poles were in full retreat. M. Grabski, the Polish Prime Minister, accompanied by the Foreign Secretary, M. Patek, appealed for Allied intervention, with the result that a proposal was framed that the Polish armies should retire voluntarily behind the Curzon line, already defined. That was only part of a peace proposal placed before both belligerents, the suggestion being that Poland's withdrawal of some 125 miles should be followed by the convocation of a Peace Conference in London, to be attended by Russia, Poland, and the various border states. The actual Note, dispatched on the 11th July, specified the Curzon line to which it was proposed that the Poles should withdraw, and then developed the proposal

'that, as soon as possible thereafter, a conference sitting under the auspices of the Peace Conference should assemble in London, to be attended by representatives of Soviet Russia, Poland, Lithuania, Latvia, and Finland, with the object of negotiating a final peace between Russia and its neighbouring States.'

The Note continued:

'The British Government, as a separate proposal, suggests that an armistice should similarly be signed between the forces of Soviet Russia and General Wrangel on the condition that General Wrangel's forces shall immediately retire to the Crimea and that during the armistice the isthmus be a neutral zone and that General Wrangel should be invited to London to discuss the future of the troops under his command and the refugees under his protection, but not as a member of the conference.'

An immediate answer to the Note was requested, and it was intimated without any language of menace that if, despite these proposals, the Soviet Government took action against Poland within Polish territory, Great Britain and the other Allies would feel bound to assist the Poles with all the means at their disposal.

To have attended a political conference in London in 1920 would have meant for the Soviet Government a rapid step towards recognition. It was, indeed, largely on that ground that the French declined to add their signatures to the British Note. There was, therefore, every reason to expect a favourable reply from Moscow, unless the military success achieved by the Red Armies led the Soviet Government to prefer other methods of settlement than conference.

(*c*) *Lenin's reply.* It was soon made apparent that Lenin and his colleagues did take that view. In a lengthy reply transmitted a week after the receipt of the British Note, the Soviet Government declined the proposals put before it. London, it was contended, was not a suitable venue for such a conference, in view of England's anti-Soviet bias. There was no point in inviting the border States, for they were at peace with Soviet Russia already. The Armistice line fixed for Poland was actually less favourable to her than the line the Soviet Government was ready to offer. And as for General Wrangel's forces, their unconditional capitulation was demanded.

In reply to this communication the British Government

telegraphed to Moscow waiving the proposal that the Conference should meet in London, and to Warsaw advising the Poles to accept the Russian offer of direct negotiations. Whether that offer was seriously meant was impossible to decide, particularly since it was both in keeping with Soviet methods generally and to the advantage of the Soviet leaders in this special case, to spin out time in abortive negotiations while their armies continued to advance. The least favourable view of Moscow's intentions was taken in Paris, and the French Government took what proved the decisive step of sending General Weygand to Warsaw as military adviser.

(*d*) *The Russian advance and defeat, July–September 1920.* The Russian advance from this time was rapid, and the Polish capital being gravely threatened, Poland, on the 30th July, appealed for an armistice. But delays and controversies followed, the Soviet troops continuing meanwhile to overrun Polish territory. The Allies now discussed the situation at a conference at Hythe and decided to help Poland with munitions but not with men. On the 10th August, the peace terms offered by Russia were made known, but procrastination still continued at Minsk, where *pourparlers* began. The Russians had, meanwhile, got within twelve miles of Warsaw, and a Polish counter-offensive began under General Weygand's direction.

A diplomatic development of some importance at this juncture calls for mention. The Russians at Minsk put forward a demand, indicated only vaguely in the statement handed to Mr. Lloyd George by the Russian representative in London that, while the Polish Army should be reduced to 50,000, there should be an armed gendarmerie of 200,000 consisting of Trade Unionists only. In view of that demand Mr. Lloyd George and Signor Giolitti, who happened at the moment to be in conference together, issued a declaration to the effect that the terms proposed were incompatible with national independence.

Such moral intervention was hardly needed by the Poles, whose armies were now driving eastwards, and fortune continuing to favour their troops they penetrated far into regions to which Poland could make no just claim on grounds of nationality. In point of fact the Polish Armies had in the course of September passed beyond Grodno, Brest-Litovsk, Kovel, and Luck, and before the month was over they had occupied

Baranovitchi and Pinsk. (Incidentally also Vilna, of which the Lithuanians had taken possession on its evacuation by the Russians in August, was seized on the 9th Oct. ostensibly without orders from Warsaw, by the White Russian General Zeligowski, an ally of the Poles and in their pay.) Poland thus succeeded at Russia's expense in practically doubling the territory the Curzon line would have given her, raising her population to an estimated 27,000,000.

(*e*) *Russo-Polish Armistice and Treaty of Riga, 12 Oct. 1920.* Under such circumstances the negotiations, which had been broken off at Minsk, were resumed in September at Riga, and there an armistice and a preliminary treaty on lines dictated, not by the Russians but by the Poles, were signed on the 12th October. A definitive treaty, by which Poland gave Russia *de jure* recognition, was negotiated, also at Riga, in the following March. With this settlement Allied contacts with Russia, through or in relation to, Poland terminated. (*v.* map, p. 283).

10. *Supreme Council and Supreme Economic Council begin to develop trade relations with Russia, January–May 1920.* The first important step towards the development of trade relations with Soviet Russia took place during a meeting of the Supreme Council in Paris in January 1920, when it was decided

'to give facilities to the Russian co-operative organizations which are in direct touch with the peasantry throughout Russia, so that they could arrange for the import into Russia of clothing, medicines, agricultural machinery, and the other necessaries of which the Russian people are in sore need, in exchange for grain, flax, &c., of which Russia has surplus supplies.'

Prior to this some attempt had been made to open up trade with the co-operative societies in the area controlled by General Denikin in South Russia, but the failure of that commander to hold the territory he was occupying brought the plan to nothing. During the Supreme Council sittings representatives of the Russian Co-operative Societies were in Paris, and there was some idea of arranging direct trade relations between them and the co-operative organizations in Great Britain and other countries. Italy, it may be observed, was already doing sporadic trade with Russia, and while always prepared to support any joint plan for the development of trade relations, never recognized any imperative necessity for such a plan, since each nation was perfectly free to take its own course in the matter.

That was emphasized at the San Remo Conference in April 1920, by Signor Nitti, who pointed out with force that, while the Allies had undertaken to make no separate peace with Germany, they were not at war with Russia, and if they could not conclude trade agreements with her jointly they had better go their several ways in independence.

The proposed arrangements with Russia were in the hands of the Supreme Economic Council, which still existed at this date, and difficulties early arose through the British Government's refusal to readmit M. Litvinoff to its soil as a member of the trade delegation it had agreed to receive. That and other matters were discussed at Copenhagen in April by members of the Supreme Economic Council with representatives of the Russian Co-operative Societies, which by this time had been taken over by the Soviet Government itself.

At this point political considerations began, as was inevitable, to blend with economic. M. Krassin, nominated by the Moscow Government to represent the Russian Co-operatives, wired that it was necessary 'in the first place to agree on broad lines on general conditions for re-establishing economic and commercial agreements between the countries in question, which require formal negotiations and definite agreements'. This and other aspects of the general question were discussed at San Remo, with the result that the Supreme Council, in the persons of Mr. Lloyd George, M. Millerand, and Signor Nitti, decided to empower the Permanent Committee of the Supreme Economic Council, subject ultimately to the Allied Governments, 'to make such arrangements with the Russian Delegation as are necessary to enable trade with Russia to be resumed as rapidly as possible'.

11. *Krassin and the Russian Trade Mission to London, May 1920.* The way thus cleared, a Russian Trade Delegation, with M. Krassin at its head, reached England at the end of May, its members undertaking on landing to engage in no form of political propaganda. M. Krassin was soon brought in touch with the Prime Minister and other members of the Cabinet, but no great progress was made towards a general agreement, much dissatisfaction being expressed in Whitehall with the Soviet Government's failure to execute duly the agreement on an exchange of prisoners negotiated between Mr. James O'Grady, M.P., and M. Litvinoff at Copenhagen in February, and with

that Government's assiduous endeavours to stir up trouble in the Middle East and elsewhere.

(*a*) *The four British points, June 1920.* The purpose of M. Krassin's mission was in the first instance merely to negotiate as to the conditions under which more or less normal trade relations between Great Britain and Russia could be resumed, but it became increasingly apparent that there could be no real severance between the political and economic aspects of the situation. By the end of June, however, four requirements were definitely laid down by Great Britain as conditions of a formal agreement, viz.:

(1) Mutual undertaking to refrain from hostile actions and subversive propaganda.
(2) Mutual return of all prisoners, civilian and military.
(3) Soviet Government to recognize its obligations to compensate private citizens to whom payment for goods or services is due.
(4) Right of each party to object to individual agents of the other as *personae non gratae*.

Small progress, however, was made on this basis owing to the intervention of the Polish offensive, the dispatch of the Allied Note from Spa proposing a conference in London, and the decision of the British Government to suspend negotiations regarding trade till these more specifically political questions had been settled or put in the way of settlement.

That detracted considerably from the importance of a telegram received from Moscow, whither M. Krassin had returned with the British terms, indicating acceptance of those terms on principle, and it was not till the end of July that the British Government signified its readiness to receive the Russian delegation. The situation meanwhile was becoming complicated as the result of indications that the Bolsheviks, by offering to subsidize *The Daily Herald* and in other ways, were endeavouring to make political propaganda in London; and in September M. Kameneff, who had joined the delegation in London earlier in the summer, was informed by the British Government, on the eve of his departure on a visit to Moscow, that he would not be permitted to return to England.

(*b*) *The Draft Trade Agreement, November 1920.* It was not till the end of November that matters were so far advanced as to admit of a draft Russian Trade agreement, prepared by the Interdepartmental Committee which had been established in Whitehall to deal with Russian commercial questions, being handed to the Soviet representative M. Krassin. Public attention was focussed mainly on the important point of whether goods 'nationalized' by the Soviet Government would be liable to attachment if imported into this country. On that Mr. Justice Roche had given an affirmative decision, which promised to impede gravely the development of trade relations, but the Law Officers gave it as their opinion that such a judgment would not lie once the Government had, by signing the Trade Agreement, recognized Russia *de facto*, and M. Krassin was informed that, if any other steps were needed to meet this difficulty, the British Government would take them.

12. *The Russo-British Trade Agreement, 16th March 1921.* Finally, on the 16th March 1921, the Trade Agreement between Great Britain and the Russian Socialist Federal Soviet Republic was signed in London by Sir Robert Horne, the Chancellor of the Exchequer, on the one side, and M. Krassin, on the other. It consisted of fourteen clauses, with an annex, the following being among the main provisions embodied:

(1) Mutual pledge against hostile action and propaganda.
(2) Mutual release of persons forcibly detained.
(3) Raising of blockade.
(4) Freedom of movement of shipping of either country in the ports of the other.
(5) Regulations with regard to the admission of trade representatives and official agents.
(6) No attachment of Russian gold or commodities in Great Britain.
(7) Soviet Government to recognize its obligation to compensate private citizens to whom payment for goods or services is due.

The preamble of the document declared that the agreement was merely preliminary to 'the conclusion of a formal general Peace Treaty' covering both political and economic relations between the two countries. On the occasion of the signature of the Trade Agreement Sir Robert Horne handed to M. Krassin a long letter enumerating in detail examples of that subversive propaganda from which the Soviet Government under the first clause of the Agreement undertook to refrain for the future.

13. *Causes of its failure.* The road was now clear of all obstacles (except *de jure* recognition) to the development of trade between Great Britain and Soviet Russia. Trade between Great Britain and Soviet Russia failed to develop. That was due partly to the impoverished condition of Russia, visited in 1921 by famine which made the demand for relief on an international scale inevitable. Most of the Western Governments made a gesture of response, but a conference of Government representatives which met at Paris in September and at Brussels in November stipulated that the acknowledgment of Russian debts must precede any movement of assistance, after which the whole proposal dropped. Active relief work was, however, initiated by the American Relief Administration and by an *ad hoc* organization created through the co-ordination of existing agencies by Dr. Nansen, acting as the agent of a conference of representatives of Governments and of private societies which had met at Geneva in August.

A more serious obstacle to the expansion of Russo-British trade was the failure of the Soviet Government to give any satisfactory assurances regarding foreign properties nationalized since the downfall of the Tsarist Government in Russia. It was manifest that trade with Russia would for the immediate future be dependent on the grant of commercial credits (since no Government was prepared to advance money to Moscow), and the private investor whose properties in Russia had been confiscated without any assurance of compensation could not be expected to engage in the operation commonly known as throwing good money after bad. That situation was not substantially improved by certain relaxations effected in March 1921 in the communistic economic system then established in Russia, and so far as Great Britain and other Western European countries were concerned trade with Russia still formed a negligible percentage of their commerce as a whole. The main outcome of the Trade Agreement diplomatically was the dispatch of a British official agent to Moscow, but without the definite status either of Minister or Consul.

14. *Cannes; the proposed Economic and Financial Conference, 6th January 1922.* These conditions persisted through 1921 and were still maintained when the Supreme Council of

the Allies met at Cannes in January 1922, to discuss primarily the new crisis then impending in regard to German reparations. The meeting had been preceded by direct conversations in London a fortnight earlier between Mr. Lloyd George and M. Briand, and though the French were far from enthusiastic regarding fresh approaches to Russia they were in no sense taken by surprise when the British Prime Minister raised the whole Russian problem in a new form at Cannes.

The essential feature of the resolution by Mr. Lloyd George unanimously adopted on the 6th January was the proposal that Russia should be invited to meet the other nations of Europe on an equal footing at a general 'Economic and Financial Conference'. The only occasion at which contacts at all comparable—and even so in a very limited field—had been established since the Russian Revolution was at a Health Conference held under the auspices of the League of Nations in March 1921.

The resolution was drafted with special reference to Russia, and its terms had so direct a bearing on what subsequently took place at Genoa that it is desirable to quote them *in extenso*, as follows:

'The Allied Powers in conference are unanimously of opinion that an Economic and Financial Conference should be summoned in February or early March, to which all the Powers of Europe, including Germany, Russia, Austria, Hungary, and Bulgaria, should be invited to send representatives. They regard such a Conference as an urgent and essential step towards the economic reconstruction of Central and Eastern Europe, and they are strongly of opinion that the Prime Ministers of every nation should, if possible, attend it in person in order that action may be taken as promptly as possible upon its recommendations.

'The Allied Powers consider that the resumption of international trade throughout Europe and the development of the resources of all countries are necessary to increase the volume of productive employment and to relieve the widespread suffering of the European peoples. A united effort by the stronger Powers is necessary to remedy the paralysis of the European system. This effort must include the removal of all obstacles in the way of trade, the provision of substantial credits for the weaker countries, and the co-operation of all nations in the restoration of normal prosperity.

'The Allied Powers consider that the fundamental conditions upon which alone this effort can be made with hope of success may broadly be stated as follows:

1. Nations can claim no right to dictate to each other regarding the principles on which they are to regulate their system of owner-

ship, internal economy, and government. It is for every nation to choose for itself the system which it prefers in this respect.

2. Before, however, foreign capital can be made available to assist a country, foreign investors must be assured that their property and their rights will be respected and the fruits of their enterprise secured to them.
3. The sense of security cannot be re-established unless the Governments of countries desiring foreign credit freely undertake :

    (*a*) That they will recognize all public debts and obligations which have been or may be undertaken or guaranteed by the State, by municipalities, or by other public bodies, as well as the obligation to restore or compensate all foreign interests for loss or damage caused to them when property has been confiscated or withheld.

    (*b*) That they will establish a legal and juridical system which sanctions and enforces commercial and other contracts with impartiality.
4. An adequate means of exchange must be available, and, generally, there must be financial and currency conditions which offer sufficient security for trade.
5. All nations should undertake to refrain from propaganda subversive of order and the established political system in other countries than their own.
6. All countries should join in an undertaking to refrain from aggression against their neighbours.

' If in order to secure the conditions necessary for the development of trade in Russia the Russian Government demands official recognition, the Allied Powers will be prepared to accord such recognition only if the Russian Government accepts the foregoing stipulations.'

15. *Genoa, 1922.*

(*a*) *The six points.* Genoa was chosen as meeting-place, and a provisional agenda of six points, the last three of them uncontroversial and the first three the reverse, drafted and circulated as follows :

(1) Examination of the methods of putting into practice the principles contained in the resolution adopted at Cannes on the 6th January 1922.
(2) The establishment of European peace on a firm basis.
(3) Essential conditions for re-establishment of confidence without injury to existing treaties.
(4) Financial subjects.
(5) Economic and commercial subjects.
(6) Transport.

At the same time the Supreme Council approved the establishment of ' an International Corporation, with affiliated

National Corporations, for the purpose of the economic restoration of Europe and the co-operation of all nations in the restoration of normal prosperity'. It was well understood that the main purpose of this body was to finance trade with Russia, but as the result of subsequent developments at Genoa it never acquired any actual importance.

(*b*) *Tchitcherin accepts the invitation; problem of recognition.* The decisions of the Cannes Conference being duly reported in the press, and through that channel transmitted to Moscow, M. Tchitcherin precipitately and enthusiastically accepted the prospective invitation before it had been officially issued at all. The United States, on the other hand, whose participation in the Genoa Meetings was greatly desired, declined to be represented.

It was manifest that the real problem before the Genoa Conference would be the recognition of Soviet Russia. The position at that date was that trade agreements had been negotiated with a number of individual nations, notably Great Britain, Germany, Italy, Norway, and Austria, and that treaties had been signed involving full *de jure* recognition with Poland, Finland, and the three Baltic Republics. Of the three principal members of the Supreme Council, Great Britain, as represented by her Prime Minister though not by the whole Cabinet, was anxious for the development of closer relations with Russia. Italy took the same view, but France showed herself markedly reluctant to move with her Allies. She had signed no trade agreement with Moscow, and representatives of the Russians of the old régime had always found a more sympathetic ear in Paris than in London or Rome.

The Genoa Conference was actually attended by representatives of thirty-four States, and though its technical commissions did work of some value, controversy centred predominantly round the question of relations with Russia. The Soviet Government was represented by its Foreign Minister, M. Tchitcherin, M. Krassin, M. Litvinoff, and M. Rakowsky, President of the Ukraine Soviet.

Day by day, from the polemic intervention of the French delegate, M. Barthou, at the opening session, down to the final collapse of the negotiations five weeks later, every point raised was vigorously and tenaciously contested. The main antagonism was between the French on the one hand and the Russians on the other, with Britain and Italy making unwearied efforts to prevent the two extremes from losing contact altogether.

(*c*) *Methods at the Conference.* On the methods adopted one word must be said, since it was claimed, with a considerable show of justice, that they were largely responsible for an unlooked-for development which in the end remained the sole political outcome of Genoa. The Conference held one plenary meeting, at which it determined to resolve itself into four Commissions, the chief of them dealing with all purely political questions. That Commission duly met and appointed a working sub-commission (consisting of the representatives of Britain, France, Italy, Poland, Rumania, Belgium, Switzerland, Sweden, Germany, and Russia), which, after holding a preliminary meeting, when an important memorandum on trade with Russia drawn up by Allied experts in London was produced, adjourned for forty-eight hours to enable the Russian delegation to study the memorandum.

At the end of that interval it failed to reassemble. Private conversations had been in the meantime initiated at the villa of the British Prime Minister, in which there participated representatives of the four Supreme Council Powers, Britain, France, Italy, and Belgium, the Russians being from time to time called into consultation. To these conversations Germany was not invited, a fact which, combined with the alleged failure of the head of the German delegation, Dr. Rathenau, to gain access to Mr. Lloyd George after repeated attempts, led the Germans suddenly to sign at Rapallo, close to Genoa, a Treaty they had for some time been negotiating with the Soviet Government.

(*d*) *German-Bolshevik Treaty of Rapallo.* The Treaty consisted of six articles, the contracting parties undertaking to renounce mutually all claims for war damages and indemnities and to assist in supplying one another's economic needs. Its signature caused an immediate sensation, and there was for a time some prospect that the French delegation would withdraw altogether, on the ground that the Germans by taking separate action had run counter to the whole spirit of the Conference. They also argued that Germany, in according diplomatic recognition to Russia, had departed from the implied conditions embodied in the Cannes invitation, which she had formally accepted. The course actually followed was that an irregular and improvised body, consisting of the four major Allied Powers, with Belgium, Czecho-Slovakia, Yugo-Slavia, Rumania, Poland, and Portugal, excommunicated Germany from the Political Sub-Commission and announced that they held themselves free to declare the Treaty of Rapallo null and void. This action could, of course, have had no effect on its validity as between the two Powers concerned.

16. *The break-down of the Conference.*

(*a*) *Russian demands.* The Rapallo episode conspired with other factors to prejudice gravely the success of the Genoa Conference, and by the time the Conference had reached its fifth week it was clear that there could be no agreement on the vital question of compensation for private property nationalized—a matter which the French and Belgian delegations declared to be of capital importance to them. In the early part of the Conference there seemed reason to hope the Russians would accept a settlement based on the following principles:

(1) Allies admit no compensation claims advanced by the Soviet Government.
(2) Allies agree to write down war debts and, in regard to other claims, to consider the postponement or even the partial remission of interest.
(3) Russia must meet fully the claims of foreign nationals in regard to debts due to them or compensation for foreign property nationalized.

Though, as has been said, the Soviet delegates replied to proposals of that nature in a Note which seemed to indicate acceptance, they insisted that *de jure* recognition must precede any recognition of Tsarist debts. It further appeared, as the discussions developed, that the Russians had understood the term 'writing-down', applied to the war debts, as meaning 'writing-off'. At all events they stood in the later stages of the Conference for—

(1) Complete cancellation of war debt.
(2) Extensive credits direct to the Soviet Government.
(3) Compensation due to Russia for damage sustained through the Allied support of Denikin, Kolchak, and other White aggressors.

(*b*) *The question of compensation for private property.* The latter demand was merely put forward for bargaining purposes, and it assumed no great prominence in the discussions. On the other two the Russians stood firm. It was, however, the question of compensation for private property which led to the final break-down of the negotiations, for on this matter the united front of the non-Russian Powers broke, Belgium being content with nothing less than the physical restoration of foreign property where it was still in existence, and France reserving her assent to the non-Russian proposals as a gesture of friendship with Belgium. The other non-Russian Powers would have been satisfied with an assurance of equitable compensation, but the Soviet delegation never went farther than undertaking to accord to former foreign owners a 'preferential right' to the recovery of their property on terms to be fixed, and it was explained, unofficially but candidly, that if some new speculator should outbid a former owner in relation to the latter's property the new-comer would enter on possession.

(*c*) *The Hague Conference and the Non-Aggression Pact.* Under those circumstances the Genoa Conference reached its last phase at a meeting consisting of the four Supreme Council Powers with Belgium, which on the 14th May drafted a reply to a lengthy Russian memorandum dated three days earlier. In the memorandum in question one loophole for the continuance of negotiations had been left. The Russians had observed that the best method after all might be for purely financial questions to be discussed as such by experts. That suggestion the Allied Powers seized on, and at the final plenary session of the Genoa Conference on the 19th May it was decided that a meeting of experts should take place at The Hague in the following month, with the understanding that, pending the conclusion of the experts' discussion, the Governments represented at Genoa should refrain from recognizing or supporting private arrangements made by their nationals with the Soviet Government. An undertaking, known as the 'Non-Aggression Pact', singular in that there was no attempt to make it more than merely verbal, was simultaneously entered into by the delegates present at Genoa. It bound the nations they represented to refrain from acts of aggression or hostile propaganda for a period of four months from the closing of the work of the Hague Commission. The pledge, for what it was worth, affected no one but Russia, all other nations being already much more effectively bound by the League of Nations Covenant or by the Peace Treaties.

Such was the output of Genoa. With regard to certain technical matters, concerning transit, financial, economic, and health questions, various problems were referred to the League of Nations, with the suggestion that representatives of such countries as Russia, not members of the League, should be given places on the League Committees dealing with these matters. Though the Russians at Genoa made formal protests against this arrangement it seemed by no means improbable that advantage would subsequently be taken of it, a certain slender contact with the Western Powers being maintained in this way.

17. *The Hague Conference, June–July 1922.* The Hague discussions of experts formed a postscript to Genoa, and constituted to all appearance the last attempt to settle with Russia through the method of international conference. The conversations continued for over a month, and at the end no progress of any consequence could be reported. Once more the question of private property proved the stumbling-block, the sub-commission appointed to deal with that baffling problem being compelled to open its report with the declaration that:

> 'The First Sub-Commission has to report with sincere regret that as a result of its labours it is plain that no satisfactory arrangement on the subject of private property can be recommended at the present Conference.'

At the final plenary session at The Hague one door was indeed half-opened, in appearance, at any rate, by M. Litvinoff, who offered to refer to Moscow a proposal that the Russian Government should acknowledge the debts due by itself and its predecessors to foreign nationals, and give compensation for property nationalized, on the undertaking that terms of payment and of compensation should be left to be arranged direct between the Soviet Government and the individuals concerned over a period of two years. That wholly inconclusive proposal was formally welcomed by the Conference, but it was impossible to regard it as justifying further discussions on the spot. When the delegates dispersed the suggestion simply lapsed.

18. *Summary and Conclusion.* The Bolshevik revolution

took place in November 1917. Five years later, in November 1922, Russia was still largely in the position of an outlaw among the nations. Her Government had of course obtained *de facto* recognition. There could be no question as to that. But it was recognized *de jure* only by Poland, Germany, the Angora Government (itself unrecognized by the Powers), Persia, Finland, and the Baltic Republics. In addition it had taken part in the Genoa Conference, on an equal footing, for that purpose, with the other nations, and it was a party to trade agreements with Great Britain, Italy, Germany, Czecho-Slovakia, and other States. It had sent delegates to a League of Nations Health Conference, but from the League itself it held resolutely aloof. In its isolation it continued to constitute not merely a European problem but a European peril.

CHAPTER IV

THE WORLD OUTSIDE EUROPE

PART I

THE BRITISH DOMINIONS

A. The Status of the Dominions before the Peace Conference

1. *Imperial Management of the Foreign Relations of the British Empire.* At the time of the armistice the British Dominions had come to occupy, with regard to the United Kingdom, a curious and anomalous constitutional position, the full significance of which was but imperfectly understood in the British Empire itself, and which was necessarily still less comprehensible to foreign powers. This was the inevitable result of the genesis of responsible government as a practical method of providing for the conduct of the affairs of large European communities in oversea settlements. The pioneers of self-government for the Colonies recognized that in the ultimate issue it was impossible to reconcile the freedom of the local government and legislature in internal affairs with subjection to Imperial authority in matters external. But they wisely disregarded difficulties which might not be of substantial importance for generations, and secured for the Colonies a measure of internal freedom which transmuted discontent and disaffection into loyalty and prosperity.

As mere colonial dependencies, in all international matters the British possessions had no status of their own, and the control of international relations affecting them lay with the Imperial Government and Parliament ; if Canadian or Newfoundland authorities interfered with the exercise of fishery rights in North American waters by citizens of the United States, it was the British, not the Canadian Government, from which the United States' administration demanded redress, and the British Government owed neither legal nor constitutional responsibility to Canada. Yet every consideration of equity and prudence demanded that, in all matters directly and vitally affecting the Colonies, their Governments should be consulted by the Imperial Government in the conduct of its policy, and in 1856 a formal pledge of consultation was given even to the small colony of Newfoundland which had just received responsible government. An obvious mode of securing co-operation was to associate colonial statesmen with British representatives in treaty negotiations, as when the Premier of Canada took part in the discussions which resulted in the Treaty of Washington of 1871. This method assured the fullest presentation and consideration of colonial views, but the final determination in each case rested with the Imperial Government, which did not hesitate to override the wishes of colonial governments, when it deemed such action necessary in the interests of the Empire as a whole. Thus in 1883 an attempt by Queensland to annex New Guinea was disavowed, and at the Colonial Conference of 1907 Australia and New Zealand protested against the failure of the Imperial Government to meet their wishes regarding the New Hebrides, while Newfoundland protested on the score of the concessions made by the United Kingdom to the United States as regards fishery rights. Notwithstanding these protests, the Imperial Government proceeded to the extreme measure of suspending the operation of Newfoundland legislation to avoid any contravention of American treaty rights, and the objections of the Government of Newfoundland were not seconded by any other colonial government.

2. *Consultation of the Dominions on Issues directly affecting them.* While, however, the Imperial Government retained final control of foreign issues affecting the colonies, its action was naturally dominated by the desire to meet the wishes of the colonies, especially in the sphere of economic policy. It was early recognized that it would be a derogation from effective self-government that the colonies should be bound automatically by commercial treaties concluded by the United Kingdom, and from 1880 steps were taken to obtain the insertion in such treaties of clauses which rendered their application to the self-governing colonies dependent on the desire of those colonies. From 1899 foreign powers were asked to concede to the colonies the right of withdrawing separately from general treaties of commerce to which they might adhere, and by 1914 the process had been carried so far that the Dominions were in a position to withdraw, if they so desired, from almost every commercial

treaty entered into by the United Kingdom. Moreover, there had grown up a practice, definitely regulated in 1895, under which special commercial arrangements were negotiated by the Imperial Government with foreign powers in the interests of individual colonies, such as that of 1893 regarding Franco-Canadian trade. The substance of such conventions was determined on the British side by the colony concerned, the Imperial Government reserving to itself the decision as to whether the terms proposed could be accepted without injury to the rest of the Empire, while every tariff concession made to a foreign power had automatically to be extended to every part of the Empire. In 1907 a further concession was made; whereas in earlier negotiations colonial representatives had acted in conjunction with British diplomats, it was now agreed that the negotiations might be left in the hands of colonial ministers, acting on the authority of powers granted by the King, and British officials be associated with them only in the signature of agreements duly arrived at. The formal and real control of the Imperial Government remained intact; it could refuse to issue the necessary powers to negotiate, without which colonial ministers could not act; no treaty could be signed until it had approved its terms; it could refuse to ratify any convention of which, even after signature, it disapproved. On the other hand, the colonial ministers had the fullest power of negotiation within the limits marked out by the Imperial Government, and were subject to effective control by their Parliaments, to which by constitutional usage they submitted the arrangements concluded, before asking the Imperial Government to advise their ratification by the King.

While commercial negotiations of this type emphasized the development of a separate individuality on the part of the Dominions, as the self-governing colonies came to be styled after 1907, there was still no breach in the diplomatic unity of the Empire. The Dominion negotiators both technically and actually were Imperial representatives, though the subject-matter of their negotiations affected only a portion of the Empire. In 1912, however, a very important departure from this practice took place; at the Radiotelegraphic Conference the Dominions were represented separately from the United Kingdom by Dominion plenipotentiaries, acting under the sole instructions of their own governments and not of the Imperial Government, and authorized to represent the views of the several Dominions only. The Imperial Government still retained the sole power of issuing the necessary authority to the Dominion representatives to act as plenipotentiaries, and it could refuse to advise the King to ratify any convention arrived at, even though ratification was asked for by the Dominions. But it had lost the right of issuing instructions to Dominion representatives as to the views they were to take in the course of the negotiations; it could no longer intervene to prevent the signature of a treaty which it disliked, and it left the Dominion representatives free to oppose British views, if they thought fit. The precedent thus created was followed in the Conference on the Safety of Life at Sea in 1914, and a model thus came into existence which was to have decisive influence on the position of the Dominions in the peace negotiations of 1919.

3. *Sole Control by the United Kingdom of General Imperial Questions.* Abundant provision thus existed in 1914 for the due influence of the Dominions in all matters directly and immediately affecting them, as opposed to questions of general Imperial concern. For almost the whole period of responsible government in the colonies before the war of 1914, such issues remained the exclusive affair of the Imperial Government. Of this anomaly there was a simple historical explanation. In the early years of responsible government there was no thought of exacting either military or naval aid in case of European wars from the struggling dependencies; indeed Imperial forces were at first maintained in them, available to safeguard internal order as well as to secure them from external attack. By 1870 it was recognized that the presence of these forces was inconsistent with the principles of responsible government; British troops were gradually withdrawn from all save naval bases, and the duty of maintaining order locally was left in the hands of the colonial governments. Each colony was also expected to assist in her own defence from external aggression, but was assured of the protection, primarily of the British Navy, and secondarily of the British Army. Reliance on this aid discouraged military preparations; it was only in 1909–12 that in Australia, New Zealand, and South Africa, limited measures of compulsory training of youths for home defence were introduced, while Canada remained content with voluntary training on a small scale. Apart from co-operation in case of actual attack, there

was no constitutional obligation for the Dominions to afford assistance to the United Kingdom in case of war. In the Boer War of 1899–1902, it was popular pressure rather than governmental initiative, which resulted in the dispatch of colonial forces to South Africa, and the Dominion Governments showed a consistent reluctance to enter into any arrangements with the Imperial Government as to affording military aid in the event of war.

4. *Dominion Claims at the Imperial Conference of 1911.* In naval matters the situation was radically similar. At the Colonial Conferences of 1887, 1897, and 1902, agreements were entered into by the Colonies, other than Canada, for small pecuniary contributions to naval funds in return for the undertaking by the Admiralty of measures of local protection in excess of those deemed necessary from the purely naval point of view. Even in 1907–14 when Australia, New Zealand, and Canada adopted the policy of developing local navies, the essential aim of these schemes was defensive, and the Dominion Governments declined to enter into any formal engagement that those forces should co-operate with the British Navy in the event of war, although they recognized that such a step would normally be taken. The development of Dominion naval interest, however, was largely prompted by the lessons of the Russo-Japanese war and the obvious growth of tension in Europe consequent on the war. These events brought home to the people of the Dominions the fact that they could not content themselves with leaving foreign affairs in general entirely in the hands of the Imperial Government, and this feeling took shape in a protest made formally at the Imperial Conference of 1911 against the conclusion of the Declaration of London in 1909 without reference to the Dominions. New Zealand, indeed, went so far as to propose at that Conference a scheme of Imperial Federation as regards foreign affairs and defence. But the other Dominions, and particularly Canada, were not prepared to accept a system which would impose on them definite obligations in respect of defence, while the actual decision in foreign affairs would still rest, by reason of her superiority in population, with the United Kingdom. The Conference, therefore, contented itself with the promise of the Imperial Government to consult the Dominions in preparation for the participation of the United Kingdom in general political

conferences such as the Hague Conferences. At the same time an important innovation in procedure was made; at a meeting of the Committee of Imperial Defence a statement on British foreign policy was made by Sir Edward Grey to the Dominion representatives, in which the principles affecting the action of the Imperial Government were explained. Shortly after the Conference there was a change of government in Canada; the new ministry evinced a greater interest in foreign relations than its predecessor, and the Premier, Sir R. Borden, after a visit to London, asked Parliament to sanction a grant of 35 million dollars to be expended on the construction of capital ships for presentation to the British Navy, a project defeated by the opposition of the Senate. The Imperial Government reciprocated this increase of interest by suggesting that each Dominion should maintain in London a resident minister from the Dominion cabinet, who would be in direct touch with the Foreign Office, and serve as a means of securing to the Dominions due influence on British foreign policy. But this suggestion was hardly acted upon prior to the outbreak of war.

5. *The Dominions in the War and the Imperial War Cabinet; the Position of India.* Hence it was that the Dominions had no share in, or knowledge of, the policy of the Imperial Government in entering into the war of 1914 other than the statements made in Parliament immediately before the declaration of war. That event automatically brought them into hostile relations, first with Germany, and then with her allies; but it left them free to decide whether to take an active part in the struggle, or to content themselves with repelling any attack made on them. In point of fact they hastened to give assurances of approval of the British decision, and of determination to lend their aid. The valuable Australian fleet and the small ships owned by Canada and New Zealand were placed at once under the control of the Admiralty, and in all the Dominions steps were taken to raise military forces for dispatch to England. These forces were at first raised on a purely voluntary basis, but, as the struggle was prolonged and the need of men increased, recourse was had to a compulsory system in New Zealand in 1916; in Canada the same step was taken in 1917, but only after a conflict between the advocates of conscription and of the voluntary system, which resulted in the formation of a coalition government, united on the principle of taking every step to secure the

reinforcement of the Canadian troops in France. Newfoundland also applied compulsion, but proposals for its acceptance were twice rejected at referenda in Australia in 1916 and 1917, and could not even be contemplated in South Africa in view of the cleavage of opinion there. Local operations were also undertaken, in co-operation with the navy, by Australia and New Zealand, resulting in the occupation of the German possessions in the Pacific south of the equator, while South African forces with naval aid reduced German South-West Africa in 1914–15, though opposition to participation in the war from Boers, anxious to recover the independence lost in 1902, led to a rebellion which was only suppressed with considerable loss of life.

The naval and military forces sent overseas by the Dominions fell under the control of the Imperial Government, but in return an assurance was given to the Dominions that they would be consulted in regard to the terms of peace when that came to be negotiated. As the war progressed and the probability of an early issue vanished, the necessity of closer relations between the Imperial and Dominion Governments became obvious, and on the change of government in the United Kingdom in 1916 arrangements were made for meetings between Dominion and British ministers to consider co-operation in war activities and the terms on which peace might be made. To these meetings in 1917 and 1918 the style of Imperial War Cabinet was given, as a parallel to the term British War Cabinet, applied to the new ministerial body created to deal with the war, but the term Cabinet in this application had a novel sense. The Imperial War Cabinet had no Prime Minister, the British Premier presiding only as *primus inter pares*; its members had no collective responsibility, and owed an account of their views to different authorities; majority decisions were impossible, as no Dominion could be required to sacrifice its freedom of action; nor had the Cabinet any direct executive authority; any action taken after discussion in this Cabinet of Governments, as Sir R. Borden styled it, had to be carried out by order of, and on the responsibility of, the several governments represented. Yet, although this body was inevitably dominated by the British ministers under whose control were the naval and military forces of the Empire, the new machinery afforded the Dominions the best available opportunity of sharing in the determination of Imperial policy for the conduct of the war and the terms of peace.

Both in 1917 and 1918 India, including the Native States, was accorded like representation with the Dominions in the War Cabinet. When the constitution of the Imperial Conference was drawn up in 1907, India was excluded on the ground that she did not enjoy responsible government, and that accordingly her interests would properly be safeguarded by the Imperial Government. The great services, however, rendered by India in the war, both in men and money, rendered it impossible to treat India on the footing of a Crown Colony; on the 20th August 1917, the Imperial Government pledged itself to the introduction of reforms leading up to self-government, and the Dominions readily conceded the right of India, even during the transition state, to take her place in the War Cabinet.

B. The Dominions at the Peace Conference.

6. *The Dominion Demand for separate Representation.* Scarcely had the sessions of the War Cabinet in 1918 terminated, than the success of the Allied offensive rendered it necessary for the Imperial Government to summon its members to consider the British attitude in regard to the terms of peace. At this juncture occurred an incident which made an unhappy breach in the harmony hitherto existing between the Imperial and Dominion Governments. The decision of the Imperial Government to express acceptance of the Fourteen Points laid down by the President of the United States as the basis of peace, subject only to a reservation as to the freedom of the seas and an interpretation of the sense of the restoration demanded for the countries invaded and occupied by Germany, was taken without consultation with the Dominions. A strong protest against this procedure was immediately made on the 7th November by Mr. Hughes as Premier of Australia, on the ground that the terms accepted did not guarantee to the Commonwealth the possession of the Pacific territories conquered from Germany, might be held to limit the autonomy of Australia in tariff matters, and did not permit of a demand being made on Germany for a full indemnity for the costs of the war. Mr. Hughes's protests were in part based on a mistaken inter-

pretation of the purport of the Fourteen Points, and were not regarded with entire favour even by his colleagues in the Commonwealth Cabinet, while they did not receive support from the other Dominions. Nor, it seems clear, could the Imperial Government have given effect to his objections at this juncture of events; but no adequate defence was forthcoming for the technical irregularity of failing to consult him, especially as such consultation might have satisfied him and convinced him of the necessity of the course of action pursued.

If, however, Canada and the other Dominions were not prepared to take exception to the general basis of the peace, they were in full agreement with Mr. Hughes as to the necessity of the adoption of such a procedure as would ensure the Dominions an effective position in the determination of the detailed conditions of a settlement. So far the Dominions had appeared to foreign Powers merely as portions of the British Empire; their forces were under British command and control, and they had no separate representation on the Supreme War Council, as established in February 1918 by the Allies fighting on the western front. That Council had taken the preliminary decision that at the Peace Conference each of the five Great Powers should be represented by five delegates, and the Imperial Government suggested that the places should be allotted to four British representatives and a Dominion or Indian delegate, chosen from time to time as the subject-matter to be discussed might dictate. The suggestion was in accordance with precedent, for at no political conference hitherto had the British Crown been represented by separate and independent delegations, and it was argued that the Dominions and India would have a more effective part in this way than if they received representation for themselves on the same basis as the minor Powers allied in the war. But this view did not commend itself to the Canadian Cabinet, which on the 4th December, urged that 'in view of the war efforts of the Dominion the other nations entitled to representation at the Conference should recognize the unique character of the British Commonwealth, as composed of a group of free nations under one sovereign, and that provision should be made for the special representation of these nations at the Conference, even though it may be necessary that in any final decision reached they should speak with one voice'. The Canadian Government also pressed for the right that a Canadian representative should take part in all the Conference proceedings, urging that Canadian opinion would not appreciate the right of five American representatives to sit throughout the Conference, while Canada was denied any representation of this kind, especially as Canada 'had as many casualties as the United States and probably more actual deaths'. The claim of Canada was supported by General Smuts, who pointed out that Canada and Australia had made a greater war effort than any other Powers below the rank of first class, and even Australia had suffered more losses than the United States, and by Mr. Hughes, although his Cabinet was decidedly doubtful as to the wisdom of insisting on separate representation as possibly injurious to Imperial unity. It was, however, obviously impossible to secure for each of the Dominions and for India representation throughout the Conference, and a compromise was devised on the initiative of Sir Robert Borden and adopted by the Imperial War Cabinet. Under this arrangement the Dominions were to have the same representation as Belgium and the other small allied nations at the Conference, but, as the representatives of these Powers were to be taken into consultation only when their special interests were under consideration, some of the representatives of the British Empire were to be drawn from a panel on which each Dominion Prime Minister would have a place.

7. *Recognition of the Dominions and India at the Conference.* The compromise had then to achieve the approval of the Supreme War Council, and naturally enough strong objections were at first raised to the proposed separate representation of the British Dominions. But the Dominion representatives with the support of the British delegates maintained their position, and the rules of the Conference as made public on the 15th January 1919, included the British Dominions and India among 'the belligerent Powers with special interests' which were to attend the sessions at which questions concerning them were discussed. Representation of two delegates each was attributed to Canada, Australia, the Union of South Africa, and India (including the Native States); New Zealand was allowed one representative, while Newfoundland was recognized to be too small to claim such treatment. Each delegation was permitted to set up a panel from which the delegates to act on any special occasion might be chosen. Under the same system, as applied to the

British Empire delegation, it was possible for Dominion or Indian representatives to be selected to serve on that delegation, though, of course, it normally was composed of representatives of the United Kingdom and the parts of the Empire which had no separate representation. In practice the value of such representation became minimal, as the exigencies of negotiation led to the supersession of the Council of Twenty-Five by the Council of Four; but the policy of the delegation was decided by the British delegates in consultation with the Dominion and Indian representatives, the activities of the Imperial War Cabinet being thus continued in a new form on French soil. Towards the close of the Conference, in the absence of the Prime Minister, the chairmanship of the British Empire delegation was held by Sir R. Borden. Dominion ministers were also freely appointed to act for the Empire on the principal Commissions and Committees appointed by the Conference to consider special aspects of the peace conditions. Mr. Hughes, as Vice-Chairman, was the leading spirit of the Commission on Reparations; Mr. Massey sat on that dealing with responsibility for offences against the laws of war; Mr. Sifton's Canadian experience marked him out for membership of the Commission on the International Control of Ports, Waterways, and Railways; and General Smuts lent great aid in the construction of the League of Nations. Sir Robert Borden sat on the Committee to deal with questions affecting Greece and Albania, while Sir Joseph Cook and General Botha dealt with the affairs of Czecho-Slovakia and Poland respectively. The extent and importance of this representation becomes obvious when it is remembered that on these bodies the Great Powers were restricted to two representatives apiece, and the other Powers were only permitted to select five of their number for representation, a fact which would normally have precluded the Dominions from representation, but for the inclusion of Dominion ministers in the British Empire delegation.

The unique position of the Dominion and Indian representatives, with their effective access to the British Empire delegation, doubtless justifies the claim of Canadian ministers that they occupied perhaps a much more important position than the representative of any of the minor Powers at the Conference. In one point, indeed, the Dominions and India were technically inferior to these Powers; in the event of any voting the British Empire delegation had the sole right to vote; but in the actual conditions of the working of the Conference formal voting was of minimal consequence, save in so far as the absence of the right might be deemed to suggest that the status of the Dominions and India was inferior to that of the minor Powers. A striking illustration of the value placed by Sir Robert Borden on the assertion of the individuality of the Dominions was seen at the second plenary session of the 25th January 1919, when announcement was made of the constitution of the Commissions which the Great Powers had decided to set up. Objection was taken to these decisions by the minor Powers both on the ground that they had not been consulted and that the representation assigned to them was inadequate, and Sir Robert Borden on behalf of Canada, as well as M. Hymans on behalf of Belgium, associated themselves with these protests, although as far as the Dominions were concerned the matter was of minimal practical interest.

8. *Dominion Representation in the League of Nations.* While there was unity among the Dominions in asserting their position at the Conference, there were, naturally, divergences in their interests. Australia and New Zealand were largely concerned with practical questions immediately affecting their national life, especially the issues of reparations and the future of the German possessions in the Pacific. Too weak to stand alone, with territories tempting Asiatic immigration, they had no special interest in asserting the independence of their position. Canada, on the other hand, secure in her friendship with the United States and the protection of the Monroe doctrine, developed a strong desire to assert her status as on an equality with any minor Power, while General Smuts was anxious to confound the Republican opposition in the Union by proving that South Africa could acquire all the advantages and prestige of independence, without severing her connexion with the British Crown and running the almost certain risk of civil war in the process. It was natural, therefore, that it should have fallen to the lot of Sir Robert Borden and General Smuts to make the only important contributions of the Dominions to the formulation of the decisive principles of the League of Nations. Indeed, the fact that the first draft of the League Covenant made no provision for the separate representation of the Dominions was due not merely to the fact that the idea of such

treatment of the Dominions was not at first acceptable to foreign Powers, but also to the reluctance of the British Empire delegation as a whole to accept a principle which might seem dangerously to menace the continued unity of the Empire. The pressure of the views of Canada and the Union, however, prevailed, although Mr. Hughes's action in supporting their position was regarded with considerable misgiving by some of his colleagues in the Commonwealth, and the Dominions were accorded a distinct position, with separate voting power, in the League alongside of the British Empire. A further struggle was necessary, again with Sir Robert Borden as protagonist, to secure that the Dominions should be eligible for election to the Council and entitled to be invited to send a representative to sit as a member of the Council during the consideration of matters specially affecting their interests; it was plausibly contended that the fact that the British Empire was permanently represented on the Council should suffice, but this contention was ultimately overridden, President Wilson, M. Clemenceau, and Mr. Lloyd George concurring formally in the view that the Dominions had the same rights in these matters as any other member of the League. Nor can it be regarded as a derogation from their position that it is understood that, if any dispute arises in which the British Empire is involved and the matter comes before the Assembly or Council under the provisions of Art. XV, the Dominion representatives will not rank as independent members for voting purposes, but will be treated as representatives of one of the parties to the dispute. Any other procedure would obviously be unjust, and the League Covenant, while it recognizes the independent personality of the Dominions, equally recognizes that they form states of the British Empire.

9. *General Smuts and the League Covenant.* Contributions of special importance towards the framing of the Covenant of the League were rendered by General Smuts. His position was, indeed, unique; representing a nationality which had been incorporated by conquest in the British Empire but had found incorporation compatible with autonomy, he could regard the issues to be faced more dispassionately than the average statesman of English race, and he had formed a conception of the relations of the portions of the British Commonwealth of Nations which suggested to him principles applicable to the

whole family of the civilized Powers. His personal experience of the necessity of conciliation in South Africa between victors and vanquished led him to realize more clearly than others the necessity for a peace which would heal as quickly as possible the grievous wounds left by the war in the fabric of European society. He insisted that the Peace Conference 'should look upon the setting up of a League of Nations as its primary and basic task, and as supplying the necessary organ by means of which most of those problems can find their only stable solution', and 'that, so far at any rate as the peoples and territories belonging to Russia, Austria-Hungary, and Turkey are concerned, the League of Nations should be considered as the reversionary in the most general sense, and as clothed with the right of ultimate disposal in accordance with certain fundamental principles'. In the future government of such territories the rule of self-determination should be applied, and any authority necessary in respect of such territories other than their own autonomy should be the exclusive function of the League of Nations. For undeveloped territories the League would appoint mandatories, but would 'directly and without power of delegation watch over the relations *inter se* of the new independent states arising from the break-up of these Empires, and will regard as a very special task the duty of conciliating and composing differences between them with a view to the maintenance of good order and general peace'. In particular he pressed 'that no new state arising from the old Empires be recognized or admitted into the League unless on condition that its military forces and armaments shall conform to a standard laid down by the League in respect of it from time to time'. This conception of the future of Austria-Hungary as a group of states under the active supervision of the League had attractions for President Wilson; had it been possible to act upon it, something might have been done to prevent the development of tariff and other barriers between the severed portions of the Habsburg dominions. In other regards also General Smuts was prepared to impose heavy burdens on the League; suggesting the abolition of conscription for all states, members of the Peace Conference, he proposed that the Council of the League should determine the numbers and training of the militia and volunteer forces which must form their means of defence; the Council was also to decide the amount of military equipment and armament requisite for the forces which it approved, and factories for the production of weapons of war were to be nationalized and their production was to be subjected to inspection by officers of the Council. In those as in other matters his proposals were too advanced for complete acceptance, but his general conceptions of the constitution of the League and of its functions in preserving world peace were largely incorporated in the Covenant as finally drafted.

10. *Canadian Criticism of Article X.* In some measure of contrast with the views of General Smuts the Canadian delegates showed some anxiety lest the acceptance of the principle of the League of Nations should interfere unduly with the autonomy of the Dominion, an idea probably prompted by the popular impression that President Wilson in his Fourteen Points had enunciated the doctrine of international free trade. It was made clear that Canada understood the Covenant to leave the right of regulation of immigration and all fiscal matters entirely in the hands of the Dominion, and a very spirited attack on Art. X was delivered both by Sir Robert Borden himself and by the Canadian Minister of Justice, Mr. C. J. Doherty, a fact which, curiously enough, remained effectively secret in the Dominion until it was brought to light by the proposal made at the first meeting of the League Assembly by Canada in favour of the deletion of the article from the Covenant. It was contended that, even as regards the territorial arrangements made at the Peace Conference, while it might be just that the Great Powers which determined the settlement should guarantee their own work, it was unjust to exact such a guarantee from Powers which had had no voice in deciding territorial changes. As regards territorial integrity, the signatories of the Covenant were in effect, Sir Robert Borden argued, 'called upon to declare (*a*) that all existing territorial delimitations are just and expedient; (*b*) that they will continue indefinitely to be just and expedient; (*c*) that the signatories will be responsible therefor. The undertaking seems to involve initially a careful survey, consideration, and determination of all territorial questions between the various states who become parties to the Covenant. Even if such a survey were practicable, it is impossible to forecast the future. There may be national aspirations to which the provisions of the peace treaty will not do justice and which cannot be permanently repressed.

Subsequent articles contemplate the possibility of war between two or more of the signatories under such conditions that the other signatories are not called upon to participate actively therein. If, as a result of such war, the nation attacked occupies and proposes to annex (possibly with the consent of the majority of the population) a portion of the territory of the aggressor, what is to be the operation of this article ? ' Stress was laid by Mr. Doherty on the distinction drawn by the Great Powers between Powers with general interests and those with particular interests, among which Canada ranked. 'Let the mighty, if they will,' he urged, ' guarantee the security of the weak. The respective positions will be more nearly equalized if no reciprocal guarantee is exacted. The burden of that reciprocal guarantee will be in many instances to the young and undeveloped state quite out of proportion to its value to the states benefiting by it, and to any benefit resulting to the burdened state from the guarantee in its favour.' Should the day come when Canada's means of defence with the support of the British Empire and the aid of the United States were insufficient to protect her territory, it might well be doubted whether the aid of the other nations of the League would avail to save her. On the other hand, public feeling in Canada would certainly resent an engagement which imposed on her a direct and absolute obligation clearly binding to military action. The arguments failed to persuade the Conference, and, when Mr. Doherty explained the Covenant to the Canadian House of Commons in September 1919, he had formed the conclusion that Art. X recognized a principle, but imposed no obligation on Canada to take any part in a war to maintain the territorial integrity or independence of any other member of the League, unless the Dominion Parliament approved of such a step.

11. *The Question of Mandates.*[1] In his proposals for a League of Nations General Smuts had emphasized the necessity of the appointment by the League of mandatories to afford assistance and guidance to undeveloped territories formerly portions of Russia, Austria-Hungary, and Turkey, which were not yet capable of standing by themselves. But neither he nor General Botha was prepared to admit that such a system could be applied to the German possessions in South-West Africa, West or East Africa, or in the Pacific. The communities there, he contended,

[1] For a full treatment *v.* Chap. VI, Part IV.

were barbarous; they were incapable of political self-determination in any sense; they might be consulted as to whether they desired the return of German rule, but the result would be a foregone conclusion. These territories should be disposed of in accordance with the principles laid down in the fifth of President Wilson's Fourteen Points, and their case be treated, like that of Alsace-Lorraine, as exceptional. This in effect meant a claim for the sovereignty of German South-West Africa for the Union, of the East and West African territories for the United Kingdom [1], and of the Pacific Islands for Australasia. Naturally enough, this claim was warmly supported by Mr. Hughes and Mr. Massey, who were determined to secure the removal from the Pacific of the menace of German fortified bases. The case of the Pacific, however, was complicated by the fact that, in agreement with the Imperial Government and with the acquiescence of the Dominions immediately concerned, Japan had assumed control of the German islands north of the Equator, which her forces had occupied shortly after the outbreak of the war. This fact ruled out of possibility of acceptance the solution regarded as ideal by Australia, the annexation of all the German Pacific possessions to the British Empire. It was fatal also to the suggestion of the United States that the islands should be subjected as a whole to an Australian mandate. The only solution, therefore, available was to acquiesce in the division of the islands, and to subject both those north and those south to mandates, the former to be allotted to Japan. But a mandatory system was wholly unacceptable to Australia and South Africa, if it were held to import the necessity of granting equal opportunities for the trade and commerce of other members of the League of Nations, and still more if it implied that the mandatory could not impose differential regulations as to immigration, since this would run directly counter to the policy of both Dominions of forbidding Asiatic immigration. A solution was ultimately found, without abandoning the principle of mandates, on which the United States laid stress. A new class of mandates was invented to cover the cases of South-West Africa and the Pacific Islands, which were to be administered under the laws of the mandatory as integral portions of his territory, subject to conditions to safeguard native interests. On this basis mandates were to be accorded

[1] Subject, of course, to such claims as France or Belgium might establish.

to Australia for the German possessions south of the Equator, save Samoa, for which New Zealand was to be responsible, while Nauru with its valuable phosphate deposits was to be assigned to the British Empire. Public opinion in New Zealand would much have preferred that the United Kingdom should have accepted the Samoan mandate, but the burden was one which clearly could not with justice be imposed on the Imperial Government. In the case of Nauru, though the mandate was assigned to the Empire, and not to Australia, arrangements were made to secure a due share in the administration and the product of the phosphate industry for the United Kingdom, Australia, and New Zealand, which together were to find the funds to expropriate the concessionary company which was working the deposits. A mandate for South-West Africa on similar terms to those for the Pacific Islands was awarded to South Africa.

12. *The Question of Asiatic Immigration.* A difficult problem, which had complicated the issue of mandates, was raised in a much more serious form by the Japanese proposal to insert in the Covenant of the League a clause requiring members of the League to accord to all aliens, nationals of states members of the League, equal and just treatment in every respect, making no distinction, either in law or in fact, on account of their race or nationality. It would have been difficult for the United Kingdom delegates, in view of the established policy throughout the Empire under Imperial administration, to dissent from this clause, but the interests of the Dominions were, of course, paramount, and the matter was remitted for consideration by the Dominion Premiers and General Smuts. Mr. Hughes remained, as was inevitable, immovable in his refusal to concur in the proposal; he contended that the doctrine of a 'White Australia' was fully as much entitled to recognition as inviolable as the Monroe doctrine to which express approval was extended by the Covenant, and all that he could offer to Baron Makino on the 11th April 1919 was the principle of equality in respect of nationals resident in Australia as opposed to would-be immigrants. This was in effect the application to Japan of the attitude towards India adopted by the Dominions at the Imperial Conferences of 1917 and 1918, but the suggestion was naturally unacceptable to Japan; no compromise was arrived at, and the issue was left over for future adjustment. None of

the Dominions was prepared to accept full rights of immigration for nationals of League states, and in their opposition they had the support of the United States, where public opinion had definitely decided against Japanese immigration.

13. *The Conflict of United States and British Empire Views on Reparation.* United on the score of mandates and immigration, the Dominions were sharply divided on the issue of reparations. Differences of material conditions accounted no less than theoretical considerations for the strong divergence of opinion between Mr. Hughes and General Smuts. Australia had suffered severely in the war through the dislocation of her trade and shipping; her generous terms to her soldiers made warfare especially costly, and, unlike Canada, her distance from the scene of operations precluded her drawing large revenues from the manufacture of munitions. South Africa, on the other hand, had spent comparatively little on the war; her trade had been less severely hampered; and, while Australia was only to obtain a number of not very valuable island possessions, South Africa was assured of the important addition of South-West Africa. It is not, then, surprising that Mr. Hughes demanded that the whole of Australia's war costs, estimated at £364,000,000, should be refunded, as well as £100,000,000 representing the capitalized value of pensions, repatriation, loss to civilians and civilians' property, &c., and urged that, as a practical measure to this end, power should be given forthwith to appropriate in reparation all German private property in the mandated territories. His views, despite their natural appeal to the other members of the Commission on Reparation, led him into sharp antagonism with the United States delegation as to the proper interpretation of the Allied terms of peace, as declared on the 5th November 1918 and accepted by Germany.

The President of the United States had included in the Fourteen Points, which formed an essential part of the terms of peace, the restoration of invaded territories; but the Allied Powers, when expressing their acceptance of the basis of peace proposed by the President, had laid it down that they understood 'that compensation will be made by Germany for all damage done to the civilian population of the Allies and their property by the aggression of Germany, by land, by sea, and by the air'. The question of the meaning to be placed on this modification of the principles enunciated by the President was obviously difficult, and admitted of legitimate divergence of opinion. One view, at first sight plausible, was that the meaning of the Allied terms as accepted by Germany was that Germany would pay in full for damage to the civilian population, but no other demand would be made in respect of war costs. This interpretation, however, was rejected without hesitation by the Commission. The United States delegation by a careful process of reasoning arrived at the conclusion that the terms of peace proposed and accepted were 'not to be construed as waiving any clear right of reparation due under accepted principles of international law',[1] but gave the Allied and Associated Powers a contractual right to compensation additional to such rights as they enjoyed under that law. This necessitated an inquiry into the rights conferred by international law, apart from convention, and the United States delegation came to the conclusion that all that could be claimed was 'damage arising from illegal acts' as contrasted with damage arising from cruel, unjust, or immoral acts. Reparation, therefore, must be confined to acts clearly violative of international law, as existing at the time of the commission of the acts, and under this category fell all the damage done to Belgium resulting from Germany's violation of her covenant not to make war upon that country, and such miscellaneous acts as the deportation of civilians, attacks on undefended towns, and sinking of merchant vessels without warning.

The British reply[2] was presented in its more technical legal aspects by Lord Sumner and from a wider point of view by Mr. Hughes. It contended against the acceptance of the United States view on two grounds. In the first place, it denied the validity of the doctrine that under the accepted principles of international law all that could be claimed from Germany was compensation for breaches of that law; no such contention could be put forward by Germany seeing that she herself in 1871 had imposed on France 'an indemnity of twice the cost of the war, an indemnity of which one-half was not reparation but penalty'. The Allies claimed no penalty, but they asked for justice in the shape of the costs of the war. In the second place,

[1] See B. M. Baruch, *The Making of the Reparation and Economic Sections of the Treaty*, p. 294.

[2] Baruch, *op. cit.*, pp. 298–315. The paragraph heading on p. 302 is misleading, as it wholly misrepresents Mr. Hughes's argument.

even admitting the United States doctrine of the limitation of liability to breaches of international law, it was maintained that 'whatever rights Belgium has under international law, by reason of her neutralization, are clearly shared by those powers who guaranteed her neutrality, and incurred fearful losses in enforcing it'. The other associated powers, e. g. the United States and Italy, who helped to defend Belgian neutrality, could also claim their war costs. In any event, therefore, it was open for the Allies to claim full war costs, and the effect of the definition in the note of the 5th November was in no way to derogate from this right, but merely to make it clear that the Allies would exact the full extent of the reparation to which they were entitled under international law, so far as it was practicable to do so.

The United States reply [1] of the 19th February 1919 to the British contention deals summarily with the first of the British arguments by asserting merely that 'it is clear that under no principle of international law has Germany become our debtor for the general costs of the war', thus ignoring the chief British argument from the German interpretation of her rights under international law in 1871. A reasoned answer, however, was given to the second British contention, that British and allied war costs were directly or indirectly due to the breach by Germany of the treaty obligation accepted by her in 1839 to respect Belgian neutrality. It was pointed out that in the case of Great Britain alone could it be argued that there was a direct causal connexion between the war costs incurred by the Empire and the violation of the treaty, since Great Britain alone had based her declaration of war on the violation of Belgian neutrality. Even in the case of Great Britain the claim could not be sustained, for the treaty of 1839 was essentially one for the benefit of Belgium alone, and any violation of it gave Belgium the right to reparation but conferred no right on Great Britain, even if it were her duty under the treaty to intervene to vindicate it against violation. Or, even if this interpretation of the effect of the treaty of 1839 were erroneous, it was clear that the British war costs must be deemed to fall under the general rule of international law, which declines to admit indirect damage as a ground for compensation. The American view, moreover, could be defended on the score of reasonableness; it recognized, as

[1] *Op. cit.*, pp. 331–7.

had Germany, the special position of Belgium and her paramount claim to full reparation for the illegality of the attack made upon her; the British contention, if logically restricted, secured a full indemnity for Great Britain alone, giving her an impossible position of advantage, a conclusion which had led to the generous but unsound attempt to extend the right to all the Powers. Further the American view would secure the maximum reparation and its most equitable distribution; to demand the gigantic total of war costs would be 'to jeopardize securing that specific reparation as to which Germany must clearly recognize her liability, and the satisfaction of which will tax her resources to the limit'.

14. *The Settlement and the Question of Pensions*. There was clearly a fundamental divergence of principle between the United States delegation and the other members of the Commission, and it became necessary to secure the decision of the Council of Four upon the issue. In the Council the American contentions, which had the support of General Smuts, finally prevailed, and the demands made upon Germany in the treaty were based on this interpretation of the rights of the allied and associated powers under the terms of the 5th November 1918. The settlement, whatever its merits in law, had important advantages; it avoided the alternative (*a*) of reducing to mere surplusage the allied declaration regarding compensation or (*b*) of relieving Germany from the obligation to make reparation for her many and heinous breaches of international law. There remained, however, for disposal one point of difficulty; could pensions to injured soldiers, their widows and families, and separation allowances to the wives and families of soldiers, be reckoned as damage to the civilian population? The United States delegation itself was divided on the point, and the final decision to accept these matters as German liabilities seems to have been at least influenced by a memorandum submitted on the 31st March 1919 by General Smuts.[1] The contention of this memorandum is that 'what was, or is, spent on the citizen before he became a soldier or after he has ceased to be a soldier or at any time on his family, represents compensation for damage done to civilians'. This is clearly true in the sense that there

[1] Baruch, *op. cit.*, pp. 29–32; *v.* Vol. V, pp. 372–4 for the text of the memorandum; Smuts has recently made a statement, *The Times*, 7th February 1923, and cp. R. S. Baker, *Wilson and World Settlement*, ii. 383, and House and Seymour, 272.

is damage, and the persons affected are civilians. But the memorandum does not answer or indeed deal seriously with the obvious objection that such items do not naturally fall under compensation as defined in the terms of the 5th November, and it enunciates the paradox that the cost of an injured soldier's maintenance in hospital before discharge is not, while the cost of his pension after discharge is, a legitimate charge on Germany. It is difficult to avoid the conclusion that acceptance of these contentions was not unmotived by the fact that the claim of the British Empire for reparation would otherwise have been minimal. General Smuts's attitude again was doubtless in part determined by consideration of conditions in the Union, which had no parallel in Australia. The presence of a large number of settlers of German origin, together with the danger of driving them into the ranks of the Nationalist party, was sufficient ground to induce the representatives of South Africa to advise and to practise moderation. Consistently with their attitude, the Union Government in 1920 decided not to exercise the power given by the treaty of peace to confiscate the property of German nationals either in the Union itself or in South-West Africa, while in Australia a diametrically opposite procedure was adopted. In Canada, again, consideration of the large population of alien origin as well as the influence of the attitude of the United States rendered the view of Sir R. Borden more akin to that of General Smuts than to the attitude of Australia, with which New Zealand was in practical accord.

15. *Punishment of War Crimes.* There was dissent also between Australia and South Africa on the vexed question of the punishment of war crimes. Mr. Hughes laid great stress on bringing to justice those persons who had been guilty of cruelty towards Australian soldiers, an attitude in strict accord with the summary punishment meted out on the capture of German New Guinea to those officials who had maltreated British subjects on the outbreak of war. General Botha, on the other hand, dissented from any proposal for the wholesale trial and punishment of offenders against the laws of war, urging instead the selection for effective treatment of a short list of the worst criminals, a suggestion which unhappily failed to commend itself to the Conference.

16. *Labour Questions.* There was, on the other hand, hearty co-operation among the Dominion representatives in

regard to the labour clauses of the treaty. Special importance naturally attached to the work of Sir Robert Borden, whose influence was invoked in the effort to attain final agreement on the essential features of the Labour Convention at a time when a deadlock was possible. To Sir Robert Borden also, acting with the cordial support of the other Dominion representatives, fell the duty of maintaining in this connexion the doctrine of the individuality of the Dominions. At his instance the suggestion that no state, including its Dominions, could have more than one representative among the twenty-four members constituting the Governing Body of the International Labour Office was rejected as a derogation from Dominion status, and the only restriction accepted was the rule that none of the eight states of chief industrial importance, which were entitled to governmental representation on the Governing Body, should take part in the election of the other four governmental representatives on that body. India, for her part, was specially concerned to secure that nothing should be included in the convention which would involve her in obligations as to hours and conditions of labour inconsistent with her backward condition of industrial development, and in the terms as finally settled due allowance was made for the needs of both India and Japan in this regard.

17. *The Territorial Settlements and the Anglo-American Pact.* The territorial arrangements for Europe, which found favour in the eyes of the Great Powers, were regarded without much enthusiasm by the Dominion representatives, and evoked strong protests from General Smuts. The occupation of German territory, and the possibility of further portions being occupied in future, though intended as guarantees for peace, merely opened up an endless prospect of future trouble, especially in view of the impossible character of the reparation demands made on Germany. The eastern settlement as regards Poland was not less objectionable, and would merely be the cause of renewed wars. It is significant that both General Botha, who had special experience in connexion with the Polish Commission, and General Smuts, who undertook in April 1919 a mission to Budapest in an effort to effect a settlement of the problems arising from the revolution in Hungary, were profoundly impressed with the danger of the Empire involving itself too closely in European affairs, a sentiment which by May 1921 had developed into General Smuts's conviction that it was essential to resume the

traditional British policy of holding aloof from entanglements in Europe. Sufficient of this feeling was present in 1919 to secure that none of the Dominion representatives desired to be associated with the Imperial Government in the compact between Britain, the United States, and France to assure France the assistance of the two powers in the event of German aggression. The agreement, therefore, expressly stipulated that no obligations under it were incumbent on the Dominions, unless expressly adopted by the Dominion Parliaments. On the other hand, tentative suggestions that France might defer to Dominion interests by ceding her rights in the New Hebrides and St. Pierre and Miquelon met with no response from the French Government.

18. *India and the Turkish Treaty.* The Turkish settlement evoked the special interest of the Indian delegation, for the Indian Government was confronted with the fact that Indian political opinion was united in claiming that no such interference with the temporal power of the Sultan should take place as would prevent the effective exercise of his spiritual authority as Caliph. It was not unnatural that Mohammedans in India should have been perturbed by the obvious danger of the destruction of the Ottoman Empire, or that a Khalifate Association should be formed, pledged to work to maintain the Sultan's authority, even if acceptance of the Sultan's claims to spiritual leadership was of comparatively recent origin. But *prima facie*, in view of the history of India, the Hindu population had not the slightest reason to wish to see anything done to preserve Mohammedan strength. But Hindu politicians, extreme and moderate, had accepted the Khalifate claims in return for promises of co-operation in the agitation for the immediate concession of a full measure of self-government to India, a matter in which the Mohammedans, as the less numerous and well educated element of the population, took scant interest for its own sake. An Indian delegation proceeded to England contemporaneously with the Conference, and pressed their views unceasingly, despite a severe rebuff at the hands of the Prime Minister in an interview of the 19th March 1919. It was claimed that the full sovereignty of Turkey over Constantinople and Thrace should be conceded, that Turkish authority should be left absolute in Asia Minor, and full control be given to the Sultan over the holy places of Islam, a demand which wholly

ignored the rights of the Arab allies of the Empire. The Dominion delegations, naturally enough, were not concerned to support the Indian claims, and Mr. Massey earnestly urged the taking over by the Empire of Gallipoli, so as to remove from Turkish control the graves of the New Zealand and Australian soldiers who fell there in the service of the Empire. But, though the fullest opportunity was afforded to the Indian delegation to present its views on this subject, the Prime Minister and the allied delegations found themselves unable to admit a claim to more than just treatment from Turkey; Turkey, it was held, could be conceded only the same consideration as Austria and Germany; she must cease to rule over non-Turkish peoples who desired freedom, as did the Syrians and the Arabs, whose right of self-determination could not be overridden in the interest of the Sultan's spiritual claims. The Indian delegation remained wholly dissatisfied with the decision, although their influence prevailed on the Conference to treat Turkey with greater leniency than her aggression merited. The sense of grievance was largely due to the interpretation placed in India on Mr. Lloyd George's declaration of the allied war aims, on the 5th January 1918; this was treated as a binding assertion of the allied aims, which could not be affected by the continuance of the war, and on the strength of which India had spared no effort to assist in the achievement of victory, while to the Allies it appeared as the basis on which peace might have been concluded with Turkey, had she accepted the chance then offered to her to make terms apart from her allies.

C. The Influence of the Peace Conference and the League Covenant on the Status of the Dominions.

19. *Dominion Status in regard to the Treaties of Peace.* The net result of the intervention of the Dominions was, as might be expected, efficacious in a high degree in attaining satisfactory results in the matters directly and immediately affecting them, while on questions pertaining to the European settlement proper their views were of much less weight. But, apart from considerations of material advantage, the Dominions and India attained the position of having a recognized place in international negotiations. Prior to the Peace Conference they had ranked merely as dependencies, without any existence in the

eyes of international law; in the main the Dominions were contented to acquiesce in that status for the time being, but, even had they desired international recognition, it would doubtless have been extremely difficult, and probably impossible, to achieve that result but for the importance of the services rendered by them in the war.

A logical consequence of the status allotted to them in the negotiations was the decision that the peace treaties and cognate conventions should be signed separately by the representatives of the Dominions and of India. In this case also the procedure adopted was devised in order to secure that there should be no breach of Imperial unity. The various representatives were authorized by their Governments to sign the treaties, but the full powers from the King conferring upon them diplomatic status were issued by the Imperial Government. After this full acceptance of Dominion status, the only logical step was that ratification of the treaties should take place after the Dominion Parliaments as well as the Imperial Parliament had approved such action; and, on the insistent demand of Sir R. Borden, this course was adopted, in preference to the suggestion of the Imperial Government that express approval by the Dominion legislatures could be dispensed with. The precedent as to signature has since been followed, and it is now constitutionally clear that political treaties to bind the whole Empire must be negotiated with the assent of the Dominions and India, and be signed and ratified on their behalf, as in the case of the Washington treaties of 1922. If the Imperial Government negotiates treaties without such assent, then it is constitutionally bound to except the Dominions and India from the sphere of their operation.

This mode of negotiation and signature, however, does not imply the existence of a separate international personality in the case of the Dominions and India. The invitation of the United States to participate in the Washington Conference was addressed to the Imperial Government alone, and, though the British delegation included Dominion and Indian representatives, it was treated as, and functioned as, a unit; it would, indeed, have been impossible for the President to adopt any other attitude in view of the strong opposition expressed by the Republican party to the acceptance of the League Covenant on the score of its recognition of the separate voting power of the Dominions and India. It is in entire harmony with this view that the New Zealand Government has intimated that it does not claim the right to enter into diplomatic communications with the United States, and that the Canadian Government has agreed with the Imperial Government that, if it is to be represented specially at Washington, this representation will take the form of a minister plenipotentiary, duly accredited to the President by the King on the advice of the Imperial and Dominion Governments, on whom will devolve the duties of the Ambassador in the absence of the latter. Canada also has decided not to attempt to appoint consular officers to represent her abroad, but to avail herself of the services of the consular officers of the Imperial Government.

20. *International Status of the Dominions and India under the League Covenant.* But under the Covenant of the League of Nations the Dominions and India enjoy a definite measure of international status, which cannot be disregarded by any signatory of the Covenant, or Power since admitted to the League. These governments in their communications with the League and in their actions at Assembly meetings are wholly independent of the Imperial Government; their representatives act without any authority other than that of their own governments, and do not receive full powers from the King through the Imperial Government. The Dominions and India, therefore, can vote in any Assembly discussion without regard to the views of the Imperial Government, a position which was not realized by foreign powers until the right was freely exercised at the Assembly meeting of 1920. The fact is hardly remarkable; although for over fifty years the Dominions had been endowed with the right of managing without interference all their domestic affairs, the mention of this commonplace by Mr. Rowell, representing Canada, on the 8th December 1920, produced a mild sensation among many of the foreign delegates, who seemed to think it heralded the dissolution of the British Empire. Still more difficult, therefore, was it to conceive that in dealing with subjects before the League the Dominions would do anything except express the views of the British Government, a consideration which was urged in the United States as a conclusive reason against accepting the separate voting power of the Dominions and India in the League. Canada, however, and South Africa, which selected Lord Robert Cecil as her chief

representative, displayed from the first marked individuality. While South Africa demanded greater publicity for League activities, a strong protest was immediately addressed by Mr. Rowell against any suggestion that the League should arrogate to itself the right of dealing with such issues as the distribution of raw materials; in Canada, as in America, there was unanimity in opposing anything suggestive of interference with their internal affairs, and the true purpose of the League must be to devote itself to the primary work of the prevention of war. The question of raw materials, he contended, did not fall within the scope of the Covenant; the League was not a super-state with power to take up any subject which it desired, but an agreement among states to co-operate for certain strictly defined purposes in a definite manner; and, even if the question could be held to fall within Art. XXIII of the Covenant, there was no right to deal with it, unless and until an international convention regarding it was agreed to by the members of the League, and then only in accord with the terms of such convention. The other Dominions and India strongly supported this view, which the British delegates were not in a position to support, since in the Council, on the motion of the Italian representative, the British representative had already concurred in the idea of an inquiry into the question of raw materials. Mr. Rowell was equally emphatic in rejecting the proposal to place on the League generally the burden of certain technical organizations which it was proposed to set up to deal with economic and financial questions and with communications and transit, insisting that these organizations should form the subject of separate conventions among such states as desired to support them, and their cost be defrayed by the contracting states. On the question of the admission of new states Canada showed equal independence; in the Commission on this topic the French and British delegates supported the refusal of the application of Albania for admission until her international status had been more clearly ascertained; this was opposed by South Africa and Canada, but was carried in the Commission; the decision, however, was reversed in the Assembly itself, when South Africa and Canada won the day, the French and British objections being withdrawn. The harmony between Canada and South Africa on this point was not repeated in the case of Armenia; Canada alone of the Dominions supported her admission, while Lord Robert Cecil felt it to be impossible since neither Art. I nor Art. X of the Covenant could be effectively complied with in her case. Canada and South Africa were also in disagreement on the subject of the South African proposal that new states desiring admission to the League must enter into engagements as to the treatment of racial minorities similar to those imposed on the new states of Central Europe in the peace treaties; Mr. Rowell objected that it was not wise to add a new condition to those laid down in the Covenant as governing the admission of states, and that, suitable as such a regulation might be for European conditions, it was inapplicable to the new world, where Canada herself was not prepared to consider favourably the maintenance of racial minorities in lieu of the creation of a single nationality. The proposal, therefore, was amended to obviate these objections and accepted, Canada refraining from voting. Canada again went so far as to suggest formally the deletion of Art. X of the Covenant, a proposal which shared the common fate of other suggested amendments in the shape of reference to the Council. The representative of Australia was especially active in demanding the revision of the absurd basis on which the expenditure of the League was apportioned; like the other Dominion delegates, he was appalled at the rates of remuneration wholly unheard of in the Dominions, and their activities resulted in a more or less satisfactory adjustment at the Assembly meeting of 1921.

21. *The Dominions in relation to the Court of International Justice and Mandates.* The discussions as to the creation of the Permanent Court of International Justice, provided for in Art. XIV of the League Covenant, emphasized the distinct personality of the Dominions and India as members of the League, and their power in their own right to refer matters to the Court and to appoint national groups empowered to make nominations of jurists for appointment as members of the Court. It was made clear for the purpose of the statute that there was a distinction between nationals of the Dominions and India and British nationals, so that the condition forbidding the appointment to the Court of more than one national of the same member of the League would not apply to prevent the selection of a British and a Canadian candidate simultaneously. Incidentally the distinction introduces a new and far-reaching conception into Imperial constitutional law, effect to which is

given by the Canadian Nationals Definition Act of 1921 so far as it concerns Canada.

Even more prominence to the individuality of the Dominions is given by the system of mandates. These they may hold direct from the League, and it is to the League direct that they owe an account of their stewardship. In their attitude towards the question there is, it is true, a marked divergence between New Zealand on the one hand and South Africa and Australia on the other. New Zealand, indeed, has doubts as to the wisdom of the separate position accorded to her in the League, being more anxious to secure effective Imperial co-operation, and a share in moulding Imperial policy, than to exercise a right of independent action which is practically to her of negligible value. She applied, therefore, to the Imperial Government for legal authority under the royal prerogative to act under the Samoan mandate, and she has deprecated direct correspondence, so far as possible, with the League. On the other hand, South Africa has asserted her independence of the Imperial Government in her treatment of the mandate for South-West Africa, and her Parliament has claimed an inherent right of legislation for that territory, which it must derive from the new status of the Union in the League, since it does not pertain to it as a Dominion legislature. Australia also has claimed an unfettered right of legislation, but in her case no constitutional difficulty is involved, owing to the wide terms of the federal legislative authority granted by the Imperial Parliament in the Constitution Act of 1900. Two difficult questions arising out of the mandate confronted Australia at the Assembly meeting of 1920; Japan was inclined to press her view that the terms of the mandate must include equal rights for the trade and commerce of all members of the League, and, although in deference to the arguments of Mr. Balfour and Senator Millen, who represented Australia, the mandate was allowed to issue without this condition, Japan reserved the right to raise the point later on, and similar views on the issues have been expressed on behalf of France and of the United States. Further, a communication was addressed to the League by Germany putting forward a claim to be allotted colonial mandates, a fact which resulted in Australia refraining from voting in favour of the admission of Austria to the League, on the ground that that state might favour German aspirations in the event of Germany's admission to the League and renewal of her colonial claims.

22. *The Reconciliation of Dominion Individuality and Imperial Unity.* The independence of action thus freely exercised in connexion with the affairs of the League by the Dominions has not gone without question in Canada, Australia, or New Zealand ; criticism, by no means following party lines, has been directed against a practice which may menace the continuance of the unity of the Empire ; and it has been suggested that the better policy would be that there should be one and the same attitude adopted by all the parts of the Empire in international matters, determined by consultation and compromise between the Imperial and Dominion Governments. The reply to this contention, as given by Sir R. Borden and General Smuts, is that the separate position of the Dominions and India in the League affords the necessary means of the expression of the individuality of these territories, while permitting the Empire still to retain some measure of unity and coherence. It is significant that the strong supporters of the position assigned to the Dominions are far from inclined to treat this status as pointing the way to the final emergence of the independence of the Dominions or India. The doctrine of the right of the Dominions to secede from the Empire, if they so desired, which seemed to be countenanced by a declaration of Mr. Bonar Law, as Leader of the House of Commons, in the debate on the Government of Ireland Bill on the 30th March 1920, has been rejected emphatically by General Smuts as applicable to the Union of South Africa.

It must, however, be admitted that the possibility of separate expression of views in international matters is not unlimited, and that the League Assembly, by reason of the nature of the matters discussed in it and its restricted sphere of action, is especially suited for the recognition of the status of the Dominions and India as *sui generis*. Apart from the impossibility of the United States recognizing the Dominions as separate entities, it would have been disastrous, had the Empire been divided in sentiment, Canada opposing, Australia and New Zealand favouring, a Pacific compact with Japan. There is, it is clear, a sphere, as yet impossible to define with accuracy, within which the Empire must act as a whole, and, where this is necessary, it becomes inevitably a matter of great delicacy to decide how far the Dominions or India should go in the expression of views which are counter to those of the Imperial Government, which, in the relative state of strength of the parts of the Empire, must at present have the final voice in the case of controversy. The Dominion or Indian Governments have clearly the right to press their views on such issues upon the Imperial Government, and to give them publicity, in order to satisfy their constituents and so far as possible to influence opinion, in other parts of the Empire. But expediency and Imperial comity set limits, not less real because difficult to define, to the measure of publicity which should be given to divergences between the members of the Empire on questions of high policy; the Government of India, for example, had clearly an absolute right to seek to induce the Imperial Government to alter its policy as to the terms on which peace should be concluded with Turkey, but it was obviously inconsiderate to desire to publish these views immediately before the holding of a conference to discuss the modification of the treaty of Sèvres, and thus to weaken the position of the British representative at the conference. The constitutional error, which involved the resignation by Mr. Montagu of his office as Secretary of State for India in March 1922, was not his support of the claims of the Indian Government, which indeed it was his duty to maintain, but the personal assumption of the responsibility of authorizing publication of those views, in lieu of consulting his colleagues whether the international situation did not render it desirable in the interests of the Empire to suggest to the Indian Government that a more opportune moment for publicity might be awaited.

The episode is sufficient to illustrate the difficulties which surround the international status achieved by the Dominions and India through their position as members of the League of Nations. Their position is not precisely parallel to any existing conception of international law, and it is not surprising that some difficulty has been felt in foreign countries in apprehending its true signification. The British Empire, however, is in itself unique in structure; it was inevitable that in its development it should necessitate the introduction of new ideas of international relationships, and it is eminently natural that these ideas should take shape simultaneously with the evolution of a new conception of international organization so remarkable as that of the League of Nations.

CHAPTER IV

THE WORLD OUTSIDE EUROPE

PART II

SHANTUNG AT THE PEACE CONFERENCE

1. *Introductory, 1897–1914.* The Shantung problem had its origin in policies pursued, acts committed, and agreements concluded during the 'scramble for concessions' which immediately preceded and which in no small measure provoked the 'Boxer Rebellion' of 1900. This was a frenzied effort on the part of the Chinese to solve the problem of foreign contact by ending it.

Germany's seizure of Kiaochow (1897) was *not* the first move in the 'scramble' of the Powers for concessions in China. The staking out of 'spheres of interest' had begun some time before; France and Great Britain had acquired concessions in the south; Japan's easy victory in the north (1894–5) had exposed China's military weakness; and the compulsory cession of Formosa and the Liaotung Peninsula to Japan[1] had given rise to widespread consideration of the possibility that China might be partitioned. Representations by Russia, Germany, and France had induced Japan to retrocede[2] the territory which she had taken in Manchuria. But scarcely had Japan moved out of this territory when Russia proceeded with plans to move in, and in the course of the next three years not only Russia and Germany but also France, Great Britain, and Japan took from China territorial leases and sundry special pledges which officially signalized the location and implied the recognition of 'spheres of interest'.

Russia began her penetration of Manchuria in 1896, railway concessions being made to serve as the entering wedge. In the same year Germany decided that Shantung was to be her sphere of action. In the next year the murder of two German missionaries by Chinese brigands gave the German Government

[1] In the Treaty of Shimonoseki, 1895.
[2] Against the retrocession China paid a cash compensation.

its opportunity. A German fleet took possession of Kiaochow Bay. Forthwith, a Russian fleet moved into Port Arthur. Before the end of 1898 Germany was established in Shantung, Russia in Manchuria, Great Britain at Weihaiwei, and France at Kuangchouwan; Great Britain had secured the lease of an additional area at Kowloon; Great Britain had specifically recognized Germany's position in Shantung; and France, Great Britain, and Japan[1] had each secured 'non-alienation' pledges with regard to regions in which each considered herself primarily interested.

2. *German Rights and Activities in Shantung, 1898–1914.*

(*a*) *German exclusive privileges.* The rights which Germany first acquired in Shantung were granted and defined in a Convention signed by China under duress on the 6th March 1898. By this Convention an area later delimited to embrace 193 square miles surrounding Kiaochow Bay, together with the bay and outlying islands, was leased to Germany for a period of 99 years. Outside this area there was established a 'neutral zone' fifty kilometres wide. Rights of sovereignty within the neutral zone were specifically reserved to China, but the right to administer within the leased territory was delegated to Germany. Germany gave the specific pledge that she would not sublet the leased territory. It was agreed that Germany might construct two lines of railway and that German subjects might 'hold and develop mining property for a distance of 30 li (10 miles) from each side of these railways' along their whole extent. Germany declared that her motives were solely 'the development of Commerce' and 'to improve the relations between the two countries'. Finally, China promised 'in all cases where foreign assistance, in persons, capital or material, may be needed for any purpose whatever within the Province of Shantung, to offer the said work or supplying of materials in the first instance to German manufacturers and merchants. . . .' This was perhaps the most important single item in the Convention—for by it Shantung Province was marked out as a sphere of interest of a single foreign Power, in terms more comprehensive and more specifically exclusive

[1] Another serious question for Japan was the Yap Controversy. On this see Chap. VI, Part IV, § 12, p. 515.

than had or have been employed and recognized by treaty in reference to any other of the spheres of interest in China.

It is to be noted that, while the lease of Kiaochow was made for a period of 99 years, no time limit was set for the duration of the other rights and privileges. Art. 29 in the Kiaochow–Tsinanfu Railway Agreement concluded two years later (21st March 1900) states that, 'It shall be the subject of further agreements when and under what conditions the Chinese Government may in future take over this railway.' So far as is known, this tentative provision was never reduced to specific terms. There was also provision that troops for the protection of the railway should be stationed by the Governor of the Province and 'therefore outside the 100 li ($33\frac{1}{3}$ miles) zone no foreign troops shall be employed for this purpose'.[1]

(*b*) *United States and the 'open door'*. In 1899 the American Government took the initiative in securing declarations by the German, the British, the Russian, the French, the Italian, and the Japanese Governments respectively that they would observe the 'open door' principle in their several spheres of interest or influence in China. During the next year, again upon the initiative of the American Government, these and other Powers declared it their intention to respect the territorial integrity of China. Great Britain and Germany, furthermore, entered into an agreement formally declaring themselves committed to both these principles.

(*c*) *German control over railways and customs.* In setting about the development of her sphere, Germany made agreements with China whereby the customs administration remained under the Chinese Maritime Customs. For the building of the railways the German Government issued a charter to a German-Chinese Company. It was formally agreed that outside the Leased Territory and the Neutral Zone the Chinese authorities should afford the protection, if necessary, of Chinese soldiers, but that no foreign troops should be used for that purpose and that no foreign troops or munitions should be transported outside the Neutral Zone. For the exploitation of mines another company was organized. In the course of the next ten years this company opened a few coal mines; in 1911 it entered into an agreement whereby all its mining rights outside specifically designated and delimited areas were

[1] Art. 16.

relinquished; and in 1912 it sold its remaining rights to the Railway Company. In 1913 and 1914 Germany and China entered into new agreements for the construction of railways: one line was to be built from a point near Tsingtao to a point on the Tientsin–Pukow Railway at the border of Kiangsu Province; another, westward from Tsinanfu to a point on the Peking–Hankow Railway in Chili Province; options were given for loans on other lines, including a third line in Shantung; but all these lines were to be constructed for, and to be the property of, the Chinese Government.

Midway in the period just covered, in 1906, the Chinese Government 'voluntarily' opened three important cities, one of them the provincial capital, as commercial 'ports', but with the provision that 'the control of all affairs therein shall pertain entirely to China'.

3. *Capture of Tsingtao by Japan, 7th November 1914.* When the War began in Europe in 1914, certain Chinese officials conferred with representatives of foreign Governments in Peking with a view to securing action whereby the belligerents should agree not to engage in hostilities either in Chinese territory and marginal waters or in the leased territories on the China coast. Before Japan issued her ultimatum to Germany there were negotiations between China and Germany looking toward voluntary return by the latter to the former of the Kiaochow Leased Territory. The President of China, Yuan Shih-kai, also considered the advisability of China joining in the war upon Germany. Yuan actually consulted foreign representatives in regard to this matter; and he was advised by at least one very influential minister not to take that step.

On the 6th August 1914 the Chinese Government issued a proclamation of neutrality. This was accompanied by certain 'Precepts of Neutrality', as follows:

'1. Belligerents are not allowed to occupy any part of the territory or the territorial waters of China; nor to commit an act of war therein, nor to make use of any place therein as a base of operations against their adversaries.

'2. Troops of any of the belligerents, their munitions of war or supplies are not allowed to cross the territory or territorial waters of China.

'In the event of a violation, the troops shall submit to the Chinese Authorities to be disarmed and interned and the munitions of war and supplies shall be held in custody until the termination of the war.

'3. If belligerent war-ships and auxiliary vessels are found in a port within the territorial waters of China where they are not entitled to remain, China may order them to disarm and detain the officers and crew until the termination of the war.'

The presentation of the Japanese Government's ultimatum to Germany on the 15th August, followed by the declaration of war on the 23rd August, put an end to negotiations intended to exclude Chinese soil and neighbourhood from the theatre of hostilities. When Japanese and British forces began their operations against Tsingtao the British troops were landed at Lao Shan Bay, within the Leased Territory, and the movements of the British forces were kept within that territory. The Japanese, however, entered China's neutral waters with war vessels and landed troops at Lungkow on the north shore of the Liaotung Peninsula, more than a hundred miles outside the boundaries of the Leased Territory, whence they marched an army southward across the peninsula. China protested, but without avail. On the 3rd September 1914 China declared a 'war zone'. This embraced an area including the whole eastern end of the peninsula, to a line drawn west of the line of the Japanese march from Lungkow and about a hundred miles west of Tsingtao. In their march toward Tsingtao the Japanese requisitioned labour and supplies from the Chinese, constructed military railways, and seized the Chinese postal and telegraph offices. Ultimately they disregarded the boundary of the 'war zone' and occupied the whole of the Tsingtao–Tsinanfu railway and its stations, including the capital city—256 miles inland.

The general bombardment of Tsingtao began on the 31st October, and on the 7th November 1914, the Germans capitulated. In the operations the Japanese had employed a land force of 30,000 men, had suffered total casualties of 1,524, and had incurred an expense of about 65,000,000 yen (6,700,000 pounds). Some 4,750 Germans were taken prisoners and were removed to Japan.

4. *The Twenty-one Demands and the Japano-Chinese Agreements of the 25th May 1915 and the 24th September 1918.* Shortly after the beginning of the Tsingtao campaign, Count (later Marquis) Okuma, then Japanese Premier, declared in an open statement to the world[1]: 'As Premier of Japan I have stated and

[1] Cabled to the New York *Independent* for publication.

I now state to the American people and to the world that Japan has no ulterior motive, no desire to secure more territory, no thought of depriving China or other peoples of anything which they now possess.' A few weeks after the fall of Tsingtao, in December, the Japanese Minister to Peking was given in Tokyo instructions with regard to a number of demands which were to be presented at an opportune moment to the Chinese Government. On the 7th January 1915 the Chinese Government gave notice of cancellation of the 'war zone' in Shantung and requested Japan to withdraw her troops. On the 18th January the Japanese Minister presented to the President of China, in secret and with the injunction that the matter must be kept secret, a memorandum containing twenty-one demands, which have occasioned much criticism ever since. After four months of diplomatic resistance on China's part, during which period Japan increased her military forces in China, the Japanese Government delivered on the 7th May an ultimatum, giving China approximately two days in which to comply with the terms of a revised edition of the demands.[1] Under these circumstances the Chinese yielded, and two weeks later the Chinese Minister of Foreign Affairs finally signed the Japano-Chinese treaties and agreements of the 25th May 1915. In an official statement concerning these negotiations, the Chinese Government declared that it was 'constrained to comply in full with the terms of the Ultimatum' but that the Government nevertheless 'disclaim any desire to associate themselves with any revision, which may be thus effected, of the various conventions and agreements concluded between other Powers in respect of the maintenance of China's territorial independence and integrity, the preservation of the *status quo*, and the principle or equal opportunity for the commerce and industry of all nations in China'. The American Government took occasion to communicate to the Chinese Government, under date of the 13th May 1915, and in identical tenor to the Japanese Government, that the United States 'cannot recognize any agreement or undertaking which has been entered into or which may be entered into between the Governments of China and Japan impairing the treaty rights of the United States and the citizens of China, the political or territorial

[1] For the text of the twenty-one demands and their embodiment in the subsequent agreements of the 25th May 1915 *v.* App. IV, Parts I–III.

integrity of the Republic of China, or the international policy relative to China commonly known as the "Open Door" policy'.

Fifteen of the twenty-one demands had been insisted on.[1] Japan had served notice that some of the others were 'postponed for later negotiation'. Among the agreements concluded, the most important were those relating to Manchuria and those relating to Shantung. Japan had by the Treaty of Portsmouth (1905) which concluded the Russo-Japanese War, and by the Treaty of Peking of the 22nd December 1905, which followed, become heir to Russia's rights, titles, and privileges in South Manchuria. In the agreements of 1915 she insisted that China should extend the period of the lease of Kwantung (which includes Port Arthur and Dairen) and of her railway and mining rights in South Manchuria. In respect to Shantung, the agreements of 1915 were made to provide in part, as follows:

'The Chinese Government agrees to give full assent to all matters upon which the Japanese Government may hereafter agree with the German Government relating to the disposition of all rights, interests and concessions which Germany, by virtue of treaties or otherwise possesses in relation to the Province of Shantung.

'The Chinese Government agrees that as regards the railway to be built by China herself from Chefoo to Lungkow to connect with the Kiaochow–Tsinanfu Railway, if Germany abandons the privilege of financing the Chefoo–Weihsien line, China will approach Japanese capitalists to negotiate for a loan.

'Within the Province of Shantung or along its coast no territory or island will be leased or ceded to any foreign power under any pretext.

'When after the termination of the present war, the leased territory of Kiaochow Bay is completely left to the free disposal of Japan, the Japanese Government will restore the said territory to China under the following conditions:

1. The whole of Kiaochow Bay to be opened as a Commercial Port.
2. A concession under the exclusive jurisdiction of Japan to be established at a place designated by the Japanese Government.
3. If the foreign powers desire it, an international concession may be established.
4. As regards the disposal to be made of the buildings and properties of Germany and the conditions and procedure relating thereto, the Japanese Government and the Chinese Government shall arrange the matter by mutual agreement before the restoration.'

These agreements having been concluded, Japan continued her military occupation in Shantung, increased her forces at

[1] *v.* Agreements of 25th May 1915 App. IV, parts I–III.

some points where she had troops in China, built new barracks, and constructed powerful wireless installations. In October 1917, the Japanese authorities established 'civil administrations' at important points along the Tsinanfu railway, outside the Leased Territory and the Neutral Zone. This provoked threats of violence on the part of the local Chinese population and led to uneasiness on the part of the Peking government. The situation was aggravated by the fact which became known that large quantities of opium and opium derivatives were passing into Shantung through the port of Tsingtao and the Japanese post offices. Finally, to relieve the tension, Peking[1] gave consent to a plan drawn up between the Chinese Minister at Tokyo and the Japanese Foreign Office, which provided that the existing railways should be made a joint Chinese-Japanese undertaking and the concessions which had been granted to Germany for the building of new lines should pass to Japan, the *quid pro quo* on Japan's part to be the withdrawal of the Japanese 'civil administration' and the advancing of funds on the credit of the railway enterprise. The substance of these agreements may be summarized as follows: The first provided that Japanese capital should build the railways in Shantung Province upon which China and Germany had agreed in 1913—and on the security of this concession the Japanese at once advanced several million yen to the Chinese Government. The second provided that: Japanese troops along the Tsinanfu railway should be withdrawn, except a contingent to be left at Tsinanfu; the Chinese Government might police the line, the railway paying a share of the expense, but Japanese must be employed at the police head-quarters, at the principal stations, and at the police training school; Chinese should be employed as 'part of the staff' of the railway administration; the railway, 'after its ownership is definitely determined', should be made a joint Chino-Japanese enterprise; and the civil administration established by Japan should be abolished. The third and fourth provided for the building by Japanese capital of four railway lines in Manchuria and in northern Chili Province. These were the agreements of the 24th September 1918, concluded in secret, protested against in China as soon as their existence became known, disclosed

[1] There is uncertainty as to the approval of the Chinese Foreign Office. The matter was handled in Peking by the Minister of Communications.

officially to the other allied powers only after the Peace Conference had begun its work in Paris, and destined to be highly damaging to the claim which the Chinese Delegation presented to the Conference for the direct restoration to China of the former German rights, titles, and privileges.

5. (*a*) *Entente Secret Agreements, 1916–17.* But other 'secret agreements' were more important, agreements to which China was not a party and of which apparently none but the contracting parties had been made cognizant.[1] In 1916, certain exchanges of view had passed between Japanese and British officials with regard to the possible ultimate disposal of former German holdings in the Pacific. In January, February, and March 1917, the Japanese Government asked the British, the French, the Russian, and the Italian Governments for formal pledges, respectively, that they would support such claims as Japan expected to make, when the Peace Conference should assemble, with regard to the disposal of Germany's rights in Shantung and in the Islands in the Pacific north of the Equator. At that moment the Allies had particular need of additional naval assistance in the Mediterranean. The British Government gave its unqualified pledge to support the Japanese claims, on the understanding that Japan would support British claims with regard to the Pacific Islands south of the Equator. The French Government agreed to give its support provided Japan would aid in persuading China to break off diplomatic relations with Germany and in making that severance of relations effective. The Russian Government pledged its support without condition. The Italian Government was thereupon approached and, on being informed of these pledges, the Italian Minister of Foreign Affairs took note and stated orally that his Government 'had no objection'.

(*b*) *The Lansing-Ishii Agreement, 2nd November 1917.* In the autumn of 1917 a Special Japanese Mission under Viscount

[1] Mr. Lansing, American Secretary of State, and member of the American Delegation at the Peace Conference, testified before the Senate Committee on Foreign Affairs on the 12th August 1919, that he had had no knowledge of these agreements until early in February 1919.

It has been asserted that knowledge of these 'agreements' was communicated by Mr. Balfour to the American Government after their entry into the War in 1917, but no documentary evidence of this has been produced. The text of these Secret Allied Agreements will be found in App. IV, Part II.

Ishii proceeded to Washington. An agreement was arrived at, confirmed by an exchange of notes between Mr. Lansing and Ishii ‘ in order to silence mischievous reports ’. The points were a recognition by the two Governments that territorial propinquity creates special relations between countries and, consequently, the Government of the United States recognizes that Japan has special interests in China, particularly in the part to which her possessions are contiguous. Both Governments denied that they had any purpose ‘ to infringe in any way the independence or territorial integrity of China’, and declared their adherence to the ‘ Open Door ’ in commerce and industry. They added that ‘ they are opposed to the acquisition by any Government of any special rights or privileges that would affect either of these principles ’.[1]

6. *The Shantung Question at the Peace Conference.*

(*a*) *Japanese and Chinese positions, 27th–28th January 1919.* On the 27th January 1919, at the Quai d’Orsai, in the presence of the leading members of the American, the British, the French, the Italian, the Japanese, and the Chinese Delegations, Baron Makino, on behalf of the Japanese Government, entered a claim for the unconditional surrender to Japan of: first, the leased territory of Kiaochow and the railways and other rights possessed by Germany in respect of Shantung Province; second, all the German Islands in the Pacific Ocean north of the Equator, with all rights and properties connected therewith. In support of this claim, Baron Makino set forth that Japan had taken these places during the war, that she held them in occupation, that Germany could not be allowed to reoccupy them, and that Japan’s contribution to the victory of the Allies rendered it only just and fair that Japan should retain them. On the next day, the 28th January, Minister V. K. Wellington Koo, on behalf of the Chinese Government, stated that the Chinese Delegation would ask the Conference for the restoration to China of the Leased Territory, of the railway, and of all other rights which Germany had possessed, before the war, in Shantung. In support of this claim Dr. Koo submitted the following considerations. The territories in question are an integral part of China; they are part of a

[1] *v.* Text in App. IV, Part III.

province whose people, numbering 36,000,000, are Chinese in race, language, and religion. The German lease had been wrung from China by force; restoration was one of the conditions of a just peace. Further, Shantung Province was the cradle of Chinese civilization, the birthplace of Confucius, a Chinese Holy Land. The province was densely populated, therefore not suited to colonization, and the introduction of a foreign power could lead only to exploitation; Kiaochow was a vital point, as it commands strategically one of the main gateways to North China and one of the shortest approaches to Peking. China appreciated what the Japanese and the British had done in driving out Germany; but China too had assisted—the population of Shantung had contributed labour and supplies for the support of the Allies' military forces.

Baron Makino thereupon stated that a friendly exchange of views had been entered into between Japan and China; Japan had already agreed to restore Kiaochow as soon as she had free disposal of it; and agreements had already been reached with regard to the railways. Dr. Koo stated that the agreements referred to were presumably the treaties and notes made in consequence of the negotiations of 1915 on the 'Twenty-one Demands'. The Chinese Government had agreed to the provisions in question only under the pressure of an ultimatum, and it looked upon them as provisional and temporary, subject to review by the Conference, inasmuch as they dealt with questions which had arisen out of the war. Moreover, China had expressly stated in her declaration of war against Germany that all treaties and conventions theretofore concluded between China and Germany were abrogated; the lease of Kiaochow was therefore terminated; but even if such were not the case, Germany was without legal right to transfer the territory to another power, because of the express provision in the lease itself against transfer.

(*b*) *The question in suspense, February to April 1919.* The Shantung question was not taken up again formally by the Council until late in April. In the interval, neither the Japanese nor the Chinese were idle with regard to it. The Japanese showed irritation over the action of the Chinese Delegation in demanding the direct restoration. They had tried before the Conference met to induce the Chinese Government to leave to Japan the presentation of Far Eastern questions.

They declared that His Excellency Lou Tseng-tsiang, Chinese Minister of Foreign Affairs and official head of the Chinese Delegation, had promised while in Tokyo on the way to Paris, that China would co-operate with Japan and would not present an independent case at the Conference. They brought pressure to bear in Peking to induce the Chinese Government to repudiate the claim which had been put forward by its Delegation. Both sides appealed to the public, through the publication of pamphlets, by interviews, by cultivation of the press, and by the issuing of 'authorized statements', affirmations, and denials. The Chinese presented to the other Delegations an official memorandum setting forth their claim, and this was given a considerable circulation. Public opinion appeared sympathetic, on the whole, to the Chinese plea. It was generally felt that from the legal point of view the Japanese could make a powerful argument, but that from the point of view of political and moral principles the Chinese had presented a strong case.

During February, March, and early April, the efforts of the Conference were directed particularly toward the production of the Covenant of the League of Nations. The Japanese Delegation made a determined effort to secure the adoption of a 'racial equality' clause. When this was eventually refused them, they concentrated on their claim regarding Shantung. It was matter of common knowledge, however, that the United States Government, traditionally the champion of the 'open door' policy and the integrity of China, recently responsible in no small measure for China's having entered the war, was sympathetically disposed toward the Chinese claim; and it was expected that President Wilson would insist that the question be considered on its merits independently of the various previous commitments cited. Although neither the Japanese nor the Chinese Delegations gave any sign of less than absolute insistence, officially, upon their respective claims, there were evidences toward the middle of April that both were considering what terms might be proposed or conceded by way of a compromise.

At a meeting of the Council of Five on the 15th April, Mr. Lansing made a proposal that Germany be made to renounce all rights, titles, and privileges in and over territory outside her European frontiers. The Japanese objected that, in view of previous commitments, the Leased Territory of

Kiaochow could not be made subject to such a disposal. President Wilson shortly thereafter suggested that the five Principal Powers act as trustees of the former German rights in Shantung. To this also the Japanese Delegation said they could not agree.

(*c*) *The question before the Three, 22nd–30th April.* On the morning of the 22nd April, the Japanese case was heard formally by the Council of Three. Baron Makino stated that what his Delegation asked involved the concession of economic, not of political privileges; that they had already promised in formal agreements to restore the Lease of Kiaochow, to 'restore sovereignty' in Shantung to China; that the railways were to be a joint Chinese-Japanese enterprise; and that the railway police were to be Chinese, with Japanese only as instructors. On the afternoon of the same day, the Chinese Delegation was called before the Council. In this hearing the Council concentrated its attention almost entirely upon inquiries and statements concerning treaties, agreements, and exchanges of notes, including the Japanese-Chinese railway agreement of the 24th September 1918 and the secret agreements which Great Britain and France had made with Japan in 1917.

On the 23rd April, President Wilson issued his manifesto with regard to Fiume. The Italian Delegation withdrew from the Conference, and the Italian people enthusiastically supported the position which their Government and its Delegation had taken. This gave the Japanese Delegation the opportunity for which they had waited. They had already intimated, and they now lost no time in letting it be understood that the Shantung question must be disposed of at once and in accordance with their claim; that if they were refused this, they would withdraw from the Conference, they would not sign the treaty, and Japan would not join the League of Nations.

On the 25th April, the Chinese Delegation submitted to the Council a proposal whereby Germany was to renounce to the Five (Principal) Allied and Associated Powers her holdings, rights, and privileges in Shantung, for restoration to China; Japan was to engage to effect the restoration to China within one year after the signing of the treaty; China was to make pecuniary compensation to Japan for the military expenses of the Tsingtao campaign; and China was to open Kiaochow

Bay as a commercial port and to provide a special quarter, if desired, as an international settlement.

Throughout the week between the 23rd April and the 30th April, the influence of the Fiume controversy, the withdrawal of the Italian Delegation, the Japanese claim for 'racial equality', and solicitude for the adoption of the Covenant of the League of Nations affected the discussion of the Shantung question. Suggestion after suggestion was made with a view to a compromise adjustment between the Chinese and the Japanese claims. Several of the technical experts urged consistently that transfer of the German rights to Japan would not be warranted and would not produce a satisfactory settlement, and some answered every inquiry with data supporting the arguments for direct or indirect restitution to China. On the 29th April, General Bliss of the American Delegation, with the knowledge and approval of his colleagues, Mr. Lansing and Mr. White, sent to President Wilson a letter cogently discussing the conflicting claims from the point of view of the 'moral right or wrong involved'.[1]

The Shantung question had, however, already been decided. It had been decided in February and March 1917, when Japan secured the individual pledges from each of four European Governments that her claims would be given their support. The British and the French spokesmen now stated and held that they were bound by these pledges. On the 30th April, the Japanese made, at a meeting of the Council, a statement declarative of their policy, in substantially the following terms: Japan would hand back the Shantung Peninsula in full sovereignty to China, retaining only the economic privileges granted to Japan, and the right to establish a settlement under the usual conditions at Tsingtao; the owners of the railway would use special police only to insure security for traffic—these police would be used for no other purpose; the police would be composed of Chinese, and such Japanese instructors as the directors of the railway might select would be appointed by the Chinese Government. With Italy gone from the Conference, with the British and the French insisting on the sanctity of their engagements, believing that the League of Nations was at stake, fearing for the Covenant and for the very

[1] Lansing, *Peace Negotiations* (1921) pp. 230–3. *v.* also R. S. Baker, *Wilson and World Settlement*, III, 311–18 for 2 documents.

life of the Conference, President Wilson yielded, and the decision which had been made in favour of Japan two years before (by agreements to which the American Government had been in no way party) was confirmed.

The text of the clauses which were to carry this decision into the Treaty had already been submitted. Slight amendments were made in the Council. In agreeing to these provisions, President Wilson placed full confidence in, and let it be understood that he considered as a binding corollary, the statement of policy which had been made by Baron Makino on behalf of the Japanese Government. He also insisted at the time, and repeatedly thereafter, that this settlement should be construed independently of the Chinese-Japanese agreements of 1915 and 1918 and without reference thereto.

7. *The Terms and Conditions of the Settlement.* The Council concluded its deliberations on the Shantung Question on the 30th April. News of the decision was given that evening to the Press and, in an informal statement, to the Chinese Delegation, by the Director of the Press Bureau of the American Delegation.

It was stated to the Chinese Delegation that the former German rights in Shantung were to be transferred without reservation to Japan; that Japan had voluntarily engaged to hand back the Shantung Peninsula in full sovereignty to China, retaining only the economic privileges granted to Germany and the right to establish a settlement at Tsingtao; that the railway police force would be composed of Chinese with Japanese instructors appointed by the Chinese Government; that the Japanese military forces would be withdrawn at the earliest possible moment; that Japan was thus getting 'only such rights as an economic *concessionnaire* as were possessed by one or two other great Powers', and the whole future relationship between China and Japan would fall at once under the guarantee of the League of Nations.

The exact terms of the agreement which was to appear in the Treaty were not communicated until some days later. The terms, which went into the Treaty as Section VIII of Part IV, were as follows:

ARTICLE 156. Germany renounces in favour of Japan, all her rights, title, and privileges—particularly those concerning the territory of Kiaochow, railways, mines, and submarine cables—which she acquired in virtue of the Treaty concluded by her with China on the 6th March 1898, and of all other arrangements relative to the Province of Shantung.

All German rights in the Tsingtao–Tsinanfu Railway, including its branch lines, together with its subsidiary property of all kinds, stations, shops, fixed and rolling stock, mines, plant, and material for the exploitation of the mines, are and remain acquired by Japan, together with all rights and privileges attaching thereto.

The German State submarine cables from Tsingtao to Shanghai and from Tsingtao to Chefoo, with all the rights, privileges, and properties attaching thereto, are similarly acquired by Japan, free and clear of all charges and encumbrances.

ARTICLE 157. The movable and immovable property owned by the German State in the territory of Kiaochow, as well as all the rights which Germany might claim in consequence of the works or improvements made or of the expenses incurred by her, directly or indirectly, in connexion with this territory, are and remain acquired by Japan, free and clear of all charges and encumbrances.

ARTICLE 158. Germany shall hand over to Japan within three months from the coming into force of the present Treaty, the archives, registers, plans, title-deeds, and documents of every kind, wherever they may be, relating to the administration, whether civil, military, financial, judicial or other, of the territory of Kiaochow.

Within the same period Germany shall give particulars to Japan of all treaties, arrangements or agreements relating to the rights, title, or privileges referred to in the two preceding articles.[1]

8. *Analysis of the Settlement.* Reuter's dispatch of the 30th April to the London *Times*, said:

'The Council of Three, after hearing both the Japanese and the Chinese Delegations . . . came to the conclusion that the Japanese demands must receive satisfaction.

'Japan receives the free disposition of Kiaochau,[2] to which she is entitled under her Treaty with China of 1915, and which was all she asked from the Conference. In the Treaty Germany will surrender the Kiaochau territory to Japan, who will, in accordance with her Treaty with China, transfer it to the latter in due course.

'The Chino-Japanese Treaty of 1915 and the agreements concluded in 1918 stand in their integrity. . . .'

This represents a view different from that of President Wilson, and from that which was conveyed, in part specifically and in part by implication, in the statement issued from the Press Bureau of the American Delegation.

To understand what really had been done, it is necessary not alone to scrutinize the provisions of the Treaty clauses, but to take careful account of the antecedents, and of the direct and indirect consequences of the decision of which those articles are the formal evidence. Attention may be directed here to only a few points.

[1] *v.* also Text in Vol. III. 186–7.

[2] Kiaochow.

The rights, titles, and privileges which Germany had possessed in Shantung were based on bi-lateral agreements between Germany and China. In one of these, the Convention of the 6th March 1898, it had been specified that Germany should not transfer the lease of Kiaochow to any other Power. The decision of the Three required that the collection of rights, titles, and privileges which China had granted to Germany be transferred and assigned to Japan. In form, the transfer was to be made by Germany; in fact, the assignment was to be made by all the Powers which signed and ratified the Treaty. It was of course assumed, when the decision was made, that all the Allied and Associated Powers, including China and the United States, on the one side, and Germany on the other, would be parties to the Treaty. Japan's title was to rest, therefore, not on a bi-lateral agreement, but on a broad, international Act.

The terms of this new and broader undertaking assigned to Japan more than Germany had possessed. Not only was Germany to 'renounce in favour of Japan all her rights, title, and privileges', but, 'all *German* rights in the Tsingtao-Tsinanfu railway', &c., together with 'the German State submarine cables', 'are and remain acquired by Japan',—i.e., the treaty provisions assigned to the Japanese Government not alone all that had been German public property, but some things which both the Chinese and the Germans contended were of private or of mixed ownership.

There was thus granted to the Japanese Government everything to which that Government might deem it advantageous to lay claim, under the terms of any or all of the German-Chinese 'arrangements relative to the Province of Shantung', regardless of the extent to which Germany had or had not exercised her rights under the agreements. From the difference in their respective situations, relations with and policies toward China, Japan might consider it to her interest to avail herself of privileges under these agreements to which Germany had not thought it desirable to give attention. The legal and political warrant for a concession of rights, titles, and privileges by one sovereign Power in favour of another must rest on the relations between the grantor and the grantee; the conditions in this respect cannot fully attach to and be carried over with a transfer of the grant to a third party;—

whence the logic and the practical intent of such provisions as that which had been written into the German-Chinese Convention of 1898 expressly prohibiting transfer of the lease. The Chinese contended that Germany could not lawfully transfer the lease. Even if there had been no specific prohibition—but there was such—there would seem to be ground for the contention that the transfer could not legally be made by one—i. e., by either—of the parties to the original agreement, except with the express consent of the other. As to consent, China had undertaken, in the agreements of 1915 with Japan, to abide by the settlement which might be arrived at between Japan and Germany. But, inasmuch as, according to the terms of the original agreement with China, Germany had undertaken not to transfer the lease, was China's agreement with Japan to be construed as an authorization to Germany to make terms with Japan without reference to that limitation? In other words, did China's agreement with Japan of 1915 cancel a part or all of the German-Chinese Convention of 1898? The Chinese had contended that their declaration of war on Germany terminated all the treaties and agreements between China and Germany. The Council of Three had not accepted that view. Arts. 156, 157, and 158 of the Treaty imply the continued binding obligation of the Chinese-German Convention of 1898 and all the agreements supplementary thereto. If, however, those agreements were and remained binding, if neither Germany nor China had been released from any of the obligations thereunder, it would certainly seem that Germany had not the right to transfer the lease; and it would follow that the assignment of the lease to Japan was in disregard of Germany's legal disability in respect thereto. On the other hand, if those agreements were, as the Chinese contended, no longer binding, the assignment to Japan of the rights, titles, and privileges for which they provided could be effected legally only by the express and immediate consent of China. That consent, the Chinese held, had not been and would not be given.

The articles in the Treaty make no mention of China or of Chinese rights. They contain no reference to any condition or any obligation entered into on Japan's part; they refer neither to the pledges in the agreements of 1915 and of 1918 nor to the explanatory statements and declaration of policy made by the Japanese Delegation in the meetings of the Council.

In the absence of any textual reference to the Japanese-Chinese agreements of 1915 and of 1918, the provisions which appeared in the Treaty seemed to imply, given the antecedents and their own sweeping character, a recognition of the validity of those agreements. The Japanese had throughout the negotiations insisted that those agreements were and must be considered binding, and, notwithstanding President Wilson's contention that the settlement must be independent of those undertakings, they had never expressly committed themselves to an assent to that view.

The statements of policy made by Baron Makino, on behalf of the Japanese Delegation, in the conversations of the Council of the 22nd April and of the 30th April, had not been reduced to the formality of an official, published declaration. No official minutes had been kept of the proceedings and hearings of the Council of Three. Sir Maurice Hankey, accompanying Mr. Lloyd George as Secretary, made notes and memoranda, and there exists, in this form, a record of the conversations; but these were not formal Conference records. The official record, the Treaty itself, expressed no conditions and laid down no limitations in reference to the provisions of Arts. 156, 157, and 158.

Under these circumstances, and in the presence of informal and abbreviated oral statements by individuals rather than an official announcement by the Council, and with a refusal by the Council to give the Chinese Delegation a copy of the informal record of the hearing at which the Japanese statement was made,[1] there was uncertainty as to the extent of the pledges and doubt as to the binding obligation of the undertakings upon which the Treaty articles were said to be conditioned.

On the 5th May, Baron Makino made a statement to the Press, in which he declared: 'Japan's policy is to hand back the Shantung Peninsula in full sovereignty to China, retaining only the economic privileges granted to Germany and the right to establish a settlement under the usual conditions at Tsingtao.' Viscount Uchida, Japanese Minister of Foreign Affairs, made on the 17th May a similar statement to the Press; and he made later, on the 2nd August, a further statement in which, after reference to the Japano-Chinese agreements of 1915,

[1] A copy was given the Chinese Delegation, 'confidentially', later.

he declared that Japan was willing to enter into negotiations with the Government at Peking as to the arrangements necessary to give effect to Japan's pledge to restore the Kiaochow Leased Territory. He said also that the Japanese Government had under contemplation plans for the establishing in Tsingtao of an international settlement instead of the exclusive Japanese settlement which it was entitled to claim. President Wilson immediately issued a public statement declaring that in the statements made by Baron Makino in Paris in reply to questions which he, President Wilson, had put, no reference was made to Japan's declaration of policy as being dependent upon the execution of the 1915 agreements, and that nothing to which he had agreed should be construed as acquiescence on the part of the American Government in the policy of the Notes exchanged between China and Japan in 1915 and in 1918.

9. *The Chinese Delegation refuses to sign the Treaty.* To the Chinese, the decision of the Council was of course a bitter disappointment. They found the provisions written into the Treaty unsatisfactory ; and they looked on the account given them of the Japanese pledges as not reassuring. The Delegation prepared a formal protest to the Conference and issued authorized statements to the Press. In these and in other statements, both written and oral, they pointed out that they had had unsatisfactory experience of the granting of 'economic privileges' to foreign governments, especially of the consequences of foreign control of ports, railways, and other instruments of communication. Referring to the 'sovereignty of Shantung' they said that Germany had possessed no right of sovereignty in Shantung, and that there could be, therefore, no restoration of 'sovereignty'. They expressed suspicion of the declared intention of Japan to 'restore the lease of Kiaochow', inasmuch as under the 1915 agreements there existed the undertaking that Japan should be allowed to choose a point on Kiaochow Bay as an exclusively Japanese 'concession'. The lease to Germany had been for a period of ninety-nine years, but a 'concession' would be without date for termination, and would amount practically to a cession in full title. If Japan chose the city of Tsingtao or the port and the railway terminals, she would retain all that was of practical value in the leased territory. They explained their apprehension as to the use which might be made of the agreements of 1915 on the score

of their painful recollection of the circumstances under which those agreements had been extorted and their knowledge of the history of similar agreements elsewhere.

At the plenary session of the Conference on the 6th May, the Chinese Delegation gave notice of a reservation on their part to that portion of the Treaty which was to contain the Shantung provisions. On the 26th May they officially notified the President of the Council that they would sign the Treaty subject to this reservation. On the 24th June they were informed by the Secretary-General that reservations to the text of the Treaty were not permissible. They then asked that they be allowed to enter their reservation as an annex to the Treaty. Permission to do this was refused. They next proposed that they should send to the President of the Council before proceeding to Versailles a separate declaration explaining that their signature would be subject to the reservation. They were informed that there could be no reservations of any kind before the signature, but that they might send a declaration *after* they had signed the Treaty. They finally made a last effort three hours before the assembling of the Conference at Versailles for signing the Treaty, proposing so to modify the wording of their reservation that it should simply state that the fact of their having signed was not to be understood to preclude China from asking at a suitable time for reconsideration of the Shantung question.—They were seeking some assurance, though merely that of a technical intimation, that the League of Nations might be expected to consider their claims.—The Secretary-General reported that none of the Council would consent to this.[1] The Chinese Delegation therefore refrained from signing the Treaty.

10. *Effects and Consequences*. The most readily discernible of the immediate effects and consequences of the 'Shantung settlement', direct and indirect, legal, political and economic, may be summarized as follows:

It left Japan in control of the most valuable natural harbour on the coast of China proper and of the main east-and-west highways within and extending westward from Shantung Province.

It conceded to Japan a 'sphere of interest', embracing

[1] Final authorization to the Delegation to refuse to sign had already been dispatched from Peking, but had not yet been received in Paris.

the whole of a rich Province, in which the preferential position of the original concessionaire power had been granted in extensive and comprehensive terms.

It strengthened Japan in the consolidation of her strategic position on the Continent and in the China Sea.

It implied, in some measure at least, a recognition of the agreements of 1915 and of 1918, both groups of which China had sought in vain to have disallowed or amended by the Conference. It thereby not only furnished an authorized basis for the consolidation of Japan's newly acquired interests in Shantung, but it also added to the strength of Japan's whole position in South Manchuria.

It further dislocated the 'balance' of interest and influence which had been established with approximate effectiveness in the years just preceding 1900 when each of five foreign Powers had more or less clearly delimited the area which it regarded as henceforth to be its 'sphere of interest'.

It amounted, practically considered, to a formal international confirmation of the 'spheres of interest' conception, giving to the Shantung type of 'sphere' the benefit of general (or at least European) conventional recognition.

It shook the confidence of the Chinese in the benevolent professions of the Western Powers.

It occasioned immediately in China a widespread boycott of Japanese goods and business.

It strengthened the position among their own people of the Japanese 'militarist' leaders, constituting as it did a crowning vindication, in terms of successful achievement, of the policy which those leaders had pursued; and it strengthened throughout the Orient the impression of Japan's military and diplomatic irresistibility.

It did more probably than did any other one thing in the Treaty to create among the American people distrust of the work of the Paris Conference; it certainly contributed very substantially to the argument and sum total of considerations which led to America's refusal to ratify the Treaty.

It injected new complications into the problem, first, of Chinese-Japanese relations, and second, of Occidental-Oriental contact.[1]

[1] For the further development of the Shantung question *v.* next page.

Editor's Note on the Shantung Treaty (4th February 1922).

Articles 156–8 of the Treaty of Versailles, relating to Shantung, are quoted in full in the text, pp. 382–3, and also in Vol. III, pp. 186–7. At the Washington Conference 'a Treaty for the settlement of outstanding questions relative to Shantung' was signed between China and Japan on the 4th February 1922. This treaty contained provisions for Japan restoring to China the former German-leased territory of Kiaochow (Art. 1), the transfer of the administration of the former German-leased territory and of public property in that territory by Japan to China (Arts. 2–8), for the withdrawal of Japanese troops (Arts. 9–11) from the territory, for the transfer to China of the Tsing-tao–Tsinanfu Railway (Arts. 14–20).

Various other articles and an annex provided generally for the opening of the Kiaochow territory and for the renunciation of preferential rights by Japan.

On the 2nd June 1922 ratifications were exchanged of the Shantung Treaty by China and Japan. By that time the Japanese troops had finally evacuated the territory in Shantung. They had evacuated Hankow (31st May), promised to withdraw from Siberia (24th June), actually withdrew at the end of 1922, and made great reductions in their army.

In addition to the Shantung Treaty signed between China and Japan, a treaty was signed on the 6th February 1922 between the United States, Belgium, British Empire, China, France, Italy and Japan, the Netherlands and Portugal, 'relating to principles and policies to be followed in matters concerning China'. A treaty between the same Powers was signed on the same day 'relating to the Chinese Customs Tariff'. In addition a number of Resolutions regarding Far Eastern Questions (3), Extra-territoriality in China (4), Foreign Postal Agencies in China (5), Armed forces in China (6), Radio stations in China (7), Unification of Railways in China (8), Reduction of Chinese Military Forces (9), Existing commitments of China or with respect to China (10), and regarding Chinese Eastern Railway (11–12) were passed by the United States, British Empire, France, Italy, and Japan. All had for their general purpose the maintenance of the territorial integrity of China and the preservation of equal opportunities of commerce to all nations.[1]

[1] The Prince Regent of Japan ratified all these arrangements on the 5th August 1922. For the text of the Shantung Treaty, for the Treaty of the 4th February 1922, and the Resolutions, *v. Bulletin of Amer. Assoc. for International Conciliation*, No. 172, March 1922, pp. 89–116, 133–45.

CHAPTER V

THE ATTITUDE OF THE UNITED STATES SENATE TOWARDS THE VERSAILLES TREATY: 1918–20

Introductory. Excepting the House of Lords, the American Senate is the oldest upper chamber in existence. Starting in 1789, with a membership then of twenty-two men representing eleven communities all east of the Mississippi River, it is to-day a body of ninety-six members from the forty-eight states which stretch from the Atlantic seaboard 3,000 miles westward to the Pacific Ocean, and southwards, from the Great Lakes and Canada to the Gulf of Mexico and old Mexico, some 1,500 miles. Its members are chosen for six years, but a third of its membership is changed every two years, and usually to some extent its political colour. Originally and for upwards of a century Senators were chosen by the legislatures of the states, but since 1913, in accordance with the seventeenth amendment to the Constitution, they have been chosen by popular vote. This comparatively recent amendment affects neither the powers nor the essential attributes of the Senate—it marks a change in the mechanism of election. To some extent already it has brought in younger and less experienced men than formerly, but it has interfered in no marked way with old traditions or modified the common belief that the Senate is our most dignified political body, wisely conservative and yet in closer touch than ever before with popular wishes and demands. The Senate reveals much of that genius for politics which Walter Bagehot thought so peculiarly characteristic of Americans, and shows moderation in action notwithstanding the superficial and often violent aspects of its oratory. One seldom fails, in following closely its proceedings, to observe an underlying regard for law and high respect for the Constitution.

1. *President and Senate as Factors in Treaty-Making.* In dealing with foreign nations the President of the United States represents in theory his country: in the absence of anyone equivalent to a prime minister, he is its chief official and spokes-

man. But it should be noted also that the Senate shares with the President the executive function in the power of making treaties. It is a co-ordinate factor, for, as the Constitution declares, the President

'shall have power, by and with the advice and consent of the Senate, to make treaties, provided two-thirds of the Senators present concur'.

It has been disputed as to whether during the negotiation of a treaty the Senate has any right to interfere or to communicate to the chief executive its views. The better opinion is that it has no right to interfere. There is, however, no doubt that Presidents from Washington's day onwards have occasionally consulted the Senate informally before negotiating treaties: at times they have sought the Senate's judgment, or that of individual Senators, as to whether negotiations should or should not be undertaken. That President Wilson was familiar with the practice is clear from his own words written many years ago—in 1908. 'The Senate', he remarked, with a backward glance at history, 'has shown itself particularly stiff and jealous in insisting upon exercising an independent judgment upon foreign affairs.' A wise President, finding the Senate 'stiff and offish' towards his policy, may himself act, according to Mr. Wilson,

'in the true spirit of the Constitution and establish intimate relations of confidence with the Senate on his own initiative, not carrying his plans to completion and then laying them in final form before the Senate to be accepted or rejected, but keeping himself in confidential communication with the leaders of the Senate while his plans are in course, when their advice will be of service to him and his information of the greatest service to them, in order that there may be veritable counsel and a real accommodation of views instead of a final challenge and contest. The policy which has made rivals of the President and Senate has shown itself in the President as often as in the Senate. . . .'[1]

The practice here brought into view reveals the mode by means of which flexibility and vital interrelations can be brought about in a government which was originally planned on the theory of rather a strict separation of powers.

2. *President Wilson's Appeal for Partisan Aid, 25th October 1918.* In the latter part of October 1918, rather more than a fortnight before the terms of the armistice were signed,

[1] Woodrow Wilson, *Constitutional Government in the United States* (N. Y., 1908), pp. 139–40.

Mr. Wilson issued an appeal addressed to his fellow-countrymen. It was not, as it might have been, an appeal to the voters of America irrespective of party affiliations to put the best possible men into Congress ; on the contrary it was a plea made avowedly to increase the Democratic majority in both Senate and House. These were his words :

> 'The congressional elections are at hand. . . . If you have approved of my leadership and wish me to continue to be your unembarrassed spokesman in affairs at home and abroad, I earnestly beg that you will express yourselves unmistakably to that effect by returning a Democratic majority to both the Senate and the House. . . .'

A Republican majority, he urged, would certainly be interpreted abroad as a repudiation of his leadership. He made the plea, he declared, neither for himself nor for his party ; it was done solely on behalf of the nation itself in order that the nation's 'inward unity of purpose' might be evident to all the world.[1]

The President's appeal was not without precedent. But it was widely felt that it might better have come from some party leader than from him. At the moment he had reached the acme of his position and was acclaimed throughout the world as the one leader who had, through a series of state papers and public addresses of marked ability, crystallized clearly the best thought of the struggling nations in their yearnings for a peace that should be based on justice and right. Neither political friends nor opponents in America could forget his clear-cut utterances of the previous May when he said :

> 'Politics is adjourned. The elections will go to those who think least of it ; to those who go to the constituencies . . . with a plain record of duty faithfully and disinterestedly performed. . . . The great days have come when the only thing they [i. e. the people] ask for or admire is duty greatly and adequately done. . . .'[2]

Discussion of the appeal was widespread and vigorous. Indeed, reference to it cropped up in the Senate debates at intervals from 1918 to 1920 over the Versailles Treaty, for it made a lasting impression.

3. *The Republican Response of the 25th October 1918.* There had been in inner party circles for several months before the appeal was issued a suspicion of some such design on the

[1] *Washington Post*, Saturday, 26th October 1918.
[2] *Congressional Record*, 65 Cong., 2 Sess. (27th May 1918), *v.* LVI, 7115.

part of the President. Republican opponents were consequently prompt in issuing a counter reply which was published almost contemporaneously. This reply was stimulated by ex-President Roosevelt's clear and public pronouncement against Mr. Wilson's series of diplomatic notes to Germany, for Roosevelt had for some time been eager for a peace based upon unconditional surrender. 'Let us dictate peace', said the ex-President, 'by the hammering gun and not chat about peace to the accompaniment of the clicking of typewriters.'[1] The counter reply called attention to Mr. Wilson's plea for Democrats irrespective of their quality. It was intimated that he would thus favour the election in Michigan of Henry Ford, the well-known pacifist, and the retention as Speaker in the House of Representatives of Champ Clark who had declared that 'there is precious little difference between a conscript and a convict'.[2] It promised that a Republican Congress would not be guilty of fixing the price of western wheat and leaving the southern planter's cotton untouched—a direct reference to Democratic partisan legislation for the benefit of the south; and it concluded with the sentiment, familiar, it assumed, to all the world, that the Republican party was opposed to diplomatic notes and would demand of the hostile armies unconditional surrender.[3]

Had not the President made a serious tactical blunder in issuing his partisan appeal? It would seem so, for the November elections resulted in a slight but controlling majority of Republicans in the Senate, raising their number from 47 to 51, and of the new members three were men from the middle western states who displaced Democratic opponents. In other words, the Democrats could reckon on simple issues, on only about forty votes after the close, on the 4th March, three months later, of the sixty-fifth Congress. The November elections were unmistakable evidence of a slight change in the party balance of power and correspondingly of public sentiment toward President Wilson and his following. In brief, the Democrats had lost control of the body which must

[1] Extract from telegram of Roosevelt, sent in triplicate, 24th October, to Senators Lodge, Poindexter, and Hiram Johnson, from Oyster Bay. Four days later (28th October), Mr. Roosevelt, in the course of an address at Carnegie Hall, New York City, on 'What Wilson did and Lincoln didn't', repeated this same sentiment to a large audience. Cp. an utterance reported in *The Times* of the 5th December 1918, quoted in Vol. I, p. 198 n.

[2] 25th April 1917. [3] *Washington Post*, 26th October 1918.

pass final judgment on anything in the shape of a treaty that Mr. Wilson might negotiate.

4. *Senate Opposition: December 1918 to 4th March 1919.* When President Wilson sailed out of New York harbour on that fateful Wednesday, the 4th December 1918, bound for France, he went as the spokesman of his country and with clear knowledge on his part that his negotiations, if resulting in a treaty, must pass finally the test of careful review by the Senate before becoming law. While there were expressions both in and outside the Senate of opposition to his departure for foreign shores, it was understood by the wiser portion of the Senate that President Wilson, in deciding to go to France for the purpose of entering upon negotiations, was entitled to exercise his judgment free from the interference of the Senate. The simple truth was well expressed by the Republican ex-President Taft when he said:

> 'There is no constitutional inhibition, express or implied, to prevent the President's going abroad to discharge a function clearly given him by the Constitution.' [1]

Addressing the Congress on the 2nd December, President Wilson spoke his final word before his departure. He was acting in accordance, he said, with his paramount duty to assist the Allied and Central Powers who had accepted the 'Fourteen Points' to interpret and apply them to the situation created by the armistice conditions as determined on the previous 11th November. 'You will', he remarked, 'know all that I do'; and he added hopefully: 'I shall count upon your friendly countenance and encouragement. . . .'

There was immediate evidence of dissatisfaction with the President in the Senate: a good deal of captious criticism was indulged in. What did the President intend to do when he reached Paris? It was assumed that his plans had been for some time 'in course', yet little enough regarding them had been clearly or definitely divulged. A considerable portion of the Senate, friends as well as enemies, was dissatisfied. The President's most voluble, if not his chief spokesman, Senator James H. Lewis of Illinois, the party whip, sounded loud and prolonged but uninforming notes about the President's designs; Senator Hitchcock of Nebraska, Democratic chairman of the

[1] *Washington Post*, 5th December 1918.

Foreign Relations Committee, not wholly sympathetic with Wilson's projects (it was believed), proved neither a strong nor an effective debater. Hence it was easy for the Republican leaders—such tried men as Senators Lodge, Knox, and Borah—to take prompt advantage of the situation and to attack vigorously the general ideal of a League of Nations on which Mr. Wilson had been dwelling for many months. Outside the Senate, Wilson had conspicuously strong defenders in the membership of the League to Enforce Peace, an organization founded in 1915, and notably in ex-President Taft who, although a Republican, rose high above partisan bias and was eager to give to President Wilson the benefits of such doubts as were easily suggested by men of a less liberal mould.

Early in December it was proposed that a committee of eight Senators, four from each party, should be dispatched to Paris, there to make itself familiar with conditions and circumstances, and to report frequently back to the Senate, making a final report 'at or before the time that the treaties growing out of the Conference are laid before the Senate for approval, rejection, or modification'.[1] Senator Pittman of Nevada, a Democrat, in a cynical mood, offered as a substitute, the suggestion that the entire body of ninety-six Senators transfer themselves to Paris to watch and wait! But the plan of a Senatorial Committee, reported upon unfavourably by the Committee on Foreign Relations, was quickly dropped.

Until the 15th February, the day after the text of the Covenant as then agreed upon in Paris had been cabled to the United States, the debates were partly concerned with vague and rather general projects for a League. It became, however, quickly clear that a large group of Senators influenced by two Republican Senators, Henry Cabot Lodge and Philander C. Knox—men very familiar with the history of foreign policy—favoured first of all a treaty of peace. As quickly as possible let there be the completion of a definite settlement. Let it be made as severe as possible—in consonance with the 'un-

[1] The narrative of this chapter, largely the result of a study of speeches and debates in the Senate, is, unless otherwise indicated, dependent for direct quotations on the language found in the *Congressional Record*, Vols. LVII–LIX, extending from 2nd December 1918, through 19th March 1920. Divided into successive 'Parts' and 'Appendices', there are actually eighteen volumes of printed matter.

conditional surrender' ideal long since enunciated by Roosevelt and men of his mind. From the 15th February to the close of the session on the 4th March the Senate had the text of the Covenant to conjure with; and the discussions were somewhat better defined, developing along the line of the covenant theme.

5. *Glimpses of the Ideal of a League of Nations: 1910–18.* The ideal of a League of Nations was, as Senator Kellogg of Minnesota pointed out on the 4th December, 'an ancient and honourable subject', one that had been discussed for a long time by publicists and journalists in the United States and abroad.[1] As far back as May 1910, ex-President Roosevelt in his Nobel Prize lecture at Christiania had advocated a League of Nations.[2] Senator Lodge, giving the commencement address at Union College in Schenectady, N. Y. on the 9th June 1915, had favoured a League.[3] President Wilson, addressing the first annual gathering of the League to Enforce Peace at Washington, D. C. on Saturday night, the 27th May 1916, announced in no doubtful fashion his adherence to the ideal of a League.[4] And Senator Lodge on the same occasion went so far as to say

> 'I think the next step is that which this League proposes, and that is to put behind international peace an international league or agreement or tribunal for force. We may not solve it in that way, but if we cannot, it can be solved in no other. . . .'[5]

[1] 'As far as I am able to judge, the consensus of public opinion among the allied nations to-day is in favour of the general principles of a League of Nations to prevent war.' *Cong. Record*, LVII, 76.

[2] See 'International Peace', esp. pp. 81–3, in Roosevelt's *African and European Addresses* (N. Y. and London, 1910).

[3] 'It may seem Utopian at this moment to suggest a union of civilized nations in order to put a controlling force behind the maintenance of peace and international order; but it is through the aspiration for perfection, through the search for Utopias, that the real advances have been made. At all events it is along this path that we must travel. . . .' p. 6. This address, entitled 'Maintenance of Peace', was printed in March 1919, as *Senate Document*, No. 443 (65 Cong., 3 sess.)

[4] Printed in the *Record* on 29th May 1916, LIII, 8854.

[5] Text as printed on Sunday, 28th May, in the *Washington Post*. In the official *Proceedings* of the League, printed later, it was slightly altered, reading: 'I think the next step . . . is to put force behind international peace', &c. Dr. George Sarton translated the volume under the title *Ligue pour Imposer la Paix* (December 1916). The Lodge sentiment read: 'Je crois que nous devons faire ce que cette Ligue propose, notamment d'appuyer la paix internationale sur une ligue ou un accord international, sur un tribunal de paix, en dernier ressort sur la force.' p. 56. [It is rather important that Wilson in his speech on this occasion excluded all reference to force (*v.* Chap. VI, p. 429), so that at this moment Lodge advocated force and Wilson did not.—*Ed. note.*]

An address by Associate Justice John H. Clarke of the Supreme Court was printed in the *Congressional Record*,[1] showing how strong for a League of Nations could be a highly trained legal expert. Admitting the difficulties of its adjustment to our government, Justice Clarke was nevertheless certain that there existed no constitutional objection to the United States joining a carefully designed League of Nations. 'Unless the league shall utterly fail of its purpose,' he declared, 'membership in it will involve a covenant on our part to join the honourable nations of the world to protect ourselves and them from nations which are predatory and false . . . it is the part of prudence, if we must make war, to make it for a just cause and in the company of honest nations.'

6. *The Treaty Ideal.* The November armistice was succeeded in the United States by a 'slump in idealism', and the Senate reflected this situation. The Republican Senators, under the leadership of such veteran statesmen as Lodge and Knox, were extremely cautious in their attitude towards a possible League. Why, urged Knox, had not the President taken steps long since to act upon authorization, given him by Congress as far back as the 29th August 1916, to invite all the great governments of the world to send representatives to a conference which should be charged with the duty of formulating a plan for a court of arbitration or other tribunal to which disputed questions between nations should be reported for adjudication and peaceful settlement?[2] The query remained unanswered. But it became clear that Knox wanted a prompt settlement by treaty distinct from any league.

On the 21st December, Senator Lodge outlined what he conceived to be the essentials of a constructive peace treaty with Germany. He was careful in conclusion to point out numerous subjects, such, for examples, as the practices of secret diplomacy, reduction of national armaments, the illusive subject of freedom of the seas, and in particular the problems

[1] LVII, 2344–7. Address delivered in August 1918, before the American Bar Association. Justice Clarke resigned from the Supreme Court in September 1922, and has since given much time to the advocacy of a League of Nations of which the United States shall be a member.

[2] The statute permitted the President 'to appoint nine citizens of the United States who in his judgment shall be qualified for the position by eminence in the law and in devotion to the cause of peace to be representatives of the United States in such a conference'. A sum of $200,000 was granted for the objects involved. U.S. *Statutes at Large*, XXXIX, Part I, 618.

associated with any effective League of Nations, all of which in his judgment should be postponed for the sake of that prolonged and studied attention requisite to the solution, or at least to the better understanding, of these difficult themes. As to a League, this was his final thought:

'The attempt to attach provisions for an effective League of Nations to the treaty of peace now making with Germany would be to launch the nations who have been fighting Germany on a sea of boundless discussion.'

In January, advocates of the League ideal in support of Wilson began to be heard in the Senate. The President's addresses abroad, quoted in the American newspapers, were bringing his projects in a clearer way before the country. Senator Porter J. McCumber of North Dakota, a Republican with twenty years' experience in the Senate and a representative citizen of the north-west, spoke out thoughtfully and definitely for Wilson's projected League ideal; and Senator Walsh of Montana, a much newer man, exceptionally discerning on legal points, was hardly less clearly for it.

After the 15th February, criticism was directed to the newly formulated text of the Covenant. A confidential dinner and meeting at the White House on the night of the 26th February, soon after President Wilson's arrival, between the President and the Foreign Relations Committee of the Senate and the Foreign Affairs Committee of the House—a gathering summoned by the President by cable from Paris—marked the first real opportunity for a small group of Senators and Representatives to obtain from the President a direct account of the Paris Conference together with first-hand knowledge of his designs. Rumours about it appeared the next morning in the newspapers, but even to-day there is no authoritative record of its colloquies in print.[1] On the last day of the month Senator Lodge once more devoted himself to a careful discussion, this time based on the definite information provided by the White House Conference and the text of the Covenant. While advocating peace with Germany first and a League at some later

[1] See *New York Times*, Thursday, 27th February 1919, for detailed story. Senators Borah and Fall, of New Mexico, and one Representative were not present. About thirty-four members of both Houses attended the dinner. The speech of Wilson, 14th February, in presenting the first draft of the Covenant is given in Vol. III, pp. 60–5, the texts of the Draft Covenant and that finally adopted are given in this volume, App. I.

time, he revealed only slight rancour and seemed inclined to fairness. His main thought was devoted to the necessity of preserving the best American traditions—matters already touched upon by numerous other Senators, mostly Republicans, since December. And these traditions, viewed as peculiarly precious to the United States, were: the avoidance of 'entangling alliances' which Washington and Jefferson had laid stress upon; the Monroe doctrine, a corollary to Washington's policy, and the importance of not surrendering any portion of our sovereignty until at any rate we knew exactly what we were doing. He was doubtful of the import of mandatories, and felt strongly that Article 10—the guaranteeing of territorial integrity and political independence to every member of the League—was likely to involve the United States in questionable if not dangerous complications in the future. On the 1st March, the next day, Senator Knox argued in a similar but somewhat more technical vein: the Covenant was likely to threaten our independence and might actually destroy our sovereignty. As for abolishing war, in the opinion of Senator Knox the League plan 'actually sanctions, breeds, and commands it'.

7. *Senator William E. Borah of Idaho.* One of the most conspicuous opponents of the League ideal at this period, and indeed throughout the months ahead—consistently against the President's ideals and plans, staunch and daring in his expressions of his views, but thoughtful and industrious in studying whatever threw light along the way—was Senator Borah of Idaho, a Republican of an irreconcilable type. Respected by his opponents, he seldom permitted much that was essentially personal or merely partisan to enter into his thought. He wanted peace with Germany and the other warring nations. In a League of Nations he had not the slightest faith. His position was thus free from complications; he appeared to be satisfied with his country's past and on that past he based his vision of its future.

8. *The Republican 'Round Robin', 4th March 1919.* On the 4th March, the closing day of the sixty-fifth Congress, Senator Lodge slipped somewhat suddenly into the *Record* [1]

[1] LVII, 4974. The names of two additional Senators made the signatories number finally thirty-nine. Reed of Missouri, a Democrat, was wholly in accord with the Republican group.

a resolution signed by thirty-seven Republican Senators, a few of them as yet only Senators elect, which has often since then been referred to as the ' round robin '. It was never acted upon—all Senators on the closing day being chiefly eager to conclude business and to depart for home—but its aim was accomplished by the mere fact of its appearance in print. The ' round robin ' was designed to clinch a point of view already familiar through Senator Knox's advocacy of it in the preceding December, for it provided the strict Republicans in the following session of Congress with a fundamental feature of policy which, in Mr. Lodge's eyes and those of his thirty-eight followers, was worth struggling for. Would the entire Republican cohort and possibly a few wavering Democrats follow this rather shrewdly devised lead ?

Assuming that he was privileged thus to express what the resolution stated as the Senate's ' constitutional duty of advice in regard to treaties ', Senator Lodge declared :

' that the negotiations on the part of the United States should immediately be directed to the utmost expedition of the urgent business of negotiating peace terms with Germany . . . and that the proposal for a League of Nations to insure the permanent peace of the world should be then taken up for careful and serious consideration.'

And furthermore :

' the constitution of the League of Nations in the form now proposed to the Peace Conference should not be accepted by the United States . . . '

The names of Lodge and Knox headed the list of signers, followed, among others, by such names as Harding of Ohio, Borah of Idaho, Lenroot of Wisconsin, and Johnson of California. It was clearly an attempt on the part of a special group in the Senate to interfere in the treaty-making process of negotiation, a function belonging solely to the President.

9. *The President returns to France : 5th–13th March 1919.* On Wednesday morning, the 5th March, Mr. Wilson left New York after a busy ten days in the United States. He must have been well informed regarding the rising tide of Republican opposition. The ' round robin ' could only exasperate any man in his position. The night preceding his departure, the 4th March, he addressed a great gathering in the Metropolitan Opera House in New York City, and with a touch of bitterness he reminded his hearers that when finally he returned to

America with a matured treaty, that document would contain not only the Covenant, but

'so many threads of the Treaty tied to the Covenant that you cannot dissect the Covenant from the Treaty without destroying the whole vital structure. The structure of peace will not be vital without the League of Nations, and no man is going to bring back a *cadaver* (corpse) with him'.

By means of a few speeches, interviews with Senators and Representatives, and a conference with Democratic national committeemen,[1] Mr. Wilson had made it clear that, in his judgment and that of his co-workers at Paris, a treaty of peace, to be truly effective and to reduce in future the probability of war, must be based upon a Covenant or general League agreement.

On the other hand, Mr. Wilson had discovered that many of his countrymen, irrespective of partisanship, were disturbed over the absence in the Covenant of definite provisions regarding at least four matters: (i) the failure expressly to recognize the Monroe doctrine as an American policy; (ii) apparent lack of any provision against permitting the League to act or to pass judgment on subjects of purely domestic concern; (iii) no clear and simple expression of the right of withdrawing; and (iv) absence of recognition of the right of Congress to have the final word or decision on such subjects, fundamental to the nation's safety, as peace and war. That he was impressed by these failures or omissions is well enough known, for the first revision of the Covenant recognized the reasonableness of them by making amends.[2] There was a widespread impression that the President had developed his projects over a short period of time and among a group of advisers in the nature of a council of oligarchs. The story of the making of the Covenant he had failed to make clear to his people. Some of his many critics were inclined to believe that it had come forth as a plan largely moulded by a few British publicists, if indeed, so far as its details were concerned, it had not been chiefly conceived by them. In any event, the dim outlines of a struggle were assuming some degree of definiteness at home.

10. *Interim (4th March–19th May) between the Sixty-fifth*

[1] See Joseph Tumulty, *Woodrow Wilson as I Know Him* (1921), 332 ff., 367–79.

[2] The text of the Covenant as adopted at the Plenary Session of the 14th February, in Paris, may be seen contrasted with that of the Final Covenant, this volume, App. I.

and Sixty-sixth Congresses. These days were filled with preparations by both political parties; and the daily atmosphere in America was alive with impressions or intimations of the grave problems and circumstances then being faced in France by the Council of three or four leaders which reacted upon our politics. Some of these problems were the troublesome Italian situation associated with Fiume and the Dalmatian coast, the question of the settlement of Shantung, the circumstances of the coming of the German emissaries to Versailles, of the presentation to them on the 7th May of the Pact, and of their crudely expressed hostility to it, with later reflections on its failure to conform in many respects to President Wilson's 'Fourteen Points' and the terms of the November armistice. There was in the United States an almost constant clash of opinion between partisans; and political leaders attempted to rally the public to one side of the issue or the other. Generally speaking, the straight Republicans wanted peace; the Democrats wanted a League of Nations based upon a Covenant. But already shades of difference were making themselves evident preparatory to the Senate struggle. Taft and Wickersham, outside the Senate and both of them Republicans, were with the Democrats for a League. So was the Republican Senator McCumber of North Dakota. On the other hand several Democratic Senators were ready to oppose Wilson at most points.

In the country at large there was not a little opposition to a League. This opposition asserted itself clearly along three or four different lines. There was the ancient prejudice to American participation in European affairs, the heritage of Washington, Jefferson, and Monroe, based to a large extent on widespread ignorance, regretfully common in the United States, of European conditions. Again, there was genuine fear lest the country should become involved in wars and squabbles arising in distant countries. There was some doubt expressed over President Wilson attempting to speak—as he often appeared to do—for one hundred millions of his fellow countrymen. 'If one man can express the mind and will of this nation,' asked a capable lawyer of Philadelphia, 'why do we have a Congress and a Supreme Court?'[1] But probably the

[1] George Wharton Pepper, now Republican Senator from Pennsylvania. *Cong. Record*, LVIII, 2579–81. Address of the 14th June 1919, before the N. J. Bar Association.

larger portion of articulate opposition rested upon the fact that Woodrow Wilson could arouse little popular sentiment of affection. Men might and often did respect and admire him, but they did not love him.

President Wilson was a man without intimates beyond a small circle. His cabinet advisers appeared not to be a very harmonious group, and at any rate were in no sense the President's intimates. His choice of commissioners to aid him at Paris startled the country and was criticized from the beginning. Secretary Lansing was of course a proper person to be selected for the peace mission; but how much had he had already to do with its work? Nobody knew or was to know until he appeared in August before the Senate Committee on Foreign Relations. Mr. House remained a man of mystery. Henry White, a Republican ex-diplomat, was regarded as one who had not been true to strict Republican traditions. The legal expert, David Hunter Miller, was a man of minor distinction in his profession; indeed, his familiarity with international problems had been of very brief duration. For a short while he had held a subordinate place in the State Department. The group of some thirteen hundred aides and experts composed of many intelligent and useful men had been gathered together, nobody knew quite how or when, and worked industriously; but they neither sought nor gained much publicity in their efforts on the President's behalf.

When the sixty-sixth Congress was assembled on the 19th May with a clear Republican majority in Senate and House,[1] there was still an opportunity for Wilson to win the great cause on which his heart was avowedly set. The country was a unit in desiring peace. It was a safe guess at that time

[1] The November 1918 elections had reduced the number of Democratic Senators from 51 to 47; the Republicans, on the other hand, gained 4 Senators, and could thus reckon on 49 members at the opening of the sixty-sixth Congress in May 1919. In the House of Representatives the Republicans numbered 237 as against 191 Democrats. It may be asserted confidently that domestic rather than foreign policy had altered the party balance. Labour was friendly to Wilson and his party. The industrial centres of such states as New York, New Jersey, and Pennsylvania revealed this fact. On the other hand Agriculture, represented by the farming communities of the north and west, had become hostile. Of 37 votes gained by the Republicans from the Democrats, 27 came from the west. To my friend, Mr. Allen R. Boyd of Washington, D.C., I owe thanks for studying out this situation, and stimulating me at various places in this chapter. For statistics, see *Congressional Directory*, 65 Cong., 3 sess., 2nd ed., January 1919. *Ibid.*, 66 Cong., 1 sess., July 1919.

that the opponents of the Covenant would seek to separate it from the body of the Treaty. On the other hand the President was sure to make their efforts difficult if not fruitless by bringing back a treaty so involved with the Covenant that the two sections could not be disentangled without dooming the instrument to destruction. The League ideal had influential friends throughout the country—as an ideal it had gained extensive, if rather vague and sentimental approval. Mr. Wilson's success or failure, many thought, would depend chiefly upon his skill in playing his game, and in particular on his ability to arouse in his favour the more or less inarticulate multitude which, in a democracy such as the United States, must always remain something of an unknown quantity. But in any event he must somehow win the Senate, at least 64 nembers of the body,[1] in order to secure the two-thirds vote necessary to ratify the Treaty. Could he do so ?

11. *First Phase of Organized Opposition: 19th May–10th July.* This phase was concluded with the presentation to the Senate by the President of the final official text of the Treaty on the 10th July. Mr. Wilson had cabled to Senator Hitchcock news of the signing of the Treaty the preceding 28th June, and then referred to it as a ' charter for a new order of affairs in the world. . . . '[2] But as early as the 9th June an unofficial text of the Treaty as originally presented to the Germans at Versailles on the 7th May had reached the Senate in a roundabout way, and through Senator Borah's efforts had been printed for senatorial use.[3] This unforeseen incident may have quickened the zeal of Senator Knox to introduce on the 10th June his resolution advocating the distinct separation of Covenant and Treaty in accordance with the well-known ideal of the ' round robin ' of the previous 4th March.[4] While it must have been understood at the time that any serious attempt to disentangle League from Treaty would mean the doom of the instrument, the Republican and anti-administration forces were already displaying bitter and partisan motives toward their minority adversaries, and sought the opportunity

In the ratification of any treaty the Constitution calls for a vote of a two-thirds majority ' of the Senators present '. The number ' 64 ' assumes of course a full Senate of 96, such as is seldom gathered even on crucial issues.

[2] *Cong. Record*, LVIII, 1952–3.

[3] *Ibid.*, 558 ff., 635, 674 ff., 733 ff., 780 ff., 802–57 (text of 440 articles)

[4] *Ibid.*, 894.

afforded by the Knox resolution to obstruct and to arouse prejudice against the President's definite plan.

Senator Lodge, chairman of the newly organized Committee on Foreign Relations, was the leader of the Republicans in the Senate. He had consulted his forces carefully before the Sixty-sixth Congress assembled,[1] hoping to assure himself and his colleagues of a strong and consistent opposition to the minority which was led by Senator Hitchcock. At the outset of the session there was much criticism of the administration over the failure on the part of the President to keep the Senate and the public informed of the course of discussions or developments in Paris—criticism, be it said, which had some degree of justification in view of Wilson's avowed and printed promises, summarized in his statement of the previous December that 'You will know all that I do'. Misinterpretations of the text of the February form of the Covenant were indulged in by various illiberal men in the Republican group. And Hitchcock and his following had much to do in trying to keep before the Senate and the outside public what they conceived to be the truth.

12. *Ex-Senator Root's Letters*. On the 23rd June Senator Lodge injected into the situation two letters written by ex-Senator Root, one of the ablest minds in the country and a man thoroughly familiar with international problems and their history. One cannot escape the impression that these letters were introduced for partisan purposes, although they were written by Mr. Root, himself a Republican, in no partisan spirit.[2] There were passages in both letters which, selected

[1] On Sunday afternoon, 27th April, the Acting Secretary of State (Polk) had given to the press the revised and final text of the Covenant. It appeared in full in many newspapers the next morning, Monday, 28th April, the day of its adoption at Paris. On Tuesday, 29th April, confident that Congress must soon be assembled, Senators Lodge and Curtis (the latter Republican whip) sent out telegrams to their senatorial colleagues requesting Republican Senators 'to reserve expressions of opinion respecting the amended League Covenant' until it could be studied and until a party conference or caucus on it could be held. For brief summary and comment, see the *New York Commercial and Financial Chronicle*, Saturday, 3rd May 1919, Vol. 108, p. 1,793; for Text, *v*. App. I.

[2] *Cong. Record*, LVIII, 1546–50. The first letter, dated 29th March 1919, had been written by Mr. Root to Will H. Hays, chairman at that time of the Republican National Committee. The second letter of 19th June was addressed to Senator Lodge. Both letters concerned the topic very vital to Americans—our attitude to the proposed Covenant—and afforded political material likely to be not merely informing, but influential.

clear of their context, would furnish excellent and telling material against Mr. Wilson's work in Paris and particularly against the text of the Covenant. These letters cannot be overlooked by any historian desirous of discovering the reasonable position at the time of many citizens opposed, but in no hostile spirit, to the League. Into the essence of the Covenant, especially in its larger bearings, they afforded insight; and they pointed to several weaknesses regarded by many Americans as fundamental. Mr. Root was not opposed to the establishment or the maintenance of a League of Nations that could be efficiently arranged. But clearly the proposed Covenant revealed to him several unsatisfactory features. Among other matters, he disapproved of Article X; he wished to have any League duly recognize and make use of the Permanent Court of Arbitration long since established at the Hague; he was in favour of international conferences at regular intervals, such conferences to state in authoritative form the prevailing principles and rules of international law; and he was opposed to the interpretation by any League of what he regarded as an essentially American policy, the Monroe doctrine.

Underlying much loose and partisan debate there were intimations, as the time for President Wilson's return to America approached, directed toward giving fair play to the President and awaiting the presentation of the official Pact to the Senate. The Knox resolution was lost. And thus a Republican and anti-Wilson effort of long standing failed. In other words, the Wilson programme won its first Senate victory. This victory was due in some measure to the skill and convictions of a few men, all outstanding figures at the time: Senator Hitchcock, leader of the Democratic minority group; Senator Walsh of Montana, a sane lawyer and earnestly bent on understanding the details of the Treaty; Senator Porter J. McCumber of North Dakota, a Republican willing for the sake of conviction in favour of the President's plan to ignore or at least to minimize partisan feelings; and Senator John Sharp Williams of Mississippi, a man liberally endowed with talent, courage, and wit. 'I do not belong', said Senator Williams,

'to the class of legalists who can see nothing in the present and hope for nothing in the future except as based upon precedent in the past. I belong to that class of men who dream . . . of a better world and want it, and, in so far as they are worthy to pray to God at all, pray to Him for it, a world . . . where nations shall govern themselves, and where . . . humanity all over the world shall govern itself by common concert of action and common accord between nations in behalf of the right and justice and peace'.[1]

13. *The Second Phase: 10th July–15th September.* On the 14th July, four days after the President had submitted the official text of the Treaty to the Senate, it was placed in printed form in the hands of the seventeen Senators—ten Republicans and seven Democrats—who constituted the Senate Committee on Foreign Relations, with Senator Lodge as chairman. The Committee was to examine it critically and, if they saw fit, to report it back to the Senate, as they did on the following 10th September. Committee hearings open to the public began on the 31st July and continued with only occasional interruptions through the 12th September. By that time a large mass of evidence had been extracted from about sixty witnesses which, when compiled and printed, formed a volume of 1,297 pages.[2]

14. *Senate Committee's Hearings.* Witnesses were as a rule summoned, although a few appeared by their own request—all of them American citizens and representatives of many nationalities. A good many had acted in official or unofficial capacities at Paris during the peace proceedings—such as the Secretary of State, Robert Lansing, Bernard M. Baruch, economic adviser, David Hunter Miller, legal expert, Thomas F. F. Millard, unofficial adviser to the Chinese delegation, and W. C. Bullitt, member of the staff of the Peace Commission. There were others summoned somewhat at random, but representing a variety of citizens more or less familiar with matters regarding which information was sought. The information was at times exceedingly valuable; but there was evidence strongly indicative of prejudice and of not a little ignorance on the part of witnesses. Included in the hearings was the result of the important interview between the Committee and President Wilson at the White House on the 19th August.

Quite the most significant and influential materials for the

[1] *Cong. Record*, LVIII, 798 (9th June). See also his vigorous characterizations of Senators Lodge and Borah in this same connexion. *Ibid.*, (796 ff.)

[2] *Treaty of Peace with Germany: Hearings before the Committee on Foreign Relations, United States Senate.* Sixty-sixth Congress, First Session . . . Washington, 1919. Senate Document No. 106.

Committee's conclusions came from the President, from Secretary Lansing, from several witnesses on the Shantung settlement, and finally from Mr. Bullitt, although in Bullitt's case the evidence came too late for use in the Committee's report. It was made clear that a large body of Irish-Americans in the United States were irreconcilably opposed to a League, regarded as tainted with British influence, and likely to take no interest in the well-known and perennial Irish claim for complete independence of Ireland from the British Empire's sway and direction.

Frequent questions were directed toward the story in its details of the mode by which Covenant and Treaty had been made. And in this connexion some members of the Committee must occasionally have turned back in thought to the Convention of 1787, when one hundred and thirty-two years earlier a comparatively small group of Americans had spent four months debating over plans for a Constitution and brought forth a slight document which can be read through aloud in less than half an hour. Here was the most formidable project ever brought to the Senate's attention for its approval, the result of heroic efforts on the part of what looked like a body of oligarchs working in more or less secret sessions, and with the aid of a small army of experts selected in ways beyond discovery, and certainly without the knowledge of the people or of the people's representatives. It was now up for the approval of the single body which could in any sense represent the American nation—the Senate.

President Wilson was unable to provide the Committee with any large number of detailed statements or official memoranda and minutes of what had occurred at Paris, where the Peace Conference was still in session. Consequently anything like an orderly view of the doings at Paris, extending over six months, could not be gained. Such knowledge as was gained came little by little and in piecemeal fashion. Only on the 19th August, at the White House interview, did the Committee discover rather incidentally that Mr. Wilson himself was the author of Article X; [1] and it was not until the last hearing on the 12th September that the Committee secured unexpectedly an enlightening variety of important official lore from Mr. Bullitt—information which should have come, if at all, from

[1] *v.* Extracts from Discussion, 19th August 1919, Vol. III, pp. 66–9.

some one higher up. Yet it is remarkable, all things considered, with what skill the Committee extracted information; and still more remarkable was their ability in getting at many of the larger and more critical aspects of the vast document.

The meaning in all its bearings of Article X, the question of safeguarding the Monroe doctrine, the problem of American withdrawal from the League, the many doubtful points suggested by the Shantung settlement, and a dozen other leading matters were explored and discussed preparatory to reaching conclusions. In the process of reading the evidence, one reaches the view that the document could be reasonably opposed, irrespective of partisanship, partly on the ground of its peculiar method of manufacture as well as on the ground of its menace to some of America's most cherished traditions. On the other hand, it was necessarily produced under extraordinary circumstances such as should be taken carefully into the account. And it appeared to be workable and in many ways the result of wisdom and statesmanship of no ordinary kind.

15. *Senate Discussion.* Throughout this second phase of the struggle the Senate in regular session listened intermittently to much discussion of the Treaty which became more and more technical and detailed, as the knowledge, obtained by the Committee on Foreign Relations at its hearings, sifted in. Lodge, Knox, Borah, and Johnson of California, all members of that Committee, were the more conspicuous leaders among the Republicans opposing the Treaty, followed closely by a group of less conspicuous men. Having had to surrender their original plan of attempting to disentangle the Covenant and the Treaty, they were now bent upon amending it; and this object they laboured hard to accomplish. Against them was the administration minority, wholly hostile to amendments, as these were reckoned to be destructive of the Treaty, and bound also to require its submission once more to the Germans as well as to the Paris Conference—an impossible act in the eyes of most reasonable Senators. Hitchcock, John Sharp Williams, Swanson of Virginia, and Walsh of Montana were the leading spokesmen of the minority. The independent Republican Senator from North Dakota, McCumber, did distinguished service for the minority, although he maintained a position somewhat distinct from that of either group, but he was with the minority in favouring the Treaty. The Senate

was not devoid of a few men, whether Republicans or Democrats, who felt and expressed honest doubts; and it was among the doubters that reservations rather than amendments were suggested as a possible way out of the impasse that seemed likely by September to occur.

16. *Amendments versus Reservations.* Reservations had, it is true, been suggested before the Treaty reached the Senate on the 10th July. On the 14th July Senator Kellogg of Minnesota gave notice that he would at the proper time draw some distinction between amendments and reservations, and nearly a month later, on the 7th August, he did so in a masterly way.[1] It is probable that a letter written by ex-Associate Justice Charles E. Hughes, and injected into Senate discussions on the 29th July, was influential in helping to alter hard and fast opinions on the same subject. Although a Republican, Mr. Hughes conceived his letter in no partisan mood. Like Mr. Root, he argued mildly for the Treaty, but with definite reservations in mind, four of which he formulated as in his judgment necessary: (i) a clear enunciation of the right of withdrawal; (ii) the differentiation of domestic matters with which no League should in any wise concern itself; (iii) strict control by the United States of the interpretation of the Monroe doctrine; and (iv) the elimination of Article X which he characterized as 'an illusory engagement'.[2]

It is true, as Mr. Lodge has pointed out, that no fewer than seventy treaties in our history have been amended by the Senate and yet have been finally adopted as satisfactory to the parties concerned. But the Versailles Treaty was as far removed as possible from all treaties heretofore known. It was, and remains, a unique instrument. And Senator Borah spoke wisely when he referred to it as 'something more than a treaty'. His conviction was thus amplified:

> 'While it passes in popular parlance by the name of a treaty, it really incorporates a scheme which, either directly or indirectly, greatly modifies our governmental powers . . . it is not in any sense an ordinary treaty.'

And this statement helped to explain Borah's uncompromising objection to it.[3]

[1] *Cong. Record*, LVIII, 2,543, 3,680–97 (*passim*).
[2] Letter of 24th July to Senator Frederick Hale of Maine. Mr. Hughes has, since March 1921, served as President Harding's Secretary of State.
[3] *Cong. Record*, LVIII, 690 (5th June), 2,730–1 (17th July).

Over one topic, the Shantung settlement, the factions raged.[1] The minority did their best to defend it; but the hearings before the Foreign Relations Committee brought into view many of the inside and diplomatic details which could be easily used against the President. When it became reasonably clear that Mr. Wilson had been forced, for fear of losing the Japanese allegiance to the Treaty, to consent to the Shantung settlement, reservations regarding it were certain to be pushed. Senator McCumber offered such a reservation early in September.

17. *Final Three Reports on the Treaty.* Three reports, dated the 10th, 11th, and 15th September respectively, marked the conclusion of the second phase of the struggle: the Majority Report of the Committee on Foreign Relations drafted by Senator Lodge, its chairman; the Minority Report, signed by Senator Hitchcock and five other Democrats; and a report independently formulated by Senator McCumber.

The Majority Report was in part devoted to an attack upon Mr. Wilson's autocratic methods in denying to the Committee any really complete records of the Paris Conference. It was written in a sharp ironic tone, and made no reference to the large objects of the League plan. It concluded with a recommendation of forty-five amendments and four reservations, the amendments of such a nature as to assure Wilson's refusal to accept them. The Minority Report was a counter attack on conclusions of the majority: it declared against any amendments, deprecated reservations, considered at some length about a dozen concessions from Germany which the United States must lose in case the Treaty failed, and concluded with a perfunctory series of statements designed to point out the significance of the League of Nations to a troubled world. Of the two reports, the Majority was distinctly the abler, bitter and prejudiced though it was. In the ears of many Republicans the Minority Report must have sounded subservient—an appeal for help at a crucial moment in a declining cause. The third Report, that of Senator McCumber, stands out as an impressive tribute to a man able to maintain independence and poise amidst party rancour. Openly deploring the failure of his colleagues on the Committee to touch upon the

[1] *v.* Extracts from Discussion, Vol. III, pp. 71–4, and for some comment on the subject this volume, pp. 381–2.

larger aspects of the Versailles Treaty, he set these aspects forth succinctly :

'The instrument is not as complete and as binding as the constitution of a state or nation. It still leaves to each nation the right of withdrawal, and depends to a great extent upon the moral sentiment of each nation to comply with its own obligations or the enforcement of such obligations upon a recalcitrant member. It is, however, a mighty step in the right direction. Every sentiment of justice and morality is on its side. Some of its provisions are yet crude and uncertain of application. But the whole purpose is most noble and worthy. And, as in our American Constitution, we were compelled, in order to form a more perfect union, to depend upon the right of amendment, so in this great world constitution experience will undoubtedly necessitate many changes in order to make a more perfect instrument that will work for the benefit of humanity. . . .'

He considered carefully two matters of special moment about which criticism raged : the six votes which the British Empire and its five self-governing Dominions were granted (an arrangement which seemed to him reasonable), and the Shantung settlement (which did not disturb his sense of justice). In conclusion he offered six reservations for the purpose of clarifying the Treaty, one of these relating to the sections on Shantung.[1]

18. *The Third Phase : 15th September–19th November.* This was a tumultuous period of debate and senatorial colloquy, lasting just over two months—to the 19th November, a date which marked the first defeat of the Treaty and concluded the session.

When it opened, President Wilson had already left Washington and at the moment was on the Pacific coast, bent on arousing the nation to its duty—as he conceived it—to enforce the acceptance of the Treaty through a general expression of opinion. Stricken by illness in Colorado on the 25th September, the weary leader returned to Washington only to fall a victim to a stroke of paralysis early in October. And he remained thereafter a maimed and broken man, living much in seclusion, but keeping in some touch by correspondence with Senator

[1] These three reports together form *Senate Report* No. 176, Parts I (Majority, p. 7), II (Minority, p. 5), and III (McCumber, p. 9). They may be found in *Senate Reports*, Vol. I (Nos. 1–306), 66 Cong., 1 sess. (1919), and are intended to accompany *Senate Document* No. 51, the text of the Treaty of Peace with Germany (ordered to be printed on 10th July 1919), p. 537, in French and English. Two editions of the text were issued, both in quarto form : a limited edition (1,773 copies) with maps, and a large edition (50,000 copies) without maps.

Hitchcock. Neither the Democrats nor the nation could afford at this critical time to lose Mr. Wilson who, of all men, was best informed about the Treaty and its relation to world affairs. There was no Democratic leader in the Senate who could carry on the fight with skill. It seems possible that, had there been one, the Treaty might yet have been saved. But the President's nature and his methods of doing business were such as to permit no understudies. Moreover, except in the far west, public opinion was not much affected by his tour. Along the Pacific coast he won great ovations.[1]

19. *Reading of the Treaty, 15th September–20th October.* Between the 15th September and the 20th October, the text of the Treaty, section by section, was duly read. There were many interruptions and almost a running fire of colloquies, a few careful speeches, and much rather grandiloquent oratory obviously designed for the consumption of constituents at home desirous of being reassured that their senatorial representatives were attending to the great business of statesmanship. Naturally a number of speakers were ill-informed about many details of the Treaty. There were a few Senators sufficiently discreet and aware of their ignorance to remain all but inarticulate. Among men earnestly seeking light or endowed with wisdom by reason of prolonged and tedious efforts to understand the Treaty—and of course taking fairly conspicuous places for these reasons—were Messrs. McCumber, Lodge, Knox, Walsh of Montana, Hitchcock, Kellogg of Minnesota, Borah of Idaho, Owen of Oklahoma, Lenroot of Wisconsin, and a few others. The strongest and ablest speech in the autumn to justify the British claim to six votes was made by Senator McCumber.[2] He made, too, an excellent appeal to leave the Shantung settlement to time to settle justly.[3] Senator Walsh of Montana was watchful over Article X from an early date, and had imbibed Mr. Wilson's point of view

[1] President Wilson left Washington, D.C., on 3rd September 1919. Beginning at Columbus, Ohio, on 4th September, he spoke in twenty-eight cities, making altogether thirty-seven speeches. He broke down at Pueblo, Colorado, on 25th September, and reached the White House on 28th September. See *Senate Document* No. 120, 66 Cong., 1 sess. ' Addresses of President Wilson . . . on his Western Tour . . . ', p. 370. Senators Borah and Johnson of California followed close on the President's trail in an attempt to minimize his influence by speaking against the League of Nations. But Senate business soon recalled them to Washington.

[2] *Cong. Record*, LVIII, 6,439 ff. (6th October), 7,369–73 (23rd October).

[3] *Ibid.*, LVIII, 6,880 ff. (14th October), 6,995 ff. (16th October).

regarding it, although he would not have made the Treaty to hang upon it. 'I want a League of Nations', declared Mr. Lodge early in the autumn. He formulated his thought in this wise:

'My idea of a League of Nations was that we should start building on the Hague conventions, which did a great and good work. I wish to see, as Mr. Root himself desired above all things, a codification of international law which has been torn to pieces and cast to the winds by Germany. I wish to see the great feature of an international court with judges. . . . We have got a document that never mentions the Hague conventions, that never says anything about international law, and the only court is pushed into one article . . .'[1]

20. *Factional Groupings.* Guided to some extent by principles, but seldom free from prejudices begotten by a long train of complicated circumstances, a number of factional groups stood out more or less clearly in the Senate by early autumn. These groups were becoming apparent even before the Committee on Foreign Relations had made its brief reports. There were (i) the group of 'Bitter-enders' or 'Irreconcilables', led by such men as Borah of Idaho and Johnson of California, all directing their energies toward defeating the Treaty. James A. Reed, Democratic Senator from Missouri, was in the group. At the other extreme was (ii) the group of administration Democrats led by Senator Gilbert M. Hitchcock of Nebraska, who accepted the Treaty as it stood and tried to be in accord with President Wilson's views. There was (iii) another small group of Senators, mostly Democrats—men such as Senators Hoke Smith of Georgia and John K. Shields of Tennessee—who, however they voted, revealed in the Senate cloak-rooms hostility to the President, to most of his policies, and to the Treaty. (iv) The 'Reservationists' were an important group in which Senator Lodge was finally to be found—many of whom probably wished secretly to defeat the Treaty without saying so directly. (v) The 'Mild Reservationists', including the Democrat, Senator Thomas J. Walsh of Montana, and such Republicans as Senators McCumber of North Dakota and Kellogg of Minnesota, argued for slight alterations in the text of the Treaty, but were eager for its acceptance.[2]

[1] Quoted in the *Record* (7th October) from a speech by Mr. Lodge, made a few days earlier before a Massachusetts audience.

[2] An amendment would require the assent of every signatory to a treaty, and in the case of the instrument under discussion, would have meant the

Arousing impatience both at home and abroad by what seemed to be inexcusable slowness, the Senate, to one willing to follow its workings during the autumn of 1919, appears to have acted neither blindly nor under the spell of partisan motives. There was within its walls opposition to President Wilson's policy and no little display of personal dislike, together with distrust, of the man. On the other hand, to an influential and obvious degree there was much judgment at work. The fact that all amendments brought forward by the Foreign Relations Committee were defeated by the 29th October through a combination of Democrats and Mild Reservationists should not be overlooked.[1] This amounted to a victory over the extremists—a victory similar, although more significant of judgment and less the result of circumstances, to the victory won in the previous summer when the Knox resolution, devised for the purpose of disentangling Covenant and Treaty and in line with the March ' round robin ', was successfully defeated.

21. *First Defeat of the Treaty, 19th November 1919.* On this day, about 10.30 p.m., the issue was decided after a long and very exciting session. At noon, the assembling hour of the Senate, ninety-three Senators (out of a possible ninety-six) had answered the first roll-call. The ratification of the Treaty with fourteen reservations already adopted by the body sitting as a Committee of the whole was twice refused : first, by a vote of 39 yeas and 55 nays, and again, after a considerable interval of debate, by a reconsidered vote of 41 yeas and 51 nays. Finally, in a resolution calling for its unconditional ratification, it failed a third time by a vote of 38 yeas and 53 nays. Thus three times the Treaty fell short of ratification by upwards of 20 votes or that two-thirds majority called for by the fundamental law.[2] The fourteen reservations, commonly called the

reconvening of the Paris Conference. The purpose of a reservation is distinct from that of an amendment, for a reservation applies to the reserving power alone and, so far as the reserving power is concerned, removes it from that portion of the contract defined or qualified by the reservation.

[1] From the 2nd–29th October 1919, at intervals, many amendments were proposed by the Foreign Relations Committee and defeated. Other amendments by individual Senators were introduced as late as the 6th November, but to no avail. Long before this latter date it was clear that reservations were certain to help to decide the issue ; and on the 7th November the struggle for qualifying reservations began in earnest. See for all reservations proposed up to the 6th November, *Senate Document* No. 150, 66 Cong., 1 sess. (p. 50).

[2] *Cong. Record*, LVIII, 8,786, 8,802, 8,803. Senator McCumber was the lone Republican who cast his vote for unconditional ratification along with

'Lodge Reservations', were designed to release the United States from certain obligations assumed by other members of the League of Nations, while they assured Americans of the benefits of the League. In brief, the reservations were supposedly a safeguard to American institutions and to certain historic policies peculiar to the American nation.[1]

A letter from President Wilson addressed to Senator Hitchcock on the 18th November and read into the Senate record the next day, may have had some slight influence on the votes. But it amounted simply to a reassurance on the President's part of his unwavering position against reservations. 'I assume', he wrote,

> 'that the Senators only desire my judgment upon the all-important question of the resolution containing the many reservations of Senator Lodge. On that I cannot hesitate, for, in my opinion, the resolution in that form does not provide for ratification but rather for nullification of the Treaty. I sincerely hope that the friends and supporters of the Treaty will vote against the Lodge resolution of ratification. . . .'[2]

At the basis of his opposition was the reservation affecting Article X, Mr. Wilson's most cherished (and probably his single) contribution to the final text of the Covenant. The sacrifice of this article was, in his language, equivalent to a 'knife-thrust at the heart of the Covenant'.[3]

22. Revival of the Issue: December 1919–January 1920. The second session of the Sixty-sixth Congress assembled automatically on the 1st December 1919. The President's

the thirty-seven Democrats. He voted also in favour of accepting the Treaty with reservations.

[1] *Cong. Record*, LVIII, 8,777–8. [2] *Ibid.*, LVIII, 8,768.

[3] In the course of discussion on this fateful day, Senator (later President) Harding thus analysed the various positions: 'In the Senate there are four distinct schools of thought in dealing with this Treaty: One is the unconditional-ratification school, those who either through their own conscientious convictions or the lash of the Executive—choose as you will—want this treaty ratified without a single modification or reservation. That is group No. 1. In direct opposition is the so-called irreconcilable group, those who are unalterably opposed to any ratification. That is group 2. The third is the group to which I choose to belong, if I may, who are agreed to bring about the ratification of this Treaty if they are convinced that reservations have been adopted which are sufficient to safeguard the interests of the United States of America. There still remains another group—popularly known as the 'mild reservationists', those who are anxious to ratify, who are anxious to safeguard the interests of this Republic, but at the same time desire to make the reservations as little offensive as possible to those who assumed to negotiate the Treaty in contempt of the Senate.' *Ibid.*, 8,792.

annual message was read the next day. It made a single accidental allusion to the League of Nations, and referred at some length to 'the widespread condition of political restlessness in our body politic', which the writer regarded as 'superficial rather than deep-seated'. The causes of this restlessness, he said, 'arise from or are connected with the failure on the part of the government to arrive speedily at a just and permanent peace permitting return to normal conditions. . . .' The message was obviously written in a mood of restraint and designed to avoid any specific references to the recent action of the Senate in the matter of the Treaty. That issue appeared to be settled.[1]

However, on the 13th December, during a discussion in the Senate of domestic economic conditions and foreign exchange rates, Senator Underwood of Alabama suddenly spoke of his desire for unconditional ratification of the Treaty. There was an immediate exchange of views—a somewhat violent colloquy—between Underwood and Lodge as to whether the Treaty was still in the Senate, Underwood claiming that it was, and Lodge declaring that technically the President must re-submit it. Other leaders spoke on the issue, which was thus summarily revived. Nearly a month had elapsed since the 19th November —the Senate was in a calmer and more reasonable mood.[2]

The outside public had never ceased discussing the subject. Such leading men as Taft, Wickersham, Lawrence Lowell, and Herbert Hoover expressed the anxious hope that some compromise could be brought about which would quiet the Senate's disputatious factions. There was a widespread impression, clearly expressed in the more liberal newspapers, that the time had come for America to join the League even though the Treaty might not prove to be in all respects satisfactory. In particular the League to Enforce Peace laboured hard in the cause of settling the difficulties by urging the acceptance by the Senate of reservations. Senatorial leaders could not escape the pressure of popular opinion. During the last fortnight in January a bi-partisan conference of nine Senators (five Democrats and four Republicans) met almost daily in Washington in formal and strictly unofficial sessions seriously to discuss the possible basis on which further discussion of the Treaty might be renewed in the Senate. Senators Lodge and Hitchcock were

[1] *Cong. Record*, LIX, 29–31. [2] *Ibid.*, 532–44 (*passim*).

naturally leaders in the two respective groups. The daily papers sought, with varying success, to inform the public of the progress of the conference. On the 31st January cautious but clear statements of the results of the conference were made public. Refraining from assertions likely to compromise the Senate, the group of nine were agreed on the desirability of modifying slightly the original Lodge reservations, but Senator Lodge made it clear that he would not consent to any, even slight, changes in the two reservations concerning Article X and the Monroe doctrine.[1]

23. *Lord Grey of Fallodon's London Letter.* By a mere coincidence on this same 31st January, Lord Grey of Fallodon published a letter in the London *Times*, which attracted attention on both sides of the Atlantic. Since September 1919—for about four months—Lord Grey had acted as British Ambassador to the United States, but at the moment he was back in England and out of office. The letter was unofficial. It came, however, from such a high source that it seemed reasonable to assume that it expressed opinions likely to meet with the approval of the British Cabinet. On the 2nd February, at the request of Senator Lodge, it was promptly printed in the Senate proceedings. Entitled 'America and the Treaty', it presented the views of a man closely observant of American affairs and was designed to clear up possible international misunderstandings as well as avowedly to help to break down the impasse then existing between the President and the Senate.

Reflecting, at the outset, upon the position of the Senate in the American plan of government, Lord Grey denied that the charge of bad faith could be brought against the United States, whatever action the Senate might finally take. Its reasons for insisting on reservations he declared to be founded on its regard for a traditional policy. The League of Nations is actually a new departure. Acceptance of it by the Senate would mean 'a plunge into something which its historical advice and tradition have hitherto positively disapproved'. Under certain conditions a conflict between President and Senate over treaties is inevitable. The success of the League

[1] *Senate Document* No. 193, 66 Cong., 2 sess., entitled 'Reservations to the Treaty of Peace with Germany. Statements made to the Press regarding the Bipartisan Conference . . . By Senator Henry Cabot Lodge and Senator Gilbert M. Hitchcock', p. 15.

would depend in his judgment upon the adherence of the United States to it. He was definite in his view that Great Britain neither could nor would accept any alteration of the text which gave to the British Empire and its five self-governing dominions a total of six votes in the League Assembly. But the greater portion of the reservations or conditions, he thought, were reasonable and must not be lightly refused at the risk of losing America's co-operation.

'Without the United States, the present League of Nations may become little better than a League of Allies for armed self-defence against a revival of Prussian militarism . . . predominantly a European and not a world organization.'

24. *The Last Stage : 2nd February–19th March 1920.* Early in February Senator Lodge, majority leader, gave notice that he would, if permitted, resurrect the Treaty together with reservations on the 9th February for further consideration. And this he accordingly did.[1] There is no evidence (or indeed any probability) to indicate that Lord Grey's impressive letter had anything to do with this move. It was the result of circumstances—in particular a growing impression in the country at large that the Senate should reach a final settlement. President Wilson, ill as he was, had already written to Senator Hitchcock, consenting to certain suggested reservations. But it was generally understood that the President had never, since his illness, seen either Lord Grey or Mr. Hitchcock. In markedly serious fashion the debate on a variety of reservations was carried on for about five weeks. On the 9th March Senator Hitchcock made public a letter from the President written the previous day. In it for the last time Mr. Wilson refused to accept the Lodge reservation on Article X which declared that the United States would assume no obligations to preserve the independence of other nations by military force, by the use of its resources, or by any form of economic discrimination, without the consent of its Congress. In brief, the economic outlawry of an offending State on which, as a means of coercion, the President placed his trust, was thus weakened and might be sacrificed to a dilatory Congress, or even wholly surrendered by a timid one. It was in this letter that the President characterized all reservations heretofore

[1] *Cong. Record,* LIX, 2,335, 2,627 ff.

proposed as amounting to a 'sweeping nullification of the terms of the Treaty.[1] Henceforth no administration Democratic Senator could have any doubt about his duty to the President when the hour for voting on the Treaty should arrive.

The final test came on the 19th March. There was less excitement in the Senate than there had been exactly four months before, on the 19th November. No longer was there any thought of unconditional ratification. If accepted by the Senate, the Treaty must carry reservations and understandings, fifteen in number. Shortly before the vote was taken, Senator Walsh of Montana made a carefully reasoned appeal to his Democratic colleagues to accept the Treaty even with reservations and in spite of President Wilson's clearly expressed opposition. He reminded his colleagues of his own consistent opposition in the past to most of the proposed reservations. He had fought vigorously against any alteration of Article X. But the modified Treaty was, in his eyes, too important to be lost. He should vote for it, for the Treaty, he acknowledged frankly, is 'supported stoutly by men as high minded as I can claim to be'.[2]

Voting in favour of the Treaty were 49 Senators (28 Republicans and 21 Democrats); voting against it were 35 Senators (12 Republicans and 23 Democrats). It failed to obtain the necessary two-thirds majority by only seven votes. In other words, the affirmative or favouring attitude of 56 Senators in a Senate that at the moment could count on a total of 84 votes, would have carried the Treaty through and thus have made the United States in all probability a member of the League of Nations. Generally speaking, Senator Walsh's attitude was typical of the 21 Democrats voting for the Treaty. The opponents of the Treaty were the small group of 'irreconcilables', 12 in number, and 23 Wilson adherents who determined, against all odds, to follow their leader. After more than eight months of strife in the Senate, reckoning from the 10th July 1919, the Treaty was lost.[3]

25. *Conclusions.* It is too soon after the events just narrated to formulate any final judgments concerning them. Behind the events is a long and complicated train of circum-

[1] *Cong. Record*, LIX, 2,622, 4,051–2, for Wilson's two letters of 26th January and 8th March 1920.

[2] *Ibid.*, 4,581 ff.

[3] *Ibid.*, 4,599.

stances that evidence, now withheld, is sure to reveal in the future. Some day the eddies and the cross-currents in the stream will be better understood. Could the Treaty have been won? On this question opinions will differ, probably always. Several conclusions, however, may be drawn which have a bearing on the question.

(i) The Democrats, losing control of the majority in the Senate after the 4th March 1919, suffered for want of really able and wise leadership. They had no such capable or thoughtful men in debate as Senators Lodge and Knox—no men so thoroughly qualified by experience and long training to understand and correctly to interpret American foreign affairs and policy. Too often they fell back upon the speeches of President Wilson instead of trusting to their abilities to study documents and, in particular, the text of the Treaty. Outside the Senate discerning leaders of public opinion—such, for examples, as ex-President Taft and ex-Attorney-General Wickersham (both Republicans in politics)—assisted their cause. Even ex-Senator Root and ex-Associate Justice Hughes were never outspoken against the cause of a carefully designed League. But it should not be forgotten that the cause was new. Against abler adversaries the Democratic group failed to make it appear that the League of President Wilson was not a dangerous scheme likely to involve the United States as a member in grave world complications.

(ii) The illness of President Wilson was a most unfortunate circumstance. The terrible strain of the war, the complicated tasks which he undertook to shoulder in Paris, the ordeal of his interview with the Foreign Relations Committee on the 19th August 1919, and lastly his speech-making tour in September following are quite enough to account for his collapse. Illness took the real leader of the Democratic cause away from any effective contact with his followers. It deprived him of cabinet consultations. It rendered an obstinate man weak at the time when, for his country's sake as well as for that of his party, he should have been strong. Indeed, it probably increased his obstinacy: he became unyielding and inflexible when many of his Democratic friends besought him to be liberal.

(iii) Senator Porter J. McCumber of North Dakota, a Republican, in the Senate since 1899, favoured the League of Nations as arranged by the Treaty. He proved himself to be a man of extraordinary courage and independence, willing for the sake of convictions carefully reached to stand at most of the points of issue with the Democratic minority. His Report of the 15th September 1919, based upon his view of the evidence obtained by the Foreign Relations Committee, is a short paper; it is likely always to afford enlightenment to any one desirous of reaching sound conclusions regarding that juncture of affairs. In the course of the debates he proved himself to be an intelligent and discerning exponent of several rather technical aspects of the Treaty text. His attitude was frequently that of a man disinclined to partisanship in the face of what he regarded as stupendously important and fateful issues. From personalities and petty flings at his opponents he was strikingly free.

(iv) During these years the work of Senator H. C. Lodge of Massachusetts can under no circumstances be overlooked. It is likely always to be sharply criticized, for Senator Lodge's bitterness toward President Wilson was often strongly expressed and sounded malicious. It impresses one as a serious blot upon his record. Furthermore, there can be no doubt about Mr. Lodge's partisan attitude and actions against his Democratic opponents of whatever hue. He was influenced by his well-known intimacy with ex-President Roosevelt, whose death on the 7th January 1919—near the beginnings of the struggle in the Senate—Mr. Lodge commemorated in an address about a month later (9th February) in the national House of Representatives. That he tried to guide himself in the matter of the Treaty by what he believed that his dead friend, Roosevelt, would have desired, is a fact in accordance with his own statement. On the 16th September 1919, Mr. Lodge said, referring to Roosevelt:

> 'The position that I have taken and now take had his full approval . . . it is a help and a strength to me to feel that I have behind me the approval, the support of the great American, the great patriot, the great man. . . .' [1]

From time to time he changed his point of view. When he found that Covenant and Treaty could not be disentangled, he turned to the policy of reservations and worked for it—just how earnestly is perhaps a question not at present to be

[1] *Cong. Record*, LVIII, 5,503.

determined from evidence thus far available. He was not greatly disturbed by inconsistencies in his own statements and thought. He took delight, however, in pointing to the inconsistencies of President Wilson.[1] That he was one of the most industrious men in the Senate there can be no doubt. He laboured hard to keep prominently before an impatient public the grave risks which, in his judgment, an unqualified acceptance of the Treaty would mean to his country. He was one among a very few men on either side of the issue whose appeals to history were made after careful investigation. As a rule these appeals are apt to be informing, and they were generally well applied. It is only fair to Senator Lodge to cite in conclusion a passage written by him in 1921, long after the issue was settled, in brief explanation of his opposition to President Wilson's tactics. The question at stake, he explains, was this:

'whether constitutional government in the United States which has been successfully maintained for one hundred and thirty years should be broken down by a single well-directed attack and replaced by the old and simple method of autocracy and the plebiscite, which would mean not only the loss of free government but a distinct retrogression to a government system of a lower type and more purely tyrannical in operation and results. . . .'[2]

(v) To the European world, President Wilson never gave any adequate conception of the limitations and bounds to his office. He was subject of course to the Constitution of the United States. He spoke at times as though he was an all-powerful autocrat. Hence it was probably never recognized generally in Europe that the Treaty, once the negotiations were completed, would inevitably be passed in review by a critical Senate as nearly as possible under the circumstances representative of the American people, but at the same time under the sway of a party out of sympathy with many of the President's ideals. In other words, as Professor Alison Phillips has pointed out, in claiming to represent the American people, President Wilson was bound to be misleading.[3]

[1] *Cong. Record*, LVIII, 5,502–4 (*passim*).
[2] *The Senate of the United States* and other Essays and Addresses, Historical and Literary. By Henry Cabot Lodge (N.Y., 1921), pp. 30–1. Cf. Senator Harding's remarks in the Senate on the 19th November 1919. *Cong. Record*, LVIII, 8,792.
[3] *Edinburgh Review* (July 1920), Vol. 232, pp. 4 ff.

(vi) The national election of November 1920 resulted in the defeat of President Wilson's party. At that time ex-Senator Warren G. Harding, the Republican candidate, won an astonishingly complete victory over a Democratic opponent and became President-elect. Was this failure of the Democrats to be ascribed to the failure in the Senate of the Versailles Treaty? An answer to this question has been well formulated by Mr. J. A. Spender as follows:

'The defeat of President Wilson in 1920 was not a repentance on the part of the American people of their action in the war; nor was it a declaration that they would retire into their continent and take no further part in world affairs. But it was very definitely a revolt against the idea that American policy should be subject to European, or that European nations should have the right to call for American intervention, apart from the decision of Congress, on a given set of circumstances arising, which might be determined in Europe and not in America. . . .'[1]

[1] *Ibid.*, (July 1922), Vol. 236, pp. 3–4.

CHAPTER VI

INTERNATIONAL DEVELOPMENTS UNDER THE LEAGUE

PART I

THE MAKING OF THE COVENANT[1]

1. *Introductory.* The circumstances in which the Paris scheme of a League of Nations was conceived and born have been outlined in a previous volume of this History.[2] It was there explained that, though much thought had gone to its making, the scheme was based on practical experience rather than abstract principles, that it was rapidly put into shape at a few meetings spread over a few weeks, and that it was not intended to be a complete constitution so much as a framework or nucleus for free development in the future. It will be shown in this chapter how the ideas in the minds of the makers of the Covenant actually took shape. It has not seemed necessary to trace the genesis of the League in ideas current before the war, or even to mark the stages of opinion during the war, except in so far as a brief summary is required to explain the making of the Covenant.

2. *Pre-war Organization for the Maintenance of Peace.* The machinery for regulating international relations before the war was fragmentary and unco-ordinated. It was designed

[1] Part I of this chapter was originally written in 1920; so far as facts are concerned, it has been brought up to date to December 1922, but the general treatment has not been changed. Authoritative information on the subject-matter of Part I is available from the following published sources: United States Senate Document No. 106, 66th Congress, 1st Session, Washington, 1919, which includes the hearings of President Wilson, Secretary Lansing, Mr. D. H. Miller, and Mr. W. C. Bullitt, with original documents; R. Lansing, *The Peace Negotiations, a Personal Narrative*, London, 1921; *What Really Happened at Paris*, edited by E. M. House and C. Seymour, London, 1921; André Tardieu, *The Truth about the Treaty*, London, 1921; *Taft Papers on League of Nations*, edited by T. Marburg and H. E. Flack, New York, 1920; R. S. Baker, *Woodrow Wilson and the World Settlement*, London, 1923. See also H. Wilson Harris, *The Peace in the Making*, London, 1919; E. J. Dillon, *The Peace Conference*, London, 1919.

[2] Vol. II, Chap. I, Part I. *v.* this Vol. App. I for Draft and Revised Covenant of 1919 and Amendments of 1921.

partly to facilitate international co-operation in peace in a general way, partly to secure a pacific settlement of disputes. It consisted on the one hand of the 'Concert of Europe', plus a number of permanent unions and commissions for special purposes, on the other of a network of arbitration conventions, reinforced from 1914 onwards by a series of so-called 'Bryan treaties'.[1] A word on these two systems may be excused.

The Concert of Europe was little more than an understanding between the six European Great Powers that on important matters of common interest they would take counsel, and possibly act, together. This understanding was disregarded by the Austro-Hungarian Government in the matter of Bosnia in 1908–9, but proved of practical value in securing the localization of the Balkan wars of 1912–13; and its success in this last case caused Sir Edward Grey to hope that, if the storm of July 1914 could be similarly weathered, 'some more definite rapprochement between the Powers' might follow. There existed at the same time several permanent international organizations, ranging from such governmental bodies as the Danube and Suez Canal Commissions to the Universal Postal Union and the International Statistical Institute.

With regard to the settlement of disputes between nations, the state of things before the war has been thus described by Sir Frederick Pollock:

> 'There was no jurisdiction to hear and determine disputes between sovereign States except by consent given either in a standing Convention of the parties, or in a special agreement to refer the case to arbitral decision. But there was a method of appointing an arbitral tribunal by selection from a standing list of competent persons, and there was the official establishment of a court, with a local habitation and records at The Hague. Most Powers were bound by a number of conventions of similar type to refer to the tribunal so provided all such disputes as did not affect their independence, honour or vital interests.'

To this we must add the so-called 'Bryan treaties', of which some thirty have been negotiated by the United States with different Powers, beginning with the United Kingdom in September 1914. These provide for the establishment of Permanent International Commissions, to which the parties undertake to refer all disputes whatever for 'investigation and report', with an agreement not to resort to war in the mean-

[1] There was, however, a limited term for all these. Germany was conspicuous in refusing to sign any of these treaties.

time; but the parties reserve to themselves full right of action after the presentation of the report.

There existed, therefore, provision for submitting justiciable issues not of a vital nature to a Court of Arbitration for definite award, and for submitting all other disputes to a Commission for investigation and report.

The events of the last days of July 1914 showed the inadequacy of all these organizations to preserve peace, and there arose a strong determination in many countries that the war must not end without the establishment of some more durable and effective machinery.

3. *Developments during the War.*

(*a*) *Early schemes.* This is not the place to describe the numerous schemes for a League of Nations put forward by societies and individuals during the war.[1] We may note in particular the schemes of the 'American League to Enforce Peace' founded in June 1915, and the British 'League of Nations Society', which published its 'Project for a League of Nations' in August 1917. The American Scheme contained the following four articles:

1. All justiciable questions arising between the signatory powers, not settled by negotiation, shall, subject to the limitations of treaties, be submitted to a judicial tribunal for hearing and judgment, both upon the merits, and upon any issue as to its jurisdiction of the question.
2. All other questions arising between the signatories and not settled by negotiation shall be submitted to a Council of Conciliation for hearing, consideration, and recommendation.
3. The signatory Powers shall jointly use forthwith both their economic and military forces against any one of their number that goes to war, or commits acts of hostility, against another of the signatories before any question arising shall be submitted as provided in the foregoing.
4. Conferences between the signatory Powers shall be held from time to time to formulate and codify rules of international law, which, unless some signatory shall signify its dissent within a stated period, shall thereafter govern in the decisions of the judicial tribunal mentioned in Article 1.

The British scheme was very similar, but went further, in that it provided that:

'All disputes arising out of questions of International Law, or the interpretation of Treaties, shall be referred to the Hague Court of

[1] An excellent summary of these is to be found in an appendix, written by Lord Phillimore, to the (unpublished) Report of the British Official Committee on the League of Nations, presented to Mr. Balfour in 1918.

Arbitration, or some other judicial tribunal, whose decisions shall be final and shall be carried into effect by the parties concerned;'

and also that there should be mutual defence against aggression from a State outside the League.

Neither scheme provides for the enforcement of an arbitral award or a recommendation of the Council of Conciliation; but the British includes, which the American does not, an obligation to obey an arbitral award, and a definition of 'justiciable questions', thus admitting in certain cases the principle of compulsory arbitration.

(b) *Wilson's early attitude, 1916.* More important than these and other unofficial schemes are the statements and suggestions of the respective governments. As early as September 1914, Mr. Asquith, then Prime Minister of the United Kingdom, pleaded for 'a real European partnership based on the recognition of equal right, and established and enforced by a common will'. But it was not till December 1916 that the question of a League of Nations was brought prominently before the belligerent statesmen as a real issue by President Wilson's Peace Note. The character and tendency of the President's earlier ideas on the subject of international relations have been considered in a previous chapter of this History.[1] It was there shown that his conception of a League of Nations was no mere war-product, but a natural part of his system of political philosophy. In January 1916 we have seen him suggesting that the states of the American continent should unite in 'guaranteeing to each other absolute political independence and territorial integrity'—words since immortalized in Art. X of the Covenant; in May 1916 he extended the application of this principle, and these very words, to 'a universal association of nations', which should 'prevent any war begun either contrary to treaty covenants or without warning and full submission of the cause to the opinion of the world'. We have seen him also in his early utterances expressing his conviction that a nation ought to submit its actions for the approval of the public opinion of mankind, and that such publicity is likely to have beneficial effects.[2] Here undoubtedly are some of the germs of the Covenant.

[1] Vol. I, p. 177 sqq.

[2] See note, Vol. I, pp. 179–80. Lansing, *Peace Negotiations*, p. 32, states that, in his address of the 27th May 1916 to the League to Enforce Peace, Wilson went over and erased all reference to the use of physical force

(*c*) *The Phillimore Report.* To the President's Note the Allied Governments replied on the 10th January 1917 that 'they associate themselves whole-heartedly with the plan of creating a League of Nations to ensure peace and justice throughout the world.'[1] As regards the British Empire, the matter was discussed in April 1917 by a Committee of the Imperial War Cabinet, which recommended the adoption of the principle that the signatories of the Peace Treaty should agree not to go to war with one another without previously submitting their dispute to a conference. In France an official Foreign Office committee was appointed to consider the organization of a League, and in March 1918 an important British committee, comprising three historians and three representatives of the Foreign Office, with Lord Phillimore as Chairman, produced a Draft Convention in eighteen Articles.[2] This Convention provided that no state, a member of the League, should go to war with another without previously submitting the dispute either to arbitration or to a Conference of all the Allied States, and (save in exceptional circumstances) awaiting the award or report; and that no state should go to war with one which complied with this award or report. A breach of any of these covenants was to be punished by an automatic severance of relations and by military and economic sanctions. The Conference, however, was only to recommend, and for a recommendation to have effect the consent of all members of the Conference, except the disputants, was required. It may further be noted, first, that there was to be no obligation on a state to accept an award or recommendation; secondly, that the League was to have no activities beyond the actual settlement of disputes, and no permanent character beyond a fixed place of meeting. A copy of the Phillimore proposals was sent to the President of the United States.

(*d*) *Wilson's pronouncements in 1918.* Meanwhile on the 8th January 1918 President Wilson had enunciated his 'Fourteen

in preventing wars. By January 1917 he had become convinced that force was the practical method of checking aggressions. The text of the speech is in J. B. Scott, *Wilson's Foreign Policy*, New York (1918), pp. 189–95.

[1] Vol. I, pp. 172–3.

[2] The other members were Sir Eyre Crowe, Sir Julian Corbett, Sir Cecil Hurst, Professor A. F. Pollard, Professor J. Holland Rose, and Sir William Tyrrell; Mr. A. R. Kennedy acted as Secretary. *v.* Vol. II, pp. 30–1. The Interim Report is published as Document 8 in Baker, *Woodrow Wilson and World Settlement*, Vol. III, p. 67.

Points', of which the last ran: 'A general association of nations must be formed under specific covenants for the purpose of affording mutual guarantees of political independence and territorial integrity to great and small states alike.' This statement he amplified in his speeches of the 4th July and the 27th September, and in the course of the summer he put on paper his first draft of a constitution for the League, or, to use his own phrase, of a Covenant. It was based partly on the Phillimore report, partly on a scheme prepared at his instance by Colonel House as an improvement on the Phillimore report, which the two friends had discussed together. In the President's speech of the 27th September he declared that 'the constitution of that League of Nations and the clear definition of its objects must be a part, in a sense the most essential part, of the peace settlement itself'. He said further: 'There can be no leagues or alliances or special covenants and understandings within the general and common family of the League of Nations. And more specifically, there can be no special selfish economic combinations within the League, and no employment of any form of economic boycott or exclusion, except as the power of economic penalty by exclusion from the markets of the world may be vested in the League of Nations itself as a means of discipline and control.'[1]

This speech of the 27th September was the President's last pronouncement before the initiation by Germany of the negotiations leading up to the armistice; it will be remembered that his addresses of this year were accepted by both sides as the basis of the peace settlement.

(*e*) *Practical organs of international co-operation.* Along with this gradual approach, official and unofficial, towards the acceptance of the League in the world of theory, the practical development of international organs of co-operation between the Allies calls for notice. Rudimentary at first, and as a rule intermittent, these efforts took on a new character with the formation in November 1917 of the Supreme War Council, composed of two statesmen from each of the chief Allied countries with permanent military and naval advisers and a permanent joint secretariat at Versailles. This organization

[1] For texts of all these speeches in 1918 *v.* Vol. I, pp. 431–8, and of some later ones in 1918 and 1919, Vol. III, pp. 58–74. The House and first Wilson drafts are published as documents 9 and 10 in Baker, *op. cit.*, Vol. III.

was modelled on that of the British War Cabinet as elaborated during the war, out of the Committee of Imperial Defence, by Sir Maurice Hankey.

The Supreme War Council dealt with high policy, but there were other Inter-Allied bodies concerned with particular sides of war organization, such as the Commission Internationale de Ravitaillement, the Inter-Allied Food Council, the Inter-Allied Munitions Council, the Inter-Allied Council on War Purchases and Finance, and, most important of all, the Allied Maritime Transport Council formed early in 1918 to allocate tonnage in the general interest. The Transport Council consisted of two ministers each of France, Great Britain, and Italy, and two representatives of the United States, and was served by a permanent secretarial organization which prepared matter for decision by the members of the Council at their occasional meetings and in the meantime supervised the execution of their decisions by the appropriate authorities.[1]

The practical experience gained in the working of these international bodies must not be overlooked as a factor in the creation of the League of Nations. It serves to explain the difference between the point of view of the statesmen who framed the Covenant and that of the many jurists, publicists, and professors who in all countries drafted schemes often of great logical and theoretical perfection. The former knew from experience what was, and what was not, possible in international co-operation, or at any rate how international official bodies actually tended to work, whereas the latter in many cases did not possess this knowledge.

4. *The League of Nations Commission.*

(*a*) *The Smuts pamphlet.* Such were the circumstances with regard to the League of Nations in the Allied countries, when the conclusion of the armistice bade the Governments prepare for a Peace Congress. In England a special section of the Foreign Office was promptly formed under Lord Robert Cecil, who had recently resigned the posts of Assistant Secretary of State for Foreign Affairs and Minister of Blockade, and who was already prominent as an enthusiastic advocate of a League

[1] *v.* Vol. I, p. 299 sqq.; Vol. II, p. 22. See also J. A. Salter, *Allied Shipping Control; an Experiment in International Administration,* and Sir M. Hankey, *Diplomacy by Conference,* No. 1, Proceedings of the Institute of International Affairs, which latter includes a diagram of the inter-allied war organization.

of Nations.[1] Both before and after the Section moved to Paris a mass of preliminary work was accomplished. In December a most valuable contribution was made by General Smuts in a confidential memorandum and in a published pamphlet which at once became famous.[2] General Smuts's proposals differed from previous suggestions of responsible statesmen in taking a much more ambitious view of the League, which he envisaged as by no means a mere organization for the settlement of disputes and the prevention of war. A wide extension of its scope was suggested by the break-up of the Russian, Turkish, and Austro-Hungarian Empires, which presented the victorious Allies with vast problems of national or international reconstruction. General Smuts proposed that the right of ultimate disposal of these territories should be regarded as vested in the League of Nations subject to the principle of self-determination, or the consent of the peoples concerned. The League was to take the form of 'a permanent conference between the Governments of the constituent states for the purpose of joint international action in certain defined respects', but was not to derogate from the independence of those states. It was to consist of a General Conference, in which all states would have equal voting power and whose resolutions would have the effect of 'recommendations' to the national Governments and Parliaments; of a Council, or executive committee, giving the Great Powers a bare majority, allowing a veto to a minority of three or more states, and served by a permanent secretariat; and of Courts of Conciliation and Arbitration. General Smuts further proposed the abolition of conscription, the nationalization and inspection of armament factories, and compulsory arbitration in justiciable causes.[3]

When the Conference finally assembled in Paris in January 1919, there were frequent conversations between members of the British and American Delegations and a general agreement as to objects and methods was arrived at.[4]

[1] Lord Robert Cecil's speech at Birmingham on the 11th November 1918 from which extracts are printed in Vol. III, pp. 51–2, was of particular importance.

[2] Extracts from the Smuts pamphlet are given in Vol. III, pp. 52–4.

[3] Extracts from General Smuts's pamphlet are printed in Vol. III, pp. 52–4. Similarities of ideas have been noticed between it and the sugges tions to be found in the *Round Table*, December 1918.

[4] See Chap. XVII (by D. H. Miller) of *What Really Happened at Paris* edited by Col. E. M. House and Professor Charles Seymour, and Baker, *op. cit.* Chaps. XVI ff.

(*b*) *Appointment of Commission ; terms of reference.* On the 25th January the Preliminary Peace Conference, as it was then styled, in plenary session appointed a Commission on the League of Nations with the following terms of reference :

1. It is essential to the maintenance of the world settlement, which the Associated Nations are now met to establish, that a League of Nations be created to promote international co-operation, to ensure the fulfilment of accepted international obligations, and to provide safeguards against war.

2. This League should be treated as an integral part of the General Treaty of Peace, and should be open to every civilized nation which can be relied on to promote its objects.

3. The members of the League should periodically meet in international conference, and should have a permanent organization and secretariat to carry on the business of the League in the intervals between the conferences.

The Conference therefore appoints a Commission representative of the associated Governments to work out the details of the constitution and functions of the League.

This Commission was to be composed of fifteen members, two representing each of the Great Powers, and five the remaining Powers. At a meeting of these last on the 27th January, Belgium, Brazil, China, Portugal, and Serbia were chosen to appoint one representative each. Representatives of Greece, Poland, Rumania, and the Czecho-Slovak Republic were added later.

The Commission thus appointed was a very strong one. It comprised besides the President of the United States, who was its chairman, a future President of Brazil, the Prime Ministers of Italy, Greece, and Czecho-Slovakia, a former Prime Minister of France, the Belgian Foreign Minister, a former Foreign Minister of Japan, and a future Foreign Minister of Italy. Lord Robert Cecil and General Smuts had both done much towards making the idea of the League of Nations appear practical in the eyes of the world, while M. Léon Bourgeois had represented France at the First Hague Conference in 1899, and stood for the tradition connected with that system.

The meetings of the Commission were held at the Hôtel Crillon. The practice was for President Wilson to sit at the head of a long table, an interpreter at his side, with Signor Orlando on his right, and beyond Signor Orlando the French delegates. On President Wilson's left sat Colonel House, and beyond him Lord Robert Cecil and General Smuts ; beyond them again were the representatives of Japan. These details are not wholly insignificant, since the harmony between the American and British delegates, on which the making of the Covenant largely depended, was distinctly favoured by the fact that they could consult together without leaving their places.

The fact, and the importance, of this harmony cannot be too much stressed. The commanding prestige of President Wilson alone, as not only the representative of the least exhausted and most disinterested of the Great Powers, but also the author of those fateful Notes which had remorselessly exposed the pretensions of the German and Austro-Hungarian Governments and appealed to the idealism of mankind, made it hard for the delegates of the Continental Powers to oppose him, had they desired to do so. It was infinitely harder when he was supported, as was nearly invariably the case, by the vigilance, the dialectical skill, the lucidity, the tact and the patent sincerity of Lord Robert Cecil. The fact that these two had agreed on the general lines of the Covenant was of inestimable value from the point of view of business-like discussion and dispatch.

(*c*) *The meetings of the Commission.* The Commission first met on the 3rd February, and decided to work on a Draft Covenant laid before it by President Wilson. Ten meetings were held before the draft, as provisionally accepted by the Commission, was presented to the full Conference on the 14th February. President Wilson then left for America. On his return two informal meetings were held, under the chairmanship of Lord Robert Cecil, with the representatives of thirteen neutral Powers. Three more meetings of the Commission followed, between the 22nd and 26th March, at which amendments were made with a view to meeting neutral and American criticisms. The Covenant so amended was referred to a drafting committee of four, and the text as it left their hands was considered at two final meetings of the Commission on the 10th and 11th April, and on the 28th April the revised Covenant was accepted unanimously at a plenary meeting of the Conference. Thus only fifteen meetings of the Commission were held in all, while the first provisional draft of the Covenant was agreed to on the 11th February—only eight days after the Commission set to work.[1]

[1] It should be said that such rapid progress could not have been possible but for the amount of preliminary work already done and the frequent unofficial meetings and redraftings which filled the hours between the formal

These facts, and these dates, show better than could any words what was the intention of the President and his chief collaborators. They might have proceeded so differently. They might have reasoned that the adoption of a document of such unique importance as the constituent instrument of the League of Nations required long and careful discussion. They might have appointed subcommittees to consider, report on, and harmonize the various schemes proposed from official and unofficial quarters. They might have invited the views of eminent diplomatists, publicists, and international lawyers. In the light of the matter thus placed at their disposal, they might have set themselves slowly and cautiously to draw up an elaborate constitution meticulously providing for every possible emergency. They did the very reverse of all this. They decided that it was all-important to produce an agreed draft at the earliest possible moment; to run no risk of the League being side-tracked and perhaps finally added as an irrelevant and incongruous appendage to a treaty complete in itself. Some at least of them were resolved that, on the contrary, the Covenant of the League must be the framework on which the whole Treaty should be built. So far as the Old World is concerned, their action was justified by the event. It would have been evidently impossible to assign rights and duties to the League—as has been done in the Treaties—if its very form and character had remained indefinite and unknown. They wished also to forestall the inevitable complaints that the conclusion of peace was being delayed by time devoted to the League of Nations. Never were complaints less reasonable. The Commission arranged its sittings so as not to clash with those of the Supreme Council, which President Wilson had of course to attend, and on one occasion at least sat on till long after midnight.[1]

The adoption of this policy—of coming to a rapid agreement on essentials—involved the avoidance of contentious matter so far as possible. Valuable time would have been lost had the Commission indulged in protracted debates on questions of principle where the minds of both sides were obviously made up.[2]

sittings of the Commission. *v.* Vol. III, pp. 56–8 for revisions of text of Covenant, and *ibid.*, pp. 60–5 for President Wilson's speech, 14th February 1919, introducing the Draft Covenant.

[1] For a strong criticism of the method adopted, see R. Lansing, *Peace Negotiations,* particularly Chaps. XII, XIV, XVI.

[2] President Wilson told the Senate Committee on Foreign Relations: 'We did not discuss ideas half as much as we discussed phraseologies.' Senate Document No. 106, 66th Congress, 1st Session, p. 508.

Such questions were reserved for private discussion between the parties chiefly concerned, in the hope that an agreement might be reached out of Court after further consideration and the consultation of principals. Often therefore the most important decisions were not come to, or only nominally come to, at the formal meetings—a concession to 'secret diplomacy' apparently essential in the interests of convenience and efficiency. These negotiations behind the scenes were sometimes successful, sometimes not. A notable case in which agreement on a difficult question was attained outside the Commission is that of the Mandate section of the Covenant. The question of Mandates (*v.* Vol. II, p. 26), 'was raised in the Council of Ten at an early meeting in January; it immediately became the subject of acute controversy, and the whole project seemed in danger of splitting on the rocks of South African and Australian nationalism. The situation was saved by a carefully drafted compromise which appears bodily in Art. XXII of the Covenant, and was left untouched by the Commission of Nineteen throughout its deliberations'.

An unsuccessful instance of this method occurred in the case of the Japanese proposal to insert in the Covenant some recognition of the principle of racial equality. Much time was spent in trying to find a formula acceptable to all the parties principally concerned, but without success, and finally the Japanese representatives carried out their intention of making a public protest against the rejection of their proposals.[1]

(*d*) *The Wilson Drafts.* It has been stated above that the Commission worked on a draft Covenant submitted by President Wilson. In August 1919 the President gave to the Senate Committee on Foreign Relations certain information as to its origin. Some months before the Conference assembled he had received a copy of the Phillimore report and had used it more or less as a basis on which to 'build a draft' of his own, 'which was quite different, inasmuch as it put definiteness where there had been what seemed indefiniteness in the Phillimore suggestion'. Later on, after his arrival in Paris, he rewrote his draft in the light of a study of General Smuts's proposals.[2] The

[1] One of the results of this lack of success was the dropping of a stipulation in the Draft Covenant approving the principle of religious equality.

[2] See Senate Document No. 106, 66th Congress, 1st Session, pp. 504, 546. Baker, *op. cit.*, Vol. I, pp. 225–8, Vol. III, p. 100.

revised version was shown to the President's advisers on the 10th January. Various modifications were made in the next three weeks as the result of discussions with them and with members of foreign delegations; on the British side a short memorandum was produced by Lord Robert Cecil, followed by a more elaborate Draft Convention, dated the 20th January. The scheme which the President finally presented to the Commission on the 3rd February had been put into shape a few hours previously, on the basis of the previous discussions and drafts, by Mr. (now Sir Cecil) Hurst, of the British Foreign Office, and Mr. David Hunter Miller, of the American Peace Commission; both in matter and wording, though not in arrangement, it was to a large extent closely modelled on the British draft convention of the 20th January. This latter document and the President's revised draft may be regarded, therefore, as the parents of the League of Nations Covenant; both of them owe much to the Phillimore Report and to General Smuts's Memorandum.[1]

(*e*) *Influence of the Smuts pamphlet on the Wilson Draft.* The revised Wilson draft consisted of a preamble, thirteen articles, and six supplementary agreements, some of which last in particular, dealing with the establishment of a mandatory system, were based on the Smuts recommendations. From General Smuts came also the dual organization of Conference and Council, the suggestion that the former should act only on the initiative of the latter, the distribution of seats on the Council among great, small, and medium Powers, and the grant of a veto to a minority of three. From the same source came the abolition of conscription and of the private manufacture of weapons of war, though President Wilson did not go so far as General Smuts with regard to the limitation of armaments. The demand for 'full and frank publicity' as to armaments and programmes is the President's own. So is the mutual guarantee, under certain conditions, of political independence and territorial integrity, and a curiously complicated suggestion

[1] See Mr. Miller's account in *What Really Happened at Paris*, pp. 403–5; also Mr. Bullitt's evidence before the Senate, *op. cit.*, pp. 1,161 ff., where the schemes of President Wilson and Lord Robert Cecil are printed; some of these are reprinted by Mr. Lansing, *The Peace Negotiations*, pp. 253 ff. See also Baker, *op. cit.*, Vol. I, pp. 229 ff. and Vol. III, pp. 117 ff., where the President's final draft and the British Draft Convention are printed as Documents 14 and 15. The former did not differ greatly from the President's second (first Paris) draft referred to above.

for an appeal in certain cases from an arbitral award. The general principles proposed for the settlement of disputes—including compulsory arbitration in justiciable causes, which are here defined—and for the coercion of the covenant-breaker are similar to those in the Smuts memorandum. The two last articles provide for the admission to the League, by a two-thirds majority of the Body of Delegates (or Conference), of any Power 'whose government is based upon the principle of popular self-government', and for the abrogation of all treaty undertakings inconsistent with the Covenant. There are, moreover, vague stipulations for the fair treatment of manual labourers and of racial or national minorities in all countries represented in the League.[1]

(*f*) *The British Plan.* The British Draft Convention has three chapters, the first dealing with the functions and organization of the League in more or less general terms, the second providing detailed machinery for the performance of one of these functions, namely the restraint of war. Other functions include the protection of the territorial integrity of Members against forcible aggression from without (with an important reservation in the case of a Member refusing to accept a modification of frontiers recommended by the League); the tutelage of backward peoples; the supervision of the arms traffic; and the study of various questions of international interest, including conditions of industry and labour, and the making of recommendations on these subjects. The organization of the League is to consist, much as suggested by General Smuts, of a general conference of 'responsible representatives' of all Member States, of a Council of the five Great Powers, with provision for co-operation, as temporary members of the Council, by other states on matters 'directly affecting' their interests, and of a permanent Secretariat under a Chancellor. The right of the British Empire to separate representation for the Dominions and India is expressly recognized. The provisions for the avoidance of war are based, like those of the schemes previously mentioned, on the principle that war is inadmissible except after the submission of the dispute either to a legal or a conciliatory body. The bodies proposed by the British draft are a Court of

[1] The President's third and final draft contained four additional supplementary agreements, dealing with religious equality, the closing of the high seas by the League, the publication of treaties, and commercial equality respectively.

International Law and the Council, or Conference, of the League. The sanctions for breach of the agreement not to go to war are substantially those of the Covenant, but are rather more elaborately defined. It is noteworthy that there is no provision for compulsory arbitration in any case, nor any obligation to carry out an award or unanimous decision, though Members do agree not to go to war with any state complying therewith. Nor does the draft say anything on the subject of disarmament, of the publication of treaties, of amendment of the convention, or of withdrawal from the League. Though much more ambitious than the scheme of the Phillimore Committee, and much less so than that of General Smuts, it is evident how much it owes to both.

(g) *The Hurst-Miller Draft.* The Hurst-Miller draft, as laid before the Commission by President Wilson, incorporates the main provisions of the British draft as to the functions and organization of the League and as to the settlement of disputes. It omits the clause making the guarantee of territorial integrity conditional on compliance with the League's recommendation, but takes from President Wilson the declaration now forming Art. XI of the Covenant, and from General Smuts the obligation to carry out an arbitral award; 'arbitration' is spoken of rather than a 'Court of International Law'. From General Smuts, too, come stipulations regarding the reduction of armaments and 'the feasibility of abolishing compulsory military service', and the acceptance of the Mandate principle and that of the Open Door in Mandate territories. From President Wilson come the preamble, stipulations for publicity of treaties and of armament programmes, a guarantee of religious equality, and the proposal that non-Members may be admitted to the League by a two-thirds majority of the Assembly. The draft consists of twenty-two articles, and contains the main features and much of the wording of the Covenant of the League of Nations.

The drafts submitted by the French and Italian delegates at the first meeting of the Commission will be touched on later. They were never considered as a whole by the Commission, which worked throughout on the English text of the President's draft, discussing it article by article.

(h) *Summary of the Work of the Commission.* On the whole, there was wonderful agreement. It was quite the exception for a vote to be taken. On some questions members of the Commission reserved their opinion till they should have consulted their Governments, and at the Plenary Conference of the 28th April protests were made on particular points by the representatives of France and Japan. But as to the general lines, and indeed most of the details, of the Covenant unanimity was attained and maintained, and it was possible to present the document to the Conference as an agreed report. This unanimity was all the more remarkable in face of the fundamental difference between two points of view represented on the Commission. This difference was not between the Great and Small Powers, as some may have supposed. After the principle that the Small Powers, or 'Powers with special interests', should be permanently represented on the Council had been accepted at the second meeting, there was a good deal of discussion as to the number of places to be given to them and the method of selection, but the nine spokesmen of the Small Powers on the Commission did not by any means all take the same side.[1] The real divergence lay between the adherents of the rigid, the definite, the logical, in other words the juridical point of view, and those who preferred the flexible, the indefinite, the experimental, the diplomatic; between those who feared human nature and wished to bind the future, and those who believed in human nature and were content to trust the future; between those who desired written guarantees, and those who desired moral obligations only; to be cynical, between those who expected to receive under the Covenant, and those who expected to give; in a word, between the continental point of view and the Anglo-Saxon. Very naturally, those states which by bitter experience knew most of the sufferings of war, and by the accident of position were most exposed to them, were not anxious to give up the protections of the old order, such as they were, except for definite promises of assistance under effective sanctions. No less naturally the great non-continental states, with their less intimate knowledge of the horrors of land-warfare and their tradition against interference and alliances, were less in bondage to fear, and, while fully

[1] The principle of differentiation between Great and Small Powers appeared in the schemes both of Lord Robert Cecil and of General Smuts; but whereas the former gave the Small Powers no representation on the Council, General Smuts—followed by President Wilson—put them in a permanent minority of one.

intending to meet the demands of duty and honour, preferred to leave particular decisions to posterity. The result was a compromise, but no is stronger than yes, and on the whole the principle of flexibility and elasticity prevailed.[1]

5. *The Principles of the Covenant.* It is impossible within the space of a single chapter to analyse the Covenant article by article, exploring the origins of the several provisions and tracing the modifications to which they were subjected. Only the principal features of the Covenant can be studied, and it will be convenient to consider them in the light of the divergence just mentioned, which became very prominent in the discussions on the delicate question of sovereignty.

(*a*) *Was the League a dissoluble or indissoluble union?* For instance, to begin with, was the League of Nations to be a dissoluble or an indissoluble union? Was it of the nature of an alliance or a federation? There was nothing said on the point in the first draft of the Covenant, nor was the question seriously raised till the President came back from the United States. But in the later series of meetings a very interesting debate occurred. On the one side it was maintained that this was the inauguration of a new world order, which, almost by hypothesis, must be permanent. How could states in an exposed position be asked to give up their age-long traditions of self-defence for a mere temporary promise of protection, which might at any moment be cancelled by the withdrawal of the more powerful guarantors? You cannot have the new world order one day, and the old diplomacy the next. On the other side it was argued that proud nations, jealous for their sovereignty, would not readily join the League unless they knew that they *could* retire from it if they so desired. A state conscious of ultimate freedom will not be nervous about its independence, and will be unlikely to exercise its right to withdraw; attempt to bind it, and it will feel distrustful and constrained. In this case the principle of permanence prevailed, though a very important saving provision was included at the end of Art. I; even this, however, failed to satisfy the Senate

[1] These sentences have been left as they were written in 1920, before it was clear that President Wilson did not represent the view of the United States. The Senate feared that the indefiniteness of the Covenant would in fact bind America, and would have preferred something at once more rigid and more narrow. Mr. Lansing always held the rigid juridical point of view, and consequently wished to limit the scope of the League; see *The Peace Negotiations, passim.*

of the United States. A suggestion that no withdrawal from the League should be allowed till after a fixed term of years was considered on the Commission but dropped.

(*b*) *Obligation as to delay in international disputes.* Let us turn to the all-important question of the extent of the obligations to be accepted by Members of the League in the matter of international disputes. The official Dutch and Swiss proposals made war at any time illegal. None of the Anglo-Saxon schemes already referred to went so far as this; nor was this view even considered on the Commission. There was general agreement that the essential thing was to secure delay; there must be no *sudden* aggression. Delay and publicity, both of which were so noticeably lacking in 1914, would give public opinion a chance to assert itself. The first paragraph of Art. XII is the keystone of the Covenant: 'the Members of the League agree that, if there should arise between them any dispute likely to lead to a rupture, they will submit the matter either to arbitration or to inquiry by the Council, and they agree in no case to resort to war until three months after the award by the arbitrators or the report by the Council.' Further negative undertakings are contained in the last paragraph of Art. XIII, and the sixth of Art. XV. They are those with which we are familiar from the various Anglo-American proposals.

(*c*) '*Justiciable*' *and* '*non-justiciable*' *disputes.* But could not more have been done? Could not more account have been taken of the essential distinction between disputes that are, and are not, justiciable? Could not the Commission have agreed to eliminate war in the case of the former, by making a judicial settlement in such case compulsory? This would, of course, have implied a definition of 'justiciable'. The answer is that here again the juridical point of view was worsted by the diplomatic. The Commission were loth to force a particular process of settlement on a reluctant state, and fought shy of compulsory arbitration in any form, even in the matter of the interpretation of the Covenant. This decision may have been necessary, but it amounted to the refusal to take a step which is essential for the establishment of the reign of law in international affairs. All that could be secured in this direction is found in Arts. XII–XIV, namely:

(i) A definition of certain issues 'generally', i. e. prima facie, suitable for arbitration: this list, which is borrowed from the First Hague Convention of 1907, is not exhaustive.

(ii) An obligation to carry out an arbitral award ' in full good faith '.

(iii) An instruction to the Council ' to propose steps ' in the case of an award not being carried out. The fact that this instruction is not given in the case of a recommendation by the Council adds somewhat to the prestige of an arbitral award.

(iv) The decision to form a Permanent Court of International Justice, to which the Council or Assembly can refer any issue for an advisory opinion.

It is to be noted that everywhere else the Covenant speaks of ' arbitration ', not of ' judicial decision ', though the latter is allowed for by the third paragraph of Art. XIII. Yet arbitral awards, it is generally agreed, can never have the force of the pronouncements of a permanent Court of Law, capable of working out a coherent system of jurisprudence. It is therefore of good augury that the Assembly of 1921 approved drafting amendments to Arts. XII, XIII, XIV, and XV, adding the words ' or judicial settlement ' after the word ' arbitration ' wherever it occurs.[1]

(*d*) *Article X and the Guarantee of Territorial Integrity.* It was said above that the prohibition of sudden aggression is the keystone of the Covenant. A similar phrase, with the same intent, has been used by President Wilson of the undertaking in Art. X ' to respect and preserve as against external aggression the territorial integrity and existing political independence of all members of the League '. We may remember that practically identical words were used by the President in 1916 to express his ideal first for a Pan-American, and later for a world-wide, union. He admitted to the Senate Foreign Relations Committee in August 1919 that he was the author of Article X ' as much as anybody '; though his own original proposal contained a significant qualification.[2] Art. III of the President's first Paris draft ran as follows: ' The Contracting Powers unite in guaranteeing to each other political independence and territorial integrity; but it is understood between them that such territorial readjustments, if any, as may in the future become necessary by reason of changes in present racial conditions and aspirations, or present social and political relationships, pursuant to the principle of self-determination, and also such territorial readjustments as may in the judgment of

[1] For matters concerned with the establishment of the Permanent Court of International Justice, and the ' optional clause ' accepting compulsory judicial settlement on condition of reciprocity, see this Chap. Part III, *passim*.

[2] *Op. cit.*, p. 546.

three-fourths of the Delegates be demanded by the welfare and manifest interest of the peoples concerned, may be effected if agreeable to those peoples; and that territorial changes may in equity involve material compensation. The Contracting Powers accept without reservation the principle that the peace of the world is superior in importance to every question of political jurisdiction or boundary.'[1] The British Draft Convention of the 20th January contained a similar qualification: 'If at any time it should appear that the boundaries of any state guaranteed . . . do not conform to the requirements of the situation, the League shall take the matter under consideration, and may recommend to the parties affected any modification which it may deem necessary. If such recommendation is rejected by the parties affected, the States members of the League shall, so far as the territory in question is concerned, cease to be under the obligation to protect the territory in question from forcible aggression by other states, imposed upon them by the above provision.'[2] Neither form of qualification, however,—and the fact may well be regretted—survived into the Hurst-Miller draft, and Art. X bore the brunt of American attack on the Covenant, as forcing on the United States an obligation to send troops to all parts of the world in defence of possibly inequitable frontiers. The Senate was not satisfied by the President's assurance that 'it is a moral, not a legal, obligation, and leaves our Congress absolutely free to put its own interpretation upon it in all cases that call for action. It is binding in conscience only, not in law'.[3] The President also explained without avail that, as he understood Art. X, 'territorial integrity' meant immunity not from 'armed intervention' but from forcible annexation.[4] In other words, the

[1] This draft article was violently criticized by members of the American Peace Commission; see Lansing, *op. cit.*, Chap. VII; Senate Document No. 106, pp. 1176 ff. Baker, *op. cit.*, I, 230, states that the words 'as against external aggression' were inserted on the advice of General Bliss. In point of fact the germ of this idea dates back to the 3rd October 1914, when House wrote to Page 'with the President's knowledge and consent' . . . 'When the War is ended and the necessary territorial alignments made, it seems to me, the best guarantee of peace could be brought by every nation in Europe guaranteeing the territorial integrity of every other nation'. To this America was later added. *Life and Letters of W. H. Page*, London, 1922, Vol. I, pp. 414–15.

[2] Baker, *op. cit.*, III, 132.

[3] Senate Document, p. 502. See also pp. 509, 514, 534.

[4] *Ibid.*, p. 538. The explanation of Art. 10 in the text is hard to reconcile with a statement of the President occurring on p. 502 of the work quoted: 'Art. 10 seems to me to constitute the very backbone of the

Article was directed against the violent transference of territory from one sovereignty to another without the consent of the League. Armed invasion was provided against by the Covenant in Art. XII quoted above, breach of which brings the sanctions in Art. XVI into force; Art. X really adds very little to this, and would seem to have received an undue share of attention. Nevertheless to the continental states in an exposed position it meant everything; one might say it was the price for which alone they were willing to barter such of their independence as they surrender under the League.[1] That there was no intention to stereotype the existing territorial settlement is clear from paragraph 2 of Art. XI and Art. XIX, while paragraphs 1, 6, and 7 of Art. XV seem to show that the guarantee is not perpetual and unconditional. For all that, Art. X is a stumbling-block to many, and its deletion was formally proposed by the Canadian Government in 1920.[2] The proposal was, however, ultimately adjourned by the Assembly in 1922.

Mr. Lansing's hostility to the Wilsonian League of Nations was largely due to his disapproval of any such 'affirmative guaranty' as that contained in Art. X. An 'affirmative guaranty' implied forcible coercion, and that in its turn implied the predominance of the Great Powers and the abandonment of the principle of international democracy or the equality of states. Mr. Lansing asserts that in the course of 1916 President Wilson became 'convinced that the use of force was the practical method of checking aggressions'.[3]

(*e*) *Limitation and inspection of armaments.* Next, as to the obligation (Art. VIII) not to exceed the limits of armaments proposed by the Council and adopted by the country concerned, and to interchange full and frank information as to programmes. Here the question was not so much as to the obligation itself, as concerning the method of its enforcement. Should there be inspection by the League of national

whole Covenant. Without it the League would be hardly more than an influential debating society.' Could this be fairly said of it if it only forbade forcible annexation? It has been suggested that his recollection of action taken by the United States on several occasions in Southern and Central America may have influenced the President's mind in this matter.

[1] France had in addition the hope of a promise of direct military assistance from Great Britain and the United States in case of unprovoked aggression. But this did not materialize, *v.* Vol. II, pp. 125–7; Vol. III, pp. 337–40.

[2] *v. supra*, pp. 349–50.

[3] *The Peace Negotiations*, p. 32. See Baker, *op. cit.*, I. 223.

armament factories and dockyards? It is no secret that the French pressed for it, and for the establishment of 'une commission chargée des constatations nécessaires'.[1]

Strong as the arguments in favour of *contrôle* appear on paper, the majority of the Commission decided against it on grounds both of expediency and practicability. It was maintained that there were proud nations which, though prepared to carry out the obligation loyally, would never allow their loyalty to be checked and verified by an international committee, and grave doubts were expressed as to whether any really secret information would ever be obtained by such a committee. At any rate in this case the advocates of logicality, definiteness, and compulsion were worsted.[2]

(*f*) *Sanctions*. With regard to the ultimate sanctions for breach of the Covenant, it was generally agreed what these should be (see Art. XVI), but there was some debate as to which of the obligations undertaken should be thus enforced. Should they apply to the obligation to comply with an arbitral award, or not to exceed the agreed limit of armaments? It was decided that they should only apply to the agreements not to resort to war contained in Arts. XII, XIII, and XV. This decision is an extreme instance of the Commission's resolve not to make more demands on national compliance than the barest minimum required to avert sudden war.

(*g*) *Their Enforcement*. On the matter of the execution of these sanctions great differences of opinion existed. There was no question of an international army, navy, or air force, but the French, not unnaturally in view of historical and geographical facts, desired permanent machinery for bringing the sanctions into force without delay. They wanted a body charged with the duty of working out in advance schemes of co-operation, and proposing definite contingents to be supplied by different Powers. At first sight this proposal seems logical and reasonable, but the majority of the Commission held it impracticable. It is an axiom of strategy that plans cannot be drawn up in the air; you must envisage a definite enemy. This leads to a

[1] See Tardieu, *The Truth about the Treaty*, p. 135.

[2] However, the French secured the adoption of Art. 213 of the Treaty of Peace with Germany: 'So long as the present Treaty remains in force, Germany undertakes to give every facility for any investigation which the Council of the League of Nations, acting if need be by a majority vote, may consider necessary.' See Tardieu, *op. cit.*, p. 140.

dilemma: either you must select a prospective enemy and exclude him from your discussions, which is contrary to the whole spirit of a universal League of Nations, or else all nations will plan against one another, which is absurd, since naturally no nation will disclose the confidential information as to its own resources which is required for concerting joint operations. As things stand, contingents and policy must be settled by agreement as each case arises. This may sound an extreme and fatal concession to national sentiment, but it should be remembered, first, that some nations would undoubtedly not agree to the French proposal; secondly, that preliminary plans of action will of course be concerted by nations fearing a threatened assault; and lastly, that everything that is practicable will really be done by the Commission to be established under Art. IX.

(*h*) *Unanimity in Council and Assembly*. The execution of the sanctions raises the vital question of agreement on the Council.[1] Was the Commission wise in generally requiring unanimity both in that body and in the Assembly to give effect to their conclusions. In fact, both in Council and Assembly a bare majority can regulate procedure; a two-thirds majority of the Assembly can admit new members; a bare majority of the Assembly, if all the states on the Council concur, can ratify amendments to the Covenant; and most important of all, the consent of parties to a dispute is not required.[2] The insistence on the need for unanimity has been more criticised than any other point in the Covenant. It is claimed that it will paralyse the action of the League. To say that it merely accepts existing diplomatic tradition is no answer. It must be considered on its merits. First, then, its assailants may be reminded that, in almost every case, what the Council and Assembly have to do, under the Covenant, is not to legislate or to order but to *recommend*. Now the force of a recommendation

[1] In the Draft Covenant presented to the Peace Conference on the 14th February, this body was styled the Executive Council. The misleading adjective was subsequently dropped.

[2] For the difficulties caused by the ambiguous wording of Art. 26, and their solution, see H. W. V. Temperley, *The Second Year of the League*, pp. 59 ff. In 1921 a compromise was agreed to by the Assembly, requiring a three-fourths majority for the acceptance and a bare majority for the ratification of amendments; in each case the Council's unanimous assent is needed. Note that it is provided that a bare majority of the Council may alter stipulations of the Minorities treaties.

depends on the power and prestige of those who recommend, and not upon legal machinery; and in practice the expressed will of the leading Great Powers is not likely to have much more force when the other Powers agree with them than when the former merely form a majority, or even are in a minority. This consideration may appear cynical, but is really the purest common sense. That it escapes notice is due to the fact that most of its critics instinctively think of the League as a kind of super-state, executive and coercive. It is not. Let us take instances. Under Art. VIII, the Council is to 'formulate' plans for the reduction of armaments, but these plans have no force until 'adopted' by the several Governments. The Council is to 'advise' how the obligation of Art. X shall be fulfilled—an obligation which, as President Wilson told the Senate 'is a moral, not a legal, obligation'. Under Art. XIII the Council is to 'propose' the steps to be taken should a state fail to carry out an arbitral award. Under Art. XVI it is to 'recommend' what armed force the members of the League are to contribute for the coercion of a Covenant-breaking state; but there is no obligation on any member to accept its recommendation, even though each member will, under paragraph 5 of Art. IV, have been invited to send a representative to 'sit as a member' of the Council during the discussion. Under Art. XVII it is to 'recommend' what is to be done in a dispute where a state not a member of the League is concerned; if both parties to the dispute are non-members and refuse to accept the obligations of the League, the Council may 'take measures' as well as 'make recommendations', but these measures can, in fact, only be recommendations. Under Art. XIX the Assembly has the right to 'advise the reconsideration' of treaties. In all the above cases, what practical difference would be made if the decision of a majority were substituted for that of all?

But we have not considered the most controversial cases, those arising under Arts. XV and XVI. Article XV provides that in the case of a dispute submitted to the Council, and not settled by it to the satisfaction of the parties, the Council shall 'either unanimously or by a majority vote' issue a report. But whereas the members of the League undertake not to go to war with a state which complies with the 'recommendations' of a report unanimously agreed to (not counting the parties to the dispute), they reserve to themselves full liberty of action if the report is not unanimous. (In neither event, we must remember, do the parties promise to comply with the recommendations of the report.) That is to say, if no unanimous report can be arrived at, not only are both parties to the dispute then at liberty to take up arms, but the other members of the League may help the party they champion. Thus a general war might come about, for, as we have seen, the Covenant does not profess to forbid war in the last resort. In this case the theoretical result of the requirement for unanimity is evident, but whether it would make much difference in practice is very doubtful.

The decision (see Art. XVI) whether any of the engagements under Arts. XII, XIII, or XV, have in fact been broken, was not entrusted to the Council under the Covenant, but was left to the individual judgment of members, each of whom undertook thereupon to break off relations with the covenant-breaker. But by one of the amendments of 1921 this decision is given to the Council, though the rupture of relations still remains a matter for the several states. The less important right of declaring a defaulting state to be no longer a member of the League is entrusted to the Council by the last paragraph of Art. XVI.

Except for this last case, the Council and Assembly have no right of deciding whether members of the League have or have not fulfilled their obligations, as President Wilson was at great pains to explain to the Senate.[1] This applies to the withdrawal clause in Art. I, to Art. VIII, to the obligation under Art. X, and to the question arising under Art. XX as to what obligations are inconsistent with the Covenant.[2] Nor is there any body whose function it is to interpret the Covenant itself. Throughout his discussion with the Senate Committee, the President insisted that the real authority of the League must be moral, not legal; it must depend on ' an attitude of comradeship and protection '; should a state be tempted to violate the spirit of its under-

[1] See Senate Document, No. 106, p. 501.

[2] Even in the most extreme instance of all, that of admission of states to the League, the independence and sovereignty of each state is preserved. States are admitted on a vote of two-thirds of the Assembly. But no state resisting this admission is obliged to give diplomatic recognition to the state thus admitted. Albania was admitted to the League in December 1920, but was not recognized by the Great Powers, who had opposed its admission, till November 1921. If the League were a ' super-state ' such collective admission would imply individual recognition.

takings, 'the only restraining influence would be the public opinion of the world'. He trusted to what he called in 1914 'the moral compulsions of the human conscience', mobilized by publicity and given time to act.

Such, indeed, was the point of view taken by the chief British and American promoters of the League of Nations, and on the whole embodied in the Covenant. The rejection of the idea of giving binding force to a majority vote is the logical fulfilment of the Anglo-Saxon principle of freedom and elasticity, the principle of not trying to bind the nations of the future, but of trusting them to be at least as wise as those of the present. Critics inclined to challenge it should ask themselves very seriously whether, with national feeling as powerful as it was known to be in the United States and the British Dominions, for example, it would have been either wise or practical to make provision for voting down a Great Power on a matter which it considered vital. May it not be more profitable to emphasize the real fact that agreement is necessary in important international questions, if harmony is to be attained in practice? That agreement is possible is shown by the experience of the League of Nations Commission.

(i) *The Functions of the League in Peace.* The most controversial and the most arresting features of the Covenant are those which have just been discussed, namely, those dealing with the avoidance of war and international action in emergencies. Fortunately, however, life does not consist wholly, or even mainly, of emergencies; while it is plain that action in emergencies depends on the instincts and habits developed in ordinary times. So it may well be that the most practically important sections of the Covenant are those dealing with the functions of the League in peace (see Arts. XXII–XXV). These activities all centre round the permanent secretariat, which is charged with their co-ordination and development. Its importance can hardly be overrated. When contempt is poured, as is so frequently the case, on the record of international action in the past, instances are usually taken in which some definitely political interest was closely involved, as in the Balkans and Morocco. The many cases of successful non-political administration are forgotten. For the future the League will provide facilities for a wide extension of common action in non-political matters, and so create a powerful tradition of co-operation between nations in the affairs of peace—a tradition which may gradually win acceptance in more controversial spheres.

6. *The French, Italian, Dutch, Swiss, Scandinavian, and German Schemes.* After this sketch of the main features of the Covenant as adopted, it may be of interest to contrast with it the other official schemes laid before the Commission. Of these the French and Italian drafts were presented at the first meeting; the Dutch, Swiss, and Scandinavian were chiefly studied in the interval after the publication of the Draft Covenant, during which the representatives of thirteen neutral Powers were heard orally; the German scheme was published on the 23rd April, and was considered by members of the Commission along with the other German counter-proposals in June.

(*a*) *The French Scheme.*[1] The French scheme, which is dated June 1918, consists of five sections:

(1) Statement of the principles to be taken as basis of a League of Nations;
(2) Diplomatic, legal, and economic sanctions;
(3) Military sanctions;
(4) Scope and functions of the International Body;
(5) Composition of the International Council and of the Permanent Delegation.

It makes plain at the outset that 'the object of the League of Nations shall not be to establish an international political state. It shall merely aim at the maintenance of peace by substituting right for might as the arbiter of disputes. It will thus guarantee to all states alike, whether small or great, the exercise of their sovereignty'. It is to be represented by 'an International Body, composed of the responsible heads of governments or of their delegates'. This body is to have the right of referring a dispute which cannot be settled amicably to an International Tribunal, or of deciding it itself. 'It shall enforce the execution of its decisions and those of the International Tribunal; at its demand every nation shall be bound, in agreement with the other nations, to exert its economic, naval, and military power against any recalcitrant nation.' For this purpose there is to be an international force; the Inter-

[1] A translation is printed as Document 17 in Baker, *op. cit.*, Vol. III.

national Body is to determine its strength 'and fix the contingents which must be held at its disposal'. There is also to be a permanent staff whose functions are thus defined:

'It shall be the duty of the permanent international staff to deal, under the supervision of the International Body, with everything relating to the organization of the joint forces and eventual conduct of military operations. It will in particular be charged with the task of inspecting international forces and armaments in agreement with the military authorities of each state, and of proposing any improvements it may deem necessary either in the international military organization or in the constitution, composition, and methods of recruiting of the forces of each state. . . . The International Body shall be entitled, at any time, to require that the member states introduce any alteration into their national system of recruiting which the staff may report to be necessary.'

The International Body is elsewhere spoken of as the 'International Council'; decisions of importance can only be taken at a plenary meeting of the Council, but there is to be a 'Permanent Delegation' of fifteen elected members of the Council to conduct its correspondence and other secondary business between meetings. It is not stated whether the Council may decide by majority vote, but, in view of the insistence on the need for 'respect for the sovereignty of states', and of the invariable diplomatic tradition, it may be assumed that unanimity is required.

The French scheme differs from the Covenant in the following important points among others: (1) The League can compel members to accept its decisions and those of the International Court. (2) The League has considerable powers over the military policy of its members; it can fix the size of their contingents to the international force, and regulate their method of recruitment, e. g. it can enforce conscription. (3) These powers are in the hands of a large body of between forty and fifty members. (4) The activities of the League are limited to the prevention of war. Thus, while (1) and (2) give the League in theory much greater powers than does the Covenant, (3) would make the exercise of these powers extremely difficult, even if national sentiment sanctioned them, which in several countries it certainly would not.

(*b*) *The Italian Scheme.* The Italian scheme begins by laying down certain fundamental principles by which international relations are to be regulated. They include control of the international distribution of foodstuffs and raw materials, and the prohibition of secret treaties. The organs of the League are to be a Conference in which all member-states have one vote, a Council composed much as under the Covenant, a Permanent Secretariat, an Economic, a Labour and a Military Commission, and a Court of International Justice. Resolutions of the Conference, which is charged with the development of the principles of International Law, require a two-thirds majority. Disputes must be submitted either to arbitration or to the Council, which can either refer them to the Court of International Justice, deal with them itself, or refer them to the Conference. 'Any solution of a dispute adopted by two-thirds of the Conference or of the Council shall be binding on the parties concerned. The minority shall in any case be accorded the right to draw up its own reasoned finding and to publish it together with the finding of the majority. Failing a two-thirds majority, the opinion of the majority shall have the weight of a simple recommendation.' If a state fails to comply with the decision of the Court or of two-thirds of the Conference or Council, the Council can subject it to penalties ranging from rupture of diplomatic negotiations to joint war. Should a state go to war without waiting for a decision, all other members become automatically in a state of war with it.

Thus the Italian scheme goes a good deal farther than the Covenant as regards the obligations accepted by members.

(*c*) *The Dutch Scheme.* The Dutch memorandum on a League of Nations takes the view that only the principles and most necessary organs of the League should be established by the original treaty, and consequently only sketches its main outlines. It is chiefly concerned with the procedure for settling disputes, and, while forbidding war and making a judicial settlement of justiciable disputes compulsory, it makes no provision for immediate discussion and action in a crisis, and does not seriously consider the question of sanctions. There is no mention of any executive council, permanent secretariat, or representative assembly, but international legislation is contemplated. Alliances are forbidden, the League is open to all states, and members may withdraw after a fixed number of years. Compared with the other schemes that we have considered, the Dutch is only a skeleton.

(*d*) *The Swiss Scheme.* The Swiss project, on the other hand, is a very full and carefully drawn up document. In it the League takes the form of an ' indissoluble alliance ' of states which engage in no case to go to war with one another, except in execution of the decisions of the League. There is consequently a very elaborate provision for the settlement of disputes by one of three methods—conciliation, judicial process, and mediation. The awards made in the two latter are in the last resort binding. Unanimity in awards and decisions is not required. The chief organ of the League is a Council of Mediation, a permanent council of resident ambassadors. Commissions of Conciliation are formed *ad hoc* out of the Council of Mediation. The representatives on the Council of Mediation of those states which undertake to guarantee the execution of the League's decisions form the Permanent Delegation, which mediates in cases where the offer of conciliation has been refused and judicial process is inadmissible. Its decisions apparently need not be unanimous. If a state is refractory, the Permanent Delegation considers the necessary measures and submits its decisions, taken by a bare majority, to the Council of Mediation, which must sanction them by a double two-thirds majority—both of the states represented on it and of their aggregate population. If the peace has already been broken, the Permanent Delegation can itself, by a bare majority, decide what measures should be taken. There is also a Conference of States, in which each state fixes the composition and numbers of its own delegation, but has only one vote. The admission of new members requires a simple majority both of the states in the Conference of States and of their aggregate population. (No state may count more than 100 millions of population.) As to amendment, certain fundamental provisions can only be altered with the consent of all the states concerned. Other important constitutional amendments require a simple majority of the states and total population represented at a Conference of States, and a two-thirds majority of the same at another Conference held from two to five years later.

The Swiss project demands a considerably greater sacrifice of state sovereignty than does the Covenant, and at the same time fails to recognize the special position of the Great Powers, on whom the chief burdens must fall. Its machinery also has the disadvantage of being very complicated, and the method of reckoning populations, which would give China greater weight than France, Germany, Italy, or Japan, is less satisfactory than ingenious. The influence of the Swiss constitution is very noticeable.

(*e*) *The Scandinavian Scheme.* The Scandinavian memorandum is the work of a joint commission representing the governments of Sweden, Norway, and Denmark. It is primarily concerned with the prevention of war by the settlement of disputes. Its proposals are based on the following general principles: (1) The legal equality of all states is recognized. (2) Members of the League undertake not to go to war before submitting their disputes either to a Permanent Court for judicial decision, to the existing Hague Tribunal for arbitration, or to a Commission of Conciliation modelled on the commissions set up under the Bryan Treaties. (3) Reference to the Permanent Court or the Hague is voluntary, not compulsory. (4) Decisions of the Court and of arbitral tribunals are binding; the recommendations of a Commission of Conciliation are not, and parties not satisfied with them may go to war after a month. (5) The sanctions of the League are regarded as a matter in which small states have no right to take the initiative, and no suggestions are made on this head. (6) International co-operation does not figure largely in the draft, and permanent organs of international administration are not proposed. (7) But there are to be international conferences, modelled on those of the Hague, every five years, to develop international law; each state is to have one vote, and is not to be bound without its own consent. (8) There is also to be an International Council, consisting of fifteen members, elected for a term of six years by a panel of electors on which each state is to have one representative. This Council is to perform some of the functions of a standing committee, and some of a secretariat, but is not intended to have the authority of the Council of the Paris scheme.

(*f*) *The German Scheme.* The German scheme is extremely elaborate. It defines the especial objects of the League of Nations as: (1) Prevention of international disputes. (2) Disarmament. (3) Assurance of free commercial relations and of general economic equality. (4) Protection of national minorities. (5) Creation of an international labour charter. (6) Regulation of colonial matters. (7) Co-ordination of existing and future international institutions. (8) Creation of a World

Parliament. The organs of the League are to be: (*a*) The Congress of States, deciding by two-thirds majority; each state has from one to three representatives, but all the representatives of one state must vote the same way, as in the Bundesrat of the German Empire. (*b*) The World Parliament, to which each national parliament is to elect from one to ten delegates. (*c*) The Permanent International Tribunal; (*d*) the International Board of Mediation; (*e*) the International Administrative Boards; (*f*) the Chancellery. In the intervals between meetings of the Congress of States, business is to be conducted by its permanent Standing Committee. All disputes must be referred either to the International Tribunal, which is given much wider powers than under the Covenant, or to the Board of Mediation, which consists of fifteen members chosen by an electoral college of four nominees of each state. The decisions of either are binding. If a state refuses to comply, or otherwise violates the constitution of the League, the Board of Mediation may decide on the application of the usual coercive measures. (The lack of authority of such a Board, as compared with the Council of the Covenant, may be noted in passing.) Disarmament is to be effected by mutual agreement, and there is to be international control over its observance. No warships are to be allowed except those of an international marine police force. There is to be freedom of transit, and no economic discrimination.

The German project, which has sixty-six articles in all, is of course far more ambitious than the Covenant, but it takes much less account of existing feeling, and, while attributing extensive functions to the League, provides no really powerful body, like the Council of the Paris scheme, capable of acting on its behalf. It is, in fact, a typical product of German liberalism.

(*g*) *Summary*. Taken together, the various Continental schemes for a League of Nations show the idealism and the ingenuity to be expected of their distinguished authors. But whereas the Covenant is the work of practical statesmen, these schemes rather express the point of view of jurists and international lawyers. They tend to pay more attention to the settlement of disputes than to the means of securing international co-operation in normal times, while with regard to disputes they are more concerned in arriving at an ideally just settlement than at one with the requisite authority to back it. The framers of the Covenant, on the other hand, approaching the subject in the light of Allied war experience, are content to establish a powerful body—the Council—representing the actual distribution of the organized political force of the world, and to trust to its wisdom and authority to preserve the peace by one means or another.

7. *Other Functions of the League of Nations under the Peace Treaties*. To return to the Paris scheme, by no means all the functions of the League are enumerated in the Covenant. The elastic nature of this document, and the speed with which it was produced, made it possible, in accordance with the hopes of its authors, for additional activities of various kinds to be assigned to the League in other parts of the peace treaties. For instance, there is the Labour Charter, with its parallel system of periodical conferences and a permanent secretariat, the latter controlled by a Governing Body. Then, by the treaty with Germany, the Council is assigned rights with regard to the extension of the period of some of the economic clauses (Art. 280), and also to the revision and extension of certain stipulations in the section dealing with Ports, Waterways, and Railways. The government of the Saar valley is assigned for fifteen years to the League as trustee, and is to be exercised through a Commission appointed by the Council. The Free City of Danzig is placed under the guarantee of the League, which is to nominate a High Commissioner. By other treaties the rights of religious and racial minorities in some of the countries of Central Europe are placed under the guarantee of the League, and the provisions establishing them are not to be modified without the consent of a majority of the Council. The government of the country agrees also to refer any dispute on these subjects between it and a member of the Council to the Permanent Court of International Justice, and to accept the Court's award. Austria moreover agrees to regard her independence as inalienable 'otherwise than with the consent of the Council.'

These are all examples of the part the League may play, under existing agreements, in the international relations of the future.

8. *Conclusion*. We should now be in a position to realize what are the essential and distinctive features of the League of Nations as constituted at Paris.

1. It is a prominent association of the self-governing nations of the world for the double purpose of ' promoting international co-operation ' and ' achieving international peace and security '. It is not an organization that will only be set in motion at seasons of crisis. Its function is far wider; it is to apply the collective wisdom and conscience of organized mankind to the settlement of all cases where national effort alone must be inadequate.

2. It works by means of periodical conferences of statesmen and a permanent secretariat of officials and experts. A permanent Court of Justice was also to be established, and is now in being.

3. Its object is to secure agreement, not to enforce decisions; to help what is good in the nations to assert itself, not to compel the nations to be good. It is a league of nations, not a world-state. In other words, it depends on public opinion in the several countries.

4. In order to facilitate agreement, its members promise not to go to war till a peaceful settlement of a dispute has been tried; they pledge themselves to regard any state that breaks this promise as a public enemy.

5. No more has been put in the Covenant than what appeared the necessary minimum to give the League a fair start; its future lines of development are left to itself.

When these principles are grasped, we can understand why the makers of the Covenant were not concerned to include much that lawyers and theorists demand.

There is no express recognition, or disavowal, of the ' equality of states '. All states are represented in the Assembly, only certain ones in the Council—both for practical reasons. Since the Council and Assembly can only ' recommend ', a declaration in either sense would seem to be irrelevant.

There is no body representing the popular, as opposed to the official, element in the several states. So long as the League can only recommend, this omission cannot be considered of vital importance. A popular assembly may perhaps be added later with advantage, but it is not required by the principles of the League.

There is no insistence on the submission of legal issues to legal or even quasi-legal decision; and there is no non-political Council of Mediation or Conciliation. Why? Because so long as all possible methods of peaceful settlement are in fact left open, as they are under the Covenant, its framers wished to make as few rules and restrictions as possible. They had no mind to tie the hands of the Council.

There is no international armed force, no international general staff, no compulsory abolition of conscription, nor inspection of armament works, nor reduction of armaments to a limit fixed by the League. Why? Because all such inroads upon national sovereignty would provoke great opposition in many countries, while they were not considered essential for the starting of the League.

There is no body entitled to interpret the Covenant, or to pronounce as to what is, or is not, consistent with it.[1] This omission would be indefensible if the Covenant were a body of legal obligations, like a national constitution; it is intelligible if we look on it as a statement of principles by which the signatories express their intention of being guided. The agreement of to-day must be repeated and consummated in the future. That is the spirit of the League. It is to be a league of free, not of fettered nations. But this is a hard saying for legalistic minds.

Indeed, there is something of a paradox in the contrast drawn in this chapter between the desire of the Anglo-Saxon statesmen for elasticity and that of the French for definiteness. For we are accustomed to think of England and America as homes of the Rule of Law, while we credit the French with a love for abstract statements of rights and duties. The fact is that the Anglo-Saxon legal and constitutional tradition teaches us to distinguish very clearly between what is and is not the sphere of positive law—to draw the line sharply, for instance, between law and convention. Where there is law, we insist that it shall rule, but we are acquainted with what we may call a non-Austinian space, where the place of law is taken by understandings and conventions. Here we are prepared for an elasticity resulting in a lack of definiteness, it is true, but allowing for organic development, and perhaps none the less effective in its results. Such is the atmosphere of the Paris Covenant. Continental statesmen may find such ideas unfamiliar or uncongenial, and may see no value in understandings with only semi-legal authority. We may not presume

[1] Except in the case mentioned on p. 450.

to judge between the two points of view. We can only hope that the operations of the League will harmonize them by succeeding.

In the success of these principles we of British nationality have a double interest ; for they are those by which the British Commonwealth exists. Its central organ is the Imperial conference, a body very similar to the Council of the Covenant, a body meeting occasionally, composed of statesmen responsible to their own peoples, and dependent on unanimous agreement. In the case of the League of Nations the bonds of common allegiance and common descent are lacking, but the bond of common interest is there, the bond of common suffering in the past, and of the certainty, if the League fails, of common suffering in the future.

CHAPTER VI

INTERNATIONAL DEVELOPMENTS UNDER THE LEAGUE OF NATIONS

PART II

THE INTERNATIONAL LABOUR SECTION OF THE TREATIES[1]

General. The genesis of the Labour Section of the Peace Treaties[2] has been explained in an earlier volume of this work.[3] It was one of the constructive experiments in the direction of creating an international comity of nations which distinguishes the work of the Peace Conference from that of previous Peace Conferences; and it was not the least audacious of these experiments. The International Labour Organization, which it created, was bred of the belief, widely if only half-consciously held at the time of the Armistice, that the solution of purely political problems would be sterile, unless some solution could also be found to the social problem, which the war had brought into sharp relief in every country, belligerent or neutral, and upon which the fires of the Russian Revolution had thrown a lurid light. Just as the League of Nations itself was designed to bring about co-operation between nations in the political sphere, the International Labour Organization was planned to promote a like international effort in the social field.

1. *The Constitution of the International Labour Organization.* The constitution of the Organization is detailed and precise. In the Preamble to Part XIII its functions and scope are clearly set out. The constitution of the General Conference and that of the Governing Body of the International Labour Office are defined.

(*a*) *Relation to the League.* It is provided by the Treaty

[1] Complete to July 1922.

[2] Part XIII of the Treaty of Versailles, Vol. III, pp. 314–28; Part XIII of the Treaty of Trianon; Part XIII of the Treaty of St. Germain; Part XII of the Treaty of Neuilly.

[3] See Vol. II, Chap. I, Part II.

(Art. 392) that 'the International Labour Office shall be established at the seat of the League of Nations as part of the organization of the League', and its expenses, together with those of the Conference and the Governing Body, are paid out of the general funds of the League. In other words, the International Labour Organization is the instrument set up to carry out Art. XXIII (a) of the Covenant, by which the members undertook to 'endeavour to secure and maintain fair and humane conditions of labour for men, women, and children, both in their own countries and in all countries to which their commercial and industrial relations extend'. It is therefore an integral part of the League, but by virtue of its constitution, as laid down in Part XIII of the Treaty, possesses an autonomous character unlike that of the other League organizations, such as those dealing with Health and Transit. The Council of the League has no control over the activities of the Governing Body and the Conference, nor is the International Labour Office part of the Secretariat. Its Director is responsible only to the Governing Body, and through them to the Conference. On the other hand, in matters of finance the Assembly of the League is of course supreme, as being alone vested with the power of voting money. In practice, the Labour Office works in close collaboration with the Secretariat, and is represented on several of the Commissions appointed by the League, notably on those dealing with Mandates and Upper Silesia.

(*b*) *Constitution of the Office.* The duties of the Office itself, the powers of its Director, and even the method of its recruitment are indicated. Finally, the procedure for giving effect to the decisions of the Conference, and for ensuring their application, is laid down in some detail. Though the difficulties of interpretation and the want of elasticity inherent in written constitutions have occasionally made themselves felt, there can be no doubt that the Organization has benefited by the possession of statutes regulating the working of its component parts. Doubts and disputes on vital questions arising at the beginning might well have raised obstacles fatal to its progress. Uncertainty or vagueness as to how the Convention and Recommendations adopted by the Conference should be made effective might have doomed them to perish of inanition. Failure to limit the scope of the Organization might have tempted it to stray into other fields, where its authority would have been open to question. It is true that the border-line dividing industrial questions from larger economic issues is sometimes hard to trace; but even where the work of the International Labour Office has brought it face to face with such issues, it is only with their industrial aspects that it has concerned itself. Generally speaking, it may be said that the framework of the Treaty has stood the test of practice. Though experience has shown the need of some modifications, its machinery has worked with smoothness and precision. Without it the idea which it was designed to carry out would in all probability have failed to produce practical results.

(*c*) *Labour Parliament.* The General Conference has held three annual meetings—at Washington in 1919, at Genoa in 1920, and at Geneva in 1921 and in 1922. At each a great deal of work was accomplished, and they exhibited a growing sense of cohesion and of parliamentary consciousness. Each country has four delegates, two representing the Government and two appointed in agreement with the 'most representative organizations of employers and workers respectively'.

This novel kind of industrial assembly has its own rules of procedure, which in spite of differences of language and parliamentary custom enable it to transact its business on regular and methodical lines. As Lord Burnham, who presided over its 1921 Session said, 'To those who have not had our experience the sum of agreement would pass belief.' Its conclusions are framed either in the form of Conventions or Recommendations requiring a two-thirds majority for their adoption, which have to be submitted to the 'competent authority' in each country within eighteen months for acceptance or rejection. If a draft Convention is accepted, ratification follows, together with the necessary legislative or administrative measures for execution. In the case of a Recommendation, no international engagement is involved, but the Members of the Organization have to inform the Secretary-General of the League of such action as they may take.[1]

2. *The Washington Conference, 1919.* What has so far been accomplished? The Washington Conference met in an atmosphere of optimism, which the critical attitude of the United States, engrossed in the Treaty fight, did little to chill.

[1] Treaty of Versailles, Art. 405.

To the 121 delegates representing 39 countries, social reform appeared necessary and urgent, not only because there were revolutionary rumblings in every industrial country, but because the community of sacrifice and effort called forth during the war had bred the idea of a like common effort to improve social conditions. Moreover, on the surface there seemed little to suggest that the world might not rapidly become richer and happier. Industry was thriving on an artificial boom which blinded most people to the stringency and impoverishment which the huge war debts, the destruction of wealth, and the shrinkage of productive power both in men and machines inevitably foreboded when the first demands for peace goods had been satisfied.

The Washington Conference went forward therefore with boldness and unity of purpose. Its first act was not its least remarkable achievement. By a majority of 71 votes to 1 it admitted Germany and Austria to membership of the International Labour Organization, a recognition of the fact, which subsequent events have abundantly emphasized, that in the economic sphere all countries are interdependent, whatever the political or sentimental barriers which may stand between them.[1] This decision, however established the principle that, although under Art. 387 of the Treaty membership of the League of Nations shall carry with it membership of the International Labour Organization, it was nevertheless possible for the Conference to admit countries before they had joined the League.

The Conference adopted six Draft Conventions and six Recommendations.

3. *The Eight Hours Convention.* First and unquestionably the most important was the Draft Convention dealing with hours of work in industry. It provided that the 8-hour day and the 48-hour week should be regarded as the normal working periods in industrial undertakings, but it was far from fixing these as absolute limits, as has sometimes been represented. Overtime was not prohibited by the Convention, but was only subjected to such limits as might be imposed by regulation after

[1] It is, moreover, interesting to record that this decision was in accordance with a Note from the Supreme Council, dated the 27th May, 1919, recommending the admission of Germany and Austria to the favourable consideration of the Conference.

consultation with the employers' and workers' organizations and to extra remuneration of not less than time and a quarter being given. Various other exceptions were provided to meet the exigencies of particular occupations, including a 56-hour week in continuous process industries and permanently longer hours for men engaged in intermittent work. There was, in fact, nothing revolutionary in the Convention, which for the most part was based on the French Eight Hours Act already in operation, and upon the proposals of the British Industrial Conference summoned by the Prime Minister in February 1919. Moreover, the 48-hour week was already the law or the practice in almost every European country, though not on the American Continent.

One other feature of the Convention calls for remark, namely, the special articles devoted to India and Japan. In framing the Treaty it had been recognized that 'differences of climate, habits and customs, of economic opportunity and industrial tradition make strict uniformity in the conditions of labour difficult of immediate attainment',[1] but the Conference felt that Western standards could not be maintained unless the rising industrial communities in the East gradually sought to adopt them. For their part the representatives of the Indian and Japanese Governments, often supported by their employers, showed themselves anxious to advance, provided that they were not driven too precipitately, as some of the European delegates ignorant of Asiatic conditions would have wished. In the end, thanks largely to the wise and patient chairmanship of Mr. G. N. Barnes, who presided over the special committee entrusted with this delicate problem, an agreement satisfactory to all parties was reached. For India the general principle of a 60-hour week was adopted, while for Japan 57 hours was to be the normal working week, except in the raw silk industry and in underground work in mines, where 60 hours and 48 hours respectively should be the rule. These provisions marked a very great advance on the existing conditions. In India the law permitted a 72-hour week, while the Japanese Factory Act permitted 13 hours work a day for seven days a week together with 120 hours overtime during the year. In the silk industry these hours, amounting to an average of 93 per week, were usual, while in other industries

[1] Treaty of Versailles, Art. 427.

an 84-hour week was customary. The importance of the Convention for the East needs no further emphasis.

Without tracing the stages by which the various articles were elaborated, it must suffice to state that in its final form the Convention was adopted by 82 votes to 2. It may further be noted that the principle of the 8-hour day and the 48-hour week was not contested even by the employers, save those of Norway and Canada. The main points on which the Employers moved amendments were concerned with widening the Convention rather than with changing its fundamental principles. Indeed, in regard to overtime they proposed a limitation of 300 hours per year, though after discussion even this limitation was abandoned by common consent. They also insisted on the necessity of the Convention being ratified by all the principal countries, a point which, as will be seen, has had a considerable bearing on the fate of the Convention.

4. *Progress in ratification.* The Eight Hours Convention was the most prominent achievement of the Conference. Its subsequent history well illustrates the difficulties which international labour legislation, to use a convenient if not altogether accurate expression, is bound to encounter, and some of the defects in the constitution of the International Labour Organization.

In March 1922 the Convention had been formally ratified by five Governments only, namely, Greece, Rumania, India, Czecho-Slovakia, and Bulgaria. This is not, however, a fortuitous or insignificant collection of states. In all of them the social problem is one of particular urgency. In Eastern Europe not only have the repercussions of the Russian upheaval made themselves specially felt, but the democratic communities which have emerged from the ruins of the Habsburg Empire have begun their career with the conviction that a programme of progressive social legislation is essential to their new national life. In the case of India similar causes have been at work. There the war has produced a great social ferment and a great industrial revolution, requiring new methods and new conditions to meet them. In a word, those countries have ratified just where public opinion in favour of social advancement is most active. The fact that the list of ratifications is as yet so short does not, however, imply that it is closed or that the Convention has definitely failed to standardize the hours of labour in industry. A consideration of some of the obstacles which have stood in the way of ratification in various countries may be briefly indicated.

The first of these obstacles consists in the shortness of the time allowed for ratification. The maximum period of eighteen months contemplated by the Treaty has proved in practice too short to permit of the necessary legislation being carried. Parliamentary time available for discussing new measures is in all countries restricted, even in normal periods. In an abnormal period like the present, emergency business of all kinds, the instability of Governments amid the recasting of programmes and the recrystallizing of parties, and the paramount urgency of fundamental political questions, have inevitably relegated social problems to a secondary place. In these circumstances it is anything but surprising that most countries have failed to live up to the rigorous time-table of the Treaty. Nevertheless, many of them have made very considerable progress towards ratification, progress which without such a time-table would almost certainly not have been realized. In nine countries besides those which have ratified, Bills have been introduced by the Government for the purpose of securing ratification of the Convention—in the Argentine, Austria, Belgium, Brazil, Chile, France, Germany, Poland, and Spain—and it may be expected that in most, if not all, of these countries, the necessary parliamentary authority for ratifying will be obtained.

5. *Difficulties experienced in securing ratification.* From this, however, it does not follow that the ratifications will be immediately deposited with the Secretary-General of the League, who under the Treaty is authorized to receive them. An international engagement being more binding and more irrevocable than a national law, many countries—particularly the smaller ones—have naturally hesitated to ratify until they were assured of ratification on the part of their principal industrial rivals. This point has been raised in the discussions which have taken place in Belgium, Poland, Holland, Italy, and Germany with regard to ratification. It is even possible that a number of countries may signify their intention to ratify provisionally subject to certain other countries following their example. This question is clearly one of fundamental importance. It not only illustrates one of the essential

difficulties of the International Labour Organization, but also demonstrates its practical necessity. If it is difficult to secure the adhesion of countries to an international agreement, which they have all accepted through their representatives, what chance would there be of progress without such an agreement to pave the way, but with every country waiting for its neighbour to take the first step ?

In the case of the Eight Hours Convention several countries have ascribed their hesitancy to the fact that Great Britain and the United States—particularly the former—have not seen their way to ratify. The case of Great Britain illustrates another difficulty which was bound to arise in connexion with the framing of International Conventions, and another point in the constitution of the International Labour Organization which seems to require amendment. For all practical purposes the 8-hour day and the 48-hour week have been operative in the great majority of industries in Great Britain since the Armistice. The Joint Committee of the National Industrial Conference further recommended the passage of a Bill legalizing the 48-hour week, but though such a Bill was introduced by the Government in 1919, it never passed into law. Consequently, save in the mines, hours of labour for men are only regulated by agreement between employers' associations and trade unions, though these cover a very large proportion of the industrial field. In fact, the British Ministry of Labour in a letter explaining the reasons for which the Government found difficulty in ratifying, stated that ' the normal hours of work in almost all industrial undertakings are 48 a week or less '.

What then are the difficulties which have hitherto prevented ratification ? The Government was advised that the terms of the Convention were not wide enough to meet the case of some existing trade agreements, notably on the railways. The International Labour Office thought that the articles in question might possibly bear a wider interpretation, but its opinion could have no legal authority. As an alternative the British Government suggested that the points in question should be cleared up by way of amendment. The Treaty, however, provides no way of amendment, except the adoption of an amending Convention, which would in turn have to pass through the whole of the prescribed procedure. This case brings out two important difficulties in the way of creating a body of international law, those of interpretation and amendment. To draft, in two languages, an international Convention which shall be sufficiently wide to meet the varying conditions obtaining in the countries of the five Continents, and at the same time so perfect in point of draughtsmanship as to need no subsequent modification or addition, is no easy task in the rush of an International Conference. Moreover, differences of view are likely to arise as to the meaning and intention even of the most perfect Acts of Parliament. The Treaty provides that recourse may be had to the Permanent Court of International Justice at the Hague in the case of dispute as to the meaning of a Convention, but it may be doubted whether this Court will depart from the well-founded judicial practice of not giving rulings on hypothetical cases. It will deal with concrete cases as they arise, but will probably refuse to give general interpretations as to the meaning of particular articles. There is no other organ which has authority to give a ruling on the meaning of Conventions. Yet without an authoritative ruling a Government may well hesitate to ratify an Article of which the interpretation appears to be doubtful. Hence the need for amendment may quickly arise. Moreover, even the most perfect draughtsmanship cannot preclude the possibility which has already occurred in the case of Switzerland and several other countries in connexion with the Eight Hours Convention, namely, that their experts may overlook some exception or some branch of industry requiring special treatment, and may accordingly omit to secure the insertion of some essential provision. Some simple method of amendment therefore appears to be called for, if Conventions are to escape shipwreck on more or less technical points.

6. *Other Results of the Washington Conference.* The history of the Eight Hours Convention has been treated at some length, as it illustrates the general procedure in connexion with ratification and the difficulties which it is liable to encounter. It would have been over-sanguine to expect that ratification, which in most cases implies Parliamentary discussion, would automatically follow a favourable vote at the Conference. Experience alone can indicate the obstacles which have to be overcome, and can teach the means of overcoming them. But when the total amount of national legislation

which has arisen out of the Washington Conference is reviewed, it cannot be contended that within the three years which have elapsed since its close important results have not flowed from its decisions. In addition to the Eight Hours Convention, other Conventions were adopted dealing with unemployment, the care of women in industry before and after child-birth, the prohibition of the employment of women at night in industry, the minimum age of admission of children to employment and the prohibition of the night employment of young persons under 18. Space does not permit of the steps already taken towards ratifying each of these Conventions being set out in detail. It must suffice to say that 54 ratifications have been deposited and 8 have been authorized for these various Conventions, and that ratification is being recommended in 48 other cases.[1]

In addition to the Conventions, Recommendations were passed to which effect has been given by legislation in a considerable number of countries. The Recommendations deal with unemployment insurance, the reciprocity of treatment of foreign immigrants, protection against lead poisoning and anthrax, and the establishment of Government Health Services. Altogether 70 legislative measures[1] have been introduced or passed to give effect to the decisions of the Washington Conference—a not inconsiderable result when the parliamentary and other difficulties outlined above are borne in mind, and when the great obstacles to social legislation raised by the economic crisis through which the world has since been passing are remembered.

7. *The Genoa Conference, 1920.* The prospects of economic and social reconstruction which seemed so bright at Washington were destined to be quickly dimmed. When the second Conference met at Genoa in June 1920 the presages of hard times were already becoming apparent, though, as yet, they were far from being fully realized. Instead of being general in character like its predecessor, this Conference was an assembly of specialists competent to deal with conditions of work at sea. As the number of countries possessing a mercantile marine is comparatively limited, the attendance was necessarily smaller, only 27 countries taking part. As at Washington, the principal question at issue related to hours of work, but in

[1] Figures correct to 31st December 1922.

the maritime sphere the ground had been much less prepared than in the industrial. In only one country (France) had legislation been adopted applying the principle of the 48-hour week on board ship, and the peculiar conditions of the seaman's calling made its application more difficult in his case than in that of the factory worker. The whole problem was therefore not only complex in itself, but largely unexplored. It gave rise to long discussions, both in Committee and in the Conference, without producing any solution which seemed likely to gain general acceptance. Finally, the Draft Convention proposing a 48-hour week with certain modifications was lost by 49 votes to 25. The necessary two-thirds majority was therefore wanting by a fraction, but the result may perhaps be considered as proving the soundness of the provision of the Treaty requiring a two-thirds majority for the adoption of a Convention. As the minority consisted not only of shipowners but also of the Government representatives of such important seafaring countries as Great Britain, Japan, Norway, Denmark, Spain, and Portugal, it is certain that the Convention would have stood little chance of being generally carried out. Nevertheless, the Conference adopted three other Conventions dealing with the means of finding employment for seamen, the payment of compensation for unemployment due to shipwreck, and the minimum age of employment of boys at sea, together with Recommendations relating to unemployment insurance, the establishment of national Seamen's Codes, the hours of work in the fishing industry, and inland navigation. Bills have been introduced to ratify all the Conventions in Belgium, Chile, Denmark, Germany, Poland, and Spain, while Great Britain, Rumania, Finland, India, and Sweden have ratified the Convention relating to the age of employment at sea, and Norway, Sweden, Finland, and Japan, that relating to means of finding employment. Ratification of the two Conventions had been authorized by Parliament in Bulgaria. Steps are also being taken in twenty-seven other countries to give effect to the Recommendations.[1]

The Conference provided for the continuance of its work by deciding on the appointment of a Permanent Joint Maritime Commission which consists of six representatives of the Shipowners and six of the Seamen's Organizations, presided over

[1] Figures correct to 31st December 1922.

by the Chairman of the Governing Body of the International Labour Office. This Commission has met from time to time in order to carry on the work of the Conference. In particular it has given further consideration to the question of hours of work. Soon after the Conference an international seamen's strike, which would have caused immense dislocation and suffering in the famished regions of Europe, was threatened in order to enforce the demand for a 48-hour week at sea. The intervention of the International Labour Office succeeded in averting such a catastrophe, and in bringing about direct negotiations on an international basis between shipowners and seamen, but in the present depressed state of the shipping industry, progress has been slow and difficult.

8. *The Geneva Conference, 1921.* Whereas the Genoa Conference was confined to a single industry, the Third Conference, which met in Geneva in October 1921, was of a more general character. As at Washington 39 countries attended, sending 69 Government Delegates, 24 Employers, and 25 Workers. They met under circumstances of undoubted difficulty. The effects of the economic crisis resulting from the War were now fully and painfully apparent. The conditions prevailing in industry had become disastrous. Many of the employers were faced with a situation far graver than any within their recollection and the number of bankruptcies during the previous 12 months was sufficient to indicate the danger which faced hundreds of establishments.

On the other side were the workers, harassed by equally pressing cares—in some countries in the shape of unemployment and in others in the guise of an interminable race between wages and prices, in which the latter always won. The setting of the Conference was therefore sombre. It was generally felt that it would be a severe test; there were many who despaired beforehand of its success.

9. *The Agricultural Question.* To these general difficulties were added others arising out of the Agenda itself. The principal questions for discussion related to the regulation of agricultural labour. This again was difficult ground. During the nineteenth century the wage-earner in agriculture was almost completely neglected, although the exodus from the land had been widely recognized and deplored. The war, however, wrought a considerable change in this, as in other

spheres. In some countries, such as the Serb-Croat-Slovene Kingdom, Austria, and Rumania, an agrarian solution of the problem had been attempted by dividing up the great estates into peasant holdings. In others, such as England, Germany, and Italy, more or less systematic attempts had been made to deal with the social conditions of agricultural labourers. In others, such as Czecho-Slovakia, a combination of both methods had been tried. Nevertheless, the instinctive conservatism of all those who have to do with the land made opposition to all such efforts inevitable. The French Government formally objected to the inclusion of agricultural questions in the Agenda, on the ground that it was inopportune to deal with them at the present time, in view of the need for increased production everywhere; and alternatively, though this contention was never put forward unambiguously, that the International Labour Organization was only competent under the Treaty to deal with matters relating to industry. The raising of such fundamental issues at the beginning of the Conference led to an animated debate. In reply (September 1920) to the Hungarian Government's objection to the Labour Section of the Treaty, on the ground that it appeared to apply to agriculture,[1] the Peace Conference clearly indicated their view that the International Labour Organization was competent to deal with agricultural questions. The majority of the Conference—including the British, Italian, and Dutch Delegations—took this view and asserted, moreover, that it could not shirk the duty of doing so. Finally, the Conference affirmed its jurisdiction to deal with the problem by 74 votes to 20, and retained all the agricultural questions on the Agenda, except that relating to the adaptation of the Washington Convention on hours of labour to agricultural conditions.[2] Once the question of principle had been removed from the path, so far as the Conference was concerned, it proceeded smoothly and agreed upon a series of Draft Conventions and Recommendations on

[1] See Vol. IV, Chap. VII, p. 427.

[2] With regard to this latter point it may be remarked that in its proposals based on the replies received from the various Governments to its Questionnaire, the International Labour Office suggested as a basis of discussion that hours of labour should be regulated by agreement between employers and workers' organizations, without indicating any limits, either weekly or daily. It had never been contended, even by the workers' organizations, that the limitations applicable in factories could be applied to agriculture without very substantial modifications.

agricultural questions,[1] which constitutes an initial attempt to apply to the agricultural labourer the principles of social protection which have long been recognized as applicable to the industrial worker.

The French Government, however, did not relinquish its opposition. It requested the Council of the League of Nations to submit the question to the Permanent Court of International Justice, in order to obtain an authoritative ruling as to the jurisdiction of the Office in agricultural matters. The case was heard by the Court in July 1922, at its opening Session. After a prolonged hearing at which arguments were presented to the Court on behalf of the French, British, Portuguese, and Hungarian Governments, as well as the International Agricultural Commission, the International Labour Office and the International Federation of Trade Unions, the Court delivered a judgement which clearly establishes the jurisdiction of the International Labour Organization to deal with matters relating to agricultural labour.

10. *Other Decisions.* Another question which aroused considerable controversy was the prohibition of the use of white lead in painting. Here the Organization was dealing with a problem which had been debated in all industrial countries for many years past. The fact that lead poisoning was responsible for considerable mortality and sickness among painters had long been generally admitted, but whether there was an effective means of combating it, short of total prohibition, was a matter still in dispute. Moreover, there were considerable economic interests involved, as a substantial portion of the business of the lead corroders and producers would be affected by the prohibition of the use of lead in the manufacture of paints. A large number of experts assembled at the Conference and a prolonged and highly technical discussion ensued. As a result general agreement was reached among all the medical men present as to the scientific elements of the problem, which paved the way to a compromise welcomed by all parties.

[1] The Draft Conventions relating to agriculture deal with (*a*) prevention of unemployment; (*b*) age of admission of children to employment; (*c*) workmen's compensation; (*d*) rights of association.

The Recommendations dealt with (*a*) social insurance; (*b*) living-in conditions; (*c*) protection of women before and after child-birth; (*d*) development of technical agricultural education; (*e*) night-work for women; (*f*) night-work for children.

A Draft Convention was eventually voted by 90 votes to 0 providing for the total prohibition of the use of white lead in interior painting, where the danger of poisoning was generally agreed to be greatest, subject to certain exceptions, and for the adoption of regulations in connexion with the exterior painting of buildings. The fact that this agreement was accepted by employers and workers alike may be regarded as a valuable achievement on the part of the Conference, and as having gone far to settle the problem of lead poisoning once and for all.

The Conference also adopted a Draft Convention for a weekly rest in industry, and others fixing the age of employment of youths as trimmers or stokers, and providing for the compulsory medical examination of youths employed at sea. Finally, it was decided to set up a Commission for the study of the prevention of anthrax—one of the most deadly of industrial diseases and one of the most difficult to combat.[1]

Apart from the actual drafting of the Conventions and Recommendations mentioned above, the Conference gave the opportunity for a general debate on the subject of unemployment which threw considerable light on the gravity of the economic situation from the employers' and workers' points of view, culminating in the adoption of a resolution proposing the urgent convocation of a general Conference to seek the means for remedying it. The meeting of the Genoa Conference in April, to which the International Labour Organization was invited to send a delegation, and which endorsed the value of its work as an element in the reconstruction of Europe, is the best justification of its attitude towards the economic crisis.

11. *Geneva Conference, 1922.* After the great activity displayed by the Third Conference, the Fourth Session, which was held in Geneva in 1922, may be regarded in the light of a breathing space. It was felt that so many Conventions and Recommendations had already been sent forward to the various Governments and Parliaments that it would be better not to add to their number at the 1922 meeting but to devote it primarily to taking stock of the constitutional machinery and improving the defects which four years' experience had shown

[1] This Commission was presided over in London in December 1922 by Sir William Middlebrook, and recommended the International Labour Conference to reconsider at an early date the question of a Convention on the compulsory disinfection of wool and hair.

to exist. There was, therefore, only one question on the agenda calling for a decision in the form of a Draft Convention or Recommendation, namely, the statistics of migration, which resulted in the unanimous adoption of a Recommendation asking for the communication to the International Labour Office at regular intervals of the available statistical and other information concerning emigration, immigration, and transit of emigrants.

Of the constitutional questions which the Conference discussed perhaps the most important was the enlargement of the Governing Body. Its composition had been the subject of some dissatisfaction ever since the days of the Washington Conference, where a Governing Body predominantly European in character was elected. This objection had, in point of fact, been met to a considerable extent by the decision of the Council of the League, given in September, to the effect that India had a right to the place previously occupied by Switzerland as one of the eight States of chief industrial importance. In spite of this, however, the general feeling of the Conference was that the Governing Body should be made more comprehensive in its character, and should accordingly be increased to 32 members, i. e., 16 Government, 8 Employers', and 8 Workers' representatives. An amendment to Article 393 of the Treaty was accordingly adopted and forwarded to the States for ratification in accordance with Article 422, this being the first instance of the amendment of Part XIII of the Treaty.[1]

A second question of no little moment was that of the periodicity of the Conference. Two alternative proposals were put forward, first that the Conference should only meet every two years, and, secondly, that it should hold alternate sessions of preparation and decision. The former of these ideas was mainly prompted by the real difficulty which the Overseas countries find in sparing their principal officials to attend annual meetings. The second was really an attempt to meet some of the difficulties in regard to the drafting of the Conventions which have already been pointed out in this Chapter (see paragraph 5). It was thought that in the case of a complicated Convention it would be better to do the preliminary

[1] Article 422 provides that an amendment cannot become operative unless it is ratified by all the States, whose representatives compose the Council of the League and by three-quarters of the Members of the Organization.

work at the first session and then before any final vote was taken refer the Draft Convention back for further consideration by the Governments during the ensuing year. Any points in which the drafting of the Convention had been found defective, or which on further examination might render it difficult of application in a particular country, could thus be brought up at the second Conference, during which the Convention would be put in a form which would render it easily and generally acceptable. This proposal was in effect adopted by the Conference, though it was left to the Governing Body to work out the precise method of applying it. On the other hand, it was decided not to alter the requirement of the Treaty that the Conference should meet annually.

Finally, the Conference considered the difficult question of amending Conventions once adopted. No definite solution was arrived at, as considerable legal difficulties were encountered, but the Office was requested to consult the Governments further on the matter and report again at the next Session.

Special attention should perhaps be called to one of the Resolutions passed by the Conference instructing the Office to make a special study of unemployment crises in collaboration with the Economic Section of the League of Nations. This problem, which has long been occupying the attention of economists in various countries, has never yet been approached from an international standpoint. It is hoped that this new method of approach may result in some light being thrown on the deep underlying causes which control the ebb and flow of production. If some measure of international forecast were made possible, methods might be adopted to diminish the violence of trade fluctuations, or at any rate to provide in time against the worst consequences of unemployment.

Of the Fourth Conference it may be said generally that, if it did not arrive at any sensational conclusions or adumbrate any important social reforms, it did much to consolidate and improve the internal working of the Organization, upon which its ultimate success must largely depend.

12. *The International Labour Office.* Such, in brief outline, is the work performed by the International Labour Conference up to date. The other branch of the Organization, the International Labour Office, which constitutes its administrative organ, now has a staff of some 350 persons, drawn from 28

different countries, under the direction of M. Albert Thomas, formerly French Minister of Munitions. In accordance with the conditions of the Treaty its principal work consists, on the one hand, of preparing the work of the Conference and of conducting the correspondence and negotiations involved in the execution of its decisions, and on the other hand of the collection and distribution of information about labour conditions all over the world by means of periodical and occasional publications, all of which are in French and English, and some of them in German, Italian, and other languages. Perhaps its most important duty is the preparation of the agenda of the Conference. On the basis of the reports prepared by the Office, the assembly when it meets, is able to go at once to the heart of each question knowing precisely how it stands in each particular country. The amount of time and irrelevant discussion saved by this procedure is incalculable. Any conference is the better for having the subjects on its agenda carefully sifted and concisely presented. An international meeting can hardly hope to overcome the numerous difficulties which naturally beset it, unless its work has been so prepared in advance. The experience of the Secretariat of the League and of the International Labour Office may be held to have proved the value of permanent international administrative organs to prepare the way for international assemblies and to follow up their decisions. They are gradually building up the technique of international administration, which is necessarily more complicated and more delicate than that of any national department, but which will in time become an indispensable cement for future international relations.

Even at the end of three years, however, it is too early to hazard any judgment as to the future of the International Labour Organization. Ideas—particularly novel ideas—are slow to penetrate and to take root in public opinion, upon which their fruitfulness must ultimately depend. To expect the rapid expansion of international co-operation into a perfect flower, despite all the material difficulties imposed by language and distance—to say nothing of the more impalpable but more blighting influences of conservative habit and mere unfamiliarity—would be to ignore all the teachings of experience. The growth and maturity of such a delicate plant must be measured by decades rather than by years. All that can be done as yet is to record what has so far been achieved in three years of exceptional difficulty, in a world thrown completely out of its economic gear, its citizens confused and often despairing, beset by immediate fears and cares which left them little inclination to seek the solution of more remote problems, however fundamental, content to escape the evils of to-day without having time to forestall the perils of to-morrow. That the International Labour Organization should not only have survived this period, but should have a not inconsiderable record of practical achievement to its credit, is the best proof that the Labour Section of the Treaties is far from being a dead letter, and the best earnest of its future possibilities.

CHAPTER VI

INTERNATIONAL DEVELOPMENTS UNDER THE LEAGUE OF NATIONS

PART III

THE PERMANENT COURT OF INTERNATIONAL JUSTICE [1]

1. *Provisions of the Covenant relating to a Court of Justice.* The Peace Conference at Paris in making its new settlement of the world did not establish a Permanent Court of International Justice. It established the League of Nations which the opinion of all civilized countries demanded as a protection against the renewal of the horrors of the Great War. But in creating the League it did not create what before 1914 everyone had agreed to be the most important institution for the promotion and maintenance of peace that could be set up. So far had ideas moved from those which dominated at the Hague in 1907.

But the idea of laying a legal foundation for a system of international justice was still strong enough to secure the insertion in the Covenant of provisions which required the subsequent establishment of the Court. This the Peace Conference itself had been unable to set up. These provisions have brought about the establishment of a Court which, within three years of the signing of the Peace, has been definitely constituted, has met twice, has established its code of procedure, has actually tried two cases, and has another pending (December 1922). The Covenant, moreover, contained some other most important provisions which indicated clearly the nature of the Court its authors intended should be set up, and which in many ways have guided, and will continue to guide, its development. These provisions and the way in which they were inserted into the Covenant are therefore of enduring and practical, as well as of historical interest.

2. *Connexion with the Covenant.* The provisions of the Covenant relating to the Court of Justice are, like most of the rest of the Covenant, a clear development from the past. It

[1] Complete till 31st December 1922.

is not generally appreciated to what a degree the institutions of the League are simply a growth from what had gone before. As has already been pointed out, the actual establishment of the League was far less of a violent revolutionary change than it appeared to be. The League Commissions, its Council, its Secretariat, and even in some degree its Assembly, are developments from the various movements towards international co-operation which had preceded the war, and from those brought about by the war itself. Just as these institutions resulted from the experience of international co-operation gained by the Allies, so the Court resulted from many years of previous effort to organize a system of international justice. It is, in a particular degree, a product of the subconscious, but almost universal, desire for the creation in international affairs of a system based on legal processes. It is, like the League itself, a forcible example of the power of opinion to create political morality and even to bring about the establishment of political institutions.

3. *Elements essential to a Court of Justice.* It may be worth while briefly to consider the history of previous efforts to establish a Court of Justice. It is only by considering the historical background of the Court, the efforts which had been made before the war to establish it, and the ideas on which those efforts had been founded, that the true significance of its actual establishment can be understood.

In every scheme for the abolition of war which had been devised by thinkers and statesmen, some form of judicial tribunal had been included. It was recognized in them all that the ideal to which they should tend was the establishment of a system under which disputes between states should be settled by judicial processes in accordance with legal rules, exactly as disputes between individual citizens within a state are settled; so that the last resort between states should be not war but law.

In the establishment of such a system there are three essential elements.

(1) There must be a judicial tribunal competent to hear any case which states may bring before it.

(2) An obligation must be imposed on every state not to resort to violence, and this must be an obligation without exception save for the exigencies of self-defence in the case of

unprovoked attack. This obligation would impose a general duty on all states not to disturb the peace, and it would be a duty on the carrying out of which every state must have the right to insist.

(3) To make the system completely effective there must be an obligation on every state to appear before the tribunal if summoned there, on the demand of any other state, and a means to enforce the verdicts which the tribunal renders.

If these three elements, which are common to the domestic legal systems of every civilized country, could be established in the law and practice of nations, they would, of course, have the necessary effect of abolishing war, and would establish the reign of justice. It is possible therefore to say that the principal ideal of the League of Nations will be achieved in proportion as these three elements become of binding effect between nations.

4. *The Hague Permanent Court of Arbitration*, 1899–1907. Before the war the efforts of statesmen and writers on international law had been concentrated on the first of these elements, that is to say, on the effort to create an international tribunal. The third of them—the obligation on every state to appear before this tribunal on the demand of any other state—had been discussed under the name of compulsory arbitration, but it could not be said that any important government had seriously considered it. The second of them, the obligation to keep the peace, had not come within the range of practical international politics. The only effort that had been made in the direction of establishing it even as a rudimentary principle had been the insertion of tentative provisions allowing for mediation as of friendly right, into one of the Hague Conventions of 1907. These provisions were themselves a development of still more rudimentary stipulations of the same sort which were inserted in the Paris Treaty of 1856. But neither in the fifty years which intervened, nor indeed until after the war, had any one observed their importance as the seed of a legal duty to be accepted by every state in the interest of all not to disturb the world's peace.

The efforts which had been made to secure the first element, the establishment of an international tribunal, had been persistent and in some degree successful. In 1899 the first Hague Conference established what was known as a Permanent

Court of Arbitration; and in 1907 the second Hague Conference approved and perfected the organization of this Court. And this Court, although still far from the ideal international tribunal, was able to try a number of cases and to settle them with complete success. It was in every important particular a true Court of international law. The difference between its working and its methods in settling the cases which were brought before it, and the methods which will be followed by the Court which has now been set up, is not nearly so profound as some writers have suggested. On this subject the remarks of Sir Frederick Pollock in the second edition of his book on the League of Nations are most illuminating.

5. *Defects of the Hague Permanent Court of Arbitration.* But although the Permanent Court of Arbitration was undoubtedly a great step in advance, it was not, even to the statesmen and jurists of the pre-war period, a wholly satisfactory tribunal. There were four features of the ideal Court of Justice in which it was notably deficient. First, it was not in any true sense a permanent court. It required for every case the special establishment of a new *ad hoc* body to be chosen by the parties from a large panel of nominated judges. It was not, therefore, immediately accessible at a moment of crisis. Second, as it was chosen by the parties and as the parties were represented upon it, it could not have the character of absolute impartiality and disinterestedness which a true court ought to have. Third, the cumbrous process of establishing the court, and the great costliness of calling together and conducting the proceedings before it, constituted a very real deterrent to states who wished their differences to be settled by arbitration. Fourth, it shared with every other system of international arbitration the defect that a decision given by any set of arbitrators is not binding on any subsequent set of arbitrators.

For these reasons and others of the same sort, the second Hague Conference endeavoured to establish, in addition to its Permanent Court of Arbitration, a new Court of International Justice, which should be definitely judicial rather than arbitral in character, which should be truly permanent, and should, as it was hoped, gradually evolve an international jurisprudence by the continuity of its decisions. It was recognized by every one that such a Court was needed; and in the course of its deliberations the second Hague Conference agreed on a complete statute for the establishment of this Court, with the exception of the provisions concerning its constitution. The conference could not agree on the question of representation, for the small countries claimed an equal right to representation, basing their claim, quite fallaciously, on the so-called principle of the legal equality of states. Even this difficulty was overcome in the similar convention for an International Prize Court. In this convention representation was given to every country by a complicated system of rotation for varying periods of time. But on the Court of Justice the smaller countries were uncompromising and the project failed.

(*a*) *The Court of Justice and the League.* The point is of more than historical interest for the reason that it was exactly this same difficulty which prevented the Peace Conference at Paris from endeavouring itself to establish a Permanent Court of International Justice. As subsequent events proved, the difficulty of constituting the Court was really insoluble until the permanent political institutions of the League of Nations were brought into being. This was observed by no one until these institutions had been actually created, and every writer, without exception, who advocated the establishment of a Permanent Court, adhered to some more or less complicated and artificial system of rotatory representation. It was only when the institutions of the League were created that it was recognized that the plan, subsequently devised, of electing the members of the Court through the Council and the Assembly of the League, was the only right and natural solution.

But although the Conference of 1907 failed to solve this problem of representation, the rest of its work on the convention of the Permanent Court of Justice was of great and enduring value. It not only made the creation of the Court a natural and necessary development, but the actual provisions of the 1907 Convention concerning procedure and other matters were in large part adopted, almost as they stood, for the Court when it was created.

6. *Views of Lord Robert Cecil and President Wilson on the Court of Justice.* But although the Hague work was still of value, the intervening period between 1907 and 1919 profoundly modified the ideas of statesmen and publicists concerning progress in the organization of international affairs. Had the League of Nations been created in 1907 the first institution

which would have been established would undoubtedly have been the Court, and it would have been in connection with the Court that all efforts to work out principles of political representation would have been made. When statesmen came practically to consider the creation of the League in 1919 the Court was not the first, it was almost the last, element which was taken into account. The history of the war, and more particularly of the origin of the war, led everyone to concentrate his attention, first, on the obligation not to break the peace, and second, on the creation of international political and co-operative institutions.

The Court of Justice, indeed, did not figure in many of the more important draft schemes which were prepared during the War and at the moment of the Armistice. Some of the official government schemes did not even allude to it. General Smuts, in his famous state paper, made no mention of it, and merely provided for arbitration more or less on the model of the old Hague system. Even the terms of reference of the Commission appointed by the Peace Conference at Paris to draft the Covenant of the League made no reference to a Court. It was recognized of course that there must be new provisions for the peaceable settlement of disputes, but the first consideration of the statesmen who had the matter in hand was to provide an obligation not to resort to war, and their hopes lay rather in political mediation than in judicial settlement.

Nevertheless, before the first Anglo-American draft was actually presented to the League of Nations Commission of the Peace Conference by President Wilson, the question of a Court had been definitely raised.[1] Lord Robert Cecil, the true

[1] *v.* App. I. Articles 13 and 14, as finally adopted and amended in 1921, are here given :

ART. 13. ARBITRATION OF DISPUTES.

* The Members of the League agree that whenever any dispute shall arise between them which they recognize to be suitable for submission to arbitration and which cannot be satisfactorily settled by diplomacy, they will submit the whole subject-matter to arbitration.

Disputes as to the interpretation of a treaty, as to any question of international law, as to the existence of any fact which if established would constitute a breach of any international obligation, or as to the extent and nature of the reparation to be made for any such breach, are declared to be among those which are generally suitable for submission to arbitration.

For the consideration of any such dispute the Court of Arbitration to which the case is referred shall be the Court agreed on by the parties to the dispute or stipulated in any convention existing between them.

The Members of the League agree that they will carry out in full good

architect of the Covenant, always held that in the long run the creation of an international jurisprudence, with an International Court of Justice to administer it, might prove to be of fundamental importance for the maintenance of peace. He was, from the beginning till the drafting of the Covenant was completed, the defender of this 'legalist' point of view against what may be called the anti-legalism of President Wilson. Before the first Anglo-American draft was finally agreed upon, therefore, he had persuaded President Wilson of the great importance of making some provision for a new supreme tribunal. He had not been able to offer any solution for the evident difficulties of the constitution, but he had brought him to accept the following provision: 'The Executive Council will formulate plans for the establishment of a Permanent Court of International Justice, and this Court will be competent to hear and determine any matters which the parties recognize as suitable for submission to it for arbitration . . .'

This was destined to remain the principal provision of the Covenant concerning the Court of Justice and was therefore a provision of great importance. It proved also to be a provision

faith any award that may be rendered, and that they will not resort to war against any Member of the League which complies therewith. In the event of any failure to carry out such an award, the Council shall propose what steps should be taken to give effect thereto.

ART. 14. PERMANENT COURT OF INTERNATIONAL JUSTICE.

The Council shall formulate and submit to the Members of the League for adoption plans for the establishment of a Permanent Court of International Justice. The Court shall be competent to hear and determine any dispute of an international character which the parties thereto submit to it. The Court may also give an advisory opinion upon any dispute or question referred to it by the Council or by the Assembly.

---

* *Art.* 13 *as amended in* 1921 *would read :*

The Members of the League agree that, whenever any dispute shall arise between them which they recognize to be suitable for submission to arbitration or judicial settlement, and which cannot be satisfactorily settled by diplomacy, they will submit the whole subject-matter to arbitration or judicial settlement.

Disputes as to the interpretation of a treaty, as to any question of international law, as to the existence of any fact which, if established, would constitute a breach of any international obligation, or as to the extent and nature of the reparation to be made for any such breach, are declared to be among those which are generally suitable for submission to arbitration or judicial settlement.

For the consideration of any such dispute, the Court to which the case is referred shall be the Permanent Court of International Justice, established in accordance with Art. 14, or any tribunal agreed.

of great wisdom, which brought about the actual establishment of the Court as quickly as the most sanguine could have hoped.

But this provision was not finally incorporated in the Covenant without some further difficulties. There was the hesitation, if not the actual opposition, of those who believed the existing 'Permanent Court of Arbitration' to be all that was required. It was for this reason that a provision was inserted in Art. XIII of later drafts of the Covenant that in any dispute between Members of the League the Court of Arbitration, to which the case was referred, should be 'the Court agreed on by the parties or stipulated in any Convention existing between them'. This provision, while comparatively harmless from the point of view of those who wished to establish a new Court with a wide jurisdiction, overcame the difficulties raised by the adherents of the Hague system. As a result of its acceptance the clause quoted above, laying a duty upon the Council to formulate a plan for the establishment of a Court, went through substantially unchanged to the final draft of the Covenant.

7. *Progress in the construction of a Court* (*1919–20*). It is clear that this result was a definite victory for the legalism of Lord Robert Cecil over the anti-legalism of President Wilson. It was all that could be obtained by Lord Robert Cecil before the first draft of the Covenant was published to the world on the 14th February 1919. But by itself it was not very satisfactory from his point of view. It did not define what sort of Court was to be established. It did not indicate, otherwise than by its title, whether this Court was to be more definitely judicial than the old 'Permanent Court'. It did not indeed make clear any way in which it was to differ from the 'Permanent Court', except that, by implication, it provided for some new form of constitution, and imposed on the members of the League the obligation to accept its verdicts whenever they brought their disputes before it for decision.

But after the publication of the first draft of the Covenant on the 14th February, and during President Wilson's visit to the United States, the current of opinion ran very strongly in favour of the legalist view of Lord Robert Cecil. It was, as has been said, natural that after the terrible events of the War the first pre-occupation of statesmen should have been the political aspects of the League. But after the 14th February, when the obligation not to resort to war and provision for the political settlement of disputes had both been, so it seemed, definitely secured, the minds of those engaged in making and in writing about the Covenant were free to examine the matter from other points of view. And not only within the Peace Conference Commission itself, but also outside, there was a strong pressure of opinion in favour of a clearer definition of the judicial character of the Court to be established, and of the jurisdiction which it was to have. Many eminent jurists published articles on the subject. A number of governments prepared and circulated definite schemes for the organization of the Court and for the definition of its character and competence. The Neutral Powers, who were called to Paris to discuss the first draft of the Covenant and to suggest changes, were all, with practical unanimity, in favour of more clearly emphasizing the judicial character of the Court.

There was, moreover, not only this general movement in favour of what has been called the legalist view of the League and the Covenant; there was also a strong opinion, particularly among the neutrals and some members of the Commission, in favour of the immediate creation of the Court. It was urged that the Court would be required almost at once after the peace settlement had been made; that after every big international settlement there arose inevitably large numbers of disputes concerning the interpretation of the new treaties; and that for the settlement of such disputes the new Court would be needed. The history of the years after the peace settlement of Vienna in 1815 was quoted in support of this view and it was urged that the work which the Court would have to do, arising out of the peace settlement, would be by far the best way of establishing permanently its authority and power.

It was not possible, however, even with the support of this body of opinion, to secure the immediate creation by the Peace Conference Commission of a Court of Justice. The difficulties of its constitution and the problem of representation were so great that every time the question arose it was decided to adhere to the device adopted in the first draft of the Covenant, of laying upon the Council of the League when it came into being the duty of drawing up a plan.

It has already been said that this in itself was a great achievement. It was, as subsequent events have proved, not only the simplest, but also the wisest, plan that could have been adopted. Seen from the standpoint of 1922 it had every advantage. It brought about the establishment of a Court as rapidly as it was needed. It enabled the neutral states to take part on a footing of complete equality in planning the constitution and in drawing up the Statute of the Court. It freed the Court from the charge of being a part of a not wholly just peace settlement—and in connexion with the Court this fact was of real importance. Most valuable of all, it gave the time which was required for the mature consideration of the very difficult questions which the Statute of the Court involved. It cannot be disputed that any scheme for a Court made in Paris during the negotiations for peace would have been hasty and probably faulty. Nor can it be disputed that the Statute, as it was finally agreed upon by the Assembly of the League, was the most carefully prepared and perhaps the most successful piece of international legislation ever carried through.

For when the preparation of the Statute of the Court was at length begun, every detail was considered with meticulous care. Every government was given the fullest opportunity of expressing its views and its objections. Every precaution was taken to leave no important point undealt with. The most eminent jurists in every country considered the matter during the year which succeeded the publication of the final draft of the Covenant. Almost as soon as it came into being the Council of the League—at its second meeting in February 1920—established a committee of eight of the most eminent legal authorities of the world to prepare a preliminary draft. The eight members of this committee individually prepared its work for four months. They then met for two months at the Hague and after fifty-nine meetings agreed upon a draft Statute.[1] Their draft was considered at three successive meetings by the Council, who approved it in its most important particulars and amended it in others before December of the same year, when they laid it before the Assembly. The Assembly created a special legal committee on which every member State was represented to consider it. This legal committee in turn appointed a subcommittee of its most distinguished lawyers. The report of this sub-committee was adopted by the full committee and by the Assembly. The resulting Statute was a more careful and com-

[1] This is printed in the *League of Nations,* Vol. III, September 1920, published by World Peace Foundation, Boston, U.S.A.

plete piece of work than had perhaps ever been done by international lawyers. In consequence of the methods adopted, the Statute was immediately accepted by practically every government in the world.[1]

The work of the Peace Conference on the Court therefore, although it seemed at the time a defeat for those who were the warmest adherents of the Court of Justice, proved subsequently to have been based on the soundest possible lines.

8. *Inconsistency of certain phrases in the Covenant with the idea of a Court of Justice.* If the 'legalists' of the Peace Conference who hoped for the immediate establishment of the Court were disappointed, in other ways the movement of opinion which took place after the 14th February brought more successful results. At the second series of meetings of the League of Nations Commission, in which the original draft of the Covenant was revised in the light of the results obtained at the meetings with the Neutral Powers, various other provisions concerning the Court were introduced. They were introduced on the initiative of Lord Robert Cecil, who still led those in the Commission who wished to lay the foundations of a true system of international jurisprudence. They were not introduced without opposition, and every single word of them was the subject of prolonged and careful consideration. When it is remembered that the Commission included, besides Lord Robert Cecil himself, such distinguished lawyers as Professor Larnaude, Doyen of the Faculty of Law of the University of Paris, and Signor Scialoja, it will be understood why the results that were achieved constituted the maximum of solid progress that it was possible to achieve. And not in the full Commission alone were these questions discussed. It was in a sub-committee, consisting primarily of distinguished lawyers, and after prolonged debate, that Arts. XIII and XIV were agreed to in their final form.

In this final form there is no doubt that the two articles constitute a real victory for the legalists. For besides laying down that the Council of the League was to prepare a plan for a Court, these articles further defined what was to be the competence of the Court and what were the sort of cases with

[1] For text of Protocol of Permanent Court of International Justice *v.* Parl. Papers. An important minor point is that, in contrast with the Covenant and the International Labour clauses of the Versailles Treaty, it is provided, Art. 37, that 'the official language of the Court shall be French'. For the general dispute about this problem in the Treaties see Vol. I, pp. 253–4.

which it was hoped that it could deal. They thus made it perfectly clear what sort of Court was intended and what sort of justice it was hoped it would secure.

But though it was a victory of substance for the legalists it was not a complete victory of form. In Art. XIII it is still stipulated that the Members of the League shall submit their disputes '. . . to arbitration'. In defining the disputes which it is thought should be settled by the Court the definition is one which declares these cases to be generally suitable for submission to arbitration. This use of the word 'arbitration' leaves it in doubt as to whether the authors of the Covenant really intended that the Court should be more strictly judicial than the previous Hague Court of Arbitration. The truth is that this use of the word 'arbitration' was a concession to the anti-legalists of the Peace Conference Commission. The fact that it introduced an ambiguity was subsequently recognized by the Assembly when, after it had drawn up the Statute of the Court, it introduced as amendments into Arts. XII, XIII, XIV, and XV of the Covenant the words 'or judicial settlement (decision)', wherever 'arbitration' was mentioned.

9. *Arbitration and Justice.* But if the Covenant as it was finally adopted by the Peace Conference Commission left this doubtful use of the word 'arbitration', the other provisions which were inserted after the 14th February into Arts. XIII and XIV substantially cleared up the point. For these provisions included, first, the definition of the cases which the Members of the League agreed should normally be submitted to 'arbitration', as this word was used in the Covenant, and, second, the definition of the jurisdiction of the Court which was to be established. Since these provisions have been, and will be, of great importance in the development of the Court and of its jurisdiction, it is perhaps worth while to say a few words about how they were introduced into the Covenant.

The definition of the cases 'generally suitable for arbitration' is as follows:

> 'Disputes as to the interpretation of a treaty, as to any question of international law, as to the existence of any fact which if established would constitute a breach of any international obligation, or as to the extent and nature of the reparation to be made for any such breach, are declared to be among those which are generally suitable for submission to arbitration.'

This definition shows beyond a doubt what was the sense in which the Commission employed the word 'arbitration'. For this definition was in fact a very well-known definition of what had come to be called by international lawyers 'justiciable' disputes. It was a definition which had been worked out by a Committee of Jurists in England, and which had been approved by Professor Oppenheim as the best definition of the class of international dispute which was capable of being settled by judicial process. The word 'justiciable' was used by Professor Oppenheim, and the original authors of this definition, as an alternative to 'arbitrable'. In other words, they regarded judicial process as different from, and more clearly legal than, arbitration.

The insertion of this definition shows, therefore, beyond doubt the sort of Court which it was the duty of the Council under Art. XIV to establish. It shows that the Commission had in view a true Court of Law, the purpose of which should be to build up, by strictly judicial procedure and on the basis of existing international law, a system of international jurisprudence.

There are one or two other points in connexion with this definition in Art. XIII which are worth noting. In the first place, in addition to its indicative value which has just been mentioned, this definition may perhaps, as will be shown later on, have a real practical value in determining, and perhaps in widening, the competence of the Court in its later development. In the second place, it is relevant to the competence of the Court, for it brought the Peace Conference Commission very near to the acute controversy concerning compulsory arbitration. Both in connexion with this Article and in connexion with Art. XIV, it was proposed by a number of Members of the Commission that the Members of the League should be placed under an obligation to submit their disputes on the demand of one party alone to settlement by the Court. This proposal was warmly defended by some of the smaller Powers; but the opposition of the representatives of the Great Powers rendered its acceptance from the first impossible. The issue arose in an intricate but acute form in connexion with the definition of Art. XIII. If at the conclusion of the definition the Members of the League had declared, not that such cases were 'generally' suitable for arbitration, but that they were simply 'suitable' this would have been, if not tantamount to giving the Court a compulsory jurisdiction, at least tantamount to a definite obligation upon Members of the League to submit their cases to it, or (in accordance with the last paragraph of Art. XIII) to some other judicial tribunal upon which they might agree. And it is not commonly known how nearly the saving word 'generally' was omitted. At one moment the decision to omit it was practically taken. It was only reinserted after a keen discussion and out of deference for the leader of those who wished to leave a greater elasticity in the development of the League.

In point of fact it may well be that both the best legal opinion and the verdict of history will be in favour of those who wished to include the word 'generally'. For the real difficulty in establishing compulsory jurisdiction for a Court of International Justice lies in this fact: that however perfect a definition of 'justiciable' disputes may be obtained, that definition cannot really solve all the difficulties which in practice are bound to arise. These difficulties must arise because the system of international law is imperfect; because in its customary and written rules there are vaguenesses and lacunae. There must, therefore, arise cases which, although they would fall within the definition of 'justiciable', yet cannot be decided by a body of judges on legal grounds alone. This, in the present state of international law, is the real difficulty about giving a compulsory jurisdiction to the Court; and it is the justification for the insertion in Art. XIII of the word 'generally'.

10. '*Compulsory Jurisdiction.*' The definition of Art. XIII, as it stood in the final drafting of the Covenant, constituted, therefore, in itself a definite repudiation of compulsory jurisdiction. Had there been any doubt remaining it was cleared up by Art. XIV, in which from the very beginning it had always been stipulated that the Court should be 'competent to hear and determine any dispute of an international character which the *parties* thereto submitted to it'. This in the earlier drafts of the Covenant, and particularly in the draft of the 14th February, constituted the whole definition given in the Covenant of the competence of the Court. In the final form of the Covenant a most important addition was made. A new sentence was added to the following effect: 'The Court may also give an *advisory opinion* upon any dispute or question referred to it by the Council or by the Assembly.'

The Court is, therefore, under the Covenant, competent to deal with two sorts of cases: first, disputes brought to it by the parties by common agreement; second, questions referred by the Council or the Assembly—but *not* by the parties—for advisory opinions. But in considering its competence it must be remembered that cases may be brought by the parties in accordance with general treaties between them, by which they undertake to submit their disputes to the Court. And in fact in this way the Court is already securing a very considerable compulsory jurisdiction. There are many general treaties, for example, which were made during the Peace Conference, and which have been made since, in which it is stipulated that disputes arising out of their interpretation or application shall be referred on the demand of *one* party to the Court for settlement. There is no need to give illustrations: disputes arising out of the labour treaties, transit treaties, and many others, contain this clause. It is evident that this clause involves none of the difficulties of unrestricted compulsory jurisdiction, for clearly a Court of Law ought always to be able to settle a case arising out of the interpretation of a treaty.

11. *The Optional Protocol.* The adherents of compulsory jurisdiction have, however, made a much more important advance than this towards their goal. It is a point worth consideration, for it illustrates how rapidly and how effectively international, political, and legal obligations may develop when the institutional basis for such development has been created. The advance which they have made consists in what is known as the Optional Protocol attached to the Statute of the Court, and adopted in this optional form by the first Assembly of the League. This Protocol provides that any state which adheres to it thereby undertakes to submit all its disputes with any other signatory to the jurisdiction of the Court. It also contains a device for avoiding what has been called above the true difficulty of compulsory jurisdiction, the difficulty, namely, of knowing whether any given case is truly 'justiciable' or not. The Optional Protocol leaves this question for decision to the Court itself. This is evidently the best solution, for the reason that, of all people able to decide whether existing international law is sufficiently clear and defined to permit of a judicial decision in any given case, the judges of the Court are clearly the most competent.

This Optional Protocol has already been signed by nineteen states, and seventeen of them have ratified their signature.[1] More than a third of the Members of the League have therefore agreed among themselves to give the Court complete obligatory jurisdiction. This is very real and very substantial progress by the adherents of obligatory jurisdiction, and it seems probable that other powers will follow this example. This is evidently an important way of perfecting the international legal system, even before the rules of international law reach the completeness and precision to which they are tending.

12. *Advisory Opinions.* There remains of those mentioned above one provision of the final draft of the Covenant concerning the competence of the Court which is worth attention. This is the provision allowing the Court to give advisory opinions on the questions submitted to it by the Council or the Assembly. Since the Court was established there has been some controversy as to whether this was a duty which the Court could properly be asked to fulfil. There have been some legal purists, and among them persons of great authority, who have held that no court of law ought to be asked to give advisory opinions on matters which may subsequently be submitted to them for definite decision. They further argue that the questions on which their opinion may be asked by the Council or the Assembly may constitute a part and not the whole of the matter at issue, and that any opinion which they give on these questions might therefore be different from the opinion which they would have given had they had the whole subject-matter under their consideration, and that in this way they might be called upon to commit legal injustice. The defenders of this theory further hold that, even if the Court agreed in principle to give such opinions it would in fact be so reluctant to do so that, in the long run, the power would be of no practical importance. They quote in support of this contention the experience of the Judicial Committee of the Privy Council, which in a hundred years has given only four opinions and these of quite secondary importance.

In reply to those who argue thus it can only be said that

[1] Austria, Brazil, Bulgaria, China, Costa Rica, Denmark, Finland, Holland, Liberia, Lithuania, Luxemburg, Norway, Panama, Portugal, San Salvador, Switzerland, Uruguay.

Sweden and Haiti have signed the optional clause or adhered to it without making it subject to ratification.

the authors of the Covenant, in adopting this provision, only did so with a view to promoting the practical utility of the Court. They believed that cases might arise in which the main substance of an international dispute might be essentially political, but in which, nevertheless, there would be legal issues on which a separate legal decision might be required. And certainly experience has already shown that there is much to be said in favour of this view. The very first dispute brought before the League—the controversy over the Aaland Islands—involved a preliminary legal question on which the Council would certainly have asked for the opinion of the Court, had it been in existence. In fact, as the Court had not then been established, they asked for an opinion of a committee of three distinguished lawyers, and based their subsequent action on this opinion.[1] In such a case as this the system of advisory opinions seems in every way legally justifiable and practically of great value. The fact that the first two cases with which the Court had to deal at its session of 1922 were both questions on which its advisory opinion was asked seems again an argument in favour of this final provision of Art. XIV.

There is, moreover, another way in which this provision may be of use in the maintenance of peace and in the securing of justice in international disputes. Under Art. XI any Member of the League may in its discretion bring any dispute with another state before the Council of the League. In the Council it can argue that any part or the whole of its dispute is strictly justiciable in nature and falls within the definition contained in Art. XIII. It may urge that the Council in considering its case cannot properly come to a decision except by obtaining a judicial opinion on the legal merits. It can request the Council, in accordance with this last sentence of Art. XIV, to refer its question to the Court for an advisory opinion. And since such a reference is evidently a matter of procedure the Council can, in accordance with Art. III of the Covenant, decide to refer to the Court by a majority vote.

Whether the Members of the League will actually utilize the provisions of the Covenant in this way cannot be foreseen. But it would seem that to do so would be perfectly justifiable and would be a valuable way of overcoming the disadvantages which admittedly result from not giving the Court full obligatory

[1] Cp. also Bolivia and Chile, 1921.

jurisdiction. It could never lead to substantial injustices. Unless the contentions of the plaintiff state were in every way valid the Council would not consult the Court. If, on the other hand, it did so and the Court gave its opinion, it cannot be doubted that both the Council and the parties to the dispute would accept this opinion as finally decisive.

13. *Summary.* We have now passed in review all the provisions of the Covenant which concern the Court of Justice and have endeavoured to give some explanation of the way in which they came to be placed in the Covenant, and of the grounds upon which their inclusion was defended. It has perhaps appeared from this account of what took place, and of the reasons for it, that these provisions of the Covenant have been, and will be, of real importance in shaping the character and the future of the Court. It is clear, in particular, that the provisions of the Covenant which concern the competence and jurisdiction of the Court will probably do much to make its jurisdiction legally or morally obligatory on any state which may be engaged in a 'justiciable' dispute with its neighbours.

But even if these supplementary provisions of the Covenant, introduced, as has been said, after the publication of the first draft on the 14th February, had not been adopted, it is probable that the jurisdiction and authority of the Court would, not the less surely, though perhaps more slowly, have been extended. For in making provision for the establishment of a supreme international tribunal and in abolishing the right of immediate recourse to war the Covenant provided the two essential elements upon which an efficacious legal system could be built. The mere abolition of the right of immediate recourse to war operates powerfully to induce states to bring every case which is capable of judicial decision to the most competent Court of Law which it can find. It was this very process which established the authority of the English Courts of Law in the fifteenth century, when Henry VII succeeded in destroying the right of the barons to resort to war. And the same process has already begun in the League of Nations itself. The case of Tunis, which has just (October 1922) been referred by Great Britain and France to the Court, is a most forcible example. After prolonged negotiations the British Government suggested that this case, which seemed to them eminently a matter of international law, should be referred to any form of arbitration which the French Government might desire. The French refused. The British Government, thereupon, laid the matter, in accordance with Art. XI, before the Council of the League. Under Art. XI the French Government could not refuse its consideration by the Council. As it was therefore necessary for them to accept international consideration and decision of the dispute in some form or another, the French Government, after a preliminary examination of the matter by the Council of the League, agreed to refer the dispute for final decision to the Court of Justice. There could be no clearer example of the way in which the giving to every state of a right to summon any other state before the Council of the League, together with the establishment of a supreme legal tribunal, will promote the development of the international legal system.

The Tunis case is interesting in another way. It illustrates another truth about the Court: that it is not an isolated institution but an essential part of the whole fabric of the League of Nations. It is as a part of the new international political system, which it is the function of the League of Nations to work out, that the Court of Justice will be of greatest value. It may well be that as part of that system, and in proportion as a world sentiment for justice is developed, the Court will become the keystone of international peace.

If this prevision is correct—as the history of the Court of Justice to the present time gives ground for hoping that it may be—the verdict of historians will be that the work of the Peace Conference in Paris on the Court of Justice was perhaps cautious, but for that very reason wise and successful.

CHAPTER VI

INTERNATIONAL DEVELOPMENTS UNDER THE LEAGUE OF NATIONS

PART IV

THE MANDATORY SYSTEM[1]

1. *Art. XXII of the Covenant.* During the progress of the War the spokesmen of the Allied countries stated on more than one occasion that the Allied war aims did not include any desire for the annexation of territory belonging to the Central Powers or to Turkey. They proclaimed in the clearest possible terms that their aim in the War was the liberation of peoples subject to German and Turkish misrule, rather than any desire for further territorial expansion on the part of the Allies. The entry of the United States of America into the War led to the further emphasis of this principle, and both in regard to the German colonies and the non-Turkish provinces of the Ottoman Empire the declared intentions of the principal Allied Powers received increased support. On the 8th January 1918 President Wilson formulated his 'Fourteen Points'. The twelfth point stated that 'the nationalities which are now under Turkish rule should be assured an undoubted security of life and an absolutely unmolested opportunity of autonomous development'. In regard to the German colonies he further stated 'that the interests of the populations concerned must have equal weight with the equitable claims of the Government whose title is to be determined'.

The defeat of the Central Powers cast upon the Peace Conference in Paris the task of giving effect to these declarations. It became necessary to provide for the unmolested autonomous development of the non-Turkish provinces of the Ottoman Empire and to provide a form of Government for the backward races of the German colonies in Africa and the Pacific which was not inconsistent with the declarations that

[1] Complete till September 1922.

had been made. The suggestion that this policy could best be carried out by associating the problem with the League of Nations came in the first instance from General Smuts. This suggestion was adopted, and the matter was discussed not only by those sections of the Allied delegations appointed to deal with the Turkish and colonial problems, but also by the authors of the Covenant of the League. From these deliberations there emerged Art. XXII of the Covenant, and the actual wording of this article is due in the main to General Smuts and Mr. Philip Kerr.[1]

Art. XXII of the Covenant of the League of Nations which appeared as Part I of each of the Peace Treaties runs as follows:

'To those colonies and territories which as a consequence of the late war have ceased to be under the sovereignty of the States which formerly governed them and which are inhabited by peoples not yet able to stand by themselves under the strenuous conditions of the modern world, there should be applied the principle that the well-being and development of such peoples form a sacred trust to civilization, and that securities for the performance of this trust should be embodied in this Covenant.

'The best method of giving practical effect to this principle is that the tutelage of such peoples should be entrusted to advanced nations who, by reason of their resources, their experience, or their geographical position, can best undertake this responsibility, and who are willing to accept it, and that this tutelage should be exercised by them as Mandatories on behalf of the League.

'The character of the mandate must differ according to the stage of the development of the people, the geographical situation of the territory, its economic conditions, and other similar circumstances.

(*A*) 'Certain communities formerly belonging to the Turkish Empire have reached a stage of development where their existence as independent nations can be provisionally recognized, subject to the rendering of administrative advice and assistance by a Mandatory until such time as they are able to stand alone. The wishes of these communities must be a principal consideration in the selection of the Mandatory.

(*B*) 'Other peoples, especially those of Central Africa, are at such a stage that the Mandatory must be responsible for the administration of the territory under conditions which will guarantee freedom of conscience and religion, subject only to the maintenance of public order and morals, the prohibition of abuses such as the slave trade, the arms traffic, and the liquor traffic, and the prevention of the establishment of fortifications or military and naval bases and of military training of the natives for other than police purposes and the defence of territory, and will also

[1] *v.* also Vol. II, pp. 234–43, for German views *v.* Vol. II, pp. 295–8, and for Allied Reply *v.* Vol. II, pp. 300–2.

secure equal opportunities for the trade and commerce of other Members of the League.

(*C*) 'There are territories, such as South-West Africa and certain of the South Pacific Islands, which, owing to the sparseness of their population, or their small size, or their remoteness from the centres of civilization, or their geographical contiguity to the territory of the Mandatory, and other circumstances, can be best administered under the laws of the Mandatory as integral portions of its territory, subject to the safeguards above mentioned in the interests of the indigenous population.

'In every case of mandate, the Mandatory shall render to the Council an annual report in reference to the territory committed to its charge.

'The degree of authority, control, or administration to be exercised by the Mandatory shall, if not previously agreed upon by the Members of the League, be explicitly defined in each case by the Council.

'A permanent Commission shall be constituted to receive and examine the annual reports of the Mandatories and to advise the Council on all matters relating to the observance of the mandates.'

2. *Origin of the Mandatory System.* The origin of the mandatory theory goes back in part to a concept of Roman law and in part to the British legal conception of 'trusteeship'. It formed an important new departure in international affairs. Suggestions had been put forward for creating international administration in the territories under consideration. Under the Sykes-Picot agreement of 1916 a proposal for the international administration of Palestine had been put forward, and similar policy in regard to the ex-German colonies had been advocated by certain sections of opinion and notably by spokesmen for the Labour Parties in the various Allied countries. However, the experience of the world in regard to international administration had shown the unsatisfactory nature of such a form of government owing to the difficulty of fixing responsibility upon any one of the participating Powers. The mandatory system created by Art. XXII provides for national responsibility subject to international criticism and supervision. The only previous analogy in history to the mandatory system is to be found in the Berlin-Congo Act of 1885 whereby the principal European Powers concerned in Africa entrusted the task of administering the Congo Basin to King Leopold II of the Belgians subject to the limiting conditions of the Berlin-Congo Act. The most notable of these limiting conditions was the securing not only in the Congo but in the whole belt of tropical Africa of equal opportunities for the trade and commerce of all nations. The unsatisfactory feature of the Berlin-

Congo Act, which Art. XXII of the Covenant seeks to remedy, was the failure to provide any effective machinery for examining and reporting upon the carrying out of the trust by the Trustee or of securing the strict observance by the Trustee of the limiting conditions of the trust. The carrying out of the policy agreed by the Peace Conference at Paris depends first and foremost upon the provisions contained in Art. XXII for the rendering by the mandatory power of an annual report with reference to the territory committed to its charge to the Council of the League, and the constitution of a permanent Commission to receive and examine these annual reports and to advise the Council on all matters relating to the observance of the mandate.

3. *The 'B' and 'C' Mandates assigned, 7th May 1919.* Under the terms of the Treaty of Versailles all German rights in her former colonies were transferred not to the League of Nations but to the Allied and Associated Powers. The selection, therefore, in the first instance, of the mandatory Powers to be appointed in connexion with the various territories in question became a matter for the supreme Council and not one for the League of Nations. As a matter of fact, in the case of the German colonies the selection of the mandatories by the Allied and Associated Powers was effected by a meeting of the Supreme Council attended by Great Britain, France, Italy, Japan, and the United States of America on the 7th May 1919, at which the following decisions were reached:

I. *Togoland and Cameroons*: France and Great Britain shall make a joint recommendation to the League of Nations as to their future ('B' Mandate).

German East Africa: The 'B' Mandate shall be held by Great Britain.

German South-West Africa: The 'B' Mandate shall be held by the Union of South Africa.

The German Samoan Islands: The 'B' Mandate shall be held by New Zealand.

The other German Pacific possessions south of the Equator (excluding the German Samoan Islands and Nauru): The 'C' Mandate shall be held by Australia.

Nauru: The 'C' Mandate shall be given to the British Empire.

German Islands north of the Equator: The 'C' Mandate shall be held by Japan.

4. '*B' Mandates: Ruanda and Urundi* (*Belgium*), *Togoland and Cameroons*,[1] *21st August 1919*. In view of representations then made by the Belgian Prime Minister, M. Hymans, the North-Western portions of German East Africa (Ruanda and Urundi) were separated from the remainder of the territory and for this Belgium was selected as mandatory. With regard to the joint recommendation to be made in regard to Togoland and Cameroons, the position is made clear by the preamble of the draft mandates for the territories in question submitted by the two Governments to the Council of the League. In each case the larger parts of the territories are allocated to France and the smaller portions to Great Britain. The preamble in question runs as follows:

'Whereas by Art. CXIX of the Treaty of Peace with Germany signed at Versailles on the 28th June 1919, Germany renounced in favour of the Principal Allied and Associated Powers all her rights over her oversea possessions, including therein Togoland; and

'Whereas the Principal Allied and Associated Powers agreed that the Governments of France and Great Britain should make a joint recommendation to the League of Nations as to the future of the said territory; and

'Whereas the Governments of France and Great Britain have made a joint recommendation to the Council of the League of Nations that a Mandate to administer in accordance with Art. XXII of the Covenant of the League of Nations that part of Togoland lying to the east of the line agreed upon in the Declaration of the 10th July 1919, of which mention is made in Art. I below, should be conferred upon the French Republic; and

'Whereas by the terms of the said joint recommendation the Governments of France and Great Britain have proposed that the Mandate should be formulated in the following terms; and

'Whereas the French Republic has agreed to accept the Mandate in respect of the said territory and has undertaken to exercise it on behalf of the League of Nations.'

[1] *v.* also Vol. II, pp. 241–6. The Belgo-British Agreement of 30th May 1919 was accepted by the Supreme Council, 21st August 1919.

5. *'A' Mandates (Syria, Palestine, Mesopotamia) assigned, 5th May 1920.* In regard to the selection of mandatories for parts of the ex-Ottoman Empire, it was provided in the Treaty of Sèvres that the only portions of such territory to which the mandatory principle should be applied were Syria, Palestine, and Mesopotamia. It had been hoped that Armenia would have been included in the mandatory system and that the United States of America would have accepted the invitation of the other Allied Powers to assume the mandate. Owing to political developments in the United States, President Wilson was compelled to intimate that his country could not see its way to undertake the responsibility, and accordingly Armenia was dropped out of the system. Further, it was decided that the mandatory system should not apply to Central Arabia, or to the four ex-Turkish provinces of Hejaz, Asir, Yemen, and El-Hasa, but should be confined to Syria, Palestine, and the three Mesopotamian vilayets. The selection of mandatories for these three territories was made by the Supreme Council at San Remo on the 25th April 1920, France being selected as mandatory for Syria, and Great Britain for Palestine and Mesopotamia, the assignment being final on 5th May.

6. *Resolutions of the Council of the League, 26th October 1920; delay in the Drafts.* The mandatory system came into effective legal being on the 10th January 1920 by the ratification of the Treaty of Versailles containing Art. XXII of the Covenant. On the 5th August 1920 Signor Quinones de Leon as President of the Council of the League addressed a letter and a memorandum drawn up by the Belgian member of the Council (M. Hymans) to the four principal Powers on the general subject of mandates. This letter requests the principal Allied Powers to inform the League officially what are the boundaries of the territories to which the mandates refer and the names of the powers appointed by the Supreme Council to act as Mandatories, and to communicate to the Council 'the terms and conditions which the principal Allied Powers propose that the Council should adopt in respect of such mandates'. This letter was followed on the 26th October 1920 by the four following resolutions adopted by the Council of the League sitting at Brussels on that day :

I. The Council decides to request the principal Powers to be so good as : (*a*) to name the Powers to whom they have decided to allocate the Mandates provided for in Article XXII; (*b*) to inform it as to the frontiers of the territories to be administered under these Mandates; (*c*) to communicate to it the terms and the conditions of the Mandates that they propose should be adopted by the Council in accordance with the prescriptions of Article XXII.

II. The Council will take cognizance of the Mandatory Power appointed and will examine the draft Mandates communicated to it, in order to ascertain that they conform to the prescriptions of Article XXII of the Covenant.

III. The Council will notify to each Power appointed that it is invested with the Mandate, and will, at the same time, communicate to it the terms and conditions thereof.

IV. The Council instructs the Secretary-General to prepare in accordance with the recommendations set forth in this report, a draft scheme for the organization of the Mandates Commission provided for by Article XXII, Paragraph 9.

These resolutions are important as they set forth the relations between the principal Allied Powers and the League of Nations in regard to mandates and define the functions of the League. From these resolutions it was clear that the terms of the mandates were to be drawn up by the principal Allied Powers in consultation with each other and were to be communicated by them to the League. It would then be the duty of the League to examine the drafts so as to ensure that the conditions laid down in Art. XXII of the Covenant were in every case complied with, and further, on its own initiative the League must proceed to organize and appoint a permanent Mandates Commission. Work on the draft mandates had been commenced in the summer of 1919 by the delegates in Paris at the Peace Conference, and an inter-allied Committee under the presidency of Viscount Milner was appointed to prepare the drafts. Unfortunately the drafts were not completed, nor had the Allied Governments given their assent to such drafts as were completed by the time the Peace Conference broke up. Consequently the further preparation of the drafts was left over for subsequent diplomatic negotiation. Difficulties had arisen in regard to certain clauses of the draft mandates for Togoland and Cameroons, while political developments of a serious character took shape in Syria and Mesopotamia.

7. *Withdrawal of the United States from the League; subsequent policy.* The chief difficulties, however, arose from the decision of the American Senate declining to ratify the Covenant of the League or the Treaty of Versailles, and the effective

withdrawal of the Government of the United States of America from the Supreme Council of the Allies. However, this withdrawal of the United States was not complete in regard to the particular question of the mandates. As one of the principal Allied and Associated Powers to whom the ex-German colonies had been transferred, America remained interested in their fate, and the American Government had from the first shown the liveliest interest in the terms of the various mandates. Immediately after the assignment of Great Britain as mandatory for Palestine and Mesopotamia by the Supreme Council at San Remo on the 5th May 1920, the American Ambassador in London addressed a letter to Lord Curzon dated the 12th May 1920 dealing in particular with the claims of the United States of America to equal treatment with members of the League in mandated territories and especially in respect to economic rights. The first two and fifth paragraphs of this letter set out very clearly the position persistently adopted by the Government of the United States throughout. They run as follows:

(*a*) *United States' letter, 12th May 1920.*

PURSUANT to the instructions of my Government, I have the honour to inform your Lordship that the Government of the United States has been unofficially informed that the mandates for Mesopotamia and Palestine have been assigned to Great Britain; the mandate for Mesopotamia being given subject to friendly arrangement with the Italian Government regarding economic rights.

2. The Government of the United States desires to point out that during the peace negotiations at Paris leading up to the Treaty of Versailles, it consistently took the position that the future peace of the world required that, as a general principle, any alien territory which should be acquired pursuant to the Treaties of Peace with the Central Powers, must be held and governed in such a way as to assure equal treatment in law and in fact to the commerce of all nations. It was on account of, and subject to this understanding, that the United States felt itself able and willing to agree that the acquisition of certain enemy territory by the victorious Powers would be consistent with the best interests of the world. The representatives of the principal Allied Powers, in the discussion of the mandate principles, expressed in no indefinite manner their recognition of the justice and far-sightedness of such a principle, and agreed to its application to the mandates over Turkish territory.

5. With this thought in mind the Government of the United States ventures to suggest the following propositions, which embody or illustrate the principles which the United States Government would be

pleased to see applied in the occupied or mandated regions, and which are submitted as furnishing a reasonable basis for discussions. In the event of such discussions, it would be assumed that the legal situation as regards economic resources in the occupied or mandated regions would remain *in statu quo* pending an agreement.

(1) That the Mandatory Power strictly adhere and conform to the principles expressed and agreed to during the peace negotiations at Paris, and to the principles embodied in mandate 'A' prepared in London for adoption by the League of Nations by the Commission on Mandatories.

(2) That there be guaranteed to the nationals or subjects of all nations treatment equal in law and in fact, to that accorded nationals or subjects of the Mandatory Power with respect to taxation or other matters affecting residence, business, profession, concessions, freedom of transit for persons and goods, freedom of communication, trade, navigation, commerce, industrial property, and other economic rights or commercial activities.

(3) That no exclusive economic concessions covering the whole of any mandated region or sufficiently large to be virtually exclusive shall be granted, and that no monopolistic concessions relating to any commodity or to any economic privilege subsidiary and essential to the production, development, or exploitation of such commodity shall be granted.

(4) That reasonable provision shall be made for publicity of applications for concessions and of governmental acts or regulations relating to the economic resources of the mandated territories; and that in general regulations or legislation regarding the granting of concessions relating to, exploring, or exploiting economic resources, or regarding other privileges in connexion with these, shall not have the effect of placing American citizens or companies, or those of other nations or companies controlled by American citizens or nationals of other countries, at a disadvantage compared with the nationals or companies of the mandate nation, or companies controlled by nationals of the mandate nation or others.

(*b*) *Lord Curzon's Reply, 9th August 1920.* Lord Curzon did not reply to this letter until the 9th August 1920. The important paragraphs of Lord Curzon's reply are 13, 14, and 15, which run as follows:

13. I will now refer to the propositions enumerated by you on which discussion is invited and which have been put forward with the object of guaranteeing to the commerce of all nations the practical fulfilment in the mandated regions of the principles of equal treatment in law and in fact. Reference is made in this connexion to the desirability of the adherence of the mandatory Power to the principles expressed and agreed to during the peace negotiations at Paris, as well as to the principles embodied in mandate (A) prepared in London by the Commission on Mandates, for adoption by the League of Nations.

14. I would first point out that in consequence of a divergence of

views, the Commission on Mandates proceeded no further with the draft of the mandate form (A), which was consequently abandoned.

15. The draft mandates for Mesopotamia and for Palestine, which have been prepared with a view to secure equality of treatment and opportunity for the commerce, citizens, and subjects of all States who are members of the League of Nations, will, when approved by the Allied Powers interested, be communicated to the Council of the League of Nations. In these circumstances, His Majesty's Government, while fully appreciating the suggestion for discussing with the United States Government the various propositions mentioned by you, with which they are in full sympathy, are none the less of the opinion that the terms of the mandates can only properly be discussed at the Council of the League of Nations by the signatories of the Covenant.

The mandate form (A) referred to in the above extracts was the general formula drawn up in Paris by the Milner Committee and is the basis for the draft mandates for Togoland, Cameroons, and German East Africa.

(c) *Reply of the United States, 20th November 1920.* The further reply of the Government of the United States is dated from Washington 20th November 1920, and was received by the British Foreign Office on the 7th December. The important paragraphs of this letter run as follows:

'It is assumed accordingly that your statements with reference to mandate "A", together with the statement that the draft mandates for Mesopotamia and Palestine have been prepared with a view to secure equality of treatment for the commerce and citizens of all States which are members of the League of Nations, do not indicate a supposition on your part that the United States can be excluded from the benefits of the principle of equality of treatment.

'This Government is pleased to find that His Majesty's Government is in full sympathy with the principles formulated in its communications of the 12th May and of the 28th July. But it is unable to concur in the view, contained in paragraph 15 of your note, that the terms of the mandates can properly be discussed only in the Council of the League of Nations and by the signatories of the Covenant. Such powers as the Allied and Associated nations may enjoy or wield in the determination of the governmental status of the mandated areas accrued to them as a direct result of the war against the Central Powers. The United States as a participant in that conflict and as a contributor to its successful issue cannot consider any of the Associated Powers, the smallest not less than itself, debarred from the discussion of any of its consequences, or from participation in the rights and privileges secured under the mandates provided for in the Treaties of Peace.

'This Government notes with interest your statement that the draft mandates for Mesopotamia and for Palestine, which have been prepared, with a view to secure equality of treatment and opportunity for the commerce, citizens, and subjects of all States which are members of the

League of Nations, will when approved by the interested Allied Powers, be communicated to the Council of the League of Nations. The United States is undoubtedly one of the Powers directly interested in the terms of the mandates, and I therefore request that the draft mandate forms be communicated to this Government for its consideration before their submission to the Council of the League. It is believed that His Majesty's Government will be the more ready to acquiesce in this request, in view of your assurance that His Majesty's Government is in full sympathy with the various principles contained in the two previous notes of this Government upon this subject.

'The establishment of the mandate principle, a new principle in international relations, and one in which the public opinion of the world is taking a special interest, would seem to require the frankest discussion from all pertinent points of view. It would seem essential that suitable publicity should be given to the drafts of mandates which it is the intention to submit to the Council, in order that the fullest opportunity may be afforded to consider their terms in relation to the obligations assumed by the Mandatory Power and the respective interests of all Governments which are or deem themselves concerned or affected.

'The fact cannot be ignored that the reported resources of Mesopotamia have interested public opinion of the United States, Great Britain, and other countries as a potential subject of economic strife. Because of that fact they become an outstanding illustration of the kind of economic question with reference to which the mandate principle was especially designed, and, indeed, a peculiarly critical test of the good faith of the nations which have given their adherence to the principle. This principle was accepted in the hope of obviating in the future those international differences that grow out of a desire for the exclusive control of the resources and markets of annexed territories. To cite a single example: because of the shortage of petroleum, its constantly increasing commercial importance, and the continuing necessity of replenishing the world's supply by drawing upon the latent resources of undeveloped regions, it is of the highest importance to apply to the petroleum industry the most enlightened principles recognized by nations as appropriate for the peaceful ordering of their economic relations.'

The two most important points in this dispatch are the demand of the United States Government for equality of treatment for the United States and its citizens with states which are members of the League and their nationals, and secondly the demand for the publication of the draft mandates before their final approval by the Council of the League. This second demand synchronized with a similar demand put forward in the Parliament and Press of the United Kingdom for such publication, and the demand was acceded to as far as the British Government was concerned in the middle of the following year. The draft mandates for Togoland and Cameroons were published in May 1921, and the draft mandates for Palestine and Mesopotamia in August 1921.

8. *Delay in the Drafts of the Mandates, 1920.* The first meeting of the Assembly of the League of Nations took place in November 1920, and, as might be expected, the delay in the coming into full force of the mandatory system gave rise to considerable discussion, more particularly on the constitutional point regarding the relation of the Council of the League to the Assembly of the League. In this as in other matters it is clearly laid down by the terms of Art. XXII of the Covenant that questions concerning mandates are reserved to the Council of the League, and that the status of the Assembly is limited in regard to Art. XXII to two functions. First, the general review which the Assembly is entitled to make each year of the work of the Council, and second, any amendment of Art. XXII as of any other article of the Covenant. The Council of the League was undoubtedly placed in a difficult position, as up to that time and even up to the 30th November, no draft mandates had been submitted to the League by the mandatories or by the Allied and Associated Powers.

Communications regarding the submission of the draft mandates were submitted by the Council of the League to the Prime Ministers of France, Great Britain, Italy, and Japan on the 5th August 1920, the 26th October 1920, and finally on the 30th November 1920. The last communication signed by M. Hymans as then President of the Council runs as follows:

'In order to give the principal Allied Powers adequate time to complete their negotiations relative to the terms and conditions of the Mandates which they are proposing for adoption by Council, the Council had decided not to present its report on this question to the Assembly until towards the end of the Session.

'As, however, so far, no draft Mandates have yet been submitted, and as this has stirred the public opinion of the world, the Council takes the liberty of urging the extreme importance of a prompt solution. However great may be its desire that the Principal Allied Powers should be in complete agreement upon the draft Mandates which they submit, the Council cannot in default of this agreement indefinitely postpone the execution of the obligations incumbent upon it.

'It is probable that the Assembly will remind the Council of the provisions of the Covenant by which the degree of authority, of control, or of administration to be exercised by the Mandatory is to be determined by the Council in the absence of a previous Agreement.

'The Council therefore urgently requests you to be good enough to communicate any draft Mandates upon which agreement may have been reached between the Principal Allied Powers at a sufficiently early date to allow the Council to give the Assembly all the necessary information before the end of the present Session.'

9. *Constitution of Permanent Mandates Commission, 1st December 1920.* This letter was written while the Council of the League was in Session, and without waiting for any drafts the Council proceeded to constitute the permanent Mandates Commission. The constitution of the permanent Mandates Commission was approved by the Council of the League on the 1st December 1920 in the following form:

(*a*) *Constitution.* The Council of the League of Nations, in accordance with paragraphs 7 and 9 of Art. XXII of the Covenant, namely,

'In every case of mandate, the Mandatory shall render to the Council an annual report in reference to the territory committed to its charge.'

'A permanent Commission shall be constituted to receive and examine the annual reports of the Mandatories, and to advise the Council on all matters relating to the observance of the mandates.'

has decided as follows:

(*a*) The Permanent Mandates Commission provided for in paragraph 9 of Article XXII of the Covenant shall consist of nine Members. The majority of the Commission shall be nationals of non-Mandatory Powers.

All the Members of the Commission shall be appointed by the Council and selected for their personal merits and competence.[1] They shall not hold any office which puts them in a position of direct dependence on their Governments while Members of the Commission.

The International Labour Organization shall have the privilege of appointing to the Permanent Commission an expert chosen by itself. This expert shall have the right of attending in an advisory capacity all meetings of the Permanent Commission at which questions relating to labour are discussed.

(*b*) The Mandatory Powers should send their annual report provided for in paragraph 7 of Article XXII of the Covenant to the Commission through duly authorized representatives who would be prepared to offer any supplementary explanations or supplementary information which the Commission may request.

(*c*) The Commission shall examine each individual report in the presence of the duly authorized representative of the Mandatory Power from which it comes. This representative shall participate with absolute freedom in the discussion of this report.

[1] It was frequently and strongly stressed that members of the Mandates Commission were in no respects the representatives of their Governments or called upon to act as such. Members were chosen as individuals though it was understood that each Mandatory Power should have one of its nationals as a member of the Commission.

(*d*) After this discussion has ended and the representative of the Mandatory Power has withdrawn, the Commission shall decide on the wording of the observations which are to be submitted to the Council of the League.

(*e*) The observations made by the Commission upon each report shall be communicated to the duly authorized representative of the Mandatory Power from which it comes. This representative shall be entitled to accompany it with any comments which he desires to make.

(*f*) The Commission shall forward the reports of Mandatory Powers to the Council. It shall annex to each report its own observations as well as the observations of the duly authorized representative of the Power which issued the report, if the representative so desires.

(*g*) When the Council publishes the reports of the Mandatory Powers and the observations of the Permanent Commission, it shall also publish the observations of the duly authorized representatives of those Mandatory Powers which have expressed such a desire.

(*h*) The Commission, acting in concert with all the duly authorized representatives of the Mandatory Powers, shall hold a Plenary Meeting to consider all the reports as a whole and any general conclusions to be drawn from them. The Commission may also utilize such a meeting of the representatives of the Mandatory Powers to lay before them any other matters connected with Mandates which in their opinion should be submitted by the Council to the Mandatory Powers and to the other States Members of the League. This Plenary Meeting shall take place either before or after the presentation of the annual reports as the Commission may think fit.

(*i*) The Commission shall regulate its own procedure subject to the approval of the Council.

(*j*) The Commission shall sit at Geneva. It may summon technical experts to act in an advisory capacity for all questions relating to the application of the system of Mandates.

(*k*) The Members of the Commission shall receive an allowance of 100 gold francs [1] per day during their meetings. Their travelling expenses shall be paid. Expenses of the Commission shall be borne by the League of Nations.

(*b*) *Personnel.* The nine countries originally invited by the Council of the League to submit names for the Commission were:

Powers Mandatory.	*Representative.*
1. France.	M. Beau, former Governor of Indo-China, ex-Ambassador to Switzerland.
2. Great Britain.	The Hon. W. Ormsby-Gore, M.P.; Sir F. Lugard.[2]
3. Japan.	M. Kunio Yanagida, formerly Secretary-General to House of Peers.
4. Belgium.	M. Pierre Orts, formerly Under-Secretary of Foreign Affairs.

[1] The amount of remuneration to the Members of the Permanent Commission has since been reduced to seventy gold francs per day.

[2] On Mr. Ormsby-Gore's becoming Under-Secretary the Colonies (1922). [Editor's Note].

Non-Mandatory.	*Foreign Affairs.*
5. United States of America.	(Spain) M. Raman Pina, ex-Ambassador.[1]
6. Italy.	Marchese Alberto Theodoli, former Under-Secretary of State for the Colonies.
7. Holland.	M. Van Rees.
8. Portugal.	M. Freire d'Andrade, former Minister of Foreign Affairs, and ex-Governor of Portuguese East Africa.
9. Sweden.	Madame Anna Bugge Wicksell, LL.D., Swedish Delegate in the Assembly.

The Government of the United States, however, felt unwilling to permit participation of a national of the United States, and eventually, as seen above, the Council selected a Spaniard to take the vacant place.

The Council of the League further appointed Monsieur W. Rappard (Swiss), Professor of Economic History at the University of Geneva, as permanent director of the Mandates Section and as Secretary of the Commission.

10. *'C' Mandates approved, 17th December 1920.* In response to the letters addressed by the Council of the League to the Principal Allied Powers the agreed drafts for the 'C' Mandates, e. g. for ex-German colonies in the Pacific and for South-West Africa, were received by the Secretary-General of the League on the 9th December 1920, and these drafts were considered and approved by the Council of the League at Geneva on the 17th December 1920. With this approval the Mandatory system came into full operation in regard to ex-German South West-Africa (Union of South Africa), New Guinea (Australia), Samoa (New Zealand), Nauru (the British Empire), and the Caroline and Marianne Islands (Japan).

(*a*) *Form of 'C' Mandate.* The form of the Mandates is almost identical and the Mandate for Samoa is given on pp. 639–40.

(*b*) *Comments on Art. II in 'C' Mandates ; Japan's protest.* The important provision to be noted in regard to the 'C' Mandates is Art. II, which permits the Mandatory to apply its own laws to the mandated territory.[2] This provision has

[1] He resigned July 1922 and was replaced by Count Ballobar, for seven years Spanish Consul at Jerusalem.

[2] ART. 2. The Mandatory shall have full power of administration and legislation over the territory subject to the present Mandate as an integral portion of the Dominion of New Zealand and may apply the laws of the

far-reaching consequences. It must be remembered that the laws of both Australia and New Zealand provide for protective measures in regard to immigration and navigation. These laws are the result of what is known as 'the white Australia policy' and are designed to prevent further Asiatic immigration. Their application to the mandated territories of New Guinea and Samoa necessarily involves the limitation of Japanese as against European rights, and consequently the Japanese representative on the Council of the League, under the instructions of the Japanese Government, deposited the following declaration with the Council of the League on the occasion of their ratification of the 'C' Mandates:

'From the fundamental spirit of the League of Nations and as the question of interpretation of the Covenant, His Imperial Japanese Majesty's Government have a firm conviction in the justice of the claim they have hitherto made for the inclusion of a clause concerning the assurance of equal opportunities for trade and commerce in 'C' Mandates. But from the spirit of conciliation and co-operation and their reluctance to see the question unsettled any longer, they have decided to agree to the issue of the Mandate in its present form. That decision, however, should not be considered as an acquiescence on the part of His Imperial Japanese Majesty's Government in the submission of Japanese subjects to a discriminatory and disadvantageous treatment in the Mandated territories: nor have they thereby discarded their claim that the rights and interests enjoyed by Japanese subjects in these territories in the past should be fully respected.'

A somewhat similar protest was made by Mr. Sastri, the Indian delegate, at the second meeting of the Assembly with regard to ex-German South-West Africa, where the laws of the Union of South Africa provided for discrimination against further Indian immigration into the territory of the Union.

11. *The Yap Controversy and Treaty, 11th February 1922.* The most serious controversy, however, that arose out of the 'C' Mandates was in regard to the Japanese Mandate for the Island of Yap, one of the Caroline Islands. It must be remembered that on the 7th December the British Foreign Office received the request of the Government of the United States, dated the 20th November, for the submission to the Government of the United States and for the publication of

Dominion of New Zealand to the territory, subject to such local modifications as circumstances may require.

The Mandatory shall promote to the utmost the material and moral well-being and the social progress of the inhabitants of the territory subject to the present Mandate.

all draft mandates before ratification by the Council of the League. The Council of the League, on the 17th December 1920, however, proceeded to dispose of the 'C' Mandates without their having been either published or submitted to the Government of the United States for their consideration. The consequence was that no little storm arose in the United States of America on this subject. Yap, which is the most westerly island of the Caroline group, is of considerable strategic importance, as it lies directly between the American Island and cable centre of Guam to the East and the American Philippine Islands on the west. Yap is in itself an important cable junction, being connected by cable not only with Guam and the Philippine Islands, but also with the Dutch East Indies. Under the laws of Japan none but Japanese subjects are entitled to own or work cables or cable stations in Japanese territory, and in view of the then state of feeling between the United States of America and Japan on all questions concerning the Pacific, and of the attitude of the greater part of American public opinion and the Senate to the League of Nations, it is perhaps not surprising that Yap became a storm-centre of public discussion. This controversy lasted for a whole year, but was finally and satisfactorily disposed of at the Washington Conference early in 1922 by the Four Power Treaty and by the special Yap Treaty dated the 11th February 1922. Under the Four Power Treaty the protection accorded is extended to the mandated islands, while at the same time 'the making of the Treaty shall not be deemed to be an assent on the part of the United States of America to the Mandates and shall not preclude agreements between the United States and the Mandatory Powers respectively in relation to the mandated islands'. This particular phrase would, however, seem to have been made inoperative by Art. I of the Yap Treaty of the 11th February 1922, whereby 'the United States of America consent to the administration by Japan pursuant to the aforesaid Mandate of all the former German Islands in the Pacific Ocean lying north of the Equator'. The greater part of the Yap Treaty consists of an assurance given by the Japanese Government to the United States of American rights and interests in the use and working of the cables.

12. *Nauru under the Mandate.* Reference should be made to the peculiar position of the Island of Nauru. Nauru is

a small island, formerly belonging to Germany, immediately south of the equator near the Gilbert Ellice group, which are administered from the Colonial Office in London. Nauru lies over a thousand miles north-west of Samoa and approximately a thousand miles north-east of New Guinea. The island contains valuable phosphate deposits formerly worked by a German company. On the outbreak of war the rights of the German company were sequestrated and vested in an English company. It will be remembered that under the decision of the Supreme Council of the 7th May 1919 it was decided that the Mandate for this valuable island should be conferred upon the British Empire as a whole. On the 2nd July 1919 an Agreement was signed by Mr. Lloyd George for and on behalf of 'His Majesty's Government in London', by Mr. Hughes for and on behalf of the Commonwealth of Australia, and by Mr. Massey for and on behalf of the Dominion of New Zealand, regarding the administration of the island and the working and utilization of the phosphate deposits. This Agreement was ratified by the Australian and New Zealand Parliaments and by the Imperial Parliament in the form of a Nauru Island Agreement Act which received the royal assent on the 4th August 1920.[1] Clause 1 of this Act sets out that 'the Agreement is hereby confirmed subject to the provisions of Art. XXII of the Covenant of the League of Nations'. The Agreement is set out in the Schedule, and provides that the administration of the island shall be vested in an administrator who shall have power to make laws and ordinances for the peace, order, and good government of the island and particularly to provide for the education of children on the island, to establish and maintain the necessary police force, and to establish and appoint courts and magistrates with civil and criminal jurisdiction. The first administrator shall be appointed for a term of five years by the Australian Government, and thereafter the administrator shall be appointed in such manner as the three Governments (parties to the Agreement) may decide.

The position thus created is peculiar when viewed in comparison with other Mandates. It is also of interest in connexion with internal constitutional problems of the British Empire. The Mandate having been conferred upon the British Empire

[1] There was some severe criticism of the Nauru Mandate in the House of Commons Debate of the 16th June 1920. [Editor's Note].

as a whole, it would appear that Canada, the Union of South Africa, and India surrendered their claim to participate both in the supervision and exercise of the mandate as well as in the advantages to be derived from the exploitation of the phosphates.

13. *Progress with Drafts and Reports, 1921.* After the decision of the Council in regard to the 'C' Mandates in December 1920 and before the next meeting of the Assembly of the League in September 1921, little further progress was made in the development of the mandatory system. The British drafts for the 'A' and 'B' Mandates were drawn up and agreed with the French Government and the boundaries between the British and French mandated areas in Togoland and Cameroons were decided, the joint recommendations of the British and French Governments as to the future of the territories being agreed on the 17th December 1920. The principal cause of the further delay in the final issue of the mandates was due to the relations between the British and French Governments on the one hand and the Government of the United States of America on the other, and the Council felt themselves unable to deal with the 'A' and 'B' Mandates as long as the negotiations with the American Government remained unsettled.

However, at the second meeting of the Assembly in September 1921 important new developments took place as a result of the initiative displayed in the Commission of the Assembly appointed to examine the position of mandates by Lord Robert Cecil and Dr. Nansen. On the 20th September 1921, Mr. Fisher on behalf of the British Government gave an undertaking in this Commission that his Government would administer the mandated territories over which they had charge in accordance with the terms of the draft mandates by then published, and, further, that although the British Government could not recognize the legal right of the Council of the League or of the Permanent Mandates Commission to receive or examine Annual Reports in respect of territories where the mandate had not been finally approved by the Council, yet the British Government were prepared to allow the permanent Mandates Commission to examine the reports which had in fact been received by the British Government in regard to these particular territories. Following this declaration by the British representative, the representatives of France and Belgium agreed to a similar course of action. The British Government immediately submitted to the League three documents which had been laid as Parliamentary papers dealing with the administration of Palestine, Mesopotamia, and Tanganyika Territory. The French Government submitted two very full reports dealing with their portions of Cameroons and Togoland, and the Belgian Government also submitted a report on Urundi and Ruanda. The permanent Mandates Commissioners were accordingly summoned forthwith to Geneva and commenced their first session before the Assembly had risen. The permanent Mandates Commission was inaugurated by Dr. Wellington Koo (China) the then President of the Council of the League and proceeded to draw up its rules of business. The Marchese Theodoli (Italy) was elected Chairman and Mr. van Rees, Vice-Chairman. In view of the fact that the reports submitted to the Commission had not been drawn up expressly for the Commission, no report was made by the Commission to the Council on the contents of the reports, but the Commission proceeded from their study of the reports to draw up full questionnaires dealing with all the points upon which it was desirous of being informed by the mandatory powers in regard to the execution of the various mandates. The questionnaires were approved by the Council and transmitted by them to the mandatory powers as a guide for future annual reports. In the course of their examination of the reports the attention of the permanent Commission was drawn to the difficulty of determining under the terms of the draft mandates the question of the national status of native and non-native citizens of mandated territories, and the Council invited the Chairman to form a special sub-committee of the permanent Mandates Commission to explore this problem in consultation with the Governments of the various mandatory powers. Accordingly the Marchese Theodoli, accompanied by M. d'Andrade and M. Rappard, visited London, Paris, and Brussels in November 1921, holding conferences with the Governments of Great Britain, France, and Belgium, and with the High Commissioners of the three interested British Dominions, and presented a report on the views thereby collected to the Council of the League at their meeting in May 1922.

14. *The Second Meeting of the Permanent Mandates Com-*

mission, July 1922. On the 12th May 1922 the Council reviewed the results of the inquiries made by the sub-committee, and invited the Permanent Mandates Commission as a whole to submit definite proposals to the Council of the League for the solution of the difficult problem that had arisen. The Permanent Mandates Commission met accordingly during the first week of August 1922 and unanimously agreed to the following proposals.

1. It is important, in order that the principles laid down in Art. XXII of the Covenant may be respected, and subject to the provision of paragraph 3 below, that the native inhabitants of 'B' and 'C' mandated territories should be granted a national status wholly distinct from that of Nationals of the Mandatory Power.

2. A special law should be promulgated by the Mandatory Power determining the status of these native inhabitants, who might be given a designation such as 'Persons administered or protected under Mandate of the Mandatory Power'.

3. It is open (*loisible*) to the Mandatory Powers to whom 'B' and 'C' mandated territories have been entrusted to make arrangements in conformity with their own laws for the individual and purely voluntary acquisition of their nationality by the inhabitants of these territories.

This third proposal arose out of a suggestion coming from the Union of South Africa regarding the naturalization *en masse* of the German inhabitants of the mandated territory of South West Africa. In explanation of their view the Permanent Mandates Commission added the following paragraph on this point.

'It seems contrary to the spirit of the Covenant and to the essence of the institution of Mandates to permit the compulsory naturalization by single act of all the inhabitants of territories under "B" or "C" Mandates. The legal relations which exist between a Mandatory Power and the territory which it administers on behalf of the League of Nations do not appear to permit of a measure which a state annexing a territory cannot apply with regard to the inhabitants annexed except by virtue of provisions expressly inserted in the Treaty of Cession. The Treaty of Versailles, by the terms of which the former German Colonies were handed over to the Principal Allied and Associated Powers, to be administered on behalf of the League of Nations by Powers called "Mandatory", contains no clause imposing the nationality of the Mandatory Power on the inhabitants of those colonies.'

15. *Council approves 'A' and 'B' Mandates except Meso-*

potamia, July 1922. The Council of the League met again in London during the last week of July 1922 and approved the terms of all the outstanding mandates except Mesopotamia, where political conditions did not permit of the matter being pressed. Accordingly, by the end of July 1922 the mandatory system came into full operation in regard to all the ex-German colonies and in regard to Palestine and Syria.

The nature of these mandates can best be understood by examination of the actual documents. The mandate for Tanganyika Territory (British), formerly German East Africa, is, with small variations,[1] the type adopted for all the six 'B' Mandates. In the 'A' Mandates the French mandate for Syria and the Lebanon follows closely, except of course in regard to the clause dealing with the Jewish National Home and the Holy Places, the British mandate for Palestine. Accordingly the terms of the mandates for Tanganyika Territory and Syria are given respectively on pp. 641–5, 645–54.

16. *Character of Mandates.*

(*a*) '*A*' *Mandates, Syria and Palestine.* Having dealt with the origin, it remains to add a few further general remarks upon the character and objects of the system. The three classes of mandate 'A', 'B', and 'C' are quite clearly differentiated. In the case of the Class 'A' Mandates it is clear that the exercise of powers by the mandatory are to be regarded as purely temporary, and that the rôle of the mandatory is to provide such protection, advice, and assistance as will enable the three countries of Mesopotamia, Syria, and Palestine to become independent States Members of the League. It is highly probable that the function of the mandatory in Mesopotamia will be of comparatively limited duration and that as soon as the Arab state of Mesopotamia is sufficiently organized to maintain itself against external aggression or absorption, and to secure internal order, the Arab state of Mesopotamia, now in its infancy, will apply to be admitted as a State Member of the League on the same footing as Persia, and, one presumes, Egypt.[2] Equally it is clear from the more difficult internal problems in Syria and Palestine that the exercise of functions by the mandatory power will in all

[1] For chief difference *v.* French Mandate for Togoland p. 642 n. [Editor's Note].

[2] *v. supra* for Syria, p. 169; for Mesopotamia, pp. 187–91. Text of draft mandate, pp. 609–13; for Egypt, pp. 203–5.

probability be more extensive and of longer duration than the mandatory functions required in the case of Mesopotamia. This is particularly true of Palestine, where in addition to the presence of important Jewish and Christian minorities there are important international interests to be safeguarded. Religious and racial difficulties arise in Palestine in intensified form in a degree unequalled in any other country in the world, and the primary function of the mandatory power will for long consist in the maintenance of internal peace and order among so mixed a population. But in Palestine the position of the mandatory is further complicated by the duty imposed upon the mandatory of carrying out a policy agreed by the Allied and Associated Powers during the War and at the Peace Conference of facilitating the creation of a Jewish national home in Palestine. The Balfour Declaration of the 2nd November 1917, to which the Governments of France, Italy, Japan, and the United States of America gave their definite adherence, imposes upon the mandatory an international task of peculiar delicacy, e. g. that of securing such social, political, and economic conditions in Palestine as will enable a renaissance of Hebrew culture and civilization to spring up once again in the land of the Bible. In view of historic, racial, and religious animosities, the carrying out of such a policy cannot be otherwise than controversial, and it must be remembered that the Balfour Declaration while supporting the Zionist movement, specifically guarantees the civil and religious rights of the non-Jewish inhabitants of the country and, further, imposes the limitation that whatever is done in Palestine should not affect the political status of Jews in other parts of the world. In the minds of most people this last provision cuts out the possibility of regarding Palestine as a potential Jewish state. In Syria, France has the difficult task of reconciling the interests and aspirations of the Lebanon, with its predominant Christian majority, with a federation of other Arabic-speaking provinces where the Mahommedans are in an overwhelming majority, and of bringing cohesion and unity to a country where local particularism has long been the distinctive feature of the country.

(*b*) '*B*' *Mandates.* In the territories under Class 'B' Mandates there live African populations of varying degrees of development, from the primitive and almost savage character to the most highly developed negro elements, amounting in all to between twelve and thirteen millions. The aim of the mandatory system is to secure disinterested and progressive colonial administration of the more backward races by experienced European Powers. Successful conduct of such an experiment may have far-reaching influences upon the character of European administration throughout Africa, and the whole world will watch with interest what is, and can be done by the application of the spirit and letter of Art. XXII of the Covenant to this great and growing problem.

(*c*) '*C*' *Mandates*. Class 'C' Mandates provide for the maintenance of a standard of administration in such territories not lower than the standard obtaining internally in the territory of the mandatory powers themselves, and for special safeguards in the interests of the indigenous native populations. Perhaps the most interesting feature of the 'C' Mandates is the fact that in the main they are conferred directly upon British self-governing Dominions, who are thereby called upon to follow the example of the parent country, Great Britain, in the task of colonial or native administration. Such a development is of peculiar interest in the constitutional development of the British Empire and the status of the British self-governing Dominions as equal members with Great Britain in the League of Nations.

Note.—Date on which Mandates came into force.

'*A*'. 24th July 1922. The Council of the League approved the mandates for Syria and Palestine, and stated they would both come into force automatically as soon as Italy and France reached agree ment on certain points in the Syrian Mandate.

'*B*'. 20th July 1922.

'*C*'. 17th December 1920 (1922.)

CHAPTER VI

INTERNATIONAL DEVELOPMENTS UNDER THE LEAGUE OF NATIONS

PART V

GUARANTEES AGAINST WAR[1]

1. *Introductory.* Clearly the best guarantee against war is to remove the causes of war. The preamble to the Covenant of the League of Nations sets forth the means by which it is proposed to achieve this result. These means are, firstly the promotion of international co-operation, secondly the acceptance of obligations not to resort to war, thirdly the recognition of the principles and understandings of international law. The methods by which it hoped to promote international co-operation have been described in a previous chapter, and they are the foundation upon which the structure of the League has been erected, for it is obvious that if the principle of such co-operation can be established the causes of war will be reduced if not eliminated. The effectiveness of those methods depends mainly upon whether the inducement to co-operate is sufficient to overcome the influence of national interests, national rivalries, and national jealousies amongst a sufficient number of nations. Effective co-operation between the Allied and Associated Powers in the Great War was slowly established as the result of bitter experience and in the presence of a common danger. The existence of a common danger and the urgent need for taking steps to readjust the balance of European Power, which was affected by the development of Germany's military and naval strength, brought about the establishment of the Entente between Great Britain, Russia, and France, and this in turn led to the immediate adjustment of interests which had long been in conflict. Agreements were satisfactorily concluded upon the Persian question, the Newfoundland fisheries dispute, the British occupation of Egypt, and other problems which had embittered relations between the Entente Powers, and which

[1] Complete till December 1922, and see note p. 538.

constituted possible causes of war. For long years the rival group of Powers which formed the Triple Alliance succeeded in adjusting their differences by agreement, despite the fact that not long before the Alliance was consummated Austria had fought both Italy and Prussia. The idea, then, of international co-operation is not new, but such co-operation has in the past been limited to groups of Powers with a common interest. The efforts of European statesmen were directed to securing peace by organizing a balance of military power sufficiently exact to make the risk of attack by the group in one scale upon the group in the other prohibitive. This procedure failed of its purpose because the members of each group constantly endeavoured to measure the weight in the opposite balance and to add to that in their own on the real or supposititious ground that the scale was being depressed against them. The result was competition in armaments and the charging of Europe with explosives for which a detonator was certain sooner or later to be found.

2. *League Machinery for the purpose.* The Covenant of the League of Nations endeavours to find a better guarantee against war by substituting for the small groups of Powers a single group so large that its authority cannot be challenged with impunity. The Balance of Power is replaced by the Concert or Concentration of Power. Omitting the United States of America as having refused membership of the League, the original group constituting the League consisted of forty-two nations, which left outside the League, in addition to the United States, Russia, Germany, Austria, Hungary, Bulgaria, Turkey, Mexico, and a number of smaller states. There was no intention of excluding these nations permanently from the League, when in the opinion of its members they were worthy of admission, and if the League was to fulfil its purpose it was obviously undesirable that so large a group should be left outside its ambit. From the time of the first meeting of the Assembly, efforts were made to increase the membership of the League, and by the end of 1921 Austria, Albania, Bulgaria, Costa Rica, Esthonia, Finland, Latvia, Lithuania, and Luxemburg had been admitted, so that the members of the League then numbered fifty-one. Until the remaining European Powers, at least, are members, there remains the possibility of the formation of a rival group which may in time become formidable. But the fifty-one

nations, including as they do four of the great Powers with a fifth as at worst a benevolent neutral, control such an enormous proportion of the world's resources that their ability to enforce any policy upon which they are agreed and prepared to act will hardly be disputed. What are the inducements held out to them to co-operate in order to prevent war? These inducements are the provision of other means than war for settling disputes, and the penalties which recourse to war will involve.

The principles of the constitution of the League have already been described, and I need not here deal at any length with the functions of its Council, Assembly, and Secretariat or of the Permanent Court of International Justice, in the settlement of disputes, but I would remind my readers that during the latter part of the war a valuable precedent was established for the operation of international machinery analogous to that which is envisaged by the Covenant. The Supreme War Council of the Allies, commonly called the Versailles Council, was an assemblage of the leading statesmen of the Allied Powers. It was not permanently in session, but came together when questions of policy affecting more than one of the Allies required decision. Its Permanent Secretariat was, with the various commissions attached to or in communication with it, so constituted as to be able to survey the whole field of Allied activities, not merely the field of naval and military activity. The various commissions were concerned with such matter as the distribution amongst the Allies of, and the resettlement of problems connected with, munitions, financial assistance, food, raw materials, and transport, though naturally, as it was a war organization, the Permanent Secretariat was largely military in composition and dealt chiefly with military problems. The Secretariat watched the situation from the standpoint of the common interest, and called the statesmen together betimes to consider problems upon which an agreed decision for common action was necessary. It prepared the agenda for such meetings and the cases for discussion, and after decisions had been reached it supervised the execution of the decisions. This procedure was a great advance upon the conferences of Allied statesmen who assembled hastily in the early years of the war, as the need for discussion arose, without the aid of any permanent organization, and it was undoubtedly fruitful in promoting Allied co-operation.

Now the machinery of the League of Nations is, if allowance be made for the fact that its prime object is the promotion of international co-operation in peace and not in war, very similar to that of the Supreme War Council during and shortly after the war. The Council of the League consists of prominent statesmen of the nations which compose it. It is not permanently in session, but has a Permanent Secretariat so organized as to be able to watch the international situation as a whole and to give warning of any difference between the nations which appears to be likely to lead to war. The Secretariat has sections of its own or commissions attached to it which are concerned with such matters as international finance, economics, labour, health, ports and waterways, naval, military, and air affairs, treaties, mandates, and international law. There is, therefore, no subject of international interest which it should not be able to survey from the point of view of the general interest of all the members of the League. By Art. XI of the Covenant any war or threat of war, whether immediately affecting any of the members of the League or not, is declared a matter of concern of the whole League, and the Secretary-General shall, on the request of any member of the League, forthwith summon a meeting of the Council.[1] Further each member of the League has the right to bring to the attention of the Assembly or of the Council any matter affecting international relations which threatens to disturb the peace. By Art. XI the members of the League agree to refer any dispute likely to lead to rupture either to arbitration or to inquiry by the Council, and they further agree not to resort to war until three months after the award by the arbitrators or the report of the Council. By Art. XVII if a dispute arise between a member of the League and a state which is not a member of the League, or between two states which are not members of the League, those states are to be invited to become members for the purpose of such dispute. In the event of refusal

[1] A remarkable example of action under this Article was furnished in the latter part of 1921. After a prolonged dispute between Albania and the Serb-Croat-Slovene state, Yugo-Slav forces crossed the frontier of Albania at the end of October. On the 7th November the British Government called the attention of the Council of the League to the situation and demanded the application of Art. 16 of the Covenant (the article instituting a blockade of an offending nation) if the Serb-Croat-Slovene state refused to execute its obligations under the Covenant. The Serb-Croat-Slovene state at once began to withdraw its troops from Albania and the risk of a serious Balkan war was averted. (*v.* also note on p. 538).

the states in question become subject to the penalties which I propose to describe later.

If the machinery which I have just described can be made operative, it will clearly provide a better guarantee against war than any which has yet existed. It provides in the first place a simpler and more direct means of communication between states than that provided by Foreign Offices and Ambassadors. It brings the responsible statesmen of the nations concerned in a dispute together to discuss the subject of difference round a table instead of by minute or by telegram. If the Secretariat of the League is watchful and efficient, and there is no reason to suppose that it will not be both, the statesmen should be brought together before an acute crisis has developed and not while it is raging. Finally it enables those parties to the dispute, who are contemplating war, to see and measure the forces which will be arrayed against them. To any one who has studied the history of the events which immediately preceded the outbreak of the Great War, it must appear at least probable that, if such machinery had been in existence in 1914, the murder of an Austrian Arch-Duke could not have become the pretext for a war of nations.

3. *Moral Sanctions and an International Army.* The large group of Powers having been formed and adequate provision made for adjusting disputes by means other than war, the questions remain whether the bonds which keep the group together are sufficiently strong to stand the strain to which they may be subjected, and whether the members of the League can be relied upon to use the means provided for them. At present the chief purpose of the League, the chief inducement to nations to join it and become loyal supporters of its principles and rules, is the avoidance of such another horror as the last war. The sceptic asserts that this is an inducement which will not always be potent, that memories are short and that a new generation will grow up to which national aspirations and rivalries will make a stronger appeal, at least in times of excitement, than will the desire for peace. It must be admitted that history gives some support for this view, but it must equally be admitted that the dread of another war of nations amongst the peoples of the principal powers is at present sufficiently strong, and is likely to last sufficiently long, to give time for new methods to be tested and to gain support if they are effective.

In the interval the obligation to support the principles of the Covenant is almost wholly moral, though material inducements are, as I will explain, not lacking. The members have pledged themselves not to have recourse to war without first applying the provisions of the Covenant for the settlement of disputes. The moral obligation will become a material obligation as and when the authority of the League becomes established and recognized.

Many critics of the League, some friendly and some hostile, have declared that the absence of material sanctions at the outset of its career is a fatal weakness in its constitution. They have asserted that it must have force under its control, if its decisions are to be respected, and that no human law can be effective unless it has force behind it. They have therefore asked for the creation of an international army under the sole authority of the League. Such a measure would involve the preparation of an entirely new Covenant fundamentally different in principle from that which has been accepted. The League as constituted is an agreement voluntarily accepted by its members, who in all essentials preserve their autonomy. It does demand some surrender of national independence in that nations aforetime, and particularly the more powerful nations, recognized as much or as little of the obligations of international law as suited their purpose. They interpreted that law themselves in accordance with their power to enforce their interpretation upon others. Just as the physically powerful individual surrenders some of his personal liberty in the general interest when he accepts the obligations of civil law and does not knock his neighbour down or seize his property, so the powerful state surrenders something of independence for the common good when it agrees to refer its disputes with other nations to discussion instead of settling them in its own way. Further than that the Covenant does not go in the direction of interference with the affairs of the members of the League, and it could not go further without setting up a super-government, a permanent organization above and more powerful than any state or group of states. The world is clearly not yet ready for such a revolution in its affairs.

It is difficult to conceive of an international force uncontrolled by an international government. Either the men composing such a force would be specially enlisted on the lines of an expanded and glorified Foreign Legion, or the force would consist of a number of contingents supplied by the members of the League. In the first case the force would tend to become a sort of praetorian guard, the commander of which would, if he were a man of strong character and ambition, possess enormous power and be the target for endless intrigue. It is not difficult to picture in such circumstances the rise of a new Napoleon, who would reorganize the governments of the world according to his taste. It is impossible to imagine the peoples of modern nations agreeing to the creation of a body with such power and beyond their control. In the second case the difficulties and dangers are almost equally great. There would still be a military force for which no permanently constituted government was responsible, since only the Secretariat of the League is permanent; there is still the difficulty of command, for a time will come before long when there is no soldier of such pre-eminence that there will be no rival claimants to his position; there is the natural unwillingness of nations to send their sons abroad in time of peace beyond their control; there are the difficulties of language and of obtaining uniformity of training, equipment, and organization in an army composed from a number of nations, and there is the difficulty of regulating the size and number of such contingents. If the armed forces of the League are limited to contingents from a few of the Great Powers, the League is open to the charge that it is nothing more than a Junta of those Powers formed by them to impose their will with a minimum of trouble and expense upon the remainder of the world. If they are composed of a large number of small contingents provided by any members of the League who may wish to be represented by military force, then they will tend to become a joke in the military world. It has been suggested that the League should have a monopoly of all the most deadly weapons of war, such as tanks, poison gas, heavy artillery, and bombing aeroplanes, and that the construction and ownership of such weapons except by the League should be prohibited.[1] Here, again, the difficulty of control arises unless a super-government is instituted, and it is easy to foresee endless differences of opinion arising as to what categories of weapons should and should not be under the control of the League. We, for example,

[1] Various proposals for limiting the use of poison gas and submarines were at the end of 1921 before the Temporary Mixed Commission of the League on Armaments. These problems, which had not then been solved, are quite distinct from that of giving the League a monopoly.

and France have great possessions bordered by uncivilized or semi-civilized peoples, not under the jurisdiction of the League. Are we to be prevented from policing our frontiers in the most efficient and economical manner? Are we to be compelled to send our men to fight without the most efficient equipment? If the League were to loan us some of the special equipment, of which it had control, for a specific purpose and for a limited time, our soldiers would be without experience of the latest methods of employing such equipment, while such equipment maintained in Europe would not be available for use in case of a sudden emergency on the North-West frontier of India or on the borders of the Sahara. On the other hand, could the League be reasonably expected to grant a special licence to Great Britain and France entitling them to use weapons denied to other powers?

4. *Articles XVI and XVII.* On all these grounds the provision of the League, as at present constituted, with special sanctions of its own sufficient to enable it to enforce its behests, appears impracticable and to involve a change in its constitution so drastic as to be far beyond anything which its members are ready to accept. This does not mean that we may not see before long a military or police force directly under the control of the League or maintained for the purpose of safeguarding some territory for which the League has itself accepted a mandate, but this is obviously very different from an international army formed to maintain the peace of the world or to punish any breach of such peace. That an international army has not been created does not mean that the League is without sanction. I have already pointed out that the machinery of the League, by which the Council is summoned *ad hoc* upon any threat, makes it possible that there will be no misconception, as there was at the end of July 1914 on the part of the German Government, of the forces which will be arrayed against a state or states contemplating war. By Arts. XVI and XVII of the Covenant, if a member of the League is guilty of a breach of the Covenant, and if a state which is not a member of the League refuses to accept the obligations of membership for the purpose of a dispute, then the remaining members of the League are pledged to place their resources at its disposal in order to protect the Covenant. It is possible to conceive that in such circumstances the armed forces at the disposal of the League might be brought

somewhat tardily into operation and that the recalcitrant state or states might imagine, as did Germany in 1914, that they could obtain an initial advantage so great as to be overwhelming. Such a sanction might therefore prove to be inadequate, but it is not the only sanction which the League possesses. By these same Arts. XVI and XVII, if a member state resorts to war in disregard of the Covenant, and if a non-member state refuses to submit itself to the jurisdiction of the League, they are *ipso facto* decreed to have committed an act of war against all other members of the League, who are pledged to sever at once with the states in question all trade and financial relations, and to prohibit all intercourse, whether financial, commercial, or personal, between their nationals and the nationals of the Covenant-breaking states. This would be in effect as terrible a weapon as was the papal excommunication in the Middle Ages. It means the immediate establishment of a blockade far more complete in its effects than was the blockade of the Central Powers during the Great War. Devastating as was the effect of that blockade it was at no time absolute, for intercourse between Germany, Sweden, and Holland went on until the very end, while in the early years of the war the Central Powers were able to draw supplies from other sources. Now recent history has shown that no nation or considerable group of nations can hope to wage a great war if it is dependent upon its own resources alone without risking utter ruin. The Great War has demonstrated the inter-dependence of civilized nations. The risks involved in facing an absolute blockade are so tremendous, therefore, that it is difficult to conceive of any state being ready to accept them. If a group of nations were formed sufficiently large to be independent of the rest of the world and to defy blockade it could impose its will without war. The threat of blockade, or as it is sometimes termed, the economic weapon, should therefore be a more effective means of preserving peace than the balance of military power. It supplies a very material inducement to members of the League to observe the terms of the Covenant and to non-members to hesitate before they reject its intervention.

The guarantees against war which the League provides are, then, first the moral obligation accepted by its members not to resort to war without recourse either to arbitration or to the machinery of the League, secondly the influence which the

League through its members and the resources of its members must exercise upon those states which are not members, thirdly, the fact that the numbers and strength of the members of the League prepared to uphold its authority will be known to those who propose to break the peace, and, lastly, there is the dread power of the economic weapon or blockade. These guarantees are not likely to prevent all war, at least until the authority of the League has become firmly established and the efficacy of its machinery for adjusting disputes is recognized. There are many parts of the world which are still uncivilized or at best in a state of semi-civilization, and there the warrants of the League will not run. It is possible that disputes may arise between small states, for example in the Balkans, in which the League may have difficulty in enforcing its commands owing to the unwillingness of its members to resort to military action in cases in which their peoples are but remotely interested. But the guarantees already provided promise to make an attempt by any one state or group of states to win by force the power to dominate its neighbours far more dangerous to its originators than it has been in the past. The war of nations which was a development arising out of the balance of power, will tend under the concentration of power to become less and less possible and may eventually become impossible.

5. *Other Effects of International Co-operation.* The Covenant inaugurates other changes in international machinery and relations, which, while they cannot be classed as guarantees against war, promise to supplement the effect of the promotion of international co-operation in reducing the causes of war. It is of the nature of treaties of peace that they are concluded while the feelings aroused by war are still high. It is therefore rare to find a treaty of peace so just, so far-sighted, and so durable that its provisions have not created a sore which has poisoned international relations and led directly or indirectly to further war. To take only recent history, the Treaty of Paris of 1856 which ended the Crimean War created a situation in Eastern Europe out of which arose the Russo-Turkish War of 1877. The Congress of Berlin which followed upon the end of that war created a number of problems in the Balkans, and those in turn produced a whole crop of wars, kept the relations of the great continental Powers almost constantly strained, and eventually contributed to the causes which led to the Great War.

The loss of Alsace-Lorraine to Germany by the Treaty of Frankfurt of 1871 kept alive in France the idea of *revanche* which in turn was a contributory cause to the formation of the modern balance of power and of the arming of Europe. Treaties of peace, once signed, sealed, and delivered, have hitherto been as the Laws of the Medes and Persians. There has been no machinery by which they could be revised as time and experience showed revision to be desirable and the cooling of passions made revision possible. The Covenant now provides such machinery, and in Art. XIX it is declared that 'the Assembly may from time to time advise the reconsideration by members of the League of treaties which have become inapplicable, and the consideration of international conditions whose continuance might endanger the peace of the world'. It is hardly necessary to point out that the power to revise the Treaty of Versailles and its subsidiary treaties which have solved a number of territorial and economic problems in a manner provocative of further problems may be a potent factor in the preservation of the world's peace.

6. *Reduction of Armaments.* The attitude of the Covenant towards armaments is regulated by the same principle which has governed its attitude towards sanctions, that is to say, it has followed upon the constitution of the League as a free association of free nations, and has avoided all dictation as from a super-government. Art. VIII of the Covenant recites that 'the members of the League recognize that the maintenance of peace requires the reduction of national armaments to the lowest point consistent with national safety and the enforcement by common action of international obligations'.

'The Council taking account of the geographical situation and circumstances of each State, shall formulate plans for such reduction for the consideration and action of the several Governments.

'The members of the League undertake to interchange full and frank information as to the scale of their armaments, their military, naval, and air programmes, and the condition of such of their industries as are adaptable to warlike purposes.'

The procedure which the Council has followed in the formulation of plans for the reduction of armaments has developed gradually and was still in process of development at the beginning of 1923. In accordance with the Covenant an

Armaments Commission, consisting of representatives of the naval, military, and air forces of certain Powers was appointed to advise the Council. It was soon found that this Commission, which consisted of regular officers of the various countries and services, was not competent to tender adequate advice on the question of the reduction of armaments which involves problems of policy and of finance. Therefore at the first meeting of the Assembly it was decided to entrust this question to a Temporary Mixed Commission composed of statesmen, financiers, and others in addition to the naval, military, and air experts. This Commission was still at the stage of inquiry when the Washington Conference was held. That conference in no way conflicted with the aims and objects of the League of Nations, and was necessary as the problems to be discussed, naval armaments and the political situation in the Pacific, concerned closely the United States of America, not a member of the League. The solution reached as regards naval armaments followed upon lines entirely compatible with the spirit of the Covenant, and the methods actually adopted, that of reduction on an agreed ratio, have been under the consideration of the Temporary Mixed Commission. That Commission has asked each of the members of the League to supply it with an *exposé* of the considerations which it deems necessary to present regarding the exigencies of its national security, of its international obligations, of its geographical position, and of its special conditions. Upon the information so obtained it proposes to prepare a proposition for the reduction of standing armies on an agreed ratio.

In the days before the war every increase in the armies and navies of one Power led to corresponding increases by other Powers, and so the race in armaments went on. In those days proposals were made by ourselves to Germany for the mutual reduction of armaments, but they proved abortive. The experience of the Washington Conference has shown that open bargaining round a table may end in more satisfactory results. But it is generally recognized that in the case of continental Powers with long and exposed land frontiers, satisfactory results are not to be expected until the problems of security have been brought nearer to solution. With that object, proposals to add to the Covenant definite pacts of guarantee were under consideration in 1923. Once the fear of aggression is reduced or removed, real progress in the reduction of armaments becomes possible. The means which the League will have of getting its views upon armaments accepted is through the influence it will be able to exercise upon public opinion. That influence will be unquestionably great. If the representatives of a state refuse to respond to the suggestions of the Council, the Council will be able to say to the world, 'We have reviewed the whole ground and are of the opinion that armaments of such size are sufficient to provide for the security of such a state. Unfortunately the representatives of this state in the League do not agree'. It will then be for the Government of this state to make good its position to its own people, who of course have to pay the bill. Modern governments will be very chary of putting themselves in such a position, and will need to be very sure of their ground before they do so.

There is a further highly important aspect of the power which the League may exercise in the reduction of armaments. By the treaties of peace imposed on our late enemies, they are required to carry out very drastic changes in the size of their armies and fleets, which become little more than armed police forces, while stringent regulations have been designed to prevent any future expansion or the accumulation of munitions of war. Now in the past attempts to secure the reduction of armaments by treaty have failed. The most conspicuous example of this is the renaissance of Prussia's military power after she had been crushed by Napoleon in 1806, when he garrisoned her fortresses and imposed upon her conditions which he believed would effectually prevent her from again placing large armies in the field. The Prussians succeeded in outwitting Napoleon, and from 1813 to the battle of Waterloo, Prussia took a great part in consummating the downfall of the French Emperor. The Treaty of Paris of 1856, to which I have already referred, prohibited Russia from placing ships of war upon the Black Sea and denied her access to the Danube. In 1871 when France was fully occupied and Great Britain indisposed to act, Russia violated both these clauses of the treaty. There are numerous other examples in history to the same effect. If a nation is determined to arm either in order to secure its safety, to right what it holds to be a wrong, and to avenge past defeats, treaties cannot be devised which will make such measures impossible for all time, even when they are backed up by what appears to be sufficient force. It is therefore very desirable that some inducement other than the fear of *force majeure* should be given to those nations whose armaments have been reduced by treaty to observe the terms of such treaties. Such an inducement would be offered to them by including them in the League, where they would obtain the same guarantees against aggression as are offered to the other members of the League, and the same facilities for the settlement of international disputes. If to these inducements is added the necessity for economy in unproductive expenditure on the part of nations which find their finances in the utmost disorder as the result of the war, the motives for observing the armaments clauses of the recent treaties will certainly be stronger than those which have existed in the case of any treaty in the past which has imposed similar conditions.

Lastly, again by Art. VIII, the Covenant proposes measures to abolish the evils which resulted in the past from the activities of great armament firms. It is notorious that great businesses such as that of Krupp commanded great political influence not only within but without their own country. It was not uncommon for Germany to grant financial facilities to small nations on the understanding that they should place orders for armaments with Krupp. Representatives of great armament firms were constantly lobbying in the legislative chambers of the smaller nations and endeavouring to influence deputies and ministers to increase armaments and to place orders with them. The arms traffic with native races was very lucrative, and was maintained despite continuous and costly efforts on our part to repress it in those parts of the world in which we are particularly interested. The times have never been more favourable than they are at present for the suppression of these evils, for as the result of the war the world is overstocked with munitions of war and armament firms have been forced in their own interests to turn their energies to the development of peaceful industries. It would appear to be a simple matter for the members of the League to agree to confine the manufacture of armaments within limits sanctioned by the League, and to make such manufacture subject to governmental licence in each state. But there are states on whom this would press hardly, seeing that they have not the resources to manufacture arms for themselves. The members of the League, while agreeing that the manufacture of arms by private enterprise is open to grave objection, have therefore left it to the Council to determine how to prevent the evil effects of such manufacture, with due regard to the interests of those members of the League which cannot provide their own armaments. A great difficulty in the solution of this problem is that the United States, one of the greatest of manufacturing powers, is outside the League. The Assembly made the proposal to overcome this difficulty by calling a general conference on the private manufacture of arms, which should include the United States. They placed the consideration of the method of calling such a conference in the hands of its Temporary Mixed Commission.

The influence of the League upon the reduction of armaments will grow gradually as it gains the confidence of its members and of their peoples, as it shows that it is able to settle international differences upon other questions than armaments, differences which in former days produced friction and sowed the seeds of war. With the growth of confidence will come an increased sense of security, greater willingness to rely upon arbitration as a means of settling disputes, and a diminishing regard for national insurance by means of armaments. These things may not come quickly, but given faith, goodwill, and a sincere desire to do everything that is possible to prevent war, they will come surely. The Covenant does not attempt to change human nature, nor does it proclaim a new era upon earth, but it does open up a prospect of obtaining better co-operation between nations and more sensible means of adjustment of conflicting interests than have yet been within reach of governments and peoples.

Note.—The case of Italian action in seizing Corfu in August 1923 is too recent for discussion here, but reference to a summary of the facts in relation to the League may be found in Wilson Harris *Greece, Italy and the League*, published by the League of Nations Union, 1923.

EPILOGUE

SOME GENERAL CONSIDERATIONS ON THE PEACE CONFERENCE AND ITS AFTERMATH[1]

I

THE WILSONIAN PRINCIPLES AND THE NEGOTIATIONS LEADING TO PEACE

1. *Survey of the Negotiations leading to Signature of the German Treaty, 28th June 1919.* The procedure by which peace was finally obtained was unique in diplomatic history. It does not remotely correspond to any previous example. A series of notes were exchanged between President Wilson and the German state, as a result of which the latter promised to give a popular and representative character to its government, and thus paved the way for the abdication of the Kaiser. President Wilson offered to make peace with Germany on the basis of the practical application of his principles, as stated in the 'Fourteen Points' and others of his addresses in 1918. His Allies concurred in this offer, with certain reservations as to Point two (Freedom of the Seas) and a definition of loss and damage. This offer was accepted by Germany, the Armistice being left by the President to military advisers (by which he meant the Allied military advisers), with the proviso that the Allied military superiority should be maintained in the Armistice conditions. This offer, as accepted, formed the basis of the pre-Armistice agreement, of which the legally binding character was subsequently admitted by the Allies in their reply to Germany of the 16th June 1919.

So far there seems to be no dispute on either side. Whether the Armistice made any difference to this agreement, particularly as regards Art. XIX of the Armistice Convention, which deals

[1] This general sketch of the results of the Peace Conference and of the prospects for the future is intended to supplement the accounts given in the text of the History by newer information when that is available, and generally to sum up the principles and aims of the Treaties, and their extension or promotion under the activities of the League and other international organizations. References are given to all the more important topics in this and the preceding volumes.

with Reparation, has been matter for some question.[1] But the fact has been recently disclosed that the Armistice was actually settled in principle by the Allies, before the 4th November.[2] On that date the Allied Memorandum was submitted to President Wilson, and presented by him to Germany on the 5th. This last formed the pre-Armistice offer of the Allies and was accepted by Germany. These facts seem decisively to prove that the Armistice was intended to be a military agreement only and that no political matter could be other than extraneous to it, or at best interpretative of, and not additional to, the terms stated in the pre-Armistice agreement. This interpretation was disputed by the French during the Conference, but seems to have been ultimately adopted by the Allies in their Reply to the German Observations, the 16th June 1919.

The difficulty of interpreting the pre-Armistice agreement lies in the fact that the basis of it consisted of the principles of President Wilson as expressed in his utterances. As has been exhaustively stated elsewhere, political speeches cannot always be the subject of exact analysis. They necessarily possess a vagueness and a generalized aspect which unsuit them for diplomatic interpretation, and Wilson's are, in point of fact, in some places inconsistent with one another.[3] These inevitable defects were rendered more serious still by the fact that they deal briefly and unsatisfactorily with the most crucial of all questions at the Conference, that of Reparation. None the less their indications, such as they are, are against punitive damages, penal indemnities, etc.[4] The inclusion of pensions in the Reparation seems hardly to agree with these utterances, and also it seems irreconcilable with the Allied definition of loss and damage in the 5th November Memorandum. This difficulty appears to have been felt by the Allies themselves. Even apart from Reparation, there can be no question that the defects of basing a diplomatic treaty on political speeches are many and grave. They contained statements about the restoration and evacuation of Belgium, Serbia, etc., the recovery of Alsace and Lorraine

[1] v. Vol. II, pp. 401–4; Vol. V, pp. 370–2.

[2] v. General Tasker H. Bliss, *American Journal of International Law*, Vol. XVI, 1921. A useful and authoritative account of the Armistice, giving new information.

[3] v. Statement of Wilson himself, Vol. IV, p. 434 n., and also Vol. I, pp. 275–7; Vol. II, pp. 366–7, 381–4, 388–93.

[4] v. Quotations, Vol. I, pp. 415–16, 437, and corrigendum of Vol. I, p. 437 on p. vii of Vol. III.

by France, the independence of Poland, and the like, which would ordinarily have been inserted in the preliminaries of peace. It is probably safe to regard the pre-Armistice agreement as the preliminaries of peace, but to admit at the same time that its character was so unusual as to increase the difficulty of arriving at an ultimate peace. There can be no doubt, at least on this head, that neither party to the pre-Armistice agreement realized at the time exactly what the adoption of the Wilsonian principles meant. Hence it was natural that they should differ infinitely in their interpretation of these principles.

In order to remedy the admitted difficulties of this new-fangled diplomacy the first endeavour of the Allied and Associated Powers was to sign what they called a Preliminary Peace, and this attempt was persisted in until the end of March and perhaps even beyond that date.[1] What the Allies meant was to make Germany sign an agreement embodying the general principles of the Treaty, leaving the details to be worked out mainly by experts in a series of subsequent agreements. In April 1919 this project was seen to be impracticable and was abandoned in favour of a general Treaty.

It is probable that, on the model of the Treaty of Vienna,[2] the Allies meant to include the five principal Treaties with the five enemy states in one great all-comprehensive Treaty. This project again proved impossible for various reasons, and the clumsy device had to be adopted of preparing five separate Treaties, each containing certain general parts (e. g. the Covenant and International Labour), which were a verbatim reproduction of those in the German Treaties, and others such as Prisoners of War, and Graves, Communications, Commerce, etc., which were only partially modified to meet each particular case. This produced striking results, forcing a whole crowd of South American states to masquerade as belligerents against all five enemies, and even causing a Great Power, like the United States, to sign the Treaty with Bulgaria against whom she had not been at war. A single Treaty might, of course, have avoided such anomalies. The cumulative effect of all these difficulties was of a very serious nature.

As regards the actual incidents leading to signature of peace

[1] Vol. I, pp. 261–2.

[2] Of course the Treaty of Vienna was preceded by the Treaty of Paris, but the latter represented terms on which all were agreed.

the procedure of the Peace Conference was unusual. It is even doubtful whether it has the right to be called a Conference (or a Congress) at all. For a Conference or Congress generally implies oral discussion of the peace terms between both parties signatory to the peace. No such verbal discussion ever took place, and every transaction was conducted in writing. It is doubtful if this procedure was wise, and it is certain that it was unusual. Written exchange of views did not prevent considerable modifications taking place in the Draft Treaties, as originally presented to the Five Enemy Powers, but it did prevent much salutary exchange of views and much verbal elucidation of ambiguities, which would certainly have had very good results in the final drafting of the articles of the treaties.

The explanation of almost all these defects lies in a single word—Passion. The rival Powers were passionately anxious to cease hostilities in November 1918. They could not wait until proper preliminaries were drawn or a proper Armistice framed. They were passionately anxious again to sign a general peace and passionately anxious to sign a final one. But finality and passion are fatal to one another, and will always be at variance.

One last point is worth mentioning. The peculiarity of the Peace Conference lay in the fact that not only were Treaties concluded, but that a permanent international organization was also created for correcting, revising, or extending the obligations of these Treaties. Thus one could not work without the other. This project met with great opposition at the time, not only from the American Senate but from European diplomats.[1] The League, said Wilson, was to be so intertwined with the tissue of the Treaty that they could not be separated. He carried this point against serious opposition and had won the day by the 21st March 1919. That day was probably the most memorable in the history of the Treaty and certainly in that of the League. Few will agree with M. Clemenceau that a 'Peace of miracles' was signed, but some may agree with President Wilson that in the Covenant he brought back from Paris 'one of the greatest of human documents'.

[1] e.g. Even so late as the 23rd June 1921 Lord Curzon voiced his regret in the House of Lords that the League had not been separated from the Treaty. Cp. this with R. S. Baker, *op. cit.*, I, 240–3.

2. *The 'final triumph of Justice and Fair Dealing'.* The expectation that Treaties could be negotiated, which would amount in substance to 'a final settlement', was widely proclaimed before and during the Peace Conference.[1] It was almost necessarily a vain hope. For, as it turned out, peace was imposed by four or five Great Powers on vanquished nations who were not allowed to debate or to discuss the terms, and on minor Powers who exercised small influence in such discussions. The Wilsonian principles did not, in themselves, comprise a body of doctrine sufficiently intelligible and precise to be interpreted in diplomatic terms. It seems, however, that the great personalities were not too well provided themselves with any far-reaching schemes of settlement; the diplomats understood the technique but were not always consulted. Even had they been, the pre-existing treaties or other obligations as to Italy or to Japan would have hindered the application of any intelligible principles whatsoever. These undesirable obligations always committed three or four of the Five Great Powers to actions and to policies to which they had been compelled under stress of need to subscribe, and which none but the interested party in fact approved. The Treaties necessarily, therefore, resulted in undesirable compromises between the vagueness of Wilsonian doctrines and the precision of the pre-existing obligations; such compromises were fatal to finality. Even had these not existed there was enough difference between the national temperaments and policies of the Five Great Powers to have rendered far-reaching and permanent agreement on many subjects impossible. Views as to law, as to commercial policy, as to military service, and as to reparation, varied almost indefinitely. The result was either an undesirable vagueness or ambiguity of phrase in the Treaties which covered irreconcilable differences, or a compromise which none of the parties concerned was likely to favour or eager to execute.

[1] *v.* quotations, Vol. I, pp. 389–90; Vol. II, pp. 344–6.

II

MR. LLOYD GEORGE'S SCHEME OF A PEACE

3. Mr. Lloyd George's Memorandum, 25th March 1919. It has often been stated that President Wilson's ideals, as propounded in the 'Fourteen Points' and other communications and addresses till September 1918, were not always embodied in the Peace Treaties. This contention is, in some respects, incontestably true, in others it is a matter of dispute. But it is less well known that the aims, to which Mr. Lloyd George committed himself after three months' experience at the Peace Conference, were by no means realized in the Treaties.

In his most remarkable Memorandum of the 25th March 1919 Mr. Lloyd George recommended to the Peace Conference a definite programme. The broad lines of his recommendations were as follows :

1. *Russian Section* [1]	*Execution.* (*References are, unless otherwise stated, to the History.*)
(1) Germany to renounce all rights under Brest-Litovsk Treaty.	(1), (2), (3) *Executed.* Art. 116–17, Vol. III, p. 177 ; Versailles Treaty, Art. 433, Vol. III, pp. 330–1.
(2) Germany to renounce all rights under Treaty of Bukarest.	
(3) Germany to renounce all arrangements by Allied and Associated Governments with reference to previous Russian territory, including special arrangements with new states.	(3) Vol. I, pp. 338–46 ; Vol. VI, Chap. III, Parts I and II.
(4) If, however, the Peace Conference is really to secure peace and prove to the world a complete plan of settlement which all reasonable men will recognize as an alternative preferable to anarchy, it must deal with the Russian situation. Bolshevik imperialism does not merely menace the states on Russia's borders. It threatens the whole of Asia and is as near to America as it is to France. It is idle to think that the Peace Conference can separate, however sound a peace it may have arranged with	(4) *Not executed.* Peace Conference separated without settling anything here, Vol. VI, Chap. III, Part II. *De facto* recognition by Great Britain of Bolsheviks, 16th March 1921, Vol. V, p. 162. Bolsheviks summoned to Genoa in 1922, where they concluded Treaty of Rapallo with Germany, 16th April 1922, Vol. VI, pp. 330–1.

[1] These extracts are from *Some Considerations for the Peace Conference before they finally draft the Terms,* D. Lloyd George, 25th March 1919, Parl. Paper, Cmd. 1614, 1922.

Germany, if it leaves Russia as it is to-day. I do not propose, however, to complicate the question of the peace with Germany by introducing a discussion of the Russian problem. I mention it simply in order to remind ourselves of the importance of dealing with it as soon as possible.

2. *The League of Nations*

(1) All high contracting parties, as part of the Treaty of Peace, to become members of the League of Nations, the Covenant of which will be signed as a separate Treaty by those Powers that are admitted, subject to acceptance of the following conditions:

(i) An agreement between the principal members of the League of Nations in regard to armaments which will put an end to competition between them.

(i) No agreed limitation of armaments arrived at before signature of Covenant.

Success achieved, as regards limiting fleets, at Washington Conference, 1922. Disarmament discussed at Council and Assembly of League, 1921–3.

(ii) The lesser members of the League of Nations to accept the limitation of armaments and the abolition of conscription.

(ii) Disarmament not effected except for Austria, Hungary, Bulgaria, Vol. IV, pp. 141, 158, 166.

(iii) An agreement to be made between all members of the League of Nations for the purpose of securing equal and improved conditions of labour in their respective countries.

(iii) *Executed.* Part XIII, Labour in Treaties. Vol. III, pp. 314–28. *v.* also Vol. II, pp. 36–9, 334–6; Vol. VI, Chap. IV, Part II.

. . . 'The first condition of success for the League of Nations is, therefore, a firm understanding between the British Empire and the United States of America and France and Italy that there will be no competitive building up of fleets or armies between them. Unless this is arrived at before the Covenant is signed the League of Nations will be a sham and a mockery. It will be regarded, and rightly regarded, as a proof that its principal promoters and patrons repose no confidence in its efficacy. But once the leading members of the League have made it clear that they have reached an understanding which will both secure to the League of Nations the strength which is necessary to enable it to protect its members and which at the same time will make misunderstanding and suspicion with regard to competitive armaments impossible between them, its future and its authority will be ensured. It will then be able to ensure as an essential condition of peace that not only Germany, but all the smaller States of Europe undertake to limit their armaments and abolish conscription. If the small nations are permitted to organize and maintain conscript armies running each to hundreds of thousands, boundary wars will be inevitable and all Europe will be drawn in. Unless we secure this universal limitation we shall achieve neither lasting peace, nor the permanent observance of the limitation of German armaments which we now seek to impose.

(2) I should like to ask why Germany, if she accepts the terms we consider just and fair, should not be admitted to the League of Nations, at any rate as soon as she has established a stable and democratic government.'

(2) *Not executed.* Germany not admitted to League (end of 1923). Vol. II, pp. 270–4.

3. *Political*

A. *Execution.*

A. *Cession of territory by Germany and the consequential arrangements*

Eastern Boundaries of Germany.

(1) Poland to be given a corridor to Danzig, but this to be drawn irrespective of strategic or transportation considerations so as to embrace the smallest possible number of Germans.

(1) Vol. II, pp. 283–93; Vol. VI, pp. 260–1.

(2) 'I am, therefore, strongly averse to transferring more Germans from German rule to the rule of some other nation than can possibly be helped. I cannot conceive any greater cause of future war than that the German people, who have certainly proved themselves one of the most vigorous and powerful races in the world, should be surrounded by a number of small states,

(2) Instead of 2,100,000 some 2,500,000 Germans transferred to Poland. Vol. II, pp. 214–15, 283–93; Vol. VI, Chap. II, Part II.

many of them consisting of people who have never previously set up a stable government for themselves, but each of them containing large masses of Germans clamouring for reunion with their native land. The proposal of the Polish Commission that we should place 2,100,000 Germans under the control of a people which is of a different religion and which has never proved its capacity for stable self-government throughout its history must, in my judgment, lead sooner or later to a new war in the East of Europe.'

(2) a. Rectification of Bohemian frontier. (Still to be decided after hearing Report of Czecho-Slovak Commission.)

(2) a. *Executed.* Vol. IV, pp. 267–77.

Western Boundaries of Germany.

(3) No attempt is made to separate the Rhenish Provinces from the rest of Germany. These Provinces to be demilitarized; that is to say, the inhabitants of this territory will not be permitted to bear arms or receive any military training, or to be incorporated in any military organization either on a voluntary or compulsory basis, and no fortifications, depots, establishments, railway construction, or works of any kind adapted to military purposes will be permitted to exist within the area. No troops to be sent into this area for any purpose whatsoever without previous notification to the League of Nations. As France is naturally anxious about a neighbour who has twice within living memory invaded and devastated her land with surprising rapidity, the British Empire and the United States of America undertake to come to the assistance of France with their whole strength in the event of Germany moving her troops across the Rhine without the consent of the Council of the League of Nations. This guarantee to last until the League of Nations has proved itself to be an adequate security.

(3) Germany west of the Rhine demilitarized and under temporary Allied occupation for 15 years, Vol. II, pp. 126–7; Vol. III, pp. 329–30—an occupation whose termination some French authorities have made to depend on Germany's fulfilment of her engagements.

(4) Germany to cede Alsace-Lorraine to France.

(4) *Ceded.* Vol. II, pp. 167–9, 280–2.

(5) Germany to cede to France the 1814 frontier, or, in the alternative, in order to compensate France for the destruction of her coal-fields, the present Alsace-Lorraine frontier with the use of the coal-mines in the Saar Valley for a period of 10 years. Germany to undertake, after the expiration of 10 years, to put no obstacle on the export of the produce of these coal-mines to France. . . . A large army of occupation for an indefinite period is out of the question. Germany would not mind it.'

(5) All of 1814 frontier not ceded to France. Saar territory under League. Mines property of France, but to be bought back by Germany if plebiscite at end of 15 years is for Germany. Vol. II, pp. 179–84, 277–80.

(6) Abrogation of Customs Union with Luxembourg and other Luxembourg questions. (Still to be decided.)

(6) Abrogated. Vol. II, p. 277.

(7) Germany to cede to Belgium Malmedy and Moresnet.

(7) Ceded. Vol. II, pp. 190–1, 275–6.

(8) Heligoland and Dune (still to be decided). Kiel Canal to be open to all nations.

(8) Demilitarized. Vol. II, pp. 151–2, 294.

Kiel Canal opened. Vol. II, pp. 200–1; Vol. III, pp. 312–13.

(9) Germany to cede certain portions of Schleswig to Denmark as provided by Danish Commission.

(9) Ceded. Vol. II, pp. 205–6, 293–5.

(10) Germany to cede all rights in the ex-German colonies and in the leased territory of Kiauchow.

(10) Ceded. Colonies, Vol. II, pp. 229–34, 295–302. Kiauchow, Vol. II, p. 301; Vol. VI, pp. 380–7, 390 n.

B. *Disposal of Magyars*

(1) 'What I have said about the Germans is equally true of the Magyars. There will never be peace in South-Eastern Europe if every little state now coming into being is to have a large Magyar Irredenta within its borders. I would therefore take as a guiding principle of the peace that as far as is humanly possible the different races should be allocated to their mother-lands, and that this human criterion should have precedence over considerations of strategy or economics or communications, which can usually be adjusted by other means.'

B. *Treaty of Trianon.*

The Magyars	
Left to Hungary	6,250,000
Transferred to Czecho-Slovakia	955,000
to Yugo-Slavia	560,000
to Rumania	1,550,000
to others	30,000
Total Magyars transferred	3,065,000
Total Magyars	9,345,000

Vol. V, pp. 151–5.

C. *Turkish Section*

(1) Germany to recognize the cession by Turkey of the whole of her territory to mandatories responsible to the League of Nations. As far as Germany is concerned, mandates to be settled by the Allied and Associated Powers.

Note.—Included in the Turkish Section also will be a number of provisions arising out of the Report of the Financial Commission, the Commission on the Breaches of the Laws of War, e. g. the surrender of Turks hiding in Germany, with their property, as well as an undertaking by Germany to be bound by terms of the treaty of peace with Turkey and a recognition of the British Protectorate over Egypt with renunciation of extra-territorial privileges and recognition of transfer to His Majesty's Government of the Sultan's rights under the Suez Canal Convention.

C. *Treaty of Sèvres.*

Mandates assigned for:

Mesopotamia (not complete). Vol. VI, pp. 187, 521.

Palestine. Vol. VI, pp. 170–7, 521.

Syria. Vol. VI, pp. 169, 521.

Hejaz, etc., independent. Vol. VI, pp. 137–8.

Egypt. British Protectorate recognized, and then independent. Vol. VI, Chap. I, Part IV.

Not executed.

Other portions of Turkish Empire returned to Turkey (e.g. Anatolia, East Thrace, and Smyrna, Cilicia, etc.).

Financial and other provisions unratified.

Position at Lausanne Treaty (24 July 1923. Vol. VI, pp. 114–7.

D. *Penalties and Guarantees*

I. *Breaches of the Laws of War*

(1) Demand and surrender of the Kaiser and all individuals responsible for the War, and also of all individuals responsible for inhuman breaches of the laws of war.

(2) Creation of Court.

(3) Jurisdiction and procedure.

(4) Punishment of offenders.

D. *Execution*

I. *Not executed.*

Articles inserted in Treaty. Vol. II, pp. 304–8, 396–7.

(1) Kaiser not surrendered by Holland.

(2) Court not created.

(3) Jurisdiction, &c., not settled.

(4) Some offenders tried in German courts, some punished.

II. *Guarantees*

Finally, I believe that until the authority and effectiveness of the League of Nations has been demonstrated, the British Empire and the United States ought to give to France a guarantee against the possibility of a new German aggression. France has special reason for asking for such a guarantee. She has twice been attacked and twice invaded by Germany in half a century. She has been so attacked because she has been the

II. *Not executed.*

Treaty of guarantee against unprovoked aggression by Germany signed with France by United States and by Great Britain, 28th June 1919, respectively. British guarantee was dependent on United States' ratification and lapsed on its not being given. Vol. II, pp. 125–7, Vol. III, pp. 337–40.

principal guardian of liberal and democratic civilization against Central European autocracy on the continent of Europe. It is right that the other great Western democracies should enter into an undertaking which will ensure that they stand by her side in time to protect her against invasion, should Germany ever threaten her again or until the League of Nations has proved its capacity to preserve the peace and liberty of the world.

E. *Economic, &c.*

(*a*) *Reparation*

Secondly, I would say that the duration for the payments of reparation ought to disappear if possible with the generation which made the war.

(Certain other proposals, the most important being the proportion of reparations: 50 per cent. to France, 30 per cent. Great Britain, 20 per cent. others.)

E. *Execution*

Nothing settled definitely on this head, end of 1922.

Proportion altered. 52 per cent. France, 22 per cent. Great Britain, 26 per cent. others. Spa Agreement, 16th July 1920.

(*b*) *Economic*

Germany to be given full access to raw materials and markets of the world on the same terms as Allies directly she signs the peace. The Allied and Associated Powers to do all they can to put her upon her legs once more. In addition we await the report of Economic and Financial Commissions, etc.

Not accepted.

Non-reciprocity commercial clauses inserted in Treaty. Vol. II, pp. 318–22; Vol. V, pp. 66–72.

4. *Success and failure of Mr. Lloyd George's recommendations as to the Peace Treaties.* To summarize this story, Mr. Lloyd George failed to achieve (1) his idea of reconciling Russia to the League of Nations and the Peace Conference. (2) He failed to obtain an agreed general disarmament previous to the signature of the Covenant or Germany's early admission to the League. (3) In matters political the Germans and Magyars ceded more territory and population, and the Turks less than he desired. (4) The Penalties on War Criminals have not been effective and the Guarantee Treaties have not been ratified. (5) Finally, the settlement of Germany's economic condition has not been made and the problem of Reparation

remains unsolved. Nevertheless, some substantial results were achieved, for which Mr. Lloyd George has not usually obtained all the credit that he deserves. In the first place it seems to have been primarily due to him that the Germans signed the Treaty and, for this purpose, his insistence on the plebiscite being applied in Upper Silesia was extremely important, as was also his solution of the Danzig problem. His attempt to get a limitation of armaments among the Allies was a failure, but his contribution to the scheme for disarming the enemy was a distinct success. Moreover, the difficulties under which he laboured should be recognized. A telegram, stated to have been signed by 370 M.P.s, reached him on the 7th April, at the moment of the gravest news of the Peace Conference, and forced him to disclaim moderation with reference to Reparation. Yet even this influence was not the most serious in defeating his views. The most important influence was that of France.

(*a*) *The influence of France.* M. Tardieu has declared that the essential guarantees for France, i. e. occupation of the left bank of the Rhine, ownership of the Saar mines, and creation of Saar valley territory, prohibition of Austria's union to Germany, and 'réparation intégrale des dommages et remboursement des pensions' were not granted till the second week in April,[1] and that even after that Mr. Lloyd George attempted to revise these conditions in the second week of June.[1] Mr. Lloyd George has himself confirmed this view. On being told 'that you brought back not a Liberal peace but a reactionary peace' in October 1920, he replied: 'Quite apart from Germany's deserts, the peace that we signed at Versailles was the minimum that France would have accepted. . . . Should England have stood out of the peace as America did?'[2] To this there is but one answer, it may have been possible for the United States to stand out. It was not so possible for Great Britain or for Italy.

(*b*) *The influence of the United States and the failure of the Guarantee Treaties.* The failure of the United States to ratify the Treaty has hampered the whole conclusion of peace. The success of the Disarmament Conference at Washington in 1922

[1] *v.* Vol. II, pp. 19–20.
[2] Interview with Harold Spender in *Lloyd George Liberal Magazine*, October 1920.

suggests that great results might have followed on a similar and more universal Conference held by the League with American co-operation. More fatal than all, however, has been the American failure to ratify the Guarantee Treaty, promising to protect France against the unprovoked aggression of Germany for ten years. For the British guarantee depended on the American being taken up, and lapsed when American ratification was refused.[1] That guarantee was a separate instrument and not part of the Peace Treaties as such. Yet its failure to materialize has most painfully affected France, and for that failure the United States is responsible. The subsequent French policy can only be understood when we realize their disillusionment and disappointment in this matter. In their eyes security was the main object of the Peace Treaties. It was obtained by the Guarantee Treaties, and these no longer exist. So long as they do not exist peace does not exist in French eyes.

III

CERTAIN PRINCIPLES IN THE PEACE TREATIES

5. *Disarmament in the Treaties.*

(*a*) *Voluntary versus Compulsory Service.* In this sphere there can be no doubt that the treaties have shown that important results can be achieved. Germany was effectively disarmed on land, on sea, and in the air,[2] so was Bulgaria;[3] Austria and Hungary were rendered nugatory[4]; even Turkey surrendered part of her armaments. This disarmament was, in the most important case of Germany, achieved without effective occupation of the capital. Germany and all the other states except Turkey have not only been disarmed, but have been rendered incapable for many years of replacing their old armaments. For a generation Europe is safe from Germany's attack, that is, if it is to be made with the same kind of weapons and munitions as were produced before or during the War. Such methods may lead her to devise subtler and more concealed weapons of destruction, such as different and deadlier aeroplanes, bombs, gases, or poisons. But Dreadnoughts and submarines and 42-inch guns cannot be manufactured in secret

[1] Vol. II, pp. 125–7; Vol. III, pp. 337–40. [2] Vol. II, pp. 129–58.
[3] Vol. IV, pp. 166–70. [4] Vol. IV, pp. 144–57, 162–5.

under the conditions which now exist. That is a great and successful achievement of the Peace Treaties, and it leaves the road open for a limitation of armaments for all nations in the next fifteen years. It must be confessed, however, that few Powers have shown any desire to avail themselves of this respite.

The enforcement of long-period voluntary service armies is a new and ingenious device for keeping the European peace.[1] It has been vitiated in practice, because the numbers of the voluntary armies assigned to Germany and to other Powers are too small to be workable. The principle works unequally, for recruits abound in industrial countries like Germany, and are not to be found in agricultural ones like Bulgaria, so that the former is likely to find herself with too many troops and the latter with too few. It will probably not work in Turkey at all, but in more civilized countries there can be no doubt that this ingenious method does limit an enemy's power for aggression or offence. Of course, neither voluntary service nor limitation of armaments can be permanently successful unless they are adopted by friends as well as by enemies. Germany cannot go on having a smaller army than that of Belgium for ever, and the combined armies of Austria, Bulgaria, and Hungary cannot always remain inferior to that of Yugo-Slavia. None the less, some progress has been achieved by inquiry and discussion of methods of limiting armaments. But the extensive scheme at the Peace Conference of limiting the armaments of all the small states broke down in practice.[2] The refusal of admission of new states to the League, unless their armaments are reasonably limited, has certainly had some effect on states desiring admission to it. Except, however, for the Washington Conference, with its great step forward in limiting naval armaments, little progress in disarmament has been made by the Great Powers. And the Washington Conference has no direct connexion with the Peace Treaties.

(*b*) *Demilitarization of Areas.* The Allies have been able to impose on the enemy the demilitarization of certain areas such as the Left Bank of the Rhine, Heligoland, the Kiel Canal. They have also prohibited the construction of new fortifications in certain parts of Germany, Austria, and Bulgaria.

[1] This was due to Mr. Lloyd George *v.* Vol. II, pp. 129–30.
[2] *v.* Vol. IV, pp. 138, 152, 170.

Some other schemes of demilitarizing areas as e. g., the boundary between Italy and the Yugo-Slav State, and elsewhere broke down.[1] None the less, one striking success has been achieved by mutual agreement between the Allies. The Mandates Commission reported in August 1922 that the mandated areas of the 'C' Mandates, i. e. various Pacific isles and South-West Africa, were 'entirely demilitarized'. The area of the Aaland Isles has also been demilitarized by the pressure of the League on Sweden and Finland. Much has also been done at Washington to demilitarize the whole area of the Pacific Ocean.

6. *Reparation in the Treaties.* The passions which modern warfare excites, and the destructiveness which it entails, presented problems to the Peace Conference of a practically insoluble character. If Mr. Lloyd George's above-quoted declaration that the Versailles Treaty represented 'the minimum demands of France' is correct, then proper settlement of the reparation question on the 28th June 1919 would seem to have been impossible. The hatred and indignation of France, very natural and intelligible in themselves, led to the formulation of impracticable demands, to their being forced both on unwilling Allies and on a reluctant and helpless Germany, and to the inevitable result of failure, disillusion, and disappointment when it came to execution. A graver matter for which British public opinion at least as much as French was responsible, was the inclusion of pensions in Reparation against the manifest intention and declared purpose of the Allied Powers themselves as expressed in the Pre-Armistice agreement. The attempt to justify it by clause 19 of the Armistice seems not really defensible, and it is clear that the Allies themselves felt the difficulty.[2]

The proof of the adverse influence of public opinion is to be found in Mr. Lloyd George's Memorandum circulated on the 25th March 1919. In that he states 'The duration for the payments of reparation ought to disappear if possible with the generation which made the war'. He further suggested that the amount 'chargeable under full reparation greatly exceeds what, on any calculation, Germany is capable of paying',

[1] Vol. IV, p. 306. Danzig has, however, been demilitarized.

[2] *v.* quotations, Vol. I, pp. 415–16; Vol. II, pp. 311–12; and comments, Vol. II, pp. 47, 401–4; Vol. V, pp. 370–4.

that ' Germany should pay an annual sum for a stated number of years ', and be allowed ' a number of years within which to work up to payment of the full annual amount ', and that a permanent commission should have power ' to postpone some portion of the annual payment ' and to ' cancel the payment of interest on postponed payments during the next few years '. The actual concrete proposals of the Treaty were really quite impossible. They fixed the total sum at some eight thousand millions, but gave the Allies power, if necessary, to decrease the annual payment, thus showing a possible desire for moderation.[1] The inability to effect this resulted almost wholly from the popular pressure brought to bear on the various Plenipotentiaries, most notably on M. Clemenceau and Mr. Lloyd George.

If the Austrian and Hungarian Reparation terms are examined it will be found that they differ from the German, slightly in the direction of moderation.[2] They are not possible terms of Reparation but they approach possibility. Those relating to Bulgaria were intended by the framers of the Treaty to be not only possible but practicable terms, and the Principal Powers were not subjected in this matter to popular pressure.[3] They include such improvements on the German Treaty as laying down a fixed lump sum for ultimate payment, and constituting the Reparation Commission on a basis which enables it to exercise great powers, and, generally speaking, to exercise those powers for the benefit of Bulgaria rather than of the Allies. Yet it is a deeply significant fact that all these improvements do not seem to have succeeded in producing a really workable scheme. It is at any rate, significant that the Commission and the Bulgarian Government, after reaching a deadlock, have definitely agreed to remit three-quarters of the debt. Thus the sum fixed was too high and even this scheme of Reparation, which was really drawn up with strict reference to the practical and real merits of the case, had no success. The fact of the matter seems to be that an essential part of successful reparation is the at least partial consent of those who are vanquished, as well as of those who are victorious. The real determining factor is not what ministers sign but what peoples consent to do. Unless the stimulus to pay and

[1] *v.* Vol. II, pp. 49–56, 66–91.
[2] Vol. V, pp. 1–16.
[3] Vol. V, pp. 39–47.

the advantage and necessity of paying are both clear to the defeated party no satisfactory reparation is likely to be obtained.

7. *Plebiscites and self-determination in the Treaties.*

(*a*) *Difference between the new and old plebiscites.* The method of deciding the allocation of important areas by plebiscite was necessarily implied in the theory of self-determination. But, while the method was not new, the principle was applied in a way that had seldom been contemplated before. The old plebiscites of Nice and Savoy and in various provinces of Italy were of a simpler character. They were usually concerned with ascertaining the desire of a defined unit or state to belong to or to revert to an old established state or nationality. The plebiscites of the Peace Conference were usually quite different from this. They were concerned with the desire of a unit not always hitherto separate or defined, such as Orava, to belong to one or other of two totally new states; or of a heterogeneous district like Klagenfurt to choose between a truncated Austria and an enlarged Balkan State. Sometimes, as in the case of Upper Silesia, they represented a political expedient destined to soften the blow to a defeated enemy, or to get over a difficult diplomatic crisis.

(*b*) *Their application in the Peace Treaties.* On the whole, plebiscites were more talked about than conceded. The Minor Powers were generally opposed to them. They were definitely refused in the case of the Slav areas annexed by Italy, of the German Brenner district annexed by Italy, and of Thrace. They were refused under a species of not very creditable camouflage in the case of Eupen and Malmedy, they were declined in all but one part of Hungary. They were deferred for a period of fifteen years in the Saar valley, East Galicia, and Smyrna. In the case of Teschen, Orava, and Spisz the dispute was settled without a plebiscite by agreement between the claimants.[1] In five cases, Schleswig, Klagenfurt, Marienwerder, Allenstein, and Oedenburg,[2] they met with definite success and

[1] Teschen, Vol. IV, pp. 362–3; Orava and Spisz, Vol. IV, p. 366.

[2] Schleswig, Vol. II, pp. 205–6; Klagenfurt, Vol. IV, pp. 379–81; Marienwerder, etc., Vol. VI, pp. 256–7. The Oedenburg plebiscite had not been held when the article on German West Hungary (Vol. IV, pp. 382–8) was written. This was for the town and environs of Oedenburg (Sopron), and on the 17th December 1921, 15,334 voted for Hungary, and 8,227 for Austria. The town, therefore, went to Hungary. The plebiscite for East Galicia was abolished in 1923 *v.* p. 283 n.

settled the fate of the area in dispute on reasonable and generally accepted grounds. The areas, however, were not of striking importance. In the most important case of all, that of Upper Silesia, the decision was a difficult one and the award by the League has not met with the approval, or with anything but the enforced consent, of the Germans.

(c) *Difficulties of plebiscites.* It will be seen, therefore, that the method has been less applied and, where applied less successful, than the logic of the Wilsonian principles demands. The fact is that the practical difficulties are as great as are the theoretical advantages. In principle such solutions are right, for they prevent peoples being bartered from sovereignty to sovereignty like chattels without their consent, they enable transfers of sovereignty to be effected without the sense of soreness which attends on mere annexation, and they give finality and permanence to a decision in the days when the sovereignty of the people is the accepted criterion of government. Moreover, in many cases, the only sure test is that of the plebiscite. For instance, in German Poland language was not always the test of nationality and, even if it had been, the statistics of language in the census had been 'doctored' and were misleading. Nor is race or ethnic identity always a test, for at Klagenfurt many Slavs voted for Austria, and at Allenstein and Marienwerder many Poles voted for Germany. Religion may be equally misleading as a test. Yet if these tests are dispensed with, and the vote decided on, many difficulties at once arise. For where populations are backward, illiterate, and easily intimidated, as in parts of Upper Silesia or at Klagenfurt, it is almost equally difficult to take the vote at once or to defer it for a long period. If the first course is adopted the result may not represent the real wishes of the majority, if the second the process involves a large number of inter-allied officials and neutral troops occupying the country for a considerable period, with opportunities for friction, intrigue, and uncertainty at every turn.[1]

(d) *Methods of holding plebiscites.* One final point is of

[1] In the case of the Saar valley there is to be a plebiscite in fifteen years (Vol. II, pp. 180–2), during which period the inhabitants are exposed to considerable propaganda owing to the French control of the mines. In the case of East Galicia, if the plebiscite had taken place after fifteen years, Polish (i.e. non-neutral) troops could have intimidated the population in the interval. At the end of such a period the results of intimidation will appear, however the plebiscite itself may be conducted.

great importance. Much depends on the methods of plebiscite which are adopted. The question actually put to the voters may be of great importance in itself. In the case of Upper Silesia the results might have been very different if the voters had had the option of voting for becoming an independent autonomous state, and the same, *mutatis mutandis*, is true of Klagenfurt. A great deal also turns on the method of voting. At Klagenfurt the voting was taken in a single zone and the total numerical majority decided the fate of the whole area. If the voting here had been by communes the southern part would have remained Yugo-Slav. On the other hand, the method of voting by communes may involve great complications and produce real injustice. It was highly successful in Schleswig where it led to a much-needed adjustment of boundary. But in Upper Silesia it caused infinite heartburnings and the event proved that better results would have been secured by another system. The fact is, the whole plebiscite system is in an experimental stage, and the experiment is now almost as likely to injure, as to benefit, those who submit or appeal to it.

(*e*) ‘*Self-determination as an imperative principle of action.*’ Self-determination as ‘ an imperative principle of action ’ was proclaimed by Wilson on the 11th February 1918, in one of the speeches which formed the legal basis of the German Treaty.[1] It was closely connected with the plebiscite and has shared, to some extent, in the relative discredit into which that system has fallen. The objection to it is the difficulty of knowing what constitutes a unit of self-determination. Trotsky is stated by some to have invented the principle in order to disrupt Europe, and Mr. Wilson, who adopted it at the Conference, was stated by Mr. Lansing to have played with ‘ loaded dynamite ’. That the principle is a disruptive, as well as a cohesive, force goes without saying. The difficulty of deciding how large an area or a population must be before it has a right to self-determination seems fundamental. Had the Slovaks a right to determine their destinies apart from the Czechs, had the Germans of Bromberg or of Bohemia a right to separate from the Poles or the Czechs, or the Serbs of Lusatia from the Saxons? Is East Galicia capable of standing alone

[1] *v.* quotations, Vol. I, pp. 398–9 ; for German and Allied views, Vol. II, pp. 266–8 ; for the principle in Austrian, Hungarian, and Bulgarian Treaties, Vol. IV, pp. 429–34.

or have the thirty millions in the Ukraine the distinguishing marks of a nation, and must East Galicia be subject to them? If self-determination is pushed far enough not only every town, but every hamlet, has the right to vote itself out of a state of which it may have been a part for five centuries. One hint has been given by the League. In admitting states into its circle it has laid down that certain states, such as Luxemburg, Lichtenstein, and San Marino, are too small to become members of the League. This is a rough and ready test which may have importance in the future, especially in more backward states. For if, let us say, a tribe in Albania, were to make good its resistance to the Central Government, its small size might deter it from being received into the League. There are other instances, however, in which the League has decided such a question on its merits without necessary reference to size. It is possible, and it is very important, that this process of judgment before the League may supply the needed criterion. A highly important case was that of Lithuania, for it is connected and separated from, Poland in much the same way as Ulster is connected with and separated from, the rest of Ireland. The League, however, decided that Lithuania had the characteristics of a state and, as such, she was admitted to its membership. Whatever be the fate of Lithuania, or its connexion with Poland in the future, the situation will never be the same again, for its right to self-determination was thus explicitly stated by an international assembly and the moral effect of that decision will be permanent.

8. *'Open Diplomacy' and Publicity.* By Point one of the 'Fourteen Points', which the Allies admitted to be binding, they pledged themselves to quite 'open covenants of peace openly arrived at'.[1] This pledge was not maintained as regards 'oral discussion' with the Germans, nor was the press or public informed at all adequately of the progress of the Peace Treaty.

At the Conference itself the publicity arrangements were generally condemned and reached a point of absurdity which can rarely, if ever, have been equalled. The secrecy of the 'Four' was perhaps necessary and right, but attempts were also made to restrain the publication of documents whose suppression cannot in any way be defended. The text of the German Treaty was denied to the press but was published

[1] *v.* discussion, Vol. II, pp. 347–8 and Vol. I, pp. 254–6.

in toto in English both by *The Times*, by the German Government, and by the American Senate before the official ban on its publication was removed. Not the minutes only, but the actual recommendations, of such bodies as the Territorial Commissions were denied to the public. They have only reached them through the garbled or coloured or restrained utterances of statesmen or journalists. The main facts have become generally known but the harm done by partial disclosures has remained.[1]

The German Observations on the Peace Treaty have never been published in France or Great Britain, though the Allied Reply has been given an extensive circulation. The British Prime Minister has stated that France has specially opposed the publication of many of these documents. If so, she has a heavy responsibility. In practice this secrecy has not paid the governments or individuals who attempted to enforce it. The most secret documents, as for example General Smuts' Memorandum on Reparation (31st March 1919, Vol. V, pp. 372–4) and Lloyd George's Memorandum of the 25th March 1919, the conversations about Fiume in January 1920 (Vol. IV, pp. 318–9), the discussions of the 'Four' on Upper Silesia and Prinkipo, the *procès-verbal* of the meeting which settled the terms of the Armistice, have all seen the light.[2] Had the Governments adopted a policy of publicity, issuing some documents after six months' delay, some after a year, etc., they would have avoided many of the difficulties and some of the censure to which they have exposed themselves. Ultimately it is quite certain that they will have to adopt some such policy, for no secrets now remain secret for long.[3] At the League

[1] Vol. I, pp. 277–8. Such recommendations were, of course, sometimes altered by the 'Four', but a reasoned statement for the alterations could have been published.

[2] The last three are in Mermeix, *Négociations secrètes*, 1919, pp. 226–77; *Le Combat des Trois*, 1922, pp. 235–55, 288–99.

[3] Cp. R. W. Seton-Watson, *The Historian as a Political Force in Central Europe*, p. 18. 'The secret conventions of 1912, upon which the Balkan League against Turkey was based, were almost certainly made known to Austria-Hungary before ever war broke out that autumn, and in the course of 1913 almost all the important facts bearing upon their conclusion became public property. . . . The essential details (of the Secret Treaty of London, 26th April 1915) did not merely become known almost instantly to the enemy, but within a week of its conclusion had reached even me, then an entirely unofficial person, from other no less unofficial sources in Petrograd and Paris.' (This is the same treaty of which President Wilson professed entire ignorance at the Peace Conference in 1919), *v.* Vol. III, p. 71.

itself some real progress has certainly been made towards publicity. The meetings of the Commissions, which report to the Assembly, were thrown open to the public in 1921, and Sessions of the Council are now not often secret. Generally speaking, the examination of any question by the League results in publicity lighting up some of the dark corners of diplomacy. It is difficult, for example, for anyone who cares to study the subject to suppose that the administration of the Saar valley satisfies its inhabitants as well as does that of Danzig; that Poland is in the right in her quarrel with Lithuania; or that Italy is enthusiastic for the registration of treaties.

It is, however, only right to add that popular influences on diplomacy both before and since the German Treaty have not always been fortunate. The demands for 'hanging the Kaiser' and 'making Germany pay' have been responsible for an immense amount of mischief without, in any way, achieving the objects at which they were aimed. The Kaiser is at Doorn and not in the Tower of London, and German reparation payments to Great Britain have so far (August 1922) not quite met the expense of her army of occupation on the Rhine. Even the most secret and undisturbed diplomacy could have accomplished as much as that. It would almost certainly have accomplished more, for, by not insisting on absurd spectacular demands, it would have obtained substantial concessions in other ways. The negotiators seem to have been helpless in the grip of the public, unable to avow the truth either to their own or to the German peoples. Under the circumstances empty verbiage or unreal demands or ambiguous (and therefore disputed) clauses in the Treaties were inevitable. Had the public attention been directed more exclusively to points like 'freedom of access to the sea', or furtherance of the activities of the League, or denunciations of all secret treaties, more valuable results would certainly have been achieved. As it is, public opinion has been almost as powerful to destroy as it has been to create. Moreover, there are many subjects—more particularly in the Treaties subsequent to Versailles—on which public opinion has been neither clear nor informed nor articulate. In somewhat earlier days when public opinion was allowed to influence foreign affairs George Canning knew how to inform and to direct it in such a way as to strengthen influences for good not only in the cause of England but in the world at large. But to-day the dangerous and subtly intoxicating influences of war-propaganda have marred the prospects of peace settlements and still continue to trouble the waters of diplomacy. As it is now, statesmen are first the inspirers, and ultimately the victims, of their own propaganda. A healthy and sane public opinion on foreign policy can only arise to-day if statesmen resolutely apply themselves to instructing and not to inciting their publics.

Registration of Treaties. In one direction certain progress has already been made. Registration of Treaties and of international engagements is prescribed by Art. 18 of the Covenant. Much discussion has taken place as to what instruments shall be registered and what shall not. On the whole the interests of all seem to be served either by arranging that all diplomatic instruments need not be registered, or by not insisting that all agreements submitted for registration should be registered *in toto*. Some portions of certain agreements clearly cannot be registered. The Franco-Belgian Military Convention is a case in point. It has been registered but its technical military details have been omitted. This practice seems reasonable enough. What the world wants to know is that there *is* such an agreement. It cannot expect to know how many divisions France will place in Belgium on the outbreak of war. Similarly there are certain classes of agreements, as e. g., certain financial or other instruments, which it is unreasonable to expect nations to disclose and which they will, in any case, not disclose. Under such circumstances it is better to try and obtain what is possible rather than to aim too high. On the whole progress in registration has been good. Some 364 treaties have already (August 1922) been registered, together with a large number of other international agreements.[1]

[1] Registration by Principal Allied Powers to December 1922: Great Britain, 103; France, 32; Italy, 1; Japan, 3; Conference of Ambassadors, 15.

IV

PROMOTION OF INTERNATIONAL CO-OPERATION SINCE 1919

9. *Diplomacy by Conference.* As regards the machinery of Conference important discoveries were certainly made. The institution of the 'Council of Four' at the end of March 1922 probably saved the situation. The essence of that system was an entire absence of formality and the settlement of all questions in a friendly and unofficial fashion by a very small number of persons. Agreement was reached by holding friendly conversations not by signing protocols. At first an interpreter only, Professor Mantoux, was present, afterwards Sir Maurice Hankey acted as Secretary. These methods, tested at the British Committee of Imperial Defence, at the Cabinet, and at Imperial Conferences, were applied with success to even more complex problems and discussions. Secrecy was also effectively preserved which certainly had not been the case when the 'Ten' ruled instead of the 'Four'.[1] But the reasons for that success were special and peculiar. 'The Four' were in a hurry to get back to their respective states, they were compelled by public opinion to decide quickly or not to decide at all. The previous discussions on the Commissions and by the 'Ten' had 'roughed out', or made more precise, many of the subjects for decision. The pre-requisities of agreement, as definition of subject, and urgency for decision, explain much of that success. Even as it was, however, some serious blunders were made, while some important problems, as for instance that of Fiume, received no solution either from the 'Four', or from the 'Five' who succeeded them.

The example from the Congress of Vienna. Arguing from the success of the various Inter-Allied organizations during the war and of the 'Council of Four', a theory has arisen that this so-called 'Diplomacy by Conference' is a method of solving all or most international difficulties.[2] This argument is, however, unhistorical, for similar attempts have been tried and have failed in the past, and it is less convincing in fact in 1922 than in 1920.

[1] Vol. I, pp. 262–6.

[2] *v. Diplomacy by Conference* by Sir M. Hankey, G.C.B., *Proceedings of British Institute of International Affairs*, No. 1, 2nd November 1920.

There are, however, important lessons to be drawn from precedents of the same kind in the past. The close informal union between the chief ministers and sovereigns established by Lord Castlereagh at Vienna in 1814–15 lasted for a few years. But the first signs of disunion appeared when the military evacuation of France began in 1818; in other words, with the removal of the need of close union for mutual protection. Fundamental differences appeared in 1820, and, just after Castlereagh's death, the Congress of Verona definitely announced the disunion of the different Great Powers. They had reached a stage at which it was safe to differ from one another, and no amount of good feeling or of old recollections of co-operation could remove those differences. Canning, in fact, took the bold step of stating that these differences rendered congresses undesirable.

If we regard the period 1914–20 as an abnormal one, like that of 1815–18, necessitating close co-operation of the Powers for common action, there is a curious analogy between the periods. The history of the Supreme Council (i. e. the meetings of the supreme controllers of the different Governments) subsequent to the year 1920 shows that no procedure, no lubricating oil of exceptional devices, will serve to produce agreement.[1] Where decisions must be quick, and when there is serious pressure on the Governments, either in the shape of a German army before Paris or of excited millions demanding a speedy peace, then agreements will be reached. When that pressure is withdrawn characteristic differences assert themselves, and cleavages correspond to those differences. One state finds its salvation in infinite delay, another in evasion of a crucial issue, a third in flat negation. Differences, which might not loom large on the paper of ordinary diplomatic intercourse, assume serious proportions when a Prime Minister has travelled hundreds of miles to a Conference and finds himself unable to go home and report its success. The methods of the Supreme Council increase in difficulty, for the agenda are not prepared by one secretariat but by several successively at Paris, at Genoa, or at London. The actual case, in which the Supreme Council broke up without coming to an agreement on the 7th August

[1] The 'Ambassadors'' Conference at Paris is merely a meeting of diplomatists, who work out the technical details of the treaty under the control of their Governments. It is not a meeting of the controllers or heads of these Governments.

1921 over Upper Silesia, showed that this method had definitely failed. The subsequent failures at Genoa and The Hague did little to suggest that the method of 'Diplomacy by Conference' was a cure for the ills of Europe.[1]

10. *Procedure of the League.* Something, however, is to be learnt from these failures. If appropriate procedure has not solved the differences between the heads of states over main problems it has done very much to promote international co-operation between the representatives of different states in lesser problems. International intercourse ceased to function after 1822 because the conferences of principal Powers ceased to meet, but to-day, whatever may be the failure of the principals, the machinery of the League provides for permanent international policies and for periodic international reunions. The procedure of the League is in reality based on the procedure of the British Committee of Imperial Defence as modified for international purposes and adapted for the use of the Supreme War Council and the 'Council of Four'. The League has imitated and improved upon these methods. Both the International Labour and the League Secretariats are alike permanent, impartial, and international in character and in aim. Their procedure is, to some extent, fixed and known. It works with a minimum of friction, for there are securities that each nation will find its peculiar ideas and idiosyncrasies respected or represented on the secretariats. The delay, conflict, and confusion so often seen at the beginning of international conferences is now a thing of the past, and, to this extent at any rate, this procedure not only saves infinite time and trouble, but does actually mark a new era. The defect is that Great Powers do not like to submit their main problems to such bodies. But the reference of so vital a problem as Upper Silesia to the Council of the League, and the agreement of England and France to abide by a decision of non-interested parties, shows that even the greatest Powers are sometimes compelled to take the line of least resistance in such matters. It is not easy to see how the matters of minor international importance can again be withdrawn from this species of international control, and there is an increasing possibility that the

[1] The Washington Conference was one at which heads of states were not present, and had those characteristics of subordinate diplomats, limited agenda and precise objects, and popular pressure which remove it from the category above mentioned.

more important matters may ultimately be drawn within this orbit.

11. *Relations of Great Powers to Minor Powers.* The minor Powers did not like their treatment at the Peace Conference, and had certainly much reason for their dissatisfaction.[1] But it is not easy to find in history, or to see in practice, any other procedure than that adopted which could have settled their affairs and concluded the Treaties in so short a time and with any fairer or more impartial results. The settlement of many problems, more particularly between Allied minor Powers, marks a definite advance on previous methods. The frontiers drawn in Hungary between Rumania and the Serb-Croat-Slovene kingdom,[2] or in Teschen between Poland and Czecho-Slovakia,[3] were genuine attempts to arrive at a fair compromise. In other cases an enemy sometimes obtained advantages from a minor Power which it could not have done, had the minor Power not been compelled to accept the award. An example of this is the frontier between Serbia and Bulgaria.[4] Further, the Minorities Treaties would certainly not have been accepted by the minor Powers without similar pressure.[5] Whatever their defects these represent a stride forward in the protection of racial and religious minorities, which can hardly fail to be of considerable value and importance for the future.

So far as the League itself is concerned the minor Powers enjoy considerable advantages which serve, in themselves, as a compensation for what they had to endure at the Peace Conference itself. Originally five and now six of them have representation on the Council and thus their representation exceeds that of the four Great Powers.[6] In the important case of altering the stipulations of a Minority Treaty decision is by a majority of the Council, and not by unanimity. Every member of the League further enjoys the privilege of criticizing the Great Powers in the Assembly, while a majority of them can actually overrule these Great Powers on so important a question as the admission of a state as a member of the League.

[1] Vol. I, pp. 269–70, 277.
[2] Vol. IV, p. 211.
[3] Vol. IV, pp. 361–3.
[4] Vol. IV, pp. 211–12, 455–6.
[5] Vol. IV, pp. 234–5 ; Vol. V, pp. 146–9.
[6] By a decision of the Council of the 19th September 1922. The four permanent members are France, Great Britain, Italy, Japan ; the six non-permanent ones are Belgium, Brazil, China, Spain, Sweden, and Uruguay (September 1922).

It was an impressive spectacle also to see the destiny of Upper Silesia, about which Great Britain and France differed, decided by the representatives of the non-interested Powers, of whom only one, Japan, was a Great Power. There are great possibilities for the influence which may be exercised by small Powers at the League, provided that they show persistence, and profit by the political experience and education in which the working of the League is abundantly rich.

12. *Admission of States to the League.* Admission to membership of the League is closely connected with the relations of the Great and the small Powers to one another. For the admission of a state to the League is decided ultimately (Art. I of the Covenant) by the vote of two-thirds of the Assembly. This means that, if they wish, the small Powers can control the Great and admit a state to membership against their wishes. This power was actually exercised in the case of Albania, which was admitted to the League in December 1920 after the preliminary opposition of Great Britain. As none of the four Great Powers recognized the Albanian Government for nearly a year it may be presumed that none of them was enthusiastic in her support. Yet Albania was admitted as a member, and her admission constituted an asset of infinite moral and material value to her. The same may be said, though in a less degree, with regard to Lithuania, whose admission was vainly opposed by France in 1921. It is apparent that the Assembly in such matters will not submit to the dictation of one, or even a group, of the Great Powers. This fact is important, for the offer to vote for the admission of a state to the League appears to be used as a resource of diplomacy. It was made to Iraq by Great Britain, and to Turkey by the three Allied Powers. It is perhaps well for such Powers to remember that the state presenting itself for submission has to pass certain tests in committee as to stability and constitutionality of government, limitation of armaments and fulfilment of international obligations, and, in some cases, protection of minorities. It is not easy to see that Kemalist Turkey has fulfilled any of these tests. But the remedy lies in the hands of the small Powers, who can refuse her permission, whatever the Great Powers may or may not have promised beforehand.

13. *General and International Clauses in the Treaties, their*

connexion with the League. Various provisions in the Treaties were directed towards laying down universal principles for the direction and control of interests and activities, which were essentially international in character, such as commerce and the means of transportation, whether by air, road, rail, or waterway. Individual interests were, in many cases, too strong to permit more than a limited success being obtained in these directions. But the importance of the ideals shadowed forth must not be neglected.

(*a*) *Commerce.* As regards freedom of commerce some progress was made and far-reaching principles laid down. There was, at one time, a fair chance that freedom for raw materials might be obtained, but this foundered on the rock of individual national interests. As regards Mandated territories of the 'A' and 'B' varieties, great and important concessions have been made permitting freedom of competition to all members of the League and prohibiting monopolies. The United States, though not a member of the League, has also obtained equality of treatment in Palestine and perhaps elsewhere, so that the area of international equality of treatment has been widened as a result of the War in these areas.

(*b*) *Communications.* As regards international rivers, the systematic extension of the principles originally laid down at the Congress of Vienna has led to the strange result that all the rivers of Germany are controlled by River Boards which are not German, and on which Germany cannot ever have a preponderant influence.[1] The extension of this principle can hardly be defended in such instances, and will ultimately have to be amended, but the securing of free zones in harbours to land-locked states is certainly an advantage and a precedent to be imitated in the future. Bound up with it is the principle of securing access to the sea for inland states, which has received an extensive application in the Treaties.[2] The general principles of transportation have received some extension since the Treaties in the Transport Conference and Convention of Barcelona. Progress has been made in such matters as promoting uniformity of passport systems and of transportation

[1] Vol. II, p. 100 n.

[2] Unfortunately while successful at Danzig and through Germany, the troubles at Fiume have hindered Austrian and Hungarian access there (Vol. IV, pp. 336–7), and nothing has been done by Greece to secure Bulgaria's access to the Aegean (Vol. IV, pp. 458–9).

rates. As economic facts are likely soon to convince even the most recalcitrant Powers of the dangers of isolation and the folly of prohibitive barriers, these principles will certainly make further progress in the future.

(*c*) *International Labour.* The progress here registered has been fully discussed in this volume (Chap. VI, Part II), and undoubtedly forms an advance on any kind of international organization that has preceded it in this direction.

(*d*) *Other international activities.* Nothing need here be said of the League itself, but certain international activities, such as the drafting of regulations and conventions for such objects as the suppression of the opium trade, of dangerous trades, of the white slave traffic, &c., as provided for in the Treaties, have already been developed and extended by the League. Other activities, such as the repatriation of prisoners from Russia, by which some 440,000 were repatriated, the campaign for the destruction of typhus, and the co-ordination and centralization of health organizations, are temporary or permanent manifestations of international efforts for which the League has been responsible. Even the United States has been unable to resist co-operating in some of these efforts, and it is probable that the League will both increase and extend these activities.

(*e*) *The Permanent Mandates Commission and the Permanent Court of International Justice.* These institutions are fully described elsewhere (Chap. VI, Parts III and IV), but certain aspects demand notice here. In each case the problem has been solved of creating a general international body qualified to pronounce on international questions, without having to appoint a representative from every member of the League. Thus a genuine international representation has been provided by an ingenious system. The Mandates Commission has a majority of members of non-interested states, and the Court of Justice contains members drawn from the different systems of law prevailing in the world. In each case the theoretical principle was preserved that members were elected for personal, and not for national, reasons. This marks an interesting ideal, and is not wholly a fiction when an American sits in an international court established by and for members of the League. Apart from the representative international character of these two bodies their functions and powers are also of great importance. Those of the Mandates Commission are, indeed, practically confined to temperate but authoritative supervision or remonstrance. Those of the Permanent Court of Justice are more extensive, for seventeen states have already submitted to 'compulsory jurisdiction' for settlement of their international differences. In these, as well as in many other, directions the power of the Court may well be extended. One thing is certain, and that is that, if it continues to exist, it will devise a more correct standard of 'International Justice' than has ever yet been attained.

14. *The Protection of Racial, Linguistic, and Religious Minorities.* The form and purpose of the Minorities Treaties signed by Allies and the minorities clauses applying to Enemy Powers has been fully discussed and explained in the fifth volume.[1] The principle has received a wider extension and application than ever before. It was hotly resisted both by Rumania and the Serb-Croat-Slovene kingdom as an infringement of sovereignty, and this fact in itself seems to show that such treaties cannot be regarded as waste paper, but imply a definite protection to minorities such as they have not before enjoyed. The fact that these questions can come before not only the Council but also the Assembly of the League has already proved to be of great importance. Czecho-Slovakia has won an honourable renown by the readiness she has displayed to give all information to the League as to her treatment of minorities, and her organization of her Ruthene autonomous province, as expounded by M. Osusky at the Second Assembly, proved that expectations had been fully realized in that area.[2] It is also clear that the German and Hungarian schools of Czecho-Slovakia are fully up to the proportionate percentage required in her Minority Treaty. A careful procedure has been elaborated for examination into complaints put forward by a minority.

It is as follows:

'This method, which consists in friendly and semi-official communications with the various Governments, was recognized by the Assembly (of 1922) as well calculated, in ordinary circumstances, to secure the establishment of good relations between the Governments and minorities concerned. The procedure consists briefly in the following steps: the Secretariat, when it receives a petition from a minority, communicates

[1] Vol. V, Chap. II, *passim*; and Wilson's speech of 31st May 1919, Vol. V, pp. 130–2.

[2] For Ruthenia, Vol. IV, pp. 272–3; for M. Osusky's speech *v. My Second Year of the League*, p. 79.

it to the Government concerned, before even passing it on to the Council, in order to permit this Government to make any remarks it considers necessary. Thereupon, the petition is studied, together with the remarks of the Government concerned, by a Council Committee consisting of the President and two Members of the Council. If this Committee considers that action should be taken on the petition, the latter is communicated to the Council, which can henceforward decide on what measures it considers suitable. This procedure was approved by the Assembly.' [1]

Every care is thus taken to provide against the premature circulation of unjust accusations. At the same time it is difficult to see how a state which is really violating its obligations in this matter can escape from embarrassment when the matter comes before the League.

(*a*) *Minority Treaties with Allied States.* The Minorities Treaties were, in effect, imposed by the principal Powers upon certain smaller ones who received part of the territories conquered and gave in return promises to protect religious and racial minorities. These stipulations are primarily guaranteed by the four Great Powers, but they are also declared 'objects of international concern and placed under the guarantee of the League'. Any member of the Council can call attention to infractions of a Minority Treaty and disputes as to law and fact can under certain conditions go up to the Permanent Court of International Justice, whose decision is final.[2]

(*b*) *Minority Clauses in the Treaties with Austria, Hungary, Bulgaria, and Germany.* Clauses protecting minorities have also been inserted in the Austrian and Hungarian, Bulgarian and Turkish Treaties.[3] These provide the same safeguards as do the Treaties, and the same possibilities of appeal to the Court of International Justice.

Recently Germany has, as a result of the Upper Silesian Award, been added to this group. She has been compelled to subscribe to the principal parts of the Polish Minorities Treaty 'at least for the transitional period of fifteen years . . . as regards those parts of Upper Silesia definitely recognized as part of Germany'.

[1] *Monthly Summary League of Nations*, Vol. II, No. 9, September 1922, p. 219.

[2] *v.* for example Art. 11 of Serb-Croat-Slovene Minorities Treaty, 10th September 1919, Text in Vol. V, pp. 451–2.

[3] Text, Austrian, Art. 62–9, Hungarian, Art. 54–60 in Vol. V, pp. 197–8; Bulgarian, Art. 49–57, Vol. V, pp. 316–17.

(*c*) *The League obtains Declarations as regards Minorities from Albania, Esthonia, and Latvia.* Thus, as the Treaties come into force, the League in effect assumes control, and that control is likely to increase. But the League has not been satisfied with watching over the observance of Minorities Treaties, etc. It has negotiated agreements of its own. Not being a state or a super-state the League has had to content itself with obtaining declarations from various Powers on their admission to the League with regard to the protection of minorities. On the 22nd September 1921 Albania signed a declaration which was, in effect, a Minorities Treaty promising, among other things, to provide ‘ an electoral system giving due consideration to the rights of racial, religious, and linguistic minorities ’, to give full detailed information, and to ‘ take into account any advice it might receive from the League of Nations with regard to this question ’. Similar declarations were obtained in 1921 from Lithuania and in 1922 from Esthonia and Latvia. In the case of Finland the Council resolved (2nd October 1921) that, under the existing internal laws, minorities were already protected, and a declaration was needless.[1] It is not clear that this principle is sound. For the advantage of a Minorities Treaty, clause, or declaration is that it gives the Government time to resist a wave, say, of anti-Semitic Chauvinism in its own country. Before any protective clauses can be abrogated in deference to popular demand the League must be consulted and give its consent. In this way the League undoubtedly strengthens Governments in their resistance to prejudice or clamour. Further, the possibility of appeal to the Permanent Court of International Justice still further lengthens the time before which any decision can be taken. The protection of minorities has certainly not been achieved, but a long step forward has been taken in providing international machinery to achieve that end. It should be noted that none of the four Great Powers has itself consented to sign Treaties guaranteeing the same protection to racial and other minorities as it is prepared to exact from the smaller Powers. Therefore it is the latter, and not the former, who are open to effective criticism by the League in this matter. The Third

[1] Except for the inhabitants of the Aaland Isles, whose Swedish population was placed under the guarantee of the League by a resolution of the Council (27th June 1921).

Assembly of the League has, however, formally 'expressed the hope that states not bound to the League by any legal obligation, such as that contained in the Minorities Treaties, would nevertheless observe in their relations with racial, religious, or linguistic minorities, at least the same degree of justice and tolerance as is required by the treaties watched over by the Council.' [1]

15. *Protection of the backward races.* Much thought was devoted to the condition of the more uncivilized races at the Peace Conference and the Mandates represent a remarkable effort to meet their needs, a result due to the insistence of President Wilson. Their objects are more fully expanded elsewhere.[2] A few observations may be here made. Even the 'C' Mandates do not represent pure annexation, and the 'A' and 'B' Mandates impose limits on the Mandatory Powers from which some of them would be glad to be exempted. It appeared to be a defect that the Mandates seemed, according to the Covenant, to be eternal, so that there was no way provided by which a 'C' Mandatory may become 'B', or 'A' become independent. More than one article in Mandates, however, now contemplates the possibility of a termination of the existing Mandate so that this objection is removed.[3] Apart from this, the League watches over the interests of the native and has the power first to pronounce the Mandate to be in accordance with the Covenant, and in succeeding years to turn the searchlight of publicity on the questionable acts of the Mandatory. It also approves changes in the terms of Mandates or their termination. So far so good. But it is regrettable that the Arms Convention has, so far, been ratified only by Siam and Greece, two powers not specially interested in supplying munitions to natives, and though liquor is prohibited in mandated territories of the 'C' order, the control of liquor elsewhere and the ratifications of the Liquor Convention are not in a wholly satisfactory state.

It is premature to pronounce on the possibilities or activities of the Mandates Commission, but an extract from the official report of their Second Session dealing with their examination

[1] *Monthly Summary of the League*, Vol. II, No. 9, September 1922, p. 219.
[2] Chap. VI, Part IV, *passim*.
[3] *v.* App. V, Part III, Art. 19 of Mandate 'A' Syria; and App. II, Part III A, Art. 20 of Mesopotamia Draft, and Part III B, Art. 18 of Iraq Treaty.

of the annual reports of the 'C' Mandated Areas will give, better than anything else, some idea of the present position. These were the only Mandates in full working order in July 1922.

'These Reports (of the 'C' Mandated Areas) [1] were examined in the presence of the accredited representatives of the Mandatory Powers: Sir Joseph Cook, for Australia; Sir James Allen, for New Zealand; and M. Matsuda, for Japan. The South African Government was not represented.

'The Commission studied these reports, taking as its basis the questionnaire sent to the Mandatories and asking their representatives to furnish explanations and additional information whenever the reports seemed lacking in clearness and precision. The Commission came to the conclusion that, in general, the provisions of the mandates were being strictly carried out: slavery, even in a domestic form, does not exist in these territories; forced labour is practically unknown and liberty of conscience is everywhere guaranteed; traffic in arms and munitions is rigorously controlled, the importation and consumption of liquor by the natives is strictly forbidden; finally, these territories are entirely demilitarized.

'On two points only did the Commission make any reservation. The first concerned the presence in all the Pacific Islands of Chinese workmen who had been brought there in order to compensate the lack of native labour. The situation of these workmen, who in most cases have signed contracts for three years, might perhaps cause some anxiety. Moreover, the Commission foresaw the possibility of social evils arising from the presence among the native population of these workmen without their wives. It therefore requested the Mandatories to keep it informed of the measures taken to protect these Chinese workmen and to prevent the social evils that might arise from their presence.

'The second question concerned the administration of Nauru, an island in the Pacific, about eight square miles in area, and containing very rich phosphate deposits. This island, the mandate for which was given to His Britannic Majesty, is at present administered by Australia. The exploitation of the phosphates is under the control of three Commissioners appointed respectively by the Governments of Australia, Great Britain, and New Zealand. The Commission wondered whether a state of affairs involving the exercise by the Mandatory of a monopoly for the exploitation of the sole natural wealth of the island, was compatible with the spirit of the Covenant. Moreover, it would appear to give the phosphates commissioners a position which might endanger the authority of the Administrator responsible for the material and moral welfare of the inhabitants. As a matter of fact, the Commissioners are appointed for an unlimited term of years by the British, Australian, and New Zealand Governments, while the Administrator of the island is appointed for five years by the Australian Government. The Commission decided to draw the attention of the Council to the situation and to ask the Mandatory for supplementary information.' [1]

[1] *League of Nations Monthly Summary*, Vol. II, No. 8, August 1922, p. 186.

16. *The Concert of Power and the Balance of Power.*

(*a*) *Leagues within the League.* There can be no doubt that one of the main inducements to the small Powers to accept the position of superiority given to the Great Powers in the organization of the League was the security and protection afforded to them by Article X. The underlying conception was simple and grand and was frequently emphasized by President Wilson. The idea was that the 'Balance of Power' represented a discredited system. Under it nations entered into competing leagues, alliances, and rivalries, which were sometimes actually intended, and were likely if unintended, to lead to warfare. To oppose this a Concert of Power was to be created, a general League in which no separate alliances were possible and which, in the case of a lawless act or act of warfare by any one member, brought down at once on the guilty party the wrath of the whole League and a universal economic boycott. This system was too advanced and too ideal to be realized at once. It was violated by President Wilson himself as well as by France and by Great Britain in the two Guarantee Treaties (respectively Franco-British and Franco-American) against unprovoked aggression by Germany. It has been violated since by such instruments as the French Military Conventions with Belgium and with Poland and by the 'Little Entente' treaties. The situation thus created is a difficult one, but a way out has been suggested by the ingenuity of Dr. Beneš, who proposed an amendment to the Covenant in 1921. It was not rejected but deferred. This would have had the effect of enabling the League to supervise proposed alliances and agreements between its members before they were contracted, and to advise as to their terms. It would thus have got over the awkward anomaly now presented by the existence of 'Leagues within the League'.[1] It was a highly interesting proposal and it may be hoped that it will be ultimately adopted in one form or another. Its acceptance would have the effect of recognizing that certain groups of states had regional interests, but that these should be pursued under the aegis of the League.[2] It is clearly better

[1] For German and Allied observations on this point *v.* Vol. II, pp. 353–4.

[2] Art. 21 of the Covenant runs: 'Nothing in this Covenant shall be deemed to affect the validity of international engagements, such as treaties of arbitration or regional understandings like the Monroe Doctrine, for securing the maintenance of peace.

The proposed Czecho-Slovak amendment was: 'Agreements between

that the League should supervise or promote such arrangements, rather than know nothing of them until they are completed.

(*b*) *Guarantee of territorial integrity under Article X and protection of Members of the League under other articles.* The obligation taken under the Covenant by Members of the League 'not to go to war suddenly and secretly' with one another, and the guarantee of territorial integrity under Article X are the two chief securities afforded by the League to its members. Neither obligation has previously ever been made the object of such extended and concerted agreement. These have been fully discussed elsewhere (Chap. VI, Part I, pp. 443–6), but it is worth while to point out that, though the tendency is to construe Article X in an elastic rather than a rigid sense, it is still considered by many states to have a very definite and positive value. Canada has shown a great and evident desire to have it defined or amended in such a way as to prevent her being under any obligations to send troops overseas on account of territorial disturbances in Europe.[1] France, on the other hand, has shown the utmost tenacity in resisting this amendment and her view has prevailed. These facts prove that the cynical sneer, that Article X is meaningless, is erroneous. If it were really so Canada would not be so anxious to amend or France so desirous of retaining its form unaltered.

The Economic Weapon, i.e. the economic boycott of a recalcitrant state under Article XVI, was relied upon by many as the chief means of preserving peace or averting war. It must be confessed that the prospect of its universality has been greatly diminished since the Assembly has expressed the view that the duty of the Council was to express the opinion as to whether a state had broken the Covenant and to invite members to apply economic pressure. But the Assembly went on to say that 'it is the duty of each member of the League to decide for itself whether a breach of the Covenant has been committed'. In other words, each state is to judge individually whether it shall, or shall not, apply the economic boycott. This ruling

members of the League tending to define or complete the engagements contained in the Covenant for the maintenance of peace or the promotion of international co-operation may not only be approved by the League, but also promoted or negotiated under its auspices, provided these agreements are not inconsistent with the covenant. Special conferences of the members of the League concerned may be summoned for this purpose by the Council or by the Assembly.'

[1] *v.* Chap. IV, Part I, § 10, pp. 349–50.

on the question was made by the Assembly in September 1921, and was regarded by many as constituting the end of the usefulness or universality of the economic blockade. Two months afterwards the croakers were confounded. Owing to various incidents on the northern frontier of Albania the threat of an economic blockade was applied to the Serb-Croat-Slovene kingdom at the instance of Great Britain. The mere threat was sufficient to cause the immediate evacuation of North Albanian territory by the Serb forces.[1] It is not easy to see how these sanctions or guarantees may be developed, strengthened or applied in the future. But the history of them to date seems decisively to show that they are neither a nullity nor a fiction. There is a real force in the 'Concert of Power', though the force exercised is more often moral than material. Yet it is material, too, for the areas directly under the protection of the League, such as Danzig and the Saar, enjoy complete immunity from the irruption of unauthorized bands from outside. Fiume, a free State, guaranteed by Italy and the Serb-Croat-Slovene Kingdom, is perpetually a prey to them. So that while the guarantee of two Powers is unreal, that of the 'Concert' is real and is enforced. Territorial integrity has really been guaranteed by the League in these two cases.

17. *The Enemy Powers and the Countries outside the League.* The comity or family of nations existed before, but the League set up a new Family of Nations, a family professing new ideals of international honour and justice and pledged to practise them towards one another, so as to attain to a closer common feeling among nations. The ultimate success of this experiment clearly depends on the character of the League becoming all-embracing. When the League has all its enemies inside the League it will no longer have enemies. It is of more than temporary significance that three of the defeated Powers—Austria, Bulgaria, and Hungary—have sought for, and received, admission within its ranks. No less important is it that a small unrecognized State, like Albania, has owed its freedom from external interference, its international status, and its very existence to the League. Yet four Powers, and each of the greatest typical importance, have hitherto stood aloof from the League and all or almost all its works.

(*a*) *The United States.* Of these the United States at present

[1] *v.* above Chap. VI, Part V, p. 527 n.

stands for the principle that the American Continent is sufficient unto itself, that the barriers set up by Washington and Monroe still remain, and that the written provisions of the Covenant are a net of ingenious devices to catch the feet of the unwary. How far this attitude will be permanent time alone can decide. But there are not wanting signs that the United States is beginning to grasp the unreality of some of her previous fears, and to see the difficulty of resisting an international movement and organization so widespread, so persistent, and, in not a few ways congenial to that pacific idealism which has struck so deep a root in American character. It is possible that the United States, while not becoming a member of the League, will become at least able to co-operate in certain ways effectively with the Court of Justice.

(*b*) *Germany*. Germany, which still stands aloof from the League, does so on the ground that the League was the creation of the men who made the Peace at Paris, and that the Covenant itself was signed at the same time as German plenipotentiaries were humiliated in the very hall where the German Empire was proclaimed. That is a bitter memory ; an even bitterer one is the award made by the League with regard to Upper Silesia. It is easy to see the feelings with which the Germans regard the League and their reluctance to associate themselves with it. Yet, in the end, it is they who will lose most by standing aloof from it. And from the very first, even in 1919, Germany was admitted to the International Labour Conference.

(*c*) *The Turks*. The Turks, like their neighbours the Bolsheviks, have hitherto stood out stiffly against the League and all its works. Their attitude is, however, different from that of the Bolsheviks and apparently from that of other Oriental nations. Chinese, Japanese, Indians, and Persians have all, in greater or less degree, shown a desire to understand Western political ideals and standards which make it possible for them not only to enter into the family of the League, but to add to it the contribution of their culture. The Turks have shown no such desire, and it must be regarded as doubtful whether they are capable of doing so. The fact that the Three Allied Powers have promised to vote for their admission must, however, argue some corresponding belief that the Turks will be able to play their part in the comity of nations. We may hope that they may. But the record of the Turks as to international engagements, either in the past or the present, is not good. They represented in the past an element of force, which no moral influence has hitherto been able to check.

(*d*) *The Bolsheviks.*[1] The attitude of the Bolsheviks was determined by their political and economic theories. Lenin from the first showed resolute hostility to the League. On the 29th March 1920 he declared that 'our enemies possessed no internal cohesion. Capitalism perverted them and converted the Allies into wild beasts.' Again on the 30th May he said there were 'two groups of world-bandits, the Anglo-French-American or the German group, they entered into an alliance with the bourgeoisie against the revolutionary struggle of the proletariat', and the League was the expression of their bourgeois and capitalistic desires. The design of the Bolsheviks was therefore to induce the workers in every capitalistic State to revolt against their masters, and both the States themselves and the League were to be discredited and broken.

That Mr. Wilson, and still more M. Clemenceau, feared the effect of this movement is well known, and the following extracts from his Memorandum of the 25th March 1919 show the danger as equally apparent to Mr. Lloyd George:

'The extreme figures of the Terror are still in command in Russia. The whole of Europe is filled with the spirit of revolution. There is a deep sense not only of discontent, but of anger and revolt, amongst the workmen against pre-war conditions. The whole existing order in its political, social and economic aspects is questioned by the masses of the population from one end of Europe to the other. . . .

'But there is a danger that we may throw the masses of the population throughout Europe into the arms of the extremists whose only idea for regenerating mankind is to destroy utterly the whole existing fabric of society. These men have triumphed in Russia. They have done so at a terrible price. . . .

'If Germany goes over to the spartacists it is inevitable that she should throw in her lot with the Russian Bolshevists. Once that happens all Eastern Europe will be swept into the orbit of the Bolshevik revolution and within a year we may witness the spectacle of nearly three hundred million people organized into a vast red army under German instructors and German generals equipped with German cannon and German machine guns and prepared for a renewal of the attack on Western Europe. This is a prospect which no one can face with equanimity. Yet the news which came from Hungary yesterday shows only too clearly that this danger is no fantasy.'

[1] *v.* Chap. III, Part 2.

To this danger he suggested the antidote of the League :

'It is not, however, enough to draw up a just and far-sighted peace with Germany. If we are to offer Europe an alternative to Bolshevism we must make the League of Nations into something which will be both a safeguard to those nations who are prepared for fair dealing with their neighbours and a menace to those who would trespass on the rights of their neighbours, whether they are imperialist empires or imperialist Bolshevists. An essential element, therefore, in the peace settlement is the constitution of the League of Nations as the effective guardian of international right and international liberty throughout the world.

Since 1921 the danger from the Bolshevik international class-war has lessened, and the fears of Mr. Lloyd George in 1919 find less of an echo to-day. In Holland, Hungary, and Italy strong anti-Bolshevik reactions have taken place, and in other countries the propaganda for a universal revolutionary class-war shows signs of weakening. As has been mentioned elsewhere, the Bolsheviks, like the later Jacobins, show some signs of recognizing the necessity of establishing relations with Governments opposed to them in political or economic principle. They have signed treaties with Germany, with Poland, and the Baltic States, and met the negotiators of Europe in conference at Geneva and the Hague. It is interesting, however, to observe that their first appearance at an international gathering was at a Health Conference of the League.

The League is thus faced with four opponents who refuse to enter it and who deny its authority. The circumstances, which may cause them to abandon their negative attitude, are so various that speculation is at this stage unprofitable. But some approach to a *modus vivendi* has, in each case, taken place.

Of one thing we may be sure. Whatever its views or ideals, a State is better within the League than without it, from the point of view, at any rate, of the League. For though the League now includes over fifty States and over two-thirds of the world, it can only be truly universal in its influence when its membership is actually world-wide.

18. *Conclusion*. The history of the Peace Conference was a disillusionment in more senses than one. There are few who do not recognize that many high hopes were disappointed and

that the aims of 'broad-visioned justice and mercy' were too often defeated. 'A supply of ideals has seldom failed the critics of peace treaties.' It does not seem wholly fair to blame the statesmen who made this peace for the evils and errors which it contained. None of them was, or even professed to be, other than the mouthpiece of his respective people. 'Statesmen', said President Wilson, 'must follow the clarified common thought or be broken.' The statesmen have been broken, but the common thought has not yet been clarified. The Peace Conference, indeed, defeated the extremer aims of the French militarists and of Yugo-Slav, Rumanian, or Polish Chauvinists. But it failed to prevent the infliction of some racial injuries, of much economic distress, and it left behind it a broad trail of bitter memories. For these results the atmosphere in which the Peace Conference worked was chiefly responsible. The issues were mingled and obscured in a seething furnace of passions. The obligation of secret pledges given at need, the strife of nationalities, the pride of victory, the bitterness of defeat, the memory of unspeakable wrongs, all these inflamed and kept open the wounds of a suffering world.

It is true, however, to say that the idea of nationality did really underlie the Peace settlement. Even the secret treaties could not prevent the spread of this influence. The 'Break-up' of Austria was one of the boldest attempts to realize the national idea that has ever been made. For the first time in history responsible statesmen denied that Austria, that swallower of nationalities, was 'a European necessity'. National aspirations were not always victorious, but progress in realizing them was actually made.

Yet those who went to the Peace Conference 'came away wiser, but they came away sadder', said Lord Grey. Of what Peace Conference cannot the same story be told? One plenipotentiary, who played a distinguished part at the Peace Conference, has said more than this. 'It was not Wilson who failed them (the people) in Paris, but humanity itself; sincerely as we believed in the moral ideals for which we had fought, the temptation of a large booty to be divided proved too great.

'And in the end not only the leaders but the peoples preferred a bit of booty here, a strategic frontier there, a coalfield or an oil-well, an addition to their population or resources—to all the faint allurements of the ideal.'[1]

One who had studied the subject more deeply than any statesman said that 'History is likely to make men wise, and is sure to make them sad'. But while history has much in it of sadness, it has something also of promise and of hope. It teaches that ideals cannot be realized at once, it tells also that, if sincerely felt, they cannot be extinguished. The world that was the world of 1914 could not be bettered or reformed at a stroke, but none the less that world will never be restored. For if there was much that was lost at Paris, there was something also that was saved, a leaven which may one day leaven the whole earth. Even General Smuts, who has taken so tragic a view of the present, has seen the promise of the future.

'What was really saved at Paris was the Covenant of the League of Nations. The Covenant is Wilson's souvenir to the world.

'The Peace Treaty will fade into merciful oblivion, and its provisions will be gradually obliterated by the great human tides sweeping over the world. But the Covenant will stand as sure as fate. It must succeed, because there is no other way for the future of civilization.'[2]

[1] General Smuts in *New York Evening Post*, 3rd March 1921. The criticisms of Mr. Keynes and Signor Nitti are even more severe.

[2] General Smuts, *loc cit.*

APPENDICES

APPENDIX I

DRAFT AND REVISED COVENANT OF 1919; AMENDMENTS OF 1921.

THE following table gives in the left-hand column the Covenant as revised, and at the bottom of this column the amendments of 1921;[1] the right-hand column gives the textual differences of the original Draft. For a brief analysis and commentary on these, *v.* Vol. III, pp. 56–7, and for Wilson's speech on 14th February 1919, *v.* Vol. III, pp. 60–65. For a full discussion *v.* Vol. VI, pp. 432–61.

THE COVENANT OF THE LEAGUE OF NATIONS (As Revised 28 April 1919; in force 10th January 1920.)	THE DRAFT AGREEMENT FOR THE LEAGUE OF NATIONS PRESENTED TO THE PLENARY CONFERENCE 14 Feb. 1919.
THE PREAMBLE.	PREAMBLE.
THE HIGH CONTRACTING PARTIES. In order to promote international co-operation and to achieve international peace and security by the acceptance of obligations not to resort to war, by the prescription of open, just and honourable relations between nations, by the firm establishment of the understandings of international law as the actual rule of conduct among Governments, and by the maintenance of justice and a scrupulous respect for all treaty obligations in the dealings of organized peoples with one another,	[Same as Revised Covenant except 'THE POWERS SIGNATORY' *for* 'HIGH CONTRACTING PARTIES'. 'secure' *for* 'achieve'.
Agree to this Covenant of the League of Nations.	'adopt this constitution' *for* 'agree to this Covenant'.]

[1] *v.* pp. 486–7.

ARTICLE 1. (MEMBERSHIP.)

The original Members of the League of Nations shall be those of the Signatories which are named in the Annex to this Covenant, and also such of those other States named in the Annex as shall accede without reservation to this Covenant. Such accession shall be effected by a Declaration deposited with the Secretariat within two months of the coming into force of the Covenant. Notice thereof shall be sent to all other Members of the League.

Any fully self-governing State, Dominion or Colony not named in the Annex may become a Member of the League if its admission is agreed to by two-thirds of the Assembly, provided that it shall give effective guarantees of its sincere intention to observe its international obligations, and shall accept such regulations as may be prescribed by the League in regard to its military, naval and air forces and armaments.

Any Member of the League may, after two years' notice of its intention so to do, withdraw from the League, provided that all its international obligations and all its obligations under this Covenant shall have been fulfilled at the time of its withdrawal.

DRAFT ARTICLE 7 (*for* Article 1, Revised Covenant).

For 1st and 2nd paragraphs in Revised Covenant, Draft gives 'Admission to the League of States not signatories to the Covenant and not named in the Protocol hereto as States to be invited to adhere to the Covenant, requires the assent of not less than two-thirds of the States represented in the Body of Delegates, and shall be limited to fully self-governing countries, including Dominions and Colonies. No State shall be admitted to the League unless it is able to give effective guarantees of its sincere intention to observe its international obligations, and unless it shall conform to such principles as may be prescribed by the League in regard to its naval and military forces and armaments.'

ARTICLE 2. (EXECUTIVE MACHINERY.)

The action of the League under this Covenant shall be effected through the instrumentality of an Assembly and of a Council, with a permanent Secretariat.

ARTICLE 1 (*for* Article 2).

The action of the High Contracting Parties under the terms of this Covenant shall be effected through the instrumentality of meetings of a Body of Delegates representing the High Contracting Parties, of meetings at more frequent intervals of an Executive Council, and of a permanent international Secretariat to be established at the Seat of the League.

ARTICLE 3. (ASSEMBLY.)

The Assembly shall consist of Representatives of the Members of the League.

The Assembly shall meet at stated intervals, and from time to time as occasion may require, at the Seat of the League, or at such other place as may be decided upon.

The Assembly may deal at its meetings with any matter within the sphere of action of the League, or affecting the peace of the world.

At meetings of the Assembly, each Member of the League shall have one vote, and may have not more than three Representatives.

DRAFT ARTICLE 2 (*for* Articles 3 and 4).

Meetings of the Body of Delegates shall be held at stated intervals and from time to time as occasion may require for the purpose of dealing with matters within the sphere of action of the League. Meetings of the Body of Delegates shall be held at the Seat of the League, or at such other place as may be found convenient, and shall consist of representatives of the High Contracting Parties. Each of the High Contracting Parties shall have one vote, but may have not more than three representatives.

ARTICLE 4. (COUNCIL.)

The Council shall consist of Representatives of the Principal Allied and Associated Powers, together with Representatives of four other Members of the League. These four Members of the League shall be selected by the Assembly from time to time in its discretion. Until the appointment of the Representatives of the four Members of the League first selected by the Assembly, Representatives of Belgium, Brazil, Spain, and Greece shall be Members of the Council.

With the approval of the majority of the Assembly, the Council may name additional Members of the League whose Representatives shall always be Members of the Council; the Council with like approval may increase the number of Members of the League to be selected by the Assembly for representation on the Council.[1]

DRAFT ARTICLE 3 (*for* Articles 3 and 4).

The Executive Council shall consist of representatives of the United States of America, the British Empire, France, Italy, and Japan, together with representatives of four other States, Members of the League. The selection of these four States shall be made by the Body of Delegates on such principles and in such manner as they think fit. Pending the appointment of these representatives of the other States, representatives of   shall be members of the Executive Council.

Meetings of the Council shall be held from time to time as occasion may require, and at least once a year at whatever place may be decided on, or failing any such decision, at the Seat of the League, and any matter within the sphere of action of the League or affecting

[1] *Article 4, as amended by Assembly,* 1921, *would have the following clause inserted here :*

The Assembly shall fix by a two-thirds majority the rules dealing with the election of the non-permanent Members of the Council, and particularly such regulations as relate to their term of office and the conditions of re-eligibility.

The Council shall meet from time to time as occasion may require, and at least once a year, at the Seat of the League, or such other place as may be decided upon.

The Council may deal at its meetings with any matter within the sphere of action of the League or affecting the peace of the world.

Any Member of the League not represented on the Council shall be invited to send a Representative to sit as a member at any meeting of the Council during the consideration of matters specially affecting the interests of that Member of the League.

At meetings of the Council, each Member of the League represented on the Council shall have one vote, and may have not more than one Representative.

the peace of the world may be dealt with at such meetings.

Invitations shall be sent to any Power to attend a meeting of the Council at which matters directly affecting its interests are to be discussed and no decision taken at any meeting will be binding on such Power unless so invited.

ARTICLE 5. (VOTING AND PROCEDURE.)

Except where otherwise expressly provided in this Covenant or by the terms of the present Treaty, decisions at any meeting of the Assembly or of the Council shall require the agreement of all the Members of the League represented at the Meeting.

All matters of procedure at meetings of the Assembly or of the Council, including the appointment of Committees to investigate particular matters, shall be regulated by the Assembly or by the Council and may be decided by a majority of the Members of the League represented at the Meeting.

The first meeting of the Assembly and the first meeting of the Council shall be summoned by the President of the United States of America.

DRAFT ARTICLE 4 (*for* Article 5).

First paragraph omitted. Next two paragraphs the same except that here, as elsewhere, *for* 'Assembly' *read* 'Body of Delegates', *for* 'Council' *read* 'Executive Council', *and for* 'Members of the League' *read* 'States represented at the Meeting'.

ARTICLE 6. (SECRETARIAT.)

The permanent Secretariat shall be established at the Seat of the League. The Secretariat shall comprise a Secretary-General and such secretaries and staff as may be required.

The first Secretary-General shall be the person named in the Annex; thereafter the Secretary-General shall be appointed by the Council with the approval of the majority of the Assembly.

The Secretaries and staff of the Secretariat shall be appointed by the Secretary-General with the approval of the Council.

The Secretary-General shall act in that capacity at all meetings of the Assembly and of the Council.

[1] The expenses of the Secretariat shall be borne by the Members of the League in accordance with the apportionment of the expenses of the International Bureau of the Universal Postal Union.

DRAFT ARTICLE 5 (*for* Article 6).

The permanent Secretariat of the League shall be established at which shall constitute the Seat of the League. The Secretariat shall comprise such secretaries and staff as may be required, under the general direction and control of a Secretary-General of the League, who shall be chosen by the Executive Council; the Secretariat shall be appointed by the Secretary-General, subject to confirmation by the Executive Council.

The Secretary-General shall act in that capacity at all meetings of the Body of Delegates or of the Executive Council.

The expenses of the Secretariat shall be borne by the States Members of the League in accordance with the apportionment of the expenses of the International Bureau of the Universal Postal Union.

ARTICLE 7. (SEAT. QUALIFICATIONS FOR OFFICIALS. IMMUNITIES.)

The Seat of the League is established at Geneva.

The Council may at any time decide that the Seat of the League shall be established elsewhere.

All positions under or in connexion with the League, including the Secretariat, shall be open equally to men and women.

Representatives of the Members of the League and officials of the League when engaged on the business of the League shall enjoy

DRAFT ARTICLE 6 (*for* Article 7).

First three paragraphs omitted.

Representatives of the High Contracting Parties and officials of the League when engaged on the business of the League shall enjoy diplomatic privileges and immunities, and the buildings occupied by the League or its officials or by representatives attending its meetings shall enjoy the benefit of extra-territoriality.

[1] ***Article* 6. *This last paragraph as amended* (1921) *would read*:**

The expenses of the League shall be borne by the Members of the League in the proportion decided by the Assembly.

The allocation of the expenses of the League set out in Annex 3 shall be applied as from the 1st January 1922, until a revised allocation has come into force after adoption by the Assembly.

diplomatic privileges and immunities.

The buildings and other property occupied by the League or its officials or by Representatives attending its meetings shall be inviolable.

ARTICLE 8. (REDUCTION OF ARMAMENTS.)

The Members of the League recognize that the maintenance of peace requires the reduction of national armaments to the lowest point consistent with national safety and the enforcement by common action of international obligations.

The Council, taking account of the geographical situation and circumstances of each State, shall formulate plans for such reduction for the consideration and action of the several Governments.

Such plans shall be subject to reconsideration and revision at least every ten years.

After these plans shall have been adopted by the several Governments, the limits of armaments therein fixed shall not be exceeded without the concurrence of the Council.

The Members of the League agree that the manufacture by private enterprise of munitions and implements of war is open to grave objections. The Council shall advise how the evil effects attendant upon such manufacture can be prevented, due regard being had to the necessities of those Members of the League which are not able to manufacture the munitions and implements of war necessary for their safety.

The Members of the League undertake to interchange full and frank information as to the scale of their armaments, their military,

DRAFT ARTICLE 8 (*for* Article 8).

The High Contracting Parties recognize the principle that the maintenance of peace will require the reduction of national armaments to the lowest point consistent with national safety and the enforcement by common action of international obligations, having special regard to the geographical situation and circumstances of each State; and the Executive Council shall formulate plans for effecting such reduction. The Executive Council shall also determine for the consideration and action of the several Governments what military equipment and armament is fair and reasonable in proportion to the scale of forces laid down in the programme of disarmament; and these limits, when adopted, shall not be exceeded without the permission of the Executive Council.

The High Contracting Parties agree that the manufacture by private enterprise of munitions and implements of war lends itself to grave objections, and direct the Executive Council to advise how the evil effects attendant upon such manufacture can be prevented, due regard being had to the necessities of those countries which are not able to manufacture for themselves the munitions and implements of war necessary for their safety.

The High Contracting Parties undertake in no way to conceal from each other the condition of naval, and air programmes and the condition of such of their industries as are adaptable to warlike purposes.

such of their industries as are capable of being adapted to warlike purposes or the scale of their armaments, and agree that there shall be full and frank interchange of information as to their military and naval programmes.

ARTICLE 9. (PERMANENT MILITARY COMMISSION.)

A permanent Commission shall be constituted to advise the Council on the execution of the provisions of Articles 1 and 8 and on military and naval and air questions generally.

DRAFT ARTICLE 9 (*for* Article 9).

A permanent Commission shall be constituted to advise the League on the execution of the provisions of Article 8 and on military and naval questions generally.

ARTICLE 10. (GUARANTEES AGAINST AGGRESSION.)

The Members of the League undertake to respect and preserve as against external aggression the territorial integrity and existing political independence of all Members of the League. In case of any such aggression or in case of any threat or danger of such aggression the Council shall advise upon the means by which this obligation shall be fulfilled.

DRAFT ARTICLE 10 (*for* Article 10).

Same except 'High Contracting Parties' *for* 'Members of the League' and 'all States Members of the League', *for* 'all Members of the League'.

ARTICLE 11. (ACTION IN CASE OF WAR OR DANGER OF WAR.)

Any war or threat of war, whether immediately affecting any of the Members of the League or not, is hereby declared a matter of concern to the whole League, and the League shall take any action that may be deemed wise and effectual to safeguard the peace of nations. In case any such emergency should arise the Secretary-General shall on the request of any Member of the League forthwith summon a meeting of the Council.

It is also declared to be the friendly right of each Member of the League to bring to the attention of the Assembly or of the

DRAFT ARTICLE 11 (*for* Article 11).

Any war or threat of war, whether immediately affecting any of the High Contracting Parties or not, is hereby declared a matter of concern to the League, and the High Contracting Parties reserve the right to take any action that may be deemed wise and effectual to safeguard the peace of nations.

It is hereby also declared and agreed to be the friendly right of each of the High Contracting Parties to draw the attention of the Body of Delegates or of the Executive Council to any circumstance affecting international intercourse which threatens to disturb international peace or the good

Council any circumstance whatever affecting international relations which threatens to disturb international peace or the good understanding between nations upon which peace depends.

understanding between nations upon which peace depends.

ARTICLE 12. (DISPUTES TO BE SUBMITTED TO ARBITRATION OR INQUIRY.)

[1] The Members of the League agree that if there should arise between them any dispute likely to lead to a rupture, they will submit the matter either to arbitration or to inquiry by the Council, and they agree in no case to resort to war until three months after the award by the arbitrators or the report by the Council.

In any case under this article the award of the arbitrators shall be made within a reasonable time, and the report of the Council shall be made within six months after the submission of the dispute.

DRAFT ARTICLE 12 (*for* Article 12).

The High Contracting Parties agree that should disputes arise between them which cannot be adjusted by the ordinary processes of diplomacy, they will in no case resort to war without previously submitting the questions and matters involved either to arbitration or to inquiry by the Executive Council and until three months after the award by the arbitrators or a recommendation by the Executive Council; and that they will not even then resort to war as against a Member of the League which complies with the award of the arbitrators or the recommendation of the Executive Council.

Second paragraph is the same.

ARTICLE 13. (ARBITRATION OF DISPUTES.)

[2] The Members of the League agree that whenever any dispute shall arise between them which

DRAFT ARTICLE 13 (*for* Article 13).

The High Contracting Parties agree that whenever any dispute or difficulty shall arise between them which they recognize to be

[1] ***Article* 12 *as amended* (1921) *would read :***

The Members of the League agree that, if there should arise between them any dispute likely to lead to a rupture they will submit the matter either to arbitration or judicial settlement or to inquiry by the Council and they agree in no case to resort to war until three months after the award by the arbitrators or the judical decision or the report by the Council.

In any case under this Article, the award of the arbitrators or the judicial decision shall be made within a reasonable time, and the report of the Council shall be made within six months after the submission of the dispute.

[2] ***Article* 13 *as amended* (1921) *would read :***

The Members of the League agree that, whenever any dispute shall arise between them which they recognize to be suitable for submission to arbitration or judicial settlement, and which cannot be satisfactorily settled by diplomacy, they will submit the whole subject-matter to arbitration or judicial settlement.

Disputes as to the interpretation of a treaty, as to any question of international law, as to the existence of any fact which, if established, would constitute a breach of any international obligation, or as to the extent and nature of the reparation to be made for any such breach, are declared to be

they recognize to be suitable for submission to arbitration and which cannot be satisfactorily settled by diplomacy, they will submit the whole subject-matter to arbitration.

Disputes as to the interpretation of a treaty, as to any question of international law, as to the existence of any fact which, if established, would constitute a breach of any international obligation, or as to the extent and nature of the reparation to be made for any such breach, are declared to be among those which are generally suitable for submission to arbitration.

For the consideration of any such dispute the Court of Arbitration to which the case is referred shall be the Court agreed on by the parties to the dispute or stipulated in any convention existing between them.

The Members of the League agree that they will carry out in full good faith any award that may be rendered, and that they will not resort to war against any Member of the League which complies therewith. In the event of any failure to carry out such an award, the Council shall propose what steps should be taken to give effect thereto.

suitable for submission to arbitration and which cannot be satisfactorily settled by diplomacy, they will submit the whole subject-matter to arbitration. For this purpose the Court of Arbitration to which the case is referred shall be the Court agreed on by the parties or stipulated in any Convention existing between them. The High Contracting Parties agree that they will carry out in full good faith any award that may be rendered. In the event of any failure to carry out the award, the Executive Council shall propose what steps can best be taken to give effect thereto.

ARTICLE 14. PERMANENT COURT OF INTERNATIONAL JUSTICE.

The Council shall formulate and submit to the Members of the League for adoption plans for the establishment of a Permanent Court of International Justice. The Court shall be competent to hear and determine any dispute of

DRAFT ARTICLE 14 (*for* Article 14).

The Executive Council shall formulate a plan for the establishment of a Permanent Court of International Justice, and this Court shall, when established, be competent to hear and determine any matter which the parties recognize as suitable for submission

among those which are generally suitable for submission to arbitration or judicial settlement.

For the consideration of any such dispute, the Court to which the case is referred shall be the Permanent Court of International Justice, established in accordance with Article 14, or any tribunal agreed.

an international character which the parties thereto submit to it. The Court may also give an advisory opinion upon any dispute or question referred to it by the Council or by the Assembly.

to it for arbitration under the foregoing article.

ARTICLE 15. DISPUTES NOT SUBMITTED TO ARBITRATION.

* If there should arise between Members of the League any dispute likely to lead to a rupture, which is not submitted to arbitration in accordance with Article 13, the Members of the League agree that they will submit the matter to the Council. Any party to the dispute may effect such submission by giving notice of the existence of the dispute to the Secretary-General, who will make all necessary arrangements for a full investigation and consideration thereof.

For this purpose the parties to the dispute will communicate to the Secretary-General, as promptly as possible, statements of their case, with all the relevant facts and papers, and the Council may forthwith direct the publication thereof.

The Council shall endeavour to effect a settlement of the dispute, and if such efforts are successful, a statement shall be made public giving such facts and explanations regarding the dispute and the terms of settlement thereof as the Council may deem appropriate.

If the dispute is not thus settled, the Council either unanimously or by a majority vote shall make and

DRAFT ARTICLE 15 (*for* Article 15).

If there should arise between States members of the League any dispute likely to lead to a rupture, which is not submitted to arbitration as above, the High Contracting Parties agree that they will refer the matter to the Executive Council; either party to the dispute may give notice of the existence of the dispute to the Secretary-General, who will make all necessary arrangements for a full investigation and consideration thereof. For this purpose the parties agree to communicate to the Secretary-General, as promptly as possible, statements of their case with all the relevant facts and papers, and the Executive Council may forthwith direct the publication thereof.

Where the efforts of the Council lead to the settlement of the dispute, a statement shall be published indicating the nature of the dispute and the terms of settlement, together with such explanations as may be appropriate. If the dispute has not been settled, a report by the Council shall be published, setting forth with all necessary facts and explanations the recommendations which the Council think just and proper for

* ***Article* 15. *The first paragraph as amended* (1921) *would read :***

If there should arise between Members of the League any dispute likely to lead to a rupture, which is not submitted to arbitration or judicial settlement in accordance with Article 13, the Members of the League agree that they will submit the matter to the Council. Any party to the dispute may effect such submission by giving notice of the existence of the dispute to the Secretary-General, who will make all necessary arrangements for a full investigation and consideration thereof.

publish a report containing a statement of the facts of the dispute and the recommendations which are just and deemed proper in regard thereto.

Any Member of the League represented on the Council may make public a statement of the facts of the dispute and of its conclusions regarding the same.

If a report by the Council is unanimously agreed to by the members thereof, other than the Representatives of one or more of the parties to the dispute, the Members of the League agree that they will not go to war with any party to the dispute which complies with the recommendations of the report.

If the Council fails to reach a report which is unanimously agreed to by the members thereof, other than the Representatives of one or more of the parties to the dispute, the Members of the League reserve to themselves the right to take such action as they shall consider necessary for the maintenance of right and justice.

If the dispute between the parties is claimed by one of them, and is found by the Council to arise out of a matter which by international law is solely within the domestic jurisdiction of that party, the Council shall so report, and shall make no recommendation as to its settlement.

The Council may in any case under this Article refer the dispute to the Assembly. The dispute shall be so referred at the request of either party to the dispute, provided that such request be made within fourteen days after the submission of the dispute to the Council.

In any case referred to the Assembly, all the provisions of this Article and of Article 12 relating

the settlement of the dispute. If the report is unanimously agreed to by the members of the Council other than the parties to the dispute, the High Contracting Parties agree that they will not go to war with any party which complies with the recommendation and that, if any party shall refuse so to comply, the Council shall propose the measures necessary to give effect to the recommendation. If no such unanimous report can be made, it shall be the duty of the majority and the privilege of the minority to issue statements indicating what they believe to be the facts and containing the recommendations which they consider to be just and proper.

The Executive Council may in any case under this article refer the dispute to the Body of Delegates. The dispute shall be so referred at the request of either party to the dispute, provided that such request must be made within fourteen days after the submission of the dispute.

to the action and powers of the Council shall apply to the action and powers of the Assembly, provided that a report made by the Assembly, if concurred in by the Representatives of those Members of the League represented on the Council and of a majority of the other Members of the League, exclusive in each case of the Representatives of the parties to the dispute, shall have the same force as a report by the Council concurred in by all the Members thereof other than the Representatives of one or more of the parties to the dispute.

ARTICLE 16. ('SANCTIONS' OF THE LEAGUE.)

* Should any Member of the League resort to war in disregard of its covenants under Article 12, 13, or 15, it shall *ipso facto* be deemed to have committed an act of war against all other Members of the League, which hereby undertake immediately to subject it to the severance of all trade or finan-

DRAFT ARTICLE 16 (*for* Article 16).

Draft is the same with a few slight verbal alterations. The last paragraph 'Any Member of the League', &c., is omitted.

* *Article* 16, *as amended* (1921) *would read :*

Should any Member of the League resort to war in disregard of its covenants under Article 12, 13, or 15, it shall *ipso facto* be deemed to have committed an act of war against all other Members of the League, which hereby undertake immediately to subject it to the severance of all trade or financial relations, the prohibition of all intercourse between persons residing in their territory and persons residing in the territory of the Covenant-breaking State, and the prevention of all financial, commercial, or personal intercourse between persons residing in the territory of the Covenant-breaking State and persons residing in the territory of any other State, whether a Member of the League or not.

It is for the Council to give an opinion whether or not a breach of the Covenant has taken place. In deliberations on this question in the Council, the votes of Members of the League alleged to have resorted to war and of Members against whom such action was directed shall not be counted.

The Council will notify to all Members of the League the date which it recommends for the application of the economic pressure under this Article.

Nevertheless, the Council may, in the case of particular Members, postpone the coming into force of any of these measures for a specified period where it is satisfied that such a postponement will facilitate the attainment of the object of the measures referred to in the preceding paragraph, or that it is necessary in order to minimize the loss and inconvenience which will be caused to such Member.

cial relations, the prohibition of all intercourse between their nationals and the nationals of the Covenant-breaking State, and the prevention of all financial, commercial, or personal intercourse between the nationals of the Covenant-breaking State and the nationals of any other State, whether a Member of the League or not.

It shall be the duty of the Council in such case to recommend to the several Governments concerned what effective military, naval or air force the Members of the League shall severally contribute to the armed forces to be used to protect the covenants of the League.

The Members of the League agree, further, that they will mutually support one another in the financial and economic measures which are taken under this Article, in order to minimize the loss and inconveniences resulting from the above measures, and that they will mutually support one another in resisting any special measures aimed at one of their number by the Covenant-breaking State, and that they will take the necessary steps to afford passage through their territory to the forces of any of the Members of the League which are co-operating to protect the covenants of the League.

Any Member of the League which has violated any covenant of the League may be declared to be no longer a Member of the League by a vote of the Council concurred in by the Representatives of all the other Members of the League represented thereon.

ARTICLE 17. (DISPUTES WITH NON-MEMBERS.)

In the event of a dispute between a Member of the League and a State which is not a Member of the League, or between States not Members of the League, the State or States not Members of the League shall be invited to accept the obligations of membership in the League for the purposes of such dispute, upon such conditions as the Council may deem just. If such invitation is accepted, the provisions of Articles 12 to 16 in clusive shall be applied with such modifications as may be deemed necessary by the Council.

Upon such invitation being given the Council shall immediately institute an inquiry into the circumstances of the dispute and recommend such action as may seem best and most effectual in the circumstances.

If a State so invited shall refuse to accept the obligations of membership in the League for the purposes of such dispute, and shall resort to war against a Member of the League, the provisions of Article 16 shall be applicable as against the State taking such action.

If both parties to the dispute when so invited refuse to accept the obligations of membership in the League for the purposes of such dispute, the Council may take such measures and make such recommendations as will prevent hostilities and will result in the settlement of the dispute.

DRAFT ARTICLE 17 (*for* Article 17).

Same with small verbal alterations. One important change is that ' League ', the last word of the first paragraph, was changed to ' Council ' in the Amended Covenant.

ARTICLE 18. (REGISTRATION AND PUBLICATION OF ALL FUTURE TREATIES.)

Every treaty or international engagement entered into hereafter by any Member of the League shall

DRAFT ARTICLE 23 (*for* Article 18

Same with small verbal alterations.

be forthwith registered with the Secretariat and shall as soon as possible be published by it. No such treaty or international engagement shall be binding until so registered.

ARTICLE 19. (REVIEW OF TREATIES.)

The Assembly may from time to time advise the reconsideration by Members of the League of treaties which have become inapplicable and the consideration of international conditions whose continuance might endanger the peace of the world.

DRAFT ARTICLE 24 (*for* Article 19).

Same with small verbal alterations.

ARTICLE 20. (ABROGATION OF INCONSISTENT OBLIGATIONS.)

The Members of the League severally agree that this Covenant is accepted as abrogating all obligations or understandings *inter se* which are inconsistent with the terms thereof, and solemnly undertake that they will not hereafter enter into any engagements inconsistent with the terms thereof.

In case any Member of the League shall, before becoming a Member of the League, have undertaken any obligations inconsistent with the terms of this Covenant, it shall be the duty of such Member to take immediate steps to procure its release from such obligations.

DRAFT ARTICLE 25 (*for* Article 20).

Same with small verbal alterations.

ARTICLE 21. (ENGAGEMENTS THAT REMAIN VALID.)

Nothing in this Covenant shall be deemed to affect the validity of international engagements, such as treaties of arbitration or regional understandings like the Monroe Doctrine, for securing the maintenance of peace.

Not in Draft.

ARTICLE 22. (MANDATORIES. CONTROL OF COLONIES AND TERRITORIES.)

To those colonies and territories which as a consequence of the late war have ceased to be under the sovereignty of the States which formerly governed them and which are inhabited by peoples not yet able to stand by themselves under the strenuous conditions of the modern world, there should be applied the principle that the well-being and development of such peoples form a sacred trust of civilization and that securities for the performance of this trust should be embodied in this Covenant.

The best method of giving practical effect to this principle is that the tutelage of such peoples should be entrusted to advanced nations who, by reason of their resources, their experience, or their geographical position, can best undertake this responsibility, and who are willing to accept it, and that this tutelage should be exercised by them as Mandatories on behalf of the League.

The character of the mandate must differ according to the stage of the development of the people, the geographical situation of the territory, its economic conditions, and other similar circumstances.

'A.' Certain communities formerly belonging to the Turkish Empire have reached a stage of development where their existence as independent nations can be provisionally recognized subject to the rendering of administrative advice and assistance by a Mandatory until such time as they are able to stand alone. The wishes of these communities must be a principal consideration in the selection of the Mandatory.

DRAFT ARTICLE 19 (*for* Article 22).

Apart from small verbal alterations the really important change from the Draft is the substitution of 'Council' *for* 'League'. *v.* below.

'B.' Other peoples, especially those of Central Africa, are at such a stage that the Mandatory must be responsible for the administration of the territory under conditions which will guarantee freedom of conscience and religion, subject only to the maintenance of public order and morals, the prohibition of abuses such as the slave-trade, the arms traffic, and the liquor traffic, and the prevention of the establishment of fortifications or military and naval bases and of military training of the natives for other than police purposes and the defence of territory, and will also secure equal opportunities for the trade and commerce of other Members of the League.

'C.' There are territories, such as South-West Africa and certain of the South Pacific Islands, which, owing to the sparseness of their population, or their small size, or their remoteness from the centres of civilization, or their geographical contiguity to the territory of the Mandatory, and other circumstances, can be best administered under the laws of the Mandatory as integral portions of its territory, subject to the safeguards above mentioned in the interests of the indigenous population.

In every case of Mandate, the Mandatory shall render to the Council an annual report in reference to the territory committed to its charge.

Last paragraph but three: 'League' for 'Council'.

The degree of authority, control, or administration to be exercised by the Mandatory shall, if not previously agreed upon by the Members of the League, be explicitly defined in each case by the Council.

Last paragraph but two: After 'Council' was added 'in a special Act or Charter'.

A permanent Commission shall be constituted to receive and examine the annual reports of the

Last paragraph runs in Draft: 'The High Contracting Parties further agree to establish at the

Mandatories and to advise the Council on all matters relating to the observance of the Mandates.

seat of the League a Mandatory Commission to receive and examine the annual reports of the Mandatory Powers, and to assist the League in ensuring the observances of the terms of all Mandates.'

ARTICLE 23. (SOCIAL ACTIVITIES.)

Subject to and in accordance with the provisions of international conventions existing or hereafter to be agreed upon, the Members of the League:

(*a*) will endeavour to secure and maintain fair and humane conditions of labour for men, women, and children, both in their own countries and in all countries to which their commercial and industrial relations extend, and for that purpose will establish and maintain the necessary international organizations;

(*b*) undertake to secure just treatment of the native inhabitants of territories under their control;

(*c*) will entrust the League with the general supervision over the execution of agreements with regard to the traffic in women and children, and the traffic in opium and other dangerous drugs;

(*d*) will entrust the League with the general supervision of the trade in arms and ammunition with the countries in which the control of this traffic is necessary in the common interest;

(*e*) will make provision to secure and maintain freedom of communications and of transit and equitable treatment for the commerce of all Members of the League. In this connexion, the special necessities of the regions devastated during the war of

DRAFT ARTICLE 20 (*for* Article 23).

The High Contracting Parties will endeavour to secure and maintain fair and humane conditions of labour for men, women, and children, both in their own countries and in all countries to which their commercial and industrial relations extend; and to that end agree to establish as part of the organization of the League a permanent Bureau of Labour.

DRAFT ARTICLE 21 (*for* Article 23).

The High Contracting Parties agree that provision shall be made through the instrumentality of the League to secure and maintain freedom of transit and equitable treatment for the commerce of all States members of the League, having in mind, among other things, special arrangements with regard to the necessities of the regions devastated during the war of 1914–18.

1914–1918 shall be borne in mind;

(*f*) will endeavour to take steps in matters of international concern for the prevention and control of disease.

ARTICLE 24. (INTERNATIONAL BUREAUX.)

There shall be placed under the direction of the League all international bureaux already established by general treaties if the parties to such treaties consent. All such international bureaux and all commissions for the regulation of matters of international interest hereafter constituted shall be placed under the direction of the League.

In all matters of international interest which are regulated by general conventions but which are not placed under the control of international bureaux or commissions, the Secretariat of the League shall, subject to the consent of the Council and if desired by the parties, collect and distribute all relevant information and shall render any other assistance which may be necessary or desirable.

The Council may include as part of the expenses of the Secretariat the expenses of any bureau or commission which is placed under the direction of the League.

ARTICLE 25. (PROMOTION OF RED CROSS.)

The Members of the League agree to encourage and promote the establishment and co-operation of duly authorized voluntary national Red Cross organizations having as purposes the improvement of health, the prevention of disease, and the mitigation of suffering throughout the world.

DRAFT ARTICLE 22 (*for* Article 24).

The High Contracting Parties agree to place under the control of the League all international bureaux already established by general treaties if the parties to such treaties consent. Furthermore, they agree that all such international bureaux to be constituted in future shall be placed under the control of the League.

ARTICLE 26. (AMENDMENTS.)

* Amendments to this Covenant will take effect when ratified by the Members of the League whose Representatives compose the Council and by a majority of the Members of the League whose Representatives compose the Assembly.

No such Amendment shall bind any Member of the League which signifies its dissent therefrom, but in that case it shall cease to be a Member of the League.

DRAFT ARTICLE 26 (*for* Article 26).

Amendments to this Covenant will take effect when ratified by the States whose representatives compose the Executive Council and by three-fourths of the States whose representatives compose the Body of Delegates.

Note. It is probable that the word 'three-fourths' in the Draft was changed to 'a majority' by a slip in the Amended Covenant. The 1921 amendment to Article 26 is designed to meet this difficulty by a compromise.

* *Article 26, as amended, would read :*

Amendments to the present Covenant the text of which shall have been voted by the Assembly on a three-fourths majority, in which there shall be included the votes of all the Members of the Council represented at the meeting, will take effect when ratified by the Members of the League whose Representatives composed the Council when the vote was taken and by the majority of those whose Representatives form the Assembly.

If the required number of ratifications shall not have been obtained within twenty-two months after the vote of the Assembly, the proposed amendment shall remain without effect.

The Secretary-General shall inform the Members of the taking effect of an amendment.

Any Member of the League which has not at that time ratified the amendment is free to notify the Secretary-General within a year of its refusal to accept it, but in that case it shall cease to be a Member of the League.

APPENDIX II

AGREEMENTS CONNECTED WITH THE TURKISH EMPIRE

INTRODUCTION

THE ALLIED SECRET AGREEMENTS

THESE are four in number and all given in the text of this volume;

(i) *The Constantinople Agreement.* 18th March 1915. pp. 4–10.
(ii) *Secret Treaty of London.* 26th April 1915. pp. 10–13.
Relevant articles, pp. 12–13, 19–20.
(Complete text in Vol. V, pp. 384–93.)
(iii) *Sykes-Picot Agreement.* 16th May 1916. pp. 16–18.
(iv) *St. Jean de Maurienne.* 17th April 1917. pp. 18–20.
(Indications only.)

The Tripartite Agreement, signed 10th August 1920, has been published, of which the general tenor is given, pp. 22, 30, 34, 87n., 90–2, 112.

APPENDIX II. PART I

THE ANGLO-FRENCH SAN REMO OIL AGREEMENT

24TH–25TH APRIL 1920

The following is the complete text [1] of the agreement on the subject of oil supplies, signed at San Remo on 24th, confirmed 25th, April 1920:

By order of the two Governments of France and Great Britain, the undersigned representatives have resumed, by mutual consent, the consideration of an agreement regarding petroleum.

2. This agreement is based on the principles of cordial co-operation and reciprocity in those countries where the oil interests of the two nations can be usefully united. This memorandum relates to the following States or countries: Rumania, Asia Minor, territories of the old Russian Empire, Galicia, French Colonies, and British Crown Colonies.

3. The agreement may be extended to other countries by mutual consent.

4. *Rumania.*—The British and French Governments shall support their respective nationals in any common negotiations to be entered into with the Government of Rumania for—

(*a*) The acquisition of oil concessions, shares, or other interests belonging to former enemy subjects or bodies in Rumania which have been sequestrated, e.g. the Steaua Romana, Concordia, Vega, etc., which constituted in that country the oil groups of the Deutsche Bank and the Disconto Gesellschaft, together with any other interests that may be obtainable.

(*b*) Concessions over oil lands belonging to the Rumanian State.

5. All shares belonging to former enemy concessions which can be secured and all other advantages derived from these negotiations shall be divided, 50 per cent. to British interests and 50 per cent. to French interests. It is understood that in the company or companies to be formed to undertake the management and the exploitation of the said shares, concessions, and other advantages, the two countries shall have the same proportion of 50 per cent. in all capital subscribed, as well as in representatives on the board and voting power.

6. *Territories of the late Russian Empire.*—In the territories which belonged to the late Russian Empire, the two Governments will give their joint support to their respective nationals in their joint efforts to obtain petroleum concessions and facilities to export, and to arrange delivery of petroleum supplies.

7. *Mesopotamia.*—The British Government undertake to grant to the French Government or its nominee 25 per cent. of the net output of crude oil at current market rates which His Majesty's Government may secure from the Mesopotamian oil fields, in the event of their being developed by Government action; or in the event of a private petroleum company being used to develop the Mesopotamian oil fields, the British Government will place at the disposal of the French Government a share of 25 per cent. in such company. The price to be paid for such

[1] Miscellaneous, No. 11 (1920). Cmd. 675, also pp. 181–3.

participation to be no more than that paid by any of the other participants to the said petroleum company. It is also understood that the said petroleum company shall be under permanent British control.

8. It is agreed that, should the private petroleum company be constituted as aforesaid, the native Government or other native interests shall be allowed, if they so desire, to participate up to a maximum of 20 per cent. of the share capital of the said company. The French shall contribute one-half of the first 10 per cent. of such native participation and the additional participation shall be provided by each participant in proportion to his holdings.

9. The British Government agree to support arrangements by which the French Government may procure from the Anglo-Persian Company supplies of oil, which may be piped from Persia to the Mediterranean through any pipe line which may have been constructed within the French mandated territory and in regard to which France has given special facilities, up to the extent of 25 per cent. of the oil so piped, on such terms and conditions as may be mutually agreed between the French Government and the Anglo-Persian Company.

10. In consideration of the above-mentioned arrangements the French Government shall agree, if it is desired and as soon as application is made, to the construction of two separate pipe lines and railways necessary for their construction and maintenance and for the transport of oil from Mesopotamia and Persia through French spheres of influence to a port or ports on the Eastern Mediterranean. The port or ports shall be chosen in agreement between the two Governments.

11. Should such pipe line and railways cross territory within a French sphere of influence, France undertakes to give every facility for the rights of crossing without any royalty or wayleaves on the oil transported. Nevertheless, compensation shall be payable to the landowners for the surface occupied.

12. In the same way France will give facilities at the terminal port for the acquisition of the land necessary for the erection of depots, railways, refineries, loading wharfs, etc. Oil thus exported shall be exempt from export and transit dues. The material necessary for the construction of the pipe lines, railways, refineries, and other equipment shall also be free from import duties and wayleaves.

13. Should the said petroleum company desire to lay a pipe line and a railway to the Persian Gulf, the British Government will use its good offices to secure similar facilities for that purpose.

14. *North Africa and other Colonies.*—The French Government will give facilities to any Franco-British group or groups of good standing, which furnish the necessary guarantees and comply with French laws, for the acquisition of oil concessions in the French colonies, protectorates, and zones of influence, including Algeria, Tunis, and Morocco. It should be noted that the French Parliament has resolved that groups so formed must contain at least 67 per cent. French interests.

15. The French Government will facilitate the granting of any concessions in Algeria which are now under consideration as soon as the applicants have complied with all the requirements of the French laws.

16. *British Crown Colonies.*—In so far as existing regulations allow,

the British Government will give to French subjects who may wish to prospect and exploit petroliferous lands in the Crown Colonies similar advantages to those which France is granting to British subjects in the French colonies.

17. Nothing in this agreement shall apply to concessions which may be the subject of negotiations initiated by French or British interests.

18. This agreement has to-day been initialled by M. Philippe Berthelot and Professor Sir John Cadman, subject to confirmation by the French and British Prime Ministers respectively.

J. CADMAN.
P. BERTHELOT.

San Remo, *24th April*, 1920.
Confirmed:
D. LLOYD GEORGE.
A. MILLERAND.
25th April 1920.

APPENDIX II. PART II A

THE NATIONAL PACT OF ANGORA[1]

Adopted by certain Turkish Deputies in Constantinople
28th January 1920, and by Angora Assembly, 1921

The following is a translation of the preamble and the six articles of the pact as published in the Official Gazette:

PREAMBLE

The members of the Ottoman Chamber of Deputies recognize and affirm that the independence of the State and the future of the nation can be assured by complete respect for the following principles, which represent the maximum of sacrifice which can be undertaken in order to achieve a just and lasting peace, and that the continued existence of a stable Ottoman Sultanate and society is impossible outside of the aforesaid principles.

FIRST ARTICLE.—Inasmuch as it is necessary that the destinies of the portions of the Turkish Empire which are populated exclusively by an Arab majority, and which on the conclusion of the Armistice of 30th October, 1918, were in the occupation of enemy forces, should be determined in accordance with the votes which shall be freely given by the inhabitants, the whole of these parts, whether within or without the said Armistice line, which are inhabited by an Ottoman Moslem majority, united in religion, in race, and in aim, imbued with sentiments of mutual respect for each other and of sacrifice, and wholly respectful of each other's racial and social rights and surrounding conditions, form a whole which does not admit of division for any reason in truth or in ordinance.

SECOND ARTICLE.—We accept that in the case of the three *Sanjaks* (Batum, Kars, Ardahan) which united themselves by a general vote to the Mother Country when they first were free, recourse should again be had, if necessary, to a free and popular vote.

[1] *v.* pp. 32, 54, 97, 102, 108–9.

THIRD ARTICLE.—The determination of the juridical status of Western Thrace also, which has been made dependent on the Turkish peace, must be effected in accordance with the votes which shall be given by the inhabitants in complete freedom.

FOURTH ARTICLE.—The security of the city of Constantinople, which is the seat of the Caliphate of Islam, the capital of the Sultanate, and the headquarters of the Ottoman Government, must be protected from every danger. Provided this principle is maintained, whatever decision may be arrived at jointly by us and all other Governments concerned with regard to the opening of the Bosphorus to the commerce and traffic of the world is valid.

FIFTH ARTICLE.—The rights of minorities as defined in the Treaties concluded between the Entente Powers and their enemies and certain of their associates shall be confirmed by us, in reliance on the belief that the Moslem minorities in neighbouring countries will have the benefit of the same rights.

SIXTH ARTICLE.—It is a fundamental condition of our life and continued existence that we, like every country, should enjoy complete independence and liberty in the matter of assuring the means of our development, in order that our national and economic progress should be rendered possible, and that it should also be possible to conduct affairs in the form of a more modernized and regular administration. For this reason we are opposed to restrictions inimical to our development in political, financial, and other matters. The conditions of the settlement of our proved debts shall likewise not be contrary to these principles.

APPENDIX II. PART II B

ANGORA AGREEMENT (FRANCE), 20TH OCTOBER 1921

Dispatch from His Majesty's Ambassador at Paris, enclosing the Franco-Turkish Agreement signed at Angora on the 20th October 1921 [1]

(Translation.)

Enclosure No. 1.

Agreement signed at Angora on the 20*th October* 1921, *between M. Franklin-Bouillon, former Minister, and Yussuf Kemal Bey, Minister for Foreign Affairs of the Government of the Grand National Assembly of Angora.*

ARTICLE 1. The high contracting parties declare that from the date of the signature of the present agreement the state of war between them shall cease; the armies, the civil authorities and the people shall be immediately informed thereof.

ARTICLE 2. As soon as the present agreement has been signed, the respective prisoners of war and also all French and Turkish persons detained or imprisoned shall be set at liberty and conducted, at the cost of the party which detained them, to the nearest town which shall be designated for this purpose. The benefit of this article extends to all

[1] Parl. Paper (Cmd. 1556), 1921. Cp. pp. 33–5, 53–4, 166–7.

detained persons and prisoners of both parties, irrespective of the date and place of detention, of imprisonment or of capture.

ARTICLE 3. Within a maximum period of two months from the date of the signature of the present agreement, the Turkish troops shall withdraw to the north and the French troops to the south of the line specified in article 8.

ARTICLE 4. The evacuation and the occupation which shall take place within the period provided in article 3 shall be carried out according to a form to be decided upon by mutual agreement by a mixed commission appointed by the military commanders of the two parties.

ARTICLE 5. A complete amnesty shall be granted by the two contracting parties in the regions evacuated as soon as they are reoccupied.

ARTICLE 6. The Government of the Grand National Assembly of Turkey declares that the rights of minorities solemnly recognized in the National Covenant will be confirmed by it on the same basis as that established by the conversations on this subject between the *Entente* Powers, their enemies and certain of their Allies.

ARTICLE 7. A special administrative régime shall be established for the district of Alexandretta. The Turkish inhabitants of this district shall enjoy every facility for their cultural development. The Turkish language shall have official recognition.

ARTICLE 8. The line mentioned in Article 3 is fixed and determined as follows:

The frontier line shall start at a point to be selected on the Gulf of Alexandretta immediately to the south of the locality of Payas and will proceed generally towards Meidan-Ekbez (leaving the railway station and the locality to Syria); thence it will bend towards the south-east so as to leave the locality of Marsova to Syria and that of Karnaba as well as the town of Killis to Turkey; thence it will join the railway at the station of Choban-bey. Then it will follow the Bagdad Railway, of which the track as far as Nisibin will remain on Turkish territory; thence it will follow the old road between Nisibin and Jeziret-ibn-Omar where it will join the Tigris. The localities of Nisibin and Jeziret-ibn-Omar as well as the road will remain Turkish; but the two countries shall have the same rights to the use of this road.

The stations and sidings of the section between Choban-bey and Nisibin shall belong to Turkey as forming parts of the track of the railway.

A commission comprising delegates of the two parties will be constituted, within a period of one month from the signature of the present agreement, to determine the above-mentioned line. This commission shall begin its labours within the same period.

ARTICLE 9. The tomb of Suleiman Shah, the grandfather of the Sultan Osman, founder of the Ottoman dynasty (the tomb known under the name of Turk Mezari), situated at Jaber-Kalesi shall remain, with its appurtenances, the property of Turkey, who may appoint guardians for it and may hoist the Turkish flag there.

ARTICLE 10. The Government of the Grand National Assembly of Turkey agrees to the transfer of the concession of the section of the Bagdad Railway between Bozanti and Nisibin as well as of the several branches constructed in the vilayet of Adana to a French group nominated by the French Government, with all the rights, privileges and advantages attached to the concessions, particularly as regards working and traffic.

Turkey shall have the right to transport troops by railway from Meidan-Ekbez to Choban-bey in Syrian territory and Syria shall have the right to transport troops by railway from Choban-bey to Nisibin in Turkish territory.

In principle no differential tariff shall be levied over this section and these branches. However, should a case arise, the two Governments reserve the right to examine by mutual agreement any departure from this rule which may become necessary.

Failing agreement, each party will resume its liberty of action.

ARTICLE 11. A mixed commission shall be constituted after the ratification of the present agreement with a view to the conclusion of a Customs Convention between Turkey and Syria. The terms and also the duration of this Convention shall be fixed by this commission. Until the conclusion of the above-mentioned Convention the two countries will preserve their liberty of action.

ARTICLE 12. The waters of Kuweik shall be shared between the city of Aleppo and the district to the north remaining Turkish in such a way as to give equitable satisfaction to the two parties.

The city of Aleppo may also organize, at its own expense, a water-supply from the Euphrates in Turkish territory in order to meet the requirements of the district.

ARTICLE 13. The inhabitants, whether settled or semi-nomadic, who enjoy rights of pasturage or who own property on one or other side of the line fixed in Article 8 shall continue to exercise their rights as in the past. They shall be able, for this purpose, freely and without payment of any duty of customs or of pasturage or any other tax, to transport from one side to the other of the line their cattle with their young, their implements, their tools, their seeds and their agricultural produce, it being well understood that they are liable for the payment of the imposts and taxes due to the country where they are domiciled.

Enclosure No. 2

Yussuf Kemal Bey to M. Franklin-Bouillon

Your Excellency, *Angora*, 20th *October* 1921.

I REJOICE in the hope that the agreement concluded between the Government of the Grand National Assembly of Turkey and the Government of the French Republic with a view to effect a definitive and durable peace will result in re-establishing and consolidating the close relations which formerly existed between the two nations, the Government of the French Republic endeavouring to settle in a spirit of cordial agreement all the questions relating to the independence and the sovereignty of Turkey.

The Government of the Grand Assembly, desirous on its part to promote the development of the material interests common to the two countries, authorizes me to inform you that it is disposed to grant the concession for the iron, chrome and silver mines in the Karshut valley for a period of ninety-nine years to a French group, which, within a period of five years from the date of the signature of the present agreement, must begin to work this concession through a company constituted in accordance with Turkish law, in which Turkish capital shall participate to the extent of 50 per cent.

In addition the Turkish Government is prepared to examine with the utmost goodwill other requests for concessions for mines, railways, ports and rivers which may be put forward by French groups, on condition that these requests are in accordance with the reciprocal interests of Turkey and of France.

On the other hand, Turkey desires to benefit from the collaboration of French specialist instructors in her professional schools. To this end, she will at a later date acquaint the French Government with the extent of her requirements.

Finally, Turkey hopes that after the conclusion of the agreement the French Government will authorize French capitalists to enter into economic and financial relations with the Government of the Grand National Assembly of Turkey.

I have, etc.
(Signed) YUSSUF KEMAL.

APPENDIX II. PART III A

MESOPOTAMIAN DRAFT MANDATE, 1921

The first draft presented to the League by Mr. Balfour, 7th December 1920, differs from the final in a few small particulars noted below.

FINAL DRAFT OF THE MANDATE FOR MESOPOTAMIA FOR THE APPROVAL OF THE COUNCIL OF THE LEAGUE OF NATIONS.[1]

THE COUNCIL OF THE LEAGUE OF NATIONS

Whereas by Article 132 of the Treaty of Peace signed at Sèvres on the tenth day of August, 1920, Turkey renounced in favour of the Principal Allied Powers all rights and title over Mesopotamia, and whereas by Article 94 of the said treaty the High Contracting Parties agreed that Mesopotamia should, in accordance with the fourth paragraph of Article 22 of Part I (Covenant of the League of Nations), be provisionally recognized as an independent State, subject to the rendering of administrative advice and assistance by a Mandatory until such time as it is able to stand alone, and that the determination of the frontiers of Mesopotamia, other than those laid down in the said treaty, and the selection of the Mandatory would be made by the Principal Allied Powers ;[2] and

[1] Parl. Paper, Cmd. 1500, 1921. This Mandate has been delayed for technical reasons. (*v.* pp. 189–91.)

[2] This preamble will now have to be altered (*v.* p. 37 n).

Whereas the Principal Allied Powers have selected His Britannic Majesty as Mandatory for Mesopotamia ; and

Whereas the terms of the Mandate in respect of Mesopotamia have been formulated in the following terms and submitted to the Council of the League for approval ; and

Whereas His Britannic Majesty has accepted the Mandate in respect of the said territories and undertaken to exercise it on behalf of the League of Nations in conformity with the following provisions ;

Hereby approves the terms of the said Mandate as follows :

ARTICLE 1. The Mandatory will frame within the shortest possible time, not exceeding three years from the date of the coming into force of this Mandate, an Organic Law for Mesopotamia, which shall be submitted to the Council of the League of Nations for approval, and shall, as soon as possible, be published by it. This Organic Law shall be framed in consultation with the native authorities, and shall take account of the rights, interests and wishes of all the populations inhabiting the mandated territory. It shall contain provisions designed to facilitate the progressive development of Mesopotamia as an independent State. Pending the coming into effect of the Organic Law, the administration of Mesopotamia shall be conducted in accordance with the spirit of this Mandate.

ARTICLE 2. The Mandatory may maintain armed forces [1] in the territories under his Mandate for the defence of these territories. Until the entry into force of the Organic Law and the re-establishment of public security, he may organize and employ local forces necessary for the maintenance of order and for the defence of these territories. Such local forces may only be recruited from the inhabitants of the territories under the Mandate.

The said local forces shall thereafter be responsible to the local authorities, subject always to the control to be exercised over these forces by the Mandatory. The Mesopotamian Government shall not employ them for other than the above-mentioned purposes, except with the consent of the Mandatory.[2]

Nothing in this article shall preclude the Mesopotamian Government from contributing to the cost of the maintenance of any forces maintained by the Mandatory in Mesopotamia.

The Mandatory shall be entitled at all times to use the roads, railways, and ports of Mesopotamia for the movement of armed forces and the carriage of fuel and supplies.

ARTICLE 3. The Mandatory shall be entrusted with the control of the foreign relations of Mesopotamia, and the right to issue exequaturs to consuls appointed by foreign Powers. It shall also be entitled to afford diplomatic and consular protection to citizens of Mesopotamia when outside its territorial limits.

ARTICLE 4. The Mandatory shall be responsible for seeing that no Mesopotamian territory shall be ceded or leased to or in any way placed under the control of the Government of any foreign Power.

[1] First draft ' troops '.

[2] In the first draft the last sentence runs ' over these forces by the Mandatory who shall not employ them for other than the above-mentioned purposes except with the consent of the Mesopotamian Government '.

ARTICLE 5. The immunities and privileges of foreigners, including the benefits of consular jurisdiction and protection as formerly enjoyed by Capitulation or usage in the Ottoman Empire, are definitely abrogated in Mesopotamia.

ARTICLE 6. The Mandatory shall be responsible for seeing that the judicial system established in Mesopotamia shall safeguard: (*a*) the interests of foreigners; (*b*) the law, and (to the extent deemed expedient) the jurisdiction now existing in Mesopotamia with regard to questions arising out of the religious beliefs of certain communities (such as the laws of Wakf and personal status). In particular the Mandatory agrees that the control and administration of Wakf shall be exercised in accordance with religious law and the dispositions of the founders.

ARTICLE 7. Pending the making of special extradition agreements with foreign Powers relating to Mesopotamia, the extradition treaties in force between foreign Powers and the Mandatory shall apply to Mesopotamia.

ARTICLE 8. The Mandatory will ensure to all complete freedom of conscience and the free exercise of all forms of worship, subject only to the maintenance of public order and morals. No discrimination of any kind shall be made between the inhabitants of Mesopotamia on the ground of race, religion or language. Instruction in and through the medium of the native languages of Mesopotamia shall be promoted by the Mandatory.

The right of each community to maintain its own schools for the education of its own members in its own language (while conforming to such educational requirements of a general nature as the Administration may impose) shall not be denied or impaired.

ARTICLE 9. Nothing in this Mandate shall be construed as conferring upon the Mandatory authority to interfere with the fabric or the management of the sacred shrines, the immunities of which are guaranteed.

ARTICLE 10. The Mandatory shall be responsible for exercising such supervision over missionary enterprise in Mesopotamia as may be required for the maintenance of public order and good government. Subject to such supervision, no measures shall be taken in Mesopotamia to obstruct or interfere with such enterprise or to discriminate against any missionary on the ground of his religion or nationality.

ARTICLE 11. The Mandatory must see that there is no discrimination in Mesopotamia against the nationals of any State member of the League of Nations (including companies incorporated under the laws of such State) as compared with the nationals of the Mandatory or of any foreign State in matters concerning taxation, commerce or navigation, the exercise of industries or professions, or in the treatment of merchant vessels or civil aircraft. Similarly, there shall be no discrimination in Mesopotamia against goods originating in or destined for any of the said States, and there shall be freedom of transit under equitable conditions across the mandated area.

Subject as aforesaid the Mesopotamian Government may on the advice of the Mandatory impose such taxes and customs duties as it may consider necessary and take such steps as it may think best to promote the development of the natural resources of the country and to safeguard the interests of the population.

Nothing in this article shall prevent the Mesopotamian Government on the advice of the Mandatory, from concluding a special customs arrangement with any State, the territory of which in 1914 was wholly included in Asiatic Turkey or Arabia.

ARTICLE 12. The Mandatory will adhere on behalf of Mesopotamia to any general international conventions already existing or that may be concluded hereafter with the approval of the League of Nations respecting the slave traffic, the traffic in arms and ammunition, and the traffic in drugs, or relating to commercial equality, freedom of transit and navigation, laws of aerial navigation, railways and postal, telegraphic and wireless communication, or artistic, literary or industrial property.

ARTICLE 13. The Mandatory will secure the co-operation of the Mesopotamian Government, so far as social, religious and other conditions may permit, in the execution of any common policy adopted by the League of Nations for preventing and combating disease, including diseases of plants and animals.

ARTICLE 14. The Mandatory will secure the enactment within twelve months from the coming into force of this Mandate, and will ensure the execution of a Law of Antiquities, based on the contents of Article 421 of Part XIII of the Treaty of Peace with Turkey. This law shall replace the former Ottoman Law of Antiquities, and shall ensure equality of treatment in the matter of archaeological research to the nationals of all States, members of the League of Nations.

ARTICLE 15. Upon the coming into force of the Organic Law an arrangement shall be made between the Mandatory and the Mesopotamian Government for settling the terms on which the latter will take over Public Works and other services of a permanent character, the benefit of which will pass to the Mesopotamian Government. Such arrangement shall be communicated to the Council of the League of Nations.

ARTICLE 16.[1] Nothing in this Mandate shall prevent the Mandatory from establishing a system of local autonomy for predominantly Kurdish areas in Mesopotamia as he may consider suitable.

ARTICLE 17. The Mandatory shall make to the Council of the League of Nations an annual report as to the measures taken during the year to carry out the provisions of the Mandate. Copies of all laws and regulations promulgated or issued during the year shall be communicated with the report.

ARTICLE 18. The consent of the Council of the League of Nations is required for any modification of the terms of the present Mandate, provided that in the case of any modification proposed by the Mandatory such consent may be given by a majority of the Council.

ARTICLE 19. If any dispute whatever should arise between the members of the League of Nations relating to the interpretation or the application of these provisions which cannot be settled by negotiation, this dispute shall be submitted to the Permanent Court of International Justice provided for by Article 14 of the Covenant of the League of Nations.

ARTICLE 20.[1] In the event of the termination of the Mandate

[1] Not in first draft.

conferred upon the Mandatory by this Declaration, the Council of the League of Nations shall make such arrangements as may be deemed necessary for securing under the guarantee of the League that the Mesopotamian Government will fully honour the financial obligations legally incurred by the Mandatory during the period of the Mandate, including the rights of public servants to pensions or gratuities.

The present copy shall be deposited in the archives of the League of Nations. Certified copies shall be forwarded by the Secretary-General of the League of Nations to all Powers Signatories of the Treaty of Peace with Turkey.

Made at the day of

APPENDIX II. PART III B

THE IRAQ TREATY, 12TH OCTOBER 1922 [1]

The following is the text of the Treaty signed at Baghdad on the 10th October 1922 between the British and Iraq Governments:

HIS BRITANNIC MAJESTY of the one part: and HIS MAJESTY THE KING OF IRAQ of the other part:

Whereas His Britannic Majesty has recognized Feisal Ibn Hussein as constitutional King of Iraq: and Whereas His Majesty the King of Iraq considers that it is to the interests of Iraq and will conduce to its rapid advancement that he should conclude a Treaty with His Britannic Majesty on the basis of alliance: and Whereas His Britannic Majesty is satisfied that the relations between himself and His Majesty the King of Iraq can now be better defined by such a Treaty of Alliance than by any other means:

For this purpose the High Contracting Parties have appointed as their Plenipotentiaries:

HIS MAJESTY THE KING OF THE UNITED KINGDOM OF GREAT BRITAIN AND IRELAND AND OF THE BRITISH DOMINIONS BEYOND THE SEAS, EMPEROR OF INDIA: Sir Percy Zachariah Cox, G.C.M.G., G.C.I.E., K.C.S.I., High Commissioner and Consul-General of His Britannic Majesty in Iraq:

HIS MAJESTY THE KING OF IRAQ: His Highness Sir Saiyid 'Abd-ur-Rahman, G.B.E., Prime Minister and Naqib-al-Ashraf, Baghdad:

Who, having communicated their full powers, found in good and due order, have agreed as follows:

ARTICLE 1. At the request of His Majesty the King of Iraq, His Britannic Majesty undertakes subject to the provisions of this Treaty to provide the State of Iraq with such advice and assistance as may be required during the period of the present Treaty, without prejudice to her national sovereignty. His Britannic Majesty shall be represented in Iraq by a High Commissioner and Consul-General assisted by the necessary staff.

ARTICLE 2. His Majesty the King of Iraq undertakes that for the period of the present Treaty no gazetted official of other than Iraq nationality shall be appointed in Iraq without the concurrence of His

[1] *v.* p. 188–91.

Britannic Majesty. A separate agreement shall regulate the numbers and conditions of employment of British officials so appointed in the Iraq Government.

ARTICLE 3. His Majesty the King of Iraq agrees to frame an Organic Law for presentation to the Constituent Assembly of Iraq and to give effect to the said law, which shall contain nothing contrary to the provisions of the present Treaty and shall take account of the rights, wishes and interests of all populations inhabiting Iraq. This Organic Law shall ensure to all complete freedom of conscience and the free exercise of all forms of worship, subject only to the maintenance of public order and morals. It shall provide that no discrimination of any kind shall be made between the inhabitants of Iraq on the ground of race, religion or language, and shall secure that the right of each community to maintain its own schools for the education of its own members in its own language, while conforming to such educational requirements of a general nature as the Government of Iraq may impose, shall not be denied or impaired. It shall prescribe the constitutional procedure, whether legislative or executive, by which decisions will be taken on all matters of importance, including those involving questions of fiscal, financial, and military policy.

ARTICLE 4. Without prejudice to the provisions of Articles 17 and 18 of this Treaty, His Majesty the King of Iraq agrees to be guided by the advice of His Britannic Majesty tendered through the High Commissioner on all important matters affecting the international and financial obligations and interests of His Britannic Majesty for the whole period of this Treaty. His Majesty the King of Iraq will fully consult the High Commissioner on what is conducive to a sound financial and fiscal policy and will ensure the stability and good organization of the finances of the Iraq Government so long as that Government is under financial obligations to the Government of His Britannic Majesty.

ARTICLE 5. His Majesty the King of Iraq shall have the right of representation in London and in such other capitals and places as may be agreed upon by the High Contracting Parties. Where His Majesty the King of Iraq is not represented he agrees to entrust the protection of Iraq nationals to His Britannic Majesty. His Majesty the King of Iraq shall himself issue exequaturs to representatives of Foreign Powers in Iraq after His Britannic Majesty has agreed to their appointment.

ARTICLE 6. His Britannic Majesty undertakes to use his good offices to secure the admission of Iraq to membership of the League of Nations as soon as possible.

ARTICLE 7. His Britannic Majesty undertakes to provide such support and assistance to the armed forces of His Majesty the King of Iraq as may from time to time be agreed by the High Contracting Parties. A separate agreement regulating the extent and conditions of such support and assistance shall be concluded between the High Contracting Parties and communicated to the Council of the League of Nations.

ARTICLE 8. No territory in Iraq shall be ceded or leased or in any way placed under the control of any Foreign Power; this shall not prevent His Majesty the King of Iraq from making such arrangements as may be necessary for the accommodation of foreign representatives and for the fulfilment of the provisions of the preceding Article.

ARTICLE 9. His Majesty the King of Iraq undertakes that he will accept and give effect to such reasonable provisions as His Britannic Majesty may consider necessary in judicial matters to safeguard the interests of foreigners in consequence of the non-application of the immunities and privileges enjoyed by them under capitulation or usage. These provisions shall be embodied in a separate agreement, which shall be communicated to the Council of the League of Nations.

ARTICLE 10. The High Contracting Parties agree to conclude separate agreements to secure the execution of any treaties, agreements or undertakings which His Britannic Majesty is under obligation to see carried out in respect of Iraq. His Majesty the King of Iraq undertakes to bring in any legislation necessary to ensure the execution of these agreements. Such agreements shall be communicated to the Council of the League of Nations.

ARTICLE 11. There shall be no discrimination in Iraq against the nationals of any State, member of the League of Nations, or of any State to which His Britannic Majesty has agreed by treaty that the same rights should be ensured as it would enjoy if it were a member of the said League (including companies incorporated under the laws of such State), as compared with British nationals or those of any foreign State in matters concerning taxation, commerce or navigation, the exercise of industries or professions, or in the treatment of merchant vessels or civil aircraft. Nor shall there be any discrimination in Iraq against goods originating in or destined for any of the said States. There shall be freedom of transit under equitable conditions across Iraq territory.

ARTICLE 12. No measure shall be taken in Iraq to obstruct or interfere with missionary enterprise or to discriminate against any missionary on the ground of his religious belief or nationality, provided that such enterprise is not prejudicial to public order and good government.

ARTICLE 13. His Majesty the King of Iraq undertakes to co-operate, in so far as social, religious, and other conditions may permit, in the execution of any common policy adopted by the League of Nations for preventing and combating disease, including diseases of plants and animals.

ARTICLE 14. His Majesty the King of Iraq undertakes to secure the enactment, within twelve months of the coming into force of this Treaty, and to ensure the execution of a Law of Antiquities based on the rules annexed to Article 421 of the Treaty of Peace signed at Sèvres on the 10th August 1920. This Law shall replace the former Ottoman Law of Antiquities, and shall ensure equality of treatment in the matter of archaeological research to the nationals of all States members of the League of Nations, and of any State to which His Britannic Majesty has agreed by treaty that the same rights should be ensured as it would enjoy if it were a member of the said League.

ARTICLE 15. A separate agreement shall regulate the financial relations between the High Contracting Parties. It shall provide, on the one hand, for the transfer by His Britannic Majesty's Government to the Government of Iraq of such works of public utility as may be agreed upon and for the rendering by His Britannic Majesty's Government of such financial assistance as may from time to time be considered necessary for Iraq, and, on the other hand, for the progressive liquidation by the Government of Iraq of all liabilities thus incurred. Such agreement shall be communicated to the Council of the League of Nations.

ARTICLE 16. So far as is consistent with his international obligations His Britannic Majesty undertakes to place no obstacle in the way of the association of the State of Iraq for customs or other purposes with such neighbouring Arab States as may desire it.

ARTICLE 17. Any difference that may arise between the High Contracting Parties as to the interpretation of the provisions of this Treaty shall be referred to the Permanent Court of International Justice provided for by Article 14 of the Covenant of the League of Nations. In such case, should there be any discrepancy between the English and Arabic texts of this Treaty, the English shall be taken as the authoritative version.

ARTICLE 18. This Treaty shall come into force as soon as it has been ratified by the High Contracting Parties after its acceptance by the Constituent Assembly, and shall remain in force for twenty years, at the end of which period the situation shall be examined and if the High Contracting Parties are of opinion that the Treaty is no longer required it shall be terminated. Termination shall be subject to confirmation by the League of Nations unless before that date Article 7 of this Treaty has come into effect, in which case notice of termination shall be communicated to the Council of the League of Nations. Nothing shall prevent the High Contracting Parties from reviewing from time to time the provisions of this Treaty, and those of the separate Agreements arising out of Articles 7, 10, and 15, with a view to any revision which may seem desirable in the circumstances then existing, and any modification which may be agreed upon by the High Contracting Parties shall be communicated to the Council of the League of Nations.

The ratifications shall be exchanged at Baghdad.

The present Treaty has been drawn up in English and Arabic. One copy in each language will remain deposited in the archives of the Iraq Government, and one copy in each language in those of the Government of His Britannic Majesty.

In witness of which the respective Plenipotentiaries have signed the present Treaty and have affixed thereto their seals. Done at Baghdad in duplicate this 10th day of October One thousand nine hundred and twenty-two of the Christian Era, corresponding with the 19th day of Sofar, One thousand three hundred and forty Hijrah.

P. Z. COX, His Britannic Majesty's High Commissioner in Iraq.

'ABD-UR-RAHMAN, Naqib-al-Ashraf of Baghdad and Prime Minister of the Iraq Government.

[*Note.*—On the 3rd May, 1923, Mr. Baldwin announced in the House of Commons what were, in fact, certain amendments to the Treaty, which have been embodied in a protocol signed by the Iraq and British representatives. The effects of these are that, notwithstanding Article 18, 'the present Treaty shall terminate upon Iraq becoming a member of the League of Nations, and in any case not later than four years from the ratification of the peace with Turkey'. The British Government offer their good offices with the League on the fulfilment of two conditions : (i) Delimitation of the frontiers of Iraq and (ii) the establishment of a stable government in accordance with the Organic Law. The Treaty was still unratified in October, 1923.]

APPENDIX III

POLAND AND GERMANY

THE UPPER SILESIAN PLEBISCITE AND AWARD[1]

PART I. ARTICLES 88 AND 90 OF THE TREATY OF VERSAILLES

The governing clauses, under which the plebiscite was taken, are here given. The fourth section of the Annex was construed as permitting out-voters to vote (i.e. persons born in Upper Silesia and resident in other parts of Germany). This conclusion prevailed, though hotly contested by the French. It increased the German vote by over 100,000 votes.

ARTICLE 88

In the portion of Upper Silesia included within the boundaries described below, the inhabitants will be called upon to indicate by a vote whether they wish to be attached to Germany or to Poland: [description of boundary follows, *v.* map opp. p. 264].

The régime under which this plebiscite will be taken and given effect to is laid down in the Annex hereto.

The Polish and German Governments hereby respectively bind themselves to conduct no prosecutions on any part of their territory and to take no exceptional proceedings for any political action performed in Upper Silesia during the period of the régime laid down in the Annex hereto and up to the settlement of the final status of the country.

Germany hereby renounces in favour of Poland all rights and title over the portion of Upper Silesia lying beyond the frontier line fixed by the Principal Allied and Associated Powers as the result of the plebiscite.

Annex

1.

Within fifteen days from the coming into force of the present Treaty the German troops and such officials as may be designated by the Commission set up under the provisions of paragraph 2 shall evacuate the plebiscite area. Up to the moment of the completion of the evacuation they shall refrain from any form of requisitioning in money or in kind and from all acts likely to prejudice the material interests of the country.

Within the same period the Workmens' and Soldiers' Councils which have been constituted in this area shall be dissolved. Members of such Councils who are natives of another region and are exercising their functions at the date of the coming into force of the present Treaty, or who have gone out of office since March 1, 1919, shall be evacuated.

All military or semi-military unions formed in the said area by inhabitants of the district shall be immediately disbanded. All members of such military organizations who are not domiciled in the said area shall be required to leave it.

2.

The plebiscite area shall be immediately placed under the authority of an International Commission of four members to be designated by the following Powers: the United States of America, France, the British Empire and

[1] *v.* p. 265.

Italy. It shall be occupied by troops belonging to the Allied and Associated Powers, and the German Government undertakes to give facilities for the transference of these troops to Upper Silesia.

3.

The Commission shall enjoy all the powers exercised by the German or the Prussian Government, except those of legislation or taxation. It shall also be substituted for the government of the province and the *Regierungsbezirk*.

It shall be within the competence of the Commission to interpret the powers hereby conferred upon it and to determine to what extent it shall exercise them, and to what extent they shall be left in the hands of the existing authorities.

Changes in the existing laws and the existing taxation shall only be brought into force with the consent of the Commission.

The Commission will maintain order with the help of the troops which will be at its disposal, and, to the extent which it may deem necessary, by means of gendarmerie recruited among the inhabitants of the country.

The Commission shall provide immediately for the replacement of the evacuated German officials and, if occasion arises, shall itself order the evacuation of such authorities and proceed to the replacement of such local authorities as may be required.

It shall take all steps which it thinks proper to ensure the freedom, fairness and secrecy of the vote. In particular, it shall have the right to order the expulsion of any person who may in any way have attempted to distort the result of the plebiscite by methods of corruption or intimidation.

The Commission shall have full power to settle all questions arising from the execution of the present clauses. It shall be assisted by technical advisers chosen by it from among the local population.

The decisions of the Commission shall be taken by a majority vote.

4.

The vote shall take place at such date as may be determined by the Principal Allied and Associated Powers, but not sooner than six months or later than eighteen months after the establishment of the Commission in the area.

The right to vote shall be given to all persons without distinction of sex who :

(*a*) Have completed their twentieth year on the 1st January of the year in which the plebiscite takes place.

(*b*) Were born in the plebiscite area or have been domiciled there since a date to be determined by the Commission, which shall not be subsequent to the 1st January, 1919, or who have been expelled by the German authorities and have not retained their domicile there.

Persons convicted of political offences shall be enabled to exercise their right of voting.

Every person will vote in the commune where he is domiciled or in which he was born, if he has not retained his domicile in the area.

The result of the vote will be determined by communes according to the majority of votes in each commune.

5.

On the conclusion of the voting, the numbers of votes cast in each commune will be communicated by the Commission to the Principal Allied and Associated Powers, with a full report as to the taking of the vote and a recommendation as to the line which ought to be adopted as the frontier of Germany in Upper Silesia. In this recommendation regard will be paid to the wishes of the inhabitants as shown by the vote, and to the geographical and economic conditions of the locality.

6.

As soon as the frontier has been fixed by the Principal Allied and Associated Powers, the German authorities will be notified by the International Commission that they are free to take over the administration of the territory which it is recognized should be German ; the said authorities must proceed to do so within one month of such notification and in the manner prescribed by the Commission.

Within the same period and in the manner prescribed by the Commission, the Polish Government must proceed to take over the administration of the territory which it is recognized should be Polish.

When the administration of the territory has been provided for by the German and Polish authorities respectively, the powers of the Commission will terminate.

The cost of the army of occupation, and expenditure by the Commission, whether in discharge of its own functions or in the administration of the territory, will be a charge on the area.

ARTICLE 90

Poland undertakes to permit for a period of fifteen years the exportation to Germany of the products of the mines in any part of Upper Silesia transferred to Poland in accordance with the present Treaty.

Such products shall be free from all export duties or other charges or restrictions on exportation.

Poland agrees to take such steps as may be necessary to secure that any such products shall be available for sale to purchasers in Germany on terms as favourable as are applicable to like products sold under similar conditions to purchasers in Poland or in any other country.

Note. The results of the plebiscite were as follows :

The Supreme Council, having failed to agree on the question of partition, appealed to the Council of the League, 12th August 1921.

APPENDIX III. PART II
OFFICIAL FIGURES OF THE PLEBISCITE

RÉSULTATS DÉFINITIFS DU PLÉBISCITE

	Inscrits.	*Votants.*	*Polonais.*	*Allemands.*
A. Districts du nord et de l'ouest :				
Kreuzburg	46,177	45,317	1,785	43,447
Rosenberg	35,976	35,108	11,150	23,857
Oppeln-Ville	22,930	21,984	1,908	20,816
Oppeln-Campagne	82,715	81,196	24,727	56,260
Lublinitz	29,981	29,195	13,679	15,454
Kosel et Ober-Glogau	88,389	86,415	16,717	67,476
Leobschutz	66,697	65,428	259	65,128
Ratibor-Ville	25,336	24,675	2,227	22,291
Ratibor-Campagne	45,900	45,052	18,516	26,354
Total	444,101	434,370	90,968	341,083
B. Districts du sud :				
Rybnik	81,985	80,435	52,347	27,918
Pless	73,781	72,277	53,378	18,675
Total	155,786	152,712	105,725	46,593

Brought forward	155,786	152,712	105,725	46,593
C. Bassin industriel :				
Beuthen-Ville . . .	42,990	40,091	10,101	29,890
Beuthen-Campagne . .	109,747	107,126	63,021	43,677
Gleiwitz . . .	41,949	40,700	8,558	32,029
Kattowitz-Ville . .	28,531	26,715	3,900	22,744
Kattowitz-Campagne .	122,390	119,458	66,119	52,892
Koenigshutte . . .	44,052	42,758	10,764	31,864
Zabrze (Hindenburg) .	90,793	89,152	43,256	45,212
Total . . .	480,452	466,000	205,719	258,338
D. Districts du centre :				
Gross-Strehlitz . .	46,528	45,590	23,046	22,415
Tost	48,106	47,435	27,198	20,098
Tarnowitz . . .	45,561	44,739	27,513	17,078
Total . . .	140,195	137,764	77,757	59,591
Total général . .	1,220,514	1,190,846	479,359	707,605

Les chiffres sont reproduits tels qu'ils figurent dans les documents officiels, bien que les totaux généraux ne correspondent pas absolument à la somme des résultats par districts.

APPENDIX III. PART III. THE RECOMMENDATION OF THE COUNCIL OF THE LEAGUE, 12TH OCTOBER 1921[1]

The question of Upper Silesia was submitted to the Council of the League of Nations in a letter dated the 12th August and signed by M. Briand on behalf of the Supreme Council of the Principal Allied Powers.

The letter announced the decision which had been arrived at by the Supreme Council 'in pursuance of Article 11, paragraph 2 of the Covenant, to submit to the Council of the League of Nations the difficulties attending the fixing of the frontier between Germany and Poland in Upper Silesia, and to request it to be so good as to inform the Supreme Council of the solution which it recommends as to the delimitation of the frontier which the Principal Allied and Associated Powers should adopt.'

In a Note on the history of the question, dated the 24th August, M. Briand added that : '. . . each of the Governments represented on the Supreme Council had, in the course of the discussions, formally undertaken to accept the solution recommended by the Council of the League.'

The Council, at its meeting on the 29th August, decided to accept this invitation. It has made the weighty problem which was submitted to it the subject of long deliberations and thorough investigation. It has endeavoured to interpret faithfully and in an equitable spirit the provisions of the Treaty of Versailles with regard to Upper Silesia. The Council, being convinced that its duty was above all to endeavour

[1] The text is from the *League of Nations Official Journal*, pp. 1224–32.
[1] *v.* pt. IV, p. 623 n.

to find a solution in conformity with the wishes of the inhabitants, as expressed by the plebiscite, while taking into account the geographical and economic situation of the various districts, has been led to the conclusion that it is necessary to divide the industrial region of Upper Silesia. Owing to the geographical distribution of the population and the mixture of the racial elements, any division of this district must inevitably result in leaving relatively large minorities on both sides of the line and in separating important interests.

In these circumstances, the Council considered that it would be desirable to take measures to guarantee, during a provisional period of readjustment, the continuity of the economic life of this region, which, owing to the density of its population, the number of its industrial undertakings, the closely-woven network of its means of communication, possesses the character of a vast agglomeration. It was also of the opinion that it would be desirable to provide for the protection of minorities.

Such are the general principles by which the Council was governed.

The Council carefully examined various solutions for giving accurate and faithful expression to the results of the plebiscite.

It recognized that solutions based on calculations of the proportion of votes would give results which would constitute an injustice for one side or the other, and it endeavoured to find a system which, when applied, would assign to each State a number of electors not differing appreciably from the total number of votes given in its favour, and which would, at the same time, as far as possible equalize and reduce the minorities.

Guided by the above considerations, as well as by the geographical and economic considerations referred to in the Treaty, the Council came to the conclusion that the most equitable solution would be obtained by the frontier line which is described in Appendix No. I,[1] and the adoption of which it unanimously decided to recommend.

The measures which the Council considers necessary in order to ensure the continuity of the economic and social existence of Upper Silesia, and to reduce to a minimum the inconveniences of the period of readjustment, are chiefly designed with the following objects:

To preserve, for a certain time, for the industries of the territory separated from Germany their former markets, and to ensure the supplies of raw material and manufactured products which are indispensable to these industries; to avoid the economic disturbances which would be caused by the immediate substitution of the Polish mark for the German mark as the sole legal currency in the territory assigned to Poland; to prevent the working of the railways serving Upper Silesia from being affected by the shifting of the political frontier; to regulate the supplies of water and electricity; to maintain freedom of movement for individuals across the new frontier; to guarantee respect for private property; to guarantee, as far as possible, to the

[1] This Appendix is not included. The Conference of Ambassadors adopted the frontier line recommended by the Council of the League (see *infra*).

workers that they shall not lose, in the portion of territory assigned to Poland, the advantages which were secured to them by German social legislation and by their Trades Union organization; and, finally, to ensure the protection of minorities upon the basis of an equitable reciprocity.

The solution of these problems should be achieved by means of arrangements effected under the form of a general Convention between Germany and Poland. The Treaty of Versailles has provided, in several analogous cases, for Conventions of this kind. As regards Upper Silesia, the Treaty has regulated certain questions by means of special provisions.

Article 92 stipulated, moreover, that 'further agreements shall regulate all questions arising out of the cession of the above territory which are not regulated by the present Treaty'.

The conclusion between the parties of a general Convention which will place Upper Silesia under a special régime during the transitional period seems to correspond to the intentions already expressed by the States concerned. Both Germany and Poland have, indeed, already considered the establishment of special institutions for this region.

With a view to facilitating the preparation and to supervising the application of the temporary measures, of which a summary has been given above, and which should be incorporated in a general Convention, the Council considers that it is necessary to set up a Commission composed of an equal number of Germans and Poles from Upper Silesia, and of a President of another nationality, who might be designated by the Council of the League of Nations. This Commission might be called the 'Upper Silesian Mixed Commission'. It would be essentially an advisory organ.

Further, it would also be expedient to constitute an arbitral tribunal to settle any private disputes which might be occasioned by the application of the temporary measures.

All disputes in connexion with the carrying out and the interpretation of the general Convention should be settled in conformity with the provisions of this Convention and, where necessary, with the Covenant of the League of Nations.

A certain time will elapse before the temporary régime referred to above can be definitively adopted and put in force. It will be for the Principal Allied Powers to take all measures necessitated by this preliminary period.

A Frontier Delimitation Commission should mark out the course of the frontier on the spot. It will be the duty of the Inter-Allied Commission already in existence to take the necessary measures for the maintenance of order during this preliminary period.

Finally, it is important that the Mixed Commission referred to above should be appointed without delay in order that it may give its assistance to the Inter-Allied Commission, which, taking into account the provisions of paragraph 6 of the Annex to Article 88 of the Treaty of Versailles, will take measures for preparing the transition from the present situation to the provisional régime.

The Council of the League of Nations has the honour to communicate to the Supreme Council a Report, which is annexed,[1] containing a statement of the principles which, in the opinion of the Council, would serve as a basis for the general Convention between the parties.

A second annexed Report deals, in the same spirit, with the problems of nationality, domicile, and the protection of minorities, the solution of which constitutes an essential condition for the maintenance of economic life in Upper Silesia.[1]

The Council considers the above proposals with regard to economic conditions as forming a unity. The Council is convinced that this scheme, taken as a whole, and after certain necessary precisions have been introduced, will safeguard the interests of the population, the sacrifices which it requires from each of the Governments being compensated for by the guarantees which it affords in favour of such of their nationals as are to be transferred to another sovereignty.

With regard to the establishment of the organization referred to, and also with regard to anything else which will facilitate the carrying out of the programme, the Council of the League of Nations remains entirely at the disposal of the Supreme Council.

PART IV. THE UPPER SILESIAN AWARD, AS CONFIRMED BY THE CONFERENCE OF AMBASSADORS, 20TH OCTOBER 1921[2]

The British Empire, France, Italy, and Japan, signatories, together with the United States of America, as Principal Allied and Associated Powers, of the Treaty of Peace of Versailles :

Whereas, by the terms of the last paragraph of Article 88 of the Treaty of Peace of Versailles, they are entrusted with the duty of fixing, in that part of Upper Silesia in which a plebiscite was to be held, the frontier-line between Germany and Poland resulting from this plebiscite ;

Whereas, on March 20 1921, a vote was taken under the conditions laid down by the Annex to the aforesaid Article ; and

Whereas, in view of the results of the voting which took place by communes, and of the geographical and economic situation of the localities, the cession of the districts concerned raises certain problems which it is important to settle ;

Now, therefore, after having obtained the opinion of the Council of the League of Nations,

Decide that :

I. The frontier between Germany and Poland, in the part of Upper Silesia described in Article 88 of the Treaty of Peace of Versailles, is defined as follows :

The frontier-line follows[3] the Oder from the point where that river enters Upper Silesia as far as Niebotschau ;

[1] These two Reports are not inserted. The text of the decision taken by the Conference of Ambassadors (see [1] pt. III, p. 620) is almost identical with that of the two Reports submitted by the Council of the League. The differences between the two texts are shown in foot-notes.

[2] The text is the decision of the Conference of Ambassadors taken the 20th October 1921. Save for the small variations noted it is identical with that of the Council of the League.

[3] Text of the Council of the League : *would follow*.

It then runs [1] north-east, leaving in Polish territory the communes of Hohenbirken, Wilhelmsthal, Raschutz, Adamowitz, Bogunitz, Lissek, Summin, Zwonowitz, Chwallenczitz, Ochojetz, Wilcza (upper and lower), Kriewald, Knurow, Gieraltowitz, Preiswitz, Makoschau, Kunzendorf, Paulsdorf, Ruda, Orzegow, Schlesiengrube, Hohenlinde; and leaving in German territory the communes of Ostrog, Markowitz, Babitz, Gurek, Stodoll, Niederdorf, Pilchowitz, Nieborowitzer Hammer, Nieborowitz, Schönwald, Ellguth-Zabrze, Sosnica, Mathesdorf, Zaborze, Biskupitz, Bobrek, Schomberg;

Thence it passes [2] between Rossberg (which falls to Germany) and Birkenhain (which falls to Poland);

Thence it runs north-west,[3] leaving in German territory the communes of Karf, Mieschowitz, Stollarzowitz, Friedrichswille, Ptakowitz, Larischhof, Miedar, Hanusek, Neudorf-Tworog, Kottenlust, Potemba, Keltsch, Zawadski, Pluder-Petershof, Klein-Lagiewnik, Skrzidlowitz, Gwosdzian, Dzielna, Cziasnau, Sorowski, and leaving in Polish territory the communes of Scharley, Radzionkau, Trockenberg, Neu-Repten, Alt-Repten, Alt-Tarnowitz, Rybna, Piassetzna, Boruschowitz, Mikoleska, Drathhammer, Bruschiek, Wüstenhammer, Kokottek, Koschmieder, Pawonkau, Spiegelhof (Gutsbezirk), Gross-Lagiewnik, Glinitz, Kochschutz, Lissau.

To the north of the latter place, it coincides with the former frontier between Germany and Russia as far as the point where that frontier joins the frontier between Germany and Poland, as laid down in Article 27 of the Treaty of Versailles.[4]

The Delimitation Commission provided for in Article 87 of the Treaty of Versailles will mark out the frontier on the spot. It will begin its work at once.

II. The German and Polish Governments will conclude, as early as possible and in accordance with the last paragraph of Article 92 of the Treaty of Peace, a Convention to give effect to the following provisions: [5]

A. *Railways.*—The administration of railway and tramway systems which belong to private concerns or municipalities shall continue to be governed by the terms of their concessions, as regards their rights and obligations. The railway system of the Schlesische Kleinbahn Aktiengesellschaft shall continue to be operated as a single unit for a period of fifteen years.

For the German State railways, both normal and narrow gauge, a joint system of operation shall be put into force in the plebiscite area,

[1] Text of the Council of the League: *it would then run.*

[2] Text of the Council of the League: *it would pass.*

[3] Text of the Council of the League: *and would take a north-westerly direction.*

[4] Text of the Council of the League: To the North of the *last* place it *would coincide* with the former frontier *of the German Empire as far as the point where the latter frontier joins the frontier already fixed between Germany and Poland.*

[5] Instead of the beginning of para. II, the text of the Council of the League has:
Transitional measures of an Economic Nature: The following provisions are designed to ensure continuity in the economic life of Upper Silesia after the partition, and to reduce to a minimum the difficulties of the period of adaptation.

for a period of fifteen years. The amount of rolling-stock allotted to the plebiscite area shall be determined in accordance with Article 371 of the Treaty of Versailles.

Railway rates shall be uniform. In conformity with Article 365 of the Treaty of Versailles, any special tariff in force between the German territory and a point within the plebiscite area shall apply to the whole plebiscite area.

The benefit of any special rate in force in the plebiscite area shall extend to goods of the same kind coming from or going to Poland, Germany or any other country.

The time-tables shall be drawn up in accordance with the needs of industry, and the delay to workers' trains crossing the frontier shall be as short as possible.

The administration of the State insurance and social insurance of employees of the Silesian railway system shall be undertaken by that system.

A single accounts office shall be set up for the whole system to deal with all revenue and expenditure, including the cost of maintenance of the permanent way and rolling-stock and sums set aside on account of depreciation. Expenses of new construction shall be charged to a separate account and shall be borne by the State on whose territory they are carried out.

The profits or deficits shall be divided between the two countries in proportion to the length of the line belonging to each and the amount of traffic.

B. *Water and Electric Power.*—In so far as the territory which comprises the existing water supply systems has not been entirely allotted to one of the two countries, in default of a special agreement between the parties, the existing systems shall be maintained. For this purpose a system of reciprocal obligation shall be established. The reserve water supply of the Tarnowitz and Olkucz district shall be at the disposal of the whole territory of Upper Silesia, under equitable conditions. The 'Oberschlesische Elektrizitätswerke' shall continue to operate as at present for a period of three years. After this the Polish Government may purchase the Chorsow power station and the system dependent thereon.

The above company shall furnish electricity on the same terms to both parts of the territory, so long as a Polish company shall not have been established.

C. *Monetary System.*—During a period which shall not exceed 15 years, the German mark shall remain the only legal unit of currency in the plebiscite area.

The two Governments may decide by common agreement to modify this system before the expiration of this period. Failing an agreement between the two Governments and in case a modification of the monetary system should become necessary, the Mixed Commission mentioned below [1] will fix the date from which the German mark shall cease to be the only legal unit of currency.

D. *Postal Services.*—During the period in which the German

[1] These *three* words are omitted from the text of the Council of the League. (*Editorial Note.* Probably *two* is meant. The note given is from League of Nations' Official Journal, December, 1921, p. 1228).

monetary system is maintained in the Polish zone, the postal, telegraph, and telephone charges shall be fixed in German currency.

E. *Customs Régime.*—The Customs frontier will be made to coincide with the new political frontier as soon as the latter has been fixed.

The German and Polish Customs law and Customs tariffs shall be applied, with the following exceptions:

1. During a period of six months, goods coming from other countries destined for the plebiscite area, on which the Customs duties levied at the German or Polish frontier have been paid before the date of the partition of Upper Silesia, shall cross the frontier free of duty.

2. During a period of fifteen years the natural products which originate in and come from one of the two zones of the plebiscite area, and are destined for consumption or use in the other zone, shall cross the frontier free of duty.

3. (*a*) During a period of six months, raw, half-manufactured and unfinished products of the industrial establishments of one of the two zones of the plebiscite area, destined to be used or finished in the industrial establishments of the other zone, shall cross the frontier free of duty. The permits issued for the entry of these products shall mention the names of the consignors and consignees.

(*b*) During a period of fifteen years, raw, half-manufactured and unfinished products originating in and coming from the industrial establishments of one of the two zones of the plebiscite area, which are to be finished in the industrial establishments of the other zone, shall cross the frontier free of duty when these products are intended for reimportation into the country of origin. The permits issued for the entry of these products shall mention the names of the consignors and the consignees.

4. In conformity with Article 268 of the Treaty of Versailles, natural or manufactured products which originate in and come from the Polish zone of the plebiscite area shall, on importation into German Customs territory, be exempt from all Customs duty during a period of three years. The period of three years shall[1] be reckoned from the notification of the delimitation of the frontier to Germany and to Poland.

With regard to the export regulations, the two countries shall undertake to facilitate during a period of fifteen years the export from their respective territories of such products as are indispensable for the industry of either zone of the plebiscite area, by supplying the necessary export licences and by authorizing the execution of contracts entered into between private individuals, it being understood that the entrance duties shall be paid by these goods upon their importation into German or Polish territory, apart from the exceptions detailed in the foregoing paragraphs.

Any arrangement with regard to the Customs régime on the new Polono-German frontier in Upper Silesia, which is not an application of the principle stated above, shall be considered as an ordinary commercial agreement between Poland and Germany.

[1] Text of the Council of the League: *should.*

F. *Coal. Products of the Mines.*—In conformity with Article 90 of the Treaty of Versailles, Poland shall permit for a period of 15 years, dating from the definitive allocation of the territory, the exportation to Germany of the products of the mines in the Polish zone of the plebiscite area.

As regards coal, account shall be taken in the application of this Article of the provisions of the different Treaties of Peace, and of the international decisions and agreements, between Germany, Poland, and the countries directly or indirectly concerned in the importation of coal from Upper Silesia, which impose obligations on Germany and Poland in respect of coal.

Germany shall permit for a period of 15 years the exportation to the Polish zone of the plebiscite area, of the products of the mines in its territory, under the conditions laid down in Article 90 of the Treaty of Versailles. The quantities of the products of the mines to which this provision shall apply shall be calculated on the basis of the average exchange of these products in the years 1911 to 1913.

G. *Employers' and Workers' Federations.*—The German and Polish Governments shall recognize for a period of 15 years the unions of employers and workers whose activities take place within the plebiscite area. These unions may enter into collective contracts throughout the whole plebiscite area.

H. *Social Insurance.*—The transfer of the funds of German social and State insurances to Poland, in so far as concerns the portion of Upper Silesia assigned to her, shall take place in conformity with the provisions and conditions of Article 312 of the Treaty of Versailles.

The beneficiaries of social and State insurance organisations will receive all the compensations and pensions which have been guaranteed to them.

The Polish Government shall establish, as soon as possible for the Polish zone, special insurance organizations and special jurisdiction for administrative matters and for the hearing of cases.

The local benefit societies, whether in the Polish zone or in the whole of the plebiscite area (Oberschlesischer Knappschaftsverein, Oberschlesische Bergbauhilfskasse, etc), shall be maintained for a period of 15 years, unless the two Governments agree to divide them at an earlier date.

I. *Movement between Zones.*—During a period of 15 years, any inhabitant regularly domiciled in the plebiscite area, or having a regular or professional occupation therein, shall receive a circulation permit free of payment, which will permit him to cross the frontier without other formalities.

J. *General Provisions.*—The provisions in force in the plebiscite area, especially with regard to mining, industrial or commercial undertakings and the existing labour—legislation including the systems of inspection—shall remain in force in the portion of the plebiscite area assigned to Poland until such time as Poland shall have passed, in regard to these matters, legislation applicable to the whole of its territory, which may be substituted for the above. Nevertheless, it is understood that Poland shall have the right to introduce in the Polish Silesian zone any modifications Germany shall see fit to adopt in her territory.

Without prejudice to Article 256 of the Treaty of Peace, the two countries shall recognize and respect, in the territory which shall be allotted to them, rights of all kinds—in particular, concessions and privileges acquired at the date of the partition by individuals, companies or other legal entities.

Poland shall renounce for a period of 15 years the powers granted by Articles 92 and 297 [1] as regards the expropriation of industrial undertakings, mines or deposits, save where, in the opinion of the Mixed Commission, such powers are indispensable to ensure continued operation.

Any dispute between the German and Polish Governments which may occur within a period of 15 years in respect of any legislative measure adopted by either of the two countries for the control of companies or industrial or commercial enterprises, and limiting in a manner contrary to justice the freedom of these companies or enterprises, as regards the nationality of their personnel, of their directors or of their capital, may be referred by the Government concerned to the Council of the League of Nations, whose decision both Governments undertake to accept.

The two countries may, by common agreement, modify or annul any of the provisions of the temporary régime.[2]

K. *Rights of Nationality and Domicile and Protection of Minorities in Upper Silesia.*—Questions relating to the nationality of persons domiciled, at the date of the definitive allocation of the territory of Upper Silesia, in the portion allotted to Poland, will be decided in accordance with Article 91 of the Treaty of Peace of Versailles, and Articles 3,4, 5, and 6 of the Treaty of the 28th June 1919 between the United States of America, the British Empire, France, Italy, and Japan of the one part, and Poland of the other part.

All persons domiciled, at the same date, in this portion of the territory, who shall have opted in favour of German nationality, in accordance with Article 91 of the Treaty of Peace of Versailles, without availing themselves of the right to transfer their domicile to Germany within 12 months after exercising the right of option, together with persons mentioned in paragraph 2 of Article 91 of the Treaty of Versailles, shall have the right to retain their domicile in Poland for a period of 15 years from the date of the definitive allocation of the territory.

All Poles over 18 years of age who are German nationals and who are domiciled, at the date of the definitive allocation of the territory, in the portion allotted to Germany, shall have the right of opting for Polish nationality within two years from this date, in accordance with Article 91 of the Treaty of Versailles.

All Poles who are domiciled, at the same date, in those parts of Upper Silesia definitely recognized as part of Germany, shall have the right to retain their German domicile for a period of 15 years from this date. This rule shall apply to Poles who, being German nationals, have opted for Polish nationality in accordance with Article 91 of the Treaty of

[1] *And 297* not in the text of the Council of the League.

[2] Text of the Council of the League: *before the expiration of the period of* 15 *years.*

Peace of Versailles, as well as to Polish nationals who have not been German nationals.

The Treaty with regard to the protection of minorities, etc., concluded on the 28th June 1919 between the United States of America, the British Empire, France, Italy, and Japan of the one part, and Poland of the other part, shall be applicable to those parts of Upper Silesia definitely recognized as part of Poland. The principles of equity and the maintenance of the economic life of Upper Silesia demand that the German Government should be bound to accept, at least for the transitional period of 15 years, dating from the definitive allocation of the territory, stipulations corresponding to Articles 1, 2, 7, 8, 9 (paragraphs 1 and 2), 10, 11, and 12 of the said Treaty, as regards those parts of Upper Silesia definitely recognized as part of Germany.

The provisions of the agreement to be concluded between the German and Polish Governments, in order to put into force the abovementioned principles, constitute obligations of international concern for Germany and Poland, and shall [1] be placed under the guarantee of the League of Nations in the same way as the provisions of the Treaty of the 28th June 1919.

Any petition addressed by one or more of the inhabitants of Upper Silesia to the Council of the League of Nations with regard to these provisions or the execution of the provisions of the Treaty of the 28th June 1919 in so far as these provisions affect persons belonging to racial, religious or linguistic minorities, shall be sent to the Government in whose territory the petitioners are domiciled. This Government shall be bound to forward them, with or without observations, to the Council of the League of Nations, for consideration.

The following bodies shall be constituted to supervise the carrying out of these measures :

1. An Upper Silesian Mixed Commission, consisting of two Germans and two Poles, from Upper Silesia, and of a President, of another nationality, appointed by the Council of the League of Nations ;

2. An Arbitral Tribunal, entrusted with the duty of settling any private disputes which may result from the application of the Convention referred to above. This Tribunal shall be composed of one arbitrator appointed by the German Government, and of one arbitrator appointed by the Polish Government. The Council of the League of Nations shall be requested to appoint the President of this tribunal.

All disputes regarding the execution and interpretation of this Convention shall be settled in conformity with the provisions of this Convention.

III. The Convention provided for by Article I above shall be concluded between a German and a Polish plenipotentiary under the presidency of a person appointed by the Council of the League of Nations, that person having a casting vote in case the parties fail to agree.

[1] Text of the Council of the League : *Should.*

The German and Polish Governments are requested to inform the Principal Allied Powers, within eight days from the date of the present decision, of the names of the plenipotentiaries whom they have respectively appointed to conclude, under the conditions laid down in the preceding paragraph, the Convention regarding economic questions and the protection of minorities, which is to be drawn up on the lines laid down in Article II. As soon as the plenipotentiaries have been appointed, it shall be the duty of the President to summon them to meet at any place which he considers suitable.

IV. As soon as the Principal Allied Powers consider that the Delimitation Commission has marked out the frontier, defined under Article I, with sufficient accuracy, and as soon as the negotiations provided by Article III have resulted in the adoption of a conventional régime in accordance with Article II, the Plebiscite Commission shall convey to the German and Polish Governments the notifications referred to in sub-paragraphs 1 and 2 of paragraph 6 of the Annex to Article 88 of the Treaty of Peace of Versailles.

V. The German and Polish Governments are requested to appoint within eight days their delegates for the Mixed Commission referred to in Article II (1). The Mixed Commission shall be immediately constituted to assist the Inter-Allied Commission in framing preparatory measures for the transition from the existing to the provisional régime.

VI. The present decision shall be officially communicated to the Plebiscite Commission and to the German and Polish Governments.

(*Signed*) HARDINGE OF PENSHURST.
JULES CAMBON.
BONIN.
K. ISHII.

PART V. EXECUTION OF THE AWARD

A Commission consisting of three: a President, M. Calcuder, a former Swiss President, nominated by the League; a German, and a Pole met at Geneva on the 23rd November 1921 to conclude a Convention on the above lines establishing the new status.

The Convention was finally signed on the 15th May 1922. Ratifications were exchanged on the 3rd June. On the 9th July the Allied troops left Upper Silesia, the Poles and Germans having already occupied those parts of the area to which they were entitled under the Award.

APPENDIX IV

CHINA AND JAPAN

PART I

THE TWENTY-ONE DEMANDS OF JAPAN, 18TH JANUARY 1915, AND CHINA'S SUBSEQUENT CONCESSIONS.

Below are the original demands of Japan and the documents agreed upon between the two States on the 25th May 1915. Demands 15–19 inclusive and 21 were not conceded by China. The demands not so realized may be considered as representing Japan's unfulfilled policy toward China at that time. The 24 Japanese demands of the 26th April 1915 were more nearly the basis of the agreements of the following May; they were formulated as the result of China's publishing the original 21 demands, and therefore do not throw as much light on Japan's intentions as their predecessors. The documents eventually signed received the assent of China after a Japanese ultimatum of the 7th May 1915 in which Japan offered the 'advice and hope that the Chinese Government, upon this advice, will give a satisfactory reply by 6 o'clock p.m. on the 9th day of May. It is hereby declared that if no satisfactory reply is received before or at the specified time, the Imperial Government will take steps they may deem necessary'.

1. JAPAN'S 21 DEMANDS, HANDED TO THE PRESIDENT, YUAN SHIH K'AI, BY MR. HIOKI, THE JAPANESE MINISTER, 18TH JANUARY 1915.[1]

The Japanese Government and the Chinese Government being desirous of maintaining the general peace in Eastern Asia and further strengthening the friendly relations and good neighbourhood existing between the two nations agree to the following articles:

Group I (Shantung)

ART. 1. The Chinese Government engages to give full assent to all matters upon which the Japanese Government may hereafter agree with the German Government relating to the disposition of all rights, interests and concessions, which Germany by virtue of treaties or otherwise, possesses in relation to the province of Shantung. [Shantung treaty, Art. 1.][2]

ART. 2. The Chinese Government engages that within the province of Shantung and along its coast, no territory or island will be ceded or leased to a third power under any pretext. [Exchange of notes B.]

ART. 3. The Chinese Government consents to Japan's building a railway from Chefoo or Lungchow to join the Kiaochow-Tsinan Railway. [*Cf.* Shantung treaty, Art. 2.]

ART. 4. The Chinese Government engages, in the interest of trade and for the residence of foreigners, to open by herself as soon as possible certain important cities and towns in the province of Shantung as commercial ports. [Shantung treaty, Art. 3.]

What places shall be opened are to be jointly decided upon in a separate agreement.

[1] China's Official History of the Recent Sino-Japanese Treaties, 18–21. Cp. Vol. VI, pp. 372–6.

[2] For Shantung Treaty (4th Feb. 1922) *v.* p. 390.

Group II [Manchuria and East Mongolia]

The Japanese Government and the Chinese Government, since the Chinese Government has always acknowledged the special position enjoyed by Japan in South Manchuria and Eastern Inner Mongolia, agree to the following articles:

ART. 5 [Art. 1]. The two contracting parties mutually agree that the term of lease of Port Arthur and Dalny and the term of lease of the South Manchurian Railway and the Antung-Mukden Railway shall be extended to the period of 99 years. [South Manchuria treaty, Art. 1.]

ART. 6 [Art. 2]. Japanese subjects in South Manchuria and Eastern Inner Mongolia shall have the right to lease or own land required either for erecting suitable buildings for trade and manufacture or for farming. [*Cf.* South Manchuria treaty, Art. 2.]

ART. 7 [Art. 3]. Japanese subjects shall be free to reside and travel in South Manchuria and Eastern Inner Mongolia and to engage in business and in manufacture of any kind whatsoever.

ART. 8 [Art. 4]. The Chinese Government agrees to grant to Japanese subjects the right of opening the mines in South Manchuria and Eastern Mongolia. As regards what mines are to be opened, they shall be decided upon jointly.

ART. 9 [Art. 5]. The Chinese Government agrees that in respect of the [two] cases mentioned herein below the Japanese Government's consent shall be first obtained before action is taken:

a. Whenever permission is granted to the subject of a third power to build a railway or to make a loan with a third power for the purpose of building a railway in South Manchuria and Eastern Inner Mongolia.

b. Whenever a loan is to be made with a third power pledging the local taxes of South Manchuria and Eastern Inner Mongolia as security.

ART. 10 [Art. 6]. The Chinese Government agrees that if the Chinese Government employs political, financial or military advisers or instructors in South Manchuria and Eastern Mongolia, the Japanese Government shall first be consulted.

ART. 11 [Art. 7]. The Chinese Government agrees that the control and management of the Kirin-Changchun Railway shall be handed over to the Japanese Government for a term of 99 years dating from the signing of this agreement.

Group III [Han-yeh-ping Company]

The Japanese Government and the Chinese Government, seeing that Japanese financiers and the Han-yeh-ping Company have close relations with each other at present and desiring that the common interests of the two nations shall be advanced, agree to the following articles:

ART. 12 [Art. 1]. The two contracting parties mutually agree that when the opportune moment arrives the Han-yeh-ping Company shall be made a joint concern of the two nations and they further agree that, without the previous consent of Japan, China shall not by her own act dispose of the rights and property of whatsoever nature of the said company nor cause the said company to dispose freely of the same.

ART. 13 [Art. 2]. The Chinese Government agrees that all mines in the neighbourhood of those owned by the Han-yeh-ping Company shall not be permitted, without the consent of the said company, to be worked by other persons outside of the said company ; and further agrees that if it is desired to carry out any undertaking which, it is apprehended, may directly or indirectly affect the interests of the said company, the consent of the said company shall first be obtained.

Group IV

The Japanese Government and the Chinese Government with the object of effectively preserving the territorial integrity of China agree to the following special article :

ART. 14. The Chinese Government engages not to cede or lease to a third power any harbour or bay or island along the coast of China.

Group V [Miscellaneous]

ART. 15 [Art. 1]. The Chinese Central Government shall employ influential Japanese as advisers in political, financial and military affairs.

ART. 16 [Art. 2]. Japanese hospitals, churches and schools in the interior of China shall be granted the right of owning land.

ART. 17 [Art. 3]. Inasmuch as the Japanese Government and the Chinese Government have had many cases of dispute between Japanese and Chinese police which caused no little misunderstanding, it is for this reason necessary that the police departments of important places (in China) shall be jointly administered by Japanese and Chinese or that the police departments of these places shall employ numerous Japanese, so that they may at the same time help to plan for the improvement of the Chinese police service.

ART. 18 [Art. 4]. China shall purchase from Japan a fixed amount of munitions of war (say 50 per cent. or more of what is needed by the Chinese Government), or there shall be established in China a Sino-Japanese jointly worked arsenal. Japanese technical experts are to be employed and Japanese material to be purchased.

ART. 19 [Art. 5]. China agrees to grant to Japan the right of constructing a railway connecting Wuchang with Kiukiang and Nanchang, another line between Nanchang and Hangchow, and another between Nanchang and Chaochow.

ART. 20 [Art. 6]. If China needs foreign capital to work mines, build railways and construct harbour-works (including dock-yards) in the province of Fukien, Japan shall be first consulted.

ART. 21 [Art. 7]. China agrees that Japanese subjects shall have the right of missionary propaganda in China.

By the treaty dealing with Shantung and South Manchuria respectively signed on the 25th May 1915 and by exchange of notes on the same day, China conceded all these demands to Japan except 11, 15–19 inclusive, and 21. Demand 11 was finally conceded by China in an exchange of notes of the 24th September 1918, *v. Chinese Official History of the Recent Sino-Japanese Treaties*, 43–4. Cp. Vol. VI, pp. 374–6.

PART II

ALLIED SECRET AGREEMENTS WITH JAPAN, 1917[1]

A. The British ambassador at Tokyo to the Japanese minister for foreign affairs

British Embassy,
Tokyo, 16th February 1917.

My dear Excellency : With reference to the subject of our conversation of the 27th ultimo, when your Excellency informed me of the desire of the Imperial Government to receive an assurance that on the occasion of a Peace Conference his Britannic Majesty's Government will support the claims of Japan in regard to the disposal of Germany's rights in Shantung and possessions in the islands north of the equator, I have the honour, under instructions received from his Britannic Majesty's principal secretary of state for foreign affairs, to communicate to you the following message from his Britannic Majesty's Government :

'His Britannic Majesty's Government accede with pleasure to the request of the Japanese Government for an assurance that they will support Japan's claims in regard to the disposal of Germany's rights in Shantung and possessions in the islands north of the equator on the occasion of the Peace Conference ; it being understood that the Japanese Government will in the eventual peace settlement treat in the same spirit Great Britain's claims to the German islands south of the equator.'

I avail myself of this opportunity, M. le Ministre, to renew to your Excellency the assurance of my highest consideration.

Conyngham Greene,
His Britannic Majesty's Ambassador.

To his Excellency, Viscount Ichiro Motono, his Imperial Japanese Majesty's Minister for Foreign Affairs.

B (i). The Japanese minister for foreign affairs to the British ambassador at Tokyo

[extract]

Foreign Office,
Tokyo, 21st February 1917.

The Japanese Government is deeply appreciative of the friendly spirit in which your Government has given assurance and happy to note it as fresh proof of the close ties that unite the two allied powers. I take pleasure in stating that the Japanese Government on its part is fully prepared to support in the same spirit the claims which may be put forward at the Peace Conference by his Britannic Majesty's Government in regard to the German possessions in the islands south of the equator.

[1] New York *Times*, 22nd April 1919. Cp. Vol. VI, 376–7.

B (ii). THE JAPANESE MINISTER FOR FOREIGN AFFAIRS TO THE RUSSIAN AND FRENCH AMBASSADORS

[EXTRACT]

FOREIGN OFFICE,
TOKYO, 19th February 1917.

The Imperial Japanese Government has not yet formally entered into conversations with the Entente powers concerning the conditions of peace it proposes to present to Germany, because it is guided by the thought that such questions ought to be decided in concert between Japan and the said powers at the moment when the peace negotiations begin. Nevertheless, in view of recent developments in the general situation, and in view of the particular arrangements concerning peace conditions, such as arrangements relative to the disposition of the Bosporus, Constantinople, and the Dardanelles, being already under discussion by the powers interested, the Imperial Japanese Government believes that the moment has come for it also to express its desires relative to certain conditions of peace essential to Japan and to submit them for the consideration of the Government of the French Republic [Russian Empire].

The French [Russian] Government is thoroughly informed of all the efforts the Japanese Government has made in a general manner to accomplish its task in the present war, and particularly to guarantee for the future the peace of Oriental Asia and the security of the Japanese Empire, for which it is absolutely necessary to take from Germany its bases of political, military and economic activity in the Far East.

Under these conditions the Imperial Japanese Government proposes to demand from Germany at the time of the peace negotiations the surrender of the territorial rights and special interests Germany possessed before the war in Shantung and the islands situated north of the equator in the Pacific Ocean.

The Imperial Japanese Government confidently hopes the Government of the French Republic [Russian Empire], realizing the legitimacy of these demands, will give assurance that, her case being proved, Japan may count upon its full support on this question.

It goes without saying that reparation for damages caused to the life and property of the Japanese people by the unjustifiable attacks of the enemy, as well as other conditions of peace of a character common to all the Entente powers, are entirely outside the consideration of the present question.

C. THE FRENCH AMBASSADOR AT TOKYO TO THE JAPANESE MINISTER FOR FOREIGN AFFAIRS

[EXTRACT]

FRENCH EMBASSY, TOKYO, 3rd March 1917.

The Government of the French Republic is disposed to give the Japanese Government its accord in regulating at the time of the peace negotiations questions vital to Japan concerning Shantung and the German islands in the Pacific north of the equator. It also agrees to support the demands of the Imperial Japanese Government for the surrender of the rights Germany possessed before the war in this Chinese province and these islands.

M. Briand demands, on the other hand, that Japan give its support to obtain from China the breaking of its diplomatic relations with Germany, and that it gives this act desirable significance. The consequences of this in China should be the following:

First, handing passports to the German diplomatic agents and consuls.

Second, the obligation of all under German jurisdiction to leave Chinese territory.

Third, the internment of German ships in Chinese ports and the ultimate requisition of these ships in order to place them at the disposition of the Allies following the example of Italy and Portugal. According to the information of the French Government there are 15 German ships in Chinese ports, totaling about 40,000 tons.

Fourth, requisition of German commercial houses established in China; forfeiting the right of Germany in the concessions she possesses in certain parts of China.[1]

D (i). M. Krupensky, Russian ambassador at Tokyo, to the Russian minister for foreign affairs [2]

Tokyo, 8th February 1917.

I never omit an opportunity for representing to the minister for foreign affairs the desirability, in the interests of Japan herself, of China's intervention in the war, and only last week I had a conversation with him on the subject. To-day I again pointed out to him that the present moment was particularly favourable, in view of the position taken up by the United States and the proposal made by them to the neutral powers to follow their example, and more particularly, in view of the recent speeches of the American minister at Peking. Viscount Motono replied that he would be the first to welcome a rupture between China and Germany, and would not hesitate to take steps in this direction at Peking if he were sure that the Chinese Government would go in that direction. So far, however, he had no such assurance, and he feared lest unsuccessful representations at Peking might do harm to the Allies. He promised me to sound the attitude of Peking without delay, and, in case of some hope of success, to propose to the cabinet to take a decision in the desired direction.

On the other hand, the minister pointed out the necessity for him, in view of the attitude of Japanese public opinion on the subject, as well as with a view to safeguard Japan's position at the future Peace Conference, if China should be admitted to it, of securing the support of the allied powers to the desires of Japan in respect of Shantung and the Pacific Islands. These desires are for the succession of all the rights and

[1] In reply Japan promised compliance with the request to get China to break relations with Germany, adding that it had spared no effort in that direction from the beginning.

At Rome, the Italian minister of foreign affairs gave the Japanese ambassador assurance that Italy would offer no objection in the matter.

[2] Manchester *Guardian*, 7th February 1918, p. 4.

privileges hitherto possessed by Germany in the Shantung province and for the acquisition of the islands to the north of the equator which are now occupied by the Japanese. Motono plainly told me that the Japanese Government would like to receive at once the promise of the Imperial [Russian] Government to support the above desires of Japan. In order to give a push to the highly important question of a break between China and Germany I regard it as very desirable that the Japanese should be given the promise they ask—this the more as, so far as can be seen here, the relations between Great Britain and Japan have of late been such as to justify a surmise that the Japanese aspirations would not meet with any objections on the part of the London cabinet.

(ii). SAME TO SAME

TOKYO, 1st March 1917.

The minister for foreign affairs asked me to-day whether I had received a reply from the Imperial [Russian] Government relating to Japan's desires on the question of Shantung and the Pacific Islands, and told me that the Japanese Government would very much like to have at the earliest a promise from us on the subject.

(iii). SAME TO SAME

TOKYO, 21st March 1917.

I communicated to-day to the minister for foreign affairs the contents of your high Excellency's telegram, and gave him a copy. Viscount Motono confined himself to the observation that he took note of my communication, and would report it to the council of ministers and the Emperor. The attitude of public opinion and the press here toward the revolution in Russia is, on the whole, sympathetic. It is regarded as a pledge of a successful prosecution of the war until complete victory has been obtained, and the end of the rule of the bureaucracy is welcomed. While paying due tribute to the Emperor's and the Grand Duke Michael Alexandrovich's patriotic acts of abdication, public opinion here expresses the hope that the new Government and the popular representatives to be summoned would not be inclined toward extreme decisions. The same attitude towards the events in Russia could be perceived in the few general words which I heard in this connexion from the minister of foreign affairs.

PART III

THE LANSING-ISHII AGREEMENT, BETWEEN THE UNITED STATES AND JAPAN, 2ND NOVEMBER 1917[1]

DEPARTMENT OF STATE,
Washington, 2nd November 1917

EXCELLENCY:

I have the honor to communicate herein my understanding of the agreement reached by us in our recent conversations touching the questions of mutual interest to our Governments relating to the Republic of China.

[1] Cp. pp. 376–7.

In order to silence mischievous reports that have from time to time been circulated, it is believed by us that a public announcement once more of the desires and intentions shared by our two Governments with regard to China is advisable.

The Governments of the United States and Japan recognize that territorial propinquity creates special relations between countries, and, consequently, the Government of the United States recognizes that Japan has special interests in China, particularly in the part to which her possessions are contiguous.

The territorial sovereignty of China, nevertheless, remains unimpaired and the Government of the United States has every confidence in the repeated assurances of the Imperial Japanese Government that while geographical position gives Japan such special interests they have no desire to discriminate against the trade of other nations or to disregard the commercial rights heretofore granted by China in treaties with other powers.

The Governments of the United States and Japan deny that they have any purpose to infringe in any way the independence or territorial integrity of China and they declare, furthermore, that they always adhere to the principle of the so-called 'Open Door' or equal opportunity for commerce and industry in China.

Moreover, they mutually declare that they are opposed to the acquisition by any Government of any special rights or privileges that would affect the independence or territorial integrity of China or that would deny to the subjects or citizens of any country the full enjoyment of equal opportunity in the commerce and industry of China.

I shall be glad to have Your Excellency confirm this understanding of the agreement reached by us.

Accept, Excellency, the renewed assurance of my highest consideration.[1]

ROBERT LANSING

His Excellency
Viscount KIKUJIRO ISHII,
Ambassador Extraordinary and
Plenipotentiary of Japan, on Special Mission

[1] To this note Viscount Ishii replied on the same day:

SIR:

I have the honour to acknowledge the receipt of your note of to-day, communicating to me your understanding of the agreement reached by us in our recent conversations touching the questions of mutual interest to our governments relating to the Republic of China. I am happy to be able to confirm to you, under authorization of my Government, the understanding in question set forth in the following terms; [the portions italicized in the Lansing Note then follow].

APPENDIX V

TEXTS OF SOME TYPICAL MANDATES

PART I

'C' MANDATES

The Terms of the 'C' Mandates were finally accepted by the First League Assembly, 17th December 1920 (Vol. VI, Chap. VI, pp. 514–20, 523). They were for German Pacific Isles north of the Equator (Japan); some south of Equator (Australia); Samoa (New Zealand), Nauru (British Empire), and German South-West Africa (Union of South Africa). The Terms of all are practically identical.

Mandate for German Samoa

The Council of the League of Nations:

Whereas by article 119 of the Treaty of Peace with Germany signed at Versailles on the 28th June, 1919, Germany renounced in favour of the Principal Allied and Associated Powers all her rights over her overseas possessions, including therein German Samoa; and

Whereas the Principal Allied and Associated Powers agreed that, in accordance with article 22, part I (Covenant of the League of Nations), of the said treaty, a mandate should be conferred upon His Britannic Majesty, to be exercised on his behalf by the Government of the Dominion of New Zealand, to administer German Samoa, and have proposed that the mandate should be formulated in the following terms; and

Whereas His Britannic Majesty, for and on behalf of the Government of the Dominion of New Zealand, has agreed to accept the mandate in respect of the said territory and has undertaken to exercise it on behalf of the League of Nations in accordance with the following provisions; and

Whereas, by the aforementioned article 22, paragraph 8, it is provided that the degree of authority, control or administration to be exercised by the mandatory, not having been previously agreed upon by the members of the League, shall be explicitly defined by the Council of the League of Nations:

Confirming the said mandate, defines its terms as follows:

Article 1. The territory over which a mandate is conferred upon His Britannic Majesty for and on behalf of the Government of the Dominion of New Zealand (hereinafter called the Mandatory) is the former German colony of Samoa.

Article 2. The Mandatory shall have full power of administration and legislation over the territory subject to the present mandate as an integral portion of the Dominion of New Zealand, and may apply the laws of the Dominion of New Zealand to the territory, subject to such local modifications as circumstances may require.

The Mandatory shall promote to the utmost the material and moral well-being and the social progress of the inhabitants of the territory subject to the present mandate.

ARTICLE 3. The Mandatory shall see that the slave trade is prohibited, and that no forced labour is permitted, except for essential public works and services, and then only for adequate remuneration.

The Mandatory shall also see that the traffic in arms and ammunition is controlled in accordance with principles analogous to those laid down in the convention relating to the control of the arms traffic, signed on the 10th September, 1919, or in any convention amending the same.

The supply of intoxicating spirits and beverages to the natives shall be prohibited.

ARTICLE 4. The military training of the natives, otherwise than for purposes of internal police and the local defence of the territory, shall be prohibited. Furthermore, no military or naval bases shall be established or fortifications erected in the territory.

ARTICLE 5. Subject to the provisions of any local law for the maintenance of public order and public morals, the Mandatory shall ensure in the territory freedom of conscience and the free exercise of all forms of worship, and shall allow all missionaries, nationals of any State member of the League of Nations, to enter into, travel and reside in the territory for the purpose of prosecuting their calling.

ARTICLE 6. The Mandatory shall make to the Council of the League of Nations an annual report to the satisfaction of the Council, containing full information with regard to the territory, and indicating the measures taken to carry out the obligations assumed under articles 2, 3, 4 and 5.

ARTICLE 7. The consent of the Council of the League of Nations is required for any modification of the terms of the present mandate.

The Mandatory agrees that, if any dispute whatever should arise between the Mandatory and another member of the League of Nations relating to the interpretation or the application of the provisions of the mandate, such dispute, if it cannot be settled by negotiation, shall be submitted to the Permanent Court of International Justice provided for by article 14 of the Covenant of the League of Nations.

The present declaration shall be deposited in the archives of the League of Nations. Certified copies shall be forwarded by the Secretary-General of the League of Nations to all Powers signatories of the Treaty of Peace with Germany.

Made at Geneva the 17th day of December, 1920.

Certified true copy.

ERIC DRUMMOND,
Secretary-General.

APPENDIX V. PART II

'B' MANDATES

The 'B' Mandates, British and French Togoland ; British and French Cameroons ; Ruanda and Urundi (Belgium), and East Africa (Tanganyika (British), were confirmed on the 1st August 1922 by the Council. With one important variation (French Togoland) [1] and certain other small ones, the Tanganyika Model may serve.

British Mandate for East Africa (Tanganyika)

The Council of the League of Nations :

Whereas by Article 119 of the Treaty of Peace with Germany signed at Versailles on June 28th, 1919, Germany renounced in favour of the Principal Allied and Associated Powers all her rights over her oversea possessions, including therein German East Africa ; and

Whereas, in accordance with the treaty of June 11th, 1891, between Her Britannic Majesty and His Majesty the King of Portugal, the River Rovuma is recognized as forming the northern boundary of the Portuguese possessions in East Africa from its mouth up to the confluence of the River M'Sinje ; and

Whereas the Principal Allied and Associated Powers agreed that, in accordance with Article 22, Part I (Covenant of the League of Nations), of the said treaty a mandate should be conferred upon His Britannic Majesty to administer part of the former colony of German East Africa, and have proposed that the mandate should be formulated in the following terms ; and

Whereas His Britannic Majesty has agreed to accept the mandate in respect of the said territory, and has undertaken to exercise it on behalf of the League of Nations in accordance with the following provisions ; and

Whereas by the afore-mentioned Article 22, paragraph 8, it is provided that the degree of authority, control or administration to be exercised by the Mandatory, not having been previously agreed upon by the Members of the League, shall be explicitly defined by the Council of the League of Nations ;

Confirming the said mandate, defines its terms as follows :

Article 1. The territory over which a mandate is conferred upon His Britannic Majesty (hereinafter called the Mandatory) comprises that part of the territory of the former colony of German East Africa situated to the east of the following line :

From the point where the frontier between the Uganda Protectorate and German East Africa cuts the River Mavumba, a straight line in a south-easterly direction to point 1640, about 15 kilometres south-south-west of Mount Gabiro ;

Thence a straight line in a southerly direction to the north shore of Lake Mohazi, where it terminates at the confluence of a river situated about 2½ kilometres west of the confluence of the River Msilala ;

If the track of the railway on the west of the River Kagera between

[1] *v.* note on next page. Cp. pp. 518–23.

Bugufi and Uganda approaches within 16 kilometres of the line defined above, the boundary will be carried to the west, following a minimum distance of 16 kilometres from the trace, without, however, passing to the west of the straight line joining the terminal point on Lake Mohazi and the top of Mount Kivisa, point 2100, situated on the Uganda-German East Africa frontier about 5 kilometres south-west of the point where the River Mavumba cuts this frontier;

Thence a line south-eastwards to meet the southern shore of Lake Mohazi;

Thence the watershed between the Taruka and the Mkarange and continuing southwards to the north-eastern end of Lake Mugesera;

Thence the median line of this lake and continuing southwards across Lake Ssake to meet the Kagera;

Thence the course of the Kagera downstream to meet the western boundary of Bugufi;

Thence this boundary to its junction with the eastern boundary of Urundi;

Thence the eastern and southern boundary of Urundi to Lake Tanganyika.

The line described above is shown on the attached British 1 : 1,000,000 map, G.S.G.S. 2932, sheet Ruanda and Urundi. The boundaries of Bugufi and Urundi are drawn as shown in the Deutscher Kolonialatlas (Dietrich-Reimer), scale 1 : 1,000,000, dated 1906.

ARTICLE 2. Boundary Commissioners shall be appointed by His Britannic Majesty and His Majesty the King of the Belgians to trace on the spot the line described in Article 1 above.

In case any dispute should arise in connection with the work of these commissioners, the question shall be referred to the Council of the League of Nations, whose decision shall be final.

The final report by the Boundary Commission shall give the precise description of this boundary as actually demarcated on the ground; the necessary maps shall be annexed thereto and signed by the commissioners. The report, with its annexes, shall be made in triplicate; one copy shall be deposited in the archives of the League of Nations, one shall be kept by the Government of His Majesty the King of the Belgians and one by the Government of His Britannic Majesty.

ARTICLE 3. The Mandatory shall be responsible for the peace, order and good government of the territory, and shall undertake to promote to the utmost the material and moral well-being and the social progress of its inhabitants. The Mandatory shall have full powers of legislation and administration.

ARTICLE 4. The Mandatory shall not establish any military or naval bases, nor erect any fortifications, nor organize any native military force in the territory except for local police purposes and for the defence of the territory.[1]

ARTICLE 5. The Mandatory:

(1) shall provide for the eventual emancipation of all slaves and

[1] In the French Mandate for Togoland there is an important addition here: *It is understood, however, that the troops thus raised may, in the event of general war, be utilized to repel an attack or for the defence of the territory outside that subject to the Mandate.* Cp. p. 521 and n.

for as speedy an elimination of domestic and other slavery as social conditions will allow;

(2) shall suppress all forms of slave trade;

(3) shall prohibit all forms of forced or compulsory labour, except for essential public works and services, and then only in return for adequate remuneration;

(4) shall protect the natives from abuse and measures of fraud and force by the careful supervision of labour contracts and the recruiting of labour;

(5) shall exercise a strict control over the traffic in arms and ammunition and the sale of spirituous liquors.

ARTICLE 6. In the framing of laws relating to the holding or transfer of land, the Mandatory shall take into consideration native laws and customs, and shall respect the rights and safeguard the interests of the native population.

No native land may be transferred, except between natives, without the previous consent of the public authorities, and no real rights over native land in favour of non-natives may be created except with the same consent.

The Mandatory will promulgate strict regulations against usury.

ARTICLE 7. The Mandatory shall secure to all nationals of States Members of the League of Nations the same rights as are enjoyed in the territory by his own nationals in respect of entry into and residence in the territory, the protection afforded to their person and property, the acquisition of property, movable and immovable, and the exercise of their profession or trade, subject only to the requirements of public order, and on condition of compliance with the local law.

Further, the Mandatory shall ensure to all nationals of States Members of the League of Nations, on the same footing as to his own nationals, freedom of transit and navigation, and complete economic, commercial and industrial equality; provided that the Mandatory shall be free to organize essential public works and services on such terms and conditions as he thinks just.

Concessions for the development of the natural resources of the territory shall be granted by the Mandatory without distinction on grounds of nationality between the nationals of all States Members of the League of Nations, but on such conditions as will maintain intact the authority of the local Government.

Concessions having the character of a general monopoly shall not be granted. This provision does not affect the right of the Mandatory to create monopolies of a purely fiscal character in the interest of the territory under mandate, and in order to provide the territory with fiscal resources which seem best suited to the local requirements; or, in certain cases, to carry out the development of natural resources either directly by the State or by a controlled agency, provided that there shall result therefrom no monopoly of the natural resources for the benefit of the Mandatory or his nationals, directly or indirectly, nor any preferential advantage which shall be inconsistent with the economic, commercial and industrial equality hereinbefore guaranteed.

The rights conferred by this article extend equally to companies and associations organized in accordance with the law of any of the Members of the League of Nations, subject only to the requirements of public order, and on condition of compliance with the local law.

ARTICLE 8. The Mandatory shall ensure in the territory complete freedom of conscience and the free exercise of all forms of worship which are consonant with public order and morality; missionaries who are nationals of States Members of the League of Nations shall be free to enter the territory and to travel and reside therein, to acquire and possess property, to erect religious buildings and to open schools, throughout the territory; it being understood, however, that the Mandatory shall have the right to exercise such control as may be necessary for the maintenance of public order and good government, and to take all measures required for such control.

ARTICLE 9. The Mandatory shall apply to the territory any general international conventions already existing, or which may be concluded hereafter, with the approval of the League of Nations, respecting the slave trade, the traffic in arms and ammunition, the liquor traffic, and the traffic in drugs, or relating to commercial equality, freedom of transit and navigation, aerial navigation, railways, postal, telegraphic, and wireless communication, and industrial, literary and artistic property.

The Mandatory shall co-operate in the execution of any common policy adopted by the League of Nations for preventing and combating disease, including diseases of plants and animals.

ARTICLE 10. The Mandatory shall be authorised to constitute the territory into a customs, fiscal and administrative union or federation with the adjacent territories under his own sovereignty or control; provided always that the measures adopted to that end do not infringe the provisions of this mandate.[1]

ARTICLE 11. The Mandatory shall make to the Council of the League of Nations an annual report to the satisfaction of the Council, containing full information concerning the measures taken to apply the provisions of this mandate.

A copy of all laws and regulations made in the course of the year

[1] The following recommendations were made at the second session of the Mandates Commission, August 1922 (*Monthly Summary of League*, August 1922, Vol. II, No. 8, p. 187).

'At its first session in October 1921, the Commission had drawn attention to a possible conflict in the application of paragraph 5 of Article 22 of the Covenant, which provides for economic equality, and the clause whereby a Mandatory Power may incorporate a mandated territory into a customs union with its own neighbouring colonies. Whilst noting that the Belgian, English, and French colonies within the conventional Congo Basin are provided with a regime of economic equality, the Commission expressed the wish to be informed whether a preferential tariff obtained in any of the mandated territories of Central Africa.

'Another special recommendation concerned Ruanda. According to the Orts-Milner agreement, the Eastern part of this territory is ceded to Great Britain to be incorporated with Tanganyika. The Commission has been informed from several quarters that this is highly detrimental to the political and economic unity of this native kingdom, which by the terms of the agreement in question, is deprived of a part of its best pasture land. The Commission decided to draw the attention of the Council to a situation which seemed likely to impair the development of the country.'

and affecting property, commerce, navigation or the moral and material well-being of the natives shall be annexed to this report.

ARTICLE 12. The consent of the Council of the League of Nations is required for any modification of the terms of this mandate.

ARTICLE 13. The Mandatory agrees that if any dispute whatever should arise between the Mandatory and another Member of the League of Nations relating to the interpretation or the application of the provisions of the mandate, such dispute, if it cannot be settled by negotiation, shall be submitted to the Permanent Court of International Justice provided for by Article 14 of the Covenant of the League of Nations.

States Members of the League of Nations may likewise bring any claims on behalf of their nationals for infractions of their rights under this mandate before the said Court for decision.

The present instrument shall be deposited in original in the archives of the League of Nations. Certified copies shall be forwarded by the Secretary-General of the League of Nations to all Members of the League.

Done at London, the twentieth day of July one thousand nine hundred and twenty-two.

Certified true copy :

SECRETARY-GENERAL.

APPENDIX V. PART III

'A' MANDATE

The Syria and Lebanon Mandate is here given as simpler and less complicated than that of Palestine.[1] The Mesopotamia Mandate is not yet issued but the final draft is published (Parl. Paper Cmd. 1500, 1921) and printed on pp. 609–13.

LEAGUE OF NATIONS, 12TH AUGUST 1922

MANDATE FOR SYRIA AND THE LEBANON

The Council of the League of Nations : [2]

Whereas the Principal Allied Powers have agreed that the territory of Syria and the Lebanon, which formerly belonged to the Turkish Empire shall, within such boundaries as may be fixed by the said Powers, be entrusted to a Mandatory charged with the duty of rendering administrative advice and assistance to the population, in accordance with the provisions of Article 22 (paragraph 4) of the Covenant of the League of Nations ; and

Whereas the Principal Allied Powers have decided that the mandate for the territory referred to above should be conferred on the Government of the French Republic, which has accepted it ; and

Whereas the terms of this mandate which are defined in the articles below, have also been accepted by the Government of the French Republic and submitted to the Council of the League for approval ; and

[1] Cp. p. 169 and n, pp. 521–2.

[2] For change in original preamble v. p. 37.

Whereas the Government of the French Republic has undertaken to exercise this mandate on behalf of the League of Nations, in conformity with the following provisions ; and

Whereas by the afore-mentioned Article 22 (paragraph 8) it is provided that the degree of authority, control or administration to be exercised by the Mandatory, not having been previously agreed upon by the Members of the League, shall be explicitly defined by the Council of the League of Nations ;

Confirming the said mandate, defines its terms as follows :

ARTICLE 1. The Mandatory shall frame, within a period of three years from the coming into force of this mandate, an organic law for Syria and the Lebanon.

This organic law shall be framed in agreement with the native authorities and shall take into account the rights, interests, and wishes of all the population inhabiting the said territory. The Mandatory shall further enact measures to facilitate the progressive development of Syria and the Lebanon as independent States. Pending the coming into effect of the organic law, the Government of Syria and the Lebanon shall be conducted in accordance with the spirit of this mandate.

The Mandatory shall, as far as circumstances permit, encourage local autonomy.

ARTICLE 2. The Mandatory may maintain its troops in the said territory for its defence. It shall further be empowered, until the entry into force of the organic law and the re-establishment of public security, to organize such local militia as may be necessary for the defence of the territory, and to employ this militia for defence and also for the maintenance of order. These local forces may only be recruited from the inhabitants of the said territory.

The said militia shall thereafter be under the local authorities, subject to the authority and the control which the Mandatory shall retain over these forces. It shall not be used for purposes other than those above specified save with the consent of the Mandatory.

Nothing shall preclude Syria and the Lebanon from contributing to the cost of the maintenance of the forces of the Mandatory stationed in the territory.

The Mandatory shall at all times possess the right to make use of the ports, railways and means of communication of Syria and the Lebanon for the passage of its troops and of all materials, supplies and fuel.

ARTICLE 3. The Mandatory shall be entrusted with the exclusive control of the foreign relations of Syria and the Lebanon and with the right to issue exequaturs to the consuls appointed by foreign Powers. Nationals of Syria and the Lebanon living outside the limits of the territory shall be under the diplomatic and consular protection of the Mandatory.

ARTICLE 4. The Mandatory shall be responsible for seeing that no part of the territory of Syria and the Lebanon is ceded or leased or in any way placed under the control of a foreign Power.

ARTICLE 5. The privileges and immunities of foreigners, including the benefits of consular jurisdiction and protection as formerly enjoyed by Capitulation or usage in the Ottoman Empire, shall not be applicable in Syria and the Lebanon. Foreign consular tribunals shall, however, continue to perform their duties until the coming into force of the new legal organization provided for in Article 6.

Unless the Powers whose nationals enjoyed the afore-mentioned privileges and immunities on August 1st, 1914, shall have previously renounced the right to their re-establishment, or shall have agreed to their non-application during a specified period, these privileges and immunities shall at the expiration of the mandate be immediately re-established in their entirety or with such modifications as may have been agreed upon between the Powers concerned.

ARTICLE 6. The Mandatory shall establish in Syria and the Lebanon a judicial system which shall assure to natives as well as to foreigners a complete guarantee of their rights.

Respect for the personal status of the various peoples and for their religious interests shall be fully guaranteed. In particular, the control and administration of Wakfs shall be exercised in complete accordance with religious law and the dispositions of the founders.

ARTICLE 7. Pending the conclusion of special extradition agreements, the extradition treaties at present in force between foreign Powers and the Mandatory shall apply within the territory of Syria and the Lebanon.

ARTICLE 8. The Mandatory shall ensure to all complete freedom of conscience and the free exercise of all forms of worship which are consonant with public order and morality. No discrimination of any kind shall be made between the inhabitants of Syria and the Lebanon on the ground of differences in race, religion or language.

The Mandatory shall encourage public instruction, which shall be given through the medium of the native languages in use in the territory of Syria and the Lebanon.

The right of each community to maintain its own schools for the instruction and education of its own members in its own language, while conforming to such educational requirements of a general nature as the administration may impose, shall not be denied or impaired.

ARTICLE 9. The Mandatory shall refrain from all interference in the administration of the Councils of management (Conseils de fabrique) or in the management of religious communities and sacred shrines belonging to the various religions, the immunity of which has been expressly guaranteed.

ARTICLE 10. The supervision exercised by the Mandatory over the religious missions in Syria and the Lebanon shall be limited to the maintenance of public order and good government; the activities of these religious missions shall in no way be restricted, nor shall their members be subjected to any restrictive measures on the ground of nationality, provided that their activities are confined to the domain of religion.

The religious missions may also concern themselves with education and relief, subject to the general right of regulation and control by the Mandatory or of the local government, in regard to education, public instruction and charitable relief.

ARTICLE 11. The Mandatory shall see that there is no discrimination in Syria or the Lebanon against the nationals, including societies and associations, of any State Member of the League of Nations as compared with its own nationals, including societies and associations, or with the nationals of any other foreign State in matters concerning taxation or commerce, the exercise of professions or industries, or navigation, or in the treatment of ships or aircraft. Similarly, there shall be no discrimination in Syria or the Lebanon against goods originating in or destined for any of the said States ; there shall be freedom of transit, under equitable conditions, across the said territory.

Subject to the above, the Mandatory may impose or cause to be imposed by the local governments such taxes and customs duties as it may consider necessary. The Mandatory, or the local governments acting under its advice, may also conclude on grounds of contiguity any special customs arrangements with an adjoining country.

The Mandatory may take or cause to be taken, subject to the provisions of paragraph 1 of this article, such steps as it may think best to ensure the development of the natural resources of the said territory and to safeguard the interests of the local population.

Concessions for the development of these natural resources shall be granted without distinction of nationality between the nationals of all States Members of the League of Nations, but on condition that they do not infringe upon the authority of the local government. Concessions in the nature of a general monopoly shall not be granted. This clause shall in no way limit the right of the Mandatory to create monopolies of a purely fiscal character in the interest of the territory of Syria and the Lebanon, and with a view to assuring to the territory the fiscal resources which would appear best adapted to the local needs, or, in certain cases, with a view to developing the natural resources either directly by the State or through an organization under its control, provided that this does not involve either directly or indirectly the creation of a monopoly of the natural resources in favour of the Mandatory or its nationals, nor involve any preferential treatment which would be incompatible with the economic, commercial and industrial equality guaranteed above.

ARTICLE 12. The Mandatory shall adhere, on behalf of Syria and the Lebanon, to any general international agreements already existing, or which may be concluded hereafter with the approval of the League of Nations, in respect of the following : the slave trade, the traffic in drugs, the traffic in arms and ammunition, commercial equality, freedom of transit and navigation, aerial navigation, postal, telegraphic or wireless communications, and measures for the protection of literature, art or industries.

ARTICLE 13. The Mandatory shall secure the adhesion of Syria and the Lebanon, so far as social, religious and other conditions permit, to such measures of common utility as may be adopted by the League of Nations for preventing and combating disease, including diseases of animals and plants.

ARTICLE 14. The Mandatory shall draw up and put into force within twelve months from this date a law of antiquities in conformity with the following provisions. This law shall ensure equality of treatment in the matter of excavations and archæological research to the nationals of all States Members of the League of Nations.

(1) 'Antiquity' means any construction or any product of human activity earlier than the year 1700 A.D.

(2) The law for the protection of antiquities shall proceed by encouragement rather than by threat.

Any person who, having discovered an antiquity without being furnished with the authorization referred to in paragraph 5, reports the same to an official of the competent Department, shall be rewarded according to the value of the discovery.

(3) No antiquity may be disposed of except to the competent Department, unless this Department renounces the acquisition of any such antiquity.

No antiquity may leave the country without an export licence from the said Department.

(4) Any person who maliciously or negligently destroys or damages an antiquity shall be liable to a penalty to be fixed.

(5) No clearing of ground or digging with the object of finding antiquities shall be permitted, under penalty of fine, except to persons authorized by the competent Department.

(6) Equitable terms shall be fixed for expropriation, temporary or permanent, of lands which might be of historical or archæological interest.

(7) Authorization to excavate shall only be granted to persons who show sufficient guarantees of archæological experience. The Mandatory shall not, in granting these authorizations, act in such a way as to exclude scholars of any nation without good grounds.

(8) The proceeds of excavations may be divided between the excavator and the competent Department in a proportion fixed by that Department. If division seems impossible for scientific reasons, the excavator shall receive a fair indemnity in lieu of a part of the find.

ARTICLE 15. Upon the coming into force of the organic law referred to in Article 1, an arrangement shall be made between the Mandatory and the local governments for reimbursement by the latter of all expenses incurred by the Mandatory in organizing the administration, developing local resources, and carrying out permanent public works, of which the country retains the benefit. Such arrangement shall be communicated to the Council of the League of Nations.

ARTICLE 16. French and Arabic shall be the official languages of Syria and the Lebanon.

ARTICLE 17. The Mandatory shall make to the Council of the League of Nations an annual report to the satisfaction of the Council as to the measures taken during the year to carry out the provisions of this mandate. Copies of all laws and regulations promulgated during the year shall be attached to the said report.

ARTICLE 18. The consent of the Council of the League of Nations is required for any modification of the terms of this mandate.

ARTICLE 19. On the termination of the mandate, the Council of the League of Nations shall use its influence to safeguard for the future the fulfilment by the Government of Syria and the Lebanon of the financial obligations, including pensions and allowances, regularly assumed by the administration of Syria or of the Lebanon during the period of the mandate.

ARTICLE 20. The Mandatory agrees that if any dispute whatever should arise between the Mandatory and another Member of the League of Nations relating to the interpretation or the application of the provisions of the mandate, such dispute, if it cannot be settled by negotiation, shall be submitted to the Permanent Court of International Justice provided for by Article 14 of the Covenant of the League of Nations.

The present instrument shall be deposited in original in the archives of the League of Nations and certified copies shall be forwarded by the Secretary-General of the League of Nations to all Members of the League.

Done at London on the twenty-fourth day of July, one thousand nine hundred and twenty-two.

Certified true Copy :

SECRETARY-GENERAL.

APPENDIX VI

TREATY OF PEACE BETWEEN THE UNITED STATES AND GERMANY[1]

A TREATY BETWEEN THE UNITED STATES AND GERMANY, SIGNED ON AUGUST 25, 1921, TO RESTORE FRIENDLY RELATIONS EXISTING BETWEEN THE TWO NATIONS PRIOR TO THE OUTBREAK OF WAR

GERMANY AND THE UNITED STATES OF AMERICA

Considering that the United States, acting in conjunction with its co-belligerents, entered into an Armistice with Germany on November 11, 1918, in order that a Treaty of Peace might be concluded ;

Considering that the Treaty of Versailles was signed on June 28, 1919, and came into force according to the terms of its Article 440, but has not been ratified by the United States ;

Considering that the Congress of the United States passed a Joint Resolution, approved by the President July 2, 1921, which read in part as follows :

'*Resolved by the Senate and House of Representatives of the United States of America in Congress assembled*, That the state of war declared to exist between the Imperial German Government and the United States of America by the joint resolution of Congress approved April 6, 1917, is hereby declared at an end.

'Sec. 2. That in making this declaration, and as a part of it, there

[1] A Treaty between the United States and Austria with similar modifications in the clauses of the Allied treaty of St. Germain (10th September 1919), was signed on the 21st August 1921 at Vienna. A modification of the Treaty of Trianon with Hungary was signed between the United States and Hungary at Budapest, 29th August 1921. The United States was not at war with Bulgaria or with Turkey, and did not therefore need to make peace with them.

are expressly reserved to the United States of America and its nationals any and all rights, privileges, indemnities, reparations, or advantages, together with the right to enforce the same, to which it or they have become entitled under the terms of the armistice signed November 11, 1918, or any extensions or modifications thereof; or which were acquired by or are in the possession of the United States of America by reason of its participation in the war or to which its nationals have thereby become rightfully entitled; or which, under the Treaty of Versailles, have been stipulated for its or their benefit; or to which it is entitled as one of the principal Allied and Associated Powers; or to which it is entitled by virtue of any Act or Acts of Congress; or otherwise.

'Sec. 5. All property of the Imperial German Government, or its successor or successors, and of all German nationals, which was, on April 6, 1917, in or has since that date come into the possession or under control of, or has been the subject of a demand by the United States of America or of any of its officers, agents, or employees, from any source or by any agency whatsoever, and all property of the Imperial and Royal Austro-Hungarian Government, or its successor or successors, and of all Austro-Hungarian nationals which was on December 7, 1917, in or has since that date come into the possession or under control of, or has been the subject of a demand by the United States of America or any of its officers, agents, or employees, from any source or by any agency whatsoever, shall be retained by the United States of America and no disposition thereof made, except as shall have been heretofore or specifically hereafter shall be provided by law until such time as the Imperial German Government and the Imperial and Royal Austro-Hungarian Government, or their successor or successors, shall have respectively made suitable provision for the satisfaction of all claims against said Governments respectively, of all persons, wheresoever domiciled, who owe permanent allegiance to the United States of America and who have suffered, through the acts of the Imperial German Government, or its agents, or the Imperial and Royal Austro-Hungarian Government, or its agents, since July 31, 1914, loss, damage, or injury to their persons or property, directly or indirectly, whether through the ownership of shares of stock in German, Austro-Hungarian, American, or other corporations, or in consequence of hostilities or of any operations of war, or otherwise, and also shall have granted to persons owing permanent allegiance to the United States of America most-favoured-nation treatment, whether the same be national or otherwise, in all matters affecting residence, business, profession, trade, navigation, commerce and industrial property rights, and until the Imperial German Government and the Imperial and Royal Austro-Hungarian Government, or their successor or successors, shall have respectively confirmed to the United States of America all fines, forfeitures, penalties, and seizures imposed or made by the United States of America during the war, whether in respect to the property of the Imperial German Government or German nationals or the Imperial and Royal Austro-Hungarian Government or Austro-Hungarian nationals, and shall have waived any and all pecuniary claims against the United States of America.'

Being desirous of restoring the friendly relations existing between the two nations prior to the outbreak of war;

Have for that purpose appointed their plenipotentiaries:

The President of the German Empire, Dr. FRIEDRICH ROSEN, Minister for Foreign Affairs, and the President of the United States of America; ELLIS LORING DRESEL, Commissioner of the United States of America to Germany;

Who, having communicated their full powers, found to be in good and due form, have agreed as follows:

ARTICLE I

Germany undertakes to accord to the United States, and the United States shall have and enjoy, all the rights, privileges, indemnities, reparations or advantages specified in the aforesaid Joint Resolution of the Congress of the United States of July 2, 1921, including all the rights and advantages stipulated for the benefit of the United States in the Treaty of Versailles which the United States shall fully enjoy notwithstanding the fact that such Treaty has not been ratified by the United States.

ARTICLE II

With a view to defining more particularly the obligations of Germany under the foregoing Article with respect to certain provisions in the Treaty of Versailles, it is understood and agreed between the High Contracting Parties:

(1) That the rights and advantages stipulated in that Treaty for the benefit of the United States, which it is intended the United States shall have and enjoy, are those defined in Section 1, of Part IV, and Parts V, VI, VIII, IX, X, XI, XII, XIV, and XV.[1]

The United States in availing itself of the rights and advantages stipulated in the provisions of that Treaty mentioned in this paragraph will do so in a manner consistent with the rights accorded to Germany under such provisions.

(2) That the United States shall not be bound by the provisions of Part I of that Treaty, nor by any provisions of that Treaty including those mentioned in paragraph (1) of this Article, which relate to the Covenant of the League of Nations, nor shall the United States be bound by any action taken by the League of Nations, or by the Council or by the Assembly thereof, unless the United States shall expressly give its assent to such action.[2]

(3) That the United States assumes no obligations under or with respect to the provisions of Part II, Part III, Sections 2 to 8 inclusive of Part IV, and Part XIII of that Treaty.[3]

(4) That, while the United States is privileged to participate in the Reparation Commission, according to the terms of Part VIII of that

[1] For text of Sect. 1 of Part IV, *v.* Vol. III, pp. 178–9; Parts V–VI, *v.* Vol. III, pp. 187–212; Parts VIII, IX, X, XI, XII, *v.* Vol. III, pp. 214–313; Parts XIV–XV, *v.* Vol. III, pp. 329–35.

[2] For text of Part I, *v.* Vol. III, pp. 111–23.

[3] For text of Parts II, III, *v.* Vol. III, pp. 124–77; Sect. 2–8, Part IV, *v.* Vol. III, pp. 179–87; Part XIII, *v.* Vol. III, pp. 314–28.

Treaty, and in any other Commission established under the Treaty or under any agreement supplemental thereto, the United States is not bound to participate in any such commission unless it shall elect to do so.

(5) That the periods of time to which reference is made in Article 440 of the Treaty of Versailles shall run, with respect to any act or election on the part of the United States, from the date of the coming into force of the present Treaty.

ARTICLE III

The present Treaty shall be ratified in accordance with the constitutional forms of the High Contracting Parties and shall take effect immediately on the exchange of ratifications which shall take place as soon as possible at Berlin.

IN WITNESS WHEREOF, the respective plenipotentiaries have signed this Treaty and have hereunto affixed their seals.

Done in duplicate in Berlin this twenty-fifth day of August, 1921.

[SEAL.] ROSEN.
[SEAL.] ELLIS LORING DRESEL.

Note. It will be observed that this Treaty makes no mention of Part VII of the Versailles Treaty which deals with the trial of the Kaiser and of German war criminals, *v.* Vol. III, pp. 212–13.

On the 18th October 1921 this Treaty was ratified by the Senate by 72–23.

By a proclamation of the President signed November 14, 1921, war between the United States and Germany was declared to have terminated July 2, 1921.

CHRONOLOGICAL LIST OF EVENTS MENTIONED IN VOLUME VI[1]

1386.	Union of Poland and Lithuania. Page 222.
1466.	Peace of Thorn. 222.
1657.	Treaty of Wehlau. 222 n.
1660.	Treaty of Oliva. 222 n.
1772.	First Partition of Poland. 225.
1774.	Treaty of Kuchuk Kainarjy. 89.
1768–74.	Russo-Turkish War. 45.
1793.	Second Partition of Poland. 226.
1795.	Third Partition of Poland. 226.
1798–1814.	Napoleonic Wars. 81.
1815.	Congress of Vienna. 220 n., 226, 489, 563–4, 568.
,,	Fourth Partition of Poland. 226.
1833.	
8 July.	Russo-Turkish Treaty of Unkiar-Skelessi (1833). 68.
1839.	Treaty guaranteeing Belgian Neutrality. 355.
1840.	
15 July.	Anglo-Austro-Prusso-Russian Agreement concerning the Pacification of the Levant. 68.
1856.	Treaty of Paris. 483, 533, 536.
1861–78.	Establishment of sovereign independent national state of Rumania. 59.
1871.	Treaty of Frankfurt. 534.
,,	Treaty of Washington. 336.
1877–8.	Russo-Turkish War. 80, 533.
1881.	
Dec.	Decree of Mouharrem. 95.
1885.	Berlin-Congo Act passed. 502–3.
1887.	Colonial Conference held. 339.
1893.	Convention regarding Franco-Canadian Trade. 337.
1894–5.	Japano-Chinese War. 368.
1895.	Treaty of Shimonoseki. 368 n.
1897.	Colonial Conference held. 339.
,,	Germans seize Kiaochow. 368.
1898.	
6 Mar.	Rights in Shantung granted to Germany and defined in Convention signed by China. 369, 378, 382, 384–5, 387.
1899.	First Hague Conference held. 434, 483.
,,	Declaration by German, British, Russian, French, Italian, and Japanese Governments that they would observe 'open door' principle in respect of their spheres of interest in China. 370.
19 Jan.	Anglo-Egyptian Convention. 204–5.

[1] A few important dates, not specifically referred to in Vol. VI, are added for the sake of completeness.

10 July. Supplementary Convention relating to town of Suakin. Page 205.
1899–1902. Boer War. 339.
1900.
21 Mar. Kiaochow-Tsinanfu Railway Agreement. 370.
1902. Colonial Conference held. 339.
1904. Anglo-French Agreement and Declaration *re* Egypt. 198.
1905. Treaty of Portsmouth. 374.
4–5 Dec. Lithuanian Convention held demanding autonomy for their country. 302.
22 ,, Treaty of Peking. 374.
1907. Colonial Conference held. 336–7.
,, Second Hague Conference held. 483–5.
31 Aug. Anglo-Russian Agreement. 6, 207–8, 211–12.
1909. Declaration of London concluded. 339.
16 July. Shah of Persia deposed. 209.
1910.
May Roosevelt's speech at Christiania advocating a League of Nations. 397.
1911. Imperial Conference held. 339, 563.
1912. Radio-Telegraphic Conference held. 337.
1913
30 May. First Treaty of London. 40 n.
1914. Conference on the Safety of Life at Sea held. 338.
13 Feb. Certain Aegean Islands assigned to Greece. 40 n. (Confirmed by Treaty of Sèvres 10 Aug. 1920, 40 n., modified by Treaty of Lausanne 24 July 1923, 117.)
28 June. Anglo-Persian Oil Company obtains from Turkish Government exclusive right to all oil in the vilayets of Mosul and Baghdad. 181.
3 Aug. Declaration of Italian Neutrality. 3, 11.
4 ,, Turkish Treaty with Germany. 2.
6 ,, China declares her Neutrality. 371.
15 ,, Japanese Ultimatum to Germany calling for surrender of Kiaochow. 372.
23 ,, Japan declares war on Germany. 372.
3 Sept. China declares ' war zone '. 372–3.
4 ,, Franco-British Treaty. 34.
5 ,, Anglo-French-Russian Declaration not to conclude separate peace. 13.
25 ,, Mr. Asquith's speech pleading for ' a real European partnership '. 429.
24 Oct. Sir H. McMahon's letter to Sherif of Mecca. 147.
31 ,, Bombardment of Tsingtao begun. 372.
,, ,, Turkey enters the War. 11.
Nov. Government of India's Proclamation to Moslems *re* Arabian and Mesopotamian Holy Cities. 122–3.
5 ,, Great Britain annexes Cyprus. 195, 205.
,, ,, Great Britain declares war on Turkey. 195.
7 ,, Germans capitulate at Tsingtao. 371–2.
10 ,, Mr. Lloyd George's speech *re* Turkey. 24.

18 Nov. Great Britain declares Protectorate over Egypt. Pages 195, 199–200.
19 ,, Proclamation deposing Abbas II and stating that succession had been offered to Prince Husein Kemal. 196.

1915.

Jan. Count Bulow's Mission to Rome. 12.
7 ,, Chinese Government informs Japan of cancellation of 'war zone' in Shantung and asks her to withdraw her troops. 373.
18 ,, Japanese Minister presents Memorandum containing the 'Twenty-One Demands' to President of China. 373, 631–3.
24 Jan. Murder of Captain Shakespeare at Riadh. 121.
19 Feb. Bombardment of Dardanelles by Allies. 5.
4 Mar. Memorandum from Russian Minister of Foreign Affairs to British and French Ambassadors *re* Constantinople, adopted by British Government 12 March and by French Government 12 April. 5, 7.
18 ,, Secret Agreement between Great Britain, France, and Russia regarding the future of Constantinople, the Straits, and Persia. 1, 4–10, 14, 16, 45.
,, ,, Telegram from M. Sazonoff to Russian Ambassador at Paris. 7.
20 ,, Telegram from M. Sazonoff to Russian Ambassador in London. 8, 208.
Apr. Treaty between Government of India and Idrisi. 124, 133.
26 ,, Italian Declaration acceding to Anglo-French-Russian Declaration of 5 September 1914. 1, 10–13. 19–20, 41 n., 560 n.
,, ,, Treaty of London.
,, ,, 21 Japanese Demands to China. 372–5, 631.
4 May. Italy denounces Triple Alliance. 3.
7 ,, Japanese Ultimatum to China, giving her two days in which to comply with revised edition of 'Twenty-One Demands'. 373, 631.
13 ,, American Note to Chinese Government. 373–4.
23 ,, Italy declares war on Austria-Hungary. 13.
25 ,, Japano-Chinese Agreements. 372–3, 378, 382–3, 385–7, 389, 631.
June. 'American League to Enforce Peace' founded. 396–7, 418, 428.
9 ,, Senator Lodge's address at Union College, Schenectady, favouring a League of Nations. 397.
Aug. Emir Husein's letter to British Government. 125, 132.
20 ,, Italy declares war on Turkey. 13.
14 Oct. Bulgaria begins hostilities against Serbia. 3.
Nov. British Government's Reply to Emir Husein's letter of August 1915. 126–7, 132, 135, 147, 153, 156, 162–3, 164.
,, Pact of London. 13, 34.
,, Treaty of Alliance between Government of India and Ibn-Saud. 24, 133.

1916. Compulsory military service introduced in New Zealand. 340.
29 Jan. President Wilson's speech suggesting that American States should unite in 'guaranteeing to each other absolute political and territorial integrity'. 429.

15 May	French Declaration *re* British Oil Concessions. 181–2.
16 ,,	Sykes-Picot Agreement. 1, 4, 7, 13–19, 21, 30, 42 n., 45, 83–4 n., 91, 128, 131–4, 137, 140–3, 145–8, 152–3, 159, 164–5, 167, 181, 502.
27 ,,	President Wilson's address to League to Enforce Peace at Washington, D.C. 397, 429.
24 June.	Lansing succeeds Bryan as U.S.A. State Secretary.
7 July.	Order in Council issued abandoning 'Declaration of London'.
17 Aug.	Rumanian Secret Treaty. 4.
27 ,,	Rumania declares war on Austria-Hungary.
29 ,,	Authority given to President Wilson by Congress to invite great governments of world to send representatives to a conference to formulate plan for court of arbitration. 398.
30 ,,	Turkey declares war on Rumania.
29 Oct.	Viviani resigns.
30 ,,	Briand becomes French Premier.
23 Nov.	Venizelist Government at Salonica declares war on Germany.
2 Dec.	Trepoff's Declaration *re* Constantinople Agreement. 9.
18 ,,	President Wilson's Peace Note. 429.
,, ,,	Mr. Balfour's Note to President Wilson. 23.
1917.	Compulsory military service introduced in Canada. 340.
,,	Independent National Republic of Erivan formed. 53.
,,	Meeting of Imperial War Cabinet. 341, 352, 430.
Jan.	Occupation of Wejh. 130.
10 ,,	Allied Reply to President Wilson's Peace Note of December 1916. 27.
Jan. & Feb.	Japan asks British, French, Russian, and Italian Governments for pledges that they would support her claims with regard to Germany's rights in Shantung, etc. 376, 634–7.
Mar.	First Russian Revolution. 285, 294, 311.
20 ,,	Ribot becomes French Premier.
Apr.	Committee of Imperial War Cabinet recommends adoption of principle that signatories of Peace Treaty should agree not to go to war with one another without previously submitting their dispute to a conference. 430.
9 ,,	Russia declares her disinterestedness in Constantinople, etc. 41–2, 48.
,, ,,	Turkey severs diplomatic relations with U.S.A.
17 ,,	Agreement of St. Jean de Maurienne. 1, 4, 13, 17–22, 25, 41, 74–5, 91.
17 May.	French Declaration of 15 May 1916 ratified by Great Britain and France. 181 n.
11 June.	Constantine of Greece, abdication demanded; signed 12 June.
27 ,,	Venizelist declaration of war on Germany becomes effective for Greece as a whole.
18 July.	Diet assumes supreme power in Finland. 286.

Aug.	British ‘League of Nations Society’ publishes its ‘Project for a League of Nations’. Page 428.
20 „	Imperial Government pledges itself to introduce reforms, leading up to self-government in India. 342.
3 Sept.	Riga evacuated. 294.
9 „	Ribot resigns, Painlevé Premier (12 September).
18–22 „	Lithuanian National Council elected. 302.
Oct.	Japan establishes civil administration at important points along Tsinanfu Railway, etc. 375.
Nov.	Bolshevik Revolution. 334.
„	Supreme War Council constituted. 431.
2 „	Balfour Declaration *re* Palestine. 86, 132, 135, 141, 170–7, 522.
„ „	Lansing-Ishii Agreement. 376–7, 637–8.
14 „	Painlevé resigns, Clemenceau becomes French Premier.
16 „	Lettish National Council constituted. 295.
24 „	Publication in Bolshevik ‘Izvestia’ of secret agreements. 16.
29 „	Count von Hertling’s speech recognizing right of Lithuania, Courland, and Poland to dispose of their own destinies. 303–4.
6 Dec.	Independence of Finland as sovereign state proclaimed by Diet. 285, 287.
11 „	Vilna recognized as capital of Lithuanian State. 304.
20 „	Publication in Bolshevik ‘Pravda’ of Russian Secret Memorandum. 5.
1918.	Allied Maritime Transport Council formed. 432.
„	Meeting of Imperial War Cabinet. 341, 352.
4 Jan.	Formal recognition of Finnish independence granted by Soviet Government. 287.
5 „	Meeting of All-Russian Constituent Assembly. 295.
„ „	Mr. Lloyd George’s speech on Allied War Aims. 23, 24, 29, 360.
8 „	President Wilson’s speech of ‘Fourteen Points’. 24, 26, 238 n., 342, 349, 351, 353, 395, 403, 430, 500, 539, 544, 559.
9 „	Lord Islington’s statement in House of Lords *re* Afghanistan. 9.
17–18 „	Lettish National Council holds its 2nd session. 295.
19 „	Publication in *Manchester Guardian* of translation of secret agreements published by Bolsheviks. 16.
„ „	Russian Constituent Assembly closed by Bolsheviks. 287.
27 „	German Government’s letter *re* Lithuanian independence. 304.
29 „	Helsingfors seized by Social Democrats. 287.
11 Feb.	President Wilson’s speech of ‘The Four Principles’. 558.
16 „	Re-establishment of independent Lithuanian State. 304.
19 „	Russian Soviet determines to accept German Peace Terms.
22 „	Publication in *Manchester Guardian* of Russian Secret Memorandum *re* Constantinople. 5.
24 „	Reval Government established. 295.
Mar.	Phillimore Draft Convention *re* League. 428 n., 430.
„	Treaty of Brest-Litovsk. 86 n., 284, 295, 304–5, 311, 544.
3 „	Germans land in Åland Islands. 288.

305, 307–8, 318–19, 335, 392, 395, 398, 403, 432, 462, 469, 486, 539, 554, 560.

11 Nov. *De facto* recognition by Great Britain of Lettish Council. Pages 297, 308.

„ „ Lord Robert Cecil's speech at Birmingham *re* League. 433 n.

13 „ Zaghlul Pasha and other Nationalists demand to be allowed to proceed to London to ask for ' complete autonomy '. 197.

18 „ Conjoint National Assembly held at Riga. 298.

26 „ Finland—Coalition Ministry under M. Ingman comes into power. 289.

„ „ Feisal lands at Marseilles. 142.

28 „ Bolsheviks cross the Narova. 298.

Dec. General Smuts' pamphlet *re* League of Nations. 347–50, 433–4, 437 and n., 438–9, 486.

2 „ President Wilson's speech to Congress before leaving for France. 395.

4 „ Canadian Cabinet urges representation of Dominions at Peace Conference. 343.

„ „ President Wilson sails for France. 395.

„ „ Senator Kellogg's speech *re* idea of League of Nations. 397.

6–10 Feisal revisits London and Paris. 142.

10 „ Agreement *re* food supplies between Mr. Hoover and Dr. Holsti. 289.

12 „ Finnish Diet elects General Mannerheim as acting Regent. 289.

21 „ Senator Lodge outlines what he considers essentials of constructive Peace Treaty with Germany. 398.

29 „ M. Pichon states French policy *re* Syria. 143.

1919. Treaty of St. Germain-en-Laye. 93, 95 n., 115, 266 and n., 571.

„ Deportation of Zaghlul. 197.

„ Washington Labour Conference held. 464–71, 477.

5 Jan. Bolsheviks enter Vilna. 308.

7 „ Death of Ex-President Roosevelt. 423.

„ „ Feisal returns to Paris from England. 144.

10 „ Revised version of ' Wilson Draft ' for League of Nations shown to his advisers. 438.

15 „ Rules of Peace Conference made public. 344.

16 „ Conversations at Quai d'Orsay between heads of Allied States *re* Russia. 312.

18 „ First Meeting of Peace Conference proper. 144, 312.

20 „ British Draft Convention of League of Nations Covenant. 438, 440, 445.

21 „ President Wilson reads to Council of Conference Mr. Buckler's Report on his conference with Mr. Litvinoff. 312.

22 „ President Wilson's proposal that Russian and Allied representatives should meet to see if a basis of agreement could be discovered. 312–13.

25 „ Plenary Session of Preliminary Peace Conference appoints Commission on the League of Nations. 346, 434.

27 „ Baron Makino's claims at Peace Conference. 377–8.

27 Jan.	Small Powers appoint representatives on League of Nations Commission. Page 434.
28 ,,	Mr. Wellington Koo's statement to Peace Conference *re* Chinese claims. 377.
30 ,,	Question of revision of Sykes-Picot Agreement discussed by Mr. Lloyd George, Sir M. Hankey, M. Clemenceau, and M. Pichon. 142.
Feb.	British Industrial Conference summoned by Prime Minister. 466, 469.
1 ,,	General von der Goltz arrives at Libau. 299.
3 ,,	Wilson Draft Covenant presented to League of Nations Commission. 435, 438.
3–4 ,,	M. Venizelos appears before Council of Ten and claims Smyrna zone. 25.
4 ,,	Feisal receives Croix de Guerre. 144.
6 ,,	Feisal states Arab case to Peace Conference. 144.
9 ,,	Senator Lodge's address in National House of Representatives on Roosevelt's death. 423.
11 ,,	First provisional draft of Covenant of League agreed to. 435.
12 ,,	Polish Commission appointed. 230 n., 247, 250-1, 256-7, 259–62, 271, 275, 345, 358.
13 ,,	Central Syrian Committee appears before Peace Conference. 145.
14 ,,	Draft Covenant of League of Nations presented to Peace Conference. 488, 491–2, 494, 498.
15 ,,	Proposed date for Prinkipo Meeting. 313.
18 ,,	Mr. Bullitt instructed to proceed to Russia. 313–14.
19 ,,	American Reply to British views *re* Reparation. 355.
26 ,,	Polish Commission instructed to report on boundary between Poland and Germany. 247.
,, ,,	Confidential meeting at White House between President Wilson and Foreign Relations Committee of U.S. Senate. 399.
4 Mar.	Close of 65th Congress. 394, 422.
,, ,,	President Wilson's New York address *re* German Treaty. 401.
,, ,,	Senator Lodge's 'Round Robin'. 400, 405.
5 ,,	President Wilson returns to France. 401.
12 ,,	Lord Allenby attends Peace Conference and advises on Syrian and Arabian Affairs. 197.
,, ,,	Report of Polish Commission completed.
14 ,,	M. Tchitcherin and M. Litvinoff draw up document containing terms Soviet Government undertook to accept if tendered not later than 10 April. 314.
19 ,,	Mr. Lloyd George receives Indian Delegation on the subject of the Turkish Treaty. 359–60.
20 ,,	Meeting of Supreme Council—question of Syria discussed. 145–8.
22–6 ,,	Meetings of League of Nations Commission. 435.
25 ,,	Lord Allenby appointed 'Special High Commissioner' of Egypt. 197.

25 Mar. Mr. Lloyd George's Memorandum. Pages 239 n., 313, 544–52, 554–5, 560, 579–80.
31 ,, General Smuts' Memorandum on Reparation. 356, 560.
Apr. General Smuts' Mission to Budapest. 358.
1–8 ,, Haller's Army transported to Poland via Danzig. 318.
3 ,, Dr. Nansen's proposal for Commission for Relief of Russia. 316.
7 ,, Telegram from 370 M.P.s to Mr. Lloyd George. 551.
10–11 ,, Amended Text of Draft Covenant considered by League of Nations Commission. 435.
11 ,, Mr. Hughes's offer to Baron Makino of principle of equality in respect of nationals resident in Australia as opposed to would-be immigrants. 352.
15 ,, Mr. Lansing's proposal at Meeting of Council of Five that Germany be made to renounce all rights, etc., in and over territory outside her European frontiers. 379.
16 ,, Colonel House's statement *re* proposal of U.S. Mandate for Constantinople and Straits. 27.
,, ,, Mr. Lloyd George's statement in House *re* Bullitt Mission. 315.
,, ,, Von der Goltz overthrows Lettish Provisional Government. 300.
18 ,, Berenger-Long Oil Agreement. 182–3.
22 ,, Japanese claims heard by Council of Three. 380, 386.
23 ,, German scheme for League of Nations published. 452.
,, ,, President Wilson's Manifesto *re* Fiume. 380.
,, ,, United States recognize British Protectorate over Egypt. 199.
24 ,, Italian Delegation leaves Paris. 25.
25 ,, Chinese Delegation submits to Supreme Council proposal that Germany should renounce to Principal Allied and Associated Powers her holdings, rights, and privileges in Shantung for restoration to China. 380.
27 ,, Revised and final text of Covenant given to U.S. Press by Acting Secretary of State. 406 n.
28 ,, Revised Covenant of League unanimously adopted at plenary meeting of Peace Conference—France and Japan protest against certain points. 435, 441.
,, ,, Baltic Commission appointed, functions enlarged 24 May. 300.
29 ,, General Bliss's letter to President Wilson on conflicting claims *re* Shantung. 381.
,, ,, Senators Lodge and Curtis's telegram to senatorial colleagues. 406 n.
30 ,, Shantung decision reached in favour of Japan. 381, 386.
May. Supreme Council's decision for Greece to take over certain military commitments in Northern Turkey. 44.
,, Viceroy of India informs British Government of Moslem feeling *re* Constantinople. 27.
3 ,, Question of recognition of Finnish independence discussed by Allied Powers. 289.

5 May. Baron Makino's statement to Press on Japanese policy *re* Shantung Peninsula. Page 386.

6 ,, British recognition of Finnish independence. 289.

,, ,, Chinese Delegation gives notice of reservation on its part to portion of Treaty which was to contain Shantung provision. 388.

7 ,, Supreme Council selects Mandatories for German Colonies. 'B' and 'C' Mandates. 503, 517.

,, ,, Draft German Treaty presented. 199, 211, 250, 261, 403, 405.

15 ,, Greek troops land at Smyrna. 25–6, 42, 45–8, 72, 74.

16 ,, Berenger-Long Oil Agreement ratified by French Foreign Office. 183.

17 ,, Viscount Uchida's statement to Press *re* Japanese policy as to Shantung Peninsula. 386.

19 ,, Sixth-sixth Congress assembles. 404.

21–22 Discussions between Clemenceau and Lloyd George *re* Mosul. 182.

22 ,, Riga captured. 300.

24 7 ,, Question of recognizing Admiral Kolchak. 316–17.

26 ,, Chinese Delegation notify President of Council that they will sign Treaty subject to their reservation *re* portion containing Shantung provision. 388.

27 ,, Supreme Council's Note to General Labour Conference recommending admission of Germany and Austria to their favourable consideration. 465 n.

30 ,, Belgo-British Agreement *re* transferring part of German East Africa to Belgium. 504 n.

4 June. New Commission for Germany's Eastern frontiers. 251, 261.

9 ,, Unofficial text of German Treaty reaches U.S. Senate. 405.

10 ,, Senator Knox's resolution advocating separation of Covenant and Treaty. 405.

13 ,, German retreat from Baltic provinces demanded by the 'Four', conveyed subsequently to Germany by Foch.

16 ,, Allied Reply to German Observations. 27, 247 n., 249 n., 250 n., 257 n., 261 n., 501 n., 539–40, 575 n.

19 ,, Poles authorized to continue advance to borders of Eastern Galicia. 272.

23 ,, Senator Lodge produces Senator Root's letter *re* Treaty. 406.

24 ,, Secretary-General of Peace Conference informs Chinese Delegation that reservations to the text of Treaty are not permissible. 388.

27 ,, President Wilson's statement to Press *re* proposed United States Mandate for Constantinople. 28.

28 ,, German Treaty signed. 93–5 and n., 115, 161, 263 n., 265 n., 275, 283 n., 405, 464 n., 466, 468–70, 474, 477 and n., 479, 491, 503–6, 520, 551, 554, 571.

,, ,, Guarantee Treaties signed. 359, 549–50, 552, 575.

2 July. Nauru Island Agreement signed. 517.

3 ,, Lettish Provisional Government concludes Armistice with Germany. 300.

10 July. Declaration *re* Togoland Mandate. Page 504.
,, ,, President Wilson lays before Senate final official text of German Treaty. 405, 411.
14 ,, Official text of German Treaty placed in printed form in hands of Senate Committee. 408.
,, ,, Senator Kellogg gives notice of intention to draw some dis tinction between amendments and reservations. 411.
16 ,, Venizelos appears before Council of Five to explain circumstances which led to Greek atrocities in Smyrna. 26.
17 ,, Bill passed giving Finland a democratic republican constitution. 290.
22 ,, Report of Baltic Commission on neutrality of Åland Isles.
29 ,, Agreement signed between M. Venizelos and M. Tittoni. 34.
,, ,, Ex-Associate Justice Hughes's letter before Senate. 411
31 ,, Senate Committee Hearings open to public begin. 408.
2 Aug. Further statement by Viscount Uchida *re* Japanese policy. 386.
7 ,, Senator Kellogg on distinction between amendments and reservations. 411.
9 ,, Anglo-Persian Agreement. 211–17.
12 ,, Mr. Lansing testifies before Senate Committee on Foreign Affairs that he had no knowledge of Japanese Secret Agreements until February 1919. 376 n.
17 ,, Mr. Cecil Harmsworth's statement *re* Persia. 214.
19 ,, President Wilson gives Senate Committee on Foreign Relations information as to origin of his Draft Covenant of League. 408–9, 422, 437, 444.
21 ,, Supreme Council approves Belgo-British Agreement of 30th May 1919 (q.v.). 504.
Sept. Mr. Bullitt's statement before Foreign Relations Committee of American Senate. 314, 409, 426 n., 438 n.
,, Mr. Doherty explains Covenant of League to Canadian House of Commons. 350.
,, Franco-British Provisional Agreement *re* Syrian questions. 152, 154, 160–1.
3 ,, President Wilson leaves Washington on his Pacific Tour. 414 n.
10 ,, Majority Report of Foreign Relations Committee. 412.
11 ,, Minority Report of Foreign Relations Committee. 412.
12 ,, Final Hearing of Foreign Relations Committee. 408–9.
15 ,, Senator McCumber's Report. 412, 423.
16 ,, Senator Lodge's speech *re* Roosevelt's attitude *re* peace. 423.
17 ,, Mr Lloyd George's speech at Sheffield *re* Turkey. 28.
24 ,, *De facto* recognition of Lithuanian Government by Great Britain. 308.
25 ,, President Wilson taken ill at Colorado. 28, 413, 414 n.
8 Oct. Avaloff-Bermondt's army marches on Riga. 301.
9 ,, General Gouraud appointed French High Commissioner for Syria and Cilicia. 154.

10 Oct. Allies' decision to force German evacuation of Baltic Provinces notified, German Reply (18).
16 ,, Report of Harbord Mission to Armenia. Pages 55–6, 72, 80 n.
21 ,, Feisal received by M. Clemenceau. 154.
30 ,, Mr. Bonar Law in House on attitude of British Government to Syrian Question. 154.
18 Nov. President Wilson's letter to Senator Hitchcock read in the Senate. 417.
19 ,, First Defeat of German Treaty in U.S. Senate, 413, 416.
20 ,, Peace Conference reaches decision on question of East Galicia. 274.
27 ,, Treaty of Neuilly. 29, 93, 115, 541, 571.
1 Dec. Second session of sixty-sixth Congress assembles. 417.
13 ,, Feisal leaves France. 157.
,, ,, Senator Underwood's speech in Senate expressing desire for unconditional ratification of Treaty with Germany. 418.
19 ,, Mr. Lloyd George in House on attitude of British Government to Syrian question. 155.
22 ,, East Galician proposals shelved. 274.
1920. Hythe Conference held. 321.
Jan. First Baltic Conference at Helsingfors convoked. 310.
,, Supreme Council's decision *re* trade with Russia. 322.
10 ,, Mandatory system comes into effective legal being. 505
20 ,, M. Clemenceau resigns. 183.
28 ,, Turkish National Pact. 32, 48, 53–4, 60, 67, 89, 97, 102, 107–8, 112.
31 ,, Lord Grey's published letter in *The Times*, 'America and the Treaty'. 419.
,, ,, Results of Bi-partisan Conference of U.S. Senators made public. 419.
2 Feb. Treaty of Peace between Russia and Esthonia signed. 301, 310, 318, 329, 580.
,, ,, Lord Grey's letter of 31 January printed in Senate proceedings. 419.
9 ,, Senator Lodge resurrects German Treaty, together with reservations, for further consideration by Senate. 420.
18 ,, Admiral de Robeck's official announcement *re* Constantinople. 28.
24 ,, Supreme Council's advice to communities bordering on Russia. 319.
27 ,, Mr. Lloyd George's speech in House of Commons *re* Constantinople. 24, 27–8.
9 Mar. Senator Hitchcock makes public letter from President Wilson of 8 March. 420.
10 ,, Congress of Syrian Notables offers crown of Syria and Palestine to Feisal. 157.
15 ,, French and British Governments repudiate action of Arab Congress. 157.
19 ,, Final Defeat of German Treaty in U.S. Senate. 421.
22 ,, Mr. Lloyd George's Declaration to Indian deputation. 24, 29.

29 Mar.	Lenin's speech *re* League of Nations. 579.
30 „	Declaration by Mr. Bonar Law *re* doctrine of right of Dominions to secede from Empire. Page 366.
Apr.	San Remo Conference—provisions of Sèvres Treaty decided on, 24 April. 29–30, 157, 323, 505, 507.
4 „	Mandate for Syria and Lebanon conferred on France by Supreme Council (confirmed 6 May). 169.
20 „	Poles enter Vilna. 308.
24 „	San Remo Conference decides that Syria and Iraq shall become independent states subject to Mandatory Power. 156–7.
24–5 „	San Remo Oil Agreement. 183, 188, 603–5.
25 „	San Remo Conference assigns 'A' Mandates, Palestine and Mesopotamia to Great Britain, Syria to France. 30, 169, 184–5, 505.
May.	Russian Trade Mission reaches England. 323.
1 „	Mr. Tschakste elected President of Lettish Assembly. 301.
5 „	Mandates for Syria, Palestine, and Mesopotamia decided by Supreme Council at San Remo. (Confirmed by League Council 12 Aug. 645).
8 „	Fall of Kieff. 319.
12 „	Letter from American Ambassador in London to Lord Curzon on the subject of Mandates. 507.
14 „	Agreement between Italy and Greece *re* certain islands. 31 n., 37.
28 „	Finnish Government authorized to request admittance of Finland to League. 292.
30 „	Lenin's speech *re* League of Nations. 579.
June.	Genoa Labour Conference held. 464, 471–3.
„	Great Britain's four requirements as conditions of a formal trade agreement with Russia. 324.
3 „	Arabs murder two British officers at Tel Afar. 185.
12 „	Peace negotiations between Russia and Finland begun. 292.
15 „	Constitution passed by Esthonian Constituent Assembly. 302.
15–16 „	Council of League discusses question of Persia's admission to League. 216–17.
16 „	Criticism of Nauru Mandate in House of Commons. 517.
20 „	British Proclamation *re* status of Mesopotamia. 185.
24 „	Mr. Lloyd George's statement in House *re* Sèvres Treaty. 31.
30 „	Finland addresses formal request to Secretary-General of League to be admitted a member. 292.
July.	Spa Conference held. 318–19, 324.
11 „	Allenstein Plebiscite held. 249, 556–7.
„ „	British Note to Poland. 319.
„ „	Marienwerder Plebiscite held. 257, 556–7.
12 „	Treaty of Peace between Russia and Lithuania signed at Moscow. 308, 318, 329, 580.
14 „	Peace Negotiations between Russia and Finland adjourned. 292.
„ „	General Gouraud sends ultimatum to Feisal. 158, 160.
15 „	Lettish Government under M. Ulmanis concludes Armistice with Germany. 301.

Nov. Draft Russian Trade Agreement. Pages 324–5.
„ Fall of Venizelos. 32.
„ First Meeting of Assembly of League. 349, 362, 365, 495, 511, 545.
„ Senator Harding becomes President-Elect. 425.
9 „ Treaty between Poland and Free City of Danzig comes into force. 260 n.
20 „ American Reply to Lord Curzon's Note *re* Mandates. 509, 515.
30 „ Communications regarding submission of draft mandates submitted to France, Great Britain, Italy, and Japan. 511.
Dec. Albania admitted to League of Nations. 363, 450, 525, 567, 577.
„ Middle East Department created, under Colonial Office. 185.
1 „ Constitution of Permanent Mandates Commission approved by Council of League. 512.
7 „ First draft of Mesopotamia Mandate presented to League by Mr. Balfour. 36 n., 609.
9 „ Draft of 'C' Mandate received by Secretary-General of League. 514.
„ „ Milner Report signed. 202.
16 „ Finland unanimously accepted as member of League. 292, 525.
17 „ 'C' Mandates approved by Council of League, and come into force. 514, 516.
22 „ Mr. Lloyd George's speech *re* Asia Minor. 32.
23 „ Franco-British Convention. 30, 164–6.

1921.

1 Jan. Peace Treaty between Russia and Finland comes into force. 292.
26 „ *De jure* recognition of Esthonia and Latvia by Supreme Council. 301.
21 Feb. Fall of Teheran. 215.
26 „ Bolshevik Treaty with Persia. 10.
Feb.–Mar. London Conference. 32, 44 n., 65–6, 86, 89.
Mar. Health Conference held, under auspices of League. 327, 334, 580.
„ Russo-Polish Treaty signed at Riga. 322, 329, 580.
16 „ Bolshevik Treaty with Kemalists. 10, 48, 53, 86 and n.
„ „ Russo-British Trade Agreement signed in London. 325–6, 544.
20 „ Upper Silesian Plebiscite held. 623.
31 „ Publication by *Manchester Guardian* of text of Bolshevik Treaty with Persia, 26 February 1921. 10.
18 Apr. Mr. Lloyd George's statement in House *re* Constantinople. 33 and n.
May. Draft Mandates for Togoland and Cameroons published by British Government. 510–11.
„ Joint Proclamation of Neutrality by High Commissioners of the Powers at Constantinople. 47.

of Covenant if Serb-Croat-Slovene State refuses to execute its obligations under Covenant. Pages 527 n., 577.

14 Nov. Proclamation signed by U.S. President declaring state of war with Germany to have terminated 2 July 1921. 653 n.

17 ,, French Reply to Lord Curzon's Note protesting against Franklin-Bouillon Agreement. 34.

,, ,, Lord Allenby's Proposals *re* Egypt. 202.

23 ,, Meeting of Commission to conclude Convention establishing new status of Upper Silesia. 630.

6 Dec. Lord Allenby's Reply to Lord Curzon *re* Egypt. 202.

11 ,, Lord Allenby's Proposals *re* Egypt. 202.

17 ,, Oedenburg Plebiscite held. 556 n.

23 ,, Zaghlul deported to Seychelles. 202.

1922. Four Power Treaty signed at Washington. 516.

,, Genoa Conference held. 328–33, 565.

Geneva Labour Conference held. 476.

Washington Disarmament Conference held. 361, 516, 535, 545, 551, 553, 565 n.

6 Jan. Cannes Conference Resolution that Russia should be invited to a general Economic and Financial Conference. 327.

12 ,, Lord Allenby asks for approval of Government for proposed statement to Sultan. 202.

3 Feb. Franco-British Agreement *re* boundaries of Syria and Iraq and Palestine, ratified by British Government (7 March 1923). 166.

4 ,, Treaty relative to Shantung signed between China and Japan at Washington Conference. 390.

6 ,, Treaty signed between United States, Belgium, British Empire, China, France, Italy, and Japan, the Netherlands and Portugal, 'relating to principles and policies to be followed in matters concerning China'. 390.

,, ,, and Treaty between same Powers 'relating to Chinese Customs Tariff'. 390.

11 ,, Yap Treaty signed. 516.

27 ,, Mr. Lloyd George's telegram to British Dominions *re* British Declaration to Sultan of Egypt. 203.

28 ,, British Declaration to Sultan. 203.

Mar. Eight Hours' Convention ratified by Greece, Rumania, India, Czecho-Slovakia, and Bulgaria. 467.

,, Paris Conference held. 35–6, 65–6, 87, 104.

,, Resignation of Mr. Montagu. 367.

1 ,, Mr. Lloyd George's speech in House *re* the Sudan. 205.

17 ,, Political Agreement signed at Warsaw between Poland, Latvia, Esthonia, and Finland. 310.

16 Apr. Treaty of Rapallo (Bolsheviks and Germany). 330–1, 544, 580.

24 ,, Italians conclude separate agreement with Constantinople Government. 36.

May. Sub-Committee of Permanent Mandates Commission's Report to Council of League of Nations. 519.

20 Nov. Lausanne Conference. Pages 39, 106.

20 Dec. *De jure* recognition of Lithuania by leading Allied Powers. 309.

1923.

Jan. Memel assigned by Principal Allies to Lithuania. 247–8, 283, 309 n.

17 ,, Poland's claim to Vilna area, to East Galicia, and to Riga-treaty frontier to East recognized by Principal Allied Powers. 283 n., 309 n.

4 April. Zaghlul released from Gibraltar on ground of ill-health. 204 n.

3 May. Baldwin announces modifications of Iraq Treaty in Commons. 192.

24 July. Treaty of Lausanne signed (ratified by Assembly of Angora 23 Aug.). 114, 115–17.

INDEX TO VOLUME VI

GENERAL SUBJECT-INDEX TO VOLS. I—VI